M_d	=	demand for money
MEI	=	marginal efficiency of investment
MSBs	=	mutual savings banks
N	=	number of workers (laborers) employed
NBFIs	=	nonbank financial intermediaries
N_{fe}	=	labor force = number of workers available for work
NX	=	net exports = $E - M$
OMO	=	open market operations
P	=	level of prices (as represented by the CPI)
$\dot{p}$	=	rate of inflation
PC	=	Phillips curve
$\dot{p}^e$	=	expected rate of inflation
P_f^k	=	keg price of foreign goods
$P_f^\$$	=	dollar price of foreign goods = P_f
P_r	=	price of raw materials
q	=	required reserve ratio
q_D	=	required reserve ratio on demand deposits
q_{ts}	=	required reserve ratio on time and savings deposits
R	=	total reserves = RR + XR = required reserve plus excess reserves
RE	=	current retained earnings
RR	=	required reserves = $q_D D + q_{ts} TS$
S	=	savings
S&Ls	=	savings and loan associations
t	=	tax rate
T	=	net taxes received by the government = taxes minus transfer payments
TS	=	time and savings deposits
u	=	unemployment rate $= \dfrac{N_{fe} - N}{N_{fe}}$
U	=	number of workers unemployed = $N_{fe} - N$
V	=	velocity of money = the ratio of GNP to the money supply
w	=	wage rate
W	=	household wealth or net worth
x_b	=	business expectations
x_h	=	household expectations
XR	=	excess reserves
Y	=	National Product or National Income = GNP
Y_d	=	disposable income
Y_f	=	foreign income
Y_{fe}	=	full-employment level of output (or income)
Z	=	miscellaneous factors affecting international transactions

---

Δ = change in

— lower case for a particular variable denotes a real (inflation-adjusted) magnitude (e.g., y = real income)

— a dot over a variable denotes a rate of change in percent (e.g., $\dot{y}$ = the rate of change of real income)

MONEY
AND THE
FINANCIAL SYSTEM

MONEY
AND THE
FINANCIAL SYSTEM

THEORY, INSTITUTIONS, AND POLICY

RAYMOND E. LOMBRA

Pennsylvania State University

JAMES B. HERENDEEN

Pennsylvania State University

RAYMOND G. TORTO

University of Massachusetts—Boston

McGRAW-HILL BOOK COMPANY

New York   St. Louis   San Francisco   Auckland   Bogotá   Hamburg
Johannesburg   London   Madrid   Mexico   Montreal   New Delhi
Panama   Paris   São Paulo   Singapore   Sydney   Tokyo   Toronto

**MONEY
AND THE
FINANCIAL SYSTEM**
THEORY, INSTITUTIONS, AND POLICY

1 2 3 4 5 6 7 8 9 0   DODO   8 9 8 7 6 5 4 3 2 1 0

This book was set in Bodoni Book by Progressive Typographers.
The editors were Bonnie E. Lieberman,
Michael Elia, and Frances A Neal;
the designer was Nicholas Krenitsky;
the production supervisor was Phil Galea.
R. R. Donnelley & Sons Company was printer and binder.

Library of Congress Cataloging in Publication Data

Lombra, Raymond E
    Money and the financial system.

    Includes index.
    1. Finance. 2. Money. 3. Fiscal policy.
4. Monetary policy. I. Herendeen, James B., joint
author. II. Torto, Raymond G., joint author.
III. Title.
HG173.L65   332   79-22204
ISBN 0-07-038607-2

TO

BOBBI
Sherri, Brian, and Todd

JOANNE
Lisa, Julie, and Joe

CAROL
Stephanie and Pamela

WITH LOVE

CONTENTS

CHAPTER 2
THE ROLE OF MONEY
23

CHAPTER 3
A FRAMEWORK FOR FINANCIAL ANALYSIS
41

PART II
A SECTORAL APPROACH TO MONETARY ANALYSIS

CHAPTER 4
THE HOUSEHOLD SECTOR
59

CONTENTS

CHAPTER 5
THE BUSINESS SECTOR
87

CHAPTER 6
THE GOVERNMENT SECTOR
115

CHAPTER 7
THE FOREIGN SECTOR
131

PART III
INSIDE THE FINANCIAL SYSTEM

CHAPTER 8
COMMERCIAL BANKING:
AN INDUSTRY OVERVIEW
157

CHAPTER 9
THE MONEY SUPPLY PROCESS:
THE ROLE OF BANK RESERVES
179

CHAPTER 10
THE MONEY SUPPLY PROCESS:
THE ROLE OF COMMERCIAL BANK PORTFOLIO BEHAVIOR
193

CHAPTER 11
NONBANK FINANCIAL INTERMEDIARIES
211

CHAPTER 12
MARKETS AND MARKET MAKERS
235

PART IV
HOW OUTPUT, PRICES, INTEREST RATES, AND EXCHANGE RATES ARE DETERMINED

CHAPTER 13
AGGREGATE SUPPLY AND DEMAND:
THE DETERMINANTS OF OUTPUT AND THE PRICE LEVEL
257

CHAPTER 14
INFLATION AND UNEMPLOYMENT
289

CHAPTER 15
THE STRUCTURE OF INTEREST RATES
319

CHAPTER 16
THE EXCHANGE RATE AND THE BALANCE OF PAYMENTS
343

PART V
STABILIZING THE ECONOMY:
MONETARY, FISCAL, AND INTERNATIONAL POLICIES

CHAPTER 17
ECONOMIC GOALS: WHAT ARE THEY, WHO SETS THEM, AND HOW ARE THEY PURSUED?
371

CHAPTER 18
THE FEDERAL RESERVE: WHO DOES WHAT
395

CHAPTER 19
THE FEDERAL RESERVE:
THE FORMULATION AND IMPLEMENTATION OF POLICY
431

CHAPTER 20
FISCAL POLICY AND THE
ELUSIVE QUEST FOR ECONOMIC STABILITY
481

CHAPTER 21
THE UNITED STATES IN THE WORLD ECONOMY
501

CONTENTS

GLOSSARY
529

INDEX
539

PREFACE

A preface is the authors' introduction to a text. The standard preface usually contains a long and often boring summary of the contents of the book and indicates how the book differs from its competitors. We will avoid this approach.

We think we can best help you gain some insight into our text by describing briefly how we came to write it. Like most people who write a text we found ourselves increasingly dissatisfied with existing texts for courses in money and banking and financial markets and institutions. Thus motivated, we started out by asking ourselves what types of questions a student should be able to answer following the completion of these courses. Our list included: Why has the inflation rate risen over the past 15 years; why have interest rates risen over the last 15 years; why has inflation persisted even during periods of sustained unemployment; why has the international value of the dollar fallen over the past 10 years; what is the role of monetary policy in determining inflation, unemployment, interest rates, and exchange rates; why has government policy failed to stabilize the economy; why have we observed so many changes in the financial system over the past decade?

Identifying the questions helped fix the objectives of the text. The courses in which the book would be used provided the focus. As the title of the text suggests, we believe answers to the above questions can be discovered by studying the functions of money and the financial system within our economy.

As work progressed, there were several principles which guided our efforts.

First, we were convinced that important economic questions cannot be answered without a firm grounding in theory, a full appreciation of the relevant institutional setting, and an understanding of the political-economic environment within which policy decisions are made. Second, we believed that models are "means" to an "end" and not ends in themselves. Accordingly, the "benefits" of modeling, in terms of increased understanding of important economic phenomena, must exceed the "costs," in terms of the time spent mastering the complexities introduced. Third, we expected the text to be accessible to students with only an introductory course in economics—even those who think they have forgotten much of that material.

Mindful of such concerns, we consciously avoided writing an "encyclopedia" which tried to cover all topics in depth. Books that try to be all things to all people often fail to separate the important from the unimportant and leave students bewildered and frustrated. In making our choices about what to include and exclude we were guided by questions like those above, by our collective teaching experiences, and by students' reactions to various topics. For example, we have observed that protracted discussions of United States monetary history and complicated derivations of formal models are not necessary to examine today's key questions and issues. Moreover these historical discussions and modeling exercises frequently dampen students' enthusiasm for what should be exciting material. Historical discussions are used only where they add to an understanding of a current issue. Our derivations and use of models is selective and tied closely to improved comprehension of public policy.

To learn more about what is in the book, read the introductions to the various parts of the text. The educational philosophy which underlies the text can be summarized by the remarks of Robert A. Gordon in his presidential address before the 88th meeting of the American Economics Association: ". . . the mainstream of economic theory sacrifices far too much relevance in its insistent pursuit of ever increasing rigor. And, . . . we economists pay too little attention to the changing institutional environment that conditions economic behavior." His credo and ours is relevance with as much rigor as possible, not rigor regardless of relevance.

Good Luck! We hope you find the reading as rewarding as we found the writing.

ACKNOWLEDGMENTS

In writing this text we have had advice and encouragement from many sources. Extremely helpful comments on earlier drafts of the manuscript were graciously provided by Will Mason, James Barth, Charles Ellard, Sheila Moore, Edward Kane, and James Gale. Their comments enabled us to clarify and correct the discussion in many places. The early drafts were typed by a cadre of patient, dedicated secretaries: Ilene Glenn, Patti Corcoran, and Nelda Sogoloff. The final drafts were typed expertly and cheerfully by Judy Buttorff and Pat Kidder. They worked under the pressure of short deadlines and scribbling that faintly resembled the written language. We are in their debt. We would also like to thank Bob Dorian,

Gale Randall, and Gayle Tauman of GROUP IV for providing ideas, inspiration, and the data for most of the figures in the text. Finally, and perhaps most importantly, we want to thank the superb professional staff at McGraw-Hill: Stephen Dietrich convinced us to sign with McGraw-Hill by emphasizing its superior editorial, production, and sales capabilities—he was right; business and economics editor Bonnie Lieberman, shepherded the book through its many stages with the kind of prodding, encouragement, and sense of dedication only the authors can fully appreciate; Mike Elia, senior editor, provided detailed comments and suggestions on the entire manuscript which improved the exposition immeasurably. In a very real sense any success the book enjoys will reflect the untiring support and efforts of Bonnie Lieberman and Mike Elia.

To all of you, and to our families, we express our profound appreciation.

RAYMOND E. LOMBRA
JAMES B. HERENDEEN
RAYMOND G. TORTO

MONEY
AND THE
FINANCIAL SYSTEM

PART
ONE

ANALYZING MONEY AND
THE FINANCIAL SYSTEM

Studying and mastering the material in this text is like constructing a building. Care must be taken in setting the foundation where inattention to details can doom the project. Once the foundation is properly and firmly in place, the rest of the building is constructed one floor at a time until it is completed. Interestingly enough, despite the critical role of the foundation, it usually cannot be seen because it is beneath the surface. Nevertheless, the foundation must be there.

Part I of this text is very much the foundation of our study of money, banking, and financial institutions. Chapters 1 through 3 outline the principles of money and finance and the direction of the text. In these chapters we provide an overview of the interaction of the financial system with the rest of the economy. Chapter 1 traces the flow of income around the economy and the role of the financial system in matching borrowers and lenders. The lifeblood of the financial system—money—is introduced in Chapter 2, where the definition, role, and relation of money to other financial assets and liabilities is presented.

We start to move into high gear in Chapter 3 which pulls together some of the pieces developed in the first two chapters. Chapter 3 presents an accounting framework that will be employed throughout the rest of the book to study the interaction of the economic and financial decisions of the various components or sectors of the economy. More generally, Chapter 3 provides the reader with an understanding of how each of the chapters in Part II is integrated into this text.

3

WHAT ARE WE GOING TO DO AND WHY?

The safest way to double your money is to fold it over once and put it in your pocket.

Frank Hubbard

1-1
DIAGNOSING THE PATIENT

It might be helpful to think of the United States economy as a human patient that we will observe and hopefully come to know and understand. Just as a human body is made up of many parts (e.g., arms, legs, torso), the United States economy is composed of many sectors (e.g., household, business, and government). The money and the financial system of our economy is analogous to the blood and the circulatory system of the body. We want to study how the behavior of money and the operation of the financial system affect the well-being of households, business firms, and—more generally—the overall economy. By focusing on money and the financial system, we shall see how the major sectors of the economy interact to produce goods and services and to generate income.

The health of the United States economy varies over time. Sometimes it

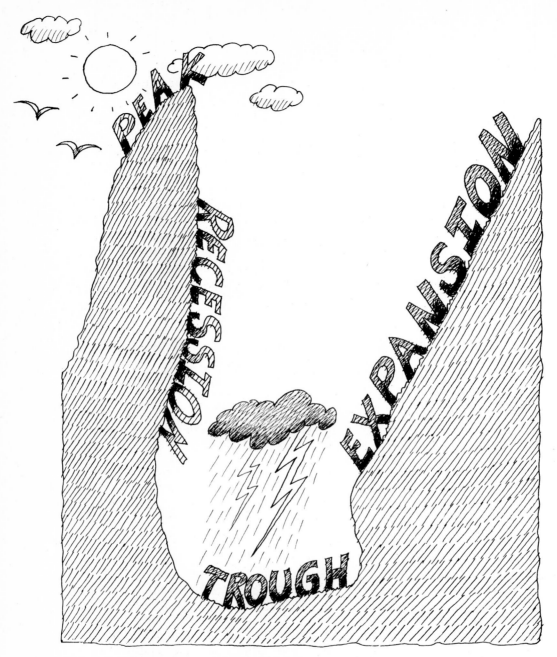

THE PHASES OF THE BUSINESS CYCLE The economy, like most of us, has its ups and downs. During an *expansion*, unemployment falls as economic activity increases. During a *recession*, unemployment rises as economic activity decreases.

To avoid confusion remember that incumbent politicians almost never admit that the economy has been, is, or will be in a recession. Like the doctor who argues that the operation was a success even though the patient died, policymakers tend to see a bright side to almost any problem.

In this text we will explore the role of money, the financial system, and policy in encouraging as well as terminating an expansion or a recession.

appears to be well, functioning normally; at others it appears listless and depressed; and at still other times it seems hyperactive—characterized by erratic, unstable behavior. By studying how all the key parts of the economy fit together, we should be able to learn something about the illnesses that can strike our patient. What causes a particular type of illness (say, inflation or unemployment)? How is the illness diagnosed? What medicines or cures can be prescribed? If there is more than one possible cure, which will work best? Are there any undesirable side effects associated with particular medications? Are the doctors who diagnose the problems and administer the treatment (the policymakers) ever guilty of malpractice?

Answers to all these questions will depend in part on "what makes the patient tick" and how we define "good health." A human patient's health is determined by the deviations (if any) from a well-established set of precise criteria involving temperature, reflexes, blood chemistry, appetite, and so forth. For the economy, however, there are no well-established, precise criteria whereby we may judge its health. Rather, there are loosely defined goals or objectives such as "full" employment, "low" inflation, and so on. If everyone agrees on these goals (including how to define them) and the economy seems to be operating in the neighborhood of the goals, then we might say the economy is in good health. If we are heading toward the goals then the economy's health would be improving. On the other hand, if the economy seems to be deviating from the agreed upon goals or objectives, then the economy is not in good health and prescriptive measures may be necessary to improve matters.

As is the case in the medical profession, before you can diagnose an ailment, considerable study is required. Accordingly, let us start out by trying to find out something about "what makes the patient tick."

1-2
HOW THE VARIOUS PARTS
OF THE ECONOMY FIT TOGETHER

We can begin our anatomy lesson with what is called a *circular flow diagram*. It presents a bird's-eye view of how the production and purchase of goods and services within the economy are interrelated. The connecting links between two major sectors of the economy—the household sector and the business sector—are shown in Figure 1-1. (There are also the government and foreign sectors, but we will keep things simple for now and ignore them.) As you can see, there are two flows from the household to the business sector and two flows from the business to the household sector. One way the household sector is connected to the business sector is by its expenditures (the money flow) on goods and services (the real flow) provided by businesses. Households buy goods and services produced by businesses and pay for them with money. The sectors are connected in a second way, because businesses buy factors of production—such as labor services—

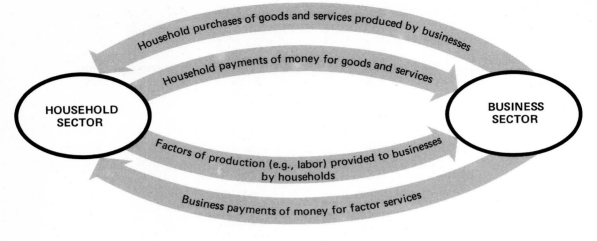

FIGURE 1-1

The circular flow of income, spending, output, and money.

from households (a real flow) and pay for them with wages and salaries (a money flow). Therefore, there is a circular flow of "real" things in one direction connecting the business and household sectors and a circular flow of money in the other direction.

The circular flow diagram in Figure 1-1 is, of course, a simplification of the real world. For instance, it ignores the possibility that the household or business sector might want to save or borrow. As the diagram is drawn, income comes into the household sector (in the form of wages and salaries) and expenditures of equal value flow out. This implies that all income earned by households is spent on goods and services and that there is no *saving*. As for the business sector, this simplified diagram assumes that there is no *investment*—that is, that firms do not spend funds to acquire new equipment or make additions to existing plants.

> **Investment** by business firms is equal to their expenditures on new plants (structures) and new equipment as well as changes in their inventories. It is important—in fact, it is crucial—to recognize that investment is *not* the buying and selling of stocks and bonds. The latter will be referred to as *financial investment*.

The picture becomes more realistic although a bit more complicated when we recognize that—within each sector—individual households or businesses (individual units) may save while others borrow. For example, you may be borrowing to finance your education while your uncle is saving for his retirement. However, in the aggregate (that is, taking all the individual units within a sector together), the household sector is a net saver or *surplus sector*, while the business sector is generally a net borrower or *deficit sector*.

> A *surplus sector* (or unit) spends less than its current income.
> A *deficit sector* (or unit) spends more than its current income.

How, you might ask, can the business sector spend more than it earns? More directly, where will it get the funds to finance its deficit? In effect, the deficit sector (the business sector), which needs funds, will want to borrow from the surplus sector (the household sector), which has funds.

For this to occur, there must be some mechanism which can transfer the funds of the surplus units to the deficit units. Obviously, there is such a mechanism and it is the financial system of the economy. Figure 1-2 is a

FIGURE 1-2

The circular flow including the financial system.

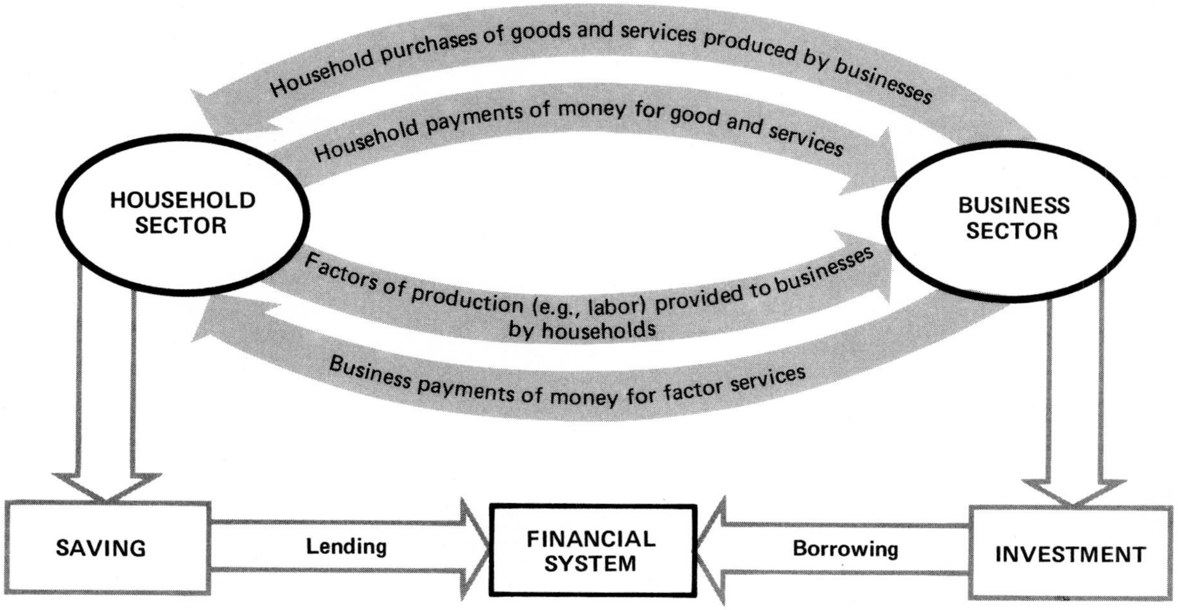

more realistic view of Figure 1-1; Figure 1-2 shows saving (the surplus funds from households), investment, and the financial system. As you can see, the financial system brings together the saving of households and channels it to firms in order to finance the deficits resulting from their investment in new plant and equipment to be used in the future production of goods and services.

1-3
MORE ON THE FINANCIAL SYSTEM

We have learned so far in our anatomy lesson that our patient, the economy, has several major parts which interact with one another. Households and firms interact directly by exchanging goods—as well as labor or other factor services—for money. The business and household sectors also interact through the financial system; the *net* surplus in the household sector is channeled to the business sector to finance its *net* deficit, through the operations of the financial system.[1]

Surplus sectors (or units) are the lenders.
Deficit sectors (or units) are the borrowers.

A well-organized, efficient, smoothly functioning financial system is an important prerequisite to a modern, highly specialized economy. The financial system provides a mechanism whereby any individual unit that saves some of its income may *conveniently* make these funds available to others that intend to spend more than their current income. The key word here is "conveniently."

The financial system has two major components. One is made up of the *financial markets* where the surplus units can lend their funds *directly* to the borrowers, or deficit units. An example would be the market for corporate bonds; IBM can sell bonds to, say, finance the construction of a new plant in Kansas, and Aunt Mary from Maine can purchase some of the bonds with the income she does not spend on goods and services. This is called *direct finance*. The other major component of the financial system comprises the *financial intermediaries*—various institutions such as banks, savings and loan associations, and credit unions—that serve as go-betweens to link up surplus (saving) units and deficit (borrowing) units.

---

[1] If we disaggregated the household and business sectors, we would find that there are, within each sector, individual units that earn more than they spend and will be induced to lend their surplus out. Likewise, there are deficit units that spend more than they earn and must borrow to finance their deficit. We are interested primarily in the *net* surplus or deficit.

Here, the linkage between saver and borrower is *indirect*. For example, a household might deposit some surplus funds in a savings account at a bank, and the bank, in turn, might make a loan to a deficit unit. This is called *indirect finance*.

You might ask, "Why do we need financial intermediaries? Why don't surplus units lend *directly* to borrowers?" To answer this, let us begin with the initial choices and decisions that would face us as, say, a household. If we are working, we have a steady flow of income coming into the household. Our choices are whether (1) to spend *all* our income, (2) to spend just *part* of our income and therefore save some of it, or (3) to spend *more* than our income. If we spend *part* of our income and save the rest, then we are a surplus household or surplus unit. If we spend *more* than our income, then we must borrow, making us a deficit household or deficit unit. Since it is pleasanter to decide what to do with a surplus than to worry about how to finance a deficit, let us assume that we spend only part of our income. Now, what should we do with our surplus or saving?

A surplus unit basically has two decisions to consider about how to employ its surplus. The first choice is between holding the surplus in the form of cash or lending it out.[1] Because cash does not usually earn interest, we would probably decide to lend out at least a *portion* of our saving to earn some interest income on it. This leads us to the second decision the surplus household must make: How and where is the surplus to be lent? We could go directly to the financial markets and purchase a *new* bond being issued by a corporation. Presumably we would not pick a bond at random. For example, we might consider selecting a bond issued by a creditworthy borrower—one who will be likely to pay the promised *interest* on schedule and also to repay the original amount lent (called the *principal*) when the bond matures in, say, ten years. In short, we would have to be able to appraise the risk of default. (Default is the failure of the borrower to pay interest, to repay principal, or both.)

To minimize the risk of our surplus being wiped out by the default of a particular borrower, we might want to spread our risks out and *diversify*. This can be accomplished by spreading our surplus out over a number of deficit units. In nontechnical terms, we would want to avoid putting all our eggs into one basket.

Most surplus units are not experts in appraising and diversifying risk. Many would prefer to rely on others, such as financial intermediaries, for such expertise. Financial intermediaries acquire the savings of surplus units by offering *claims* on themselves. What this means is that the saver has really made a loan to the financial intermediary and therefore has a financial claim (holds an IOU) on the intermediary in the amount of the savings. A savings and loan association is an example of a typical financial

---

[1] There is another option. If we owe back debts, we could employ the surplus funds to pay off those debts.

intermediary, and a savings deposit is an example of a claim on an intermediary. Claims on intermediaries are sometimes called *indirect* or *secondary* claims; you will see the reason for this in a moment.

The financial intermediaries use the funds they acquire to make loans to businesses and households, to purchase bonds, and so forth. In doing so, the intermediaries are actually lending out the savings they accept from individual surplus units while also appraising and diversifying the risk associated with lending directly to the deficit unit. Because they specialize in this kind of work, it is reasonable to presume that they know what they are doing and, on average, do a better job than individual surplus units could do.

An additional factor which helps explain why surplus units often entrust their funds to financial intermediaries is that the secondary claims (or indirect claims) offered by intermediaries are often more attractive (have more desirable characteristics or attributes) to many surplus units than are the primary (or direct) claims available in financial markets. One reason is that, in many cases, the secondary claims of intermediaries are insured by an agency of the federal government;[1] therefore less risk of default is associated with holding a secondary claim than a primary claim. Another reason for the attractiveness of secondary claims is that their *liquidity* is often greater than that associated with primary claims. "Liquidity" refers to how easy or difficult it is to exchange a financial claim for cash. Different types of claims possess varying degrees of liquidity. A claim easily exchanged for cash, such as a savings deposit, is highly liquid; a claim not easily exchanged for cash (where "easily" is defined in terms of the time and cost involved in exchange) is illiquid.

Suppose you lent funds directly to a small, obscure corporation and the loan's term of maturity (the time from when you gave them the funds until they must pay back the principal) was two years. You have their IOU in the form of a loan contract and they have your surplus funds. What would happen if, after one year, you suddenly needed the funds back for some emergency expenditure? One possibility would be to ask the corporation to pay you back at once, before the due date (final maturity) of the loan. If this option is closed because the borrower is unwilling or unable to pay off the loan immediately, you might try to sell the claim on the borrower to someone else who is willing to hold the claim until maturity. While organized markets do exist for the trading (buying and selling) of certain types of *ex-*

---

[1] The government agencies (such as the Federal Deposit Insurance Corporation) enable the public to feel confident that funds on deposit at a bank, for example, are safe. If the bank fails, the FDIC will step in and pay off the depositors. When financial institutions were failing daily during the Great Depression (beginning in 1929), the government became convinced that there was a pressing need for such agencies. The idea of having the government insure primary claims issued by, say, corporations has been discussed from time to time but rarely implemented. (There are exceptions: during the 1970s the United States government agreed, in effect, to insure the debt of the Lockheed Corporation.) In general, such suggestions are viewed as a threat to private enterprise and an unwarranted expansion of government's role.

isting financial claims (corporate bonds, for example), such markets do not exist for all types of claims. The hassle associated with unloading the loan contract in a time of crisis should be obvious. Given its illiquidity, exchanging such a financial claim for cash might involve considerable time, costs, or both. To avoid such inconvenience, many surplus units would prefer to hold claims on financial intermediaries.

1-4
MORE ON FINANCIAL INTERMEDIARIES

There are many types of financial intermediaries that surplus units can choose from, and the menu of secondary claims is quite varied. Surplus units primarily interested in liquidity and safety might prefer to hold claims on banks, credit unions, and similar types of financial institutions. Some intermediaries offer specialized claims. For example, insurance companies offer financial protection against early death (life companies) or property losses (casualty companies), while pension plans provide financial protection for one's old age. All these specialized intermediaries collect savings in the form of premium payments or contributions from those who participate in the plans. Each intermediary then uses the funds acquired to purchase a variety of primary claims.

Within the financial sector, there is one type of financial intermediary which requires our special attention—the commercial bank. In fact, financial intermediaries are usually broken down into two groups: *banks*, a category occupied solely by commercial banks; and *nonbank* financial intermediaries, comprising every other type.[1] There are many important reasons for the special attention given to commercial banks. To begin with, they are by far the largest type of intermediary. They also provide about three-quarters of the nation's money supply. In particular, commercial banks provide demand deposits, more commonly called checking accounts, which represent the main component of the money supply. Since one of our main objectives is to understand the nature and role of money in our economy and commercial banks provide the most important component of the money supply, we will focus on the behavior of commercial banks and the process of intermediation in order to learn how these lead to increases or decreases in the money supply. By examining how money is provided, what it costs to obtain money when we need it, and what we can earn when we have enough of it to lend out, we will learn much about how money and the financial system affect the economic well-being of households, businesses, governments, and foreigners.

---

[1] This nomenclature is sometimes confusing for a student. In everyday language, the term "banks" refers to commercial banks as well as savings and loan associations and mutual savings banks. This usage is to be resisted, however, since these intermediaries do differ from one another. In this text and in financial writing generally, "banks" mean commercial banks only.

1-5
WHERE DOES THE
FEDERAL RESERVE FIT IN?

The way in which commercial banks serve as intermediaries and affect the money supply is greatly influenced by the Federal Reserve System. The Federal Reserve System is a quasi-independent government agency that serves as our nation's central bank. The "Fed," as we will affectionately refer to it, indirectly controls the behavior of commercial banks through its influence on interest rates and bank reserves. For now, think of bank reserves as the essential input for banks—as gasoline is for a car. Without reserves, the banking system cannot operate.

The Fed can affect commercial bank reserves, which directly affect demand deposits and, in turn, the money supply. This influence on commercial bank reserves spreads through a number of channels to other nonbank financial intermediaries (such as savings and loan associations and credit unions), and more generally to the transfer of funds from surplus units to deficit units. Figure 1-3 pulls together our discussion to this point. Surplus units lend funds; they can acquire indirect (secondary) claims from financial intermediaries or they can acquire direct (primary) claims in financial markets. Deficit units borrow funds by issuing claims in financial markets

FIGURE 1-3

The financial system in more detail.

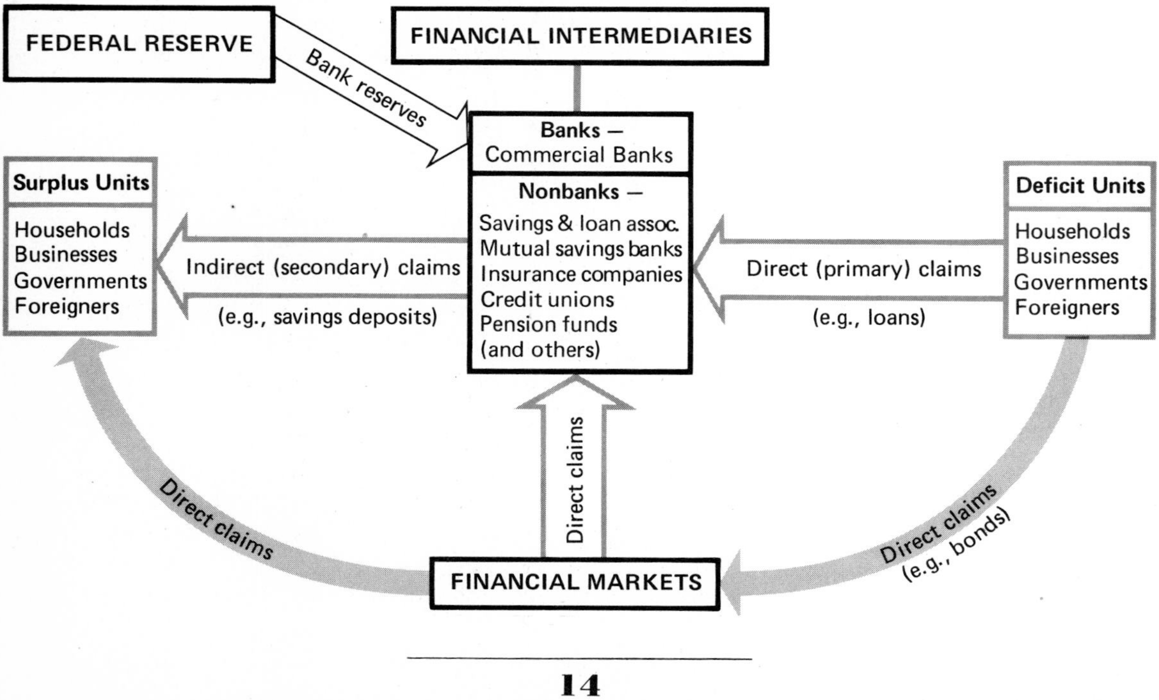

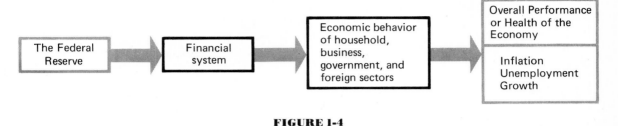

FIGURE 1-4

How the Fed fits in.

or to financial intermediaries. Individual units (for example, individual households or businesses) within sectors can be surplus units or deficit units, and financial intermediaries can deal in the financial markets. Monitoring and reacting to all this activity is the Fed.

By affecting interest rates and the volume of funds transferred from surplus to deficit units, the Fed can influence the level of total aggregate demand in the economy and, hence, spending and saving and the overall health of the economy. A general representation of this relationship is shown in Figure 1-4. The middle of this figure represents the essential anatomy or structure of the economy. The task before us is to learn how each part of it operates and how the collective activity of the parts is affected by monetary policy.

1-6
LOOKING AHEAD AND LOOKING BACK

In Parts I through IV of this text (Chapters 1 through 16), we will study how our economy and financial system work, with special emphasis on the *financial* side of spending and saving decisions. In particular, we want to identify the factors affecting decisions to save, lend, and borrow and to see how these decisions affect the health and performance of the economy. In Part V we will study the policymakers. They are the doctors who look at the health indicators to determine the current condition of our economy. We need to understand the cures or tools (i.e., alternative policy actions) that are available to the doctors and to understand what their effects on the patient may be. It is in Part V that we graduate from anatomy to the study of diagnostic and prescriptive medicine.

Unfortunately, cures for all the economic ills we may encounter are not known. The 1970s have vividly demonstrated this, since the remedies that have been tried have not worked very well. The rate of inflation has averaged about 7 percent in the 1970s as compared with 2½ percent in the 1960s; the rate of unemployment has averaged 6¼ percent in the 1970s as compared with only 4¾ percent in the 1960s. While this illness is apparently chronic, we do not believe that it is terminal.[1] A fair question, however, is "Why does it persist?" The complex answers are tackled in Part V; they fall into three possible areas. First, the illness might persist because the diagnosticians fail to understand *all* its causes. What this really means is that we do not understand enough about how the economy functions. Second, the policymakers tend to be reluctant to use the currently known medicines to cure the patient, most probably because of the undesirable side effects associated with particular remedies. They may, in fact, see the side effects as being worse than the disease. Third, the illness may not be curable as yet, so that more research will be needed to find a useful therapeutic approach.

Thus far we have assumed that the illness can only be cured by the doctors and their medicines. But could the patient get better by itself? And what about possible malpractice?

Prior to the Great Depression, many economists tended to see the economy as inherently stable, having strong self-correcting tendencies. The prevailing belief was that the economy would never shift away from full-employment *equilibrium* for long.

> ***Equilibrium*** **is a concept used by economists to help analyze the economy. It refers to a state of the economy from which there is no tendency to deviate—a state of rest. Of course, in reality, the economy is constantly being bombarded with disturbances and is hardly ever "at rest." The concept of equilibrium, then, is an analytic device which helps us sort out the influences of many different factors which, in the real world, are often all changing at the same time.**

Any disturbance or shock which pushed the economy away from full employment would automatically set in motion forces tending to move the economy back to full-employment equilibrium.

Before the Depression, it was felt that there was no need for corrective government action when the economy was disturbed—that any movement away from equilibrium would be temporary and self-correcting. This view of the economy, depicted by the pendulum in Figure 1-5, provided an economic rationale for the government to pursue a laissez faire, hands-off policy (or nonpolicy).

---

[1] There are some economists, most particularly those of the Marxist school, who do indeed believe that the illness is terminal and that capitalism will, in one way or another, totally collapse. Then, they maintain, society will eventually regroup around a socialist system.

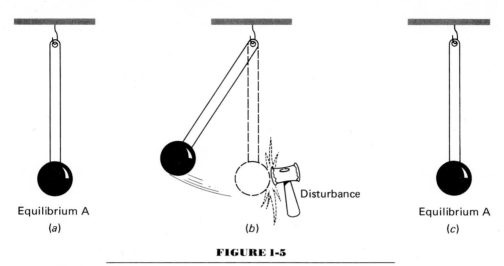

FIGURE 1-5

Predepression view of the economy. Visualize a pendulum hanging at rest from a hook on the ceiling (*a*). Now suppose someone comes along and disturbs the pendulum—hits it with a sledgehammer (*b*). It will swing back and forth (that is, it will oscillate), but the forces of gravity will cause it eventually to come to rest—return to equilibrium—at exactly the same place as it was before it was disturbed (*c*).

The Great Depression altered this view of the economy's internal dynamics. Between 1929 and 1933, the unemployment rate increased from about 3 percent to about 25 percent. Few could argue, in the face of such evidence, that the problem was correcting itself. The work of John Maynard Keynes, Michael Kalecki, and others suggested that once the economy's full-employment equilibrium was disturbed, its self-correcting powers were likely to be overwhelmed by other forces. The net result, depicted in Figure 1-6, would be that the economy could settle at a new "equilibrium" well below full employment.

This new perspective gave the government an economic rationale for attempting to stabilize overall economic activity. A consensus was forming that a highly developed market economy, if left to itself, would be highly unstable. As a result, stabilization policy has been practiced by both Democratic and Republican administrations since the mid-1930s. Until recently, there has been relatively little debate as to whether or not the government should intervene. Rather, the debate has been when, how, and to what degree the government should use its policies to help reestablish the economy's full-employment, low-inflation equilibrium.

It would be fair to say that the economy's performance in the 1970s has given rise to doubts about the government's ability to stabilize the economy. Does the government know precisely how to proceed in trying to restore

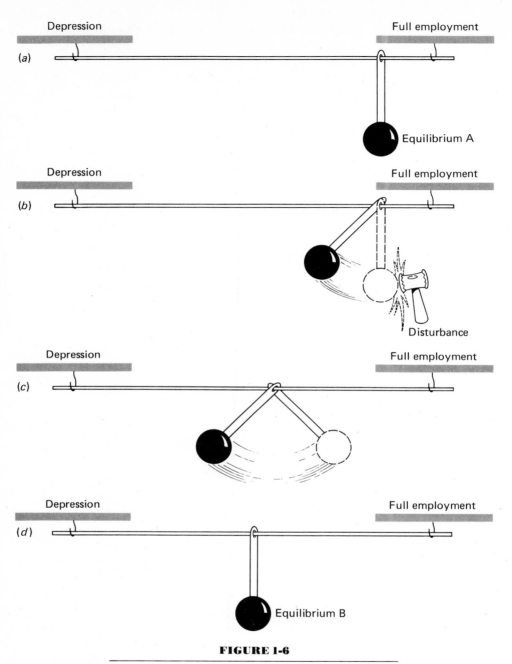

FIGURE I-6

Postdepression view of the economy. Now visualize a pendulum as hanging from a thin rod hung between two hooks—one hook representing full employment and the other hook representing depression (a). If the pendulum is at the full-employment hook and is disturbed (the sledgehammer again), two things will occur: it will begin to move to and fro (oscillate) as before (b) and it will be displaced along the rod (c)—that is, the point from which it hangs will move away from the full-employment hook. The result will be that when the pendulum settles back down, it will be in an equilibrium position somewhere along the rod between the two hooks (d).

the patient's health? We will explore questions like this further in the next chapter, where we will examine in greater detail the significant role of money in the government's attempts to stabilize the economy.

1-7
SUMMARY OF MAJOR POINTS

1

Our central concern in this book is how money and the financial system function in the economy and affect the volume of economic activity.

2

The volume of economic activity includes the production of goods and services and the generation of income with which to purchase these goods and services.

3

Spending units that spend less than their current income are called *surplus units*. Spending units that spend more than their current income are called *deficit units*.

4

Financial markets and financial intermediaries channel funds from surplus units to deficit units.

5

Direct finance involves lending directly to deficit units. Indirect finance involves lending to a financial intermediary who, in turn, lends to a deficit unit.

6

Financial intermediaries exist because they perform certain functions that lenders or borrowers may be unwilling or unable to perform for themselves. For the lender, financial intermediaries furnish liquidity, safety, and the ability to diversify and appraise the creditworthiness of borrowers. Financial intermediaries can tailor loans to fit the needs of the borrowers; they can also furnish other financial services.

7

Banks are important among financial intermediaries because they issue to depositors claims that are called *demand deposits* (more popularly referred to as *checking-account balances*), which make up about 75 percent of the United States money supply.

8

The government agency responsible for controlling and regulating the financial system is the Federal Reserve System, popularly known as the "Fed."

9

The Fed affects the financial system through its influence on the supply of reserves available to commercial banks. The supply of reserves in turn influences the level of interest rates.

10

Government policy designed to stabilize the economy was not always considered necessary or desirable. The Great Depression, however, gave rise to a revolution in economic thinking which resulted in the pursuit of an active stabilization policy by the government. The poor performance of the economy in recent years has led some skeptics to question the skill of policymakers in administering their doses of economic medicine to the economy.

1-8
REVIEW QUESTIONS

1   Provide a short discussion or your definition of the following terms: investment, financial investment, surplus and deficit sectors and surplus and deficit units, direct versus indirect finance, risk of default, diversification, financial claims, intermediation, liquidity, equilibrium, stabilization policy.

2   Some people have money; some people need money. Explain how the financial system can allocate money from those who have it to those who need it.

3   Explain why many lenders and borrowers prefer indirect finance to direct finance.

4   Why are banks considered important in relation to other financial intermediaries?

5   In general, how does the Fed's behavior affect the overall health of the economy?

6   Make a list of questions you think this course might help you to answer. (Have your professor look them over.)

1-9
SUGGESTED READINGS

1 While we do not want to give too much help to our competition, it is sometimes useful to have another text to refer to from time to time if a particular point needs clarification. We would suggest *Money and Banking* by Dudley Luckett (New York: McGraw-Hill, 1980) and *Money, the Financial System and the Economy,* by George Kaufman (Chicago: Rand McNally, 1977).

2 If the material covered in the text is to come alive and make real sense to you, we suggest you try to read the *Wall Street Journal* and *Business Week* regularly. In fact, hardly a day goes by without a report on an issue that is in some way relevant to our subject. The importance of this cannot be overstated. You might also consult the *New York Times, Washington Post,* or the *Los Angeles Times;* all have good financial sections.

3 The Federal Reserve System pumps out thousands of pieces of data each month. Go to the library and thumb through the *Federal Reserve Bulletin.* A half-hour investment here will reveal the types of data collected and distributed (contained in the second half of the *Bulletin*) and the range of issues the Fed concerns itself with (contained in the first half).

4 For further discussion of the circular flow of income and money, see Campbell McConnell, *Economics* (New York: McGraw-Hill, 1978), chap. 3; and Paul Nadler, *Commercial Banking and the Economy* (New York: Random House, 1979), chap. 1.

THE ROLE OF MONEY

Certainly there are lots of things in life that
money won't buy, but it's very funny—Have
you ever tried to buy them without money?

Ogden Nash

2-1
FIRST FIDDLE OR SECOND FIDDLE?

Economists do not agree on precisely how money affects the economy.
Some economists believe that money matters more than anything else in determining the overall health of the economy; they are appropriately called
monetarists.[1] Others believe that money is only one among many factors affecting the economy.[2]

---

[1] Milton Friedman, now retired from the University of Chicago; Karl Brunner of the University
of Rochester; and Allan Meltzer of Carnegie-Mellon University are usually viewed as the leading
spokesmen for the monetarists.

[2] Such economists carry various labels—nonmonetarist, Keynesian, neo-Keynesian, post-
Keynesian, and so forth. Just as with beer, there is often something to be gained by differentiating
one's product from that of the competition! Prominent economists frequently viewed as marching
under one of these banners include Paul Samuelson (MIT), Franco Modigliani (MIT), James Tobin
(Yale), Arthur Okun (The Brookings Institution), Paul Davidson (Rutgers), Sidney Weintraub
(Penn), Robert Clower (UCLA), and many others. We listed these names in this and the previous
note to encourage you to read articles (in newspapers or magazines) written by or referring to such
economists so that you will develop some appreciation for various alternative points of view.

This controversy is somewhat like trying to determine whether or not the coach is the key to a team's success. Some will argue that the team won in spite of poor coaching, while others will attribute the team's triumphs to the insight and intelligence of the coach. It is difficult to resolve such debates. The only evidence to go by is the team's record. A team that continues to win over a number of years, even though its talent has varied noticeably, will convince even skeptics that the coach was responsible for its successful record.

The controversy over the role of money in the economy is similar. Although not everyone agrees on exactly how and to what degree money matters, no one disputes the contention that money has an important influence on spending, production, inflation, and unemployment.

2-2
DEFINING MONEY

Understanding *how* money matters will be quite difficult unless we are clear on *what money is* and what, in fact, serves as money. Economists define money in terms of its specific function within the financial system—that is, by what it does. By specifying precisely what it does, we should be able to distinguish money from everything else we observe in the financial system, even those things which at first glance appear quite similar. We are most interested in what, if anything, makes money unique; what does it do that other things do not?

> The primary function of *money*, and the function which distinguishes it from all else in the financial system, is that it *serves as a generally acceptable means of payment (or medium of exchange)*.
>
> Money represents immediate purchasing power. It represents a direct, general *claim* on goods, services, bonds, and so forth, which can be exercised on demand.

The importance of money's function as a means of payment is so obvious that it is often overlooked. Imagine a world where all material things were exchanged by barter—that is, by trading goods for goods. If you worked in a steel factory, you might be paid in slabs of steel, which would not only be extremely difficult to exchange for other goods or services but also rather cumbersome to carry around. To buy groceries, for example, you would have to persuade the grocer to accept your slabs of steel for payment. Certainly, there would be no reason for the grocer to do so unless he or she had a use for them or knew someone else who did and would therefore be willing to accept the steel in exchange for something the grocer wanted. Since uncovering such *coincidences of wants* would be extremely difficult, exchange under a barter system would be costly in terms of search time—that is, in terms of time spent looking for someone who has groceries *and* wants slabs of steel—and it would clearly be cumbersome and inefficient for virtually all goods. Because of these costs of barter, the volume of exchange in the economy would be considerably less than with money as the medium of exchange.

There is something else about barter that would make the total volume of exchange less than with money. With barter, families would need to produce most, if not all, the products they consumed. For example, instead of shopping in grocery stores and supermarkets, millions of people would all be on their own farms producing the food they needed. Without a coincidence of wants, everyone, independently, would have to produce the things they needed. The result: an economy involving very little exchange.

Fortunately, all this is not necessary since we do have something that serves as a medium of exchange: money. People can exchange goods for money and money for goods.

Something which becomes acceptable as a means of payment in exchange for goods and services will also function as a *store of value*.[1] Money must serve as a store of value or purchasing power because people receive money and spend it at different times.[2] If, today, you are paid for the sale of your labor and do not need to purchase anything until tomorrow, you would presumably be unwilling to accept in payment anything that is likely to decline in value before you spend it. Thus it is necessary for anything which functions as money to store value; general acceptability of a means of payment depends on the population's confidence in its ability to store value. Hence, people will accept something as a means of payment in exchange for goods when they believe that they can easily exchange it for something else of like value in the near future.

For monetary exchange to proceed in an orderly fashion, there must be some method of specifying the quantity of money required to pay for a given quantity of a particular good. In other words, there is a need for an accounting unit, commonly referred to as a *unit of account*. Because all prices and financial records in the United States are expressed in dollars, the dollar serves as the monetary unit of account—that is, the measure of value. Thus the grocer and the steel worker can keep records of their transactions in terms of dollars. The grocer can add up the dollar value of various goods

---

[1] As we shall see more clearly later on in this chapter, many things in our economy store value. Thus storing value is not unique to money and does not differentiate it from all else in the economy; that is, storing value does not differentiate money from other financial assets which store value.
[2] That is, there is a difference between the time pattern of people's money receipts and expenditures.

sold to get total receipts, add up the dollar value of various expenses to get total expenses, and calculate the difference as the dollar value of net income. A unit of account makes it possible for transactors across the economy to keep records and compare the relative values of different goods and services.[1]

Whatever circulates in a modern economy as a generally acceptable means of payment will also function as a store of value, and its unit of measurement will naturally become the accounting unit and measure of value.

2-3
HOW MONEY RELATES TO
OTHER FINANCIAL CLAIMS

Money is a *direct*, general financial claim on goods and services—a claim that can be exercised on demand. Other types of financial claims (for example, bonds or loan contracts) are, in effect, claims on money. As a result, financial claims other than money are *indirect* claims on goods and services. Indirect claims represent potential purchasing power; these claims must first be converted into money before that purchasing power can be exercised.

In Chapter 1 we saw that surplus units usually lend their surplus to the deficit units through the financial system (financial markets and financial intermediaries). Put another way, *purchasing power* is transferred from those who have it to those who need it. What is transferred, in fact, is money in exchange for another financial asset which is a *future claim* on money. In effect, the surplus units "rent out" their surplus money to deficit units for a given period of time, much as a landlord rents out an apartment. The landlord gets a lease—that is, a written promise by the renter to return the premises in good shape at the termination of the lease contract and to pay a monthly rental fee for the use of the apartment—and the renter gets the use of the premises. In the financial world, the lender (surplus unit) acquires a financial asset, which is a claim or IOU issued by a deficit unit. This asset (which may or may not be in the form of a written contract) is analogous to the lease. Suppose you agree to make a loan directly to a friend. Your friend, the borrower, will agree to return the funds borrowed at some future time and to pay you some "rent" or *interest*. In effect, you use your surplus funds to buy a financial claim, which is an asset for you and a liability for the borrower; in return, your friend gets to use your funds for a specified period of time. In the future, when the term of the loan ends, your friend will repay the original amount borrowed (the principal) and, in effect, buy back (or redeem) the claim (IOU) you have been holding. Assuming that your friend is trustworthy and does not skip town (that is, does not default),

---

[1] To appreciate why it is convenient to have a standardized unit of account, imagine the poor grocer and the customers who would have to remember that one slab of steel equals two sacks of flour, one crate of oranges equals 4 quarts of milk, and so forth.

you now have back your surplus money plus interest and can spend it on goods and services or lend it out again.

Financial claims other than money are issued (supplied or sold) by deficit units or financial intermediaries. The latter issue claims on themselves and then, in turn, lend to deficit units. Financial claims are acquired by lenders with surplus funds who want to store and "rent out" purchasing power until some future date. Surplus units can also store value by holding money. However, the interest available (that is, the rent to be earned) by holding other types of financial claims makes holding money a relatively unattractive way of storing value. There are many different types of financial claims, reflecting the wide variety of borrowers and lenders and the tendency to tailor particular types of claims to match the preferences and needs of the surplus and deficit units. Since all financial claims are claims on money, they can in some sense be compared with one another as well as with money. One traditional standard of comparison is the liquidity of various claims, a concept discussed briefly in Chapter 1.

> The *liquidity* of a financial claim (or asset) is determined by how easy or difficult it is to convert the claim (or asset) into money. Liquidity has two dimensions: the *cost* and the *time* associated with converting the claim (or asset) into money. If the costs are high and/or it takes considerable time to convert a particular type of asset to money, it is usually referred to as "illiquid." As the costs and time required to exchange a particular asset approach zero, the liquidity of an asset increases.

By definition, money is at one end of the liquidity spectrum, representing perfect liquidity.[1] At the other end of the spectrum might be real estate, which is a rather illiquid asset. For example, suppose you owned a house and you wished to sell it immediately for cash. On the basis of other recent sales of similar houses in the neighborhood, your house appears to have an approximate market value of $70,000. To turn your house into cash in a single day would be quite difficult and probably costly. For one thing, you would be quite unlikely, in only a day, to find a buyer willing to pay the market price. Instead, you would probably have to contact a real estate

---

[1] D. H. Robertson, an eminent British economist, points out in his book, *Money* (Chicago: University of Chicago Press, 1957) p. 2, n. 1, that during the middle of the nineteenth century coal miners' wages in Staffordshire were paid partly in beer! Commenting on this practice, Charles Fay, a historian, remarked: "This currency was very popular and highly liquid, but it was issued to excess and difficult to store" (*Life and Labour in the Nineteenth Century*, Cambridge: Cambridge University Press, 1920), p. 197.

broker who would try to locate a willing and able buyer; then mortgage financing would have to be arranged; and you would also have to get a lawyer to attest to the validity of the current title to the house, to prepare the necessary papers, and so forth. All this takes time. Presumably the time could be cut if you were willing to pay the lawyer and others something extra to speed things along, but this would increase the costs of *liquidating* the asset—that is, converting it to money. You could cut the price by $10,000 in the hope that this would attract a buyer more quickly. But then you would suffer a *capital loss*—another cost often associated with liquidating an illiquid asset.[1] Clearly, real estate is not a liquid asset, since the time and costs associated with converting it to cash are often significant.

Different types of financial assets (claims) have different degrees of liquidity. In Chapter 12, we will find out that the liquidity associated with many individual claims (such as municipal bonds, corporate bonds, and Treasury bills) depends very much on the organization of the market in which the claims are traded.

In general, liquidity and the whole process of monetary exchange—that is, the exchange of financial assets, goods and services, or factors of production for money—will depend on the nature and efficiency of our payments mechanism and financial system. Accordingly, the ongoing evolution of this payments mechanism, our financial system, and what, in fact, functions as money in the United States is the next item on our agenda.

2-4
THE ONGOING EVOLUTION OF MONEY, THE FINANCIAL SYSTEM, AND THE PAYMENTS MECHANISM

The payments mechanism is the means by which transactions are consummated—that is, how money (purchasing power) is transferred among transactors. As we have pointed out, a monetary system offers great advantages over a system of barter. However, our payments mechanism has not always functioned as it does now. Like the human race, it has evolved from a very primitive state and will continue to evolve in the future. For example, things that, in the distant past, once functioned as money—such as beads among the American Indians and gold and silver coins among the colonists—are no longer generally acceptable as means of payment and therefore are not money today. Similarly, things that function as money today may not be a generally acceptable means of payment in the future. The point is that whatever functions as a means of payment is money, and these things tend to change over time. This tendency to change

---

[1] A *capital loss* results when the price at which one purchases an asset exceeds the price at which the asset is subsequently sold. A *capital gain* results when the subsequent selling price exceeds the original purchase price.

also applies to the technology used to consummate transactions; presumably, it will evolve and improve.

If someone asked you what made up the United States money supply, you would probably answer currency (consisting of coin and paper currency issued by the government) and demand deposits at commercial banks (more commonly referred to as checking accounts). These deposits are payable on demand to third parties (the first two parties are you and the bank); the check you give somebody in payment for, say, goods is an order for the bank to debit (subtract) a certain number of dollars from your deposit account and to credit (add) these dollars to the demand deposit of the third party who sold you the goods. Thus, a demand deposit is a means of payment and the check is a means of transferring ownership of the deposit among parties to a transaction.

Ongoing technological innovations may soon make checks obsolete as a means of transferring purchasing power. In the most widely discussed innovation, the *electronic funds transfer systems* (EFTS for short), payments (transfers of purchasing power) are made to a third party in response to *electronic* instructions rather than instructions written on a paper check. To pay your grocery bill, for instance, your account would be debited by the amount of your bill, and the grocer's account would be credited by the same amount at the time of the exchange. The whole system would be computerized, so that no written checks would be necessary. All you would need would be an account number and a *debit card*, which you would present to the grocer. The grocer, in turn, would enter the prices of your purchases into a computer terminal, and you, at the end of the month, would receive a statement giving your current balance and a record of all the charges and deposits in your account. This would be just like a checking account statement, but you would not have to write all those checks. Currently, many employers, in cooperation with banks, pay salaries by automatically crediting their employees' bank accounts rather than by issuing the customary weekly or monthly check. This is a form of EFTS.

Basically, EFTS is nothing more than the application of available modern computer and communication technology to the entire area of financial transactions and services. Its aim is to reduce the physical handling of an ever-expanding volume of paper checks as well as to provide increased convenience and services to the public. While the general public is not yet using EFTS widely, it is used in various forms by some international, national, and regional payment networks.[1]

Historically, commercial banks had been at the center of the payments mechanism because they were the only financial intermediaries permitted to offer demand deposits to the public. Such deposits represent claims on banks—that is, they are liabilities for the banks and assets to the deposit

---

[1] EFTS does not eliminate the need for deposit accounts; they are merely a more efficient way of transferring funds from one deposit account to another. Selected readings on EFTS are provided at the end of Chapter 2.

holders.[1] Since 1972, however, there have been a number of innovations in the financial system which have allowed institutions other than commercial banks to offer what are, in effect, interest-bearing demand deposits. Let us take a brief look at some of these innovations.

NOW ACCOUNTS

Since 1972 in Massachusetts and New Hampshire and since 1976 in the rest of New England (Maine, Vermont, Rhode Island, and Connecticut), there has been a payable-on-demand account called a NOW account—an acronym for *negotiable order of withdrawal*. These accounts allow the customer to withdraw or transfer funds by writing a negotiable order of withdrawal payable to a third party. The maximum interest rate payable is 5 percent (at this writing), and NOW accounts can be offered by commercial banks, mutual savings banks, and savings and loan associations. Since NOW accounts are limited to New England and New York and by law can only be held by households, NOW account deposits are not yet very large by comparison with demand deposits. (At the end of 1978, NOW accounts totaled $3.8 billion, while demand deposits totaled $272 billion.) If, however, NOW accounts are legalized nationwide as the result of several pending bills in Congress, then they would become a much more significant part of the nation's money supply.

CREDIT UNION SHARE DRAFTS

Beginning in August 1974, credit unions in some states were permitted to offer their customers share drafts to transfer funds from their accounts to third parties. By the beginning of 1978, virtually all credit unions could offer this service to customers. Share drafts are simply checklike instruments written against accounts that are interest-bearing. Thus they operate very much like NOW accounts. As of the end of 1978, share draft accounts amounted to only $700 million.

THRIFT INSTITUTION CHECKING ACCOUNTS

In some states, thrift institutions (savings and loan associations and mutual savings banks) have been granted the authority to offer non-interest-bearing checking accounts. These, too, are relatively small, amounting to $950 million at the end of 1978.

All these innovations were, to some extent, prompted by the economic environment and the increasingly competitive relationships among the various types of financial intermediaries (banks and nonbanks). We shall postpone a more detailed discussion of these changing relationships and their implications until Chapters 8 and 11. However, it is important to recognize that these innovations are relatively small in volume at present;

---

[1] Such deposits are fully negotiable in that the holder need not seek the banks' permission to transfer the funds to a third party.

therefore, most of the United States money supply is still made up of currency plus demand deposits at commercial banks.

FINANCIAL INNOVATION AND
THE MONETARY AGGREGATES

Among the jobs carried out by the Federal Reserve is the collection of data measuring a number of important monetary variables. In fact, the Fed regularly publishes data on several different monetary measures, usually referred to as *monetary aggregates* (that is, collections of financial or monetary assets). Figure 2-1 shows the composition of M1, M2, and M3, the monetary aggregate measures most frequently mentioned in discussions of monetary policy. These aggregates, which we will explain in a moment, comprise several different types of financial assets, some of which are currently money. That is, some serve as means of payment (currency and demand deposits), some are clearly not money (time deposits at banks and thrift institutions), and some are already or are on the verge of becoming

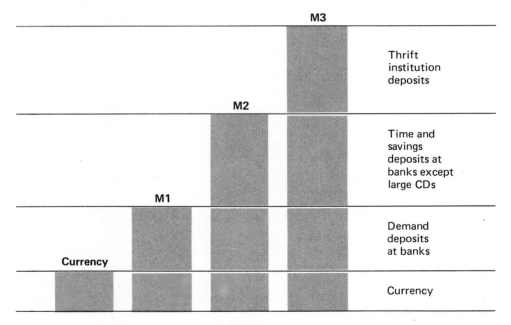

FIGURE 2-1

Composition of various monetary aggregates. M1 = currency plus demand deposits at banks. M2 = M1 plus time and savings deposits at banks (negotiable certificates of deposits over $100,000—called large CDs—at the large banks are excluded). M3 = M2 plus all deposits at thrift institutions (savings and loan associations, mutual savings banks, and credit unions).

money (savings deposits at banks and thrift institutions). As of this writing, customers of banks and thrift institutions are permitted to make payments from their savings accounts by calling the intermediary and instructing it to debit their account and credit the account of the payee. To the very limited extent that such "telephone transfers" (also a form of EFTS) have thus far been used to mediate exchanges, savings deposits are functioning as money. Along the same line, in 1978 the Fed permitted banks, on behalf of customers, to make *automatic transfers* from savings deposits to demand deposits to cover a customer's overdraft. In effect, this arrangement allows customers to earn interest on their money balances. If the bank were not to charge for such transfers, there would be no incentive for customers ever to hold a non-interest-bearing demand deposit balance (legislation passed in the mid-1930s prohibited the payment of interest on demand deposits). All funds would be held in interest-earning savings deposits until checks drawn on customers' demand deposits appeared. At that point, the banks would transfer the funds; the public would be earning interest on their money balances and savings deposits would be money. At the end of 1978, this automatic transfer service (ATS) was beginning to catch on; the Fed estimated that about $3 billion of the $220 billion of saving deposits held by banks were ATS accounts.

The definition of each monetary aggregate as of this writing is as follows: M1 = currency plus demand deposits at commercial banks; M2 = M1 plus time and savings deposits excluding large ($100,000 and over) negotiable certificates of deposit (CDs); M3 = M2 plus deposits at thrift institutions (savings and loan associations, mutual savings banks, and credit unions). The measure which currently corresponds most closely to our definition of money as developed above is M1, and this is the measure we shall have in mind throughout the text when we refer to "the money supply." All the components of M1 are means of payment. This is not true of M2 and M3; time deposits at banks and thrift institutions are not means of payment. The Fed recognizes that M1 does not contain all the means of payment in the economy. For example, NOW accounts (which clearly are means of payment) at banks are counted in the savings deposit component of M2 and NOW accounts at thrifts are part of the thrift deposit component of M3. Such inconsistencies have crept into the data over time because of the innovations mentioned above and the difficulty the Fed has encountered in getting timely data from the intermediaries it does not regulate directly, such as the thrifts. By the time you read this the Fed may have redefined M1—as well as the other monetary aggregates—to take account of changing institutional developments. In late 1978 the Fed invented M1+ (equal to M1 plus saving deposits at banks plus all "checkable" deposits at thrift institutions (such as NOW accounts and credit-union share drafts). Although more representative than M1 of the means of payment in the economy, this measure also has flaws; not all savings accounts at banks are functioning as a means of payment.

All this is not semantics or simply a problem in classification such as one might encounter in biology. As we will see in Chapter 19, the Fed in part guides its policy actions by what is happening to the money supply. To avoid error, the Fed will strive over time to improve measurement of the money supply. In the meantime, it is sensible for them to look at all the various available measures—recognizing that each is in some way flawed. But fear not! One thing you can be sure of is that our financial system will continue to evolve; therefore whatever serves as a means of payment will continue to change.

2-5
HOW MONEY MATTERS:
SOME FIRST PRINCIPLES

To get some feel for how money fits into the financial system and the rest of the economy, you will find it helpful to view money as an asset, such as an apartment house. Let us suppose that you wanted to understand what determined the rental fee of apartment units and the *quantity* of units produced and rented. One promising way to proceed would be to identify and analyze the factors affecting the *supply* of apartments produced by builders as well as the factors affecting the *demand* for apartments by renters. The analysis of money proceeds in a similar fashion. By identifying and analyzing the factors affecting the supply of and demand for money, we shall gain considerable knowledge of the determinants of the quantity of money supplied and demanded and the "rental rate," or interest rate, associated with borrowing or lending it.

The *interest rate* is the *cost* to borrowers of obtaining money and the *return* (or yield) on money to lenders. Thus, just as rent is the cost to apartment dwellers and the return to the owner when apartments are rented, the interest rate is the rental rate when money is borrowed or lent.

The demand for money by households, businesses, governments (federal, state, and local), and foreigners is primarily determined by their spending plans and thus by their need to pay for their spending. The supply of money will be shown to be determined primarily by reserves, which are regulated by the Fed, and the profit-maximizing behavior of commercial banks. The interaction between the supply of and demand for money will determine the quantity of money and "the interest rate."[1]

---

[1] As you are undoubtedly aware, there are many interest rates in the economy; so speaking of "the interest rate" as if there were only one is an obvious abstraction from reality. We shall limit the number of interest rates we discuss until Chapter 15, so as to keep our analysis as simple and tractable as possible. Once the fundamentals are developed, it will be much easier to extend our analysis to take account of the many different interest rates.

Changes in the supply of or demand for money will affect the interest rate just as changes in the supply of or demand for apartments will affect the rental fees of apartments. To illustrate the point, suppose that the Fed (through a stepped-up provision of reserves to banks) succeeded in increasing the supply of money relative to the demand. One would expect the *initial effect* of this action to be a fall in the interest rate.[1] The fall in interest rates—or reduction in the cost of borrowing—would probably encourage some spending units in the economy to borrow more money and use it to purchase more goods and services. More specifically, *the increase in the supply of money would lead to an increase in the demand for goods and services.* The increased demand for goods and services, given the supply, may lead to both an increase in goods and services produced (supplied) in the future and an increase in the general level of prices. (Even if you do not immediately see how this happens, trust us.) The rise in the general level of prices (that is, the average prices of all goods and services in the economy) represents a decline in the value of money.

The *value of money*, or its purchasing power, is equal to $1/P$, where $1 represents the face value of a dollar and P is the level of prices as expressed by a price index, say, the consumer price index.

You have probably heard people say the dollar is not worth very much today. Intuitively, you realize that the value of money is equal to the value of the goods and services it can buy. Over time, the value or purchasing power of money will change as the prices of goods and services change. Thus, if last year $1 bought 2 quarts of beer (50 cents per quart) and today it buys only 1 quart ($1 per quart), then the value of the dollar has halved. In general, the value of money and the price level of goods and services vary inversely; the higher the level of prices, the lower the value of money.

In general, changes in the supply of or demand for money will affect interest rates as well as the demand for goods and services in the economy. This, in turn, will affect the level of output, unemployment, and the general level of prices. The latter, of course, affect the value of money. We will see that the behavior of various spending units in the economy will be affected by the value (or purchasing power) of their money, the cost of borrowing to finance a deficit, and the return or yield on lending. The precise nature of these relationships is the subject of Parts II through IV of the text.

---

[1] Note that the analogy continues to hold: an increase in the supply of apartments, given demand, would be expected to result in a fall in rental fees.

Constructing a price index and calculating the rate of inflation.
The major price indexes in the United States—the consumer
price index and the wholesale price index—are computed and
published monthly. In general, a certain group of goods and services are selected—this is usually called the "market basket" of
goods and services—and each month the price of each item
around the country is surveyed. The hypothetical example in the
table below illustrates how the resulting index and the rate of
change in the index (that is, the rate of inflation or deflation) are
computed.

YEAR	NUMBER OF ITEMS IN MARKET BASKET	TOTAL COST OF GOODS IN BASKET	PRICE INDEX	RATE OF INFLATION
1980	10	$50	1.00	
1981	10	$52	1.04	4%
1982	10	$60	1.20	15.4%

The year 1980 is the base year in that prices in future years will be
compared to prices existing in 1980. Accordingly the price index
for 1980 is equal to 1.00. In 1981, the total cost of the goods in the
market basket rose to $52. To compute the index, the total cost in
1981 is divided by the total cost in the base year ($52/$50 = 1.04).
In their published form, the actual indexes are multiplied by
100; thus 1.04 would appear as 104. To compute the rate of inflation during 1981, the change in the price index for that year is divided by the price index for the previous year (4/100 = .04). This
is referred to as *annual rate of inflation of 4 percent.* See if you
can calculate and explain the next row.*

* Note that this is an annual inflation rate computed from
yearly data. To get the annual rate of inflation in any given
month, you take the change in the index in that month, divide it by the level of the index in the previous month, and
multiply by 12.

2-6
SUMMARY OF MAJOR POINTS

1

The primary function of money, and the function which makes it unique, is that it serves as a generally acceptable means of payment.

2

Something which becomes a generally acceptable means of payment will, of necessity, function as a store of value.

3

The unit of account in the United States is the dollar. It serves as a common denominator or standardized unit of measure in which all prices are quoted.

4

Money is a direct financial claim on goods and services. Other financial assets are claims on money; thus they represent indirect claims on goods and services.

5

The payments mechanism is the means used to transfer money among transactors. Checks, for example, transfer ownership of demand deposits. Innovations now being developed, such as electronic funds transfer systems (EFTS), will undoubtedly lead to changes in the payments mechanism over time.

6

The Fed publishes data on a number of monetary aggregates. While each suffers from some conceptual problems, M1 (currency plus demand deposits at banks) is the best measure of the money supply currently available.

7

The demand for money is determined by the behavior of households, firms, governments, and foreigners. The supply of money is primarily determined by the behavior of the Fed and commercial banks. Changes in the supply of and demand for money will affect the interest rate—the cost of borrowing and the return for lending.

8

Changes in the interest rate affect the demand for goods and services in the economy and, therefore, the level of output, unemployment and prices. The value (purchasing power) of money is inversely related to the level of prices.

2-7
REVIEW QUESTIONS

1   Discuss or define briefly the following terms or concepts: illiquidity, store of value, unit of account, means of payment, the interest rate, the value of money, electronic funds transfer systems, monetary aggregates, barter.

2   What are the functions of money? In what way is money similar to other financial assets? How can money be distinguished from other financial assets?

3   How does the Fed calculate M1, M2, and M3? Are these all money? Why or why not?

4   Credit cards are not money. Explain why.

5   What is the "payments mechanism"? What changes are occurring in this mechanism and how does this affect what actually serves as a means of payment in our economy?

6   Distinguish between the value of money and the cost or yield on money and then show how they relate to one another.

7   Explain how a price index, such as the consumer price index, is computed.

2-8
SUGGESTED READINGS

1   More information on the evolution of money—that is, the transition from barter to monetary exchange—may be found in Arthur Nussbaum, *A History of the Dollar* (New York: Columbia University Press, 1957) and John Kenneth Galbraith, *Money: From Whence It Came and Where It Went* (Boston: Houghton Mifflin, 1975). Students may find the latter especially entertaining and enlightening.

2   One of the most comprehensive reviews of monetary developments in the United States is contained in the monumental work by Milton Friedman and Anna Jacobson Schwartz, *A Monetary History of the United States, 1867–1960* (National Bureau of Economic Research, Princeton: Princeton University Press, 1963). While you should be aware of the monetarist slant in the way this book interprets various events, it should give you considerable background on a variety of issues discussed throughout our text. For example, we would highly recommend Friedman and Schwartz's discussion of the evolution of the Federal Reserve System in conjunction with our

Chapters 18 and 19; their discussion of the Great Depression could usefully be read now.

3   Considerable elaboration on EFTS can be found in the recent report of the National Commission on EFTS, *EFT in the United States: Policy Recommendations and the Public Interest* (Washington, D.C., 1977). You might also consult the *Annual Report* of the Federal Reserve Bank of Cleveland for 1977, which reviews the growth of EFTS.

4   The Fed releases data on the monetary aggregates each Thursday night. Start reading the Friday edition of *The Wall Street Journal* (or the financial page of another leading newspaper) to become familiar with the ways in which these data are analyzed.

5   There are twelve Federal Reserve Banks within the Federal Reserve System. They are located in Boston, New York, Philadelphia, Cleveland, Chicago, Minneapolis, St. Louis, Kansas City, San Francisco, Dallas, Atlanta, and Richmond. Most publish a monthly, bimonthly, or quarterly document which reviews recent economic and financial developments and also analyzes key issues affecting money and the financial system. These publications are among the most readable, informative sources you can find anywhere. Your library should have current and past issues. You can receive future copies free simply by writing to the public information department at any of these banks and asking to be put on the mailing list.

6   For a lucid discussion of recent financial innovations and how they may affect the Fed's monetary aggregate measures, see Thomas Simpson, "Redefining the Monetary Aggregates," *Federal Reserve Bulletin* (January 1979), 13–42.

3

A FRAMEWORK FOR FINANCIAL ANALYSIS

Money may not buy friends but it certainly
gives you a better class of enemies.

Metropolis News (Illinois)

3-1
THE TREES VERSUS THE FOREST

There is a constant danger that you will find the details of the analysis to
follow overwhelming. This would be unfortunate for it might obscure the
broader story we are trying to weave. The problem is akin to getting lost in a
forest; by paying too much attention to the individual trees you become dis-
oriented and lose your way, forgetting where you came from and where you
are going.

The purpose of Chapters 1 and 2 was to introduce the roles money and
the financial system play in the American economy. Of particular importance were the circular flow diagrams (Figures 1-1 and 1-2), the figure on
monetary policy (Figure 1-3), and the accompanying discussion, which provided an overall view of how the sectors of the economy, the financial
system, and the policymakers fit together. Prepared by that general back-

ground, we can now begin to develop some methods of analysis and conceptual issues common to most sectors operating in the financial system. We will develop a general framework for financial analysis that will guide our more detailed inquiry into the behavior of various sectors in coming chapters. However, in economics, as in other disciplines, we do not yet have all the answers to the problems that plague us. Nevertheless, by asking the right questions and knowing how to apply a general mode of analysis to a particular problem, you will often find yourself on the path toward the correct solution. If, despite our best efforts, you still become lost, call the chairman of the Federal Reserve System—try collect—and ask for directions.

Let us begin with some key concepts.

3-2
SOME KEY CONCEPTS

Individual spending units (or economic units) in the economy—that is, individual firms, households, organizations, financial intermediaries, or government agencies—will *over time* receive and spend income. For example, a household may receive a salary of $1500 each month and then use all or part of it to purchase goods and services.[1] At any particular *moment* in time, the household will probably own an automobile, a house, a savings deposit, and so forth, and it will also have some debts. This collection of assets and liabilities is called a *portfolio*. It is composed of *real assets* such as autos, houses, and washing machines; *financial assets* such as money, bonds, and time deposits; and *financial liabilities* such as mortgage, auto, and education loans.

The budding accountants among you will immediately recognize that the portfolio is analogous to the *balance sheet*. A balance sheet for a household would measure the *monetary value* of its *stock* of assets, liabilities, and net worth at a specific time (say, the last day of a year).[2] It represents a snapshot of the household's portfolio at that particular moment. In this text, we shall be primarily concerned with what happens between snapshots—that is, how and why the size and composition of the spending unit's balance sheet or portfolio changes from one time to another. For example, if the value of a household's real asset holdings at the end of 1981 is $50,000 and it was only $40,000 at the end of 1980, we would want to know what accounted for the increase. More specifically, how did the real assets increase? Was the increase attributable to spending current income, borrowing (a rise in lia-

---

[1] For consistency, we shall use households throughout most of the chapter for our examples.
[2] The fundamental balance-sheet identity is that assets A equal liabilities L plus net worth NW. Rearranging, $NW = A - L$. If each dollar of assets is matched by a dollar of liabilities, net worth is zero; if the value of liabilities exceeds the value of assets, call the bankruptcy lawyer.

bilities), liquidating financial assets (selling bonds), or realizing capital gains (a rise in the value or price) on particular assets held (such as a house)?

In general (if we ignore capital gains and losses), changes in the composition of portfolios over time reflect decisions by economic units to spend, save, or borrow. We want to know how these *portfolio decisions* affect and are affected by developments in the financial system and the rest of the economy.

It is important to understand that a portfolio is a *stock* concept—it measures the value of assets and liabilities held at a particular moment. In contrast, consumption spending, saving, investment spending, income, borrowing, and so on are *flows*—they are variables measured over an *interval* of time. To illustrate, the value of your real assets would be a stock concept—it could be measured only at a moment in time ($63,542.66 at 3 a.m., November 11, 1980, for example). On the other hand, your earnings last year (income) is a flow concept because it is a magnitude that can have meaning only if it is measured over an interval of time ($50 a day, $250 a week, $1000 a month, $12,000 a year).

If we are interested in changes in portfolios over time, it follows that we should focus our attention on flows, since *changes in stocks occur because of flows*. Some examples will illustrate this point: investment is a flow which adds to the stock of plant and equipment held by firms; household spending on autos, furniture, appliances, and so on (typically referred to as "consumer durable goods") represents consumption—a flow which adds to the stock of real assets held; the stock of federal debt outstanding will rise when the flow of federal expenditures exceeds the flow of federal receipts (the federal deficit is a flow).

The relationship between stocks and flows, which is akin to the relationship between the balance sheet and income statement in accounting parlance,[1] is one of the basic building blocks in our study of economic behavior. In general, it is assumed that economic units adjust their spending (consumption and investment, for example), saving, and borrowing—that is, their flows—to bring their actual portfolios into line with their desired portfolios (stocks).

---

[1] The *income statement* is a summary of a unit's receipts (sources of funds) and expenditures (uses of funds) over a given period of time, say a year. For a household, income and borrowing are *sources* of funds, while consumption and saving (the purchase of financial assets) are *uses* of funds. As pointed out in Chapter 1, a surplus unit spends less on goods and services than it receives in income over a given period of time. The surplus (saving) will be used to accumulate various types of financial assets. On an income statement, since sources of funds must equal uses, the surplus unit would register on the receipts or sources side a particular level of income which was matched on the uses side by some combination of spending on real and financial assets. The latter would represent the change in the unit's balance sheet (portfolio) over the year. See if you can explain how a deficit unit's income statement would relate to its balance sheet.

3-3
MAKING PORTFOLIO DECISIONS: SOME FIRST PRINCIPLES

In the economy, selection of a desired or planned portfolio will be governed by an objective or a set of objectives. These objectives will, in turn, guide an economic unit's spending, saving, and financing decisions—all actions designed to attain the desired portfolios and achieve the specified objectives.

Each spending unit in the economy is presumed to pursue some objective or set of objectives. For *households,* we assume that they wish to *maximize utility or satisfaction* over time. But what does this mean? If, as seems sensible, it is presumed that *people prefer more assets to less*—two cars to one car, five suits to three suits, $200 to $100, and so on—it means that (1) people desire to increase their holdings of real and financial assets and (2) faced with a choice, people will first select those assets which provide the most utility or satisfaction. Imagine trying to choose between two identically priced goods you think you need—say, a new color television set and a new couch. Of course, you would prefer to have both, but if you can only have one, it is assumed that you will choose whichever is most useful to you now—that is, the one that yields the most utility or satisfaction. (More on this in Chapter 4.) For *business firms,* we assume that their portfolio decisions are guided by the desire to *maximize profits.* Logically, this means that firms will try to maximize the difference between their costs of production and their revenues from sales. After all, profits equal revenues minus costs. In general, firms will make hiring decisions, investment decisions, and pricing decisions by assessing the impact of alternative courses of action on costs and revenues and thus ultimately on their profits. More on firms in Chapter 5.) As for *government* policymakers, we assume that they are guided by a desire to *maximize their political support* and also, perhaps, *society's welfare.*[1] (In Chapter 6, we will discuss how such considerations affect their decisions to spend and to tax.[2])

In general, economic units are assumed to be guided by their own "enlightened" self-interest; they are all attempting to maximize something for themselves. Unfortunately, however, there are limits to what economic units can attain. The practical world that we all live in does not allow us to achieve unlimited utility or unlimited profits. The fundamental economic problem is that we have infinite wants while our means or resources are limited. This means, in effect, that there are *constraints* which limit the maximum degree of satisfaction, profits, and so on that economic units

---

[1] Sometimes these dual objectives go in tandem and sometimes they diverge. We will study these aspects of policymaker behavior in later chapters.
[2] Thus far we have not mentioned foreigners. Fret not. Foreign participants in the United States economy will be either households, firms, or governments and thus will pursue the same objectives as their domestic counterparts. This is the subject of Chapter 7. It should also be pointed out that the framework being developed above is most directly applicable to the behavior of households, firms, foreigners, and financial intermediaries. Governments must be viewed in a somewhat different light.

Our couple would love to have $1000; he could buy a new skiing outfit and she could take a long overdue vacation to the Bahamas. Unfortunately, they only have $500; this means a choice will have to be made between the two possible purchases.

can attain. The existence of such constraints forces economic units to choose among alternative courses of action. For example, as mentioned above, you might prefer to purchase both a new television set and a new couch. However, if you can afford only one—if you are constrained by your available funds—you must make a choice between two alternative courses of action. Thus, every economic unit will choose the mix of assets (engage in portfolio decisions) that are most consistent with its objectives *subject to* the constraints it faces.

But what are these constraints? It has often been said that the first rule of economics is "there is no such thing as a free lunch." *All purchases of real or financial assets must somehow be financed.* More specifically, you must part with money to consummate transactions. This being the case, the constraint on an economic unit's spending can be defined in terms of its access to means of payment.

An individual economic unit that does not have money can generally get it in one or more of the following ways: (1) the unit can earn income by selling its labor (households) or its products (firms); (2) the unit can liquidate (sell) some of its holdings of real or financial assets; or (3) the unit can borrow. These three options are not freely available to all spending units: General Motors can borrow $100 million by picking up the telephone and

Money, income, and wealth are terms often confused; this misunderstanding should be resolved before we go further. Although related, these three terms are conceptually distinct from one another. *Wealth* or net worth is a balance-sheet concept. It represents the difference between the value of the stock of assets and the value of the stock of liabilities. Since it is measured at a given moment, wealth is a stock concept. *Money* is a particular type of financial asset and—assuming wealth is positive (assets exceed liabilities)—is part of the economic unit's wealth. *Money* held is a stock concept, since such holdings are measured at a particular moment. *Income*, on the other hand, is a *flow* of earnings over a period of time, say a week. It is true that in the first instance a flow of income (received in the form of a check, which is credited to your demand deposit) results in an equal increase in your money holdings. This is perhaps the reason why we so often hear people say "How much money do you make?" In fact, people earn income and use it to add to their holdings of real assets and financial assets (including money). Note, however, that there is no reason to expect income to equal the change in money holdings. This would only occur if people did not use their income to acquire real assets or other financial assets.

calling its bank, or it can issue a bond; you may be able to borrow $2000 (if your credit rating is good) from your bank or credit union. The reason for the disparity is perhaps obvious. We shall see in coming chapters that constraints on spending are ultimately related to past, current, and expected future income and the current "health" of a spending unit's balance sheet. Past income is relevant because some of it might have been used to accumulate financial assets which can now be liquidated. Current income is relevant because it can be used directly to finance spending. Expected future income and the current health of the balance sheet (net worth, debt outstanding, and so forth) are relevant because a unit's borrowing power will be directly related to its ability to service new debt (that is, meet the scheduled payments of interest and principal) and its ability to furnish collateral in the form of existing assets.

To sum up what we have said so far, spending, saving, and financing decisions are, in effect, *flow* decisions to alter portfolios. To achieve its desired portfolio, a spending unit must decide how much to add to its stock of assets over any given period of time and how to finance the acquisition of these assets (that is, use current income, increase liabilities, or sell assets). We shall say more on portfolio decisions in later chapters. Now it is appropriate to see how the millions of individual portfolio decisions and the resulting flows of saving, spending, investing, and borrowing throughout the economy can be pulled together into a coherent framework.

3-4
PULLING THINGS TOGETHER

Thus far in this chapter we have developed concepts and discussed behavior in terms of individual units in the economy. The time has now come to look at these units in the aggregate, that is, in broad sectors—the household sector, the business sector, the government sector, and the foreign sector. In essence, we are assuming that most individual units within a sector are more alike than different and that summing all their individual spending, saving, borrowing, and lending decisions will not introduce significant analytic problems.[1] In addition to looking at the aggregate of each of the four sectors, we will also sum up all four of them to arrive at the spending, saving, and financing decisions for the economy as a whole (that is, for the aggregate of the entire economy).

[1] This is the "aggregation problem." The questionable legitimacy of the above procedure lies at the core of the fuzzy relationship between microeconomics (which focuses on the determinants of behavior by individual firms and households) and macroeconomics (which focuses on the determinants of consumption spending by all households taken together, aggregate investment spending by firms, and so forth). This is a major unresolved issue in economics and accounts for considerable recent research into the microfoundations of macroeconomics.

The standard way to finesse the problem is simply to ignore it. Given the current state of knowledge, we will grudgingly follow the same practice. At least we "tell it like it is." (Howard Cosell, are you listening?)

Table 3-1 presents a number of details on sectoral and overall economic concepts. Let us first talk through each row. The household sector supplies factors of production (labor, land, and financial capital) to other sectors. In return, it receives wages and salaries, rent, interest, and dividends. Out of this gross income, the government will take some taxes. What is left after taxes is net household receipts—*disposable income* Y_d. Households use this income to purchase goods and services—that is called *consumption C*. Whatever is left over is *saving S*—the surplus in the household sector.

The business sector produces and sells goods and services. From its gross revenue must be subtracted the costs of producing and selling its products (wages paid employees and interest paid on outstanding debt, for instance), dividends paid to shareholders (the owners of the corporation), and taxes. The result is net business receipts (current *retained earnings* RE). Additional expenditures by business will involve additions to its capital stock (plant, equipment, or inventories) in the form of *investment I*. If investment exceeds retained earnings (as is often the case), the business sector will run a deficit D_b.

Net final receipts for the government sector consist of their tax collections (income taxes, excise taxes, sales taxes, social security taxes, and so on) minus transfer payments. Transfer payments involve such items as unemployment compensation, welfare, veterans' benefits, and social security benefits. In general, transfers are payments by the government to various economic units where no goods or services are provided in return. We shall refer to net government receipts—that is, taxes minus transfers—as *net taxes T*. The government's purchases of goods and services (federal, state, and local government combined) include outlays on education, national defense, police protection, highways, and so forth. We shall refer to this as *government spending G*. If government spending exceeds net taxes, the government will incur a deficit D_g.

Finally, we have the foreign sector. Foreign gross receipts consist of rent, interest, dividends, and so on paid to foreigners by United States domestic sectors. To get net foreign earnings FE, we must subtract any dividends, interest, and so on that United States citizens receive from foreigners. To arrive at net expenditures by foreigners, we take foreign purchases of United States goods and services (United States exports) and subtract from it United States purchases of foreign goods and services (United States imports). The result will be referred to as net exports NX. The difference between net exports and net foreign earnings is the foreign surplus or deficit D_f.

Now that we have reviewed each row of the table which summarizes the behavior of all units within a sector, we can add up the columns to arrive at some important accounting relationships. Equation (3-1) represents the sum of the expenditures column.

(3-1)
$$Y = C + I + G + NX = PQ$$

TABLE 3-1
AN ACCOUNTING FRAMEWORK

SECTOR	RECEIPTS	−	EXPENDITURES	=	SECTOR DEFICIT OR SURPLUS
Household	Y_d = disposable income of households		C = consumption expenditure of households		S = saving = household surplus = $Y_d - C$
Business	RE = net retained earnings of business		I = net investment of business (including inventory accumulation)		D_b = business deficit (or surplus)
Government	T = net taxes (taxes minus transfers)		G = government expenditures on goods and services		D_g = government deficit (or surplus)
Foreign	FE = net foreign earnings		NX = net exports (exports minus imports)		D_f = foreign deficit (or surplus)
Total for economy (sum of sectors)	Y = national income		Y = national product		$Y - Y = 0$

National product Y, or national output, is equal to the total value of all *final goods* and services produced during a given time period, say one year.[1] The total *value* of all goods and services provided is equal to the *price P* of each good or service multiplied by the *quantity* produced Q. In terms of our expenditure column, national product is equal to all goods produced and sold to the various sectors (reflecting household consumption, business spending on plant and equipment, government spending, and net exports) plus goods produced but not sold. Goods produced but not yet sold are additions to business inventories. The sum of the expenditure column is commonly called *gross national product* (GNP), although we shall continue to refer to it as Y because it is a simpler notation. Although Equation (3-1) is an identity, which means that it must be true by definition, it will be useful to think of it as reflecting the *demand* for goods and services in the economy.

The next hurdle is to add up the receipts column. This is accomplished in Equation (3-2).

$$(3\text{-}2) \qquad Y = Y_d + \text{RE} + T + \text{FE}$$

Like Equation (3-1), this is also an identity. It shows that national income Y is equal to the net receipts in each sector over a specific period of time. These receipts are the result of the production and sale (that is, the *supply*) of goods and services in the economy.

Now comes the interesting part. National income Y must, by definition, be equal to national product or national output Y.[2] Total expenditures on goods and services will accrue to various sellers of goods and services in the economy. The sellers receive these expenditures as gross receipts. But the sellers must pay taxes to the government, wages to the labor hired to produce and sell the goods, interest on outstanding debt, and so forth. In general, total receipts will be distributed across the various sectors and must add up to total expenditures. This is just another way of showing the relationships embedded in the circular flow diagram (Figure 1-1) in Chapter 1. There, by definition, the dollar flow of household spending and business receipts was exactly equal to the dollar flow of business payouts for factor services.

The last column of Table 3-1 is of particular interest in this text. As mentioned earlier in the chapter, individual sectors can incur either deficits (when expenditures exceed receipts) or surpluses (when receipts exceed expenditures). However, all spending must be financed, and thus all defi-

---

[1] We say "final" because all "intermediate" goods produced by one firm and sold to another firm are excluded. For example, if U.S. Steel sells sheet metal to General Motors to build a car, we do not count the steel twice. Instead, we count the car which includes the steel. This procedure avoids double counting. The sheet metal produced by U.S. Steel and purchased by General Motors is considered an intermediate good.

[2] In actuality, there is a minor difference between national product and GNP involving the treatment of depreciation. For those who will not be able to sleep until they learn more about this and other details of our national accounts, see the suggested readings at the end of this chapter.

cits must be financed. This means the sum of the deficits and surpluses for the various sectors must equal zero.

$$(3\text{-}3) \qquad\qquad S + D_b + D_g + D_f = 0$$

Equation (3-3) is merely another way of saying that for every borrower (deficit), there must be lender (surplus). As introduced in Chapters 1 and 2, the financial system provides the means by which the deficits get financed by the surpluses.[1] Sectors with surplus funds acquire claims on financial intermediaries or on final borrowers. Sectors with deficits issue and sell claims in financial markets or borrow from financial intermediaries. In general, surpluses give rise to a demand for financial assets (claims) and a supply of funds, while deficits give rise to a supply of financial liabilities (claims) and a demand for funds.

To show that the details really hang together, Table 3-2 presents the actual figures in the various categories for 1978. Note that the household and foreign sectors were surplus or saving sectors while the business and government sectors had net deficits.

3-5
THE RELATIONSHIP BETWEEN PORTFOLIO DECISIONS AND ECONOMYWIDE ACCOUNTING IDENTITIES

Now that we know how to define various aggregate measures of economic and financial activity, we want to find out how these data relate to decision-making by the various economic units in society. At the end of a given time period, say a year, the total amount of funds lent (supplied) must be equal to the total amount of funds borrowed (demanded), just as the total value of goods demanded (purchased) must be equal to the total value of goods supplied (sold). These are ex post (after the fact), *realized* accounting relationships. Table 3-1 shows how these relationships are derived from the *actual* spending, saving, producing, borrowing, and lending decisions of the various sectors. These ex post relationships and decisions must be distinguished sharply from ex ante (*before the fact*), *planned decisions*. To illustrate the difference and how it matters, let us, for the sake of simplicity, ignore the government and foreign sectors. We shall assume that the business sector, based on its objectives and desired portfolio, *plans* to run a $10 billion deficit; however, the household sector *plans* to save only $8 billion. In this case, the planned demand for funds by business (supply of financial liabilities) would exceed the planned supply of funds (demand for financial assets) by households. What happens when the demand for any good ex-

---

[1] We *could* treat the financial system as a separate sector. However, it is better to view the financial system as the network—the circulatory system—that ties together all the other sectors of the economy.

TABLE 3-2
RECEIPTS, EXPENDITURES, DEFICITS, AND SURPLUSES FOR 1978
(In billions of dollars)

SECTOR	RECEIPTS	−	EXPENDITURES	=	SECTOR DEFICIT OR SURPLUS
Household	Disposable income = 1416.4		Consumption = 1339.7		Saving (household surplus) = 76.7
Business	Retained earnings = 243.6		Investment = 344.5		Business deficit = −100.9
Government	Net taxes = 432.7		Government spending = 434.2		Government deficit = −1.5†
Foreign	Foreign earnings = 13.0		Net exports = −11.8		Foreign surplus = 24.8
Total for economy (sum of sectors)	National income = 2106.6‡		National product = 2106.6		Sector deficits or surpluses = 0‡

† In calendar year 1978, the federal deficit was about $29 billion, while state and local governments had a combined surplus of 27.5 billion.

‡ These columns do not add exactly to the numbers shown. There is a $1.1 billion "statistical discrepancy," which represents accounting errors made by the government in estimating the various entries.

SOURCE: Unless otherwise noted, sources for data in all figures and tables throughout the text are the *Economic Report of the President*, the *Survey of Current Business*, and the *Federal Reserve Bulletin*.

ceeds the supply? Let us hope you guessed that the price would rise, because that is what would happen. In this case, the interest rate would rise, and here comes the key point: as the interest rate (the cost of borrowing and the return for lending) rises, we would expect households and business to *revise their plans.* In particular, the rise in the interest rate might discourage some firms from investing; thus, in the aggregate, the business deficit might shrink to, say, $9 billion. At the same time, the rise in the interest rate might encourage households to save more and thus enlarge their surplus to, say, $9 billion. Thus, ex post funds supplied will equal funds demanded, even though this was not the case before the fact. The rise in the interest rate encouraged adjustments in planned portfolio decisions which equated actual demand and supply.

The type of adjustment process discussed above is an important part of our story, and its importance cannot be emphasized too strongly. In Parts II and III of the text we shall analyze the behavior of each sector and that of the financial system. Then, in Part IV, we shall pull the behavior of each sector together again as a prelude to discussing the impact of policy on the economy. As we proceed, it is important that you not lose sight of the general way in which all the various parts of the economy interact and hang together.

3-6
SUMMARY OF MAJOR POINTS

1

A portfolio is composed of a spending unit's holdings of real assets, money, other financial assets, and financial liabilities. It is akin to a balance sheet which measures the monetary value of the stock of assets, liabilities, and net worth at a particular time.

2

Portfolio decisions—that is, decisions to alter holdings of assets and/or liabilities—are determined by spending units' objectives. We assume that households attempt to maximize utility, firms attempt to maximize profits, and governments attempt to maximize political support as well as, perhaps, society's welfare.

3

Desired changes in the composition of portfolios result in decisions by economic units to spend, save, or borrow. These are all flows which occur over time. Changes in stocks of assets held occur as the result of spending and saving flows.

4

Economic units face constraints which limit the level of utility or profits attainable. Constraints force economic units to make portfolio choices among alternative goods, services, and financial assets.

5

A fundamental constraint is that all spending must be financed with money. Typical sources of financing are current income, the liquidation of assets held, and borrowing.

6

The actual portfolio decisions made by the economic units within each sector in the economy (household, business, government, and foreign) can be summarized in terms of their receipts, expenditures, and deficit or surplus.

7

Taking all the sectors together—that is, the aggregate of the economy—total receipts equal national income and total expenditures equal national product. Further, national product must, by definition, equal national income.

8

Individual sectors may incur surpluses or deficits. For the economy as a whole, however, the total amount of funds actually demanded by deficit sectors (liabilities supplied or issued) must be equal to the total amount of funds actually supplied (assets demanded) by surplus sectors. Thus the sum of the actual surpluses and deficits is zero.

9

If planned deficits do not equal planned surpluses, an adjustment process will be set in motion involving changes in interest rates and induced revisions in planned portfolio decisions. This process will, in the end, result in the equality of planned and actual deficits and surpluses.

3-7
REVIEW QUESTIONS

1   Provide a brief discussion or definition of the following terms: portfolio, balance sheet, income statement, disposable income, retained earnings, net taxes, net foreign earnings, consumption, net exports.

2   Distinguish between stocks and flows. Give some examples of each.

3   Explain what is meant by the statement that "economic units maximize subject to constraints."

4   Explain why the sum of sector surpluses and deficits must be zero.

5   What is a "portfolio decision?" What influences such decisions?

6   Explain what might happen in the economy if planned surpluses exceeded planned deficits.

7   Distinguish between money, income, and wealth.

3-8
SUGGESTED READINGS

1   For a more in-depth discussion of national income accounting, see William Abraham, *National Income and Economic Accounting* (Englewood Cliffs, N.J.: Prentice-Hall, 1969), chaps. 1–3. You might also check Paul Samuelson, *Economics* (New York: McGraw-Hill, 1978), chap. 10.

2   The basic data for national income and product and their components are published monthly in the *Survey of Current Business* (as well as the *Federal Reserve Bulletin*) and summarized annually in the *Economic Report of the President*, an especially valuable source of historical data. Consult also *Business Conditions Digest*, published monthly by the U.S. Department of Commerce; its many charts place the relevant data in historical context.

3   A whole separate accounting system has been developed to detail the relationship between sector deficits and surpluses. This system is called the "flow of funds accounts." For a helpful discussion of these accounts, see Lawrence Ritter, *The Flow of Funds Accounts: A Framework for Financial Analysis* (New York: New York University, *The Bulletin*, Institute of Finance, 1968); *Introduction to Flow of Funds* (Washington, D.C.: Board of Governors of the Federal Reserve System, 1975); and Lawrence Ritter and William Silber, *Principles of Money, Banking, and Financial Markets* (New York: Basic Books, 1977), chap. 26.

PART
TWO
A SECTORAL APPROACH TO MONETARY ANALYSIS

The first part of this text was designed to introduce money and the financial system, develop some key concepts, and prepare you for the analysis that is to come. Part II focuses on the behavior of each key sector in the economy. While a separate chapter is devoted to each sector—household, business, government, and foreign—there are common themes running through them all. In general, our major objective shall be to identify and analyze the major determinants of decisions by economic units to spend, save, or borrow. Since the emphasis will be on the financial side of economic behavior, these chapters will explore the role of interest rates, supplies and demands for money and securities, and expectations of future economic and financial conditions and their influence on the portfolio decisions within each sector. We must develop an understanding of these things before we can analyze the interaction among the sectors (Part IV) and the way in which policy—particularly monetary policy—affects portfolio decisions (Part V).

4
THE HOUSEHOLD SECTOR

Saving in season,
spending with reason,
makes a good household.

Robert Bland

4-1
THE BIG ENCHILADA

The household sector comprises every man, woman, and child in the United States. Each one of us is a member of a household *unit* and all household units together make up the household *sector*. Our goal is to analyze the spending, saving, and borrowing behavior of all households taken together. Your reaction to this approach may be that each household is different from every other, and therefore trying to analyze their collective behavior must surely be doomed to failure. Do not be pessimistic. Hang in there with us. Our aim is *not* to analyze and *not* to predict, or explain the behavior of each *individual* household. Rather, our aim is to examine and explain central tendencies and key elements in the behavior of *all* households, especially with respect to the financial system.

In order to see where the household sector fits into the financial system, let us look at the major functions of households in a modern industrial economy.

First, households demand and *consume goods and services*. The total expenditure by households on goods and services is usually referred to as *consumption*. The goods and services demanded and consumed by the household sector are produced and supplied by the other sectors (business, government, and foreign). What this simply means is that the household sector is linked to the other sectors by the relationship between supply and demand (or that between production and consumption). The *second* major household function is to *supply labor* to other sectors. This labor is combined with the other factors of production—land and capital—to produce goods and services.

The household sector plays a key role in the economy—households are an important part of the production or supply process, and their consumption decisions are a key determinant of the aggregate demand for goods and services. Furthermore, the production and consumption functions are interrelated. If your mother were a vice-president of Ford Motor Co., she would be contributing to the production of autos and trucks. In return, she would receive income (in the form of wages), which would, presumably, have an important effect on her spending or consumption.

The *third* major function performed by many households is that they *supply financial capital*—that is they lend money—to other households and other sectors. This is accomplished by acquiring financial claims (IOUs) on others. The financial capital may be lent directly to borrowers (deficit units); for example, the household can purchase a U.S. Treasury security. Or the household may lend money indirectly through a financial intermediary. For example, a household might open a savings account at a local bank—thus, in effect, lending funds to the bank—and the bank might, in turn, lend these funds, along with those deposited by a number of other households, to a firm. The reward for being a creditor (a lender) comes in the form of interest payments, dividend payments, and perhaps capital gains.

Last but not least is the *fourth* function—households may *borrow financial capital* (money). For example, a household considering the purchase of a car may find that it does not have enough money on hand to pay for the car. If the household decides to go ahead with the purchase, part of the cost will have to be financed by borrowing. In all likelihood, this will entail a loan from a financial intermediary (usually a bank, finance company, or credit union). This loan will be a claim on the household, increasing its liabilities, as well as an interest-earning asset for the financial intermediary.

If this functional breakdown does not convince you of the importance of the household sector, check out these data. In 1978, total spending on goods and services by households accounted for almost two-thirds of total GNP in the economy. The surplus in the household sector financed 75 percent of the deficits in the economy (see Table 3-2). Obviously, the behavior of households will have a profound effect on the health of the economy. Accordingly, identifying and analyzing the determinants of household behavior is an important item on our agenda.

4-2
HOUSEHOLD PORTFOLIO DECISIONS:
CONSUMPTION, BORROWING, AND SAVING

As discussed briefly in Chapter 3, household decisions to spend, borrow, and save are guided by certain objectives. Households aiming to achieve such objectives (whether or not they are in fact achievable) are said to be acting so as to *maximize* utility or satisfaction (that is, get as close to the maximum as possible). Operationally, this means that households have *desired* portfolios; they spend, save, borrow, and work so as to move their actual portfolios toward such desires.

Household decisions to purchase goods and services—that is, decisions to add to the stock of real assets—represent the single most important component of aggregate demand for goods and services in the economy. This component of aggregate demand, called *consumption*, is one of the uses of current household receipts—that is, disposable income (or "income" for short). As discussed earlier, the *sources* of disposable income (Y_d) are wages and salaries, interest, and dividends minus net taxes. The *uses* of Y_d are expenditures on goods and services—consumption C—plus income not spent on goods and services—saving S. Equation (4-1) expresses the identity that disposable income must be either consumed or saved.

(4-1) $$Y_d = C + S$$

This equation summarizes the first general portfolio decision a household must make—should current income be consumed or saved?[1]

THE RELATIONSHIP
BETWEEN INCOME AND CONSUMPTION

Households spend to consume, and all spending must be financed. In the majority of cases, consumption spending is financed out of current income. It is for this reason that our consumption story begins with the simple notion that consumption demand (which is simply another way of saying "con-

---

[1] We will try to answer the above question by examining a host of factors affecting consumption and saving decisions. Since, by definition, a decision to save is a decision not to spend, we could proceed by analyzing only, say, consumption. However, since our focus is on the financial side of portfolio decisions, we shall find it useful to supplement our consumption story with an analysis of saving behavior.

Assuming that income is a given, $C = Y_d - S$ or $S = Y_d - C$. These two expressions are simple algebraic transformations of Equation (4-1). The assumption that income is given will be used until at least the next chapter, where firm decisions to hire labor are analyzed.

sumption spending") is a function of the current level of income. Equation (4-2) summarizes this elementary relationship:

(4-2)
$$C = f(\overset{+}{Y}_d)$$

The symbol f means "a function of." More specifically, it means that the variable inside the parenthesis determines or helps explain movements in the variable on the left-hand side of the equation. The plus sign above Y_d (disposable income) means that consumption is a positive function of income: when income rises, we would expect consumption to rise; similarly, when income falls, we would expect consumption to fall.

Equation (4-2) expresses the *general* mathematical relationship between consumption and income; it does not express the *specific* mathematical relationship. While for the most part we will work with general mathematical expressions in this text, it is important to recognize that the relationship could be expressed more specifically. As a hypothetical example, consider Equation (4-3).

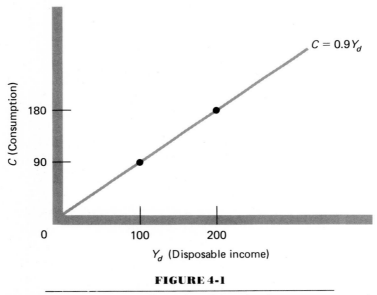

FIGURE 4-1

This consumption function shows the relationship between consumption and disposable income. In this example, following Equation (4-3) 90 cents of every dollar of disposable income is consumed. The "independent" variable Y_d is plotted on the vertical axis. The line (which is called the consumption function) emanates from the origin (where income = 0 and consumption = 0). We know this from substituting $Y_d = 0$ in Equation (4-3) and solving for the dependent variable. This is called the *intercept*. The *slope* of the line is 0.9. When $Y_d = 100, C = 90$, and so forth.

(4-3) $$C = 0.9Y_d$$

Translated literally, it says that for every dollar of income Y_d earned, 0.9 × $1 = $.90 is consumed.[1] Figure 4-1 is a graphical representation of the same relationship.

Equation (4-3) can be rearranged to show what *fraction* of disposable income is consumed in spending on goods and services.

(4-4) $$C/Y_d = 0.9$$

Let us see how our hypothetical ratio $C/Y_d = 0.9$ relates to the real world. Figure 4-2 shows the ratio of actual consumption to income for each quarter during the 1957–1978 period. Note that if the ratio were constant (at 0.9 or any other level) during this period, the line in Figure 4-2 would be perfectly horizontal. Obviously the ratio is not constant. Why is there variation in the proportion of income that households consume?

A LOOK AT THE
COMPONENTS OF CONSUMPTION SPENDING

Consumption spending can be divided into the large categories of spending on nondurables and services and spending on durables. All of us need food,

[1] Given Equation (4-1), how much of each dollar is saved?

C/Y_d (Consumption divided by disposable income)

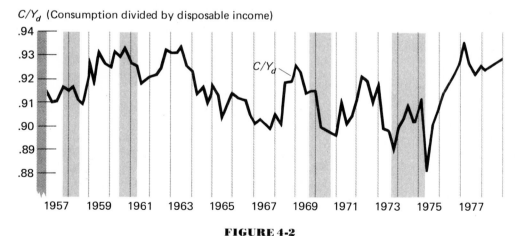

FIGURE 4-2

The ratio of consumption to disposable income varies over time. The periods of time between business cycle *peaks* and *troughs* are shown as shaded areas on this and most other figures in the text. These periods are highlighted because when economic activity slows and eventually declines—that is, as the economy slides into a recession—we will want to identify what contributes to the eroding health of the economy. Similarly, we shall be interested in what contributes to the economy's improving health as economic activity bottoms out (the trough) and begins to rise.

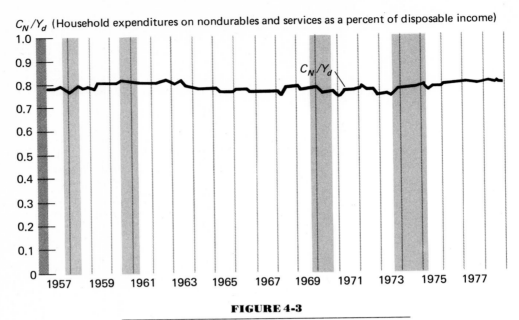

FIGURE 4-3

Consumption of nondurable goods and services is a relatively
constant proportion of disposable income.

clothing, shelter, medical care, and so on—these are basic necessities
which economists refer to as *nondurable goods and services*. As Figure 4-3
illustrates, the relationship between income and consumption spending on
nondurables C_N varied very little each year over the 1957–1978 period. This
means that C_N changes at about the same rate as Y_d changes.

If consumption spending for necessities does not vary much with income and total consumption spending does vary, what explains the variation in total spending? It must be consumption spending for durables C_D.

By contrast with nondurable goods and services, *durable* goods (autos,
furniture, appliances, etc.) are usually not biological necessities. This means
that the *timing* of expenditures for durable goods is, for the most part, under
the household's control—that is, the household has some choice about when
to make these expenditures. Assuming that a household desires to acquire
durables—that is, it desires to add to its portfolio holdings of real
assets—what will influence the timing of this spending?

Figure 4-4a shows the ratio of spending on durables C_D to disposable income Y_d.

Note that the C_D/Y_d ratio displays considerable variance. This suggests
that it is changes in spending on durables relative to income which lead to
much of the fluctuation in the C/Y_d ratio in Figure 4-2. This can be seen
more clearly by examining the growth rates of real disposable income $\dot{y}_d$ and

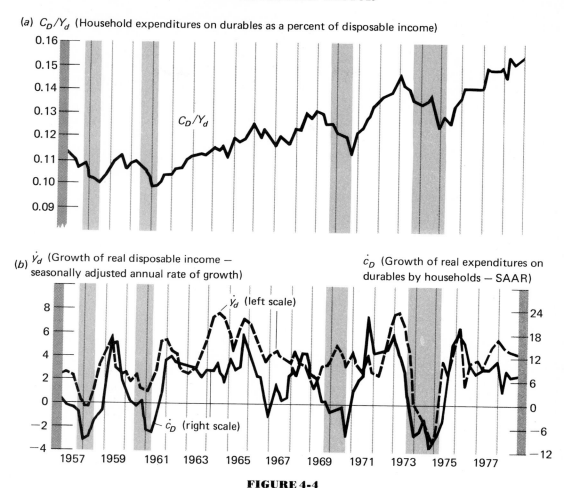

(a) C_D/Y_d (Household expenditures on durables as a percent of disposable income)

(b) $\dot{y}_d$ (Growth of real disposable income — seasonally adjusted annual rate of growth)

$\dot{c}_D$ (Growth of real expenditures on durables by households — SAAR)

FIGURE 4-4

(*a*) The ratio of consumer spending on durable goods to income shows considerable cyclical movement. (*b*) When the growth in real disposable income picks up (as is generally true during economic recoveries), consumer spending on durables also picks up. In fact, spending on durables often grows faster than income during this phase of the business cycle as expectations about the future pace of economic activity improve.

real expenditures on durables $\dot{c}_D$.[1] These data are plotted in Figure 4-4*b*. As one would expect, the growth of real income accelerates during economic recoveries and decelerates, or becomes negative, during recessions. Since people often tend to extrapolate current trends into the future, it is reason-

[1] As discussed in the insert on the next page, we shall use lowercase letters to refer to real (inflation-adjusted) magnitudes and a dot over a variable to denote the growth rate of a particular variable.

able to expect that as the growth rate of current income rises, households become more optimistic about the future pace of income growth and therefore become more willing to purchase durables. Conversely, as income falls, households become pessimistic and less willing to purchase durable goods. As we see in Figure 4-4*b*, purchases of durables are positively related to the growth rate of income and both show considerable cyclical variance. We may note further that when income growth picks up (as in 1958, 1961, 1975), the growth in spending on durables often rises even faster. This suggests that consumption, particularly of durables, is a function not only of current income but also of expectations about future income. When households expect their income to rise, they feel more comfortable making large purchases.

SOME IMPORTANT CONCEPTS

The growth rate in real disposable income is plotted quarterly and expressed as a seasonally adjusted annual rate of growth (SAAR) in Figure 4-4*b*. If you go to the *Survey of Current Business* or other data sources we have referred you to, you will find that this method is commonly used to present data.

Seasonal adjustment is a statistical procedure applied by statisticians to the raw data collected by the various government agencies. The objective of this adjustment is to remove the normal, recurring, seasonal movement in the data so as to get at the underlying trends and cycles which are of more lasting significance. For example, if Y_d usually rises by about $1 billion in December (because of overtime and so forth associated with Christmas) and in December 1981 Y_d rises by only $500 million, the seasonal adjustment procedure would produce a Y_d series that showed a decline in December 1981 of about $500 million, rather than the $500 million increase in the raw, unadjusted series. The implications for policymakers are obviously quite different when income declines instead of rising.

For the most part, economists are interested in the *growth* of consumption, income, investment, and so forth, not the absolute *level* in dollars. This is because we are interested in changes in particular variables over time. Accordingly, data are often presented in terms of *annual rates of growth* (or decline). If the level of Y_d (seasonally adjusted) were $100 billion in November and it declined to $99.5 billion in December, the annual rate of growth would be minus 6 percent. This is computed by taking the

change between the two months ($99.5 - 100 = -.5$), dividing it
by the level in the previous month ($-.5/100 = -.005$), and multiplying by 12 ($-.005 \times 12 = -.06 = -6$ percent). The monthly
rate of change in December is $-.5$ percent. To get the annual rate
of change (that is, what the percent change would be if the change
in December occurred every month for a year), the monthly percent change is multiplied by 12. If you had quarterly data, you
would compute the percentage change in the quarter and multiply
by 4. This is how the quarterly data in Figure 4-4b are calculated.
We shall use a dot over a particular symbol to denote the growth
rate of a particular variable.

Recall that in Chapter 2, it was pointed out that the value of
money could be measured by $\$1/P$, where $\$1$ is the *nominal*
value of a dollar and P is a price index which measures the general level of prices of goods and services that can be purchased
with a dollar. When the nominal value of anything is divided by a
price index, the result is referred to as a *real* magnitude. Data
can be expressed in nominal terms (in terms of current dollars)
or in real terms (in terms of dollars that adjust for the changing
purchasing power of the dollar which results from changes in
prices). The latter method of expressing data is usually referred
to as "constant dollars"—dollars of constant purchasing power.
To illustrate, suppose that nominal disposable income (that is,
the income actually received by households) rose by 4 percent in
a given year but prices rose by 6 percent in the same year. In
real terms, households are worse off—the purchasing power of
their income has declined, not risen, as suggested by the increase
in nominal income. To express a series in real terms, the nominal series is divided (*deflated*) by the appropriate price index.
(The deflated series would then be used to compute the growth
rate.) We shall use a lowercase script character to denote a real
magnitude. Thus y_d is real disposable income and $\dot{y}_d$ is the annual
rate of growth in real disposable income.

It would be incorrect to presume that increased spending on durables or
other goods and services is financed only by rises in current real income.
Many households purchasing durable goods find it necessary or desirable to
finance their purchases by borrowing from, say, a bank or credit union. Borrowing is an important aspect of household behavior. Let us look at it in
more detail.

FACTORS AFFECTING HOUSEHOLD BORROWING

Suppose a household has no existing stock of money or other financial assets but desires to consume more now than it earns; that is, since $C > Y_d$, the household's desired consumption exceeds its current income flow. Will it be rational[1] for the household to borrow and pay interest to consume some of its future income before it is earned? The short answer is that it will be rational if the cost of borrowing is at least offset by the benefits derived from the spending. Here are some examples.

Example

1

If current income is low and future income is expected to be high (think of a student in medical school), the household may desire to equalize consumption over time, raising it now relative to current income by borrowing and lowering consumption in the future relative to income then by paying off the debts accumulated now. In other words, the doctor might buy golf clubs now instead of later and pay for them with future income.

2

The household may wish to accumulate real productive assets which will furnish it with a higher future income stream. It may also borrow to acquire labor skills (get an education) that will raise its future income stream. In either case, if the rate of return on the "investment" exceeds the cost of borrowing, the household can increase its income stream by borrowing.[2]

3

The household may wish to borrow to increase the quantity and/or quality of the flow of services yielded by its stock of

---

[1] By "rational" we mean that a household will choose the most efficient (lowest-cost) path or means to achieve its objectives (ends).

[2] The household may also borrow to accumulate financial assets (stocks, bonds, etc.). As above, this will be rational if the *expected* gain exceeds the cost of borrowing. An example of such behavior by households is provided by the margin accounts that many have with brokerage firms. The investor who buys stock is required to put up a certain proportion of the total cost. This "margin requirement" is set by the Federal Reserve and is discussed briefly in Chapter 18. The rest of the purchase price can be borrowed. The investor will engage in such a transaction if the expected appreciation of the stock exceeds the interest charges on the borrowed funds.

durable goods. Households buy houses, autos, appliances, and furniture because they yield a flow of services—shelter, transportation, and so forth—that provide utility or satisfaction. If the *implicit* yield on such goods (that is, the value of the service flow) exceeds the cost of borrowing funds (the interest rate), the household will increase its overall welfare by purchasing these goods and financing them by borrowing (that is, increasing its liabilities as well as its assets).

All this makes borrowing sound relatively painless. If this is the way things are, why not borrow continually? The answer, of course, is that the household, like the business firm, will not be able to borrow an unlimited volume of funds at the prevailing interest rate. Here come those constraints again! The impediment to continuous borrowing comes from both the lenders (banks and credit unions, for example) and borrowers (the households). It is generally believed that as the ratio of debt or debt repayments (that is, the regular interest and principal payments made on outstanding debt) to income rises, the ability of the household to "service" or pay off the debt is eroded. Have you ever taken your monthly income and added up your nondiscretionary expenses (rent, food, auto-loan payment, insurance, etc.) and found that there was very little left over?

Historical experience suggests that as the volume of debt repayments relative to income rises, the probability of default or delinquent payments on a loan also rises. This, of course, is what makes lenders cautious in granting new loans to heavily indebted borrowers; it also leads to a greater reluctance on the part of households to borrow. The forms you fill out when you apply for a loan and the credit checks that lenders make are designed to gauge the riskiness of lending you funds. In general, risk is presumed to be related to the balance-sheet position of the household and some key characteristics of the borrower's income stream (that is, the current and future flow of income). As for the balance sheet, the lender will be interested in the stock of assets owned and/or the assets to be acquired with the prospective loan, since these may serve as collateral for the loan, existing liabilities, and—ultimately—net worth.

On the income side, the expected *size of the income stream* relative to "nondiscretionary" payments out of income—that is, spending on food, shelter, and payments on existing debt—will be important, since the interest and principal payments on the new loan will come from the remaining income, which is called "discretionary" income.[1] The top panel of Figure

---

[1] Analytically one could divide total disposable income into nondiscretionary income (income you *must* spend on necessities) and discretionary income (income you are free to spend or save). As suggested above, spending on durables and the willingness and ability to borrow to finance such spending is directly related to the expected growth in discretionary income over time.

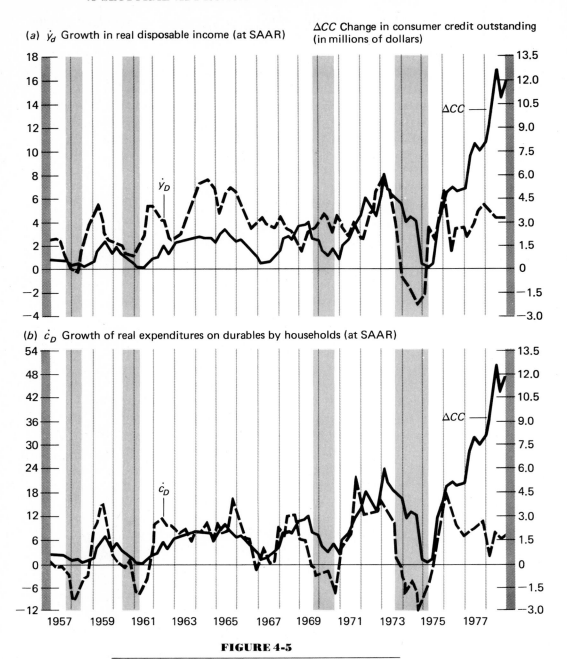

(a) $\dot{y}_d$ Growth in real disposable income (at SAAR)

ΔCC Change in consumer credit outstanding (in millions of dollars)

(b) $\dot{c}_D$ Growth of real expenditures on durables by households (at SAAR)

FIGURE 4-5

(a) When the growth of income picks up, households find they have more "discretionary" funds to spend. The growth in income will make it easier to service increased debt. (b) This encourages them to acquire durable goods and makes them more willing to borrow.

4-5 shows the growth in real disposable income and the change in consumer installment credit outstanding ΔCC. The lower panel shows changes in consumer installment credit and consumer spending on durable goods.[1] We use the change in consumer credit outstanding rather than the total amount outstanding because we are interested in relating borrowing to spending, both of which are flows. In this case, the flows are a change in the stock of liabilities (the change in consumer credit outstanding) and a change in the stock of real assets (spending on durables). When income growth accelerates, "discretionary" income also grows and consumer expectations about future income improve. As a result, households become more willing to spend and to increase their borrowing.

With income the key to servicing the debt, lenders will also try to evaluate the uncertainty associated with the size of the expected income stream. This is usually measured by the *variability of income* in the recent past. To illustrate, suppose your income had been $15,000 in three of the last five years and $20,000 in the other two, reflecting extensive overtime worked during those years. If a $20,000 income in the future would be needed to service the new loan, the lender may be reluctant, given the variability in past income.

The *expected* rate of growth of the income stream will also be an important factor influencing a household's willingness or desire to borrow and the lender's willingness to lend. As a specific example, consider physicians who borrow extensively during the time spent in medical school and training, expecting their income to grow over time. So long as there is a valid basis for expecting income to grow steadily, rising debt levels need not be a problem. However, if income growth levels off or falls, as it often does in a recession, households may have some difficulty servicing existing debt and will be reluctant to increase their debt. In general, as income growth falls, the household becomes less willing to borrow—its ability to service debt is reduced, as is its confidence (outlook) about the future—and lenders become more selective. This is the message contained in Figure 4-5.

FINANCIAL VARIABLES AND CONSUMPTION

We have saved the discussion of financial influences on consumption for last—the *price* and *nonprice terms* of borrowing will also influence household decisions to consume or not to consume. The price of borrowing is the interest rate charged. The nonprice terms include the down payment required[2] and the repayment term (that is, the number of years over which the loan is to be repaid). When a given sum is borrowed, the higher the interest

---

[1] Installment credit includes all consumer credit that is scheduled to be repaid in two or more payments. The four principal classes of installment credit are automobile, other consumer goods, home improvement, and personal.

[2] The down payment will determine the loan-to-value ratio, that is, the proportion of the value of goods purchased which will be financed by the loan. For example, if the required down payment is 25 percent, the loan-to-value ratio will be 75 percent.

rate charged by lenders and the shorter the repayment term, the higher will be the monthly interest and principal payment. If the minimum down payment is raised, say, from 10 percent of the value of the good to 20 percent, this increases the lump sum of money a household must have before going ahead with the purchase. We would expect that higher interest rates, shorter repayment periods, or increases in required down payments all would have some dampening effect on consumer purchases of durables.

If this is the case, what is it that causes lenders to alter the price and nonprice terms of lending to households? As for the interest rate charged on borrowed funds, we might expect it to move in the same direction as market interest rates. A rise in market interest rates (such as the rate on Treasury bills due to mature in three months) means that financial intermediaries will have to pay more to acquire funds from surplus units in the economy. If an intermediary wants to remain competitive—that is, continue to attract funds from lenders—it will have to offer a rate of return on its liabilities (assets to the holders) that is attractive when compared with alternative assets (such as Treasury bills) that surplus units might acquire. Thus a rise in market rates will tend to raise the cost of funds (inputs) to the intermediary. This, in turn, will encourage the intermediaries to raise the rate charged borrowers.[1]

What about nonprice terms of credit? And why do lenders use them to affect borrowing demand? We will have to analyze nonprice terms against the background of the state laws that set a maximum interest rate that can be charged on consumer loans. These maximum rates are called *usury ceilings*.[2] The existence of such ceilings in many states means that as market interest rates rise, rates on consumer loans will also rise, but they can only rise to the rate set by the usury ceilings. After that point, if the demand for loans by consumers exceeds the available supply, lenders will attempt to *ration* the supply by tightening the nonprice terms; for example, they may raise required down payments and shorten the maturity of loan contracts. Such actions will make the financing of planned purchases unattractive and cause some borrowers to postpone their spending. Figure 4-6 shows three things: (*a*) the movement in the short-term interest rate (in this case, the rate on Treasury bills with a 90-day maturity i_{90}); (*b*) the percent of income spent on durables; and (*c*) the net increases or decline in consumer installment credit. As the discussion above suggests, when interest rates rise and as nonprice terms of lending are tightened (that is, made more restrictive), consumers become less willing to borrow. As a result, the growth in consumer credit outstanding slows or actually turns negative, and spending on durables as a percent of income moderates.

---

[1] This is only one of several ways in which the rate charged households for borrowing can rise. A more complete discussion of the determinants of rates charged by financial intermediaries is contained in Chapter 10.

[2] Let us assure you the authors are not in favor of high interest rates. However, we believe that such ceilings represent counterproductive government interference in the market. The attempts by policymakers to affect the cost and volume of credit available to specific types of borrowers are usually referred to as "selective credit controls" (more on this in Chapter 19).

(a) Treasury bill rate (90 day maturity)

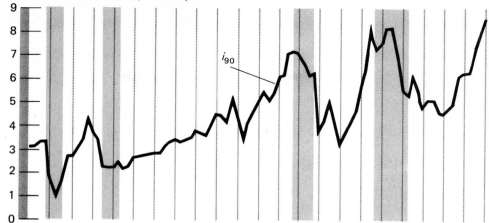

i_{90}

(b) Consumer expenditures on durable goods as a percent of disposable income

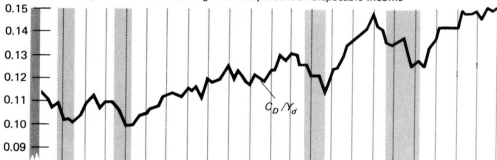

C_D / Y_d

(c) Net change in consumer installment credit outstanding (in millions of dollars)

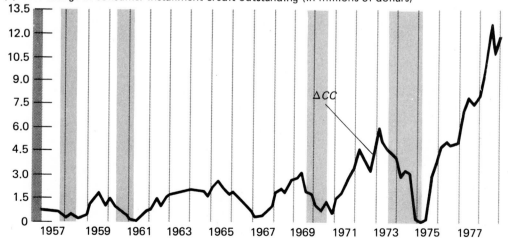

ΔCC

FIGURE 4-6

When interest rates rise and nonprice terms of credit are tightened, customers become less willing to borrow. As a result, spending on durable goods relative to income declines and the increase in borrowing slows.

Now let us consider how interest rates viewed as the return for lending influence household decisions whether to spend or save. If interest rates rise, this raises the cost of borrowing, and it also raises the return for lending. Intuitively, we should expect both effects of rising interest rates to lower borrowing and to decrease consumption (particularly of durables); this, of course, leads to an increase in saving.

Recognizing that interest rates are only one factor affecting saving decisions, let us look at saving in more detail.

FACTORS AFFECTING HOUSEHOLD SAVING

In the aggregate, the household sector is a *surplus* sector of the economy, meaning that its current receipts exceed its current expenditures. Within the household sector, some households will be net borrowers while others will be net savers and, therefore, lenders. While changes in the variables discussed previously (income, interest rates, the level of outstanding debt, and so on) will affect the degree of borrowing by the net borrowers and may induce some households to switch from borrowing to saving or vice versa, it is a fact that, in the aggregate, households are net savers. Indeed, over the last fifteen years, saving—or income that is not spent—has for the most part amounted to 5 to 8 percent of household disposable income.

So why do households save? What motivates households to forego current consumption? To get at the answer, recall the general objectives (mentioned earlier in this chapter) that guide household behavior: households will act (spend, save, and borrow) so as to maximize utility and/or increase the value of their income stream over time. But how can saving contribute to utility or future income?

Saving (a flow) is the method by which households accumulate wealth (a stock) and thereby increase their net worth. If the value of your liabilities exceeds that of your assets, you possess negative net worth—better call a good lawyer specializing in bankruptcies! If the value of your assets exceeds that of your liabilities, you have positive net worth. By allocating part of your income to saving and accumulating financial assets, you can increase your net worth (or wealth).

The assets acquired in the saving process would probably include bonds, equities (common stock), and other types of financial assets. The household would hope and expect to earn interest or dividends on the assets as well as to see the value of the assets appreciate reflecting capital gains. Even without capital gains, the household could expect the interest and dividends earned on bonds, stocks, and so forth to supplement income received in the form of wages and salaries, or pensions when retirement begins. The latter suggests a strong motive for saving; by accumulating income-earning assets now, a household will be able to maintain consumption in its retirement years when there will be no income from wages and salaries.

The pattern of a household's income, consumption, saving, and dis-

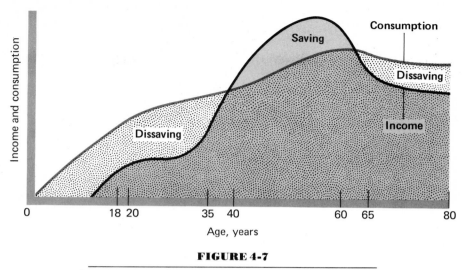

FIGURE 4-7

The relation between consumption, saving, and income over the lifetime of a typical household shows that in the early and late years a household typically dissaves (it borrows or liquidates assets); it saves in the middle years.

saving (borrowing) over a lifetime is illustrated in Figure 4-7. Note that in the early income years—say to age 35—households are depicted as net borrowers (dissavers). This is a period when durable goods and homes are being purchased, children are being reared, and so forth. Also important is the fact that many households will expect their incomes to rise over time as they gain experience and move up in their jobs. This encourages households to consume some future income before it is earned. In the years of middle age—say from ages 38 to 60—the household is depicted as a net saver. Assets are being accumulated to support consumption in the retirement years and perhaps to leave an estate for the heirs. Debts accumulated in earlier years are also being paid off. In the final stage—at about age 60—income drops relative to consumption and households again become dissavers, liquidating assets to finance expenditures.

Of course, retirement is not the only thing that motivates households to save. Equally important is the fact that we live in an uncertain world—you can get laid off from your job, the frost-free refrigerator can break down, a medical emergency can occur, and so on. These possibilities mean people will make portfolio choices which minimize their exposure to such risks. The combination of risk aversion and uncertainty over the future suggests that a household will desire to maintain a stock of *liquid* assets.[1] These are assets that can be turned into money quickly with no hassle and little or no

[1] Risk aversion is discussed in more detail in Chapter 15.

change in their market value. Examples are savings deposits and Treasury bills.[1] This stock of assets would be held to serve as a buffer for the household, insulating it to some degree from the adverse effects of unforeseen financial needs and emergencies. A common expression for this type of behavior is "saving for a rainy day."

Nearly all households hold some financial assets in their portfolios. Savers in the process of accumulating net additions to wealth must decide in what form to hold it. Savers and borrowers must decide in what form to hold existing assets. Should the portfolio mix be altered by, say, lowering bond holdings and increasing stock holdings? Households can hold many types of financial assets—money, time and savings deposits (these are liabilities of banks, savings and loan associations, mutual savings banks, and credit unions), equities, and bonds (we use bonds as a catch-all term for all market securities that yield interest). To complete our overview of household behavior, we will now examine the factors that influence the way in which households choose financial assets.

4-3
THE DEMAND FOR MONEY
AND OTHER FINANCIAL ASSETS

In our discussion of asset choice, we have mentioned the role of the expected rate of return and the expected risk associated with holding particular assets. Accordingly, we find that household choice among alternative assets is governed by the rate of return and risk on one type of asset compared with that on another. Since this text is about money, the household's demand for money will be examined first.

Why does a household need to hold cash? Basically, there are two reasons. *First,* households need money to consummate financial *transactions.* Someone who purchases real assets, bonds, and so on must supply in exchange a means of payment that is generally acceptable to the seller, and money is *the* means of payment. Since financial transactions occur frequently (probably several times a day) and income is typically received less frequently (usually monthly, biweekly, or weekly), a household must hold an *inventory of money* to get from one income-receiving period to the next. A typical relationship between income receipts, financial transactions, and money holdings is depicted in Figure 4-8. The peaks in money holdings every two weeks represent paydays, and the gradual decline in money holdings between paydays reflects spending on goods, the payment of bills (rent, loans), and so forth.

---

[1] Illiquid assets take time to liquidate—that is, exchange for money—and often necessitate a capital loss if they must be disposed of quickly. To illustrate, suppose you own stock in an obscure, small firm whose equity issues are not actively traded or listed on any of the major stock exchanges. It may take some time to find a buyer at what you consider to be the actual value of the stock. More on this in Chapter 12.

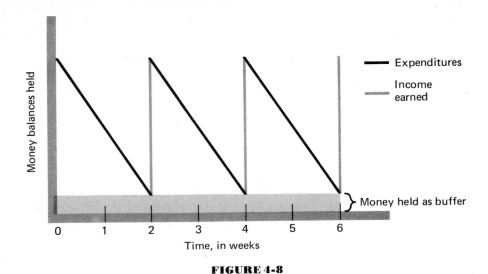

FIGURE 4-8

If income is received every two weeks and a household makes an equal amount of expenditures each day and, in addition, always maintains some small amount of money as a buffer (or shock absorber for unforeseen contingencies, the quantity of money balances held over time will fluctuate as shown above.

Note our assumption that the household will have some money left over at the end of each two-week period.[1] This reflects the *second* motive for holding money: households will try to hold some money as a *precaution* against unforeseen developments. Money is the most liquid asset there is. Unlike other assets, it is immediately spendable—there is no need to exchange it first for an acceptable means of payment. (Money is *the* means of payment.)

We can think of money balances as yielding a stream of services to households. These services are defined in terms of the time, resources, and other costs saved by having money in hand when it is needed to consummate a transaction. Suppose a household holds *all* its financial assets in the form of bonds. This means that when it wants to purchase a good, it must first sell bonds and acquire money. The household must call a broker, pay a

[1] The authors admit that their own inventory of money is often zero and the relationship between their income and expenditures looks more like the graph at the right. (Just shows you how theory and practice can differ.)

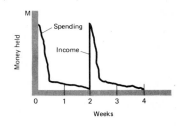

brokerage fee, and wait several days for the money actually to arrive. The cost associated with purchasing the good—economists refer to these as *transactions costs*—are both monetary (the brokerage fee) and nonmonetary (the time and inconvenience). *Holding money minimizes the transactions costs associated with making transactions.*

Most households also earn some interest on those money balances that are held in the form of demand deposits (checking accounts). This interest can be explicit, as with NOW accounts, or implicit, as in the case of the silverware, toasters, and other premiums offered to depositors. More commonly, "free" checking accounts (no service charges) also carry implicit interest. If the bank does not fully charge a depositor for all the costs associated with servicing the account (bookkeeping, preparation and mailing of monthly statements, etc.), then, in effect, the depositor is earning implicit interest on the deposit. The amount of implicit interest would be equal to the actual costs incurred by the bank for each deposit dollar minus whatever charges are paid by the depositor.

How much money should a consumer hold? This figure ought to be related in part to the rate of return on money balances compared with the rate of return available on other assets. The latter is referred to as the *opportunity cost* of holding money.[1]

To illustrate, as market interest rates rise relative to the return on money i_M, we would expect households to reduce their money holdings somewhat and increase their holdings of near-monies, such as time and savings deposits or short-term market securities (for example, Treasury bills). Figure 4-9 plots the expected relationship between the demand for money and the rate on 90-day Treasury bills i_{90}, holding i_M and other factors affecting money demand constant. As i_{90} rises, the quantity of money demanded by households would be expected to fall.

The household's problem in deciding how much money to have on hand is akin to the problem faced by the manager of a department store in selecting the optimal inventory of goods to hold. The holding of inventories is not without cost—it must be financed. If too much inventory is held, extra costs are incurred. If too little is held, sales may be lost. If a household holds too much money, it loses the interest that could have been earned on higher-yielding assets. If too little money is held, extra transactions will be required to convert other financial assets to money when cash is needed.

Households desire to earn as much income on their asset holdings as possible. But one of the constraints most households face in selecting asset portfolios is the need for liquidity and the preference for safe (that is, low-risk) investments. This gives rise to a need to hold not only money but also some relatively safe liquid assets, such as savings accounts (such assets are sometimes referred to as *near-monies*), as well as higher-yielding,

---

[1] In most empirical work on the demand for money, this opportunity cost is considered equal to the rate that could be earned on a short-term market asset, such as the rate on Treasury bills due to mature in ninety days (i_{90}).

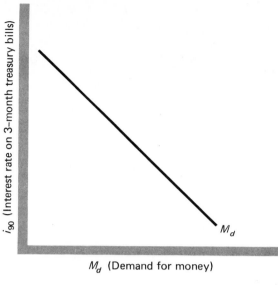

FIGURE 4-9

The demand for money is inversely (or negatively) related to the opportunity cost of holding money (here measured by the rate on three-month Treasury bills). As the bill rate (opportunity cost) rises, the quantity of money demanded falls, and vice versa.

less liquid assets (such as stocks and bonds). As discussed earlier (with more detail to come in later chapters), diversification of asset holdings can help to minimize risk and at the same time help the household to meet its income and liquidity objectives.

4-4
A GENERAL MODEL
OF THE HOUSEHOLD SECTOR

The preceding discussion has examined various important factors that affect household demand for goods, services, money, and other financial assets. Figure 4-10 summarizes the two-stage decision process we have been examining. Given disposable income, households must first decide whether to consume or save and how much of each to do. Once that decision is made, the next decision involves allocating savings across different types of financial assets and determining what to consume. The set of equations presented in Table 4-1 provides a useful summary of many of the issues covered thus far.

Equation (1) is the household-disposable-income identity. It indicates

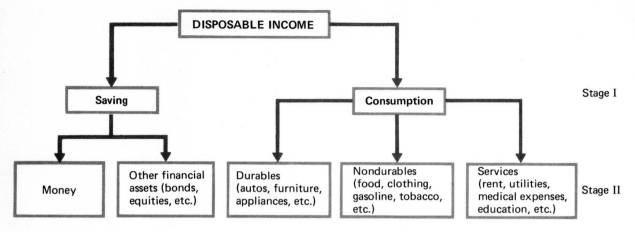

FIGURE 4-10

Given disposable income, a household can be viewed as going
through a two-stage decision process. It must decide, first,
whether the income should be consumed or saved and, second,
what goods and services should be consumed and what financial assets should be acquired.

that household income is equal to income spent on goods and services (consumption) plus income not spent (saving).

Equation (2) is the aggregate-household-consumption function. Included in the parenthesis on the right-hand side of this equation are the primary factors that affect household consumption. Above each of the factors
is a plus or minus sign, indicating how each factor affects consumption. For
example, as income Y_d goes up, so does consumption; as interest rates i go
up, consumption decreases. A question mark indicates that the direction of
influence is uncertain.

We expect consumption to be a positive function of income, and we
hope that this needs little further explanation.[1] Rises in income provide
funds for current consumption and facilitate the servicing of debt that consumers may incur in order to spend now.

As for the interest rate, we would expect changes in it to be negatively
related to consumption. A rise in market interest rates is likely to lead to
some rise in the rate charged on consumer loans and/or a tightening of the
nonprice terms of lending. This, in turn, will discourage borrowing and also

---

[1] What may need explaining is that since, in the aggregate, the household sector saves, it must follow
that for any given dollar increase in income, consumption rises by less than a dollar because part of
the increase will be saved. The relationship between the change in consumption and the change in
income is known as the *marginal propensity to consume*. Note that the fraction of each dollar of income consumed depends on all the variables listed on the right-hand side of Equation (2), not just
on Y_d. For example, if household expectations about the future are bright, many will be willing to
consume a somewhat larger share of current income.

TABLE 4-1

(1) $$Y_d = C + S$$

(2) $$C = f(\overset{+}{Y_d}, \overset{-}{i}, \overset{+}{W}, \overset{?}{x_h})$$

(3) $$S = f(\overset{+}{Y_d}, \overset{+}{i}, \overset{-}{W}, \overset{?}{x_h}) = \Delta M_d + \Delta B_d$$

(4) $$M_d = f(\overset{+}{Y_d}, \overset{+}{i_m}, \overset{-}{i}, \overset{?}{x_h})$$

(5) $$B_d = f(\overset{+}{Y_d}, \overset{-}{i_m}, \overset{+}{i}, \overset{?}{x_h})$$

where Y_d = disposable income
C = consumption spending
S = saving
i = short-term market interest rate
W = household wealth or net worth
x_h = household expectations concerning future income, interest rates, etc.
i_m = rate of return on money
M_d = demand for money
B_d = demand for other financial assets which are, for simplicity, all lumped together and called bonds
Δ = "change in"

discourage some household spending, particularly on durables. Also, when there is an increase in the interest rate (viewed now as the reward for saving), households will tend to save more, decreasing their consumption. Hence, there are two reasons for the negative relationship between consumption and the interest rate.

The third factor in our consumption equation—household wealth (net worth)—has a positive effect on consumption. Over the long run, as wealth is accumulated from saving, the need to save out of current income may decline somewhat. Thus, as wealth rises, consumption is encouraged. In the short run, most changes in wealth occur through changes in the market value of assets held, with the major change occurring in capital gains and losses on equities. Figure 4-11 shows movements in the Dow Jones index of stock prices for thirty large industrial corporations; it also shows consumer spending on durables as a percent of income. As you can see, the pattern of spending on durables relative to income is similar to the pattern of changes in stock prices. Presumably, when the stock market crashed in 1929, the erosion in household wealth considerably reduced household spending.

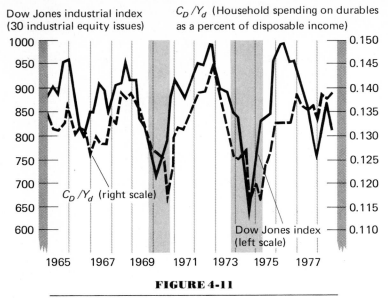

Dow Jones industrial index
(30 industrial equity issues)

C_D/Y_d **(Household spending on durables**
as a percent of disposable income)

C_D/Y_d (right scale)

Dow Jones index (left scale)

FIGURE 4-11

A rise in equity prices increases the value of household wealth.
This, in turn, tends to encourage household spending on durables relative to current income.

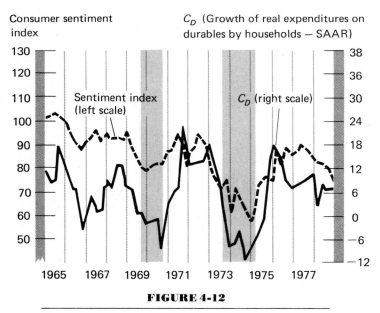

Consumer sentiment
index

C_D **(Growth of real expenditures on**
durables by households — SAAR)

Sentiment index
(left scale)

C_D (right scale)

FIGURE 4-12

When household expectations about the future course of economic activity improve, consumers are willing to spend more on durable goods.

Finally, household expectations about future income, interest rates, and wealth will have an important effect on decisions to spend or save. Figure 4-12 shows movements in the index of consumer sentiment produced by the Survey Research Center at the University of Michigan. This index is drawn from cross-sectional surveys of United States households regarding their expectations. Note that when the index moves up (indicating that consumer sentiment—and therefore expectations about the future—has improved), consumption of durables also rises.[1,2]

Since a decision not to consume a certain proportion of one's income is, in effect, a decision to save that portion, it should not be surprising that saving is a function of the same variables as is consumption; we can see this in Equation (3). Further, ignoring income for the moment, the other variables have an effect on saving that is opposite their effect on consumption. Given income, if a rise in the interest rate discourages consumption, it must encourage saving. This follows from the identity shown as Equation (1). As for income, rises in income permit more saving as well as more consumption. Thus, holding the other variables constant, rises in income are expected to increase saving.[3] Since all saving results in additions to the stock of financial assets held, we can also view saving as being equal to the sum of the change in household demand for money and for other financial assets such as bonds.

The major factors affecting the demand for money are summarized in Equation (4). Rises in the rate of return on money (equal to the flow of services money yields plus any implicit or explicit interest it earns) are expected to increase the quantity of money demanded, while rises in the re-

---

[1] It is important to understand that the various graphs presented in this chapter (as well as in others in the text) do not prove, for example, that changes in consumer sentiment *cause* changes in spending. All the graph shows is that those variables tend to move together—that is, they are correlated with one another (in the case of consumer sentiment and consumption, the correlation is positive). In most cases in economics, the relationship among two or more variables is quite complex, with the direction of causation between two variables often running both ways. For example, while improvements in consumer sentiment probably encourage more consumption, it is also true that increases in consumer spending will raise income and this, in turn, will probably improve consumer sentiment. Against this background, understand that comments made in the text are designed to summarize and simplify, to the extent possible, the vast amount of empirical research on the relationship and directions of causation among various key variables in the economy.

[2] Sharp-eyed readers will note that movements in the Dow Jones index (Figure 4-11) and movements in the index of consumer sentiment are also correlated. This phenomenon is often explained as the "trickle-down effect." A relatively small proportion of the United States population directly holds stock in its portfolios. As a result, when stock prices rise, nothing happens to the wealth positions of many households. However, each day on the evening news, the day's happenings in the stock market are reported. It seems quite possible that as people observe, say, a rise in stock prices, they infer that the economic environment is improving, and this, in turn, makes them more optimistic. Thus the rise in stock prices affects not only wealthy shareholders but also "trickles down" and affects the psychological outlook of other households.

[3] There is a counterpart to the "marginal propensity to consume" discussed in footnote 1 on page 80. The "marginal propensity to save" is that part of any increase in income that is saved as opposed to being consumed. From Equation (1), it must follow that the marginal propensity to consume plus the marginal propensity to save equals 1—all income is either consumed or saved.

turn on other assets (as measured, or "proxied," by a short-term interest rate) encourage people to reduce the quantity of money held.

Another factor that affects households' demand for money is disposable income. Recall from the discussion of the consumption function that spending on goods and services is influenced in a major way by changes in disposable income. As spending rises, transactions rise; therefore, the need for money balances increases.

Finally, the expectations of households will affect the quantity of money held for contingencies (precautionary motive).[1]

The last equation (did you think it would never come?) is Equation (5), the demand for other financial assets (bonds). Money is a substitute for bonds in consumer portfolios. Therefore, a rise in the return on money will lead people to hold more money and less bonds, while a rise in the return on bonds will lead to an increase in bond holdings. Income and holdings of financial assets are positively related because as income rises it tends to increase saving, and an increase in saving implies an increased accumulation of financial assets.

You have now fought your way through a detailed examination of household portfolio decisions. A quick check on your understanding of the key structural underpinnings can be made by looking back at Figure 4-10 in this chapter and Figures 1-2 and 1-3 in Chapter 1. You should find that you now have a broader understanding of what affects consumption, saving, borrowing, and lending decisions.

4-5
SUMMARY OF MAJOR POINTS

1

The functions performed by households include the following: (*a*) purchasing goods and services from other sectors; (*b*) supplying factor services (such as labor) to the other sectors; (*c*) lending funds to the other sectors; and (*d*) borrowing funds.

2

Household portfolio decisions—that is, decisions to spend, save, or borrow—are guided by a desire to maximize the satisfaction or utility derived from the portfolio over time and to maximize the value of the stream of income accruing to the household.

3

The fraction of income consumed by households fluctuates over time, mainly reflecting changes in consumer demand for durable goods.

[1] If households expect interest rates to rise, they may be encouraged to hold money now and buy bonds later, when rates rise. This is usually referred to as "the speculative motive" for holding money.

4

Consumer demand for durables, especially if financed by borrowing (consumer credit), is affected by current and expected income, the present balance sheet, and the terms of credit.

5

The volume of household borrowing is not unlimited. It is constrained by lender behavior and by household willingness to incur debt.

6

Households save to accumulate wealth. The decision to accumulate wealth may reflect a desire to consume at a later date, leave an estate for heirs, or guard against unforeseen developments.

7

Households demand money primarily for transactions and for precautionary purposes.

8

Household money and bond holdings and, more generally, household decisions to consume or save are affected by interest rates.

9

The economic behavior of the household sector can be summarized by five equations: the disposable income identity, the consumption function, the savings function, the money demand function, and the demand for bonds (other financial assets).

4-6
REVIEW QUESTIONS

1 Provide a short discussion or definition of the following terms: nondurable goods and services, seasonal adjustment, nonprice terms of credit, implicit return on money holdings, opportunity costs as they apply to money holdings.

2 Distinguish between real and nominal magnitudes. Why is this distinction important?

3 Discuss the primary factors limiting the availability of credit to households.

4 How do interest rates affect household portfolio decisions?

5 Over the past 10 years the ratio of household money balances to disposable income has declined significantly. Can you explain why?

6   Suppose a state government imposed a usury ceiling on the rate lenders could charge borrowers and this rate were below that which would equate supply and demand. Explain what motivates legislators to impose usury ceilings and show what, in fact, their effect is on consumers.

7   Explain how a fall in stock prices may affect household behavior.

4-7
SUGGESTED READINGS

1   For an excellent although advanced survey of consumer theory, see Robert Ferber, "Consumer Economics: A Survey," *Journal of Economic Literature* (December 1973), 1303–1342. See Campbell McConnell, *Economics* (New York: McGraw Hill, 1978), and Rudiger Dornbusch and Stanley Fischer, *Macroeconomics* (New York: McGraw Hill, 1978) for introductory and intermediate textbook treatments, respectively, of consumption and saving.

2   A sample of very useful Federal Reserve publications on the topic includes the following: *Consumer Spending and Monetary Policy: The Linkages*, proceedings of a conference sponsored by the Federal Reserve Bank of Boston, 1971; "Household Borrowing in the Recovery," *Federal Reserve Bulletin* (March 1978), 153–160; James O'Brien, "The Household as a Saver," *Business Review*, Federal Reserve Bank of Philadelphia (June 1971), 14–23.

3   Important recent academic papers which emphasize the financial side of household spending and saving decisions include the following: Friederic Mishkin, "What Depressed the Consumer? The Household Balance Sheet and the 1973–75 Recession," *Brookings Papers on Economic Activity*, 1 (1977), 123–174; and Michael Boskin, "Taxation, Saving, and the Rate of Interest," *Journal of Political Economy* (April 1978), 3–27.

THE BUSINESS SECTOR

The business of America is business.

Calvin Coolidge

5-1
WHAT'S GOOD FOR GENERAL MOTORS IS
(A) GOOD, OR (B) BAD FOR THE REST OF US[1]

Who or what constitutes the business sector? Some people think of business as a nonhuman entity, as if an office building or a computer could make decisions about hiring, pricing, output, and other business matters. It is, of course, *people* who own and manage a business and people who directly contribute to the goods and services that are produced by business.

Our aim in this chapter is to analyze business decisions about output, employment, investment, and financing. As in our discussion of households in the previous chapter, we shall not concern ourselves about the behavior of individual units. Instead, we will concentrate on the behavior of the entire business sector—that is, on the aggregate behavior of all firms taken together.[2]

[1] Cross out either (A) or (B) after reading this introductory section.
[2] When we speak of "firms," we implicitly assume that all firms behave more or less like a single "representative" firm.

The business sector produces goods and services sold to households, other businesses, governments, and foreigners. To produce these goods and services, the business sector hires and purchases land, labor, capital (plant and equipment), and raw materials. Labor and managerial skills are hired from the household sector; raw materials are acquired from other firms or imported from the foreign sector; and so forth. To function, firms must have funds to finance their operations. These funds can be acquired by earning a profit from previous production or by borrowing. A firm borrows funds by issuing (selling) bonds or equities (common stocks) to the public or through borrowing from banks or other financial intermediaries. A firm earns profits by selling its output for more than it costs to produce. As discussed in Chapter 3, we assume that firms are in operation to earn profits and that everything they do (hiring, pricing, etc.) is guided by the desire to maximize the stream of profits over time.

This is the story in a nutshell. As we proceed with a more detailed examination of the business sector, recognize that increases and decreases in demand for a firm's output will affect the number of workers the firm hires and the wages and salaries it is willing to pay. In addition, the increases and decreases in demand may contribute to increases and decreases in profits as well as in dividends. Since wages, salaries, and dividends accrue to households, it is obvious that household income depends critically on the behavior of firms and the economic environment within which they operate.

5-2
HOW MUCH TO PRODUCE?
HOW MUCH LABOR TO HIRE?

To keep our investigation as simple as possible at this point, let us hold all prices and wages in the economy constant. For the same reason, we shall be concerned in this section with the decisions firms must make over the *short run* (think of it as the current production period.)[1] Obviously, the shorter the period of time we are talking about, the more realistic our initial assumption of constant wages and prices. Analytically, the short run is a period of time over which firms have certain factors of production in place which cannot easily be increased or decreased (plant, equipment, and land). These are the *fixed* inputs. Firms can, however, vary the volume of other inputs, particularly labor, to increase or decrease production. These are the *variable* inputs.

Given output prices, firms must make two basic assessments in deciding how much output to produce:

---

[1] The production period will differ across industries. For a dressmaker the production period may be one month. For a computer manufacturer, it may be one year.

1

How much output will the public demand—that is, how much will the public buy at the prevailing price level?

2

How much will it cost to produce any particular volume of output?

The volume of output Q the public demands at a particular price level P will determine total revenue TR for firms.

$$\text{(5-1)} \qquad \text{TR} = P \cdot Q$$

The total costs TC of producing any volume of output Q will be equal to the cost per unit of inputs c multiplied by the quantity of inputs (or factors of production) required F. The quantity of inputs hired will be a positive function of the quantity of output produced.

$$\text{(5-2)} \qquad \text{TC} = c \cdot F\ (\overset{+}{Q})$$

Profits before taxes π are equal to total revenues minus total costs.

$$\text{(5-3)} \qquad \pi = \text{TR} - \text{TC}$$

We assume that in each production period firms will choose to produce the output volume Q expected to maximize profits—that is, the Q that maximizes the difference between expected total revenues and total costs.[1]

To determine the output volume Q that is expected to yield maximum profits, firms use the following rule of thumb: *Adjust production until the extra costs of producing an additional output unit are just equal to the extra revenue from selling that additional output unit.*[2] To see intuitively why this is so, suppose the extra revenue from selling the last unit of output produced exceeded the extra costs of producing it. Since total revenue increased more than total costs, profits rose. Given that firms are trying to maximize profits, there is an incentive to expand production so long as the increase in total revenue *exceeds* the increase in total costs.

Will production expand without limit? The answer is no. Most empirical studies suggest that as firms expand production, there will be a point at

---

[1] Notice we say "expected." We live in an uncertain world. Firms can never be absolutely sure how much output the public will purchase at prevailing prices; costs of certain raw materials essential to the production process may rise unexpectedly, and so forth. We shall sidestep the role of uncertainty until later and assume for now that firms have reasonably good estimates of what they can sell at prevailing price levels and what it costs to produce alternative quantities of output.

[2] Note we did not say adjust output until *total* costs equal *total* revenue. When total costs equal total revenue, profits equal zero—a strategy hardly consistent with maximizing profits. In general, firms should expand production until expected marginal costs (the change in total costs for producing one more unit of output) equal expected marginal revenue (the change in total revenue for selling that one more unit of output). See the suggested readings at the end of the chapter for more formal treatments of the determinants of production decisions.

which the increase in total revenue does not exceed the increase in total costs. On the demand side firms would eventually find that the public would buy additional output only if prices fell. When prices fall, the extra revenue from additional production will also fall. On the cost side, it seems to be true that as production increases, after a point, the extra costs of producing additional output begin to rise. These rising costs result from the lower productivity (that is, the lower volume of output produced) of additional workers relative to existing workers and the reduced productivity of existing workers who work longer hours. The latter is perhaps easier to see. If a worker's day expands from eight hours to ten hours, it seems reasonable to expect that the worker will be somewhat less productive (that is, produce less output per hour worked) over the two extra hours than over the first eight hours (because of fatigue and so on).[1]

To grasp the effect of additional workers on costs and productivity, assume that, as the personnel manager for a large firm, you were interviewing applicants for an opening as a lathe operator. How would you make your decision? Cutting through all the details, you would probably choose the applicant who could do the job best—that is, the one who could work most quickly, safely, and efficiently. A more formal way of making the point is to say you would pick the applicant who was likely to be most productive.

The relationship between costs and productivity is straightforward. Given wages and the fixed factors of production, the cost of producing any particular volume of output will be determined by the number of workers required to produce it. The more (less) productive each worker, the smaller (larger) will be the number of workers required, and therefore the lower (higher) will be the costs of production per unit of output. The relationship between output and inputs is referred to as the *production function*. It is a technological relationship which specifies the inputs required to produce various levels of output.

Suppose that, after hiring the best lathe operator, the firm decides to expand output, so that you must now hire ten more operators. In general, it will be true that the additional workers hired will be at least slightly less productive than the first one (and the tenth one may be considerably less productive than the first). After all, you picked the best first. This being the

[1] An even more obvious effect on costs results from the fact that, in general, when existing employees work longer hours, "overtime" pay per hour is usually some multiple (say $1^{1}/_{2}$) of regular pay. Thus the firm pays a higher cost per hour worked.

case, it will follow that the extra costs associated with expanding output will eventually rise.[1]

If the extra revenue from selling the last unit of output exceeds the extra costs of producing that unit, firms will expand output. However, as production and sales expand, firms will experience rising extra costs of production due to reduced productivity and perhaps, as prices fall, the additional sales will yield reduced extra revenue. When the increase in total revenue falls to a point where it equals the increase in total costs, the firm will have reached the optimal quantity of output produced.[2]

Go back and look at Equations (5-1), (5-2), and (5-3). Note that when firms choose to produce a particular quantity of output Q given the price level and factor costs c, they also choose a particular quantity of inputs F to use in the production process. Also note that—since we are treating labor as the chief variable input to the production process—when firms decide on what Q to produce, they also decide on how many workers to hire and the number of hours they will work. Figure 5-1 demonstrates the key relation-

[1] Another reason for the increasing costs of producing additional output is that each new unit of labor will have proportionally less of the other factors (such as capital) to work with.
[2] You might work through the opposite case. Suppose the extra costs of producing the last unit of output exceeded the extra revenue received from selling it. With total costs rising more than total revenue, profits would be lowered by the production of that last unit. How would the firm adjust?

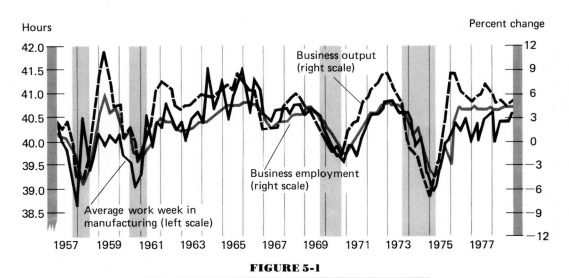

FIGURE 5-1

When firms expand production (output), they will hire new employees and lengthen the work week for existing employees. Similarly, when firms reduce production, as is the case during recessions, they will hire few new workers, lay off some existing workers, and shorten the work week for remaining employees.

ship among growth in business output, growth in employment, and the length of the average work week. When firms decide to increase output, existing employees work longer weeks and new employees are hired.

In summary, firms decide on the quantity of output to produce by comparing the costs and revenues associated with alternative quantities of production and picking the one that is expected to maximize profits. As costs change (perhaps because wage rates change) or as revenues change (perhaps because the public's demand for output changes, thus causing prices to change), the output level that yields maximum profits will also change. Over the short run, decisions to expand or contract output will be associated with increases or decreases in employment. This last point represents an essential linkage among the sectors in the economy. Write it on the back of your hand for swift recall!

5-3
BUSINESS PORTFOLIO BEHAVIOR:
THE FINANCING OF CURRENT OPERATIONS

A firm's production of goods and services generates a variety of financial transactions, which are the concern of the firm's financial department. In other departments of a corporation, there are production managers concerned with minimizing costs of production and marketing managers concerned with maximizing sales revenue. The financial managers have similar aims. As a result, they will engage in portfolio decisions designed to minimize the quantity of non-interest-bearing financial assets held, maximize the profit on invested funds, minimize the cost of borrowing any particular volume of funds, and so forth. In other words, they will choose the mix of financial assets and liabilities that will maximize profits subject to the constraints imposed by their attitude toward risk.

Over the past few years, as universities have produced large numbers of highly capable graduates trained in the intricacies of money, banking, and finance and as the use of new technology (such as computers) has become more widespread, cash management has become highly sophisticated. Nevertheless, the basic factors determining business holdings of financial assets can still be viewed in fairly simple terms. Firms decide how much money to hold in much the same way that households decide; they take account of their transaction needs, the rate of return on money, and the rate of return on alternative assets. Basically, the cash manager will want to reduce money holdings, which do not generally earn explicit interest,[1] and maximize the revenue on invested funds (without subjecting the firm's portfolio to undue risk) while at the same time minimizing the cost of making transactions. Sounds easy, right?

In general, corporate financial officers exist because firms experience

---

[1] NOW accounts, discussed in Chapter 2, are by law available only to households.

two flows of cash in the production and sale of their output—expenditures (outflows) and receipts (inflows)—which are not perfectly synchronized.[1] This lack of synchronization means that if receipts exceed expenditures over a given period—say a week—a portfolio decision must be made. Should the surplus be held as money? Or should it be used to acquire some other financial asset? The decision will most likely be based on the future cash needs of the corporation (is the surplus permanent or temporary?), the rate of return on financial assets, and so forth. When expenditures exceed receipts, firms must either have money on hand or have immediate access to it.

Firms, like households, need (demand) money to consummate transactions. Examples of such transactions would be regular, expected payments for factor services (such as wages and salaries) and tax payments. In addition to these regular payments, firms need money for transactions that cannot be perfectly anticipated. The timing of some transactions may be uncertain (when will the steel be delivered, and when does it have to be paid for?) or the transactions may be totally unexpected (a bill for repairing an equipment breakdown). Expenses, whether anticipated or not, must be paid. As a result, firms will need some money and/or liquid assets (Treasury bills or savings deposits, for example) as a precaution against these contingencies.

Shown in Figure 5-2 are business money holdings and business output.

[1] To see if you have your act together, draw a diagram for firms like the one presented in Chapter 4 for households (Figure 4-8). How does the one diagram relate to the other?

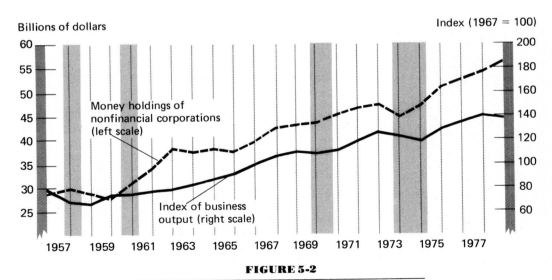

FIGURE 5-2

As business output rises and transactions increase in number and value, firms' need for cash balances also rises.

We would expect that as businesses expanded output, transactions would increase, thus giving rise to increased needs for money. This positive relationship appears to be borne out by the data. It should be noted, however, that recent research strongly suggests business's money holdings have generally risen less than might have been expected as output and sales rose. Can you explain why? Perhaps the most important reason is that over the 1957–1980 period, interest rates have generally trended up. Higher interest rates increased the opportunity costs of holding money balances and encouraged firms to economize on their cash positions. The result was that the increase in business money holdings was proportionally less than the increase in the value of business transactions. Presumably, the funds that normally would have been held as money balances were used to expand operations, acquire other financial assets, pay off existing debts, and so forth.

COMPENSATING BALANCES

Do not get the idea that MBA's with sharp pencils have pared all firms' money balances to the bare minimum needed to consummate day-to-day transactions. Research suggests many firms still tend to hold money balances that are somewhat in excess of day-to-day transactions needs. An important reason for this is that firms and bankers set up arrangements called *compensating balances* which require firms to maintain a certain volume of demand deposits at banks. These deposits are balances that, in effect, are lent to the banks to compensate the banks for services rendered to firms. Such services could involve extension of a line of credit to be drawn upon when needed, payroll services, assistance in making foreign transactions, and the actual granting of a loan. The latter is perhaps the most familiar case.

When a firm secures a loan from a bank, it will be required to pay a particular rate of interest and certain nonprice terms may be imposed as well, such as the maintenance of a compensating balance equal to 10 to 20 percent of the loan. As the following example illustrates, compensating balances raise the cost of borrowing for firms as well as the rate of return on lending to banks.

Example

Suppose a firm needed $800,000 to finance its inventories, the posted interest rate was 8 percent, and the compensating balance requirement was zero. The total interest paid (per annum) would be $64,000, and the true interest cost would be 8 percent. Compare this with another situation which is identical except that the compensating balance requirement is 20 percent. Now the firm would have to borrow $1 million and hold $200,000 in a non-interest-bearing demand deposit (remember, it needs $800,000). The total interest paid would be $80,000, and even though the posted interest rate is still 8 percent, the cost of borrowing the $800,000 the firm needs is really 10 percent (80,000/800,000 = .10). The cost of borrowing is clearly higher. Can you see why the bank is better off? The bank has the $200,000 available to relend to someone else and thus can, in effect, earn interest on the same money twice. Pretty good deal, right?

Corporations are not fooled by this razzle-dazzle. They simply look at the true cost of borrowing and decide whether to borrow or not. Here is a handy formula: the true cost of borrowing is equal to the posted interest rate divided by 1 minus the compensating balance requirement (case one, .08 = .08/1; case two, .10 = .08/.80). In sum, compensating balance requirements can lead firms to hold money balances that are not directly needed for day-to-day transactions. Such balances earn an implicit rate of return for corporations to the extent that the corporations receive services or actual loans from the banks.[1]

Firms, like households and other participants in our economy, experience periods when their operating expenditures exceed their receipts plus their existing stock of money and other financial assets. (The financial assets would have to be liquidated to finance spending.) As a result, firms have a need to borrow funds. This can be accomplished by issuing (supplying) debt directly to the financial markets or by entering into a loan agreement with a financial intermediary (such as a bank or an insurance company). For example, if payments for goods sold (accounts receivable) are lagging, a firm would need temporary financing to pay for the cost of producing these goods. Similarly, firms often need to borrow temporarily to finance inventories of raw materials, goods in production, and finished goods. Inventories are an important part of the dynamics of economic activity. Let us look at them in more detail.

---

[1] A trend gaining some momentum in the banking system is the substitution of explicit fees for compensating balance requirements. Rather than requiring firms to hold deposit balances in return for lines of credit or other services, a growing number of banks are now charging explicit fees for these services. This development may be another factor enabling firms to pare their money holdings.

BUSINESS INVENTORIES

Businesses need inventories of raw materials to produce output; businesses also keep on hand inventories of finished goods to satisfy consumer demand. We will see that changes in these inventories have significant effects on the overall economy. We are primarily interested in the *change* in inventories held by business, because such changes are usually the most volatile component of GNP. If firms hold $200 billion of inventories this quarter and $200 billion next quarter, there will be no net change in the stock of inventories held. Thus, even though inventories are constantly being turned over (that is, sold and being replaced by new goods), the stock of inventory is the same. The result is no increase in spending and thus no net increase in GNP. On the other hand, if firms plan to add to their inventories, this will raise output (GNP) in the current period. To increase output, firms would probably lengthen the work week, increase employment, and perhaps increase their business borrowing to finance all this activity.

But why would firms decide to add to their inventory stocks? Figure 5-3 shows the growth in inventories and the growth of sales (expressed in constant dollars). As might be expected, they seem to be positively correlated over time. Think of a retail department store. When sales pick up, there is a need to restock shelves more frequently so as to avoid losing sales. If a sup-

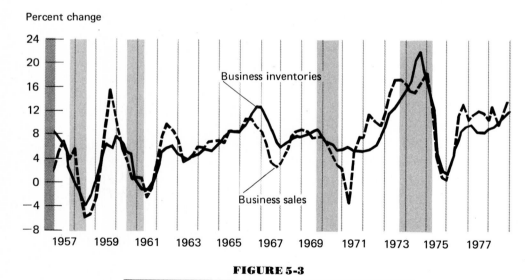

FIGURE 5-3

When sales rise and firms expect the growth to continue, they will raise their holdings of inventories into line with the growth in sales. Similarly when sales fall, as they do in a recession, firms will lower inventories. *Note:* Sales are lagged six months to reflect firms' adjustment of inventories to changes in sales.

plier delivers goods to the store only once a week, the store will need to hold more inventories to bridge the gap between deliveries.

A close look at Figure 5-3 shows that inventories and sales both show considerable cyclical movement. Note in particular that sales and inventory growth tend to pick up as the economy approaches a business-cycle peak. Similarly, sales and inventories fall off as the economy approaches a trough.

The manager of a firm's inventories is never certain about future sales. Nevertheless, the manager must forecast sales and try to manage inventories accordingly. In the real world, of course, these sales forecasts can often be wrong. If sales turn out to be stronger (or weaker) than forecast, the result will be that inventories will turn out to be lower (or higher) than originally planned. If inventories turn out lower (or higher) than desired because of strong (or weak) sales which are *expected to persist*, the manager will have to raise (or lower) planned inventories in the next production period to make up for the actual shortfall (overshoot in inventories). This "inventory cycle" is an important part of the short-run adjustment process in the economy.

Note on Figure 5-3 that sales growth slowed during the last part of 1973. Inventories initially rose as sales fell short of forecasts and managers tried to decide whether the slowdown in sales was temporary or likely to persist. When the managers turned pessimistic about the economic outlook, they cut back sharply on their inventory holdings; this was the final push of the economy downward to the recession trough in March 1975. As sales recovered in late 1975 and early 1976, partly in response to stimulative monetary and fiscal policies, firms were cautious about increasing their inventories. As sales maintained an upward momentum, more businesses became convinced that the economic recovery would continue and they rebuilt their inventory stocks. Production resumed its upward trend, and unemployment began to fall. Here again we have another important linkage in the relationship between firms and households and the economic health of the economy.

Holding inventories, like other things in life, is not free. Firms must finance their inventory stocks out of past earnings, current receipts, or borrowing. Traditionally, borrowing to finance inventories has taken one of two forms: loans from banks or commercial paper. Loans we already know about. Commercial paper represents IOUs or financial claims (promises to pay in the future) sold directly to surplus units or to financial intermediaries.[1] Figure 5-4 shows the change in inventories held by businesses and the change in short-term borrowing (bank loans plus commercial paper) by businesses.

As inventories rise, financing needs also rise. Thus business decisions to add to inventory will increase borrowing. As borrowing demand increases, this will put upward pressure on interest rates.

---

[1] Commercial paper is discussed in more detail in Chapter 12.

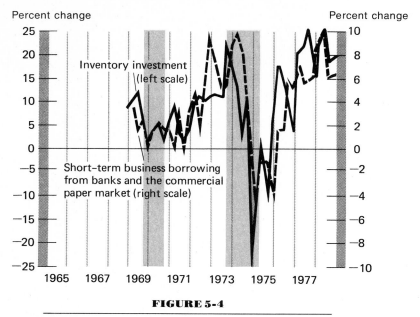

FIGURE 5-4

When firms decide to add to their stock of inventories, such acquisitions must be financed. This often gives rise to an increased demand for funds by firms.

5-4
DETERMINANTS OF BUSINESS INVESTMENT IN NEW BUILDING STRUCTURES AND EQUIPMENT

To this point we have been dealing with *short-run* business decisions: how much output to produce, how much labor to hire, what quantity of inventories to maintain, how to finance current operations, and what amounts of money and financial assets to hold. While all this is going on, firms must also make a variety of decisions that will have an impact on their *long-run* profitability and survival. Almost all producers of goods and services face some competition. This means that producers will constantly strive for ways to improve their existing products; they will attempt to develop new products; and they will search for ways to produce more efficiently. If there are two competing firms and one firm succeeds in one or more of these areas while the other does not, we would expect the successful firm's profits and market share to increase while the unsuccessful firm suffers a corresponding decrease in profits and market share. As was the case in our examination of firms' *short-run* decisions, the desire to maximize profits over the longer run will encourage firms to consider adding to their stock of capital (real assets).

We shall see that if new equipment or a more modern plant (structure) can be expected to raise profits over time, firms will invest in these things.

Business spending on new structures and equipment is usually referred to as "fixed investment," to differentiate it from inventory investment. We shall simply refer to it as investment I.[1] From an economywide perspective, investment plays two roles:

1

As discussed in Chapter 3, it is an important component of current aggregate demand—that is, a significant part of aggregate spending on goods and services goes into the production of fixed investment. Policymakers are interested in this role because business decisions to invest or not to invest will have important effects on GNP, unemployment, and prices, all of which affect the current health of the economy.

2

The flow of investment spending adds to the nation's capital stock, which increases firms' productive capacity and thus affects the long-run health of the economy.

To improve our standard of living and to compete in the world economy, the productive potential of business in the United States will have to rise. This can happen only if capital inputs (as well as other inputs) to the production process are improved and increased.

At any given time there are usually a variety of potential investment projects a firm could undertake. In determining which of these to pursue, a firm's decision maker must consider a number of factors. But the very first thing to be considered is the extent to which the firm's current fixed capital is being utilized. For example, if firms are using only about half their existing capital, it would seem unlikely that investment spending would be high on their corporate priority lists.

The top panel of Figure 5-5 shows the relationship between the growth in business output and the capacity utilization rate.[2] Note that when output

---

[1] We shall focus on net investment—that is, gross investment minus depreciation. As a firm's existing capital wears out (depreciates), it must decide whether or not to replace it. If a firm's investment spending is only as large as depreciation, this does not increase the capital stock but only maintains it. Net investment increases the capital stock. Since the factors affecting decisions regarding replacement are essentially the same as those affecting net investment, there is no real need for a separate analysis of investment spending which replenishes worn-out capital.

[2] The capacity utilization rate is compiled and published by the Federal Reserve. The nation's factories, mines, and utilities are surveyed regarding their stock of capital, the volume of output which could be produced given the current stock of capital (capacity output), and their current production. These data are then used to derive the percentage of capacity being utilized. The closer the percentage is to 100, the closer the nation is to its productive capacity. In practice, as Figure 5-5 shows, 92 percent is the record high for capacity utilization. This suggests that some portion of the existing capital stock is economically unusable. Remember also that the index shown is an average figure for all industries taken together. Thus, when the average is 92 percent, some firms and industries will be operating at utilization rates well above this figure while others are below it.

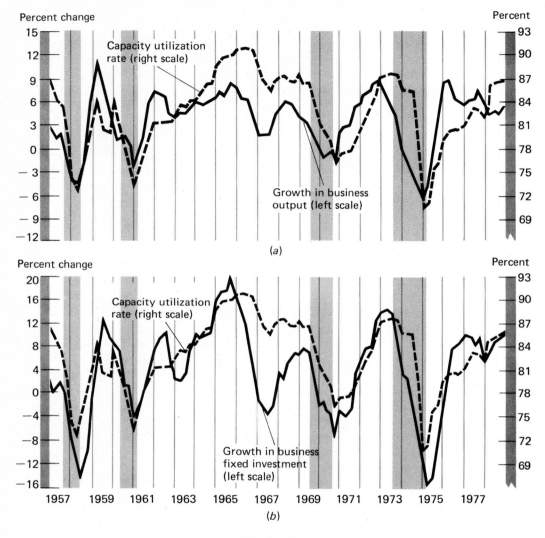

FIGURE 5-5

(*a*) As firms increase production, the rate at which existing
productive capacity is utilized also rises. (*b*) When capacity
utilization rises, this encourages firms to invest and thereby
expand productive capacity.

growth picks up, the rate at which existing capacity is being utilized increases; as output growth slows down, the capacity utilization rate falls.

The bottom panel of Figure 5-5 shows the relationship between capacity
utilization and business investment (expressed in real terms). As capacity
utilization rises and falls, so also does the growth in investment. In gen-

eral, output rises when sales rise and firms find they can make more profits by expanding production. When the rate of capacity utilization is high, firms will be likely to consider investment spending.[1]

Once a firm decides to increase investment in fixed capital, the next step, as in virtually all business decisions, is to consider, with an eye toward maximizing profits, the cost and revenues (or net returns) associated with various investment projects. Specifically, firms will compare the rate of return on a project with the cost of financing it. To make this comparison, both the rate of return and the cost of financing a project are expressed in annual percentage rates.

The cost side can be kept fairly simple at this point. Suppose a firm were considering a project that would cost $1000 to purchase. The firm could borrow the funds to finance the project, or it could use profits accumulated from past sales.

If the firm borrowed the $1000, the cost of funds would be the prevailing interest rate. If the firm used past profits, the cost of using the profits should be measured by the return the firm could earn if it lent out the profits instead of spending them on the new project. Since the firm could lend out the profits at the prevailing interest rate, the interest rate is the cost of using the profits even though the firm is spending and not lending them. This is an application of the notion of opportunity costs, discussed earlier when we examined the demand for money by households; the cost of holding or spending money is the return you could have earned by using it in the next best alternative or opportunity. So, whether the firm borrows or uses profits accumulated from past sales, the cost of funds is the prevailing interest rate.

Given the interest rate and the cost of the project, we can compute the returns that could be earned by taking the available funds and compounding by the interest rate. (*Compounding* is discussed in Section 5-6). These earnings, which can be expressed in dollar terms or in annual percentage terms, represent what the firm gives up when it uses its available funds to purchase new capital goods. Whether or not firms are willing to do this depends on a comparison of the *cost of capital* with the returns expected on the purchase of new capital goods.

In general, the business outlook is the key to how firms assess the expected returns on any particular investment project. Let us define R_j as the stream of dollar returns expected to be associated with any project. The subscript j refers to the relevant period: $j = 0$, the current period; $j = 1$, the next period; $j = 2$, etc. Therefore, R_j refers to the stream of returns in the current and future periods over the useful life of the capital good (R_0, R_1, R_2, R_3, etc.). What determines the R_j? Or, more specifically, what will

---

[1] The major exceptions would be changes mandated by government environmental or safety regulations in a firm's plant or equipment. Such changes might have to be undertaken even if capacity utilization were not high.

determine a firm's expectations of the stream of returns likely to be associated with a particular project? The value of the R's will be determined by the expected net revenue, or the profits, a project generates.[1] Therefore, the way the business outlook affects the values of the estimated R's should be obvious: If the outlook is good, firms will expect demand for output to continue to grow, prices to rise, and, therefore, revenues to increase. On the other hand, if the rates of capacity utilization, sales, and profits are now high but firms expect a long-lasting recession to begin within the next few months, the situation and outlook will not be conducive to investment: Lower expected future sales will mean lower future values of the R's.

You should recognize that the values of the R's are really a firm's guesses or expectations about the future. As such, the R's are governed by the economic outlook and the confidence business has in the ability of government policymakers to maintain the economy's health.

Once the stream of a project's R's is estimated, the firm then calculates the rate of return—usually referred to as the *marginal efficiency of investment* (MEI)—on alternative investment projects.[2] These projects can then be ranked by their MEIs. A firm should then invest in the project or projects up to the point where the MEI is just equal to the cost of borrowing additional funds i_c. If MEI $> i_c$, the profit-maximizing firm can raise profits now and in the future by investing. Figure 5-6, using some hypothetical numbers, plots the relationship between the cost of funds and total investment spending in the economy.

Firms rank alternative investment projects in order of their MEIs from the highest MEIs to the lowest. In Figure 5-6, we have $50 billion of projects yielding at least 10 percent, another $50 billion yielding from 7 to 10 percent, and so forth. Given an interest rate of, say, 5 percent (which represents the cost of funds to firms in this example), firms will invest to the point where $i_c =$ MEI. This equilibrium is defined at point A, where investment spending totals $150 billion.

To keep things simple, we have assumed that the cost of financial capital is constant. In reality, of course, the cost of funds is not constant. Also, we have not yet said much about the way investment is financed. Even at the level of the individual firm, important portfolio decisions must be made regarding the financing of investment spending. Should the spending be financed *internally* or *externally*? Internal financing is simply the spending of retained earnings. There are two kinds of external financing: expanding equity or borrowing. External financing through the expansion of equity involves issuing additional shares of common stock, thus expanding the ownership interests in the firm. If the firm chooses external financing through

---

[1] Net revenue will be a function of the productivity of the capital good (how much output it will help produce), the price of the firm's output, costs associated with operating and maintaining the capital good, and taxes. The effects of depreciation allowances and investment tax credits on investment are discussed in the context of overall fiscal policy in Chapter 20.

[2] The details of such a calculation are discussed in Section 5-7.

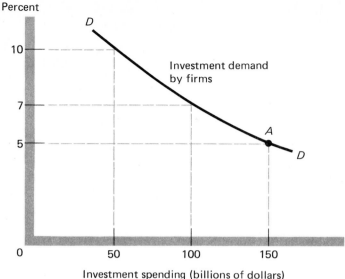

FIGURE 5-6

The investment demand function (DD) is derived by ranking investment projects from those with the highest MEIs (rates of return) to those with the lowest. Given the cost of capital, firms will then choose all those projects with MEIs greater than or equal to the interest rate (cost of capital). This means that investment demand by firms and interest rates are negatively related. As interest rates rise, some investment projects that firms had planned to undertake will be canceled, since they will no longer be profitable; their MEIs will be less than the now higher cost of capital. Similarly, when interest rates fall—other things equal—firms will increase their investment spending. Projects which had been unprofitable will now be worth undertaking, since their MEIs will be greater than (or equal to) the now lower cost of capital.

borrowing, it must then consider whether to issue long-term bonds or short-term commercial paper or whether it should borrow directly from a financial intermediary (take out a loan). In general, the answer to all these questions is that the profit-maximizing firm will choose the option that minimizes the cost of borrowing any particular volume of funds.[1] For each firm, the cost of alternative sources of financial capital will be influenced by several things: (1) the firm's own financial structure (that is, its balance sheet), (2) the tax laws, and (3) the overall financial environment.

A common measure of financial structure is the firm's ratio of debt to

---

[1] This means that the firm will equate the marginal cost of each type of financing to the marginal return on investment.

equity—the so-called *leverage ratio.* Debt costs are financial obligations which must be paid irrespective of current earnings. Equity is the owners' financial investment in the firm. Other things equal, the higher the leverage ratio (that is, the ratio of debt to equity), the greater the risk to potential bondholders and stockholders. As a result, the higher the leverage ratio, the more vulnerable the firm is to declining earnings. In the limit, a substantial decline in earnings for a highly leveraged firm could force it into bankruptcy, cause it to default on its debt obligations, and leave its stockholders with nothing. Recognizing the relationship between leverage and risk, risk-averse investors will demand a higher yield on funds they lend to highly leveraged corporations. Hence firms that already have considerable debt will find their cost of external financing to be relatively high.

The tax laws are also relevant to the costs of financing because, as of this writing, United States law tends to bias the financing decisions of business firms toward debt and away from equity. The reason is that interest costs on debt are a deductible cost of doing business and thus are subtracted from gross revenues before the corporate income tax is computed. Not so for equity. Corporations cannot deduct dividends paid stockholders; dividends must be paid out of after-tax earnings.[1] Thus we have a paradox: Debt financing will initially be cheaper on average than equity financing, in part because of the tax laws. But increasing debt will increase leverage, expose the firm to more risk, and ultimately raise the overall cost of capital as suppliers of funds require higher expected returns to compensate them for the additional risk they must bear.

[1] Thus there exists the so-called double taxation of dividends; they are taxed as part of business income and taxed again as part of household income.

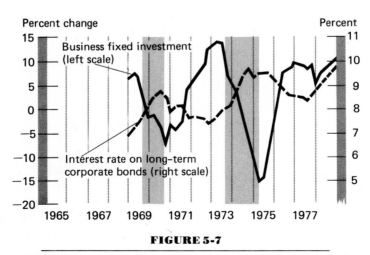

Percent change

- Business fixed investment (left scale)
- Interest rate on long-term corporate bonds (right scale)

Percent

FIGURE 5-7

When interest rates rise and thus the cost of financial capital increases, the growth of investment tends to decline.

The third significant factor affecting the cost of capital to firms is the overall financial environment. Viewed in very general terms in the overall economy, the demand for funds relative to the supply will determine the interest rate and the cost of capital to individual firms. We know from Figure 5-6 and the accompanying discussion that when the cost of capital rises or falls, business spending on investment would be expected to fall or rise, respectively. The relationship among interest rates, the cost of financial capital to firms, and investment spending is a key linkage between the financial system and aggregate demand for goods and services in the economy. Recognize that if monetary policymakers can affect the supply of funds and the level of interest rates, they can have some effect on investment spending. As shown in Figure 5-7, when interest rates on corporate bonds have risen, the growth in investment has tended to decelerate. Similarly, as interest rates fell, investment growth picked up. Isn't it nice to see that theory and practice are not totally divorced from one another?

5-5
A GENERAL MODEL
OF THE BUSINESS SECTOR

We have covered a number of different aspects of business behavior. The equations in Table 5-1 are presented to help summarize the essential features of business decision making in relation to overall economic activity.

The message in Equation (1) is that business demand for labor N_d is a function of the volume of output to be produced Q and the wage rate w. In the short run, the major variable input in the production process is labor. If firms want to alter the volume of output, they will probably alter the amount of labor in the same direction. An increase in the wage rate, other things remaining the same, will lead firms to employ fewer workers.

Just like the rest of us, firms need money balances M_d to finance transactions. Equation (2) tells us that their transactions and financing needs will be related to three factors:

1 The value of output being produced.
2 The rate of return on financial assets other than money.
3 The rate of return on money.

The greater the value of output produced, the greater the number of transactions, and hence the greater the firms' demand for money. The higher the market interest rates i, the greater the incentive for firms to reduce their cash balances. Hence an inverse relationship exists between money demand and i. On the other hand, if firms receive services in return for holding demand deposits at banks (remember the story on compensating balances), this will tend to encourage businesses to hold more money in their checking accounts than might be needed for day-to-day transactions.

TABLE 5-1

$$(1) \qquad N_d = f(\overset{+}{Q}, \overset{-}{w})$$

$$(2) \qquad M_d = f(\overset{+}{Y}, \overset{-}{i}, \overset{+}{i_m})$$

$$(3) \qquad I = f(\overset{+}{CU}, \overset{?}{x_b}, \overset{-}{i_c})$$

$$(4) \qquad i_c = f(\overset{+}{i}, \overset{+}{L}, \overset{?}{t})$$

where
N_d = business demand for labor
M_d = business demand for money
Q = output
w = wage rate
Y = value of output produced and sold $(P \cdot Q)$
i = market interest rate
i_m = implicit rate of return on money balances
I = business investment
CU = capacity utilization
x_b = business expectations about future profits
i_c = cost of financial capital
L = leverage ratio = ratio of debt to equity on firms' balance sheets
t = government tax policy

Economic growth and the growth of individual firms is directly related to the growth in the capital stock. In practice, the growth in the capital stock ebbs and flows over time as the flow of business spending on new plant and equipment picks up or falls off. Equation (3) summarizes the major influences on investment spending. Investment is encouraged by increases in sales and the resulting rise in production and capacity utilization CU, business expectations of a bright economic outlook x_b, and stable or falling costs of financial capital i_c.

Note that it is the business outlook, against the background of the degree of capacity utilization, which will influence firms' projections of the returns which may be associated with additions to the capital stock. The decision to invest or not to invest, as shown in Figure 5-8, will then turn on a comparison of these returns with the cost of financing. As Equation (4) shows, the cost of financial capital i_c will be a function of market interest rates i, leverage L, and the government tax policy t. Policymakers thus have several ways to affect investment spending: they can do something to raise current

A recession cometh and projected expansion goeth! If current sales and capacity utilization are high but a recession is expected to begin soon, many firms will be reluctant to push ahead with their investment plans. A deterioration in the economy would probably reduce sales and capacity utilization and thus reduce the expected profitability of investment. Such an outlook will lead firms to cancel or postpone planned additions to their plant and equipment.

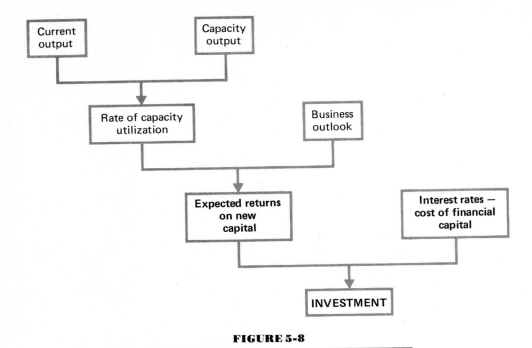

FIGURE 5-8

In deciding whether or not to invest firms will assess the business outlook and their rate of capacity utilization. This will enable them to compute the returns expected on proposed additions to their capital stock and to compare these returns to the cost of financing.

sales and/or improve the business outlook; they can influence interest rates; and they can legislate liberal depreciation allowances and/or investment tax credits which will lower the cost of capital and raise the expected returns.

5-6
APPENDIX A—COMPOUNDING*

Literally, "compounding" means to combine, add to, or increase. In the financial world, it refers to the increase in the value of funds that results from reinvesting the principal (original amount invested) and interest earned on a financial asset. Let us take a simple example to see how compounding works. Assume you purchase a financial asset that will mature in one year—say a time deposit at a bank—which costs $1000 (the face value or principal) and pays 10 percent interest each year. The value of the funds invested at the end of one year is $1000 + .10 ($1000) = $1100.

* This section contains optional material which can be omitted without loss of continuity throughout the rest of the text.

Expressed symbolically:

(a) $\qquad V_1 = V_0 + iV_0 \qquad$ or rearranging, $V_1 = V_0(1 + i)$

where $\qquad V_1$ = value of our funds at end of one year
V_0 = value of our funds at beginning of year
i = rate of interest

Now assume nothing changes except that our asset will mature in two years and the interest earned after one year is reinvested. The value of our funds at the end of two years would be:

$$\$1000 + .10(\$1000) + .10[\$1000 + .10(\$1000)] = \$1210$$

The value at the end of two years V_2 is the original value ($1000) plus the interest on the original value ($100) plus interest on the value at the end of one year [$1000 + .10(1000) = \$1100$]. Notice the implication of the last term that interest is earned on interest—this is compounding. In the second year, we earn interest not only on the principal but also on the reinvested interest.[1]

Expressed symbolically:

(b) $\qquad\qquad V_2 = V_0 + iV_0 + i(V_0 + iV_0)$

Using some simple algebra, this equation can be simplified to:

(c) $\qquad\qquad V_2 = V_0(1 + i)^2$

Happily, Equation (c) can be generalized for any asset with any maturity.

(d) $\qquad\qquad V_N = V_0(1 + i)^N$

The value of a sum of money invested for N years V_N is equal to the original sum V_0 compounded by the interest rate $[(1 + i)^N]$. Note that we are talking about how the nominal value of the funds invested grows over time.

5-7
APPENDIX B—DISCOUNTING AND THE
MARGINAL EFFICIENCY OF INVESTMENT*

Assuming that firms have estimates of the stream of R_j's associated with a capital good, how is the rate of return on a project (or group of alternative

---

[1] The posted annual interest rate is 10 percent (sometimes called the simple rate). If you withdrew the interest earned on the time deposit after one year (but left the principal), your total return over two years would be $200, or $100 each year, and your average annual rate of return would be 10 percent ($.10 = 200/1000 \div 2$). If, as in the example, you reinvested the interest earned after one year, your total return would be $210 and your *compound* annual rate of return would be 10.5 percent ($.105 = 210/1000 \div 2$). The compound rate will always be greater than the simple rate due to the interest earned on interest.

* This section contains optional material which can be omitted without loss of continuity throughout the rest of the text.

projects) to be calculated? One approach would be to first sum the R's

$$\sum_{j=1}^{N} R_j$$

a complicated-looking mathematical notation that merely means:

Summation (Σ) of the net returns (R)
on a project from the current period ($j = 1$)
to the end of the project's useful life ($j = N$)

Therefore

$$\sum_{j=1}^{N} R_j = R_1 + R_2 + \cdot \cdot \cdot R_N$$

After summing the R's, divide the sum by the present cost of the project, both expressed in dollars. This approach treats all the R's equally—no discrimination here—and, as we shall see below, for this reason this approach must be rejected.

The opportunity to earn interest on money lent over time means that a given sum of money lent today will yield a larger sum of money in the future (the original volume of funds invested plus the interest earned).[1] Analytically, this means $1000 received or earned today is implicitly worth more than $1000 earned one year (or one day, one week, etc.) from now. The reason, of course, is that $1000 received today could be lent out. If the annual rate of interest is 10 percent, the $1000 received today and lent out would be worth $1100 in one year, $1210 in two years, and so forth (refer back to the discussion on compounding). As a result, if the R's associated with a project are, say $1000 per year, the returns in the future are worth less than the current returns. Put more formally, the future stream of returns associated with a project must be *discounted* to take account of the fact that $1000 received today is worth more than $1000 received tomorrow.

Discounting is a process that is essentially the opposite of compounding. Compounding tells us the *future* value of a sum of money N years from now V_N invested today at the going rate of interest i. Discounting tells us the *present* value V_0 of a sum of money due to be received N years from today.[2]

Take our example in Appendix A (Section 5-6). Compounding told us that two years from now, the value of $1000 lent today with the interest rate at 10 percent, would be $1210. Discounting tells us that the present value of $1210 received two years from now will be $1000 if the rate of interest is 10 percent.

The general formula for calculating V_0, the present value of a given

[1] Again, we are ignoring the effect of inflation on the real value of money and the possibility of a default by the borrower.
[2] For the mathematicians among us, the relationship between discounting and compounding is akin to the relationship between differentiation and integration in calculus.

amount of money V_N to be received N years in the future, is a straightforward rearrangement of Equation (d) in Appendix A.

(e)
$$V_0 = \frac{V_N}{(1 + i)^N}$$

If we are interested in the present value of a *stream* of returns (R_j) to be received over time, the relevant formula can be modified to[1]:

(f)
$$V_0 = \sum_{j=1}^{N} \frac{R_j}{(1 + i)^j} = \frac{R_1}{(1 + i)} + \frac{R_2}{(1 + i)^2} + \cdots + \frac{R_N}{(1 + i)^N}$$

where R_1 through R_N represent the stream of net returns expected to be received in each time period.

In terms of an investment project, the discounted present value PV of the stream of returns R_j can be written[2]:

(g)
$$PV = \sum_{j=1}^{N} \frac{R_j}{(1 + i)^j}$$

The decision rule for profit-maximizing firms to follow is to engage in any investment project where the present value of a project's expected stream of returns is greater than its present cost. (This is just another way of saying "Expand operations so long as marginal revenue exceeds marginal cost.") Of course, firms are presumed to invest first in those projects with the largest difference between present value over present cost.

An alternative but formally equivalent investment criterion is to compare the marginal efficiency of investment (MEI) on alternative projects with the cost of capital. The MEI—or rate of return—on a project is computed by solving for the rate r which makes the discounted present value of the stream of returns associated with a project just equal to its present cost PC.

(h)
$$PC = \sum_{j=1}^{N} \frac{R_j}{(1 + r)^j}$$

The firm should invest so long as $r > i$. Note by comparing Equations (g) and

---

[1] Note that even if $R_1 = R_2 = R_N$—that is, if the stream of returns are all equal—the present values are not equal: The present value of R_1 is greater than the present value of R_2, which, in turn, is greater than the present value of R_N. Mathematically, the future returns are discounted by a factor $(1 + i)^j$, which must, by definition, be greater than 1 and grow as j increases. Thus the value of $R_j/(1 + i)^j$ must fall as j, and hence the denominator, increase in value. This means that the R's cannot simply be summed to get the present value of the stream of returns. The R's must be discounted to take account of the *time value of money*—that is, the fact that money received now is worth more than money received later.
[2] The interest rate (or the cost of financial capital) to the firm is traditionally used as the discount rate in this calculation.

(h) that if $r > i$, then PV > PC. Thus, the investment criteria are equivalent.[1]

5-8
SUMMARY OF MAJOR POINTS

1

Business firms serve important economic functions: They produce goods and services to sell to the other sectors, they purchase factor services from the other sectors, and they borrow funds from other sectors either directly through financial markets or indirectly through financial intermediaries.

2

The objective of business decisions is to maximize profits.

3

Firms should increase production and expand output until the extra costs of producing an additional unit of output are just equal to the extra revenue from selling that additional unit of output.

4

Labor is the major variable input to the production process in the short run. As a result, decisions to alter production affect both the hours worked by workers currently employed and the number of workers to be hired or fired.

5

Firms hold money in order to make transactions, to meet contingencies, and to compensate financial intermediaries for services provided.

6

Firms often borrow in the short term to finance current operations or to finance inventories. These borrowings, typically in the form of loans from banks or commercial paper, are a significant component of the overall demand for funds in the economy and can affect interest rates.

7

Firms hold inventories of raw materials to facilitate production; they keep inventories of finished goods to facilitate sales. When sales do not go according to plan, inventories are initially affected (they rise when sales fall and fall when sales rise). The adjustment of firms to unex-

---

[1] There are times when the two methods can yield conflicting signals. Such nuances are covered in the texts on corporate finance listed at the end of this chapter.

pected rises or falls in inventories affect production, employment, and borrowing demands and thus are an important part of the dynamic adjustment process of the overall economy.

8

Business investment spending is a major component of aggregate demand. And because of the way it affects the capital stock over the long run, business investment spending is an essential ingredient of economic growth.

9

Firms will invest until the expected returns on new capital are just equal to the cost of funds.

10

Policymakers can affect investment by influencing expected returns—that is, affecting current and expected sales, capacity utilization, taxes, and so forth—and by affecting the cost of funds.

5-9
REVIEW QUESTIONS

1 Provide a short discussion or definition of the following terms: production function, compounding,* discounting,* marginal efficiency of investment,* compensating balances, inventory cycle, capacity utilization, leverage ratio.

2 Suppose most firms in the economy are currently operating at about 75 percent of capacity and they all experience an unexpected increase in sales.

    a What will be the initial effects on inventories, production, and employment?

    b What will be the more enduring effects if the growth in sales continues and capacity utilization moves to a high level?

3 From mid-1977 until mid-1978, long-term interest rates rose significantly. Over the same period, investment spending by corporations also grew. Does this mean that interest rates and investment are positively related? Why or why not?

4 Why might business firms hold more cash balances than they need for day-to-day transactions?

5 The leverage ratio for many firms has risen over time. Can you explain why?

* Refers to the Appendix (optional material).

6   Suppose you were in charge of planning for a large automobile manufac-turer. How would you go about forecasting sales in the coming year? (Think back to Chapter 4.)

*7   Show how an improved business outlook can increase the discounted present value of the stream of returns expected to be associated with an in-vestment project and raise the project's expected rate of return or marginal efficiency of investment.

5-10
SUGGESTED READINGS

1   An excellent supplement to this chapter would be selected readings from a good book on corporate finance. Among the best are Lawrence Schall and Charles Haley, *Introduction to Financial Management* (New York: McGraw Hill, 1977) and Fred Weston and Eugene Brigham, *Manage-rial Finance* (Hinsdale, Ill.: Dryden Press, 1975).

2   For an excellent discussion of the determinants of investment spending, see the articles by Richard Kopcke in the November–December 1977 issue of the *New England Economic Review,* published by the Federal Reserve Bank of Boston.

3   For a complete discussion of the theory of the firm and the determinants of output, price, and employment decisions, see Roger LeRoy Miller, *Inter-mediate Microeconomics* (New York: McGraw Hill, 1978).

* Refers to the Appendix (optional material).

THE GOVERNMENT SECTOR

Everyone is always in favor of general economy
and particular expenditure.

Sir Anthony Eden

6-1
"OF THE PEOPLE,
BY THE PEOPLE,
AND FOR THE PEOPLE"

Look at the front page of your local newspaper on any day, and you will find
a number of articles on what your federal, state, or local government is
doing or failing to do. While we have not yet reached the social condition
described by George Orwell in his insightful novel *1984*, it is clear that more
and more the effects of government actions pervade our day-to-day lives.
These effects include environmental regulations which affect the air we
breathe and the water we drink, laws which govern how fast we can drive,
the price of gasoline and more general actions affecting the pace of economic
activity.

Our aim in this chapter is to understand the impact of government decisions on economic activity. In particular, we want to learn how the government affects economic decisions (spending, saving, borrowing, etc.) made by the other sectors. Our investigation will begin in this chapter with an examination of the economic role of government and recent trends in governmental policymaking activity. Later in the text, government policy will be linked directly to overall economic activity (Chapters 13 and 14), and we will examine specific aspects of the government's attempts to keep the economy in good health (Chapter 20).

As we proceed, it is imperative for you to recognize that government economic policy cannot be understood within a purely idealistic framework. In theory, the government is supposed to make decisions that are in the public interest. Loosely defined, this means the government should act in a way that is consistent with the will (desires) of the majority of the people. To the extent that government actually does behave in this way, it is said to be acting so as to maximize *society's welfare*. Unfortunately, such a view of policymaking is seriously deficient, for it fails to recognize political realities. Leaders of democratic societies are elected, and they usually hope to be reelected. What that means in the simplest terms of practical politics is that the elected leaders may make economic policy decisions designed to maximize *political support* rather than the welfare of society. We shall have much to say on the "political economy of policymaking"—a term designed to account explicitly for the interaction between politics, economics, and the needs and desires of society.

6-2
THE ECONOMIC ROLE OF GOVERNMENT

Government expenditure and taxation policies affect the economy in many ways and are designed to serve a variety of purposes. The effects and objectives of the various policies can be distinguished from one another if we look at the three functions performed by the government. (For now, we shall focus on the federal government.) These are the *allocation function*, the *distribution function*, and the *stabilization function*.[1]

ALLOCATION FUNCTION

When we speak of the allocation function, the focus is on how government activity affects the allocation of resources in the economy. First, the government is a major producer of goods and services. The production of these goods—for example, national defense and the provision of a judicial system—requires resources (labor, capital, and land). The resources the

[1] This classification system was developed by Richard Musgrave in his seminal text *The Theory of Public Finance* (New York: McGraw-Hill, 1959).

government uses are, of course, unavailable to the other sectors. This has an obvious, direct effect on the allocation of resources within our economy. A second, less obvious effect on the allocation of resources stems from the role the government plays as a regulator of economic activity in various industries and markets. There are many, many government agencies whose purpose is to regulate the price, quality, or quantity of specific goods produced. Examples are the Food and Drug Administration, which regulates the quality and availability of various foods and drugs; the Interstate Commerce Commission, which regulates interstate trucking rates; and the Federal Trade Commission, which regulates the advertising and promotional activities of many industries. In addition, the Department of Agriculture administers many farm programs designed to regulate the output of specific farm products.

A third way the government affects resource allocation is through its taxing policy. Tax credits, deductions, and exemptions applied to, say, investment spending by firms or housing purchases by consumers will stimulate spending in these areas. This, in turn, encourages more production, which requires that additional resources be allocated to these endeavors.

DISTRIBUTION FUNCTION

Perhaps a more familiar effect of government actions on the economy is their impact on the distribution of income. Within the private sector (households, businesses, and foreigners), the distribution of income is initially determined by the wages and salaries, rent, interest, and profits earned by furnishing factor services to the production of goods and services. Government then comes along and, through its system of taxes and transfer payments, redistributes income. For example, many of us have social security taxes withheld from our regular paychecks. The government takes these funds and transfers them to the retired who are receiving social security benefits. Less obvious forms of redistribution occur when the government takes the proceeds of the income tax and makes payments to welfare recipients or to veterans.

STABILIZATION FUNCTION

For the purposes of our study of the financial system, the most important economic function of government is the stabilization function. This involves the taxing and spending policies of the government—usually referred to as *fiscal policy*—designed to improve or maintain the overall health of the economy, as measured by the rate of inflation, the unemployment rate, the pace of economic growth, and the relationship between the United States and world economies.

Most government programs are aimed at objectives related to the allocation of resources or the distribution of income. However, virtually every program enacted by the government will also have some macroeconomic effects (which are often unintended) on the overall state of the economy (for example, inflation and unemployment). In fact, we shall see in later chapters that the government's failure to recognize the macroeconomic effects of allocative and distributive policies has been one of the factors contributing to economic instability. Consider, for example, United States agricultural policy. In recent years the government paid farmers of various crops substantial sums of money to restrict the acreage they planted. In addition, the government has raised the support prices (the minimum prices farmers receive) on some crops. Under pressure from special-interest groups (lobbyists), legislators responded with these kinds of policy actions, which are designed to increase farm income. Whatever the merits of these policy actions from the farmer's viewpoint, they have contributed to the overall rise in food prices that has plagued all of us in recent years. In general, the government's stabilization function (e.g., lowering the rate of inflation) has to some extent been undermined by policies related to its other functions.

6-3
GOVERNMENT
POLICYMAKING: WHO CALLS THE SHOTS?

Perhaps, from the way we have just described the role of the government sector in our economy, you might imagine that the government's policies issue automatically from an enormous white building in Washington, D.C., much as toll tickets are automatically dispensed by the machines at the entrances of turnpikes. Not so—especially not in our democracy. Policies are formulated and implemented through compromises among four centers of power within the government.

First, there is the *President*—the elected representative of all the people—whose continued political success requires careful balancing of the interests of many large and diverse groups of people. Second, there is the *Congress*—explicitly, the elected representatives of a specific regional constituency (their voters); implicitly, the representatives of special-interest groups from the private sector and from portions of the federal bureaucracy. That members of Congress do represent special-interest groups and the federal bureaucracy becomes a bit easier to see when you realize that Congress is organized around a committee system which specializes in certain functional areas (defense, education, banking, commerce, etc.). Members of these committees often receive campaign contributions and organizational support from various groups that are interested in influencing the policies formed by the committees. Third, there is the *government bureaucracy* (made up of political appointees and career civil service workers) which manages day-to-day policy and which interacts with regulatory agencies and the groups that the agencies are supposed to regulate (for example, the interaction between the Civil Aeronautics Board and the airlines). Fourth, there are the *organized* special-interest

Politicians tend to be shrewd, diplomatic, and crafty. In attempting to appease various constituencies, they will often support increased government spending on specific programs and cuts in taxes. How many politicians regularly support cuts in spending or increases in taxes and get reelected? You might begin to think about what all this has to do with budget deficits and economic instability.

THE POLITICIAN

groups (the AFL-CIO, American Medical Association, National Rifle Association, etc.), which have access in varying degrees to the first three groups and thereby can affect governmental policies. (Love those lobbyists!)

To illustrate how these groups can affect policies, let us assume that there is a piece of proposed legislation regarding bank regulation. The interacting power groups would include (1) the relevant Congressional committees—the House and Senate banking committees; (2) the interested government agencies—the Federal Reserve System, the Office of the Comptroller of Currency, and the Federal Deposit Insurance Corporation; and (3) the organized special-interest groups—the American Bankers Association and organizations representing other financial intermediaries which might be affected by the legislation (such as the United States League of Savings Associations).

In addition to the four power centers discussed above, there is the general *electorate*—the voters—who may or may not be aware of or concerned with particular policy issues. On issues with strong public appeal or extensive publicity, the general electorate acts as a fifth force in determining the outcome of policy decisions. If there is strong voter support on an issue, Congressional representatives might resist the pressures of organized interest groups and the government bureaucracy. Members of Congress are concerned ultimately with the sentiments of their voters. On issues involving little public awareness or interest, the policy decisions are the result of *compromise* among the competing pressures of the organized special-interest groups, the government bureaucracy, the Office of the President, and the congressional committees.

6-4
SOME BACKGROUND ON GOVERNMENT EXPENDITURES AND RECEIPTS

You may or may not be surprised to learn that about 20 percent of GNP is accounted for by *government purchases* of goods and services. What may surprise you, though, is the fact that this percentage has remained relatively stable over the last twenty-five years. Figure 6-1 shows a few more interesting things about government spending during these past twenty-five years: Although total government spending has risen, as shown in Figure 6-1*a*, the ratio of *federal* purchases to GNP has fallen, as shown in Figure 6-1*b*; also note in Figure 6-1*b* that the ratio of *state and local* purchases to GNP has risen. The growth in purchases of goods and services by state and local governments relative to those by the federal government reflects the demographic changes in our population, such as the baby boom in the 1950s and 1960s. That rapid increase in population—as well as the population shift to the suburbs—generated a need for schools, highways, medical care, police and fire protection, sanitary services, and recreational facili-

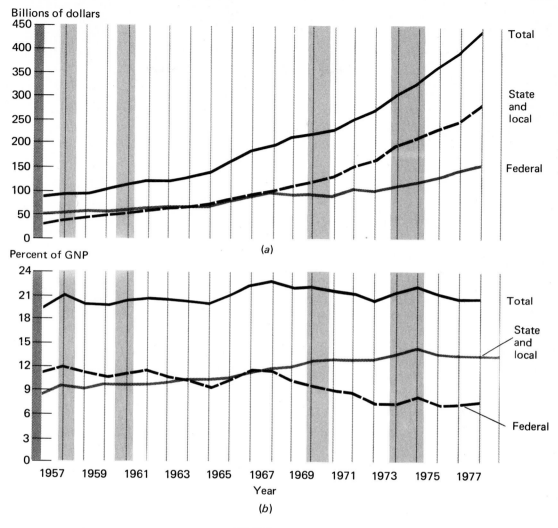

FIGURE 6-1

(a) Government purchases of goods and services. (b) Government purchases of goods and services as a percent of GNP.

ties. State and local governments provided these things in response to the political process, and, as a result, state and local spending increased.

The perception of many people is quite different from the real facts represented by the data in Figure 6-1. Many people believe that the government, particularly the federal government, has grown in size. How can we reconcile these data with such perceptions? Total *outlays* by the federal government consists of (1) *purchases* of goods and services (a component of

GNP), (2) *transfer* payments, (3) *grants* in aid to state and local governments, (4) *interest* paid on the federal debt, and (5) *subsidies*. Thus federal *outlays* include *purchases* (or *spending*) on goods and services and a variety of other things. The top part of Figure 6-2 shows each of the five categories as a percentage of total federal outlays; the bottom panel shows total outlays and purchases of goods and services as a percentage of GNP. Note that total federal government outlays have risen relative to GNP, largely as a result of the growth in transfer payments (social security, medicare, and so forth) and the growth in grants to state and local governments. The increase in

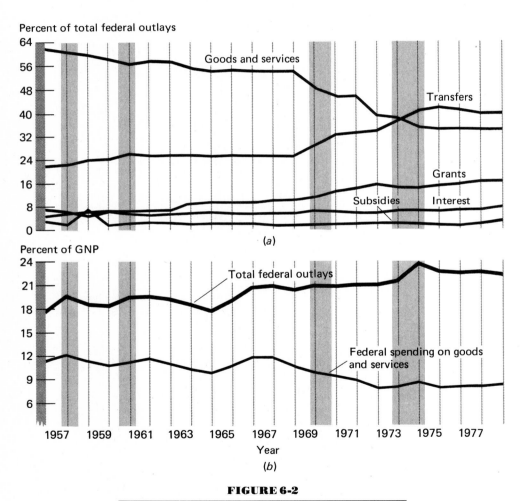

(a)

(b)

FIGURE 6-2

(a) Federal expenditure categories as a percent of total federal outlays. (b) Federal spending on goods and services and federal outlays as a percent of GNP.

grants, of course, has helped to finance the growth in state and local government spending on goods and services. Thus the federal government *has* increased in size as measured by total outlays. The increase mainly reflects government programs that redistribute or transfer income between groups in society.

The federal government spends directly on goods and services and redistributes purchasing power to others who, in turn, purchase goods and services. All this activity must be financed by either taxing or borrowing. The top part of Figure 6-3 shows the sources of federal receipts in 1978. The individual income tax, corporate income tax, and social security tax (paid by both employers and employees) accounted for over 90 percent of federal revenues. The bottom part of Figure 6-3 shows the sources of state and local

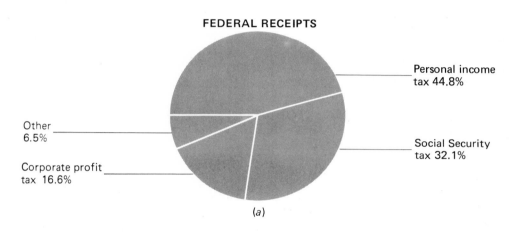

(a)

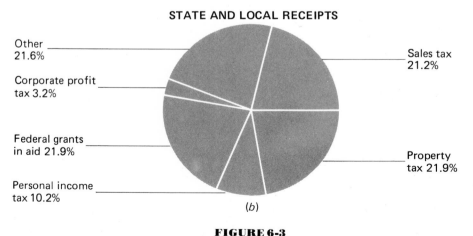

(b)

FIGURE 6-3

Sources of (*a*) federal and (*b*) state and local receipts, 1978.

revenues. Note the wider variety of taxes imposed by state and local governments and that over a fifth of their total receipts come from the federal government.[1]

Most of the complaints about government are generated by the burden of all these taxes. The more the government takes, the less income firms and households have left to spend. In mid-1978, the taxpayers in California finally said "Enough!" They overwhelmingly approved "Proposition 13," which called for a substantial cut in property taxes. This so-called taxpayers' revolt, which has to some degree spread across the nation, is an indication that the general electorate, normally apathetic and passive, is increasingly dissatisfied with the performance of government and the cost of financing government. Leaving aside until later the interesting issue of how the government has performed, let us take a closer look at how government operations are financed.

6-5
FINANCING THE GOVERNMENT

Despite their various sources of revenue, governments, and particularly the federal government, have generally found it impossible to balance their budgets; that is, they do not take in enough revenue to finance their expenditures. When outlays exceed receipts, the result, of course, is borrowing to finance the deficit.

At a very simple level, it is not hard to understand why government deficits have persisted for so long. When it looks as though there will be a deficit, the government has three options: (1) cut some type of spending to eliminate the deficit; (2) increase taxes to eliminate the deficit; or (3) borrow to finance the deficit. Option 2 will often be unpopular with the voters. Option 1 will also be unpopular but not with all the voters — only those who feel the effects of the cuts in spending. For example, cutting defense spending will be unpopular among defense contractors and Pentagon employees. Cuts in the grants to state and local governments for primary and secondary education will be unpopular among schoolteachers and parents of school-age children. Wherever the cuts are suggested or contemplated, special-interest groups will organize and lobby against changes that would leave them worse off. The result of the lobbying will be pressure on the politicians to minimize spending cuts. This leaves option 3 and budget deficits as an attractive alternative, at least in the short run.[2]

---

[1] For two decades federal aid to state and local governments has risen at a faster clip than state and local revenues raised from state and local sources. This is particularly true for local governments. Thus municipal governments are becoming increasingly dependent on federal assistance.

[2] It should be noted that many state constitutions require state and local governments to balance their budgets. This means that when it looks as though there will be a deficit, it *must* be eliminated by cutting spending, raising taxes, or both. Some state governments faced with impending deficits proved they could innovate around regulations just as households and businesses do — they created various borrowing authorities or agencies whose sole purpose was to get around constitutional barriers to deficit financing.

But what has actually happened is that governments at all levels have tended to raise taxes, increase spending, and increase borrowing all at the same time. (Who said politicians could not walk and chew gum at the same time?) The public was willing to go along for a while. However, the ongoing attempts by policymakers to remedy various social ills has inevitably led to a proliferation of programs and increases in spending which outstripped the government's revenue base. The result: chronic budget deficits, mushrooming government borrowing, and fed-up voters and taxpayers.

The top panel of Figure 6-4 shows the federal budget deficits and surpluses over the 1957–1978 period; the bottom panel shows the resulting increase in the level of federal debt outstanding.

Let us try to put all this together with some simple mathematical expressions. We shall define net taxes, as in Chapter 3, as total taxes minus total transfer payments (including grants and subsidies). Equation (6-1) tells us that if no new tax policies are enacted (that is, if there is no change in tax rates or transfer programs), the dollar amount of net taxes T is a positive function of the level of GNP.

$$(6\text{-}1) \qquad\qquad T = f(\overset{+}{Y})$$

There are two reasons for this positive relationship. First, both corporate and personal tax payments are directly tied to income. As firm and household incomes rise, so do their tax payments. Second, many transfers are negatively tied to income. An increase in GNP (employment, production, and income) will reduce unemployment compensation payments and, perhaps, welfare payments; therefore transfers will be reduced. Since transfers are subtracted from government receipts, a reduction in transfers means an increase in net tax receipts for the government.

The difference between net government tax receipts T and government spending G on goods and services will determine the government's surplus or deficit. Equation (6-2) depicts the more familiar case—government spending G minus tax receipts T equals the government's deficit D_g.

$$(6\text{-}2) \qquad\qquad G - T = D_g$$

To finance this deficit, the government will issue (sell) bonds in the financial market. Analytically, this means that the government's deficit will be equal to the change Δ in bonds supplied by the government B_{sg}.

$$(6\text{-}3) \qquad\qquad D_g = \Delta B_{sg}$$

Government borrowing and the deficit which accounts for it can have a considerable and direct impact on the availability and cost of funds to other borrowers and ultimately on overall economic activity and the rate of inflation. A rise in government borrowing represents an increased demand for funds. If this increased demand is not met by an increase in the supply of funds, the effect of the government borrowing will be to raise interest rates. As interest rates rise, some private borrowers might be

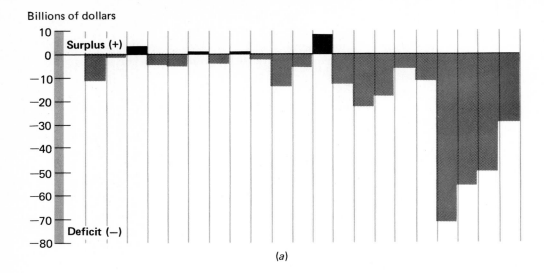

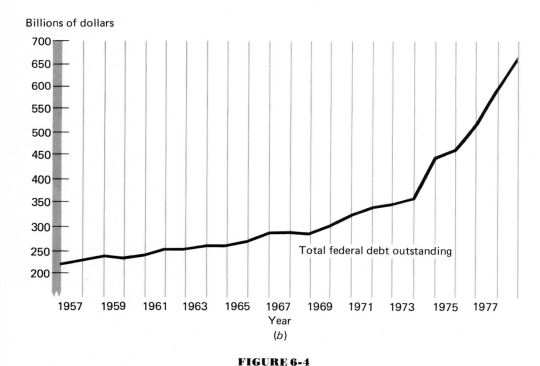

FIGURE 6-4

(a) Federal budget deficits and surpluses, 1957–1978, in billions of dollars. (b) Total federal debt outstanding, 1957–1978.

"crowded out" or rationed out of the market. For instance, the higher interest rates mean a higher cost of capital—a cost that may exceed the expected return on planned investment for some firms. Accordingly, these firms will postpone or cancel their borrowing and spending. Higher interest rates will also raise the cost of household borrowing as the interest rates on mortgage and consumer loans rise. The net result is that a rise in government spending, which is financed by borrowing, can increase interest rates which, in turn, causes some reduction in consumption and investment.

To avoid these undesirable side effects of deficit financing by the federal government, the Fed can increase the supply of money. As the money supply expands, there will be less upward pressure on interest rates. This induced expansion in the money supply also has an undesirable side effect: over the long run, it appears to contribute to inflationary pressures in the economy. More on this in Chapter 20.

STATE AND LOCAL GOVERNMENT BORROWING

For the most part, borrowing by state and local governments is limited to the financing of capital expenditures—schools, highways, sewer systems, and so forth. Many state constitutions impose limitations on the volume of borrowing, the types of projects which can be financed by borrowing, and the cost of borrowing. Other states are not bound by these limitations and, of course, their indebtedness has increased over the years. Debt issued by state and local governments totaled $65 billion in 1960; in 1978 that debt had risen to $277 billion.

What accounts for the rapid rise in state and local borrowing? Given the demographic changes mentioned earlier, the public's demand for government services and facilities increased and state and local governments responded by building, spending, and borrowing. Once capital expenditures are made, they are accompanied by a continuing stream of current expenditures necessary to operate them. Examples would be salaries paid to teachers, expenses associated with maintaining highways, and so forth.[1]

In the inflationary environment of the last decade, such operating expenses rose quite rapidly. At the same time, people were moving from the large cities of the eastern part of the country (Cleveland, New York, Boston, Philadelphia) to the suburbs, thus eroding the property-tax bases in the cities. The resulting budget squeezes and the public's resistance to higher taxes induced city governments to try to cut spending and to lobby the federal government for financial aid. Some officials of city government thought that it would be relatively easy to cut local spending. For example, since the decline in the birthrate reduced the need for many schools, education costs could be pared. However, attempts to shut down neighborhood schools met significant resistance—everyone favors reduced spending as

---

[1] It appears that the growth of state and local governments due to the demographic changes of the 1950s and 1960s might be reversed in the 1980s, as the emerging trend toward smaller families reduces the need for increases in spending on education and other services provided by municipal governments.

long as they are not hurt by the reduction! As the data on federal grants to state and local governments presented above show, state and local politicians were more successful in soliciting federal funds. Unfortunately, even an increase in federal funds cannot help overcome the budget deficit in some cities. For example, New York City continued to run large budget deficits which required further borrowing to finance current operating expenditures. As the public became more and more aware of increasing borrowing and the deteriorating financial condition of the cities, buyers of municipal bonds—and the buyers are the suppliers of funds—became more and more scarce. Without willing buyers of municipal bonds, there was no one to finance further deficits. Municipalities that faced reluctant lenders had to offer higher interest rates to bond buyers, while others that could not get buyers even at the higher rates had to make massive cuts in expenditures. These are dramatic examples of how financial conditions can affect spending in our economy.

6-6
SUMMARY OF MAJOR POINTS

1

Government policy actions serve three primary functions: the allocation function, the distribution function, and the stabilization function.

2

Any government policy may have an impact on all three functions. Our primary concern is with government policy designed to stabilize economic activity.

3

There are four centers of power within the government and they all affect the formation of government policy: the Office of the President, the government agencies responsible for administering and implementing policy, the congressional committees with jurisdiction over particular policy areas, and the organized special-interest groups. Lurking in the background is the general electorate which can elect or reject the political decision makers.

4

Although government policymakers are often presumed to be acting so as to maximize society's welfare, they frequently make decisions designed to maximize political support.

5

Spending on goods and services by all levels of government has accounted for about 20 percent of GNP during each of the past twenty-five years. What this steady share of *total* government spending does not show is the rise in municipal government spending and decline in federal government spending relative to GNP.

6

Federal government outlays—which include transfers, grants, subsidies, and interest paid on the debt as well as purchases of goods and services—have risen rapidly relative to GNP, reflecting spectacular growth in grants and transfers.

7

The federal government relies on the individual income tax, the corporate income tax, and the social security tax for over 90 percent of its revenues. Municipal governments rely on these taxes as well as sales and property taxes.

8

Government outlays are financed by taxing or borrowing. For most of the past quarter century, federal government receipts have fallen short of outlays. The resulting budget deficits were financed with considerable borrowing and large increases in the volume of federal debt outstanding. Many municipal governments, in the face of rising expenditures and eroding tax bases, also stepped up their borrowing and have encountered reluctance among lenders in financial markets.

6-7
REVIEW QUESTIONS

1 Provide a brief definition or discussion of the following terms: special-interest groups, balanced budget, crowding out.

2 How does the government affect the allocation of resources in society?

3 Present some examples of government policies aimed at allocative or distributive objectives which also have important effects on economic stability.

4 Distinguish between government outlays and government purchases of goods and services.

5 Why has state and local government spending risen so fast over the past twenty years?

6 Why do government budget deficits persist, especially at the federal level?

7 Why was the federal budget deficit so large in 1975?

6-8
SUGGESTED READINGS

1   Readers interested in theories of political behavior and how the political process affects and is affected by the economic environment are referred to Joseph Schumpeter, *Capitalism, Socialism and Democracy* (New York: Harper & Row, 1950); Mancur Olson, *The Logic of Collective Action* (New York: Schocken, 1968); James Buchanan and Gordon Tullock, *The Calculus of Consent* (Ann Arbor, Mich.: University of Michigan Press, 1967); Anthony Downs, *An Economic Theory of Democracy* (New York: Harper & Row, 1957); Randall Bartlett, *The Economic Structure of Political Power* (New York: Basic Books, 1973); and James Buchanan and Richard Wagner, *Democracy in Deficit: The Political Legacy of Lord Keynes* (New York: Academic Press, 1977).

2   A variety of excellent texts exist in the field of public finance. Among the best are Richard Musgrave and Peggy Musgrave, *Public Finance in Theory and Practice*, 3d ed. (New York: McGraw-Hill, 1980); Jesse Burkhead and Jerry Miner, *Public Expenditures* (Chicago: Aldine, 1971); and Joseph Pechman, *Federal Tax Policy* (Washington, D.C.: Brookings, 1977).

3   For an anatomy of the financial problems faced by New York City and other municipalities, see Roger Alcaby and David Mermelstein, eds., *The Fiscal Crisis of American Cities* (New York: Vintage, 1976). For a general discussion of municipal finance, see James Maxwell and J. Richard Aronson, *Financing State and Local Governments* (Washington, D.C.: Brookings, 1977).

7

THE FOREIGN SECTOR

That world was easier.

Paul Volcker

7-1
WHY NOT IGNORE IT?

Not long ago, the interactions between the United States economy and the economies of other countries were ignored by most bankers, stock market analysts, economists, accountants, corporate treasurers, policymakers—and textbook writers. The reason was simple: trading between the United States and the rest of the world accounted for only a small percentage of total output (or income) in the United States. Many economists assumed that because foreign trade was so small, it had an insignificant effect on the United States economy. They also assumed that they could analyze the United States economy in isolation, that is, within a purely domestic frame-work (economists call this a closed-economy model) and lose very little information on how prices, income, and interest rates, among other things, are determined. Clearly, as Paul Volcker, chairman of the Fed, suggests, "That world was easier." However, as the contents of any major daily newspaper will reveal, all this is no longer true. It is not possible to ignore the foreign sector in the belief that it has relatively unimportant effects on the United States economy.

Foreign producers—especially in the auto, textile, electronics, shoe, and steel industries—are becoming increasingly more competitive in the United States. Similarly, United States producers of agricultural and manufactured goods are finding opportunities to expand profits in foreign markets. Many United States firms now have plants and large sales forces in countries throughout the world. These firms are known as *multinational firms* (firms with offices or plants in many nations). Table 7-1 shows the 1977 domestic and foreign sales and profits for a number of United States multinational firms. Although the table shows only manufacturing firms, there are also many multinational service firms. For example, Citibank (of New York City), the second largest bank in the United States, has offices in over a hundred countries and makes more loans to foreigners than to United States residents.

For more evidence of the significant effects of the foreign sector, consider the following: the quadrupling of the price of imported oil in 1973, the large purchases of United States wheat by the Soviet Union in 1972–1973, and the monetary and fiscal policies of governments around the world during the early 1970s—all these events contributed to the inflation and recession in the United States and the rest of the world between 1973 and

TABLE 7-1
THE IMPORTANCE OF THE FOREIGN SECTOR TO UNITED STATES MULTINATIONAL FIRMS

COMPANY	1977 Sales, Percent		1977 Operating Profits, Percent	
	UNITED STATES	FOREIGN	UNITED STATES	FOREIGN
Caterpillar Tractor	81	19	90	10
Coca-Cola	56	44	42	58
Colgate-Palmolive	44	56	37	63
Dow Chemical	55	45	65	35
Du Pont	77	23	87	13
Ford Motor	65	35	56†	44†
General Electric	79	21	78†	22†
General Motors	79	21	89†	11†
Gulf Oil	45	55	NM‡	NM‡
I.B.M.	50	50	55†	45†
I.T.T.	49	51	48	52
Johnson & Johnson	59	41	50	50
Pfizer	47	53	36	64
Standard Brands	66	34	65	35
Standard Oil (Indiana)	75	25	73†	27†
Xerox	56	44	65†	35†

† Company provided net income rather than operating profits.
‡ NM = not meaningful.
SOURCE: *Business Week*, April 24, 1978.

1975. More recently, the large rise in oil prices in 1979 aggravated inflation and raised the probability of a 1979–1980 recession.

The main thing we will examine in this chapter is the interaction between the foreign sector and the domestic United States economy. We will look at the spending, saving, and borrowing decisions of domestic and foreign economic units engaged in international transactions. The United States is part of the world economy and is affected by world economic developments. This carries implications for the United States which cannot be ignored. If you are still not convinced about this, look at the manufacturer's label on your stereo equipment.

7-2
RELATING INTERNATIONAL
AND DOMESTIC TRANSACTIONS

In earlier chapters we assumed that households and firms held in their portfolios real assets, financial assets (including money), and financial liabilities. Furthermore, we assumed that all these assets and liabilities originated in the United States. Some typical United States assets and liabilities—for example, a Ford Thunderbird (real asset) made in Detroit and a bond (financial asset) issued by American Telephone and Telegraph—are shown in Figure 7-1. In this chapter, we will widen the scope of a typical portfolio; we will consider that firms and households can also acquire assets and liabilities produced in the rest of the world. These are shown in the dark boxes in Figure 7-1.

Let us consider Figure 7-1 for a moment. We know that United States residents buy Sony television sets, Swiss watches, and bonds issued by Volkswagen of Germany. What factors influence American residents to choose among United States and foreign goods and assets in their portfolios? And how do such choices ultimately affect United States economic activity and financial markets?

We shall begin with a very simple model, *initially assuming that the prices of all goods, services and interest rates (both domestic and foreign) are constant.* This does not mean that we are assuming that the prices of goods in Japan, for example, are equal to the prices of goods in the United States—all we are assuming is that the prices in each country initially remain unchanged. *We shall also assume at this point that the dollar is accepted as a means of payment (or medium of exchange) in the whole world.* This means that we will not have to distinguish between money in the United States and the monies used in the rest of the world.[1]

---

[1] Given this assumption, the analysis developed is analogous to an examination of the determinants of financial flows and trading between, say, New York and California.

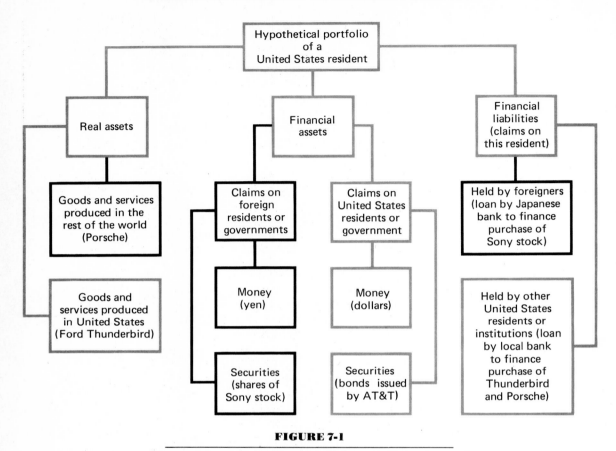

FIGURE 7-1

The portfolio of a United States resident can include assets and liabilities acquired in international transactions as well as assets and liabilities reflecting strictly domestic transactions.

TRADING GOODS

National expenditure (or national output) in the United States is equal to the following sum:[1]

Total United States output (or expenditure)
    = Domestic expenditures   +   Exports   —   Imports
        C, consumption E, purchases by M, purchases by
        I, investment   foreign residents   United States residents
        G, government   of goods and   of goods and services
                               services produced   produced in
                               in United States   foreign countries

[1] Imports must be subtracted because when a United States household, for example, purchases goods produced in foreign countries, such purchases are already counted in consumption. Thus to eliminate double counting, imports are subtracted out of total expenditures.

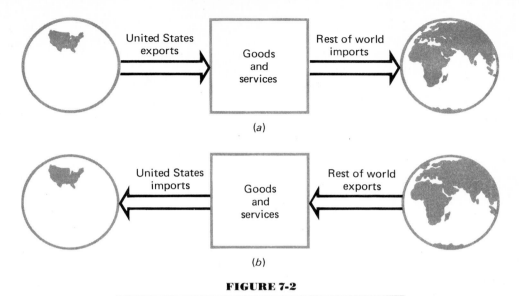

FIGURE 7-2

United States exports of goods and services are what the rest of
the world imports. United States imports of goods and services
are what the rest of the world exports.

It is important to understand that *United States exports E* are that part
of the United States *output* of goods and services demanded by the rest of
the world. As a result, *exports generate payments* from the rest of the world
to the United States. *United States imports M* represent purchases of output
from the rest of the world and therefore *generate payments by the United
States to the rest of the world.*

The dollar value of exports (sales receipts) minus the dollar value of im-
ports (expenditures or payments) will be referred to as net exports NX:[1]
*If the United States exports more than it imports, net exports are positive.
If the United States imports more than it exports, net exports are negative.*
To summarize:

$$NX = E - M$$
$$NX \text{ is positive if } E > M$$
$$NX \text{ is negative if } E < M$$

The dollar value of NX is one of the key components of the nation's GNP accounts; it is the indicator of what the foreign sector contributes to domestic
economic activity.

Figure 7-2 shows that what the United States imports, the rest of the
world exports, and what the United States exports, the rest of the world im-

---

[1] The appendix to this chapter will discuss various accounting conventions associated with the data
on international transactions. For international buffs already familiar with the data, what we are
calling *net exports* is often called the *balance on goods and services.*

ports. This relationship means that if exports exceed imports in the United States, then imports exceed exports in the rest of the world by an *equivalent* amount. The converse is also true. Therefore, anything which affects the propensity of the United States residents to buy foreign goods or to sell goods to foreigners must also, by definition, affect foreign economic activity.

Although exports represent only about 9 percent of GNP in the United States, exports account for much larger percentages of GNP in many foreign countries (29 percent in England, 15 percent in Japan). Furthermore, although United States imports (foreign exports) amount to only about 14 percent of total imports among all countries in the world, the United States is the major importer of goods produced in many countries. Perhaps our imports of petroleum are the best example: daily consumption of oil in the United States amounts to about 20 million barrels, of which we import about 9 to 10 million barrels from OPEC (the Organization of Petroleum Exporting Countries); the value of these United States imports (OPEC exports) represents about 20 percent of GNP for OPEC. Similar stories apply to other trading partners; 30 to 35 percent of Japan's exports are United States imports. Is it any wonder that foreign countries have a keen interest in the United States economic and financial outlook?

Figure 7-3 presents net exports NX for the United States from 1960 to 1978. Note that, over most of the period, United States exports exceeded imports, meaning that NX was positive and GNP was raised by the net purchases of United States goods and services by foreigners. However, this situation has reversed in recent years, when the United States experienced huge increases in imports and NX turned negative. The following analysis should help explain why these recent developments occurred.

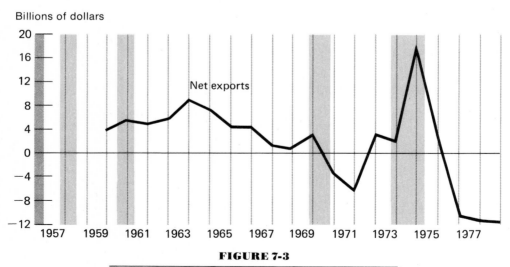

FIGURE 7-3

In recent years, the net exports of the United States have become negative.

To understand what causes changes in NX, it is necessary to identify the determinants of United States demand for foreign goods (imports) and foreign demand for United States goods (exports).[1]

Imports United States *imports*—that is, the demand by United States residents for foreign goods—are a function of three factors:

1

The dollar price of goods produced in the United States P_{us} *relative* to the dollar price of *similar* goods produced in foreign countries P_f

2

The income of United States residents Y_{us}

3

All other factors Z influencing import demand, such as the nonavailability of certain goods or raw materials in the United States, tastes for particular foreign goods, etc.

The first factor, the relative price of *similar* domestic and foreign goods, needs little explanation. If a Toyota produced in Japan sells for less dollars than a Ford Pinto produced in the United States—$P_f < P_{us}$—and the quality of construction, dealer service, gas mileage, and so forth, are comparable in the consumer's mind, there is an obvious price incentive to purchase the foreign good, the Toyota. In general, as P_{us} rises and United States goods become relatively more expensive, we would expect United States demand for foreign goods to rise. The result will be an increase in imports.

But what would cause United States prices to rise? Suppose monetary and fiscal policy in the United States causes a higher rate of inflation in our country than in foreign countries. This means that P_{us} will rise faster than P_f.

The role of the second factor, income, can be seen by recalling our earlier discussion of household behavior. If United States income rises, part of the increased income will be used to purchase goods and services (consumption). Surely, part of the increased income will be used to purchase United States goods and part to purchase foreign goods. Thus, we would expect that as Y_{us} rises, import demand will also rise.

The third factor is actually a variety of miscellaneous influences affecting import demand. United States residents desire or have a need for certain goods that are in limited supply in the United States or for which there are no domestically produced substitutes. Obvious examples of such foreign goods are the coffee beans we import from South America, Rolls Royce cars, petroleum, etc. The demand for such foreign goods is probably

---

[1] We shall usually refer to goods so as to save words, but the analysis generally applies to both goods and services.

not influenced very much by changes in relative prices and domestic income; it is probably influenced more by consumer tastes and habit and by the availability of fairly good domestically produced substitutes.

To summarize, we can write down the following expression where import demand M is a function of the factors P_{us}, P_f, Y_{us}, and Z; the plus or minus sign above each of the factors indicates the direction of the influence of each variable on M.

$$(7\text{-}1) \qquad M = f(\overset{+}{P}_{us},\ \overset{-}{P}_f,\ \overset{+}{Y}_{us},\ \overset{?}{Z})$$

The demand for imports M is positively affected by income in the United States Y_{us}. As Y_{us} rises, the demand for imports rises. Similarly, prices in the United States P_{us} and M are also positively related, while foreign prices P_f and M are negatively related. If P_{us} increases or P_f decreases, then M will increase. If P_{us} falls or P_f rises, then M will fall. Finally, import demand is also a function of other factors Z, which cannot be quantified or measured directly.

Exports   Just as we explained United States demand for foreign goods (imports), we can similarly explain foreign demand for United States goods—that is, United States *exports* of goods and services to the rest of the world. Foreign purchases of United States goods will depend on:

1

The dollar price of United States goods P_{us} relative to the dollar prices P_f of similar goods produced by foreigners

2

The income of residents in foreign countries Y_f

3

Other miscellaneous factors Z influencing foreign demand

We can relate United States exports to prices, income, and other factors in the same way we related United States imports to these things.

$$(7\text{-}2) \qquad E = f(\overset{-}{P}_{us},\ \overset{+}{P}_f,\ \overset{+}{Y}_f,\ \overset{?}{Z})$$

If foreign income Y_f rises, we would expect foreign consumption of all goods including goods produced in the United States to rise. On the other hand, if United States prices rise relative to foreign prices, we would expect exports to fall as foreigners shift their spending away from goods produced in the United States to goods produced in their own countries. Thus, E and P_{us} are negatively related. If foreign prices P_f rise, United States goods become more attractive to foreigners and E will rise. Thus E and P_f are positively related.

Net Exports To facilitate later discussions it will be helpful to combine Equations (7-1) and (7-2), recognizing that NX $= E - M$. Anything that raises exports will be positively related to NX, while anything that raises imports will be negatively related to NX. Similarly, anything that lowers exports will be negatively related to NX, while anything that lowers imports will be positively related to NX. Keeping the resulting function very general yields the following useful expression for United States net exports NX$_{us}$:

$$(7\text{-}3) \qquad NX_{us} = f(\overset{-}{Y}_{us}, \overset{+}{Y}_f, \overset{-}{P}_{us}, \overset{+}{P}_f, \overset{?}{Z})$$

The determinants of United States net exports are United States income (positively related to import demand and therefore negatively related to NX), foreign income (positively related to export demand and therefore positively related to NX), United States prices (negatively related to export demand, positively related to import demand, and therefore negatively related to NX), foreign prices (positively related to export demand, negatively related to import demand, and therefore positively related to NX), and other miscellaneous factors. To be certain that you understand this expression, convince yourself that if NX$_{us} = 0$ initially, and P_{us} rises while other things remain the same, this will lead NX to turn negative.

Refer back to Figure 7-2. Now that you know some of the determinants of NX, you should be capable of some intelligent analysis of the causes of the decline in NX in the United States in the latter part of the 1970s. As the 1974–1975 recession worsened, United States monetary and fiscal policymakers undertook a variety of actions designed to improve the economy's health. In retrospect, it appears that these actions, along with the natural recuperative powers of the economy, stimulated economic activity and therefore the growth of GNP far more than was the case in foreign countries. The greater rebound in our GNP (in comparison to our trading partners) led Y_{us} to rise faster than Y_f, thus contributing to a decline in United States net exports.

This tendency was reinforced by the more rapid rate of inflation in the United States as compared with that in many foreign countries with which we trade. The resulting rise in P_{us} relative to P_f made United States goods less attractive in foreign and domestic markets. The other major factor was oil. United States energy policy, such as it was, tended to encourage imports of high-priced foreign oil. This miscellaneous factor Z, along with the growth in income and rise in prices in the United States, shifted the NX from a positive figure to a record negative figure.

Do not think of negative NX as bad and positive NX as good. Any particular NX reflects portfolio decisions by domestic and foreign residents. Value judgments ought not be attached to such decisions. It would be more correct to view the inflation or the energy policy which causes such deficits as "bad."

In general, since United States monetary and fiscal policies have some impact on United States income and prices, it must also be true that policy will affect the demand for exports and imports and therefore NX in the United States. This being the case, policy in the United States will have important effects on the United States economy and the economies of our trading partners. As the next section shows, these effects are not limited to the trading of goods and services.

TRADING SECURITIES

A simple way to think of trading securities between the United States and foreign countries is to think of United States residents as exporting and importing securities. To analyze the determinants of trading securities, we will look at the demand or lending side (the purchase of securities) and at the supply or borrowing side (the selling or issuing of securities).

The Demand for Securities When, earlier, we examined household portfolio behavior, we pointed out that financial asset holdings are related to savings which, in turn, are related to income. We also saw that households choose financial assets according to their rate of return and risk. It is no different for buying securities originating in foreign countries. For example, a household in the United States may decide to purchase bonds issued somewhere in the rest of the world because the rate of return on the foreign bonds is significantly higher than the rate of return available on United States bonds (assuming that the risks associated with the foreign bond and United States bond are approximately equal). This international transaction—the purchase of a foreign bond by a United States resident—is referred to as a *capital outflow*. In effect, the United States imports bonds from abroad and, as in importing goods, generates payments (our outflows) of funds to the rest of the world. (Do not think that the phrase "outflow of funds" means that dollar bills are being loaded on boats or planes and shipped to foreign countries. Rather, the phrase refers to a change in ownership of funds from United States residents to ownership by foreigners. More on this later.)

The Supply of Securities How might United States corporations that are planning to borrow (to add to their existing stock of plant and equipment) be affected by an interest rate in the United States that is well *above* the interest rate abroad? Keep in mind that the interest rate is income to lenders (it is the rate of return) but a cost to borrowers. It seems reasonable to assume that United States corporations will make financing decisions based on the lowest cost of funds. That is, their decisions on where to borrow will be affected by the cost of funds in the United States relative to the cost of funds abroad. If the interest rate is lower abroad, then United States corporations (chiefly the very large, multinational corporations) will borrow abroad, where the interest rate (cost of capital) is lowest. This, in effect, results in the exporting of bonds and therefore generates payments to the United States or inflows of financial capital, referred to as *capital inflows*.

To summarize: interest rates in the United States vis-à-vis interest rates in the rest of the world affect the inflow and outflow of financial capital in two ways. First, a *higher* rate of interest in the United States will attract financial capital from investors in the rest of the world. Second, a higher rate of interest in the United States will encourage borrowers (United States and foreign) to raise funds in the rest of the world. Both effects will increase the flow of payments (funds) into the United States from the rest of the world. This means that there would be a net inflow of funds into the United States and that the United States would be a net exporter of financial claims to the rest of the world. If United States interest rates were well below world interest rates, then we might expect the United States to experience capital outflows and be a net importer of financial claims.

Balance on Capital Account The actual *net* change in *financial claims* on the United States is referred to as the *balance on capital account* (BKA) or *capital account balance*. The following expression summarizes the major determinants of the BKA:

$$(7\text{-}4) \qquad BKA = f(\overset{-}{Y}_{us}, \overset{+}{Y}_f, \overset{+}{i_{us}/i_f}, \overset{?}{x})$$

where Y_{us} = income in the United States
  Y_f = foreign income
  i_{us}/i_f = interest rate in United States relative to interest rate in foreign countries
  x = expectations

The higher is income Y_{us} in the United States, the larger are the number of dollars saved and the more likely it is that United States residents will purchase foreign bonds—that is, import foreign bonds. As was true when United States residents imported goods, importing securities generates payments to foreigners—outflows of funds or financial capital—causing the BKA to move toward deficit (a negative BKA). In contrast, when foreign incomes rise, the increased saving by foreign residents will raise the demand for United States bonds. The resulting export of bonds generates payments to United States residents—inflows of funds or financial capital—which move the BKA toward a surplus (a positive BKA).

As discussed above, the rate of return on financial assets in the United States relative to the rate of return on foreign assets—i_{us}/i_f—is also a key determinant of the net flow of financial capital into or out of the United States. If the rate of return on United States securities rises relative to foreign rates, this will raise world demand for United States financial assets and encourage United States borrowers and others—that is, suppliers of bonds—to raise funds in foreign countries. Both effects will tend to attract financial capital to the United States and thus positively affect the BKA—that is, increase the outflow (exporting) of financial claims and increase capital inflows.

Over the short run (day to day, week to week, and month to month), the net inflow or outflow of financial capital is influenced to an important degree by the expectations x of borrowers and lenders in the United States and abroad. These expectations typically relate to such things as the risk of default and liquidity of financial instruments, future movements in interest rates, and anticipated rates of inflation. To illustrate, suppose foreigners hold bonds issued by a United States corporation and *The Wall Street Journal* reports that this corporation's earnings are negative and bankruptcy is a possibility. Regardless of the current rate of return on this corporation's bonds, the increased risk of default associated with holding these securities may induce foreigners to liquidate their bond holdings. There are other examples of the effects of expectations on BKA: government pronouncements, recent movements in key macroeconomic variables, and so forth will affect expectations which, in turn, will affect portfolio choices by domestic and foreign households and firms. More on this later in the text.

THE TRADING OF
GOODS AND SECURITIES TAKEN
TOGETHER—THE BALANCE OF PAYMENTS

We have now examined the determinants of export demand and import demand for both *goods* and *securities*. We have also seen how these determinants affect net exports NX and the balance on capital account BKA. Now we shall look at the net difference between *payments from* the rest of the world for United States goods and securities purchased by foreign residents and *payments to* the rest of the world for foreign goods and securities purchased by United States residents. This net difference is called the *balance of payments* (BOP). The way we get the BOP is to add NX (net exports)

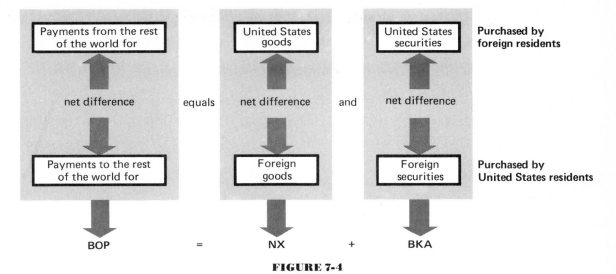

FIGURE 7-4

The net difference between *payments from* the rest of the world—representing purchases of United States goods and securities by foreigners—and *payments to* the rest of the world—representing purchases of foreign goods and securities by United States residents—is the balance of payments.

and BKA (balance on capital account). Therefore, the total balance of payments is[1]:

$$(7\text{-}5) \qquad BOP = NX + BKA$$

What lies behind Equation (7-5) is illustrated by Figure 7-4.

If payments *to* the rest of the world exceed payments *from* the rest of the world, then the United States has a balance of payments deficit. This deficit, like all others, must be financed. Of course, a deficit is not the only possible state of affairs. For example, it is possible that the portfolio choices of domestic and foreign residents—that is, firms and households (we are ignoring domestic and foreign governments for now)—could be such that the $BOP = 0$. This could occur, for example, if the excess of imports of goods and services over exports (negative NX) were exactly equal to the excess of exports of securities over imports of securities (positive BKA). In this case, the net payment *to* foreigners for imports of goods and services (negative NX) would in effect be financed by the net payments *from* foreigners to domestic residents resulting from the exports of bonds (positive BKA) by domestic residents.

[1] Carrying this summation one step further, one can aggregate the behavioral equations for NX (7-3) and BKA (7-4) to yield the behavioral equivalent of (7-5):

$$BOP = f(\overset{-}{Y_{us}}, \overset{+}{Y_f}, \overset{-}{P_{us}}, \overset{+}{P_f}, \overset{+}{i_{us}/i_f}, \overset{?}{x}, \overset{?}{Z})$$

The Balance of Payments and the Financing of International Transactions The following example should help to illustrate how the BOP and various international transactions fit together.

Example

Bert is a resident of the United States and plans to import goods worth $100 from Joan, who resides in country Y; Bert intends to pay for—that is, finance—these imports by selling bonds in the United States financial market. Now suppose the interest rate on the bonds sold in the United States is so attractive that Ernie, who lives in country Y and has funds to invest, buys them. Bert takes the proceeds from the bond sale and pays off Joan.

Table 7-2 represents the international transactions described above. Note that the NX in the United States are negative by an amount which is exactly equivalent in dollar terms to country Y's positive NX. Further, the positive capital account balance in the United States is matched by a negative BKA in country Y; as a result, the BOP of both equals zero. The excess of imports over exports in the United States, in effect, is financed by the

TABLE 7-2
INTERNATIONAL TRANSACTIONS

	United States		Country Y	
	EXPORTS	**IMPORTS**	**EXPORTS**	**IMPORTS**
Goods		$100 (Bert)	$100 (Joan)	
Securities	$100 (Bert)			$100 (Ernie)
Summary	NX = −100 $\begin{cases}\text{\$0 goods exported,} \\ \text{\$100 goods} \\ \text{imported}\end{cases}$		NX = +100 $\begin{cases}\text{\$100 goods} \\ \text{exported,} \\ \text{\$0 goods imported}\end{cases}$	
	BKA = +100 $\begin{cases}\text{\$100 securities} \\ \text{exported,} \\ \text{\$0 securities} \\ \text{imported}\end{cases}$		BKA = −100 $\begin{cases}\text{\$0 securities} \\ \text{exported,} \\ \text{\$100 securities} \\ \text{imported}\end{cases}$	
	BOP = 0		BOP = 0	

willingness of residents of country Y to acquire financial claims on United States residents.[1] A subtle but important concept that is revealed by this example is that the trading of goods and securities *need not* be directly related to one another—Ernie and Joan are different people and there is no reason to believe the spending, saving, or borrowing decisions of one depend on what the other does. Remember the function of financial markets and financial intermediaries—they transfer funds from surplus units (lenders) to deficit units (borrowers). This is true *between* countries as well as *within* countries.

International Reserves So far, so good. Be careful though—just when you have this all figured out we have to zing you by making the example more realistic and therefore a bit more complicated. The first realistic and complicating factor is perhaps obvious. Suppose Ernie is unwilling to acquire financial claims on residents of the United States, perhaps because the rate of return on bonds in country Y is higher than the rate in the United States. Then what happens? Suppose Bert possesses a stock of assets which he accumulated previously and that these assets are generally acceptable as a means of payment throughout the world. Let us call these generally acceptable assets *international reserve assets*. Let us also remember the simplicity of our uncomplicated world where we are assuming that the dollar is the only means of payment. This means that Bert's money balances are in fact international reserves. If his payment ($100) for imports of goods and securities exceeds his receipts ($0) from exports of goods and securities, Bert must finance the excess by transferring his previously acquired dollars to Joan. What is happening is that he is reducing his holdings of international reserves (money) and increasing hers. In this case, the BOP deficit in the United States will be equal to the decline in United States holdings of international reserves (IR). In general:

$$(7\text{-}6) \qquad \qquad BOP = NX + BKA = \Delta IR$$

[1] You may wonder what, in addition to relative rates of return, influences the willingness of foreigners to acquire United States financial assets. In general, the dollar is an important international money which many foreign governments, firms, and even households desire to hold: the dollar sometimes serves as a means of payment internationally between two foreign countries (some refer to this as the dollar serving as a *vehicle* currency—a vehicle facilitating the trading of goods and securities between countries); the United States possesses highly developed, multisectored financial markets, making holding and investing in United States financial assets an attractive and relatively safe endeavor; and with the United States being an important producer of goods in the world, accumulating dollar balances or United States financial assets allows various countries to purchase goods from the United States at a later date even if they are not exporting enough to pay for such purchases at the time. In addition to the above factors, the relatively stable political-social environment in the United States and the comparatively decent inflation performance in the United States over the 1950s and early 1960s—which limited the erosion of the purchasing power of the dollar claims foreigners accumulated—contributed to the catch-all factor called "confidence" which encouraged foreigners to hold dollars and other United States financial assets.

The message in Equation (7-6) is that if, for example, the United States incurs a BOP deficit (United States expenditures on foreign goods and securities), the deficit will be financed with a means of payment that is acceptable to foreigners. International reserve assets are an acceptable means of payment to all foreigners.

Suppose Bert, or more generally the United States, continually runs BOP deficits. What happens? Let us reexamine for a moment the spending, saving, and financing behavior of a single individual, discussed in Chapter 4. By definition, an individual's income is either consumed or saved ($Y = C + S$). If $Y > C$, an individual will save, that is, accumulate money and other financial assets (claims). However, if $C > Y$, then saving is negative, which means consumption expenditures are greater than current income. This requires (1) liquidation of some part of the individual's stock of money balances or financial assets accumulated from past saving to finance C minus Y and/or (2) borrowing—that is, the issuance of an IOU—to pay for the difference between consumption and current income.

It is quite unlikely that an individual will be able to spend more than is earned and to finance the difference by liquidating assets and/or borrowing for any prolonged period. For one thing, the stock of assets held by this individual or by anyone is finite—continued liquidations of assets must eventually exhaust a person's stock. For another thing, lenders of funds to this individual will sooner or later become concerned with the individual's mounting volume of IOUs relative to income; thus the lenders will reach a point where they will refuse to accept any more IOUs. As debt rises relative to income, the debtor's ability to pay off the debt is reduced. An individual whose stock of accumulated assets is depleted and whose ability to borrow more funds becomes exhausted will be forced to make an adjustment in his or her consumption expenditures. The most obvious adjustment is, of course, a reduction in current consumption expenditures to the point where $C \leq Y$. Countries, like individuals, find such adjustments —reductions in their standard of living—painful, and they often try to postpone the required changes in their spending, saving, and financing behavior. Perhaps you can begin to see why the international monetary system has been subjected to continual tension and crisis.

How does all this relate to the United States? In our Bert-Ernie-Joan example, we assumed that the dollar was generally acceptable as a means of payment throughout the world. As a result, we assumed that an individual's dollar holdings were international reserves. In reality, the dollar is *not* universally acceptable as a means of payment in other countries. As discussed later in the text (Chapter 21), there are three kinds of assets that qualify as international reserves acceptable in foreign countries for the settlement of debts: (1) holdings of gold, (2) Special Drawing Rights (SDRs) issued by the

International Monetary Fund, and (3) foreign monies (which can include dollars).[1]

During most of the 1950s, 1960s, and early 1970s, payments by United States residents to the rest of the world for imports of goods and securities and for military expenditures exceeded payments received by United States residents for exports of goods and securities. That is, the United States experienced BOP deficits. Given the preceding discussion, you should not be surprised to learn that United States international reserves declined significantly over this period. How the United States government and foreign governments came to finance these BOP deficits in the United States and the consequent impact on the international value of the dollar will be examined in Chapters 16 and 21.

7-3
APPENDIX: INTERNATIONAL TRANSACTIONS—
AN OVERVIEW OF THE DATA*

The balance of payments (BOP) for the United States is defined as the record of transactions between United States residents and foreign residents over a given period of time (say, a quarter or a year). The accounting scheme underlying the BOP is based on the principle of double-entry bookkeeping, which is quite similar to that used by business firms. In principle, this means that *each* international transaction involves a credit and a debit. The purchase or importation of real or financial assets from a foreign resident is recorded as a debit (or minus) entry in the BOP; the sale or exportation of real or financial assets is recorded as a credit (or plus) entry in the BOP.[2] Thus, if the United States exports computers to Germany, for example, this transaction would be recorded as a credit, while the payment received for the computers, which in effect involves the importation of a financial asset, would be recorded as a debit.

Since a debit entry is, by definition, always accompanied by a credit entry, total debits must always equal total credits. This being the case, the *entire* BOP cannot ever show either a deficit (debits > credits) or a surplus

---

[1] SDRs are often referred to as "paper gold." They represent international money created by the International Monetary Fund. This is discussed in more detail in Chapter 21.

* This section contains optional material which can be omitted without loss of continuity throughout the rest of this text.

[2] This, of course, follows standard accounting practice; a debit entry reflects an increase in assets or a decrease in liabilities, while a credit entry reflects a decrease in assets or an increase in liabilities.

(debits < credits); the BOP always balances. If this is so, why do we always read and hear about deficits (or surpluses) in the BOPs of various countries? More importantly, why did we discuss BOP surpluses and deficits in the main part of this chapter? The answer is that there is no bookkeeping requirement that the sum of credits and debits for a *particular subset* of the many accounts which make up the entire BOP must be equal.

A summary of the major accounts comprising the balance of payments and various examples of transactions within each account are presented in Table 7-3. Note that the principle of double-entry bookkeeping ensures that *total* receipts or credits are identically equal to *total* debits. For any given account, say the goods account, receipts can exceed payments (or vice versa). This imbalance between credits and debits can also occur when several accounts are combined—say the goods, services, transfers, and capital accounts.[1]

In this chapter we analyzed a *partial* BOP concept which combines several key accounts. We divided the entire BOP into three broad components: net exports (NX), the rough equivalent of accounts 1 through 3 in Table 7-3; the balance on capital account (BKA), the equivalent of account 4; and the international reserve account (IR), the equivalent of account 5. By focusing on these three components of the BOP, we can emphasize the important financial transactions in the foreign sector and see how they affect the economy in the United States:

Net exports (NX), the sum of receipts minus payments from the goods and services accounts (in Table 7-3), is an important component of national income in the GNP accounts.

The *balance on capital account* (BKA) traces the net inflow or outflow of financial assets (liabilities) not including government transactions.

The *international reserve account* (IR) traces financial transactions in gold, SDRs, or foreign currencies undertaken by the United States or foreign governments (that is, changes in IR reflect policy actions).

---

[1] For more detailed discussion of the various accounts, see John Pippenger, "Balance of Payments Deficits: Measurement and Interpretation," Federal Reserve Bank of St. Louis, *Review* (November 1973), 6–14; Norman Fieleke, "What is the Balance of Payments?" Federal Reserve Bank of Boston, *Special Study* (July 1976); and Donald Kemp, "Balance of Payments Concepts—What Do They Really Mean?" Federal Reserve Bank of St. Louis, *Review* (July 1975), 14–23.

TABLE 7-3
SUMMARY OF BALANCE OF PAYMENTS ACCOUNTS

ACCOUNT	Entries	
	RECEIPTS FROM FOREIGN SECTOR (CREDITS)	PAYMENTS TO FOREIGN SECTOR (DEBITS)
1. Goods	Exports	Imports
2. Services	Military sales to foreigners	Military purchases from foreigners
	Interest and dividends on United States foreign investment	Interest and dividends on foreign investment in the United States
	Tourism in the United States by foreigners	Tourism by United States residents
3. Transfers	Gifts to United States residents	Gifts to foreign residents United States foreign aid
4. Capital	Increases in foreign ownership of United States financial assets	Increases in United States ownership of foreign financial assets
	Decreases in United States ownership of foreign financial assets	Decreases in foreign ownership of United States financial assets
5. International reserves (sometimes referred to as the "official account," reflecting reserve transactions by governments)	Decreases in (sales of) international reserves held by the United States government	Increases in (purchases of) international reserves held by the United States government
	Increases in United States assets held by foreign governments	Decreases in United States assets held by foreign governments
	Total credits (plus items)	= Total debits (minus items)

From our discussion above we know that:

$$BOP = NX + BKA + \Delta IR = 0$$

The entire BOP must equal zero. However, by rearranging terms, we know that:

$$NX + BKA = \Delta IR$$

This particular grouping—which is the partial BOP concept referred to in Chapter 7 of this text—is intended to focus attention on movements in IR.[1] As is discussed in the appendix to Chapter 18, United States holdings of IR are a component of the reserve base of the United States banking system;

[1] See Kemp, op. cit., for a detailed discussion of and justification for this particular BOP concept.

therefore changes in IR can affect the supply of money and credit in the United States. Furthermore, as is discussed in Chapter 21, if the United States buys or sells foreign currencies to affect the dollar exchange rate, this will be reflected in IR. Thus, since this is a text on money and the financial system (domestic and international), it seems warranted to focus on this BOP concept.[1]

7-4
SUMMARY OF MAJOR POINTS

1

Net exports represent the difference between the dollar value of United States exports of goods and services to the foreign sector and the dollar value of United States imports from the foreign sector.

2

The primary determinants of net exports are United States income Y_{us}, foreign income Y_f, United States prices P_{us} relative to foreign prices P_f, and certain miscellaneous factors Z.

3

The balance on capital account represents the net change in financial claims on the United States. More specifically, it is the difference between capital inflows resulting from "exports" of bonds (increases in financial claims on the United States by foreigners) and capital outflows resulting from "imports" of bonds (increases in financial claims on foreigners by United States residents).

4

The primary determinants of the balance on capital account are United States income Y_{us}, foreign income Y_f, the rate of return in the United States relative to the rate of return in foreign countries i_{us}/i_f, and expectations.

---

[1] Over the years, government statisticians and analysts have found one (or more) subsets of the entire BOP useful for a variety of purposes. The objective was to find a single number—the net of credits and debits in a selected number of accounts—that could provide a reasonably accurate indication of the international economic position of the United States with regard to the competitiveness of our industry, the "strength" of the dollar abroad, and so on. For a detailed review of the deficiences inherent in various BOP concepts, see the sources cited above and *Report of the Advisory Committee on the Presentation of Balance of Payments Statistics* (U.S. Government Printing Office, 1976).

5

The balance of payments is the difference between payments received from the rest of world for United States goods and securities and payments made to the rest of the world for foreign goods and securities purchased by United States residents. Formally, the balance of payments is equal to net exports plus the balance on capital account.

6

If United States payments to the rest of the world exceed payments received from the rest of the world, there is a balance of payments deficit in the United States (and a balance of payments surplus in the rest of the world).

7

As is the case for domestic deficits incurred by households, firms, and governments, all international (balance of payments) deficits must be financed. In an international context, the financing of deficits will entail reductions in holdings of international reserve assets (gold, special drawing rights or SDRs, and foreign currencies), or borrowing—that is, the issuing of financial claims to foreigners.

8

Over most of the last twenty-five years the United States incurred balance of payments deficits. As a result, United States holdings of international reserves fell dramatically and foreign financial claims on the United States rose to unprecedented levels. With the United States at the center of the international monetary system, this unhealthy economic climate bred the eventual breakdown of the prevailing system.

9*

The data on the balance of payments (published by the Commerce Department) are a record of the transactions between the United States and foreigners over a given period of time. Since the accounting scheme underlying the balance of payments is based on the principle of double-

* Refers to the Appendix (optional material).

entry bookkeeping, total debits equal total credits; that is, the balance of payments always balances. Reference to deficits or surpluses in the balance of payments results from analysts focusing on the net of credits and debits in a selected number of balance of payments accounts. The objective of such analysis is to uncover a single number, summarizing United States international transactions, that provides a reasonably accurate indication of the international economic position of the United States with regard to the competitiveness of our industry, the international value of the dollar, and so forth. Given the focus of this text, we have adopted a balance of payments concept that highlights changes in international reserves held by the United States.

7-5
REVIEW QUESTIONS

1   Briefly discuss or define the following terms: imports, exports, capital inflows, capital outflows, international reserves.

2   Despite the fact that net exports are only a small share of total GNP, the foreign sector still has very important effects on the domestic economy. Explain why.

3   Discuss the major determinants of United States net exports. Explain how each determinant affects NX and show how an acceleration of inflation in the United States would affect net exports.

4   Discuss the major determinants of the United States balance on capital account. Explain the direction of influence of each determinant on the balance on capital account and show how it would be affected by a rise in United States interest rates.

5   Discuss the relationship between net exports, the balance on capital account, and the balance of payments.

*6   List the major accounts comprising the balance of payments and provide examples of transactions within each account.

* Refers to the Appendix (optional material).

7-6
SUGGESTED READINGS

1   There are a number of outstanding texts in international economics. Among the best are Richard Caves and Ronald Jones, *World Trade and Payments* (Boston: Little, Brown, 1977); Delbert Snider, *Introduction to International Economics* (Homewood, Ill.: Irwin, 1979); and Klaus Friedrich, *International Economics* (New York: McGraw-Hill, 1974).

2   Data on international transactions can be found in sources cited earlier—*Survey of Current Business, Economic Report of the President, Federal Reserve Bulletin,* and the *Treasury Bulletin*—and in *International Financial Statistics*, published by the International Monetary Fund. Useful data on employment, prices, and output in various key countries are published regularly by OECD (Organization for Economic Cooperation and Development). Consult the card catalog in your library for the titles of various OECD publications. You might also look at (and get on the mailing list for) the *International Letter*, published by the Federal Reserve Bank of Chicago, and several releases on the international economy published by the Federal Reserve Bank of St. Louis.

3   A very readable review of United States interactions with the world economy can be found in *The U.S. Balance of International Payments and the U.S. Economy* (Washington, D.C.: Congressional Budget Office, February 1978).

4   The dramatic increases in oil prices engineered by OPEC have contributed to a rise in the value of United States imports. This is a two-way street, however—with more income, OPEC has more to spend. See Norman Fieleke, "Trade with the Oil-Exporting Countries," *New England Economic Review*, Federal Reserve Bank of Boston (May–June, 1977), for a review of how OPEC spends its income.

PART
THREE

INSIDE THE
FINANCIAL SYSTEM

In Part I, we presented an overview of the financial system, discussed the role of money in the economy, and developed a framework for financial analysis. In Part II, we studied the behavior of the four sectors of the economy: the household, business, government, and foreign sectors. We saw that we could classify spending units in our economy as either surplus units (lenders) or deficit units (borrowers). Surplus units consume less than their current income and thus have funds to lend. Deficit units spend more than their current income and therefore need to finance the difference. The financial system serves as the mechanism which transfers funds from the surplus to the deficit units; we shall analyze the financial system in more detail here in Part III.

The main components of the financial system are the financial intermediaries and the financial markets. There are two types of financial intermediaries: *commercial banks*, the largest, most important, and most diversified of all financial intermediaries; and *nonbank financial intermediaries*, which include all financial institutions except commercial banks.

As the following table shows, commercial banks are by far the largest type of financial intermediary, more than twice as large as savings and loan associations, the largest nonbank financial intermediary. Accordingly, we shall devote three chapters to commercial banks, developing and analyzing in detail their role in the financial system. This discussion will reveal, among other things,

MAJOR FINANCIAL INTERMEDIARIES

	TOTAL FINANCIAL ASSETS, 1978 (BILLIONS OF DOLLARS)
Commercial banks	$1158.9
Nonbank financial intermediaries	
Savings and loan associations	523.6
Life insurance companies	376.4
Private pension funds	207.2
Mutual savings banks	158.4
Government pension funds	148.5
Property-casualty insurance companies	124.6
Credit unions	58.2

that nonbank financial intermediaries are competing more and more with commercial banks. In fact, some nonbank financial intermediaries have grown more rapidly over the past twenty years than commercial banks! Such growth indicates the increasing importance of nonbank financial intermediaries in our financial system. The reasons for this growth and what this growth implies are the subjects of Chapter 11. Chapter 12 wraps up our investigation of the financial system with a description and analysis of financial markets and the brokers and dealers who "make" markets.

Before going on, we suggest you review Chapter 1 and especially Figures 1-2 and 1-3. This review should help you to renew your focus on the main objective of this book, which is to link the financial system to the real economy (and the behavior of the various sectors) on the one hand and to the behavior of policymakers, particularly the Federal Reserve, on the other.

8

COMMERCIAL BANKING: AN INDUSTRY OVERVIEW

A bank is a place where they lend you an umbrella in fair
weather and ask for it back again when it begins to rain.

Robert Frost

8-1
THE BIGGEST INTERMEDIARY IN TOWN

The word "bank" is derived from the Italian word *banca*, which refers to
the table, counter, or place of business of a moneychanger.[1] In the United
States, as in many foreign countries, there are many different types of
moneychangers, which in more modern terms are called *financial intermediaries*. Since banks are by far the largest type of intermediary, we will
begin our study of financial institutions by examining the essential aspects
of commercial banking.

[1] We debated whether or not it was important for the student to be exposed to the derivation of the
word "bank." On a 2-to-1 vote, it was decided that the explanation of the Italian derivation would
be included in this text. (If you have trouble understanding the voting pattern here, expect trouble
understanding the chapters on the political economy of policymaking.)

The large size of the commercial banking industry relative to other types of nonbank financial intermediaries implies that banks play a predominant role in transferring funds from surplus units in our economy to deficit units. In effect, banks function as arbitragers: that is, they borrow funds from surplus units and pay interest costs on the borrowed funds; they then lend these funds to deficit units and earn interest on the loaned funds. The excess of the interest earned on the loaned funds over interest costs on the borrowed funds is the profit earned from intermediation.

The intermediation process requires commercial banks to make decisions regarding the interest rate they will pay to borrow funds and the interest rate they charge to lend funds. These decisions on interest rates affect the public's demand for funds (borrowing) from banks and their supply of funds (lending) to banks, which in turn affects economic activity.

The focus of the next three chapters is on how bank behavior affects interest rates, the money stock, the volume of credit extended by banks, and economic activity. We begin by examining the commercial banking industry. It should be emphasized that this industry is continually changing and attempting to innovate, just like many other industries in our society. As a result, many institutional details change somewhat as time passes. Nevertheless, we can provide a snapshot of the current state of affairs; we will suggest why banks have evolved into this current position; and we will highlight the key aspects of bank behavior regarding the macroeconomy. Through our examination of these things, we will also be able to see many of the factors that lead to innovation by banks.

8-2
THE STRUCTURE OF THE COMMERCIAL BANKING INDUSTRY

Banking is a heavily regulated industry. Entry into the industry is controlled at both the federal and state levels. In fact, the American commercial banking system is unlike others in the world. Commercial banks in the United States are chartered—that is, they are given permission to engage in the business of commercial banking—by *either* the federal government or one of the fifty state governments.

THE DUAL BANKING SYSTEM

If a bank's charter is granted by the federal government—the Office of the Comptroller of the Currency is the federal government agency charged with this responsibility—the bank is called a "national" bank. For example, the First National Bank of Boston is a federally chartered bank. Banks can also be chartered by a state banking authority. This system, in which commercial banks are chartered and regulated either by the state or federal government, is usually referred to as the *dual banking system.*

At the end of 1978, there were about 14,700 commercial banks in the United States. Of this number, only about one-third were chartered by the federal government. However, while state-chartered banks are more numerous, the federally chartered banks are generally larger. The one-third of the banks that were federally chartered—that is, the national banks—held about 55 percent of all assets (and therefore liabilities) in the banking system.

WHO REGULATES WHOM?

While the dual banking system has little direct effect on the formulation and implementation of monetary policy, it does play a role in the regulatory and supervisory aspects of commercial banking. In fact, the dual banking system is one of the things that makes the American banking system so complex. Banking practices that are legally permitted in one state may be prohibited in another, and practices permitted for state banks in a particular state may not be permissible for national banks, even in the same state. The complexity of the banking system and its regulatory guidelines provides a rewarding living for bank lawyers.

Commercial banks which are federally chartered *must* belong to the Federal Reserve System, and all Federal Reserve member banks must subscribe to Federal Deposit Insurance. As a result, national banks are subject to the regulatory and supervisory authority of the Comptroller of the Currency, the Federal Reserve, and the Federal Deposit Insurance Corporation (FDIC). A state-chartered bank will be regulated by its state banking authority; if it chooses to join the Federal Reserve, it will also have to deal with the Fed and FDIC. One of the interesting and probably unique features of the system is that *those being regulated can choose the regulator.* By this we mean that banks can shift from state charter to federal charter or vice versa. Also, state-chartered banks need not be members of the Federal Reserve System, and they can decide whether or not they want to insure their deposits with the FDIC. In practice, nearly all banks belong to the FDIC.

There are some people who believe that the profusion of regulations, supervisory authorities, and statutes of the dual banking system leads local banks to adapt themselves and structure their services so as to fulfill local banking needs. For instance, the defenders of the dual banking system believe that state-chartered banks will be induced by the regulatory guidelines to meet local needs, while guidelines for federally chartered banks may relate to national needs. They also argue that the dual banking system fosters competition and innovation among banks. Opponents of the dual banking system argue that the overlapping of regulatory agencies breeds considerable confusion and leads to laxity in enforcement; they maintain that all this really gives banks considerable freedom to do whatever they want.

In the first half of the 1970s, several large banks failed. The Congress questioned the various agencies that were responsible for regulating these banks and wanted to know how such failures could occur if regulation and supervision were adequate. The unsatisfactory responses led to the introduction of several bills in Congress to place all responsibility for regulation and supervision in one federal agency. Guess what happened? The various agencies that would lose power argued against the proposal and the state banks that were not members of the Fed were violently opposed, preferring to be regulated by the generally friendlier state authorities. This political coalition has thus far held off any significant changes in the laws governing banks.

FED MEMBERSHIP

One of the more important aspects of the dual banking system is that many state-chartered banks that are not Fed members face different regulations than Fed members regarding the amount and type of reserves they are required by law to hold. All commercial banks are required to hold some part of their assets in the form of reserves. National banks, by law, must be members of the Federal Reserve System, and the Fed requires that the banks must hold reserves either as cash in their own vaults or as funds deposited at their local Federal Reserve bank. Reserves held in this way are *nonearning* assets; this means that they do not earn explicit interest income. By contrast, nonmember state banks come under state laws which often require lower levels of reserves; furthermore, state-chartered banks are usually allowed to use certain kinds of interest-earning assets (for example, United States government securities) to satisfy the legal reserve requirements. This latter feature makes state charters more attractive to banks than federal charters—banks are businesses and they want to maximize their profits; one way of doing this is to earn interest on their reserves.

The attractiveness of state charters helps explain why most banks are not members of the Federal Reserve System and why many banks have left the system in recent years. As of the middle of 1978, only about 32 percent of all commercial banks (5621 of 14,698) belonged to it. However, while the member banks may be outnumbered by the nonmembers, the former are larger by far—accounting for about 73 percent of all commercial bank assets.

As the final draft of this text was being prepared, the Fed had submitted to the Congress a plan designed to stem the steady erosion in Fed membership and allow members and nonmembers to compete on a more equitable basis. The following is excerpted from the August 1978 issue of *Voice*, published by the Federal Reserve Bank of Dallas:

A plan to provide greater competitive equality among financial institutions and to halt the withdrawal of member banks from the Federal Reserve System has been sent to Congress by the Board of Governors of the Federal Reserve System. Two key elements in the plan are the proposal to require all financial institutions to hold reserves with the Federal Reserve and the proposal for interest to be paid on these required reserve balances. The purpose of the proposed program is to make membership in the Federal Reserve System more attractive to the growing number of banks that are questioning whether the benefits of membership outweigh the costs. Over the past ten years, 551 banks have withdrawn from membership in the Federal Reserve System. Not only are more banks withdrawing, but there is also a growing trend for larger member banks to withdraw. Because of the decline in membership, the proportion of total commercial bank deposits held by member banks has fallen to 72 percent nationwide. This trend has eroded the effectiveness of monetary policy, a key responsibility of the Federal Reserve. It is this problem, as well as the inequity of the competitive situation between member banks and other financial institutions, that the Federal Reserve proposal addresses.

Note that, in the second sentence, the proposal refers to *all* financial institutions. Can you guess who was against the proposal?

Figure 8-1 summarizes how our banking system breaks down in terms of type of charter, Fed membership, and FDIC insurance. Most banks that are not members of the Fed are small. In 1978 there were 12,219 banks with total deposits of $50 million or less; 33.9 percent belonged to the Fed. At the same time, there were 228 banks with deposits exceeding $500 million; 84.2 percent belonged to the Fed. Why do the big banks tend to belong while the small banks do not?

The larger banks derive from Fed membership benefits which represent an implicit return on the non-interest-bearing reserves the Fed requires them to hold. The benefits include the value of a variety of services provided by the Fed—check collection, coin and currency pickup and delivery, wire transfers (telegraphic transfers of funds), safekeeping of securities, and access to the Fed's discount window (to be discussed in Chapter 18). Finally, there is also the value of *correspondent banking relationships*.

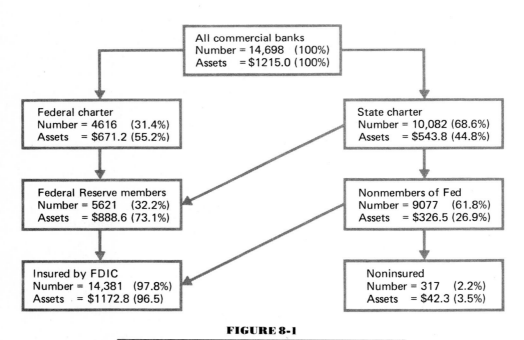

FIGURE 8-1

Commercial banking system as of June 1978. Dollar figures are in billions and figures in parentheses are percentages of total number of banks or total assets for all banks.

A *correspondent relationship* between two banks is a situation in which one bank, usually a larger bank, maintains a business relationship with another bank, usually a smaller bank. The larger bank provides the smaller bank with a wide range of services—check clearing, advice on portfolio strategy, access to various financial markets (such as the foreign currency market), and so forth. Like other customers, banks utilizing these services must pay for them by maintaining compensating balances with the seller of the service or by making explicit payments. Research suggests that smaller banks cut costs by operating through larger correspondent banks and being nonmembers, while larger banks increase their earnings by selling access to services provided by the Fed and themselves to a large network of smaller banks.* The profit motive at work again!

* See Robert Knight, "Comparative Burdens of Federal Reserve Member and Nonmember Banks," *Monthly Review*, Federal Reserve Bank of Kansas City (March 1977), 13–28; and R. Alton Gilbert, "Utilization of Federal Reserve Bank Services by Member Banks: Implications for the Costs and Benefits of Membership," *Review*, Federal Reserve Bank of St. Louis (August 1977), 2–15.

Besides helping to explain why large banks tend to be Fed members, correspondent banking relationships also help to explain how the banking system is linked or hooked together. To illustrate, a small bank in, say, Wichita, Kansas, might have a correspondent relationship with a bank in Kansas City, which in turn has a correspondent relationship with a bank in Chicago, which in turn has a correspondent relationship with a bank in New York City—the financial capital of the world. In effect, these networks of correspondent banking relationships hook these banks together and, in general, hook all banks together. Why is this worth noting? As you may know, Federal Reserve open-market operations—the major monetary policy tool—are carried out in New York City. The immediate effects of these operations are felt by the large banks located there. However, these effects are diffused or transmitted through the network of correspondent banking relationships to the rest of the banking system. In fact, since many large United States banks maintain working relationships with foreign banks, the effects of policy operations are also transmitted abroad to some degree.

TABLE 8-1
STATE BRANCHING RESTRICTIONS

TYPE	NUMBER OF STATES	NUMBER OF BANKS AFFECTED
Unit banking—no branching permitted	12	6,696
Limited branching—usually permits branching into contiguous counties within state	16	6,070
Statewide branching	22	1,944
	50	14,710

SOURCE: The Federal Reserve. Data are for June 1978.

COMPETITION IN THE BANKING INDUSTRY

In the process of outlining the structure of the banking system, we have uncovered evidence of a large number of small banks, a small number of large banks, and fairly close working relationships between large and small banks. What does all this imply for the degree of competition present in the banking industry?

In introductory economics courses, it is suggested that one of the things that indicates a competitive industry is the presence of a large number of firms within it. Since there are about 14,700 banks, should we conclude that banking is a very competitive industry? Unfortunately, such a conclusion would not be warranted. If anything, the large number of banks is a testimony to the lack of competition in a variety of areas. As we pointed out above, the majority of banks are relatively small. The main reason for this is that many states limit the degree of branching—that is, the opening of additional offices—a bank can engage in. As shown in Table 8-1, over half of all banks in the United States are located in states that prohibit branching. Most of these banks are quite small, they are located in small towns, and they face little competition.

What about the small number of large banks? There is obvious concentration in the industry (see Table 8-2). The twenty biggest banks account for only one-tenth of 1 percent of all banks. But these twenty banks control over one-third of total banking industry assets and deposits. Does their size mean that competition is severely restricted? The answer to this question is a definite "Yes and No"!

TABLE 8-2
THE GIANTS

BANK	TOTAL DEPOSITS AS OF DECEMBER 31, 1978 (BILLIONS OF DOLLARS)
1. Bank of America, San Francisco	$76.8
2. Citibank, New York	61.6
3. Chase Manhattan Bank, New York	49.5
4. Manufacturers Hanover Trust Co., New York	32.1
5. Morgan Guaranty Trust Co., New York	28.6
6. Chemical Bank, New York	24.9
7. Continental Illinois, Chicago	20.9
8. Bankers Trust Co., New York	18.4
9. First National Bank, Chicago	17.5
10. Security Pacific National Bank, Los Angeles	16.8
11. Wells Fargo Bank, San Francisco	14.8
12. Marine Midland Bank, Buffalo	11.4
13. Crocker National Bank, San Francisco	11.2
14. United California Bank, Los Angeles	10.2
15. Irving Trust Co., New York	9.5
16. Mellon Bank, Pittsburgh	8.5
17. First National Bank, Boston	7.6
18. National Bank of Detroit	7.0
19. Bank of New York	5.9
20. Republic National Bank, Dallas	5.3

SOURCE: *American Banker* (February 23, 1978), p. 2.

For a small number of banks to restrict competition, they must be able to exercise *market power*—that is, they must impose their will to some degree on customers in a specified market, such as the markets for large loans or small loans or the markets for savings deposits or demand deposits. Besides competing in many different markets defined by the type of asset or liability, banks also compete in a geographic market. For the smaller banks, their geographic market is generally local. Their competition, say, for deposits is largely with other local banks and other local nonbank financial intermediaries. For larger banks, the geographic market is more national. Competition for, say, large negotiable CDs (certificates of deposit), is with other large banks located in New York, Chicago, or San Francisco.

In fact, banks compete in all the markets we have just mentioned. Banks are multiproduct firms; they "produce" many different products, such as business loans and consumer loans. They also acquire funds in a variety of markets, like the markets for demand deposits, savings deposits, and CDs. These funds are "factors of production" (or "inputs") to the banks. Hence, banks compete in many different markets and in each of these markets they face competition in varying degrees. Sometimes this competition will come from other banks and sometimes it will come from nonbank financial intermediaries. For example, banks may compete with one another for demand deposits, they may compete with savings and loan associations for saving deposits, and they may compete with credit unions for consumer loans.

When General Motors is negotiating a loan with a bank, it is unlikely the bank can exercise much market power. GM has many alternative sources of funds—it can borrow from many other banks, sell commercial paper, and issue bonds or equities. An individual bank negotiating with GM therefore faces considerable competition. Contrast this situation with that involving a loan being negotiated between the bank and Barbara's Dress Shop (assume that annual sales total $100,000). Since Barbara's range of alternatives is probably much narrower than GM's, the individual bank faces less competition and can exercise some market power—that is, the bank can get away with charging a higher interest rate to the borrower than it could if it faced more competition.[1]

It is generally true that more competition is better than less; in an economy like ours, competition helps resources to be used as efficiently as possible, and that reduces costs to all of us. There is considerable competition in many of the markets that banks operate in; unfortunately, however, some banking regulations, such as the one restricting branching, tend to inhibit competition.

8-3
SOURCES OF BANK FUNDS:
AN EXAMINATION OF BANK LIABILITIES[2]

Commercial banks are multiproduct firms. Their products (or output), which can be found on the asset side of their balance sheets, consist primarily of loans and securities. The inputs which banks need to produce their output can be found on the liability side of the balance sheet, where the volume of funds the bank has hired (or borrowed) are recorded. It is these inputs or sources of funds that are employed to produce the output or uses of bank funds. The relationship between the sources of bank funds (the inputs) and the uses of bank funds is illustrated in Figure 8-2.

---

[1] Do not get the idea that a lack of competition is the only reason Barbara may be charged a higher rate than GM. As discussed in more detail in Chapter 15, risk may also play a role.
[2] In this section and the next, the term "commercial bank," or simply "banks," will apply to those banks who are members of the Federal Reserve System. This simplifies our discussion of the sources and uses of bank funds.

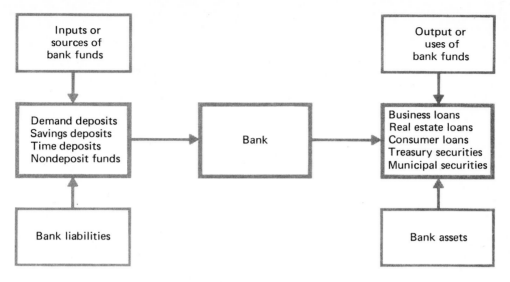

FIGURE 8-2

Banks are multiproduct firms. Their products, or output, which can be found on the asset side of their balance sheets, consist of loans and securities. The inputs, or sources of bank funds, which can be found on the liability side of their balance sheets, consist of deposits and nondeposit funds.

A bank's success depends largely on its ability to attract deposits, since deposits are by far the principal source of bank funds. Any bank will continually strive to increase its deposits. How well it succeeds depends on the population and level of economic activity in the area the bank serves. The growth in deposits also depends on the bank's ability to attract deposits away from competing banks and nonbank financial intermediaries. Banks compete for deposits by offering more attractive rates and services. In a more general sense, the growth of deposits in the banking system will depend on three things: monetary policy, interest rates, and the overall pace of economic activity.

DEMAND DEPOSITS

In 1978, demand deposits constituted about 31 percent of bank liabilities and capital (net worth) and were the largest single source of bank funds. Interestingly, as shown in Table 8-3, these deposits represented about 60 percent of their liabilities in 1961. The decline in demand deposits as a proportion of total liabilities and capital does not mean that the absolute dollar volume of deposits has declined or that banks have shrunk in size. In fact, both have grown significantly. The implication of the declining percentage share of demand deposits as a source of bank funds is that there has been an increase in other liabilities used by banks to attract funds. These include savings deposits, CDs, federal funds, and Eurodollars, to mention a few major ones. We will turn to these other sources of funds momentarily, after we continue with a bit more on demand deposits.

From an economywide viewpoint, demand deposits are quite important because they account for about three-quarters of the existing money supply. As detailed in earlier chapters, households and businesses hold demand deposits so as to mediate transactions—that is, to consummate the purchase and sale of goods and services. While the volume of demand deposits has grown since 1961, why has this volume grown less rapidly than many other major sources of bank funds?

TABLE 8-3
COMMERCIAL BANK LIABILITIES AND CAPITAL: 1961–1978
(Billions of dollars)

	1961		1978	
	BILLIONS OF DOLLARS	PERCENT OF TOTAL	BILLIONS OF DOLLARS	PERCENT OF TOTAL
Liabilities				
Deposit liabilities	**$209.6**	**89.2**	**$701.2**	**77.5**
Demand	142.2	60.5	282.4	31.2
Saving	52.0	22.1	152.2	16.8
Time	15.4	6.6	266.5	29.5
Deposits with denominations of less than $100,000			116.3	
Deposits with denominations of $100,000 or more (including negotiable certificates of deposit—CDs)	NA		150.2	
Nondeposit liabilities	**6.9**	**2.9**	**139.8**	**15.5**
(Including Eurodollars, borrowing from the Federal Reserve, federal funds borrowed, and commercial paper)				
Equity capital	**18.6**	**7.9**	**63.2**	**7.0**
Total liabilities and equity capital	235.1	100.0	904.2	100.0

SOURCE: *Federal Reserve Bulletin.* Details may not add to totals because of rounding. Data are for member banks only. NA = not available.

The slower growth of demand deposits reflects the combined effect of two factors. First, during the period between 1961 and 1978, commercial banks were prohibited by law from paying explicit interest on demand deposits. (This prohibition has been in effect since 1935. As of this writing, the pressure to lift the prohibition is growing.) Second, in the 1960s and 1970s, the general trend of interest rates was up. With the explicit rate of return on demand deposits frozen at zero while interest rates on all other kinds of assets were rising, households and businesses were induced to reduce the volume of their funds held in demand deposits. Anyone who kept funds in a demand deposit lost the interest income that could have been earned if the funds had been placed in interest-bearing time and savings deposits or other financial assets such as Treasury bills. The public adjusted their portfolios in response to changes in the rate of return on other assets relative to the rate of return on demand deposits. As the public shifted from demand deposits to, say, time and savings deposits, banks, of course, found the composition of their liabilities changing.

SAVINGS DEPOSITS

Savings deposits (sometimes called *passbook savings accounts*) earn explicit interest. After demand deposits and currency, they are generally the next most liquid type of financial instrument in our economy. The small print in a depositor's account book, often called a passbook, usually indicates that depositors must give a thirty-day notice before withdrawing their funds. But this thirty-day-notice requirement is universally waived. Thus, although savings deposits are not yet generally a means of payment, they function as safe, liquid, interest-earning stores of value or purchasing power.

As we write the final draft of this text, the distinction between savings deposits and demand deposits was becoming more blurred with each passing day. Banks are now permitted to offer customers the following services: transfer of funds from savings deposits to demand deposit by telephone; preauthorized bill paying out of savings deposits; and, as of November 1, 1978, banks were allowed to offer customers automatic transfers of funds out of savings accounts to demand deposits to cover overdrawn accounts. In effect, these developments mean that savings deposits are, in many cases, essentially functioning as money.*

* The development of ATS (automatic transfer from savings) accounts raises the likelihood that Congress will approve NOW accounts nationwide.

TIME DEPOSITS

Unlike savings deposits, *time deposits* are issued in designated denominations and have fixed maturity dates ranging from thirty days to eight years. It is useful to divide time deposits into two components—those with denominations of under $100,000 and those with denominations of $100,000 and over. The former, sometimes referred to as consumer-type time deposits or small CDs (certificates of deposit), can be redeemed prior to maturity if the holder is willing to give up a substantial portion of interest already earned on the deposits. These penalties reduce the liquidity of time deposits relative to savings deposits. As you might expect, the depositor is compensated for the lower liquidity of time deposits by an interest return that is generally higher than the interest earned on savings deposits.

The other component of time deposits consists of "large CDs." These deposits, available in denominations of $100,000 and over, are issued in nonnegotiable and negotiable form (hence the term "negotiable CDs"). The negotiable feature means that the principal and interest on the deposit are paid at maturity to the bearer, who need not be the original holder. Beginning in 1961, large banks began offering these deposits more aggressively to large corporations, well-heeled foreign investors, and state and local governments. The marketability that flows from the negotiability of these instruments makes them quite liquid and attractive to investors with large volumes of funds.

GOVERNMENT REGULATION AND
SHIFTS IN THE SOURCES OF BANK FUNDS

With the gradual shift in the public's preferences away from demand deposits and toward time deposits and savings deposits, banks found that they had lost some of the advantages they once held vis-à-vis other financial intermediaries. In particular, banks were at one time the only type of financial intermediary with the power to offer to the public claims—demand deposits—that functioned as means of payment in the economy. They faced no competition in the market for demand deposits. However, when the public's preferences shifted toward time and savings deposits, banks found that they had to compete directly with nonbank financial intermediaries, especially the thrift institutions—that is, savings and loan associations, mutual savings banks, and credit unions—who also could offer the public time and savings deposits.

Unfortunately, the government imposed ceilings on the maximum interest rates that banks and thrift institutions could offer the public on time and savings deposits. These limitations, known as the *Regulation Q ceilings*, stifled much of the competition that one might have expected.[1] In fact, Congress under heavy pressure from lobbyists mandated that the interest-rate ceilings should be higher for thrift institutions. It justified these higher

---

[1] The ceilings are set by the Fed for member banks, by the FDIC for state nonmember banks, and by the Federal Home Loan Bank Board for member savings and loan associations. An interagency committee meets regularly to coordinate the ceiling-setting process.

ceilings for thrifts on the premise that commercial banks can offer depositors "one-stop banking"; that is depositors can get demand deposits, savings deposits, and time deposits services in one place. It was argued that since thrift institutions could not offer demand-deposit liabilities to the public, one-stop banking depositors must be induced to make two stops, the commercial bank and a thrift institution. The placement of a higher ceiling on time and savings deposits at the thrifts would provide the necessary inducement for a depositor to stop at a thrift institution as well as a commercial bank. The social good this was supposed to generate is related to the fact that thrift institutions provide a large share of the total volume of funds (mortgages) that finance housing in the United States. It was thought such ceilings would maintain or increase the flow of funds to thrifts and thus benefit the housing market.

The economic implications of these changing competitive relationships will be examined in more detail in Chapter 11. However, it should be clear that banks found themselves in a new ball game, having lost some previously held competitive advantages. Of course, banks did not concede defeat. They fought back. To encourage the public to maintain and add to their demand deposits, commercial banks lowered service charges, extended hours of operation, and—where possible—opened new branches. The inducements offered the public were often more tangible—toasters, dinnerware, and similar premiums were offered to those who opened or added to their deposits (demand deposits as well as time and savings deposits). Lowered service charges, increased services, and inducements are really ways of increasing the implicit return on deposits. Although these things were moderately successful as demand, savings, and time deposits grew in absolute terms over time, the growth was not enough to enable banks to fully accommodate their customers' rising demands for loans. As rising demand for funds pushed interest rates available from nonbank investments well above the Regulation Q ceilings, many depositors were induced to switch from time and savings deposits at banks (or thrifts) to market assets—that is, they bypassed the intermediaries. As a result, banks found themselves faced with potentially profitable loan opportunities and security acquisitions but with a relatively smaller volume of funds (inputs) available to lend.

NONDEPOSIT FUNDS

Given the opportunity to raise profits if only additional sources of funds could be found, banks innovated around the Q ceilings and developed a variety of nondeposit sources of funds which carried interest rates not constrained by the ceilings. Examples of such nondeposit sources of funds (discussed in Chapter 12) include borrowing in the Eurodollar market and issuing commercial paper. By 1978, nondeposit sources of funds accounted for about one-seventh of total bank liabilities and capital. This rise in nondeposit sources of funds, from only 3 percent in 1961 to about 15 percent of bank liabilities and capital in 1978, means that all kinds of deposits in general and demand deposits in particular have become relatively less important as sources of funds to banks.

LIABILITY MANAGEMENT

Many bank managers used to be relatively passive in their pursuit of liabilities. However, during the 1960s and 1970s portfolio shifts by the public and various regulations (such as Regulation Q) contributed to a slowdown in the growth of traditional sources of bank funds, such as demand and savings deposits. This situation forced bank managers to become more aggressive in seeking existing types of liabilities (like large negotiable CDs) and in developing new sources of funds (Eurodollars and federal funds, for example).[1] This liability management, in the face of a changing competitive and economic environment, accounts in large part for the change in the composition of bank liabilities over the past twenty years.

8-4
USES OF BANK FUNDS:
AN EXAMINATION OF BANK ASSETS

Banks must decide on how best to use their funds to meet their objectives. One obvious objective is to maximize profits—the stockholders will see to it that the bank's management will not lose sight of this goal. Banking can be a risky business, however, and the management and stockholders will want to minimize the risks faced in the pursuit of profits. In particular, banks will try to diversify their portfolios in a way that will ensure a considerable margin of *liquidity* and *safety* for the bank. They seek safety because they are *highly leveraged* institutions—that is, their assets are overwhelmingly supported by borrowed funds.[2] As Table 8-4 shows, borrowed funds (including deposits) accounted for 93 percent of bank liabilities in 1978, capital funds accounted for only about 7 percent. As we learned in Chapter 5, the more highly leveraged a firm is, the more vulnerable it is to adverse developments. It is the same with banks. If, for example, some of a bank's larger loans go sour—that is, borrowers default and fail to pay the principal and interest due—this will reduce the cushion provided by the bank's capital base and push the bank toward insolvency. The capital base represents the funds provided by the bank's shareholders and funds retained from past earnings.

Bank concerns about liquidity are generated in part by the nature of their sources of funds. For example, demand deposits in a given bank, which are obviously payable on demand, can and often do fluctuate widely. When demand deposits fall, banks must have a cushion of liquidity to

[1] See Table 12-1 for a brief description of Eurodollars and Federal funds.
[2] Borrowed funds include all deposit and nondeposit sources of funds except equity capital. Equity capital represents the funds furnished by the stockholders (owners) of the bank.

TABLE 8-4
COMMERCIAL BANK ASSETS 1961–1978
(Billions of dollars)

	1961		1978	
	BILLIONS OF DOLLARS	PERCENT OF TOTAL	BILLIONS OF DOLLARS	PERCENT OF TOTAL
Reserves	**$ 19.7**	**8.4**	**$ 36.9**	**4.1**
Vault cash	2.8		8.9	
Deposits with Federal Reserve	16.9		28.0	
Loans	**106.2**	**45.2**	**500.8**	**55.4**
Business (commercial and industrial)	40.9	17.4	171.8	19.0
Consumer	22.9	9.7	110.9	12.3
Real estate	23.9	10.2	138.7	15.3
Other (loans to farmers, financial institutions, etc.)	18.5	7.7	79.4	8.8
Investments (securities)	**73.4**	**31.2**	**173.2**	**20.8**
United States government	53.9	22.9	61.6	6.8
State and local government	16.7	7.1	83.7	9.3
Other	2.8	1.2	27.9	3.1
Other assets (includes cash items in the process of collection, bank premises, etc.)	**35.8**	**51.1**	**193.3**	**21.4**
Total assets	**235.1**	**100.0**	**904.2**	**100.0**

SOURCE: *Federal Reserve Bulletin.* Details may not add to totals because of rounding. Data are for member banks only.

enable them to meet these payment demands.[1] Such liquidity needs can be satisfied by the holding of some highly liquid assets, such as Treasury bills, and non-interest-bearing cash reserves. If profits were all that mattered, a bank would never hold Treasury bills yielding, say, 6 percent if another asset yielding, say, 8 percent were available. However, the liquidity of Treasury bills provides, in effect, an *implicit* return to banks in addition to its explicit yield.

Guided by its liquidity, safety, and earnings objectives, a bank must make portfolio decisions regarding the optimal mix of loans, securities, and reserves it will hold. What this means is simply that the bank must decide on the best way in which to use its funds. The output of a bank, which is the loans and securities it holds, can be broken down into several major categories, as shown in Table 8-4.

BUSINESS LOANS

Business loans, commonly referred to as *commercial and industrial loans,* usually make up the largest individual category of earning assets held by banks. Since businesses are not a homogeneous group of borrowers, the rate charged on business loans varies from customer to customer. The larg-

[1] Banks may also hold liquid assets so that they will be able to accommodate unexpected loan demands from valued customers.

est and most creditworthy customers are charged *the prime rate*. Smaller and less creditworthy customers will be charged some markup over the prime rate. This markup reflects the greater risk of lending to such borrowers as well as the market power banks can exercise over borrowers with lower credit ratings and relatively few financing alternatives. Banks are the largest source of business funds. As we learned in Chapter 5, business loans play a major role in financing working capital, particularly inventories.

REAL ESTATE LOANS

These loans are generally made in the form of mortgages which are backed (or collateralized) by real estate—land as well as structures. Nearly two-thirds of these loans are for residential real estate (single-family houses, apartment buildings, condominiums), while the rest are for commercial and agricultural real estate. This is the second most important use of funds by banks; and banks are the second largest provider of funds to the mortgage market (savings and loan associations are the largest).

CONSUMER LOANS

Bank loans to consumers come in many forms. The largest category are installment loans that enable consumers to finance purchases of autos and other durable goods. While the rates on these loans vary somewhat, they generally exceed the loan rate charged most large, highly rated businesses. Can you explain why? (Hint: consider the relative risk, the market power possessed by banks, and the administrative costs per dollar of loan incurred by banks on each type of loan.)

UNITED STATES GOVERNMENT SECURITIES

As discussed in Chapter 6, these securities are issued by the United States government to finance budget deficits (the excess of expenditures over receipts). Given that they are highly liquid and free of the risk of default (assuming that the government does not collapse), such securities help banks meet their liquidity and safety objectives. The quantity of Treasury securities held by banks often varies, but in a cyclical way. As the economy enters a recession, loan demands fall, the federal budget deficit increases (as taxes fall and transfers rise), and the supply of Treasury securities accordingly rises. In this environment, banks tend to purchase relatively large amounts of Treasury securities. As the economy improves, loan demand rises, and the federal deficit generally shrinks. Banks then slow their acquisition of Treasury securities and increase their volume of loans. This pattern suggests that Treasury securities are in many cases a residual use of funds by banks, rising when loan demand falls and falling when loan demand rises.

STATE AND LOCAL
GOVERNMENT (MUNICIPAL) SECURITIES

These securities are issued by state and local governments and are attractive to banks for several reasons. First, unlike other securities, interest payments on municipal securities are exempt from federal income taxes. Since banks are subject to the 46 percent corporate income tax, the effective rate of return on, say a municipal bond yielding 6 percent is higher than the effective after-tax return on a Treasury security yielding 10 percent (6 percent on the municipal bond is greater than 10 percent minus taxes (.46 × 10%), or an after-tax yield of 5.4%). The second, more subtle attraction is that banks often find it in their best interests to purchase some securities issued by municipalities in their immediate geographic area. When a considerable portion of a bank's funds (deposits especially) come from the local economy, the bank is considered to have made an investment in good will. (Cynics see it as a necessary political investment.)

RESERVES

We have saved perhaps the most familiar of a bank's assets for last. Why do banks hold reserves? One reason is to help meet their liquidity and safety objectives. Another reason is that the Fed *forces* banks to hold reserves. Both reasons are correct. As we will discuss in more detail in Chapter 9, the Fed sets reserve requirements which specify that a certain percentage of each dollar of deposits a bank acquires must be held by banks as *required reserves*. Any funds that banks choose to hold over and above this figure are referred to as *excess reserves*. Banks that belong to the Fed hold reserves in two forms: the first is called *vault cash* —currency and coin held by banks to accommodate customer needs; the second, held at Federal Reserve banks, is called *deposits*. The sum of the two is called *total reserves*.

Note that total reserves can be defined in terms of the form in which they are kept—vault cash or deposits at the Fed—or by how they are being used—required reserves or excess reserves. Why all the fuss about reserves? Simply put, *the Fed can affect the volume of deposits in the banking system and the volume of credit extended by banks (loans and investments)—and therefore interest rates and ultimately economic activity—by altering the quantity of reserves in the banking system or the reserve requirement.* The details of this process are the subject of the next two chapters and Chapter 19.

8-5
SUMMARY OF MAJOR POINTS

1

Banks are by far the largest and most important type of financial intermediary. They are important in our study of money and the financial system because of their size and their ability to issue demand deposit liabilities. Also, the behavior of banks has important effects on the overall economy because banks are a major supplier of the money and credit demanded by households, firms, governments, and foreigners.

2

In the United States, we have a "dual banking system." Banks can be chartered by either the federal government (national banks) or by the various state governments (state banks). National banks must become members of the Federal Reserve System; state banks may decide for themselves whether or not they want to be members. Since the reserve requirements imposed by the Fed on member banks are in many cases more stringent than those imposed by state banking authorities, more and more banks are leaving the Fed or choosing not to join. In general, small banks prefer not to be members, while the larger banks, which can offer the smaller banks correspondent banking services, are members.

3

The banking system is characterized by varying degrees of competition. Banks are multiproduct, multi-input firms. They lend and borrow in many different types of markets. Some of these markets are local (for example, the consumer loan market), some are regional (such as the market for loans made to medium-sized businesses), and some are national (like the government securities market). Some markets are highly competitive, while other markets are relatively less competitive. The large number of banks is not a good guide to the degree of competition which exists in the banking industry. In general, restrictive branching laws in many states and various regulations (such as Regulation Q) tend to inhibit competition in the banking industry.

4

Bank managers make portfolio decisions based on several objectives. One objective is to maximize profits while at the same time satisfying the need for liquidity and the need to minimize the risk associated with borrowing and lending large sums of money. The need for liquidity flows from the "payable on demand" characteristic of a large portion of bank liabilities; the need for safety flows from the high leverage with which banks operate.

5

The major sources of funds for banks are demand deposits, savings deposits, time deposits, and various nondeposit sources of funds. Rising interest rates, rising competition from other financial institutions, and the interest rate ceilings mandated by the Congress have all contributed to the declining proportion of bank funds in the form of demand deposits over the past twenty years.

6

The major uses of bank funds are business loans, real estate loans, consumer loans, state and local securities, federal government securities, and bank reserves.

8-6
REVIEW QUESTIONS

1　Discuss briefly or define the following terms: correspondent banking, the prime rate, the dual banking system, savings deposits, time deposits, required reserves, liability management, excess reserves, nondeposit sources of funds.

2　Explain why in recent years many banks have been dropping their membership in the Federal Reserve System.

3　"Since there are about 14,700 banks, it is obvious that the banking system is characterized by considerable competition." Analyze this statement.

4　Explain why banks have increasingly relied on nondeposit sources of funds as opposed to deposit sources over the past twenty years.

5   As an introduction to the next two chapters, visualize yourself as the portfolio manager of a medium-sized bank. Make a list of the issues you and your staff might consider in assessing various alternative portfolio decisions affecting the bank's assets and liabilities.

6   Generally, GM can borrow funds at banks at interest rates several percentage points below the interest rate banks would charge you. How might this differential be explained (assuming that loan officers are not violating federal law and discriminating against students, women, and so forth)?

7   Why might a bank acquire a Treasury bill yielding 8 percent if instead it could make a loan to Mary's law firm yielding 10 percent?

8-7
SUGGESTED READINGS

1   There are many excellent books on the commercial banking system and the management of commercial banks. Among the best are Paul Nadler, *Commercial Banking in the Economy* (New York: Random House, 1979); Howard Crosse and George Hempel, *Management Policies for Commercial Banks* (New York: Prentice-Hall, 1973); Edward Reed et al., *Commercial Banking* (Englewood Cliffs, N.J.: Prentice-Hall, 1976); and George McKinney et al., *American Commercial Banking* (New York: Lexington, 1978).

2   For an excellent series of readings on varied aspects of banking, see Thomas Havrilesky and John Boorman, *Current Perspectives in Banking: Operations, Management, and Regulation* (Arlington Heights, Ill.: AHM Publishing, 1976).

3   Commercial banks have also become multinational firms. For a review of United States banks' development abroad, see Andrew Brimmer and Frederick Dahl, "Growth of American International Banking: Implications for Public Policy," *Journal of Finance* (May 1975), 341–364; and *Key Issues in International Banking* (Boston: Federal Reserve Bank of Boston, 1977).

4   Nearly every year since 1967 the Federal Reserve Bank of Chicago has published the proceedings of its annual conference on bank structure and competition. The papers in those volumes cover many of the key issues in banking.

THE MONEY
SUPPLY PROCESS:
THE ROLE
OF BANK RESERVES

Money is like manure, if you spread it around
it does a lot of good. But if you pile it up in one
place it stinks like hell.

Clint Murchison, Jr.
Texas Financier

9-1
WHERE DOES THE MONEY COME FROM?

When we examined the commercial banking system (Chapter 8), we were
mainly concerned with the institutional, regulatory, and marketing environ-
ments within which banks must operate. In this chapter and the next, we
will explain those aspects of bank behavior that will help you to see and
understand the linkages between monetary policy and economic activity.
As we mentioned earlier, demand deposits—a liability of commercial
banks—represent about three-quarters of the money supply in the United

States. The commercial banking system can effect increases or decreases in the amount of credit available in the United States—that is, it can expand or contract its loans—and, therefore, increase or decrease the availability of money in the economy. All this happens through the supply of reserves in the entire banking system. In this chapter we shall examine how the reserves in the banking system can affect the money and credit in the economy. Later on, in Chapter 19, we will show how the Fed can influence the supply of reserves in the banking system. Establishing these linkages between the actions of the Fed and the behavior of banks is a key step in identifying the relationship between monetary policy and economic activity.

As we have done before, we shall start with a very simplistic model and gradually introduce the real but complicating factors of the real world.

It should be emphasized that the analysis presented in this chapter is only a first step—the model developed is extremely simple and thus abstracts from some important aspects of the problem. Our motto is, "You have to learn how to walk before you can run." Accordingly, once you master this first approach, you will be ready for the more complete (and, unfortunately, more complicated) analysis developed in subsequent chapters.

9-2
DEPOSIT AND LOAN
CREATION BY BANKS: A SIMPLE MODEL

To understand how commercial bank reserves determine the money supply and bank credit (the quantity of loans and securities held by banks), let us begin with a simple balance sheet for an individual bank. Recall that a balance sheet measures stocks of assets, liabilities, and net worth at a particular time and that a balance sheet must always balance; total assets must equal total liabilities plus net worth. Any change in assets must be exactly offset by a change in the sum of liabilities and net worth. We will work with a simplified balance sheet called a *T account*. On the asset side, there are reserves, loans, and securities; we shall assume that there are only demand deposits on the liability side. In the example which follows, the accounts will show only changes in these assets and liabilities.

There are seven columns in Table 9-1. The first column at the left shows a T account for the HLT First National Bank. Let us assume that $1000 in new deposits has just been acquired by the HLT Bank (for now, we will not worry about where it came from). This will show up as $1000 in demand deposits on the liability side and $1000 of vault cash (reserves) on the asset side (stage I). However, HLT National is not in business to hold idle cash; it uses cash deposits to acquire assets that earn interest income—remember the stockholders! If the Fed insists that HLT keep 10 percent of its deposits as required reserves, the remaining 90 percent—excess reserves—can be lent out. (Excess reserves can also be used to buy securities. But in our example we will ignore security purchases. This will not affect the analysis and it simplifies matters.) Suppose Charlie Brown needs $900 to insulate his house for the coming winter. HLT agrees to lend Brown $900; Brown signs a loan contract and HLT credits $900 to his checking account balance. Stage II of Figure 9-1 shows the T accounts for HLT and Brown after this transaction. At this stage, we now see that HLT's balance sheet has assets of $1000 in cash reserves plus $900 in loans. On the liability side it now has $1900, since it has gained the new $900 deposit in Brown's account. In other words $900 of money has been "created." A great game while it lasts!

Unfortunately, things are not that simple for the individual bank. Brown will use his $900 to pay his insulation contractor who, we will assume, is not a customer of HLT National. Thus, when Brown writes a check for $900 against his account at HLT, this will reduce HLT's deposits and reserves by $900. Stage III of Table 9-1 shows this result. Now HLT's balance sheet shows +$900 of loans and +$100 of cash reserves on the asset side. HLT cannot, in general, assume that new deposits created in conjunction with loans will remain (be redeposited) in its coffers. This means that an individual bank can lend out only its excess reserves and can, by itself, only create additional deposits equal to its excess reserves.

However, the process has not ended. The insulation contractor will presumably deposit the $900 in his account at another bank. Let us call this the Second National Bank. The middle of Table 9-1 (stage IV) shows how the Second National's balance sheet would change as a result of this deposit. As above, the Second National Bank will react to the deposit inflow by lending out that portion of the cash received which is left over after the Fed's reserve requirement has been met. Let us assume that it also has to comply with a legal reserve ratio of 10 percent on demand deposits. In this case, it will have to keep $90 as reserves and will have $810 of excess reserves to lend out to, say Jill Mason, who happens to need exactly that much to buy new furniture for her house (stage V). Again, let us assume that Ms. Mason gives a check to the furniture dealer, who then deposits it in another bank. Again, Table 9-1 shows (stages VI and VII) the balance sheets of Second National and the other bank (Third National) after these transactions have occurred.

WHAT DOES ALL THIS MEAN?

In general, we have shown that each individual bank was able to increase its *earning assets* by the excess reserves that resulted from a deposit inflow. As the output—that is, the loans—of one bank increased, the use of the proceeds of the loan by the borrower led to a deposit inflow—an increase in inputs—at another bank. A deposit inflow at an individual bank increases the bank's total deposits and reserves. The bank will adjust to the inflow of reserves and deposits by expanding its loans or securities and "creating" additional deposits. Subsequently, the individual bank will lose reserves (assets) and the additional deposits (liabilities) as the borrower uses the pro-

TABLE 9-1
BALANCE SHEET CHANGES: BANKS AND THE PUBLIC

Stage	HLT National Bank Assets	Liabilities	Charles Brown A	L	Insulation Contractor A	L
I	+1000 reserves [+900 excess reserves +100 required reserves]	+1000 deposits				
II	+900 loan to Brown	+900 deposits due Brown	+900 deposits at HLT	+900 loans due HLT		
III	−900 reserves	−900 deposits due Brown	−900 deposits at HLT +900 insulation		−900 insulation materials +900 check from Brown	
IV						
V						
VI						
VII						
VIII						
Net Changes for Banks	+100 reserves (all required) +900 loans	+1000 deposits				

Second National Bank		Jill Mason		Furniture Dealer		Third National Bank	
A	L	A	L	A	L	A	L

Second National Bank

+900 reserves
[+810 excess reserves
+90 required reserves]

+900 deposits due contractor

+810 loan to Mason

+810 deposits due Mason

−810 reserves

−810 deposits due Mason

+90 reserves (all required)
+810 loans

+900 deposits

Jill Mason

+810 deposits at 2d National

+810 loan due 2d National

−810 deposit at 2d National
+810 furniture

Furniture Dealer

+810 check from Mason
−810 furniture

Third National Bank

+810 reserves
[+729 excess reserves
+81 required reserves]

+810 deposits due furniture dealer

+729 loans
[We have not explained this change --can you?]

+729 deposits

183

ceeds of the loan to pay for something. However, since another bank gains the previous bank's loss in reserves and deposits, the total volume of reserves in the banking system does not change. What does happen at each stage is that deposits rise and the composition of total reserves in the banking system changes—required reserves rise and excess reserves fall. In our example, the size of these changes can be stated precisely. As deposits flow from bank to bank, the change in deposits at each bank can be represented as the change in required reserves (this is equal to 10 percent of the deposit inflow) plus the change in excess reserves (which is equal to 90 percent of the deposit inflow). The change in loans and deposits "created" by the bank is equal to 90 percent of the inflow. This is shown in the bottom part of Table 9-1, where the sum of the changes in deposits for each bank is presented. The $1000 increase in deposits at HLT is followed by a $900 increase in deposits at Second National, which is followed by a $810 increase in deposits at Third National. Taken together (that is, adding up the changes in each bank's balance sheet), the increase in total deposits in the banking system at each stage is 90 percent of the new deposits "created" at the previous stage. If we look at only two stages for simplicity, we see that new deposits = $1000; increase in total deposits at subsequent stages = $900 + $810. This means that, ultimately, the new deposits created at subsequent stages approach zero and the process ends.[1]

THE MULTIPLIER MODEL
OF THE MONEY SUPPLY PROCESS

The relationship between reserves and the money supply can be viewed from a different perspective. In our simple example, the process of creating money and credit from increases in reserves will end when all reserves in the banking system become required reserves—this is sometimes referred to as a situation in which the banking system is fully "loaned up." This situation is reached when the banking system "creates" deposit liabilities and at the same time increases its assets (loans and securities).

Required reserves RR are by definition equal to the required reserve ratio q multiplied by the amount of deposits.

(9-1) $$\text{RR} = qD$$

Excess reserves XR are by definition equal to total reserves R minus required reserves.

$$\text{XR} = R - \text{RR}$$

If total reserves equal required reserves, there are no excess reserves to be lent out since XR = 0, and therefore

(9-2) $$R = \text{RR} = qD$$

---

[1] To illustrate: $.9 \times 1000 = 900$, $.9 \times 900 = 810$, $.9 \times 810 = 729$, $.9 \times 729 = 656.10$, $.9 \times 656.10 = 590.49$, etc.

Rearranging terms yields

(9-3)
$$D = \frac{R}{q} \quad \text{or} \quad D = \frac{1}{q} \times R$$

Total deposits are equal to the quantity of reserves multiplied by the reciprocal of the required reserve ratio. We shall refer to $1/q$ as the *reserve multiplier* (sometimes called the "money multiplier.")

To find the total *change* in deposits for any *change* in reserves, we can rewrite Equation (9-3) with a delta (Δ) to signify "change in":

(9-4)
$$\Delta D = \frac{1}{q} \times \Delta R$$

Since we assumed that q was fixed at 10 percent (.1) in our example, the reserve multiplier = $1/0.1 = 10$. Therefore, the increase in deposits resulting from the $1000 increase in reserves will be $10,000.

We have pointed out all along that the change in deposits is, by definition, accompanied by a change in bank earning assets (EA). The total change in EA will be equal to the total change in deposits minus q multiplied by the change in deposits. Remember, after the process is over, total assets must equal total liabilities. If D (a liability) increased by $10,000 and R (an asset) increases by $1000, then EA can rise by only $9000.

In general, $\Delta EA = \Delta D - q\,\Delta D$. Since $\Delta D = 1/q\,\Delta R$, we can substitute for ΔD: $\Delta EA = 1/q\,\Delta R - q(1/q\,\Delta R)$ or $\Delta EA = (1/q - 1) \times \Delta R$. In the example above, $\Delta EA = (1/.1 - 1) \times 1000 = (10 - 1) \times 1000 = \$9000$. Check Table 9-1 to convince yourself that the change in EA for each bank, and therefore the banking system, is .9 of the change in deposits.

Even though we have abstracted from many details, several policy implications flow from the above analysis. First, if the Fed wants to affect the demand deposit component of the money supply and bank credit, it must be able to influence the quantity of reserves in the banking system or reserve requirements. We know from Chapter 8 that the Fed sets reserve requirements for member banks. In Chapter 18, we will show how the Fed can influence the supply of reserves throughout the entire banking system. For now, take our word for it—the Fed can, in effect, control the supply of reserves. The second implication is that a given dollar change in reserves will lead to a larger change in the money supply and bank credit.

THE MULTIPLIER PROCESS: MAGIC OR REAL?

Sometimes students come away from the preceding analysis with the feeling that they do not really understand how an injection of reserves into the banking system by the Fed leads to multiple increases in the money supply. For those of you who fall into this category, we can illustrate this phenomenon without resorting to the technical analysis above. The multiplier process is a reflection of what is called the *fractional reserves banking system.* Individual banks must hold some *fraction* (between 0 percent and 100 percent) of any increase in deposits they experience in the form of reserves. The fraction they must hold is determined by the reserve requirements set by the Fed. Imagine a world where the reserve requirement is 100 percent. Any increase in deposits experienced by a bank would at the same time also be, dollar for dollar, an increase in required reserves. In this case the reserve multiplier, shown in Equation (9-4), would equal one. If the reserve requirement is less than one, however, the bank experiencing a given dollar increase in deposits will be required to hold only some fraction of the increase in deposits as required reserves. The remaining fraction (excess reserves) can be lent out. In this latter case, the total change in deposits is greater than in the 100 percent required reserves case and, therefore, the multiplier is greater than one. In general, the change in deposits and bank credit which accompanies a given change in reserves will be larger the lower are reserve requirements.

The whole process can be viewed as an inverted pyramid (∇). The original injection of reserves and deposits by the Fed provides individual banks with excess reserves. They adjust to this abundance of reserves by expanding loans and deposits. The deposits, when spent by loan recipients, flow to other banks (higher up on the pyramid), who, in turn, expand loans and deposits. The process continues because profit-maximizing banks are in general not interested in holding non-interest-earning excess reserves. As a result, the original injection of reserves (the foundation of the inverted pyramid) can support a multiple expansion in loans and deposits. The whole process is not unlike one's family tree. A husband and wife have children, who in turn have children, and so forth.

9-3
SOME COMPLICATIONS

Let us take a look at the simplifying assumptions we made in developing the preceding model of how money is created.

First, we assumed that banks never hold any excess reserves—when deposits flow in, banks lend out all the excess reserves. As Figure 9-1 shows, banks *do* hold excess reserves, and the excess reserves they hold fluctuate over time. If banks hold *some* part of an increase in total reserves in the form of excess reserves, this is a *leakage* from the flow of increases in deposits and bank credit. The effect of this leakage is similar to the effect of an increase in reserve requirements. The loans and deposits created at each stage will be reduced by the volume of excess reserves held. The net effect will be to lower the reserve multiplier.

Second, we have ignored currency. If the furniture dealer in the example in Table 9-1 holds, say, one-quarter of the funds received from Ms. Mason in the form of currency, then the funds received by Third National in the form of a deposit to the dealer's checking account will be three-quarters of the figure shown. This will reduce the flow of reserves and deposits to subsequent banks and hence reduce the overall expansion of the money supply.

Third, we have ignored the fact that there are time deposits and savings

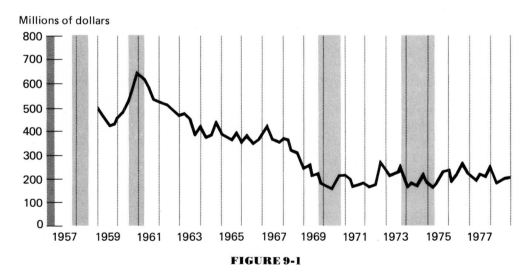

FIGURE 9-1

Excess reserves held by commercial banks. Bank holdings of excess reserves declined from about $700 million in 1961 to $200 million in 1969 and have fluctuated around the latter figure since then. In Chapter 10, some of the reasons for this decline will be discussed. (*Source:* Federal Reserve; data are for member banks.)

deposits and that banks have to hold required reserves against these deposits. The insulation contractor may decide to hold one-fifth of the proceeds from his sale in the form of time deposits. This can also be viewed as a leakage, since the resulting change in demand deposits and therefore the money supply will be smaller.

MODIFYING THE MULTIPLIER MODEL

The actual reserve multiplier is clearly not as simple as the one presented in Equation (9-3). We can develop a somewhat more realistic reserve multiplier by taking into account some of these items. Let us see what happens when we recognize that banks offer time deposits and savings deposits as well as demand deposits (we shall continue to assume banks do not hold excess reserves). Now total reserves are reserves held against demand deposits R_D plus reserves held against time deposits and savings deposits R_{ts}.

$$(9\text{-}5) \qquad R = R_D + R_{ts}$$

Let q_D be the required reserve ratio for demand deposits and q_{ts} be the required reserve ratio for time deposits and savings deposits. We can then rewrite equation (9-5) as follows:

$$(9\text{-}6) \qquad R = q_D D + q_{ts} TS$$

where TS = total time deposits plus savings deposits and D = total demand deposits. Next, for simplicity, assume that the public prefers to hold time deposits and savings deposits as a constant proportion of demand deposits. Thus we can define $TS = sD$ where s = the ratio of time deposits plus savings deposits to demand deposits. Substituting this expression into Equation (9-6) yields:

$$(9\text{-}7) \qquad R = q_D D + q_{ts} sD$$

Solving this equation for D yields

$$(9\text{-}8) \qquad D = \frac{1}{q_D + q_{ts}s} R$$

and in terms of changes in reserves and deposits, we have

$$(9\text{-}9) \qquad \Delta D = \frac{1}{q_D + q_{ts}s} \Delta R$$

Equation (9-8) defines our new relation between demand deposits and bank reserves. Note that the reserve multiplier in Equation (9-8) $\dfrac{1}{q_D + q_{ts}s}$ is smaller than the reserve multiplier $1/q_D$ in Equation (9-4). For example, if $q_D = .10$, $q_{ts} = .05$, and $s = 2.0$, the multiplier now is $\dfrac{1}{.10 + .05(2.0)} = 1/.2 = 5.0$. The multiplier has been cut in half!

Recall that the total money supply M is equal to demand deposits plus currency. Let us assume that the public also desires to maintain its currency holdings as a constant proportion of its demand deposits. Thus let $C = cD$ where C = total currency held by the public and c = the desired ratio of currency to demand deposits. Thus we can write

(9-10) $$M = D + C = D + cD = (1 + c)D$$

Substituting the equivalent of D from the right-hand side of Equation (9-8) for D in Equation (9-10), redefining reserves to take account of currency drains,[1] and combining terms gives

(9-11) $$M = \frac{1 + c}{q_D + q_{ts}s + c} R$$

and

(9-12) $$\Delta M = \frac{1 + c}{q_D + q_{ts}s + c} \Delta R$$

Equation (9-11) defines the total money supply in terms of our new multiplier and the supply of reserves.[2] Equation (9-12) shows the change in the money supply for a given change in reserves.[3]

THE FED'S CONTROL OVER THE MONEY SUPPLY

Compare Equations (9-12) and (9-4). Note that in Equation (9-4) the determinants of the money supply, R and q, were both under the control of the Fed. In Equation (9-12), the Fed's control of the money supply is not so straightforward. The public rather than the Fed controls c, and banks and the public together will determine the volume of time and savings deposits. Further, the public's holdings of currency and time and savings deposits are in reality not a constant fraction of demand deposits but rather vary over time in response to movements in interest rates and economic activity. This means that the multiplier in Equation (9-12) is not perfectly stable or predictable.[4] And what does that mean? It means even if the Fed can control the

---

[1] Reserves would now be redefined as

$$R - cD = q_D D + q_{ts}sD$$

since a rise in currency holdings will (other things equal) drain reserves from the banking system. Rewriting yields

$$R = q_D D + q_{ts}sD + cD$$

or

$$D = \frac{1}{q_D + q_{ts}s + c} R$$

[2] If $c = .3$, $q_D = .10$, $q_{ts} = .05$, and $s = 2.0$, the multiplier becomes $1.3/2 = 2.6$.
[3] We have still ignored excess reserves. Although quite volatile, as Figure 9-1 indicates, they are a very small fraction of total deposits on average. Thus little is lost as a result of this omission.
[4] An alternative approach to the money supply process preferred by some economists is to define the money supply in terms of a multiplier relationship with the *monetary base*, where the monetary base is defined as total member banks' reserves plus currency held by the public; $B = R + C$, where B is the monetary base. See the book *The Money Supply Process*, by Albert Burger (listed at the end of the chapter), for an in-depth treatment of this approach.

supply of reserves in the banking system, it may find controlling the money supply somewhat more difficult.

The simple model presented above yields many insights into the money supply process and the interaction among banks. You should recognize, however, that it is really a "sausage grinder" model—the reserves go in one end, you crank the handle, and loans and deposits come out at the other end.[1] What is missing from the simplified model is the notion that *banks are firms* and, like other firms, they are interested in maximizing profits. As we saw in Chapter 5, such an objective will lead firms to consider the marginal costs and marginal revenues associated with alternative courses of action. The multiplier model simplifies away such notions. In particular, the cost of deposits and the return on loans—in other words, interest rates—were ignored. It was simply assumed that banks always had customers ready, willing, and able to borrow, regardless of the level of interest rates. The next chapter will fill this void by relaxing some of our simplifying assumptions and pursuing a more analytic, more realistic approach to the relationship between bank reserves, bank behavior, and the money supply.

9-4
SUMMARY OF MAJOR POINTS

1

In our simple model (where we ignored excess reserves, currency, time deposits, and savings deposits), we showed that a given injection of reserves into the banking system would result in a multiple increase in the money supply (demand deposits) and bank credit. Written in general form, the money supply function derived from this model is[2]:

$$M = f(\overset{+}{R}, \overset{-}{q})$$

The money supply is a positive function of the quantity of reserves R in the banking system and a negative function of the reserve requirement q on demand deposits. The larger q is, given R, the smaller the reserve multiplier and thus the smaller the money supply.

---

[1] Some call it a "hot potato" model—banks get reserves and treat them like a hot potato, getting rid of them as fast as possible by expanding loans.
[2] In effect, $M = R \times$ multiplier, where the multiplier $= f(\bar{q})$.

2

In a more elaborate model, where currency as well as time and savings deposits are taken into account, the money supply function becomes:

$$M = f(\overset{+}{R}, \overset{-}{q_D}, \overset{-}{q_{ts}}, \overset{-}{s}, \overset{-}{c})$$

The money supply is a positive function of the quantity of reserves R and a negative function of the ratio of currency to demand deposits c. The money supply is a negative function of the reserve requirement on demand deposits q_D, time and savings deposits q_{ts}, and the ratio of time and savings deposits to demand deposits s. The reserve multiplier in this model is considerably smaller than in the simple model above because there are now several leakages from the multiplier process which reduce the quantity of money that can be supported by a given volume of reserves.

3

It should be clear from summary points 1 and 2 that the Fed can *affect* the money supply through its reserve requirements. However, once you take account of currency, time deposits and savings deposits, excess reserves, and nonmember banks, you can see that (*a*) banks and the public can also affect the supply of money and (*b*) the multiplier is volatile and not precisely predictable. In general, this means that the Fed's control over the money supply is not as precise as you might imagine.

4

The multiplier approach to the money supply process does not explicitly take account of the profit-making behavior of banks and the role of interest rates. In effect, the multiplier approach summarizes, without analyzing, the portfolio decisions of banks and the public and their implications for the money supply.

9-5
REVIEW QUESTIONS

1 What is meant by a "fractional reserve banking system" and what does it have to do with the reserve multiplier?

2 Suppose banks desire to hold a constant fraction of their demand deposit liabilities as excess reserves. Show how this would affect the reserve multiplier. (We would recommend a derivation like those in the text.)

3   "Since the Federal Reserve can set reserve requirements and the quantity of reserves in the banking system, controlling the money supply is relatively easy." Comment on this statement.

4   In early 1929 commercial banks held average excess reserves equal to about $50 million (less than one-quarter of 1 percent of deposits). In ensuing years, banks raised their holdings of excess reserves considerably in response to the deteriorating business situation and the failure of thousands of banks (in late 1933 and early 1934 excess reserves averaged about $2 billion). Given the analysis developed in this chapter (and your answer to question 2), what do you think happened to the money supply? Friedman and Schwartz, *Monetary History of the United States*, examine what actually happened. What could the Fed have done to reverse what happened?

9-6
SUGGESTED READINGS

1   For a detailed discussion of multiplier models of the money supply process, see Albert Burger, *The Money Supply Process* (Belmont, Calif.: Wadsworth, 1971). See also Dwayne Wrightsman, *An Introduction to Monetary Theory and Policy* (New York: Free Press, 1976).

2   An excellent review of the money supply process and some issues covered in later chapters is available in *Modern Money Mechanics*, published by the Federal Reserve Bank of Chicago. If you write a cordial letter to their publications department, they will send you a free copy.

10

THE MONEY SUPPLY PROCESS: THE ROLE OF COMMERCIAL BANK PORTFOLIO BEHAVIOR

Lend less than thou owest.

William Shakespeare
King Lear

10-1
ANOTHER CHAPTER ON BANKS?

Banks are business firms, and like the business firms examined in Chapter 5, the drive for profits guides their behavior. For banks, profits are equal to the difference between the revenue generated by acquiring loans and securities (the output of the bank) and the costs associated with acquiring various deposit and nondeposit sources of funds (the inputs to the bank). Even with this simple definition of how a bank makes its profits, we can identify a number of portfolio decisions bank managers must make: How many loans should be made in total? How many of these should be consumer loans and business loans? What rate should be charged on the loans? How many securities (municipal and Treasury, for example) should be purchased? What rates should the bank offer on its time deposits and savings deposits?

Banks are complex institutions continually involved in borrowing and lending funds. To see how their various portfolio decisions ultimately affect the money supply, interest rates, and the overall level of economic activity, we need to examine the key factors which guide their portfolio decisions. To gain insight into the relationship between banks and the rest of the economy, including the Federal Reserve, we will develop an *analytic* model of bank behavior in this chapter. The previous chapter presented a simplistic approach to the analysis of bank behavior and what determines the money supply. With this background, we are now in a position to examine more closely the determinants of commercial bank behavior and the money supply.

10-2
A MODEL OF INDIVIDUAL BANK BEHAVIOR

In Chapter 5 we developed the theory of the firm and firm behavior. To get at the core of commercial bank behavior, we will extend that theory to include banks. We will assume that banks seek to maximize profits and that there are two types of assets, *reserves* (a nonearning asset) and loans and securities (*earning assets*), and one liability, *deposits*. Since assets must equal liabilities, we can write the balance-sheet identity as follows:

BALANCE SHEET FOR COMMERCIAL BANKS

ASSETS	LIABILITIES
EA	D
R	

$$\text{Assets} = \text{Liabilities} \quad \text{or}$$
$$\overbrace{EA + R} = \overbrace{D}$$

or, rearranging terms

(10-1)
$$EA = D - R$$

$$\underbrace{\text{Earning assets}}_{\text{Output}} = \underbrace{\text{deposits} - \text{reserves}}_{\text{Input}}$$

where EA = earning assets (loans plus securities)
$\quad\ R$ = reserves
$\quad\ D$ = deposits

In general, we can view earning assets EA as the output of the banking firm and deposits less reserves $D - R$ as the *net* inputs to the firm. The bank's *profits* will be the difference between the *revenue* received on the output, that is, earning assets, and the costs associated with producing this output. To maximize its profits, the bank should behave so as to equate the *marginal costs* (in this case the change in total cost for a \$1 change in earning assets produced) *to marginal revenue* (in this case the change in total revenue resulting from the acquisition of \$1 of earning assets).

A CLOSER LOOK AT BANK MARGINAL COST

Banks hold reserves partly because the Fed requires them to. The reserves the Fed requires banks to hold are called *required reserves*. Banks may also hold more reserves than those required by the Fed to hedge against unexpected deposit outflows and other contingencies. The reserves held above the amount required by the Fed are called *excess reserves*. We know that the level of required reserves is determined by multiplying the Fed's reserve requirement by the level of deposits banks hold. Thus required reserves are a function of the Fed's reserve requirement and the level of deposits. Let us assume that the excess reserves held by banks are also a function of the level of deposits. For example, the Fed's reserve requirement could be 9 percent of total deposits and excess reserves held by banks could, on average, be equal to 1 percent of total deposits. As a result, for every dollar of deposits acquired by a bank, it would hold 10 cents—9 cents required reserves plus 1 cent excess reserves—and it would therefore have 90 cents to lend out. Put another way, for every dollar of deposits received, the bank will be able to obtain only 90 cents of earning assets.

A bank attracts deposits by offering depositors a rate of return on their deposit holdings. The bank then sets aside some part of each dollar of deposits in the form of non-interest-bearing reserves—required reserves plus excess reserves—and lends out the rest $(D - R)$. As a result, the cost associated with "producing" \$1 of earning assets c_{EA} is a function of two things: the rate paid on deposits i_D and the fraction of each dollar held as reserves.

Reserves and Bank Costs   Let us see what effect total reserves has on the cost of earning assets. Let us assume that K is the ratio of total reserves to total deposits, expressed in percent. In the previous example, K is the sum of the Fed's required reserve ratio q expressed in percent (9 percent) and the bank's ratio of excess reserves to total deposits expressed in percent (1 percent). Therefore K would equal 10 percent in our example.

If the Fed raises reserve requirements q from, say, 9 to 11 percent, then K would equal 12 percent and every dollar of deposits will produce only 88 cents of earning assets instead of 90 cents. Put another way, when q was equal to 9 percent, $K = 10$ percent, and it took about \$1.11 of deposits to get \$1 of earning assets. [Since $EA = D - R$ and $R = KD$, then $EA = D - KD$; or, using some simple algebra, $EA = D(1 - K)$. This is solved by dividing through by $1 - K$, yielding $D = EA/(1 - K)$. Thus if $K = 10$ percent, then $\$1/(1 - K) = \$1.11$.] If $K = 12$ percent, it would take about $\$1.14$ in deposits to produce $\$1$ in earning assets.

How does this affect the cost of earning assets? When $K = 10$ percent, banks need $\$1.11$ of deposits to produce $\$1$ of earning assets; when $K = 12$ percent, banks need $\$1.14$ of deposits to produce $\$1$ of earning assets. As K (the ratio of total reserves to deposits) rises, banks need more deposits per dollar of earning assets. This means banks must "borrow" more deposits to produce a given amount of earning assets. Since banks must pay interest on each dollar of deposits i_D, this means that the cost of producing a given amount of earning assets rises.[1]

If $K = 0$, the cost of producing $\$1$ of earning assets c_{EA} would be equal to the cost of acquiring $\$1$ of deposits i_D. If $K > 0$, then $c_{EA} > i_D$. The appropriate formula is:

(10-2)
$$c_{EA} = \frac{i_D}{1 - K}$$

As K rises, c_{EA} rises.

The Interest Rate on Deposits and Bank Costs So much for the effect of reserves on bank costs. What about the other key factor affecting bank costs—the interest (both explicit and implicit) paid on deposits i_D? It does not take much training in economics or finance to figure out that a rise in i_D will raise bank costs. This being the case, what determines the rate banks must pay to attract deposits?

The rate of interest i_D banks must pay to attract deposits can be derived from the supply of deposit funds available to banks. We assume that a bank cannot attract an unlimited volume of funds at a given interest rate. This means that a bank must raise its interest rate on deposits if it wishes to attract additional deposit funds. Intuitively, the analysis is similar to the discussion of the labor market in Chapter 5; if a firm wants to hire more labor, it must raise its wage offer. The willingness of households to supply additional labor to firms and thus additional deposits to banks is positively related to the reward: the wage rate in the case of supplying labor and i_D in the case of supplying deposits. Thus, as the interest rate i_D on deposits increases *relative* to the rate of return on alternative financial assets (close substitutes such as Treasury bills), the supply of funds to banks will increase. As people increase their deposits with banks, the banks will have increased funds to lend out. In sum, banks can expand output, or earning assets, but only by increasing inputs, or deposits. To expand inputs, banks must raise i_D, and the raising of i_D raises bank costs.

---

[1] The argument here is exactly analogous to the argument contained in Chapter 5 on how compensating balances affect the cost of borrowing for a firm. As the requirements for compensating balances rise, the cost of borrowing a given dollar sum rises because the firm will have to borrow more than the needed sum in order to satisfy the requirement. Since the firm must pay interest on the entire amount, the cost of borrowing the funds actually needed rises.

Bank Costs—A Numerical Example   The following example should help to nail down the relationship between the supply of deposits to banks and the cost of producing earning assets. Table 10-1 presents figures depicting the relationship between total costs, average costs, and marginal costs for a hypothetical banking firm. Columns 1 and 2 together represent the supply function for deposits faced by banks; as banks raise the rate paid on deposits i_D, the dollar volume of deposits the public is willing to supply banks increases. We shall assume that the reserve ratio K is 10 percent. Given K, we can multiply each of the levels of deposits in column 1 by $(1 - K) = .90$ to get the level of earning assets the bank could acquire at each level of deposits. Refer back to Equation 10-1 [EA $= D - R$ and $R = $ KD, so EA $= D(1 - K)$]. This is shown in column 3.

To find the average cost per dollar of earning assets, shown in column 4, the rates in column 2—the cost per dollar of deposits—are divided by .90. Refer back to Equation (10-2); $K = .1$, so $(1 - K) = .9$. The average cost of producing \$1 of earning assets is equal to the volume of deposits needed to produce \$1 of earning assets—\$1/(1 - K)—multiplied by the rate on deposits i_D. If EA = \$1, then $D = $ \$1/(1 - K)$ and the cost per dollar of EA $= i_D \times$ \$1/(1 - K) = i_D/(1 - K)$. Multiplying the average cost per dollar of earning assets by the level of earning assets (column 3 multiplied by column 4) yields the total costs associated with acquiring (or producing) each level of earning assets; this is shown in column 5.

Column 6, derived from column 5, presents the change in total costs as we vary the level of earning assets (column 3). Column 7, derived from column 3, shows the dollar changes in earning assets. Dividing column 6 by column 7 yields, in column 8, the marginal cost per dollar of earning assets—that is, the change in total costs as earning assets change.

Using the figures in Table 10-1, the average cost of deposits (column 2), the average cost of earning assets (column 4), and the marginal cost of earning assets (column 8) are plotted in Figure 10-1.

A CLOSER LOOK AT BANK MARGINAL REVENUE

Firms generate revenue (income) by selling their output. The revenue a firm receives for selling a given quantity of output depends on the price the public is willing to pay to purchase this particular quantity of output. Generally, we assume that the lower the price, the larger the quantity the public will be willing to buy. Banks generate revenue by lending funds—that is, by acquiring assets (loans and securities) that earn interest income. The price banks charge for their output is an interest rate. Based on earlier discussions in Chapters 4 and 5, we would expect that the public's willingness to borrow is negatively related to the interest rate the bank charges; that is, the higher the rate, the lower the quantity of funds the public is willing to borrow.

Table 10-2 presents a hypothetical set of revenue figures corresponding to the various levels of earning assets depicted in Table 10-1 and Figure

TABLE 10-1
COSTS OF DEPOSITS AND EARNING ASSETS FOR A HYPOTHETICAL BANKING FIRM

(1) D = TOTAL DEPOSITS HIRED (MILLIONS OF DOLLARS)	(2) i_D = AVERAGE COST OF HIRING (ATTRACTING) DEPOSITS = RATE PAID ON DEPOSITS	(3) EA = EARNING ASSETS = $(1-K) \times D$ (MILLIONS OF DOLLARS)	(4) $c_{EA} = i_D(1-K)$ = AVERAGE COST OF EARNING ASSETS PER DOLLAR	(5) $TC_{EA} = c_{EA} \times EA$ TOTAL COST OF EARNING ASSETS (MILLIONS OF DOLLARS)	(6) ΔTC_{EA} = CHANGE IN COST OF EARNING ASSETS (MILLIONS OF DOLLARS)	(7) ΔEA = CHANGE IN EARNING ASSETS (MILLIONS OF DOLLARS)	(8) $\frac{\Delta TC_{EA}}{\Delta EA}$ = MARGINAL COST OF EARNING ASSETS PER DOLLAR
0	.04	0	.044	0			
50	.045	45	.05	2.25	2.25	45	.05
100	.05	90	.056	5.04	2.79	45	.062
200	.06	180	.067	12.06	7.02	90	.078
300	.07	270	.077	20.79	8.73	90	.097
400	.08	360	.089	32.04	11.25	90	.125

TABLE 10-1

Supply of deposits to banks by the public

i_D / D

TABLE 10-2
RETURN ON EARNING ASSETS FOR A HYPOTHETICAL BANKING FIRM

(1) EA = TOTAL EARNING ASSETS (MILLIONS OF DOLLARS)	(2) i_{EA} = AVERAGE RETURN ON EARNING ASSETS PER DOLLAR	(3) $TR_{EA} = i_{EA} \times EA$ = TOTAL REVENUE ON EARNING ASSETS (MILLIONS OF DOLLARS)	(4) ΔTR_{EA} = CHANGE IN TOTAL REVENUE (MILLIONS OF DOLLARS)	(5) ΔEA = CHANGE IN EARNING ASSETS (MILLIONS OF DOLLARS)	(6) $\frac{\Delta TR_{EA}}{\Delta EA}$ = MARGINAL REVENUE ON EARNING ASSETS PER DOLLAR
0	.15	0			
45	.145	6.5	6.5	45	.144
90	.14	12.6	6.1	45	.136
180	.13	23.4	10.8	90	.120
270	.12	32.4	9.0	90	.100
360	.11	39.6	7.2	90	.080

TABLE 10-2

Public's demand for bank output—earning assets—e.g., loans

i_{EA} / EA

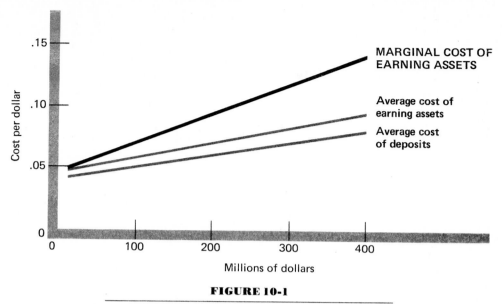

FIGURE 10-1

Average cost of deposits, average cost of earning assets, and marginal cost of earning assets for an individual bank (columns 2, 4, and 8 from Table 10-1).

10-1. We assume that as the bank expands its loans, it must lend funds at lower rates in order to induce the public to borrow. Columns 1 and 2 represent the public's demand for loans. As loan rates decline, the public will be more willing to borrow from banks. At the same time, however, the revenue banks receive per dollar of funds lent also declines. Note that the levels of earning assets in column 1 correspond to the various levels of earning assets in column 3 of Table 10-1. Multiplying the yield—the interest income—on earning assets by the level of earning assets gives the total revenue on earning assets, which is shown in column 3. Column 4 presents the change in total revenue between each level of earning assets, that is, the differences between the figures in column 3. Column 5 shows the change in earning assets calculated from column 1. Dividing the change in revenue by the change in earning assets yields the marginal revenue per dollar of earning assets, presented in column 6.

Figure 10-2 plots the average revenue (column 2) and marginal revenue (column 6) on earning assets that are shown in Table 10-2.

COSTS AND REVENUES TAKEN TOGETHER

Figures 10-1 and 10-2 are pulled together in Figure 10-3. Note that the marginal-revenue curve crosses the marginal-cost curve at point A at a rate of approximately .10 (or 10 percent) and about $225 million dollars of

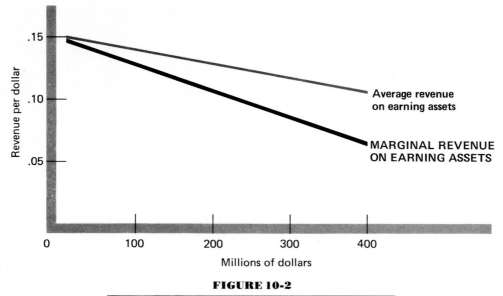

FIGURE 10-2

Average and marginal revenue per dollar of earning assets for
an individual bank (columns 2 and 6 from Table 10-2).

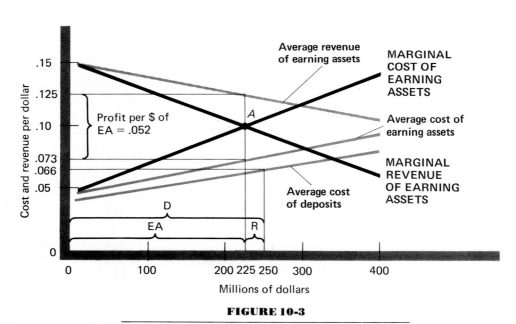

FIGURE 10-3

The profit-maximizing solution for the individual bank.

earning assets. This is the profit-maximizing level of earning assets for the bank.

Note from Figure 10-3 that the average cost of earning assets at $225 million of earning assets is about 7.3 cents per dollar and the average revenue is 12.5 cents per dollar. Thus profit per dollar of earning assets is 5.2 cents (12.5 − 7.3) and total profit is $11.7 million (.052 × 225). Note also that total deposits are $250 million dollars (225 ÷ .90).[1]

As interesting as this solution may be, the really important question we want to focus on is this: What causes banks to *change* the rate they pay on deposits, the quantity of deposits they have, the rate they charge for loans, the quantity of loans they extend to borrowers, and so forth? In general, anything which affects the underlying cost and revenue functions will induce a bank to alter its portfolio and adjust the rates on its assets and liabilities. Accordingly, the next section summarizes the key determinants of banks' costs and revenues and their resulting impact on bank portfolio decisions.

THE DETERMINANTS OF BANK
COSTS AND REVENUES—A SUMMING UP

We may summarize the above discussion by writing generalized equations containing the determinants of bank costs and revenues:

$$(10\text{-}3) \qquad \mathrm{MC_{EA}} = f\,(\overset{+}{D},\ \overset{+}{K},\ \overset{+}{i})$$

where $\mathrm{MC_{EA}}$ = marginal cost per dollar of earning assets
    D = level of deposits hired
    K = banks' reserve ratio (which is the sum of the Fed's required reserve ratio plus the bank's own desired excess reserve ratio)
    i = market yield on financial assets (say, 90-day Treasury bills or commercial paper)

The positive sign over each variable indicates that $\mathrm{MC_{EA}}$ will change in the same direction as a change in that variable.

An increase in the level of deposits hired D will require banks to increase the rate paid on deposits, and that accordingly will raise the cost of deposits. For any given reserve ratio, this increased cost of deposits will increase both the average and marginal cost of earning assets $\mathrm{MC_{EA}}$, as we saw in our preceding example.

An increase in K means that more of every dollar of deposits will be set aside as reserves. Therefore, when K increases, more deposits will be needed to get the same amount of earning assets as before the increase in K. The cost of deposits will increase, and that will increase average and

---

[1] To convince yourself that point A in Figure 10-3 is, in fact, the profit-maximizing solution for this hypothetical bank, assume that the bank selected a position different from point A. You should be able to show that the bank could increase profits by moving toward point A.

marginal cost per dollar of earning assets. The relationship between K and the average cost of earning assets is given by $c_{EA} = \dfrac{i_D}{1 - K}$.

An increase in market interest rates i means that some depositors will be lured away from the bank, given the existing rate being paid on deposits i_D. For example, if the rate on Treasury bills rises relative to the rate on deposits, the public would be expected to increase their demand for Treasury bills and decrease their demand for deposits; that is, the public will become less willing to supply banks with its funds. Remember, portfolio choice is a function of relative rates of return on alternative assets. If the bank kept paying the prevailing rate on deposits while close substitutes paid higher rates, the bank would lose deposits. Accordingly, to "compete" with the higher return on alternative assets, the bank would have to offer a higher rate on deposits. The rise in i_D induced by the rise in i will raise marginal costs.

We may write the marginal revenue function as

$$
(10\text{-}4) \qquad\qquad \mathrm{MR}_{EA} = f\,(\overset{-}{\mathrm{EA}},\ \overset{+}{i})
$$

where MR_{EA} = marginal revenue per dollar of earning assets
$\quad\quad\ \mathrm{EA}$ = level of earning assets acquired
$\quad\quad\quad\ i$ = market yield on financial assets

If a bank attempts to expand its earning assets, say its loans, it will have to lower the rate it charges borrowers to induce them to borrow additional funds. As the loan rate or, more generally, the yield on earning assets falls, marginal revenue (the extra revenue received by expanding earning assets) falls also. Thus, the level of earning assets and MR_{EA} are negatively related; when EA rises, MR_{EA} falls.

Changes in the market yield on financial assets and the marginal revenue banks earn per dollar of earning assets are positively related for two reasons. First, banks can purchase market securities and hold them in their portfolios. Thus, as the rate on this type of earning asset rises, the marginal revenue per dollar of earning assets also rises. The second reason is more subtle. Some large business firms have a variety of methods they can use to finance their operations. For example, they can issue commercial paper, or they can expand their loans from banks. In general, corporate financial officers will choose that means of finance which minimizes the cost of capital. When the rate on market assets i rises, the cost of financing in the open market (of issuing commercial paper, for example) rises relative to the rate banks are charging on business loans. Businesses respond by raising their borrowing demands at banks, and banks respond to the rising demand like any firm; they expand output and raise price. In this case, they raise the loan rate and expand loans. Thus MR_{EA} and i move in the same direction (that is, they are positively related).

HOW DO BANKS RESPOND
TO CHANGES IN THE UNDERLYING
DETERMINANTS OF COSTS AND REVENUES?

We might show what happens to the optimum level of deposits and earning assets if the public's demand for loans from banks increases.[1] Suppose the initial equilibrium for the bank is defined at point A in Figure 10-4. The

[1] Please keep in mind that the public's demand for loans at banks is determined by a wide range of factors in addition to the interest rate on bank loans relative to the interest rate on loans from other sources. Business firms will need funds if they are adding to their inventories, purchasing new equipment, and so forth. Presumably, the current and anticipated pace of economic activity will play a key role in determining the extent of spending by firms and therefore their demand for funds to finance their spending. Similar arguments would hold for the household sector. The effect of changes in expectations and changes in economic activity (GNP), for example, will be to shift the demand function for loans that banks face. For example, if sales are rising and firms decide to add to their stock of inventories, the demand function in Figure 10-3 (average revenue function) would shift upward and to the right, indicating that the public now desires to borrow more from banks given any particular interest rate.

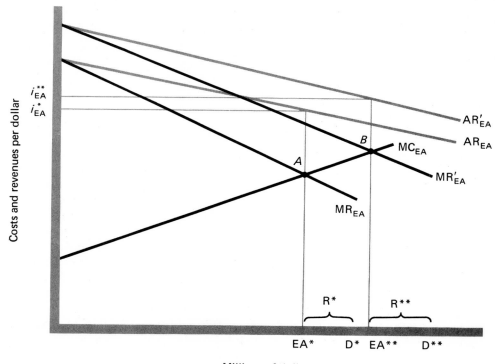

FIGURE 10-4

Changes in earning assets, deposits, and reserves for an individual bank as a result of an increase in the public's demand for funds.

bank earns (or charges) i^*_{EA} on earning assets and acquires EA* of earning assets and D^* of deposits. Now assume that economic activity picks up as a result of some dose of fiscal policy (a cut in taxes and/or an increase in government spending). The result should be a rise in the demand for funds from banks; the government will need to sell securities to finance this larger budget deficit and the public may raise its spending plans and loan demands as a result of the improved economic outlook. Such developments are depicted by the upward shift in the marginal-revenue curve along the marginal-cost curve facing our hypothetical bank from MR_{EA} to MR'_{EA}. The increase in demand will induce the bank to increase its earning assets and will raise the rate on earning assets. This expansion in earning assets can occur only if banks attract additional deposits. The way to attract additional deposits is to increase the rate paid on deposits; therefore marginal costs will rise. The new profit-maximizing position for the bank is defined at point B. The bank will increase its holdings of earning assets from EA* to EA** and will increase its deposit liabilities from D^* to D^{**}, where $D^{**} = EA^{**} \div (1 - K)$. Reserve holdings will also rise from R^* to R^{**}, where $R^{**} = KD^{**}$. The rate on earning assets will rise from i^*_{EA} to i^{**}_{EA}.

In general, the rise in the demand for funds induces banks to expand earning assets and increase the rate on them. Since expanding output requires an expansion in inputs, banks increase the deposits they "borrow" from the public by raising the rate paid on deposits.

10-3
MANY ASSETS AND MANY LIABILITIES

The preceding model was developed on the assumption that there was only one type of deposit and one type of earning asset on a bank's balance sheet. In reality, of course, there are a variety of sources of bank funds, both deposit and nondeposit, and a variety of earning assets such as loans and securities. The portfolio problem for bank management is to choose the best mix of consumer loans, business loans, Treasury securities, municipal securities, and so forth on the asset side and demand deposits, savings deposits, CDs, Eurodollars, and so forth on the liability side. This mix should maximize profits and provide for adequate liquidity and safety. In the preceding model, we found that a bank maximized profit when the marginal revenue from acquiring the last additional dollar of earning assets was equal to the marginal cost of obtaining that last additional dollar of loanable funds. If there are many assets and liabilities, this rule is easily generalized: *the marginal revenue from each earning asset should be equal to the marginal cost on each liability.*[1]

---

[1] More specifically, the marginal revenue on each asset must be equal to the marginal revenue on any other asset, the marginal cost of each liability must be equal to the marginal cost of any other liability, *and* therefore the marginal revenue on any asset must be equal to the marginal cost on any liability.

To convince yourself this is true, assume that the marginal cost of each liability is equal to 5 cents per dollar and the marginal revenue from consumer loans is 10 cents per dollar, while the marginal revenue from all other earning assets is 5 cents per dollar. In this case the bank will be able to raise its profits by increasing its consumer loans and reducing its other earning assets. It will even be worthwhile to expand liabilities (which will raise MC). The point is that so long as MR on any asset exceeds MR from other assets and/or the marginal costs of acquiring funds, profitable portfolio changes are possible. A similar argument holds on the liability side: if the MC of any liability is less than the MC of other liabilities, it will be worthwhile to expand the former and reduce the latter.

10-4
BANK INNOVATION:
A RATIONAL RESPONSE
TO GOVERNMENT REGULATION
AND PROFITABLE LENDING OPPORTUNITIES

In Chapter 8 we pointed out that the Federal Reserve (and other regulatory agencies) set maximum *explicit* rates of interest (the Regulation Q ceilings) that banks may pay depositors on certain types of liabilities. We also suggested that banks had been induced to innovate around such regulations. We are now in a better position to see why this happens. Suppose we begin from a situation where the marginal revenue from all types of earning assets is equal to the marginal costs of all types of liabilities. That is, this is the profit-maximizing position for banks described above. Now suppose that the demand for loans increases. This will raise expected marginal revenue on loans and the bank will find it profitable to expand its loan portfolio and raise the rate on loans. The expansion of loans will require more liabilities, such as deposits. However, suppose that the current rate banks are paying on savings deposits and other types of deposits is the maximum permitted under Regulation Q. As a result, banks would not be able to attract more deposits by raising the *explicit* return on such deposits. What will banks do?

There are at least two possibilities. First, banks will find ways of paying *implicit* interest on deposits. They will lengthen hours, open more branches, give out toasters for new deposits, and so forth. Such actions will raise the rate of return to depositors (which is the sum of explicit and implicit interest paid), raise bank costs, and presumably attract more deposits. A second possibility is that banks will try to find or invent sources of funds not subject to the ceilings of Regulation Q and will bid aggressively for such funds by raising the explicit rate of return that is available to lenders. Examples of liabilities not subject to the ceilings are borrowings in the Eurodollar, commercial paper, and federal funds markets ("nondeposit sources of funds") and negotiable CDs.

Over the late 1960s and 1970s, market interest rates periodically rose well above the Regulation Q ceilings (most notably in 1969, 1974, and 1979). This induced holders of demand, savings, and time deposits to "disintermediate"—that is, bypass financial intermediaries (in this case, banks) by withdrawing their funds from intermediaries and purchasing securities directly in the open market.

In order to compete for funds, banks responded by increasing implicit interest paid and by expanding liabilities not controlled by Regulation Q.[1]

10-5
WHAT DETERMINES THE PRIME RATE?

Having generalized the relationship between marginal costs and marginal revenue to all assets on the bank's balance sheet and having discussed bank

[1] See Donald DePamphilis, "The Short-Term Commercial Bank Adjustment Process," *New England Economic Review* (May–June 1974), 14–23, for a blow-by-blow description of banks' response to rising market interest rates and government regulation.

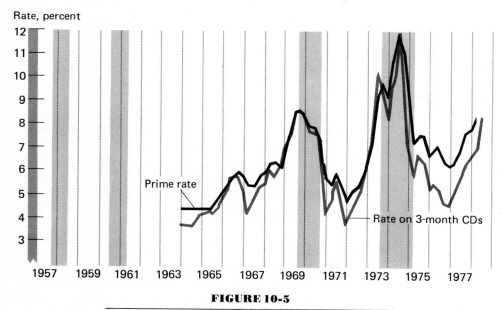

FIGURE 10-5

The rate on CDs and the prime rate are highly correlated. This reflects two related aspects of bank behavior. If short-term interest rates rise, banks will have to increase the rate they are willing to offer on CDs in order to remain competitive. The increase in the cost of funds will induce banks to raise the prime rate. On the other hand, if loan demand rises and banks decide to expand their earning asset portfolio, they will have to attract more deposits to support the expansion of assets. The rise in costs and demand will both lead to rises in loan rates.

responses to regulations, we might focus briefly on the actual determinants of bank loan rates. In Figure 10-5 we have plotted two things: the prime rate (the rate banks charge their most creditworthy business customers) and the rate of return banks pay on negotiable three-month CDs. As discussed in Chapter 8, certificates of deposit are an important *source* of bank funds and business loans are an important *use* of bank funds. Figure 10-5 shows how these two rates have risen and fallen together for the past two decades. What might explain the high correlation between these two rates? One possibility is that when the CD rate rises, this increases the cost of funds to banks and banks respond by raising the prime rate.[1] Another possibility is that when loan demands rise, banks will try to expand their loans and raise the prime rate on them; at the same time, banks expand their CDs (and other liabilities) by raising the rate offered on them.[2]

10-6
EXTENDING THE MODEL FOR ONE BANK TO A MODEL FOR THE BANKING SYSTEM

The banking system consists of all the banks in the country. By making a few adjustments in the model for a single bank, we can obtain a model for the entire banking system. The major adjustment is this: *within the commercial banking system, when one bank gains deposits (and reserves), another bank usually loses deposits (and reserves).* Why does this matter? In developing the determinants of the cost of funds to the individual bank, we assumed that each individual bank could acquire more deposits and, therefore, more earning assets by raising the rate paid on deposits. However, for the banking system as a whole, the supply of deposits must be considerably more "inelastic" with respect to changes in the deposit rate than the "elasticity" we assumed for the supply of deposits for individual banks. The supply of deposits in the overall banking system is inelastic because changes in deposit rates by individual banks within the banking system will primarily change the *location* of deposits rather than have much effect on the total quantity of deposits.

If the quantity of reserves in the entire banking system is held constant, changes in the interest rate on earning assets will have some expansionary (elastic) effect on the supply of funds extended by banks to borrowers. This elasticity will result mainly from the combined effect in two possible areas. First, *if* individual banks are holding some excess reserves, a rise in interest rates on earning assets may induce them to lend out these excess reserves.

---

[1] We might also expect banks to expand other liabilities with lower costs. However, if market rates are already above the Q ceilings, the expansion of demand, savings, and "small" time deposits will be quite limited.

[2] Some of the largest banks in the country (Citibank, for example) instituted formulas in the '70s that set the prime rate as a markup over certain money market rates (for example, the CD rate and/or the commercial paper rate). This, of course, makes the linkage between the cost of funds and the revenue on loans even more explicit.

With these reserves no longer lying idle on a particular bank's balance sheet, the total supply of deposits in the banking system will rise. Thus, the increase in interest rates first causes an increase in the use of available reserves and then that causes an eventual increase in loans and deposits. A second, related possibility is that a rise in interest rates on nondeposit sources of bank funds may induce the public to switch from deposits to various types of nondeposits. Since many types of nondeposits have no reserve requirements or have reserve requirements that are lower than the reserve requirements on deposits, the net effect of an increase in nondeposits is to generate some increase in excess reserves. Reserves previously required to be held against deposit liabilities are now free to be lent out. Thus the total quantity of reserves in the banking system need not change for the supply of earning reserves available to banks to rise.

BANKING SYSTEM BEHAVIOR
AND THE MONEY SUPPLY FUNCTION

In Chapter 9 we developed the following money supply function

$$(10\text{-}5) \qquad M = f(\overset{+}{R}, \overset{-}{q_D}, \overset{-}{q_{ts}}, \overset{-}{s}, \overset{-}{c})$$

where R = total reserves
$\quad q_D$ = required reserve ratio against demand deposits
$\quad q_{ts}$ = required reserve ratio against time and saving deposits
$\quad c$ = ratio of currency to demand deposits
$\quad s$ = ratio of time and saving deposits to demand deposits

We can simplify Equation (10-5) to

$$(10\text{-}6) \qquad M = f(\overset{+}{R}, \overset{-}{q})$$

where R = total reserves
$\quad q$ = required reserve ratio against all deposits (demand, time and savings)

We assume in Equation (10-6) that c and s are constant and thus changes in the money supply are determined by two policy variables q and R, both of which are under the control of the Federal Reserve System.

In light of our discussion in this chapter, we can modify Equation (10-6) to

$$(10\text{-}7) \qquad M = f(\overset{-}{K}, \overset{+}{R}, \overset{-}{i_D}, \overset{+}{i_{EA}})$$

where i_D = cost of deposits to the banking system
$\quad i_{EA}$ = yield on earning assets in the banking system
$\quad K$ = ratio of reserves banks hold (both excess and required) to deposits

In this equation the money supply is determined by the reserves supplied by the Federal Reserve R and by the portfolio decisions of banks and the public in response to changes in the rates on deposits i_D and earning assets i_{EA}.[1] Although more complicated than the "multiplier" model, this model is also more realistic. More specifically, it makes explicit the role of interest rates in the money supply process.

10-7
SUMMARY OF MAJOR POINTS

1

Bank portfolio decisions are guided by a desire to maximize profits. This is accomplished by equating the marginal revenue on earning assets (loans and securities) to the marginal costs incurred in "producing" (or acquiring) such assets.

2

The marginal cost of producing earning assets will depend mainly on the costs associated with attracting deposit liabilities and the ratio of reserves to deposits. In general, the cost of producing earning assets will rise as the reserve ratio rises, the volume of deposits "hired" rises (because the rate paid on deposits will rise), and as the rate available on alternative financial assets rises.

3

The marginal revenue earned on assets will depend on the public's demand for funds. In general, if banks want to expand earning assets, they will have to reduce the rate they charge customers to induce the public to borrow. Thus marginal revenue will decline, other things equal, as earning assets expand. The demand for funds from banks and therefore marginal revenue will also depend on the cost to the public of borrowing from sources other than banks. When such costs rise, the public's demand for funds at banks will increase, and thus marginal revenue will be raised.

4

In the more realistic multiasset, multiliability world, banks will hire each source of funds and extend each use of funds to the point where

[1] For reference in later chapters, the reader might note that the rates on deposits and earning assets are themselves a function of and positively related to the rate on close substitutes for bank deposits and for loans from banks. An example of the former is the Treasury bill rate, while an example of the latter is commercial paper rate. Since movements in the bill rate and paper rate are in fact highly correlated with one another, we have used i in the text to represent "the market interest rate."

marginal revenues and marginal costs are equal for all sources and uses of funds.

5

In the aggregate, the money supply depends on the supply of reserves to the banking system, reserves held by banks (which are largely determined by the reserve requirements set by the Fed), and the general level of interest rates on loans and deposits.

10-8
REVIEW QUESTIONS

1 Identify and explain the decision rule that banks ought to follow if they desire to maximize profits.

2 Identify the factors affecting bank costs. Explain how the public, the Federal Reserve, and the overall environment in the financial system affect bank costs.

3 Identify the factors affecting bank revenues. How does the public's demand for funds and nonbank sources of funds affect the revenue from bank lending?

4 Over the last twenty years, banks have continually innovated around government regulations. Explain how Regulation Q induced bank innovation.

5 Explain why the prime rate is highly correlated with the rate on CDs.

6 Explain why the supply of deposits available to the banking system is more insensitive (inelastic) to changes in the rate banks pay on deposits than is the supply of deposits to individual banks.

7 Explain how reserves supplied by the Fed, the reserve ratio, and the rate on earning assets and deposits affect bank portfolio decisions and the money supply.

10-9
SUGGESTED READINGS

1 For a very readable supplement to some of the material covered in this chapter, see T. Havrilesky and J. Boorman, *Monetary Macroeconomics* (Arlington Heights, Ill.: AHM Publishing, 1978), chap. 3 and the appendix to chap. 3.

2 We would also recommend Oliver Wood, *Commercial Banking: Practice and Policy* (New York: Van Nostrand, 1978).

11

NONBANK FINANCIAL INTERMEDIARIES

Presume not that I am the thing I was.

William Shakespeare
Henry IV

11-1
THE TIMES THEY ARE A-CHANGIN'

We pointed out in Chapter 7 that it was once common practice to ignore the rest of the world when studying the United States economy. There was also a time when nonbank financial intermediaries (hereafter called NBFIs) were similarly ignored because commercial banks overwhelmingly dominated the financial system. Over the past decade, however, the force of economic events has made NBFIs impossible to ignore. In general, a variety of NBFIs entered into active competition with commercial banks; NBFIs competed with banks to acquire the savings of the surplus units and also to make loans to the deficit units.

While this competition has evolved over some time, 1972 is seen by many as a watershed year. In that year Massachusetts and New Hampshire allowed mutual savings banks and savings and loan associations to offer households negotiable orders of withdrawal (NOW) accounts. These NOW accounts, which are interest-bearing demand deposits, removed what was *once* the unique feature of commercial banks: that is, commercial banks were no longer the only ones to offer depositors a liability—non-interest-bearing demand deposits—that functioned as money. Thus, the emergence of NOW accounts blurred the distinction between banks and NBFIs and, perhaps more importantly, brought to light a variety of issues surrounding the competitive relationships among all financial intermediaries.

In this chapter we will examine the growth, development, and key characteristics of NBFIs. The factors contributing to the competition between banks and NBFIs and to the growth of the latter will require special attention.

11-2
AN OVERVIEW OF NBFIs

The key word in NBFI is "intermediary"; NBFIs (as well as commercial banks) serve as intermediaries between surplus units and deficit units in the economy. Of course, there are many different types of NBFIs in the United States. In general, the various types of NBFIs can be analyzed in terms of the range of financial services each provides.

It is convenient to classify an NBFI according to the nature of its liabilities. As we shall see, the nature of a particular NBFI's liabilities is a major factor in determining the nature of the assets that NBFIs will acquire. In general, the maturity, stability, riskiness, and liquidity of liabilities affect the need for liquidity and the safety of assets held by the NBFIs.

Based on the nature of their liabilities, NBFIs can be classified into five categories. These are:

1

Deposit-Type NBFIs. These institutions issue liabilities that are almost identical to the deposit liabilities issued by commercial banks. Like banks, they issue time and savings deposits which, from the public's viewpoint, are safe, liquid, interest-earning assets. In addition, the advent of NOW accounts and credit-union share drafts means that these NBFIs also issue liabilities that are nearly identical to demand-deposit liabilities of banks. This category of NBFIs includes mutual savings banks, savings and loan associations, and credit unions.

2

Contractual-Type NBFIs. As the name suggests, the liabilities of these institutions are defined by contract. In general, these contracts call for regular payments into these intermediaries in exchange for future payments from these intermediaries under specified conditions. Examples would be insurance companies and pension funds, which require the public to make regular premium payments in exchange for insurance coverage (life or casualty) or retirement benefits.

3

Investment-Type NBFIs. The major types of intermediaries in this category are mutual funds—also known as investment companies—and trust funds. The latter are normally managed by the trust departments of commercial banks. The liabilities of these intermediaries are trust agreements executed by the people setting up the trusts or the ownership shares purchased by the public.

4

Finance Companies. Finance companies (for example, the Household Finance Corporation or Beneficial Finance, and the General Motors Acceptance Corporation) lend funds to households and businesses. Their major liabilities include bank loans, commercial paper, and long-term bonds.

5

Other. These NBFIs, which include government agencies and investment and brokerage houses, do not fit neatly into any particular category. More on the institutions in this catch-all category later.

Table 11-1 shows the major characteristics of the most important NBFIs in each of these five categories. Notice that the composition of assets (and of liabilities) differs significantly from one type of financial intermediary to another. This is shown more vividly in Figure 11-1, where the asset composition of the largest and most important NBFIs are displayed.

The composition of the assets of each type of financial institution reflects three main influences. These are the nature of the institution's liabilities; any legal constraints on the institution's asset portfolio; and tax considerations. For example, life insurance companies have a relatively steady and predictable inflow of premium payments, and—given the life expectancy tables—they have a fairly predictable stream of liabilities distributed over time. This allows life insurance companies to hold long-term assets which generally provide higher yields than short-term assets but, of course, are not as liquid. As for savings and loan associations and mutual savings banks, which are very similar to each other, they can reap substantial tax savings by maintaining a large volume of their assets in the form of mortgage loans.[1] The tax incentive to acquire mortgages is reinforced by

---

[1] See K. Biederman, J. Tucillo, and G. Viksnins, *The Taxation of Financial Intermediaries* (Washington, D.C.: 1974) for details.

TABLE 11-1
INFORMATION ON MAJOR NBFIs*

CATEGORY	MAJOR ASSETS AS A PERCENTAGE OF TOTAL ASSETS		MAJOR LIABILITIES AS A PERCENTAGE OF TOTAL LIABILITIES		NOTEWORTHY INSTITUTIONAL DETAILS
DEPOSIT TYPE					
Savings and loan associations	Mortgages	83%	Time and savings deposits	89%	Originally known as "building and loan associations"; the principal assets of savings and loan associations are still mortgages; recent legislation permits savings and loans to offer NOW (negotiable order of withdrawal) accounts, which function like demand deposits; four-fifths are members of Federal Home Loan Bank System (FHLB).
Mutual savings banks	Mortgages Corporate bonds	60% 15%	Time and savings deposits	98%	State-chartered, state-supervised, nonstock deposit institutions; also permitted to offer NOW accounts; exist in only seventeen states, mostly in the northeastern United States; permitted to invest only in an approved list of loans and securities.
Credit unions	Consumer credit	72%	Credit union shares	100%	Cooperative thrift and loan organizations composed of individuals bound together by some tie, such as a common employer; assets are mainly consumer credit; now permitted to offer credit union share drafts, which function like demand deposits; supervised by state banking departments and National Credit Union Administration.
CONTRACTUAL TYPE					
Life insurance companies	Corporate bonds Mortgages	41% 28%	Life insurance reserves Pension fund resources	53% 31%	Purchase of life insurance involves an agreement to save. Savings used to pay for insurance at older ages when probability of death is larger and to furnish funds to be paid back to the insured later. Also sell annuity contracts and pension plans which require accumulation of savings. Asset portfolios restricted to higher-quality instruments, although laws have been liberalized in recent years. Regulated by state insurance departments.
Property-casualty insurance companies	State and local bonds Corporate equities Corporate bonds	44% 16% 16%	Policy payables	99%	Payments are not as easily predictable as those of life insurance companies hence these companies have a need for higher liquidity; regulated by state insurance departments.
Private pension funds	Corporate equities Corporate bonds	55% 25%	Pension benefits	100%	Funded principally by employer contributions. Granted tax-exempt status (contingent upon fulfillment of certain safety criteria): tax-exempt securities, therefore, are not an important part of their asset portfolios; regulated by the Department of Labor.
Government pension funds	Corporate bonds Corporate equities	57% 23%	Pension benefits	100%	Includes Railroad Retirement, Civil Service, State and Local Governments, Federal Old Age and Survivors, and Federal Disability Insurance Funds.

INVESTMENT TYPE

Type	Assets	Liabilities	Description
REIT	Total assets = $15.8 billion (includes residential and nonresidential structures and mortgages held on commercial and multifamily real estate)	Bank loans 50%	Make loans to construction companies (principally for multifamily units).
Mutual funds	Corporate equities 68%; Credit market instruments 26% (e.g., Treasury bills, CDs, and commercial paper)	Outstanding shares 100%	Most are "open-end"—they issue new shares of stock to anyone who desires to purchase them. Owners of shares may redeem them for cash at any time. Amount paid on redemption depends on market value of company's portfolio at that time.
FINANCE COMPANIES	Consumer credit 44%; Loans to business 44%	Corporate bonds 37%; Open market paper 33%	Includes sales finance companies which finance purchases of consumer durables; consumer finance companies which specialize in small consumer loans; and commercial finance companies which specialize in loans to business firms; because finance companies borrow in both the short-term money market and long-term capital market, they are an important link between these markets and short- and long-term interest rates. Regulated at both federal and state level.
MISCELLANEOUS Federally sponsored credit agencies	Housing credit (e.g., loans to savings and loan associations by the Federal Home Loan Bank Board, or the outright purchase of mortgages by the Federal National Mortgage Association) 56%; Agricultural loans 38%	Note and bond issues 86%	Perform two major functions: encourage flow of credit from private sources into "socially desired" channels and extend government credit directly. Principally active in aid to agriculture and to homeowners. Includes Federal National Mortgage Association (FNMA, or Fannie Mae); Government National Mortgages Association (GNMA, or Ginnie Mae); and Federal Home Loan Mortgage Corporation (Freddie Mae).

* All data are as of the end of 1977 and were taken from the flow-of-funds data published by the Federal Reserve.

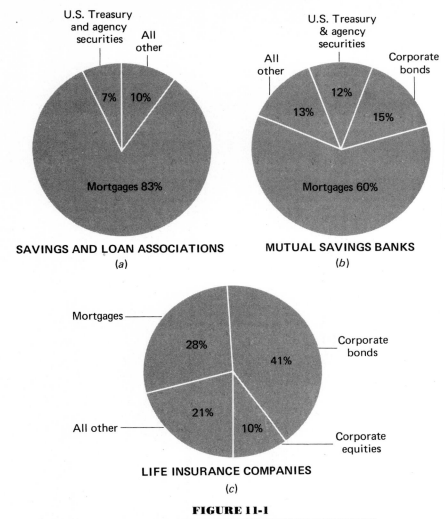

FIGURE 11-1

Composition of assets held by major NBFIs.

laws which, for example, prohibit S&Ls from making consumer loans or acquiring corporate bonds or equities.

The data we have looked at show commercial banks as the largest type of intermediary within the financial system. But NBFIs are growing rapidly and their growth rate is a function of the many types of financial claims they have made available to surplus and deficit units. To illustrate the growing importance of some NBFIs over the period 1967–1978, total assets at all commercial banks grew at an average annual rate of 9.4 percent, while assets at savings and loan associations grew 11.4 percent, and credit union

TABLE 11-2
TOTAL FINANCIAL ASSETS HELD BY SELECTED FINANCIAL INTERMEDIARIES
(Billions of dollars)

	1967	1978	AVERAGE ANNUAL GROWTH RATE, PERCENT 1967–1978
Commercial banks	$395.5	$1158.9	9.4
Major NBFIs			
Savings and loan associations	143.5	523.6	11.4
Mutual savings banks	67.2	158.4	7.4
Credit unions	13.2	58.2	13.2
Life insurance companies	172.6	376.4	6.7
Property-casualty insurance companies	40.9	124.6	9.7
Private pension funds	89.4	207.2	7.3
Government pension funds	42.6	148.5	11.0

assets grew 13.2 percent. Table 11-2 lists the major NBFIs and also commercial banks and the corresponding growth rates of their assets.

11-3
WHY NBFIs HAVE GROWN AND WHAT THEIR GROWTH IMPLIES

If an NBFI wants to expand its assets (uses of its funds), it must, of course, find a way to expand its liabilities (sources of funds). In general, the liabilities of financial intermediaries grow along with the savings (surpluses) of the general public. If some NBFIs have grown faster than commercial banks, this means that the growth of these NBFIs' liabilities (inputs) and assets (outputs) has exceeded the growth of bank assets and liabilities. Since more inputs are required to expand output, the question is what has induced the public to lend relatively more funds to (acquire claims on) these NBFIs than to banks.

We pointed out earlier that rising market interest rates over the past twenty years have induced the public to economize on its money balances. The resulting demand for *near-monies*—many of which are liabilities of NBFIs (for example, time and savings accounts at S&Ls, mutual savings banks, and credit unions)—aided the growth of NBFIs and contributed to innovations in the NBFI industry designed to attract larger shares of the public's savings.

As discussed in Chapter 2, the term "near-monies" refers to financial claims which possess many but not all of the characteristics of money. For example, regular savings deposits at mutual savings banks are very liquid and virtually risk-free because of deposit insurance, and they earn an explicit interest return. Given these characteristics, regular savings deposits store value (or purchasing power) as well as or better than money. While

Surplus units (lenders) have many options in deciding where to place their surplus funds. Since intermediaries must attract surplus funds to function (that is, to lend to deficit units), competition in the financial intermediation industry has been heating up in recent years.

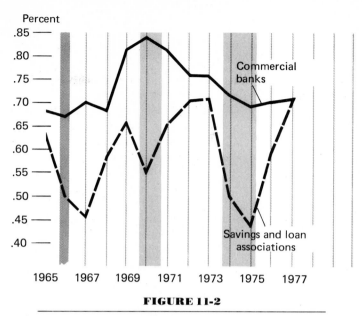

FIGURE 11-2

Average return on assets, 1965–1977. The rate of return on
assets for savings and loan associations (the ratio of net income
to total assets) has generally been lower and more variable than
the return on assets for banks.

most liabilities of NBFIs cannot function as a substitute for money held to
mediate exchanges, they can substitute for money held for other reasons.[1]
These near-monies can therefore affect the portfolio decisions of households and businesses. In particular, we might expect households and businesses to substitute liabilities of NBFIs (near-monies) for certain bank
liabilities (demand deposits). The NBFIs take the funds they acquire as a
result of this substitution and lend them out to deficit units in the economy.

In competing for the savings of the public, the *thrift institutions* (this is
shorthand for credit unions, mutual savings banks, and S&Ls) have had a
considerable competitive advantage vis-à-vis banks. As discussed earlier
(Chapter 8), the regulatory authorities set interest rate ceilings (Regulation
Q) which permitted thrift institutions to pay interest on time and savings
deposits ¼ percent higher than the interest banks could pay. This *rate differential*, which has been the subject of much political controversy over the
past several years, has contributed significantly to the rapid growth of
NBFIs; the public knows a better deal when it sees one!

The difference in profitability of commercial banks and NBFIs also had
a lot to do with the competition between them for the public's savings. Look
at Figure 11-2, where the rate of return on assets for commercial banks and

[1] The exceptions are NOW accounts at savings and loan associations, share drafts at credit unions,
and so forth. As of this writing, they account for a relatively small share of these institutions' liabilities.

the rate of return for savings and loan associations (the largest type of NBFI) are shown. Notice that the rate of return for commercial banks (a proxy for profitability) has generally been higher and less variable than that experienced by savings and loan associations. If you owned an S&L and knew the bank across the street was earning more than you were, what would you do? You would probably try to compete more effectively by developing a liability structure closer to that of banks (that is, demand deposits). You would also attempt to increase your assets by trying to obtain the power to make consumer loans and other types of loans. Such *diversification* would presumably help boost income earnings and maintain a consistent profit rate. This, of course, is exactly what many NBFIs tried to do.

NBFIs can now offer to savers a wide variety of assets and to borrowers many kinds of financing alternatives. Savers (lenders) can select for their portfolios deposits at thrift institutions, mutual fund shares, pension fund contributions, insurance premiums, and so forth. We would expect lenders' portfolio decisions to be guided by the expected rate of return and risk. The returns could be explicit in the form of current payments (for example, interest on deposits at thrift institutions) or promised future payments (such as a pension upon retirement) or perhaps implicit, in the form of a flow of services (for instance, the protection and peace of mind afforded by insurance). The availability of such claims on NBFIs and the various characteristics of each (the rate of return and risk) influence saving in the economy, and therefore the accumulation of wealth, as well as the allocation of wealth across the spectrum of financial assets.[1]

Borrowers have also benefited from the growth in NBFIs and the wide range of financing alternatives now available from them. For example, credit unions are now financing a growing share of auto purchases in the United States. Commercial banks and finance companies were once the traditional sources of auto loans, but consumers have been shifting toward the attractive terms and rates on auto loans from credit unions. Many corporations have found life insurance companies and pension funds an attractive source of long-term funds relative to bank loans or issuing securities in the open market.

In general, the activity of NBFIs has affected the behavior of commercial banks, intensified the scramble for market shares in the financial intermediary industry, and affected the cost of borrowing and the return from lending; it has also had an effect on the allocation of funds in the economy. As a result of all these effects, NBFIs have become an important part of the linkages between monetary policy and the economy.

The next two sections will analyze in some detail how the behavior of NBFIs affects our financial system.

---

[1] For the pathbreaking work in this area, see John Gurley and Edward Shaw, "Financial Intermediaries and the Savings-Investment Process," *Journal of Finance* (March 1956), 257–276, and their book *Money in a Theory of Finance* (Washington, D.C.: Brookings), 1960.

11-4
THE MONETARY
IMPLICATIONS OF NBFI BEHAVIOR

Let us suppose Mary, a keen observer of the financial scene, notices that interest rates are rising and she decides to reduce her average holdings of money balances. Assume Mary accomplishes this by shifting $10,000 (she is obviously well heeled) from her demand deposit in a commercial bank to a savings deposit at an S&L. After this transfer of funds, the aggregate balance sheets of the commercial banking industry, the savings and loan industry, and the public would be as in the "T" accounts in Figure 11-3a. The commercial banking industry would have lost $10,000 in reserves and the same $10,000 in demand deposits; concurrently, the savings and loan industry would have gained $10,000 in reserves and the same $10,000 in the form of saving deposits. As for Mary's transactions, shown on the public's balance sheet, she now has reduced her holdings of demand deposits by $10,000 and increased her holdings of savings deposits by a like amount. Of course, the process would not stop here.

The S&L would use the reserves to acquire income-earning assets. Let us suppose the S&L uses the funds to finance someone's dream home—that is, the S&L invests in a mortgage.[1] The $10,000 would go initially to the

[1] For simplicity, we assume that the S&L does not hold any "reserves." In actuality, the S&L might hold 5 to 8 percent of the deposit as liquid reserves—in the form of Treasury bills and cash, for example—and lend the rest out to the home buyer.

	COMMERCIAL BANKING SYSTEM		SAVINGS AND LOAN INDUSTRY		PUBLIC	
	Assets	Liabilities	Assets	Liabilities	Assets	Liabilities
(a)	−$10,000 bank reserves	−$10,000 demand deposit due Mary	+$10,000 reserves	+$10,000 savings deposit due Mary	−$10,000 Mary's demand deposit +$10,000 Mary's savings deposit	
(b)	+$10,000 bank reserves	+$10,000 demand deposit due home builder	+$10,000 mortgage loan −$10,000 reserves		Home-builder +$10,000 demand deposit	+$10,000 mortgage loan
(c) Net changes	0	0	+$10,000 mortgage loan	+$10,000 savings deposits	+$10,000 savings deposit	+$10,000 mortgage loan

FIGURE 11-3

Balance-sheet effects of Mary's portfolio shift.

buyer of the home who, in turn, would use it to pay the builder. The builder deposits the $10,000 in a commercial bank. Thus the buyer has a house (an asset) and a mortgage loan (a liability). The balance sheets in Figure 11-3*b* show us the relevant transactions. At this point, what has Mary's portfolio decision led to? The net result of these transactions, in Figure 11-3*c*, shows that the commercial banking system experienced no net change in assets or liabilities. The savings and loan industry has a net increase of $10,000 in savings deposits and mortgage loans. Mary is the proud owner of a 10,000 savings deposit and an unknown individual has a new home (albeit a small one) and a loan to pay off. But what has really happened here is that the same $10,000 has moved from Mary's checking account to her S&L, where it helped someone buy a house. The money *moved* through the economy. Let us consider this movement of money—the velocity of money.

The dictionary defines "velocity" as "quickness of motion, or movement; rapidity; rate of turnover." The velocity of money measures the movement of money—that is, the number of times the money supply moves through the economy over the course of, say, a year, to finance any particular level of GNP.

Thus velocity is the rate at which each dollar "turns over" or circulates around the economy.

The following equation, which is an identity (it is true by definition) highlights the role of the money supply M and its velocity V:

(1) $$MV = Y$$

All spending on goods and services—GNP(Y)—involves transactions where money is exchanged. Thus the money supply multiplied by its velocity must be equal to the level of GNP. Note that this means GNP can rise because of a rise in M or V.

We can rearrange Equation (1) to focus explicitly on velocity:

(2) $$V = Y/M$$

The velocity of money V is equal to GNP(Y) divided by the money supply M.

Some economists suggest that V is stable or that if V does change, the changes are predictable. If V is stable or if it changes in some systematic fashion, increases in M will be matched by predictable increases in GNP. More specifically, since GNP is equal to the average price level P multiplied by the real value of output produced y—and assuming the economy is at full employment (y is fixed)—increases in M will be matched by proportionate increases in P. The policy prescription which flows from this hypothesis is perhaps obvious: *if V is stable* (or *if changes in V are predictable*), the Federal Reserve can control GNP *if* it can control the money stock. Crucial to this approach is the stability (or predictability) of velocity which, in turn, depends on the stability of the demand for money.

The relationship between the velocity of money V and money demand may not be obvious. Suppose (1) we hold the money supply constant, (2) assume money supply is equal to money demand, and (3) hypothesize that the demand for money by the public is equal to some fraction k of GNP. We may then write down the following equation:

(3) $$M = kY$$

The actual value of k will be determined by the factors mentioned in earlier chapters which determine the public's demand for money—the rate of return on money, the rate of return on other financial assets, expectations, and so forth. Now compare Equations (1), (2) and (3). Since $V = Y/M$ and $k = M/Y$, it must follow that $V = 1/k$. This is significant; since V is the inverse of k, *changes in the velocity of money V depend on the public's demand for money.*

The view that changes in the money supply will lead to proportional changes in prices is known as the *quantity theory of money*. This theory is a central tenet of monetarism, discussed briefly in Chapter 2 and in more detail in Chapter 19.

In the preceding example, the velocity of money increased. More goods were produced and sold (the house) with the same stock of money. How is this accomplished? It is accomplished by people engaging in transactions (with NBFIs, for example) to reduce their money holdings and increase their holdings of other assets (such as savings deposits). The NBFIs, in turn, lend the funds acquired in these transactions to deficit units that plan to finance expenditures. The result is a more intensive use of the existing money stock—an increase in the velocity of money—and increases in GNP.

Rising interest rates over the post-World War II period, along with technological advances which have increased the efficiency of the payments mechanism, have led the public to minimize the money balances they need to conduct transactions. The rising demand for near-monies, including the

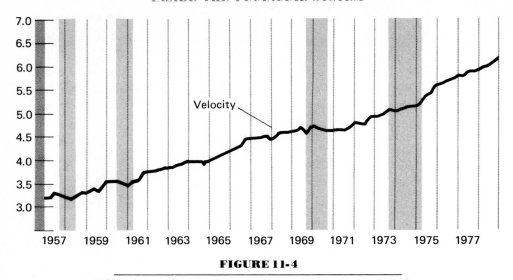

FIGURE 11-4

The velocity of money. Because rising interest rates induce the
public to economize on their money holdings, velocity (equal to
GNP divided by the money supply) rose significantly over the
past two decades. Improvements in the payments mechanism
facilitated the rise, since the public was able to conduct more
transactions per dollar of the money supply.

liabilities of NBFIs, aided the growth of NBFIs *and* has contributed to increases in the velocity of money. Figure 11-4 shows the rising trend in
money velocity since 1957.

In sum, NBFIs are crucially important in the linkage between money,
its velocity, and economic activity. Changes in the volume of near-monies,
with their implications for velocity, will affect the spending decisions of
economic units, as does the money supply. Hence, we see that NBFIs as
well as commercial banks both contribute importantly to the stability or
instability of the economy.

11-5
NBFIs AND THE MORTGAGE MARKET

Intermediation—that is what the financial intermediaries, banks, and especially NBFIs do in the saving-investment process. An interesting question
to ask is what happens when the process of intermediation is bypassed?
This would happen when surplus units withdraw their surplus funds from
the financial intermediaries and place their surplus *directly* into the financial markets. This process is called *disintermediation*, and it can have significant effects on the economy, most particularly in the housing market.

The effect is more pronounced in the housing or mortgage market be-

THE MORTGAGE MARKET

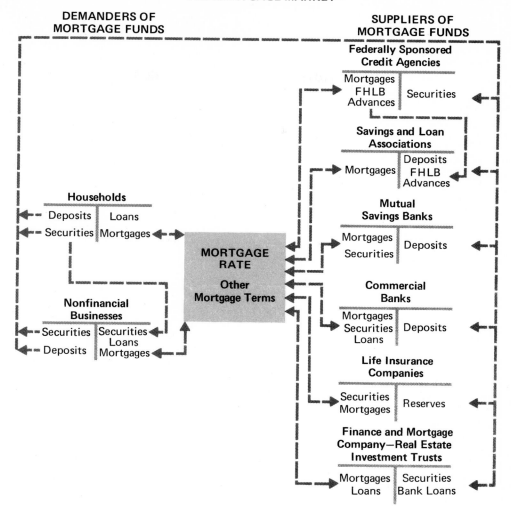

FIGURE 11-5

The mortgage market. NBFIs are major *suppliers* of funds in the mortgage market. The most important are savings and loan associations and mutual savings banks. These intermediaries acquire deposits from households and businesses and in turn extend mortgage loans to other households and businesses. The federally sponsored credit agencies, particularly FNMA, GNMA, and the FHLBB are also important on the supply side: FNMA and GNMA issue securities in the open market and use the proceeds to purchase mortgages from other intermediaries; the FHLBB also issues securities in the open market and uses the proceeds to make loans (advances) to savings and loan associations. (*Source:* Timothy Cook, "The Residential Mortgage Market in Recent Years," *Economic Review*, Federal Reserve Bank of Richmond, September–October 1974, p. 5.)

cause NBFIs are significant suppliers of funds to this market. As we have seen earlier in this chapter, S&Ls and mutual savings banks allocate a large portion of their asset portfolios to mortgages. The mortgages of these NBFIs tend to be on single-family dwellings, while life insurance companies tend to invest in mortgages on multifamily dwellings (like apartments and condominiums) and commercial establishments (like office buildings).

A schematic of the mortgage market is presented in Figure 11-5. Major suppliers of mortgage funds are the NBFIs that we have discussed, while households and nonfinancial businesses are the demanders of mortgage funds. The two sides of the market come together to determine the mortgage rate and the other mortgage terms.

Let us pause for a moment and recall that in this text we are interested in linking up monetary policy and GNP. What does the mortgage market or, more generally, the housing market and NBFIs have to do with this? Figure 11-6a shows the percent change in housing starts and the percent change in expenditures on residential structures since 1957.[1] Not surprisingly, these series are highly correlated. The important thing to learn here is that expenditures on residential structures is a component of GNP.

Figure 11-6b shows the percent change in time and savings deposits at S&Ls (liabilities) and the percent change in mortgages held (assets) by S&Ls, which are a major lender of funds to the mortgage market. Again note the high correlation. Comparing the top and bottom panels, we see a fairly close positive relationship among all the various variables.

To determine some of the factors that link these variables together, let us first recall the factors affecting spending (consumption) decisions by households. We would expect household spending to be affected by income, interest rates, nonprice terms of credit, wealth, and expectations. In particular, we would expect housing demand to be a function primarily of the price of homes, income, the mortgage interest rate, and the nonprice terms associated with a mortgage loan.[2]

Given the demand for housing and the fact that the overwhelming portion of housing purchases are financed by mortgage loans, we can view the demand for mortgage credit faced by potential lenders as a "derived demand"—derived directly from the public's demand for housing. The willingness of lenders to supply mortgage loans will be a function of the expected return on the loans compared with the cost and availability of deposits to the lender. As was the case in Chapter 10, we would expect the profit-maximizing lender to equate the marginal return on loans to the marginal cost of acquiring funds from depositors. If the costs of funds rise,

---

[1] The reader should note that residential construction is considered to be part of investment (rather than consumption) in the GNP accounts.
[2] Over the longer term, we might also include some demographic variables such as population size, the rate of family formation, and so forth. For instance, the housing boom of the late '70s and early '80s resulted from the fact that those born during the post-World War II "baby boom" had now reached adulthood and were forming their own households.

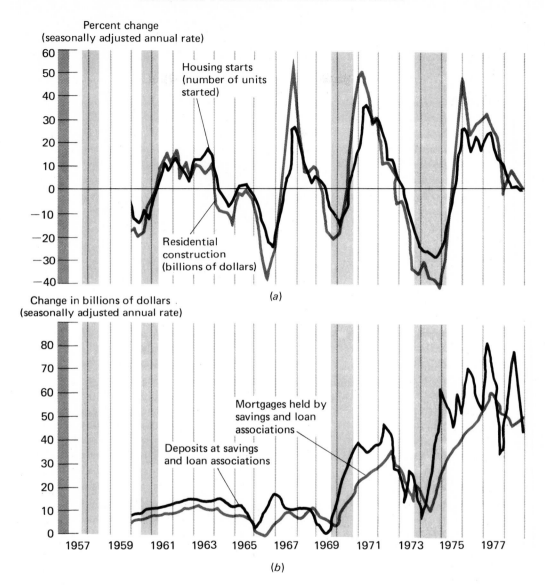

FIGURE 11-6

(a) When the *number* of houses started rises (or falls), the component of GNP known as residential construction rises (or falls). (b) When deposit flows to savings and loan associations rise (or fall), their willingness to add to their holdings of mortgages increases (or decreases).

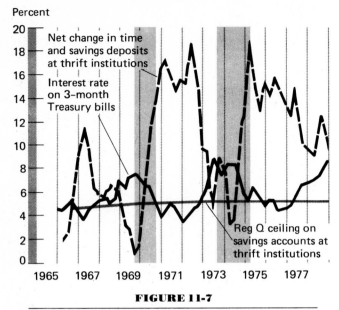

Percent

FIGURE 11-7

When interest rates rise above the Regulation Q ceilings,
disintermediation begins and deposit flows to thrift institutions
slack off.

NBFIs would respond by requiring a higher rate mortgage loans. Presumably, the rising mortgage rate will, in turn, reduce demand for housing.

All this is a rather normal part of the intermediation and credit allocation process. However, there is one major factor that affects NBFIs (and commercial banks). This is Regulation Q.

As market rates rise above the Q ceilings, banks, S&Ls, and mutual savings banks are prevented from bidding competitively for funds. Regulation Q prevents them from offering higher explicit rates of return to depositors for their funds. Thus, the supply of funds to these institutions is cut off to a significant degree. Figure 11-7 shows the difference between the Regulation Q ceiling on passbook savings accounts at thrift institutions and the interest rate on three-month Treasury bills. We would expect these instruments—both near-monies—to be good substitutes for one another in the portfolios of many surplus units, especially the larger ones. As a result, if the three-month Treasury bill rate, for example, moves above the rate thrifts are offering on savings deposits (which has most often been the maximum permitted by Regulation Q), we should expect the public to shift their funds out of savings deposits and into Treasury bills and also to allocate their new savings flow toward Treasury bills. This is called *disintermediation*—the intermediaries are bypassed in the saving-investment process. This process is illustrated in Figure 11-8. Figure 11-7 shows that when the rate on three-month Treasury bills (and other market rates) move above the Regulation Q ceilings, deposit growth at major mortgage lenders declines. This decline contributes to a rise in the mortgage rate and a tightening of nonprice terms of lending. What happens as a result? The growth of the supply of housing falls, as does the demand for housing; residential construction slows also, as shown in Figure 11-6.

For most of the last quarter century, when interest rates have swung in one direction, the demand and supply of housing has swung in the opposite direction. The resulting instability in the housing and mortgage markets, which contributed to the poor earnings performance of S&Ls shown in Figure 11-2, often led to the charge that the housing sector bore a disproportionate share of the burden of monetary restraint. That is, when policy was "tightened," economic activity in the housing sector fell more than activity in other sectors. Such "discriminatory" effects of monetary policy, it was argued, were in conflict with the social goal of upgrading the nation's housing stock so that all Americans could find a decent place to live. These arguments, which were often made by special interests tied to the industry (like

INTERMEDIATION

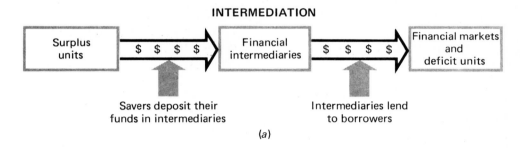

(a)

DISINTERMEDIATION

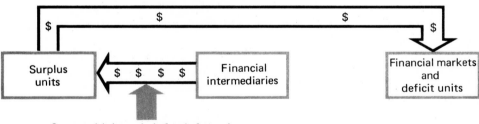

(b)

FIGURE 11-8

When disintermediation occurs, the intermediaries are bypassed. Since some deficit units such as households cannot borrow by issuing debt directly in the financial market, disintermediation reduces the supply of funds available to such borrowers.

the National Association of Home Builders and the United States League of Savings Associations), were reinforced by major studies suggesting that existing institutional regulations and arrangements were inequitable and inefficient (that is, some groups in society suffered relative to others and the regulations were costly) (see Section 11-8).

MONEY MARKET CERTIFICATES

As a result of a decision by Federal regulators, banks and thrift institutions are now allowed to offer the public time deposits with six-month maturities carrying maximum rates tied to the prevailing rate on six-month Treasury bills.* These deposits are referred to as *money market certificates*. This amounts to a partial repeal of the Regulation Q ceilings. It was motivated by sharply rising interest rates during the first half of 1978 and—you guessed it—sharply decelerating growth in deposit flows to thrift institutions. The threat to the housing industry and to economic recovery induced the regulatory response in order to stave off runaway disintermediation. Are you surprised that, by mid-1979, the public held about $175 billion of these new financial claims?

VARIABLE-RATE MORTGAGES

Until a few years ago all mortgages carried fixed rates of interest. When you bought a house, if the prevailing mortgage rate on a 25-year mortgage loan was 6 percent, this was the rate you paid for the life (maturity) of the loan. As interest rates have risen over the past decade and as Regulation Q has gradually been relaxed, the rates financial intermediaries have had to pay to attract funds (deposits) have also risen. Keeping in mind that financial intermediaries earn their profits by borrowing at one rate and lending at a higher rate, you can visualize the difficulties that mortgage lenders, particularly the thrift institutions, found themselves in; the cost of funds was rising with market interest rates, but the return on mortgage loans in their portfolios was fixed (new mortgages carried higher interest rates but accounted for only a small portion of the total portfolio). One way out of this profit squeeze was to offer home-buyers variable-rate mortgages (VRMs) carrying an interest rate adjusted up or down over time as the cost of funds to the lenders moves up or down. The VRMs and other alternative mortgage contracts are becoming more popular and will probably grow, relative to conventional fixed-rate mortgages.

MONEY MARKET MUTUAL FUNDS

In 1974 interest rates on short-term securities rose significantly above the Regulation Q ceilings for the third time in nine years. A group of perceptive entrepreneurs recognized that the high minimum denominations on such securities prevented a large number of Americans from taking advantage of these higher returns. As a result, money market mutual funds were born. Small investors purchased ownership shares in these funds for as little as $100 and the funds pooled the money to buy CDs, commercial paper, Treasury bills, and so forth. The interest earned, minus a small management fee, is then shared by the owners of the fund. By 1978–1979, as interest rates again rose above the Regulation Q ceilings, the public had become more familiar with these institutions, which experienced spectacular growth. In the year ending in mid-1979 total assets of money market mutual funds had more than doubled—amounting to $30 billion.

> * If the prevailing rate is 9 percent or less, banks are allowed to pay as much as the prevailing rate, while S&Ls and mutual savings banks are allowed to pay ¼ percent more. The "differential" remains in force. If the prevailing rate is more than 9 percent, all institutions are allowed to pay the prevailing rate; the differential disappears. If you think there is a logical explanation for this regulation, you have not yet developed the cynicism necessary to analyze money and the financial system.

Attempts to insulate the housing industry from the brunt of monetary policy led to a stepup in the mortgage market activities of federally sponsored credit agencies such as the Federal National Mortgage Association (FNMA), the Federal Home Loan Bank Board (FHLBB, the equivalent of the Federal Reserve for S&Ls), and the Government National Mortgage Association (GNMA). In addition, various and mostly abortive attempts at "financial reform" were initiated by the Congress and others. Progress toward reform of the financial system has been slow because any change will inevitably have some adverse effects on particular special interests. A detailed discussion of these issues would take us too afield. However, it is clear that the traditional distinctions between banks and NBFIs are becoming blurred. The growing similarities are the result of the force of economic events which have bred innovation and changes in our financial structure. Some of the innovations that are changing our financial system are described in the following examples: development of money market certificates, variable-rate mortgages, and money market mutual funds. A sure bet is that such changes will continue.

11-6
SUMMARY OF MAJOR POINTS

1

Nonbank financial intermediaries, like banks, link up surplus units and deficit units in the economy. A NBFI can be classified by the type of assets and liabilities it holds. A NBFI's assets and liabilities are governed by regulations, tax laws, and custom. The most important NBFIs are the so-called thrift institutions—savings and loan associations, mutual savings banks, and credit unions. Since many of these thrift institutions can now offer the public liabilities which function as means of payment (NOW accounts, for example), the traditional distinctions between NBFIs and banks are becoming increasingly blurred.

2

The growth of many NBFIs has exceeded the growth of banks over the past two decades. Rising market interest rates over this period induced the public to economize on their money balances and raised their demand for near-monies. Near-monies are liabilities of NBFIs. This contributed to the growth of NBFIs and intensified competition among financial intermediaries for the public's savings.

3

An important implication of the growth in the public's demand for near-monies and the growth of NBFIs has been the increase in the velocity of money. This means that rises in GNP were facilitated by rises in velocity as well as rises in the money supply ($MV = Y$).

4

The thrift institutions are an important part of the mortgage market. Therefore, they have important effects on the demand for and supply of housing. Since residential construction is an important component of GNP, the behavior of thrift institutions can have considerable effects on the overall economy. For example, if thrift institutions experience changes in their cost of funds, this will have an impact on terms of mortgage loans (loan-to-deposit ratio, maturity, interest rate, etc.). The terms of mortgage loans affect the cost and availability of funds to builders and home buyers.

5

For much of the last fifteen years, Regulation Q contributed to instability in the housing sector. Whenever market interest rates rose above the maximum rates that thrifts could offer the public on time deposits and savings deposits, disintermediation occurred. Disintermediation reduced the supply of funds available for mortgage lending, which led to reductions in the volume of new construction. The view that housing bore a disproportionate share of the burden of monetary restraint led to various attempts to insulate the housing and mortgage markets from the perceived "discriminatory" effects of monetary policy. This helps to explain the increased mortgage market support provided by federally sponsored credit agencies (like the FNMA and GNMA) and the 1978 decision to ease Regulation Q.

6

The evolution and growth of NBFIs has done the following: (*a*) affected the behavior of commercial banks and intensified the scramble for market shares in the intermediation industry; (*b*) widened the variety of assets for lenders and the variety of liabilities for borrowers; and (*c*) affected the cost of borrowing and the returns from lending. As a result of all these things, NBFIs have had a significant impact on the allocation of funds in the economy. Thus they are an important part of the linkage between monetary policy, the financial system, and the rest of the economy.

11-7
REVIEW QUESTIONS

1   Define and briefly discuss the following terms: near-monies, the Regulation Q rate differential, velocity of money, the quantity theory of money, disintermediation, money market certificates.

2   Discuss some of the reasons for the rapid growth of NBFIs over the past twenty years.

3   What are the key implications of the growth of NBFIs?

4   Explain the relationship between the demand for money and the velocity of money.

5   Why are some NBFIs apparently trying to become more like banks?

6   Discuss the role of NBFIs in the housing and mortgage markets. In particular, explain the reasons for the collapse of housing in 1974, its resurgence in 1975–1977, and why it did not collapse in 1978–1979 even though short-term interest rates in the open market rose to record levels.

11-8
SUGGESTED READINGS

1 Considerable institutional detail on NBFIs is contained in Doris Harless, *Nonbank Financial Institutions*, published by the Federal Reserve Bank of Richmond. This very readable booklet will be sent to you free of charge if you write to the bank's publications department.

2 For a textbook treatment of some of the analytic issues discussed see Benton Gup, *Financial Intermediaries*, 2d ed. (Boston: Houghton Mifflin, 1980).

3 The evolving institutional environment governing the changing competitive relationships between banks and NBFIs is discussed in Jean Lovati, "The Growing Similarity Among Financial Institutions," *Review*, Federal Reserve Bank of St. Louis (October 1977), 2–11. Several papers offering a perspective on the current and future structure of the financial system are available in Thomas Havrilesky and John Boorman, *Current Perspectives in Banking* (Arlington Heights, Ill.: AHM Publishing, 1976), part IX.

4 For a more detailed discussion of the money market certificates, see Paul Kasriel, "New Six-Month Money Market Certificates—Explanation and Implications," *Economic Perspectives*, Federal Reserve Bank of Chicago (July–August 1978), 3–7.

5 A more detailed analysis of the housing market can be found in Roger Starr, *Housing and the Money Market* (New York: Basic Books, 1975) and *Housing in the Seventies* (Washington, D.C.: U.S. Department of Housing and Urban Development, 1976).

6 A readable, informative review of the behavior of nonbank thrift institutions in recent years is contained in an article in the December 1978 *Federal Reserve Bulletin* (Sherry Atkinson, "Nonbank Thrift Institutions in 1977 and 1978").

MARKETS AND MARKET MAKERS

He that gets money before he gets wit, will be but a short while master of it.

Thomas Fuller

12-1
GAME TALK!

When the quarterback reads a blitz (or red-dog) and man-to-man coverage, it is critical to check off and automatic at the line of scrimmage and hit the flanker on a fly pattern. Of course, if the blitz does not materialize, the quarterback may find that he has thrown the pass into the teeth of zone coverage where the free safety could easily pick off the ball.

Such is the jargon of football. Most of this jargon is understood only by players, coaches and Howard Cosell.

Similarly, to understand the role of money in the financial system, we must first understand the jargon employed by market makers or "insiders" when they discuss the "action" in financial markets. In this chapter, we will learn some things about the structure of financial markets (chiefly in the United States), and we will also learn the "language" of financial markets.

12-2
INTRODUCING FINANCIAL MARKETS

Considerable ambiguity surrounds the definition of a "market." For example, a market may be a place where trading occurs. The New York Stock Exchange is a market where corporate stock is traded—hence the term "stock market." However, there are less formal notions of what constitutes a market. In general, the market for any real or financial asset can be viewed as the process or mechanism which connects the buyers and sellers (the traders) of particular assets regardless of where they happen to be physically located.

There are obviously many different kinds of financial markets reflecting the multitude of financial instruments. Before looking at some of these markets, it will be helpful to classify the financial markets into two distinct categories—the *primary market* and *secondary market*. The primary market is the market where a security is traded for the first time. For example, if a deficit unit (like a firm) needs to sell some new bonds (or stocks) to finance investment in new equipment, the *initial* sale of these new bonds occurs in the primary market. The primary market is where the public (individuals or institutions) buys the bonds or stocks from the firm which issues them.

Once the firm has sold the bonds or stocks, further trading—selling and buying—occurs in the secondary market. Most of the transactions in financial markets occur in the secondary market. It will be helpful to think of these financial transactions in the secondary market as occurring in the "used-car lots" of our financial system.

The distinction between the primary and secondary markets is purely conceptual. In practice, the trading of "new" securities (primary market) and "used" securities (secondary market) occurs side by side; there are few distinctions.[1]

If this is so, why bother to distinguish analytically between primary and secondary markets? To understand why we do distinguish between them, we must first understand something about the *quality* of secondary markets. The quality of secondary markets is measured by the cost and inconvenience associated with trading existing securities. High-quality secondary markets (low trading costs and little inconvenience) contribute to an efficient allocation of financial resources and facilitate the saving-investment process. In particular, smoothly functioning secondary markets facilitate shifts in portfolios that result in the sale and purchase of existing securities.

---

[1] An analogy may help. The market for autos is made up of the market for new autos and the market for used autos. However, if you go to a GM dealer looking for these parts of "the" auto market, the only real distinction you will observe is that the used and new cars are located on different sides of the lot.

To gain some insight into the relationship between primary and secondary markets in our economy, imagine a financial system (like those in many less developed countries) where formal secondary markets do not exist. Assume now that you want to sell a security you purchased several years ago when it was first issued, say, by ABC Peanut, Inc. The absence of a secondary market implies that you would first have to search for someone willing and able to purchase your ABC Peanut security and then negotiate a price with that person. This is obviously inefficient (time-consuming and inconvenient) and might discourage you from saving part of your income in this way in the future. Most likely, you would not buy ABC Peanut's bonds again. If other people who own securities have similar experiences, ABC Peanut, Inc., will encounter some difficulty in financing future deficits generated by planned additions to its plant and equipment. Without this investment, there will be little future growth of output and employment in the peanut industry.

The message in this example is that the lack of a smoothly functioning secondary market will inhibit the financing of planned deficits in the primary market and thus have an adverse effect on investment and economic growth over time. In general, the viability of primary markets is a function of the quality of secondary markets. The $64 question is what determines the quality of secondary markets for various types of securities.

Some markets, such as the Treasury securities market, are characterized by high-quality secondary markets, while others, such as the municipal securities market, are characterized by lower-quality secondary markets. To understand some of the reasons for these differences and what they imply for our financial system, we will examine some of the details (see Table 12-1) of the structure of financial markets and the role of the firms who act as brokers and dealers in financial markets—the market makers.

12-3
THE FINANCIAL MARKETS: SOME SPECIFICS

There are many different ways to distinguish among the many sectors or markets that make up the entire financial system in the United States. One approach is to divide the financial system into a *money market* and a *capital market*. The money market includes those markets where securities with original maturities of one year or less are traded; examples of such se-

TABLE 12-1
FINANCIAL INSTRUMENTS*

INSTRUMENT	DESCRIPTION	DENOMINATION	MATURITIES	AMOUNT OUTSTANDING	MAJOR HOLDERS
Federal funds and repurchase agreements	Immediately available funds; involves trading of deposit balances of commercial banks (i.e., reserves) held with the Federal Reserve	Typically traded in units of $1 million	Usually 1–15 days; a large proportion are for 1 day	$100 billion	Corporations, commercial banks
Commercial paper	Unsecured promissory notes issued by corporations	$5000 to $5 million; $100,000 basic trading unit	15–270 days; average maturity about 30 days	$85 billion	Dealers, institutional investors, other corporations, banks
Negotiable certificates of deposit	A marketable time deposit issued by banks for a specified period of time at a specified rate of interest	$100,000 and up	Usually 1–12 months, occasionally up to 18 months; average maturity about 3 months	$96 billion	Corporations; state, local, and foreign governments; individuals
Bankers' acceptances	Obligation of bank against which draft is drawn and which "accepts" draft; commonly used to finance imports and exports	Odd denominations	30–180 days	$33 billion	United States banks, foreign bank and nonbank institutions
Treasury securities					
Bills	Obligations of United States government to pay bearer a fixed sum in specified number of days after issue	Five denominations from $10,000 to $1 million	91, 182, and 365 days	$162 billion	Commercial banks, corporations, nonbank financial intermediaries, Federal Reserve System
Notes and bonds	Obligations of United States government to pay bearer a fixed sum each year (the coupon) and the face value in a fixed number of years after issue	$1000 or $5000 depending on the issue	Notes 1–10 years and bonds 10–40 years	$326 billion	Federal Reserve System, commercial banks, insurance companies, state and local governments

Federal agency securities	Obligations of United States agencies (e.g., Federal Home Loan banks, Federal National Mortgage Association, etc.)	$1000 to $100,000	30 days–40 years	$130 billion	Federal Reserve System, commercial banks
Eurodollars	Deposits placed with banks outside the United States which are denominated in United States dollars	Odd amounts	Usually relatively short, but may be up to 5 years	Total size of the market is estimated at $500 billion. Outstanding United States banks' borrowings in Eurodollar market $20 billion at the end of 1978.	Multinational corporations, foreign governments
Corporate bonds	Long-term debt issued by corporations	Usually $1000	Typically 10–30 years	$320 billion	Life insurance companies, state and local governments, retirement funds, households, private pension funds, mutual savings banks
Corporate stock	Equity (ownership) shares issued by corporations	Depends on market price	As long as the firm survives	$990 billion (market value)	Households, private pension funds, life insurance companies, state and local governments, retirement funds
Municipal securities	Debt obligations issued by state and local governments	Usually $1000	Mostly long-term	$275 billion	Commercial banks, property and casualty insurance companies, households
Mortgages	Residential and non-residential loans, secured with real estate	Odd amounts	Usual maturity is 20–30 years (actually tends to be 7–8 years for single-family houses because of early payoffs when property is sold)	$1,150 billion	Savings and loan associations, commercial banks, mutual savings banks, life insurance companies, federal agencies

* All data refer to 1978.

curities would be Treasury bills, commercial paper, and negotiable certificates of deposit (CDs). As you might guess, the capital market includes those markets where securities with original maturities of more than a year are traded. Examples here would be corporate bonds and government bonds. Not surprisingly, some refer to the money market as the "short-term market"—that is, the market for financial instruments with short terms to maturity—and refer to the capital market as the "long-term market."

The money-capital market distinction is only one way to differentiate among the various parts of our financial markets. Another way is to disaggregate the financial markets into individual submarkets according to the instrument traded—the corporate bond market, the municipal bond market, the Treasury bill market, the commercial paper market, and so forth. Table 12-1 lists and briefly describes noteworthy aspects of the major types of financial instruments traded in United States financial markets. For example, the table indicates that the certificate of deposit is a financial instrument in which some of us may be able to invest our surplus funds for a short period of time. Maturities on CDs are usually fairly short—one to three months. Unfortunately, the minimum denomination is $100,000. Obviously, such a high-minimum denomination will mean that those of us with modest surpluses will have to find another place to invest.

FINANCIAL MARKETS
ARE INTEGRATED

Although the various sectors of our financial markets each have their own characteristics, the underlying factors affecting the price (or interest rate) and quantity demanded and supplied in each market are more alike than different.

The network linking the various markets together can be seen if we focus on the activities of commercial banks. A bank in need of extra funds has several choices: it can issue CDs, borrow in the Eurodollar market or federal funds market, or sell assets (such as Treasury bills). A bank with funds to lend also has several choices: for example, it can purchase Treasury bills, sell funds in the Eurodollar market or federal funds market, or buy commercial paper. Banks have choices and will buy and sell, regularly making changes in their portfolios to minimize cost and maximize returns. This guiding principle may lead them to borrow in a particular market one day and lend in the same market the next day. Through such borrowing and lending activities, banks link up the supply of and demand for various financial instruments which are *substitutes* for one another in bank portfolios.

What this means, then, is that if banks can substitute one instrument, such as Treasury bills, for another, such as commercial paper, the markets for these instruments are not independent; indeed, they are linked to one another. For example, suppose the rate on three-month Treasury bills is 5 percent and the rate on three-month commercial paper is 6 percent, reflecting the higher risk associated with holding the commercial paper. Now, what would happen if something caused the rate of Treasury bills to fall to 3 percent? We would expect banks to rearrange their portolios by selling Treasury bills and purchasing commercial paper in order to increase the overall rate of return on their portfolios. Such actions by banks will raise the interest rate on Treasury bills (lower the price) and lower the interest rate on commercial paper (raise the price).

THE INVERSE RELATIONSHIP BETWEEN SECURITY PRICES AND INTEREST RATES

A security such as a bond is an IOU which represents a contractual obligation between the issuer of the bond (the borrower) and the purchaser of the bond (the lender). The contract calls for the borrower to pay C interest per year (where C is the coupon yield) and to redeem the bond at maturity by repaying the principal ($1000 per $1000 of par or face value). When a bond is issued at par, as is frequently the case, an investor pays $1000 for each $1000 par value of the bond. The coupon yield and the current yield then have the same value.

Between the time the bonds are issued and when they mature, some of the initial holders of the securities may decide to sell them in the secondary market. The question is: What price will our original investor get for the bond? The answer is that it will depend on what has happened to interest rates since the time the bonds were issued. In general, if interest rates have risen, our investor will have to accept a price below $1000—that is, below the price originally paid; if interest rates have fallen, the investor can sell the bond for more than the $1000 originally paid.

To see this, let us begin by assuming that a $1000 bond is issued with a contractual promise to pay 7 percent interest each year. Whoever buys this bond for $1000 receives $70 a year in interest. The $70 divided by the bond price of $1000 shows that the bond *yields* 7 percent.

Now assume that, a year or so later, another $1000 bond is issued by the same company with the same maturity date. However, assume that the prevailing level of interest rates in the economy has risen so that the new bond will have to pay $80 a year in interest—that is, provide an 8 percent yield—in order to be competitive. Clearly the new bond is now a better investment than our one-year-old 7 percent bond. Suppose the owner of the 7 percent bond wants to sell it. Who would want a 7 percent bond when you could acquire an 8 percent bond for the same price? The older bond can only compete if it can somehow be made to yield 8 percent. A change in its price is the key to competing.

The older bond cannot change the fact that it pays $70 a year in interest. This is a contractual arrangement. However, the older bond *can* sell for a lower price. If the price dropped to $875, then $70 a year interest would represent a current yield of 8 percent on an investment of $875 (70/875 = .08).

In the example in the text, investors sell bills because the new prevailing yield on bills is not competitive with (is less attractive than) the higher yield on commercial paper. As investors try to sell the bills, most people will be unwilling to purchase them unless the price falls and therefore the yield rises back to a level that is competitive with the yield on commercial paper.

In general, there is an inverse relationship between the price of *outstanding* bonds and the *prevailing* level of market interest rates.

As a result, one can say that bond prices are rising or interest rates are falling (or bond prices are falling and interest rates are rising); these are different ways of saying the same thing. Go to the "Bond Markets" column in *The Wall Street Journal* (usually found about ten pages from the back) and read the story. You should now be able to follow the description of the happenings in the market without difficulty. For a more formal development of the relationship between bond prices and interest rates, see the discussion of "yield to maturity" in the appendix to this chapter.

In sum, the attractiveness of commercial paper vis-à-vis Treasury bills would lead banks to substitute commercial paper for Treasury bills in their portfolios. Thus different markets are linked together by the portfolio behavior of borrowers and lenders. As a result, although there are indeed individual markets for financial instruments as listed in Table 12-1, they are interrelated and cannot be meaningfully viewed as separate entities.

12-4
THE ROLE OF MARKET MAKERS

Our financial markets are operated by the market makers—the specialists who serve as the intermediaries between buyers and sellers of financial instruments. They may make markets in only one type of security, say Treasury bills, or they may make markets in several different types of securities. Who are these market makers, where are they located, and why do they exist?

Many students have probably heard of large Wall Street firms such as Merrill Lynch, Salomon Brothers, Morgan Stanley, and Goldman Sachs. The main offices of these financial firms are located in New York City—the financial capital of the world. These home offices are linked by telephone and Telex to other major cities in the United States and the rest of the world, where branch offices and regular customers are located. Like most enterprises, these firms are in business to earn profits. In this industry the profits are earned by providing financial services to the public. These services include investment advice and trading facilities for buyers and to sellers of securities in the secondary market and advice and marketing services to issuers of new securities in the primary market.

Market makers are important because of the trading services they provide. Their services affect the transaction costs and therefore the liquidity associated with various securities. Because a security's transactions costs and liquidity will affect investors' portfolio decisions, market makers can influence the allocation of financial resources in our economy. For this reason, the market-making function is a key part of our study of the financial system.

THEY FACILITATE
TRANSACTIONS IN FINANCIAL MARKETS

There are two kinds of market makers: *brokers* and *dealers*. A broker is an agent who simply arranges trades between buyers and sellers. Note that a real estate salesperson is often referred to as an agent or broker. A dealer, on the other hand, in addition to arranging trades between buyers and sellers, stands ready to be a principal in a transaction. The dealer will take title to securities sold by investors, will hold them—that is, carry an inventory (sometimes called the dealer's "position")—and then sell them to other investors. When we refer to market makers in this text, we will be referring to dealers.

A market maker posts a price on a particular security and stands ready to buy that security *and* to sell it at the posted price. The market maker holds an inventory of securities and is prepared, over the short run, to decrease inventories if more securities of a given type can be sold at a particular price than are bought at that price; or the market maker's inventories will increase if more securities of a particular type are bought at a given price than can be sold at the same price. If the posted price leads the market marker to buy much more than are sold, there will be a considerable rise in inventories. If inventories become larger than the market maker desires to hold, what will the market maker do? It would seem logical to lower the posted price, since this ought to reduce purchases and increase sales, thereby reducing inventories.

As a trader in financial markets the market maker has an important role in our financial system. What is the specific role of the market maker? Let us assume that there are 100,000 shares of a security for sale at a particular price. Let us further assume that buyers take only 80,000 shares at that price. What happens to the balance, 20,000 shares? The market maker buys them at the posted price.

In the very short run, the market maker facilitates the ongoing shuffling and rearranging of portfolios by standing ready to run up or run down his or her inventory position if there is not a buyer for every seller or seller for every buyer. This serves to increase market efficiency and contributes to an orderly, smooth functioning of our financial system.

THEY FACILITATE
AN ORDERLY ADJUSTMENT
OF PRICES IN FINANCIAL MARKETS

In addition to the above, market makers continually receive, process, and disseminate information which influences the current structure of securities prices. Prices can be influenced by such information as the outlook for monetary and fiscal policy, newly published data on inflation, unemployment, and output, or fresh information on international economic conditions. Prices are also affected by information on the profits of individual firms or analyses of trends and market shares in various industries. As all this information is digested by holders of outstanding securities and by potential issuers of new securities, it can bring about a change in the current structure of interest rates and securities prices. For example, if the people who trade in the various financial markets believe that the Federal Reserve is likely to take actions that will soon raise interest rates, they will expect the prices of outstanding securities to fall. Accordingly, many will sell to avoid the impending capital losses, few will buy, and market makers' inventories of outstanding bonds will rise. At the same time, potential issuers of new securities will be encouraged to issue them now rather than later. This also will lead to inventory increases for market makers. Of course, market makers will not be willing to hold increasing inventories of securities for very long. This would cost them dearly in terms of impending capital losses and financing costs; hence, they would seek to sell off at least some of their undesired inventory. The overall impact, then, of an expected rise in interest rates on holders of outstanding securities, issuers of new securities, and market makers will be to increase the supply of securities relative to the demand, resulting in a lower price and higher interest rate on securities.

Conversely, if new information leads to the view that the interest rates on bonds are "high" and that the rates may go down (that is, that bond prices may increase), many people will buy bonds now, few will sell, and inventories will fall. The response by market makers to such portfolio actions will be to adjust the structure of bond prices up and interest rates down. The market makers will continue to adjust prices and rates until they are satisfied with their inventories. In general, when something affects the supply of or demand for a good, we know the price of that good will be affected. In financial markets, when something affects the supply of or demand for a security, the market makers facilititate the adjustment of that security's price to a new level. As a quick perusal of the newspaper will reveal, security prices change nearly every day. Reflecting the activity of market makers, these changes occur in an orderly and efficient manner.

CRACKING THE CODE:
DAILY BOND MARKET INFO

Here is a typical example of the way bond market information appears in the newspaper. In this case we have clipped the quotations below from *The Wall Street Journal.*

Let us pick a company's bond to study. How about A.T.T. (American Telephone and Telegraph)? Notice that A.T.T. has a number of different types of bonds outstanding. They were issued at different points in time to finance their operations. Accordingly, all these issues are "used" (or "seasoned") bonds trading in the secondary market. Let us focus on the last one listed.

BOND	CUR YLD	VOL	HIGH	LOW	CLOSE	NET CHG
ATT 8⅝s 07	8.8	16	97½	97⅜	97½	+⅛

First you see the company's name—A.T.T. The "8⅝s" next to the name is the *coupon yield.* It appears on the face of the bond and is the amount of interest that A.T.T. will pay the holder of the bond. In this case, A.T.T. will pay the holder 8⅝ percent (8.625 percent), or $86.25 annually (usually in semiannual installments) per $1000 of face (or par) value of bonds held. Next we see "07"—this means the bond will mature in the year 2007. At that time, A.T.T. will give the holder of the bond the last interest payment and $1000 of principal per $1000 of face (or par) value. It is called the "face value" because it appears on the face of the bond.

CORPORATION BONDS

Volume, $11,140,000

Bonds	Cur Yld	Vol	High	Low	Close	Net Chg.
ATO 4⅜s87	cv	5	71⅞	71⅞	71⅞	.....
ATO 10⅜98	11.	17	97⅞	97	97	−1
AddM 9⅜95	9.6	20	98	98	98	.....
AetnCr 8¾83	8.8	17	99½	99½	99½	−1½
AlaP 9s2000	9.6	15	93⅞	92⅛	93⅞	+ ¾
AlaP 7⅞s02	9.6	35	83	82	82	− ½
AlaP 9¾s04	9.7	16	100⅜	100¼	100⅜	+ ⅛
AlaP 10⅞05	10.	1	107	107	107	−1
AlaP 9½08	9.6	5	99⅛	99⅛	99⅛	+ ⅛
AlaP 9⅝08	9.7	1	99½	99½	99½	− ⅛
AllgL 4s81	cv	10	88	88	88	+ ½
AllgL 9s89	9.4	5	95⅜	95⅜	95⅜	.....
Allen 11½94	cv	2	130	130	130	+3
AlldC 8⅜83	8.5	10	98¼	98¼	98¼	+ ¼
AldSu 5¾87	cv	11	53½	53	53½	+ ¼
Alcoa 5¼s91	cv	60	98	97	98	.....
Alcoa 9s95	9.0	105	100¼	100	100¼	− ¼
Alcoa 7.45s96	8.5	5	87⅜	87⅜	87⅜	+ ¼
AMAX 8s86	8.6	23	93⅜	93⅛	93⅛	− ¼
AForP 5s30	9.2	1	54⅛	54⅛	54⅛	.....
AAirl 4¼s92	cv	15	60½	60	60	− ⅝
ABrnd 9⅝79	9.6	10	100⅜	100⅜	100⅜	+ ¼
ACan 4¾s90	6.1	15	78	78	78	+1½
ACred 7.95s92	8.7	3	91⅝	91⅝	91⅝	−1⅜
ACyan 8⅜06	8.9	5	94½	94½	94½	.....
AGnIn 6½94	6.4	20	101½	101½	101½	+ ¾
AHosp 5¾99	cv	10	108¼	108	108¼	.....
AMF 4¼s81	cv	1	91¾	91¾	91¾	.....
AmMot 6s88	cv	16	77	76½	76½	− ½
ASug 5.3s93	7.2	1	74	74	74	.....
ATT 2¾s80	3.0	5	91¾	91¾	91¾	.....
ATT 3¼s84	4.2	20	77¾	77¾	77¾	+ ¾
ATT 4⅜s85	5.5	27	80	79⅛	79¼	− ¾
ATT 4⅜s85r	5.5	5	80	80	80	.....
ATT 2⅝s86	3.8	7	69½	69¼	69¼	+ ¼
ATT 3⅞s90	5.7	36	67¾	67¾	67¾	− ¼
ATT 8¾00	8.8	48	100¼	100	100	.....
ATT 7s01	8.4	30	83¼	82½	82⅞	− ⅛
ATT 6½s79	6.7	9	97⅛	97⅛	97⅛	.....
ATT 7⅛s03	8.5	24	83¾	83½	83½	− ¼
ATT 8.80s05	8.9	100	99	98½	98⅝	− ⅛
ATT 7¾s82	7.9	30	97¾	97½	97¾	+ ¼
ATT 8⅝s07	8.8	16	97½	97⅜	97½	+ ⅛
Ames 10s95	10.	14	99½	99½	99½	.....
Ampx 5½94	cv	10	68½	68½	68½	− ⅛
Anhr 6s92	6.7	1	89½	89½	89½	+4
AppP 11s82	11.	1	103⅛	103⅛	103⅛	+ ⅜
Arco 8.70s81	8.7	20	99⅞	99¾	99¾	− ¼
Arco 8s82	8.2	10	97⅛	97⅛	97⅛	− ⅜
Arco 8⅜s83	8.6	25	97⅝	97⅝	97⅝	− ⅝
Arco 8s84	8.3	85	96¼	96⅛	96⅛	− ⅜
Arco 7½82	7.9	5	95	95	95	+ ¼
ArizP 9½s82	9.4	20	101¼	101	101¼	+ ¼
ArlnRlt 5s86	cv	5	62½	62½	62½	+2¼
ArmS 8.7s95	9.1	10	97⅜	95¾	95¾	−1⅝

New York Exchange Bonds

Wednesday, October 11, 1978

Total Volume $11,400,000

SALES SINCE JANUARY 1

1978	1977	1976
$3,625,541,000	$3,687,232,000	$4,106,276,900

	Domestic Wed	Domestic Tues	All Issues Wed	All Issues Tues
Issues traded	661	840	673	853
Advances	228	294	229	297
Declines	250	323	256	329
Unchanged	183	223	188	227
New highs	12	7	12	7
New lows	14	27	16	28

Dow Jones Bond Averages

−1976− High	−1976− Low	−1977− High	−1977− Low	−1978− High	−1978− Low		WEDNESDAY −1978−	WEDNESDAY −1977−	WEDNESDAY −1976−
93.20	85.70	93.87	90.69	90.86	86.73	20 Bonds	88.21 − .07	92.50 − .30	89.20 + .12
98.56	87.46	99.10	94.98	95.00	90.05	10 Utilities	91.30	96.70 − .32	95.60 + .09
87.85	78.58	89.18	85.31	86.79	83.30	10 Industrial	85.13 − .14	88.31 − .27	84.00 + .14

Bonds	Cur Yld	Vol	High	Low	Close	Net Chg.
Dow 8½s06	9.0	5	94	94	94	−1¾
duPnt 8s81	8.1	13	98¾	98½	98¾	− ¼
duPnt 8s86	8.3	18	96⅜	95⅞	95⅞	− ½
duPnt 8½06	8.7	50	97⅝	97⅝	97⅝	−1
DukeP 6.85s78	6.9	10	99½	99½	99½	.....
DukeP 7⅜01	8.9	4	83	83	83	.....
DukeP 7¾02	9.0	7	86	86	86	.....
DukeP 9¾04	9.5	2	103	103	103	+ ⅜
DukeP 13s79	13.	30	103 1-16	103 1-16	103 1-16	+1-16
DukeP 9⅜08	9.4	23	100⅞	100	100	− ⅞
EasAir 5s92	cv	9	62¾	62¾	62¾	− ¼
EasAir 4¾93	cv	15	63¾	63¾	63¾	− ½
ElPas 6s93A	cv	34	100½	100½	100½	− ½
Exxon 6s97	7.7	20	77½	77⅜	77½	− ⅜
Exxon 6½98	8.0	90	81⅞	81¼	81½	− ⅜
ExxP 8.05s80	8.2	7	98½	98	98½	.....
FMC 4¼92	cv	15	77⅛	77⅛	77⅛	+ ⅝
Fairch 4⅜92	cv	17	136	135	136	+3
FairFd 9s96	cv	12	100⅜	100¼	100¼	− ¼
Farah 5s94	cv	5	49¼	49	49¼	+ ¼
Feddr 5s96	cv	14	52⅞	52½	52½	− ⅛
FstChi 7¾86	8.3	20	93¼	93⅛	93¼	− ⅜
FtNSt 8⅞88	9.0	15	99	99	99	.....
FstSec 8½99	8.5	1	100½	100½	100½	.....
FlexiV 4¾97	cv	5	90½	90½	90½	.....

Bonds	Cur Yld	Vol	High	Low	Close	Net Chg.
MGM 10s94	10.	1	97⅝	97⅝	97⅝	− ⅞
MichB 8⅛15	8.9	10	91½	91½	91½	+ ⅝
MidMt 8s80	9.9	21	81	81	81	−4
MidlBk 8⅞84	9.0	4	98⅛	98⅛	98⅛	− ⅞
MMM 8.20s	8.4	20	98	98	98	− ⅛
MKT 4s90	8.2	25	49	49	49	.....
MPcCp 8s94	cv	2	207¼	207¼	207¼	.....
MPac 4¾20f	..	7	52¼	52⅛	52⅛	.....
MPac 4¾30f	..	9	51⅜	51⅜	51⅜	.....
MPac 5s45f	..	1	52¾	52¾	52¾	.....
Mobil 8½01	8.9	71	96⅛	95⅞	96	+ ¼
MobO 7⅜01	8.5	23	87	87	87	.....
Mons 9⅛00	9.0	5	101¼	101¼	101¼	+2¾
Mons 8s85	8.4	5	95¼	95¼	95¼	−1
MntWC 9s89	9.0	9	100½	100½	100½	.....
Morgn 4¾98	cv	52	80	79	80	+1⅛
Morgn 8s86	8.3	20	96⅛	96	96	+ ¼
MtSTl 7¾13	8.9	5	87½	87½	87½	−1
MtSTl 8⅝18	9.0	15	96⅛	96⅛	96⅛	.....
NCR 9s85	8.9	21	100¾	100¾	100¾	.....
NarE 10½80	10.	6	102½	102½	102½	.....
NCan 5s93	cv	17	79½	79½	79½	+1
NCash 4¾85	5.7	1	83⅜	83⅜	83⅜	+ ½
NCity 5½88	cv	6	66½	66½	66½	+1⅜
NCity 6½91	cv	50	68¾	68¾	68¾	− ¼
NDist 4½92	cv	3	86	86	86	− ⅛

Let's skip over to the "High," "Low," "Close," and "Net Change" columns, which all refer to the price of the bond. The price of a bond fluctuates as supply and demand in the bond market change. Accordingly, bond prices can move up or down each day. To conserve space in the paper, bond prices are stated as percentages of 100, with 100 representing $1000 face value. Hence, the high price for the day was 97½, which means $975 (each point is equal to $10, so "½" of a full point is equal to $5). The low price was $973.74, and the closing price was $975. The closing price was up ⅛ from the previous day's closing price, or $1.25 ($1.25 = ⅛ × $10). Do not spend your "capital gain" all in one place!

The volume ("Vol") column is simple; sixteen of these bonds were traded on October 11; a pretty slow day! Not so simple is the *current yield* ("Cur Yld") column. This bond pays $86.25 annually to its holder. At the close on this day, someone could have bought the bond for $975. As a result, the current yield on the investment—that is, the bond purchased—would be 8.8 percent (86.25/975 = .088 = 8.8 percent). If a bond is selling at 100, the coupon yield will be equal to the current yield. Look at the Alcoa bonds—9s 95—the coupon yield is 9 percent and, with the price very close to 100, the current yield is also 9 percent. If the price of the bond is below (above) 100, the current yield will be above (below) the coupon yield. In general, the current yield is equal to the coupon yield divided by the price.

WHY DO MARKET MAKERS MAKE MARKETS?

The willingness of a market maker to make a market for any particular security will be a function of the risk and expected profits associated with buying, selling, and holding that security. The profits earned by a market maker will flow mainly from the revenue generated by the transactions and any capital gains or losses associated with the market maker's inventory of securities. Generally, a market maker will charge a fee—sometimes called

CRACKING THE CODE:
DAILY STOCK MARKET INFORMATION

Here is a typical example from the stock page of a major newspaper. In this case it is again from *The Wall Street Journal*. To understand the code, go down the list and look at Aetna Lf, which stands for Aetna Life Insurance Co.

52 WEEKS										
HIGH	LOW	STOCK	DIV	YLD %	P-E RATIO	SALES 100S	HIGH	LOW	CLOSE	NET CHG
45¾	31	Aetna Lf	2.20	5.2	5	317	42⅜	41⅝	42⅜	+¼

First, after the name of the company is the annual *dividend* paid by Aetna Life. In this case it is $2.20. The dividend is usually compared with the price of the stock to get the current

NYSE-Composite Transactions

Wednesday, October 11, 1978

Quotations include trades on the New York, Midwest, Pacific, Philadelphia, Boston and Cincinnati stock exchanges and reported by the National Association of Securities Dealers and Instinet.

52 Weeks High	Low	Stock	Div.	Yld %	P-E Ratio	Sales 100s	High	low	Close	Net Chg.
			—	A—A—A	—					
39½	28⅞	ACF	2.10	5.8	9	28	36¼	36	36¼	+ ⅛
23⅝	15⅝	AMF	1.24	5.2	11	1003	23⅝	22⅜	23⅝	.....
15¾	9⅜	APL	1	8.5	16	67	11⅞	11¼	11¾	+ ¼
48⅜	32⅜	ARA	1.64	3.8	10	22	43¼	43	43⅛	− ⅛
31⅜	19	ASA	1	3.3	..	505	31	30½	30½	− ⅛
14⅞	7¾	ATO	.48	4.0	7	44	12⅛	12	12⅛	+ ⅛
40	29	AbbtLb	.84	2.4	16	1374	35⅝	34⅞	35⅛	− ⅛
23½	11	AcmeC	1	4.5	8	10	22¼	22⅛	22¼	− ¼
6¼	2¾	AdmDg	.04	.7	8	37	5⅝	5⅜	5⅜	− ⅛
13	11¼	AdaEx	1.11	8.8	..	32	12⅞	12⅝	12⅝	− ⅛
8½	4	AdmMl	.20e	2.9	9	11	7⅛	7	7	.....
32⅞	12½	Addrsg	.28	1.0	11	201	28⅜	27⅝	28⅜	+ ⅜
45¾	31	AetnaLf	2.20	5.2	5	317	42⅜	41⅝	42⅜	+ ¼
26¾	15⅞	Ahmans	1	4.0	5	22	24⅞	24¾	24¾	− ⅜
4	2¼	Aileen		..	..	32	3⅜	3¼	3¼	.....
31⅞	22½	AirPrd	.60	2.1	11	715	28½	28¼	28¼	− ¼
26¾	13⅝	AirbFrt	1	4.3	13	61	23¼	23	23¼	+ ⅜
15¼	11¼	Akzona	.80	5.4	18	36	14¾	14½	14¾	+ ⅛
18	15¾	AlaGas	1.40	8.5	5	4	16⅜	16⅜	16⅜	+ ⅛

yield. The price of the stock at the close of the day's trading was 42⅜ or $42.375. (There is no place dropped from the price here as was the case in the bond price quotations.) The dividend of $2.20 divided by the closing price ($42⅜) gives a current yield of 5.2 percent on the stock.

The next column tells us that the ratio of the *price* per share to the *earnings* per share of the company is 5—that is, the price-earnings (P-E) ratio. The higher the earnings per share of the company (given the price of the stock), the lower the ratio.

The sales column tells us the number of shares traded (in hundreds) on the given day. On this particular day 31,700 shares of Aetna Life were traded. Also, the high price during the course of the day was $42⅜, the low price was $41⅝, and the price of Aetna closed at $42.375—its high for the day and up 25 cents (last column) a share from the close of the previous day.

The final thing to notice is that to the left of the listing of the stock's name are two columns headed "High" and "Low." These are the high and low prices of the stock for the current calendar year. Aetna had traded at a low price of $31 and as high a price as $45.75. Those of you who bought in at $31 are allowed to smile.

a *brokerage fee* or *commission*—for each trade. The fee may be per item, such as 10 cents per share of stock, or perhaps a specified percent of the total value of the trade, such as 1 percent of the total proceeds received from a sale of bonds. Market makers also collect a fee in some markets by being ready to buy a particular security at one price—the "bid price"—and selling the security at a slightly higher price—the "offer" or "asked price." In this case, the revenue received by a market maker will be a function of the spread between bid and asked prices and the number of transactions the market maker and the public engage in.[1] If the number of transactions has an important effect on the revenue earned by making a market in a particular type of financial instrument, then we would expect that a market where there is a substantial number of transactions would attract a substantial number of market makers. The increased number of market makers and, therefore, the greater competition in providing the public with financial services would lower the trading costs in such a market. Since transactions are, by definition, a function of the volume of securities in existence, perhaps you can understand why there are so many market makers (about thirty-five) in the Treasury security market and why trading costs are so low relative to, say, the trading costs that are charged in the municipal bond market.

To sum up, the market makers play a key role in facilitating the buying and selling of securities by the public. First, market makers assist in raising funds to finance deficits by marketing the borrower's new securities through the primary market. Second, they advise potential buyers and sellers of securities on the course of action likely to minimize costs and maximize returns. Third, they stand ready to buy or sell outstanding securities through the secondary market.

Another important but less obvious role played by market makers is that they help to integrate the various financial markets. Figure 12-1 shows the trading room at Salomon Brothers—one of the most important market

---

[1] Economic theory would predict that the actual costs and risks associated with making a market and the competitive environment in the market-making industry would determine the size of the fee or revenue per trade. Since the computer and efficient wire transfer systems make the actual costs associated with any trade quite small for the market maker, it turns out that the risk associated with making markets is a major determinant of trading costs. Most market makers operate with considerable leverage (that is, a high ratio of debt to equity). This means that their inventories of securities (assets) are financed almost exclusively with borrowed funds. To see why this matters, suppose a market maker holds a $700-million inventory of securities and the price of the securities falls 50 cents for each $100 of securities held. The resulting $350,000 capital loss ($700 million/$100 × $.50) would wipe out a lot of revenue earned from trading and could erode the net worth of the firm. The dilemma facing the market makers is that they need inventories to function effectively, yet holding inventories exposes them to capital losses and requires them to borrow to finance the inventories. Not surprisingly, then, the cost of financing inventories and the expected movement in securities prices will strongly influence the level of inventories market makers are willing to hold. More specifically, high financing costs and/or an expected decline in securities price will encourage market makers to pare their inventories.

FIGURE 12-1

Salomon Brothers trading room. (Courtesy of Salomon Brothers and Adams & Rinehart Inc.)

makers in the world. As you can see, it is a busy place. On the floor of the trading room the specialist in Treasury bills sits near the corporate bond specialist, who in turn is no more than 20 feet from the municipal bond specialist. Assuming that these people talk to one another (not a bad assumption!), the activity in one market is known to those operating in other markets. With each specialist disseminating information to customers via telephone and continually monitoring computer display terminals, a noticeable change in the Treasury bill market (say a drop in the three-month bill rate of ¼ percent), will quickly become known to buyers and sellers in other markets. This may influence their trading decisions and thus will affect interest rates on other securities.

Note one other aspect of the picture. In a prominent place high on the walls where all can see, there is an electronic sign which shows many details on current interest rates and securities prices. Among the many lists of data displayed on the wall, and watched closely by everyone on the trading floor, is information relating to the operations of the Federal Reserve. In fact, if you asked these traders which type of information they considered most important, they would probably answer, "Information on Federal Reserve policy."

12-5
APPENDIX—YIELD TO MATURITY

The yield to maturity is the average annual rate of return (sometimes called the internal rate of return) on an investment (or security) if it is held to maturity. It is based on the coupon payment, price, and the length of time to maturity. Formally, it is the rate of discount i — see Appendix B in Chapter 5 — which makes the present value of future coupon payments C plus the present value of the par value of the bond at maturity VM just equal to the prevailing price of the bond P.

$$P = \sum_{n=1}^{m} \frac{C_n}{(1 + i)^n} + \frac{VM}{(1 + i)^m}$$

For any outstanding bond two things are fixed—the amount of the coupon payment (C dollars per year) and the term to maturity in years (which runs from 1 to m). The above formula can be used to solve for either the current price of the bond P or the yield to maturity. Suppose we had a bond due to mature in one year paying C = $80 per year with a value at maturity of VM = $1000. Suppose further that we knew its current price P = $1000. What would be its yield to maturity? By rearranging the above equation, we would get:

$$(1 + i)^m = \frac{C + VM}{P} \qquad \text{where } m = 1$$

$$(1 + i) = (80 + 1000)/1000 = 1.08$$

Therefore,

$$i = 0.08 \text{ or 8 percent}$$

Suppose the current price of the bond P were $981.82, what would be the yield to maturity i? Your trusty calculator should show 10 percent.

$$(1 + i) = (80 + 1000)/981.82 = \frac{1080}{981.82}$$

$$(1 + i) = 1.10$$

$$i = .10 = 10\%$$

The yield to maturity rises because the purchaser of the bond would get the $80 coupon payment *and* a capital gain of $18.18 ($1000 − $981.82) for every $1000 par value of bonds purchased at maturity. Thus, when the price of existing bonds falls, their yield to maturity rises. Conversely, when price rises, yield falls. You might work out some simple examples when the yield to maturity is known and you need to solve for the price.

If the term to maturity were more than a year, the calculations required by the formula above would be quite tedious. Fortunately there are bond tables (available in any library) which, given the coupon payment, show the relationship between the price of an outstanding bond and its yield to maturity. You might glance at these tables. When we speak of "the interest rate" in financial analysis, we are generally referring to the yield to maturity.

12-6
SUMMARY OF MAJOR POINTS

1

The primary markets are where new securities, issued to finance current deficits, are bought and sold.

2

Secondary markets are markets where outstanding issues of securities ("used" securities) are bought and sold.

3

Secondary markets are important for an efficient financial system. Well-organized and smoothly functioning (that is, high-quality) secondary markets facilitate the trading of securities at relatively low cost and with little inconvenience. The liquidity of a financial instrument will be a function of the quality of the secondary market.

4

Financial markets can be divided into the money market and the capital market. In the money market securities with maturities of less than one year are bought and sold. In the capital market securities with maturities of more than one year are bought and sold.

5

The markets for various securities are closely linked because many marketable securities are relatively close substitutes for one another.

6

Market makers are the financial market specialists who act as intermediaries for buyers and sellers of securities. They serve three important functions. First, they disseminate information about market conditions to both buyers and sellers. Second, they connect the various markets by buying and selling in the markets themselves. And third, the quantity of financial services they provide and the price the public must pay for these services determine the quality of primary and secondary markets, which, in turn, affects the ease or difficulty associated with financing deficits, lending surpluses, and more generally shifting into and out of various financial instruments.

12-7
REVIEW QUESTIONS

1 Distinguish between primary and secondary markets and between money and capital markets.

2 Why are well-developed secondary markets important for a highly developed and efficient financial system?

3 Discuss the major functions of market makers in the securities markets.

4 If you call a local brokerage firm, you will find that the commission or brokerage fee charged for purchasing $10,000 of Treasury bills is below the charge associated with purchasing $10,000 of, say, municipal bonds issued by the city of Cincinnati. Explain why.

5 Explain why prices of existing securities fall when interest rates rise.

6 Explain why it would be incorrect to view the various sectors of the financial markets as totally separate entities.

7 Why do market makers pay so much attention to Federal Reserve policy?

12-8
SUGGESTED READINGS

1 Several textbooks pursue some of the issues raised in this and earlier chapters of Part III in more detail. See Herbert Dougall and Jack Gaumaitz, *Capital Markets and Institutions* (Englewood Cliffs, N.J.: Prentice-Hall, 1975); Charles Henning, William Pigott, and Robert Scott, *Financial Markets and the Economy* (Englewood Cliffs, N.J.: Prentice-Hall, 1979).

2 There are a number of helpful guides to the financial markets published by the big market-making firms (such as Merrill Lynch, Pierce, Fenner, and Smith; First Boston Corporation; and Salomon Bros.). If you call a local office or write them in New York City, they will probably send you a copy.

3 For more details on the money market (short-term securities) an outstanding book is now available: Marcia Stigum, *The Money Market —Myth, Reality and Practice* (Homewood, Ill.: Dow Jones-Irwin, 1978).

4 We highly recommend the Federal Reserve Bank of New York's effort to improve the public's understanding of the financial system in a series of articles in its *Quarterly Review*: "Repurchase Agreements and Federal Funds," Summer 1977; "Corporate Bonds," Autumn 1977; "Negotiable CDs," Winter 1977–1978; "Dealers in U.S. Government Securities," Winter 1977–1978; "Equities," Winter 1978–1979.

PART

FOUR

HOW OUTPUT, PRICES, INTEREST RATES, AND EXCHANGE RATES ARE DETERMINED

At this stage of our study of money and the financial system, let's step back for a moment to review the bigger picture that we are trying to help you to understand.

In Part II (Chapters 4 through 7), we studied the behavior of each of the sectors of the economy. We studied the flow of expenditures and receipts for the household, business, government, and foreign sectors. We learned that when a sector's receipts are greater than its expenditures, funds are lent to other sectors; when a sector's receipts are less than expenditures, funds are borrowed from other sectors.

In Part III (Chapters 8 through 12), we saw how the workings and behavior of financial institutions facilitate the exchange of funds between deficit and surplus sectors as well as between deficit and surplus units. We discussed the behavior, structure, and workings of financial intermediaries—particularly the commercial banks—as well as the workings of the financial markets.

Now that you have some understanding of the various sectors of our economy, we can show you how these sectors interact. In particular, we will analyze the spending, saving, and borrowing decisions of these sectors and give you some idea of how they determine national output, prices, employment, interest rates, and exchange rates. This is the intent of Part IV.

We have four chapters in Part IV. Chapter 13 presents the structure of the economy and shows how aggregate demand and aggregate supply interact to determine the level of real output, employment, and prices. In addition, we show how the financial system is related to expenditure decisions through both the bond and money markets. By establishing this relationship, we can also show how output, employment, and the price level are determined simultaneously with the level of interest rates. The analysis will show how monetary and fiscal policy can influence the level of aggregate demand and therefore also the level of real output, employment, prices, and interest rates. Chapter 13 is a theoretical chapter. Its mastery calls for careful study and hard work. But careful, prudent efforts here will pay off as you read later chapters and in future courses in economics and finance.

Chapter 14 builds on the theoretical model developed in Chapter 13. It presents an analysis of the relationship between the rate of inflation and the rate of unemployment. Chapter 14 is also theoretical and also needs careful study, but the policy implications drawn from this analysis are extremely important.

Chapter 15 shifts the focus a bit. In Chapters 13 and 14, we discuss the level of "the" interest rate—an obvious abstraction from reality. In Chapter 15, we drop this abstraction and look at the many interest rates that prevail in the financial markets. We also study the determinants of the structure of these interest rates.

Chapter 16 shifts our discussion to the international realm. Here the determinants of the exchange rate between currencies is presented. You will discover that exchange rates are also affected by factors affecting the aggregate demand for and supply of output in the United States.

The chapters in Part IV prepare us for the grand finale of our study, the role of policymakers in the economy, which is the subject of Part V.

13

AGGREGATE SUPPLY AND DEMAND: THE DETERMINANTS OF OUTPUT AND THE PRICE LEVEL

The roots of education are bitter but the fruit is sweet.

Aristotle

13-1
THEORY AND PRACTICE:
THE AGONY AND THE ECSTASY

To this point we have been examining the factors affecting the spending, saving, and financing decisions within the primary sectors of the economy. In a series of behavioral equations, we showed the factors affecting each of these decisions for each sector. In this chapter and the next, we will bring these equations together to show how the sectors interact to determine the overall level of output, employment, and prices in the economy.

Mastering these chapters represents an investment which may not appear to provide an immediate payoff; perhaps, therefore, our motto should be "Pain before pleasure!" Students often resist exercises in theory—and not just in economics. Their complaint is that the theory is not realistic and/or that time spent on theory would be better spent on examining current real-world issues. Our guess is that many medical students also go through this same stage—bring on the heart patient and save the chemistry, anatomy, and pharmacology courses for later! Poor basic knowledge makes for poor heart surgeons. Likewise, inattention to economic theory gives us poor economic decision makers.

In this chapter we will focus on the market for bonds (securities), the market for goods and services, the labor market, and the role of money—which is traded in each of the markets we just mentioned (as well as others). And because money is, in effect, the lifeblood of the economy, circulating among the various markets, we will begin our analysis of the aggregate economy by bringing together the determinants of the demand for and supply of money.

13-2
THE DEMAND FOR AND SUPPLY OF MONEY

The demanders of money are households, businesses, financial institutions, and foreigners. We saw in earlier chapters that they demand money for two main reasons: (1) Because income receipts are periodic (monthly, weekly, seasonal) and expenditures are often daily, money is used to bridge the gap between receipts, this is the transactions demand for money. (2) Many households and businesses do not know precisely what their income or expenditures will be over a given period; therefore they want to hold some money for unforeseen contingencies. This is the precautionary demand for money. In sum, money is held because, as a means of payment, it is *immediately* spendable.

MONEY DEMAND

The behavioral equation expressing the aggregate demand for money in the economy is as follows:

$$(13\text{-}1) \qquad\qquad M_d = f(\overset{+}{i_m}, \overset{-}{i}, \overset{+}{Y})$$

where M_d = demand for money
$\quad\quad i_m$ = implicit and explicit yield on money balances
$\quad\quad i$ = market rate of interest
$\quad\quad Y$ = aggregate income or expenditures

Equation (13-1) indicates that the aggregate demand for money depends on the implicit yield on money balances, the market rate of interest, and the aggregate level of income or expenditures. The sign above each variable indicates how an increase or decrease in that variable will affect the demand for money. The return on money balances i_m is the value per dollar of the services money yields plus the rate of return actually earned on money balances. An increase in i_m would lead the public to hold more money and therefore less money substitutes; therefore M_d would increase.

The demand for money M_d is a negative function of i because an increase in i, other things equal, represents an increase in the yield on money substitutes relative to the return on money. People will then reduce the amount of money they hold, converting some of their money into substitutes (financial assets that yield higher returns). Money demand is a positive function of Y because increased expenditures mean increased transactions, which require higher levels of money balances.

MONEY SUPPLY

On the supply side, we can write a simple version of the money supply equation developed earlier in Chapters 9 and 10:

(13-2)
$$M_s = f(\overset{+}{i}, \overset{+}{R}, \overset{-}{q})$$

where M_s = supply of money
$\quad\quad i$ = market rate of interest
$\quad\quad R$ = total bank reserves
$\quad\quad q$ = average reserve requirement against demand, time and savings deposits at commercial banks

We expect that an increase in i will lead to an increase in the supply of money because banks will reduce their holdings of excess (or idle) reserves and increase their holdings of earning assets when the opportunity cost of holding excess reserves increases. The rise in earning assets will be matched by a rise in deposit liabilities. What all this means is simply that the higher the interest rates banks can earn on their loans, the more loans they will make, thus increasing the money supply M_s.

We know that increases in total reserves R will increase the supply of funds to banks. Therefore increases in total reserves R will increase the amount of loans that the banking system is able to extend and hence the money supply.

An increase in q lowers the effective supply of funds banks have available to lend; a rise in q raises required reserves and reduces the quantity of loans and deposits banks can "create."

EQUILIBRIUM

Figure 13-1 shows the demand for money as a function of the market interest rate, as given by Equation (13-1); it also shows the supply of money as a function of the market interest rate, as given by Equation (13-2). In drawing

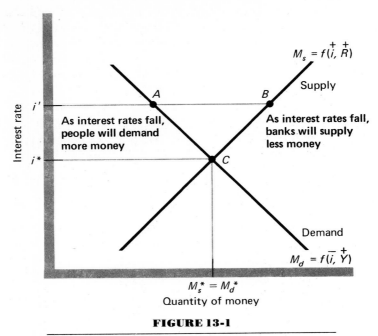

As interest rates fall, people will demand more money

As interest rates fall, banks will supply less money

$M_s = f(\overset{+}{i}, \overset{+}{R})$

Supply

Demand

$M_d = f(\overset{-}{i}, \overset{+}{Y})$

$M_s^* = M_d^*$

Quantity of money

FIGURE 13-1

The supply of and demand for money. The interaction of the supply and demand for money determines the equilibrium interest rate i^* at point C. If the interest rate was at i', the supply of money would be greater than the demand for money. An excess supply of money would lead to a reduction of the interest rate to i^*.

this figure, we assume that i_m and q are unlikely to change in the short-run; therefore we drop them from our money supply equation. This assumption appears plausible because research suggests that i_m is adjusted infrequently by banks, and the Fed has also not changed q frequently.

When the supply of money equals the demand for money, we have an equilibrium interest rate i^* and equilibrium money balances of $M_s^* = M_d^*$. This is shown at point C in Figure 13-1. If the current interest rate is above i^*, say at i', the supply of money at point B exceeds the demand for money at point A. This means that people currently have more money balances than they desire to hold at existing interest rates. Holders of excess balances will use the funds representing the excess to acquire other financial assets. This will increase the demand for money substitutes (such as Treasury bills) and therefore reduce interest rates. As interest rates fall, the banking system will supply less funds moving down the supply function from B toward C. Also as interest rates fall, the demand for money will rise, moving us from point A toward point C. At point C, the amount of money balances demanded will equal the amount supplied. If interest rates are below the equilibrium level, the demand for money will exceed the supply. People will move out of money substitutes and into money. Then interest rates will rise, moving us again toward point C.

Another way of showing the determination of the equilibrium interest rate is to derive an equation which combines money demand and money supply—a "reduced-form equation."

DERIVING A REDUCED-FORM EQUATION

Suppose we had the following explicit money demand and money supply functions:

$$M_d = \alpha_1 Y - \alpha_2 i$$

$$M_s = \alpha_3 R + \alpha_4 i$$

where α_1, α_2, α_3, and α_4 are fixed coefficients (parameters)

We know in equilibrium $M_d = M_s$. Therefore, it must follow that the right-hand sides of the above equations are equal to one another:

$$\alpha_1 Y - \alpha_2 i = \alpha_3 R + \alpha_4 i$$

Solving for i yields:

$$i = \frac{\alpha_1}{\alpha_4 + \alpha_2} Y - \frac{\alpha_3}{\alpha_4 + \alpha_2} R$$

The latter is a reduced-form equation. It expresses i as a function of Y and R when $M_d = M_s$.

At the point of equilibrium where the supply of money equals the demand ($M_s = M_d$), we can express the interest rate as a function of Y and R.[1]

(13-3) $$i = f(\overset{+}{Y}, \overset{-}{R})$$

This equation indicates that the interest rate depends on the aggregate level of income (expenditures) Y and total reserves R. The level of income determines transactions and thus the need for cash balances, and bank re-

---

[1] For those familiar with intermediate macroeconomics and the IS-LM model, this equation represents the LM curve. See William Branson and James Litvak, *Macroeconomics* (New York: Harper and Row, 1975), 65–71, or Rudiger Dornbusch and Stanley Fischer, *Macroeconomics* (New York: McGraw-Hill, 1978), 103–111.

serves determine the funds available to banks. Of these variables, Y is determined by aggregate spending in the economy and R (a policy variable) is under the control of the Federal Reserve System. Given a fixed value for R, we can expect a positive relationship between i and Y. In other words, an increase in income will lead to an increase in the demand for money (a shift to the right of the M_d curve), and this will bid up interest rates for any given supply curve of funds.

The relationship between R and i is negative. This follows from the money supply function in that an increase in total reserves R will lead to an increase in the supply of money available to banks; an increase in money, other things equal, will lower interest rates. We have discussed the process in much greater detail in Chapters 9 and 10.

Of course, at any given point in time, both Y (and therefore money demand) and R (and therefore money supply) may be rising. The interest rate will then depend on the growth in demand *relative* to the growth in supply: if demand grows faster than supply, interest rates will rise; if supply grows faster than demand, interest rates will fall. This is important to remember.

13-3
THE AGGREGATE DEMAND
FOR GOODS AND SERVICES

In addition to money, each sector also demands goods and services. In Chapter 3 we developed a table of the receipts and expenditures for the four sectors of the economy. Table 13-1 repeats that table, which we will discuss further here. In the table, the sectors are listed in the first column, receipts and expenditures for each sector are listed in the second and third columns respectively, and the difference between receipts and expenditures (deficits or surpluses) for each sector is shown in the fourth column. The last row of the table shows the aggregation of the receipts, expenditures, and deficits for each of the sectors. Hence, the sum of the receipts for all the sectors is national income Y. The sum of the expenditures for all sectors is national expenditures Y. And the aggregate of the surpluses minus the deficits for all sectors taken together adds up to zero.[1]

From the second and third columns in this table, we can extract two equations which are important to us here:

$$(13\text{-}4) \qquad C + I + G + \text{NX} = Y$$

$$(13\text{-}5) \qquad S - D_b - D_g - D_f = 0$$

Equation (13-4) represents sector expenditures which add up to total expenditures Y, or the aggregate demand AD for all goods and services in the economy. Equation (13-5) shows that the total deficits and surpluses of

---

[1] Remember the circular flow; national income = national expenditures, so we use the symbol Y to represent both flows.

TABLE 13-1
AN ACCOUNTING FRAMEWORK

SECTOR	RECEIPTS	– EXPENDITURES	= SECTOR DEFICIT OR SURPLUS
Household	Y_d = disposable income of households	C = consumption expenditures of households	S = savings = household surplus
Business	RE = net retained earnings of business	I = net investment of business (including inventory accumulation)	D_b = business deficit (or surplus)
Government	T = net taxes (taxes minus transfers)	G = government expenditures on goods and services	D_g = government deficit (or surplus)
Foreign	FE = net foreign earnings	NX = net exports (exports minus imports)	D_f = foreign deficit (or surplus)
Total for Economy (sum of sectors)	Y = national income	Y = national product (national expenditures)	$Y - Y = 0$

the sectors must add up to zero; the surpluses will be positive, the deficits negative. Any sector having a surplus will use that surplus to accumulate assets; thus a surplus sector will have a net accumulation of financial assets. A sector having a deficit will issue financial liabilities (IOUs).

For the economy as a whole, the aggregate surpluses and deficits must sum to zero. Hence, for every borrower there must be a lender; in other words, every deficit must be offset by a surplus.

The equation showing aggregate demand—Equation (13-4)—is, of course, just the sum of the expenditures column in Table 13-1. To transform this equation from an identity to a behavioral relationship, we need to specify the determinants of expenditure decisions in each of the sectors. As you will recall, we did this in earlier chapters by presenting equations which essentially summarized the determinants of sector demand. Table 13-2 lists simple versions of the behavioral equations from each of the sectors; it also lists the definitions of symbols to refresh your memory. It should be noted that, for the moment, we are ignoring the price level as a determinant of spending. This will be considered later.

The equations in Table 13-2 list factors which influence the spending behavior in the sectors over the short run. When we analyze anything in a short-run context, we can assume that the factors affecting behavior in the long run are constant and therefore do not affect the analysis.

Thus, if we rewrite Equation (13-4) with the important short-term determinants for each sector, we obtain:

$$(13\text{-}6) \qquad \text{AD} = Y = C(\overset{+}{Y}, \overset{-}{i}, \overset{-}{t}) + I(\overset{-}{i}, \overset{-}{t}) + G_0 + \text{NX}(\overset{-}{Y}).$$

In this behavioral equation, we see that aggregate demand AD is the sum of

TABLE 13-2
THE BEHAVIORAL EQUATIONS FOR
EXPENDITURES IN THE SECTORS

SECTOR	EQUATION
Household†	$C = f(\overset{+}{Y}, \overset{-}{i}, \overset{-}{t})$
Business	$I = f(\overset{-}{i}, \overset{-}{t})$
Government	$G = G_0$
Foreign	$NX = f(\bar{Y})$

where C = consumption expenditures
I = investment expenditures
i = market rate of interest
t = tax rate
G_0 = government expenditures, which are assumed to be a policy variable
NX = net exports (exports minus imports)
Y = aggregate income (which equals aggregate expenditure in the United States)

† Recall that in Chapter 4 we wrote

(1) $C = f(Y_d, i, W, z)$

where W = net household wealth; z = household expectations about future income, prices, etc.; and Y_d = household disposable income, which is equal to gross income received minus taxes. For now, we can assume that W and z are constant. Thus we have

(2) $C = f(\overset{+}{Y_d}, \overset{-}{i})$

Also we can write

(3) $Y_d = f(\overset{+}{Y}, \overset{-}{t})$

where t = the average tax rate on personal income, Y_d = disposable personal income, and Y = aggregate expenditures. This equation indicates that disposable income depends on aggregate expenditures and government tax policy. Again, the sign over each variable shows the direction of influence. An increase in aggregate expenditure means an increase in aggregate income Y. However, part of this increased income will accrue to business as retained earnings, to foreigners as net foreign earnings, and to government as net taxes. Assuming that the relations between retained earnings, net foreign earnings, and aggregate expenditures are given, we can write disposable income as a function of aggregate expenditure and the tax rate. An increase in the tax rate reduces disposable income of households, a decrease in the tax rate increases disposable income of households. Substituting Equation (3) into Equation (2), we can get

(4) $C = f(Y, t, i)$

This is the relation given in the text.

the demand from the individual sectors and that the important variables determining the level of expenditures are income Y, the interest rate i, the tax rate t, and government spending G_0. Of these variables, two—Y, i—are determined by interactions within the economic system and two—t, G_0—are determined by policymakers.

Equation (13-6) represents aggregate demand in the economy as a function of the determinants of expenditures for each sector. However, look carefully at Equation (13-6) and you will note that Y appears in three places: it determines net exports NX and consumption C, which in turn determine aggregate demand and thus Y. This is not circular reasoning but merely represents the fact that Y, NX, and C are *simultaneously determined*. What we want to do is rewrite this equation in such a way that we reduce the number of determinants of aggregate demand to only those variables which are *not* simultaneously determined. The first step in deriving the reduced form of Equation (13-6) is shown below:[1]

$$(13\text{-}7) \qquad \qquad \text{AD} = Y = f(\overset{-}{i}, \overset{-}{t}, \overset{+}{G_0})$$

Equation (13-7) tells us that Y is determined by three variables, two of which—t, G_0—are determined by fiscal policymakers and one of which, i, is determined "endogenously" within the economic system. All this means is that i is determined by the behavior of households, firms, foreigners, financial intermediaries, *and* government policymakers. The spending, saving, borrowing, and lending decisions by each sector interact with each other and all affect i. If we want to focus on how policy, particularly monetary policy, affects i, and we do, we can make use of Equation (13-3)—$i = f(Y, R)$—which we developed in the previous section. If we substitute this expression into Equation (13-7), we get:

$$\text{AD} = Y = f[(Y, R), t, G_0]$$

Combining terms yields:

$$(13\text{-}8) \qquad \qquad \text{AD} = Y = f(\overset{+}{R}, \overset{-}{t}, \overset{+}{G_0})$$

In Equation (13-8) we have derived a reduced-form equation which expresses aggregate demand as a function of the policy-determined variables in our model.

We have seen in the chapters on the sectors how these policy-determined variables influence spending decisions. Let us quickly summarize these effects. First, there is the tax rate t which, if increased, will reduce disposable income Y_d of households and the retained earnings RE of business. This will, in turn, reduce consumption C and investment I and

---

[1] This is the expression for the IS curve in the IS-LM model. See Branson and Litvak, op. cit., 61–64, and Dornbusch and Fischer, op. cit., 92–103.

thus reduce aggregate demand. Second, there is the level of government expenditures G_0. If government expenditures for goods and services increase, this will increase aggregate demand. Third, there are bank reserves. An increase in reserves through Federal Reserve actions will increase the availability of funds and reduce the marginal cost of funds to the banking system. This will lead to an increase in loans and an increase in demand deposits. The increase in the supply of loans and of money will lower interest rates, and this fall in borrowing costs will increase investment by businesses and expenditures on consumer durables by households.

13-4
RELATING AGGREGATE DEMAND AND
AGGREGATE FINANCING: THE BOND MARKET

There is one inviolable principle in finance that all of us must live by: expenditures must be paid for. If receipts are less than expenditures, you can still spend by selling off some of your assets (you might pawn your stereo!) or by borrowing ("Dear Mom and Dad . . ."). In this section, we want to examine the relationship between a sector's expenditures and the way in which it finances those expenditures or *borrows*. We will ignore the option of selling off assets.

Earlier—in Equation (13-5)—we wrote an identity for the sum of the deficits and surpluses for each sector. This is reproduced here:

$$(13-9) \qquad S - D_b - D_g - D_f = 0$$

The sum of the deficits and surpluses for the economy must be zero because for every borrower there must be a lender; thus every deficit must be offset by a surplus. While Equation (13-9) states the condition that sector surpluses minus deficits must equal zero, it does not demonstrate *how* a sector's deficit is actually financed. What needs to be shown is that there exists a financial counterpart for each sector's surplus or deficit—more specifically, *surpluses must be associated with net increases in financial assets and deficits must be associated with net increases in financial liabilities.* To simplify matters, let us assume that all deficits are financed by issuing bonds and all surpluses are used to purchase bonds. Given this assumption, the financial equivalent of Equation (13-9) is:

$$(13-10) \qquad \Delta B_{dh} - \Delta B_{sb} - \Delta B_{sg} - \Delta B_{sf} = 0$$

where ΔB_{dh} = net change in demand for bonds by household sector (household surplus)

ΔB_{sb} = net change in supply of bonds by business sector (business deficit)

ΔB_{sg} = net change in supply of bonds from government sector (government deficit)

ΔB_{sf} = net change in supply of bonds from foreign sector (foreign deficit)

Equation (13-10) is written on the assumption that only the household sector is running a surplus, the excess of household receipts over expenditures will give rise to an increase in the *demand* for bonds, while deficits incurred by the other sectors will give rise to an increase in the *supply* of bonds.[1]

We can rearrange Equation (13-10) to represent the condition that demand equals supply:

Demand = Supply

(13-11)
$$\Delta B_{dh} = \Delta B_{sb} + \Delta B_{sg} + \Delta B_{sf}$$

This simply states that the change in the demand for bonds must equal the sum of the changes in the supply of bonds if the deficits of the deficit sectors are to be financed.

THE SUPPLY OF BONDS

We have shown above that sector expenditures are primarily determined by a few important variables. In turn, we have assumed that when a sector's expenditures are greater than its receipts, that sector issues bonds to finance its deficits. This means that the supply of new bonds is determined by financing needs which, in turn, are determined by expenditures and receipts in each sector. It follows, therefore, that the supply of bonds from the business sector depends negatively on interest rates: if interest rates rise, investment (expenditure) plans of business fall and hence the supply of bonds (borrowing) is cut back due to the higher cost of financing those expenditures. Therefore, for the business sector, both investment demand and the supply of bonds are inversely related to interest rates.

For the government sector, the supply of bonds will be a negative function of the level of income. The reason for this is that an increase in national income will increase tax receipts which, in turn, will reduce the government deficit for a given level of spending G_0. Therefore, the government will reduce the amount of bonds it issues because its deficit is reduced. The supply of bonds will be a negative function of the tax rate, since increases in the tax rate, for a given level of spending G_0, will decrease the deficit and reduce the need for financing. Finally, the supply of government bonds will be a positive function of the level of government expenditures. An increase in G_0, all other variables held constant, will require additional bonds to finance the deficit.

[1] Note that we are talking about a net change in bonds demanded (or supplied). This allows for the possibility that some individual units within, say, the household sector are in deficit, while others are in surplus. Our focus is on the net surplus or deficit and, therefore, the net demand for (or supply of) bonds. It should also be noted that the equation is written in terms of changes (first differences). This is because a difference between the *flow* of receipts and expenditures for a sector must be associated with a *change* in the *stock* of financial assets held by surplus sectors and the *stock* of liabilities issued by deficit sectors. If household receipts (income) exceed expenditures (consumption), the difference represents the household surplus (saving), which will, in the example above, be equal to the change (increase) in household demand for bonds.

THE DEMAND FOR BONDS

The demand for bonds comes from the household sector's surplus. Hence, the demand for bonds is a positive function of income (as income rises, so also does saving); the demand for bonds is a positive function of interest rates (a rise in interest rates increases the return on saving); and the demand for bonds is a negative function of the tax rate (higher taxes would reduce disposable income and therefore also reduce saving).

EQUILIBRIUM

All this can be summarized by rewriting Equation (13-11) as follows:

$$(13\text{-}12) \qquad \Delta B_{dh}(\overset{+}{Y}, \overset{-}{t}, \overset{+}{i}) = \Delta B_{sb}(\overset{-}{i}) + \Delta B_{sg}(\overset{-}{Y}, \overset{-}{t}, \overset{+}{G_0}) + \Delta B_{sf}(\overset{-}{Y})$$

Equation (13-12) relates the changes in the supply and demand for bonds to the interest rate i, the tax rate t, government spending G, and the level of income Y. All these variables are major determinants of the aggregate demand AD for goods and services. Hence, one way to view Equation (13-12) is as the financial equivalent of Equation (13-6), the aggregate expenditure equation above.

Now we are prepared to bring together the supply and demand for new bonds and the supply and demand for money. Figure 13-2 relates the demand for and supply of both money and bonds to the interest rate.[1] In these

[1] Note here that we are being careful to talk about *new* bonds, which represent an addition to the stock of all bonds outstanding.

Note that the supply of new bonds slopes downward and the demand for new bonds slopes upward. The supply curve slopes down because, as the interest rate (the cost of borrowing) falls, borrowers will issue new bonds to finance additional investment. The demand curve slopes up because, as the interest rate (the return for lending) rises, households will, at any given level of income, be induced to acquire more financial assets by saving more and spending less on goods (particularly consumer durables). The demand and supply for money have opposite slopes because they are plotted against the interest rate on bonds (which are a substitute for money). When the interest rate on bonds rises, the public will reduce its demand for money and increase its demand for bonds.

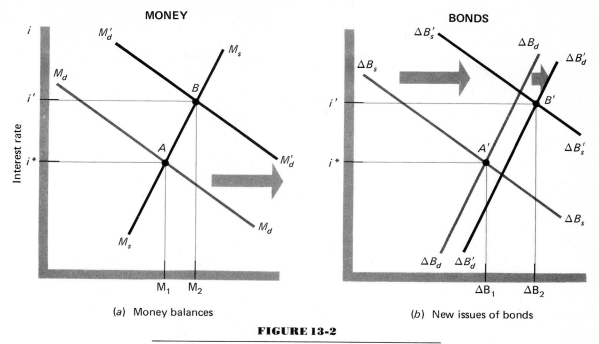

FIGURE 13-2

The money market (*a*) and the bond market (*b*) with an increase
in expenditures.

diagrams, the determinants of supply and demand other than *i* are treated
as variables that would shift the respective demand and supply curves. The
major point we wish to demonstrate with Figure 13-2 is that the particular
level of the interest rate which equates the demand for and supply of money
will also equate the demand for the supply of new bonds.[1] As it is drawn,
the interest rate that equates demand and supply in both markets is *i*** (points
A and *A'*).

Now let us suppose that one of the sectors wishes to increase its
expenditures and that these expenditures will be financed by selling bonds.
This would be represented in Figure 13-2 by a shift to the right in the supply
schedule of bonds from ΔB_S to $\Delta B'_S$. The increased expenditures would lead
to an increase in income, which would increase the demand for money from
M_d to M'_d and the demand for bonds from ΔB_d to $\Delta B'_d$. The reason the de-

---

[1] We are ignoring differences in maturity, risk, and liquidity between different types of bonds.
These are discussed in Chapter 15.

mand for bonds would shift is that as income rises, so does saving, and the additional saving will be used to purchase new bonds. Thus the increase in expenditures will lead to an increase in interest rates, in the quantity of money, and in the supply of new bonds (points B and B').

13-5
PRICES AND AGGREGATE DEMAND

Conspicuously absent from our discussion so far in this chapter (as well as the discussion in the chapters on the individual sectors) is the role of prices in influencing aggregate demand. Increases or decreases in prices do affect consumption, investment, net exports, and government spending. This means that changes in prices affect aggregate demand.

Changes in the price level have several effects on aggregate demand. First, an increase in prices will reduce the real wealth of households. Real wealth is simply actual wealth divided by the price level; as prices rise, the real value (or real purchasing power) of wealth falls. Recall that households are net savers. To the degree that households hold government bonds or currency, an increase in the price level will reduce the purchasing power of bonds and currency. A decrease in the net wealth of households should have a negative effect on household consumption. Hence, an increase in the general level of prices will reduce households' real wealth and reduce household consumption.

Second, an increase in the level of prices will increase actual taxes paid by the public. This is true because of the way our tax system works: as nominal income rises, the public is forced into progressively higher tax brackets, thus increasing their average tax rate. This so-called "inflation" tax is easily shown with the aid of Table 13-3, where a hypothetical progressive tax schedule and a rise in prices combine to produce a decline in real disposable income even though nominal income doubles, as do prices.

Third, even if we ignore taxes, an increase in prices may reduce the real disposable income of households. Much of household income is fixed in current dollars in the short run due to relatively fixed wage contracts and fixed income on various financial assets. Thus, if prices rise but wages (and therefore nominal income) do not rise as much, real income falls.

Fourth, an increase in prices reduces the real value of government expenditures. Government expenditures are approved by Congress and the President in current dollars. If prices rise, $20 billion will necessarily buy less tanks, and so forth.

Fifth, an increase in prices will reduce the real value of money. Any given quantity of money will purchase less goods and services at a higher level of prices![1]

Last, if we assume in the short run that the price of foreign goods is independent of the price of domestic goods, then an increase in our price

---

[1] If you do not believe us, just think what happens when the price of a glass of beer rises from 40 cents to 50 cents. When that happens, beer drinkers find that $2 then buys four glasses instead of five.

TABLE 13-3†

YEAR	GROSS INCOME	TAX	DISPOS-ABLE INCOME	PRICE INDEX	DISPOSABLE INCOME / PRICE INDEX	=	REAL DISPOSABLE INCOME
1	100	10	90	1.0	90/1	=	90
2	200	(10 + 20) = 30	170	2.0	170/2	=	85

† The hypothetical schedule of tax rates is: 10 percent on the first $100 of income and 20 percent on higher levels of income. Now suppose that between year 1 and year 2 both prices and gross income double. What happens to real disposable income? As you can see, the rise in gross income makes the wage earner subject to a higher tax rate. This, in combination with the rise in prices, *reduces* real disposable income by $5.

level relative to prices in the rest of the world will result in the following: foreigners will reduce their demand for our exports and we will increase our demand for foreign imports. The overall result is a reduction in net exports.

In sum, increases in the price level will lead to a reduction in aggregate demand because the higher price level depresses the real value of each of the components of AD; that is, it reduces C, I, G, and NX.

The relationship between AD and the average price level P is plotted in Figure 13-3. This diagram shows that the amount of real output demanded

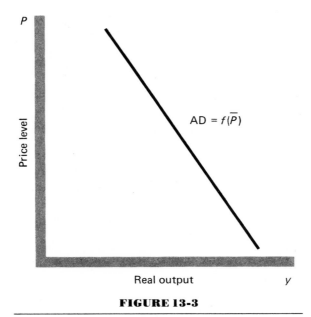

FIGURE 13-3

The aggregate demand curve. This curve tells us the quantity of real output demanded at alternative price levels. In general, as the price level rises, the demand for real output by households, firms, governments, and foreigners falls.

is a negative function of the price level. We will refer to this diagram as "the aggregate demand curve for real output." We can summarize aggregate demand in equation form as follows:

$$(13\text{-}13) \qquad AD = Y = f(\overset{-}{P}, \overset{-}{t}, \overset{+}{G}, \overset{+}{R})$$

Aggregate demand will be a negative function of the price level—higher prices will reduce demand. Aggregate demand will also be a negative function of the tax rate. An increase in taxes reduces aggregate demand because increased taxes reduce retained earnings of business firms as well as the disposable income of households. An increase in G will increase AD because increased expenditures generate additional income for firms and households. An increase in reserves R in the banking system will lower interest rates, which leads to an increase in investment spending by businesses and in spending by households on consumer durables.

13-6
THE AGGREGATE SUPPLY CURVE

What the economy produces is the aggregate supply AS of goods and services. Therefore, to determine the aggregate supply curve, we will first have to examine and understand the aggregate production function for the economy. As discussed in Chapter 5, a production function is a technical relationship between inputs and output. It assumes a given level of technology. For our purposes we will write the aggregate production function as:

$$(13\text{-}14) \qquad AS = Y = f(\overset{+}{N}, \overset{+}{RM}, \overset{+}{K_0})$$

where AS = aggregate supply of real output in the economy
  N = total number of workers employed in the economy
  RM = total quantity of raw materials employed in the economy
  K_0 = total stock of capital goods (such as plant structures and equipment)

This equation tells us that the aggregate supply of real output AS is a function of the number of workers employed N and the quantity of raw materials RM used, given the stock of capital (the existing stock of plant and equipment). Aggregate supply is also a function of K_0, but we assume that K_0 is fixed because, as previously discussed, the equation and our analysis focus on the short run; K_0 is a factor which changes only in the long run because of the time needed to increase the amount of plant and equipment.[1] The relationship between aggregate output and each of these variables is positive. This, of course, makes intuitive sense; if we increase the amount of labor or the amount of materials in the production process, we would expect real output to increase.

Assuming that K_0 is fixed, the two variables in the production function which can be altered in the short run are N and RM. However, we know that as we increase a variable input—say, labor N—with a fixed supply of capital K_0, there will be a point where output per unit of labor will begin to decline. (We have discussed this relationship in Chapter 5.) The important thing is what happens to costs per unit of output as output rises.

In Chapter 5 we learned that for the individual firm, marginal costs per unit of output rise as additional input units are added in the production process. If each new unit of labor is less productive than existing workers, it will take more units of labor per unit of output than previously to expand output. Hence, costs per unit of output will rise as output rises. This reveals *the relationship between input costs and the quantity of output.* To derive an aggregate supply function, however, we need to establish the relationship between output prices and the quantity of output. To get this relationship, we will first have to derive a relationship between input *costs* and output *prices*.

To simplify matters, let us assume that all firms in the economy are profit maximizers. This means that we can expect each firm to produce where its marginal (or extra) revenue from additional output sold is equal to its marginal (extra) cost of additional output produced. To maximize profits, a firm must operate where its marginal revenue equals its marginal cost. When additions to revenue exceed additions to costs, profits rise; when additions to revenue fall below additions to costs, profits fall. Thus, when the additions to revenue just equal the additions to cost, profit must be at a maximum; firms will produce that quantity of output where marginal revenue equals marginal cost. But what will be the price charged for such output? The price charged will obviously be greater than the firm's marginal cost.[2] In general, the price can be viewed as some proportionate markup factor m multiplied by marginal cost. This is given in Equation (13-15):

(13-15) $$P = m \cdot \text{MC}$$

---

[1] We must be careful in conceptualizing K_0. It is the amount of capital potentially *available* in the short run but not necessarily the amount *in use*. In the short run, there could be idle or excess capital available with accompanying high levels of unemployment. In such a situation, both the amount of labor and capital *in use* could be increased through policy actions. More on this later.

[2] This statement assumes that firms face downward sloping demand curves. As a result firms cannot sell an unlimited volume of output at a particular price, but must lower price to induce the public to purchase additional output. This means that marginal revenue, which is less than price (average revenue), declines as price falls and output sold rises. Since we know marginal revenue = marginal cost in equilibrium, this means price exceeds marginal cost. See the numerical example for the banking firm in Chapter 10.

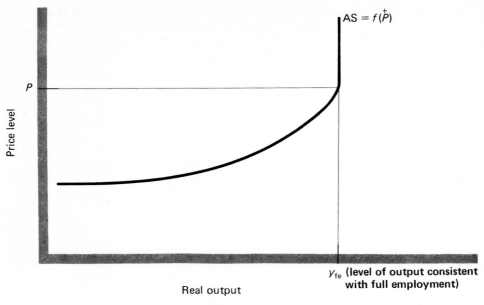

FIGURE 13-4

The aggregate supply curve. This curve tells us what price firms require to produce alternative levels of output. In general firms will require higher prices to expand output because costs of production per unit of output rise as output expands. Once the full-employment level of output is reached, firms will not be able to respond to rises in price by expanding output; all inputs to production are fully employed.

For instance, if $m = 1.2$ (that is, if price will be 120 percent over marginal cost) and MC = \$1, then P would be \$1.20.

Thus far in this section we have shown several things: the determinants of real output in the production function, the factors to be considered in assessing the costs of producing this output, and the relationship between costs and price. With this background, we can now develop a relationship between the general price level and real output, which is represented by the aggregate supply curve. *The aggregate supply curve captures the behavior of firms. It tells us what price firms require to produce alternative levels of output.* The supply function can be written as follows:

$$(13\text{-}16) \qquad AS = f(\overset{+}{P}, \overset{-}{m}, \overset{-}{w}, \overset{-}{P_r})$$

where AS = aggregate supply of output
  P = price level
  m = markup over marginal cost
  w = wage rate
  P_r = price of raw materials

If we assume that w, m, and P_r are given (fixed in value) in the short run, we can trace out the relationship between P and AS as shown in Figure 13-4. This is the aggregate supply curve. You will note that the aggregate supply function slopes upward to the right until y_{fe}, which is the output level at which all the input factors are fully employed. y_{fe} is the level of output consistent with full employment. At this point, y_{fe}, the aggregate supply function becomes vertical, indicating that output cannot be increased in the short run. What this means is that supply cannot be increased beyond y_{fe} and that at y_{fe}, increases in demand cause only increases in the price level.

THE LABOR MARKET

Underlying the aggregate supply curve and firm decisions to expand or contract output are firm decisions to increase or decrease the number of workers they hire. In general, labor is the major variable input to the production process. Accordingly, whenever firms decide to expand output, employment rises and unemployment falls. Whenever firms decide to reduce output, employment falls and unemployment rises. This means that unemployment U is a function of the level of output being produced. The closer actual output produced, or y_{actual}, is to y_{fe}, the lower is unemployment. In equation form:

$$U = f(\overset{+}{y_{fe}} - y_{actual})$$

You will note also that even prior to point y_{fe}, the aggregate supply curve slopes upward to the right at an increasing rate. This is a reflection of our earlier discussion of the relationship between output, costs, and price. Remember that costs per unit of output rise at an increasing rate as output rises in the short run. More specifically, marginal costs will rise as more labor is added to a given capital stock. As shown in Equation (13-15), if MC increases at an increasing rate and m is a constant, then P must also increase at an increasing rate. To be induced to expand output, firms will require higher selling prices for the output produced. This means that aggregate supply and the price level are positively related.

Firms' markup over marginal cost, the wage rate, and the price of raw materials are all *negatively* related to the aggregate supply of output. If

m, w, or P_r rise, firms will supply less output at any given price level than before the rise. For example, assume a firm is currently in equilibrium (marginal revenue = marginal cost) and producing 1000 units of output. Now suppose the wage rate rises, increasing marginal cost. The firm would respond by cutting output (lowering marginal cost) until equilibrium is re-established. In general a rise in m, w, or P_r will reduce AS.

13-7
AGGREGATE SUPPLY AND DEMAND

We can combine our aggregate supply curve with our aggregate demand curve to determine the output level and price level for the economy as a whole. This is shown in Figure 13-5. We have drawn the aggregate demand and aggregate supply curves intersecting at P^* and y^*, which give us the price level and real output level equating the supply of and demand for goods and services in the economy. The point of intersection indicates that the price level at which consumers are willing to buy aggregate real output is equal to the price level at which producers are willing to supply aggregate real output.

At the output level y^*, which is shown in Figure 13-5, firms would have unused capacity and labor would not be fully employed because the short-run level of equilibrium output is not at the full-employment level. If the economy is not at full employment, there are two general ways of getting there. One way is to shift the supply curve down and to the right and the other way is to shift the demand curve up and to the right. For our model, the important variables determining aggregate supply in the short run are m, w, and P_r. Hence the supply curve would shift down with cuts in profit margins, wage costs, or raw material costs.[1] The important variables determining aggregate demand are R, G, and t, which are policy variables. A rise in reserves or government spending or a cut in taxes will shift demand up. In general, there is no guarantee in the short run that aggregate supply and aggregate demand *will be equal* at the full-employment level.

We will discuss in more detail in the next chapter why the economy may not adjust automatically to full employment. At this point, we will merely point out the major reasons why it does not do so.

The first reason is that many costs on the supply side are rigid or fixed in the short run. Wages are fixed in the short run because most wages are based on fixed contractual or quasicontractual arrangements. Also, raw material costs are determined in part by conditions in international markets. Remember that in the short run, international prices are relatively independent of domestic demand. Thus, if demand intersects supply at less

---

[1] Long-run variables that could accomplish the same objective are changes in technology which increase the productivity of labor, growth in the stock of capital, and growth of the labor force. These variables are ignored in our short-run model above but are examined in the next chapter.

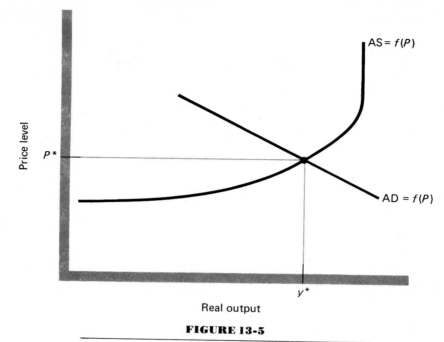

FIGURE 13-5

Aggregate supply and demand. The intersection of aggregate demand and aggregate supply determines the equilibrium level of prices and real output.

than full employment, there is no reason to believe that the supply curve will shift down to bring full employment.

What about the demand side? Unless profits of businesses and incomes of households are increased, leading to an increase in consumption or investment spending, there is no reason for the demand curve to shift rightward. Under conditions of unemployment, both profits and income will be relatively low; in the short run, there is little reason for expecting an increase in demand.

All this suggests that when the price-output equilibrium is not at the full-employment level, we have to do something to get the economy to full employment. Another way of putting this is to say that we need policy to get the economy to full employment. And we already know that monetary policy and fiscal policy can shift aggregate demand.

It is important that you understand the mechanics so as to develop some intuition for what is behind the graphs and the equations. The section that follows works through the effects of shifts in supply and demand; it also provides several fairly detailed examples.

13-8
MANIPULATING THE
AGGREGATE SUPPLY-AND-DEMAND MODEL*

Recall that the aggregate demand curve traces out the levels of real output that will be demanded as the price level is varied but the policy variables—the tax rate, government expenditures, and bank reserves—are held constant. Thus, changes in taxes, government spending, or bank reserves will shift the demand curve. Table 13-4 lists these "shifters" and the direction in which each will shift aggregate demand.

The policy variables include government spending, taxes, and reserves: fiscal policy involves changes in government spending and taxes; monetary policy involves Federal Reserve operations—increasing or decreasing reserves available to the banking system in order to influence interest rates and the money supply.

Also listed in Table 13-4 are the supply shifters: The short-run shifters include wages, raw material prices, and profit margins. The long-run shifters are the growth of the capital stock, growth of the labor force, technological change, and profit expectations. Anything that increases firms'

TABLE 13-4
SHIFTERS OF AGGREGATE DEMAND AND SUPPLY

SHIFTERS OF AGGREGATE DEMAND	AN INCREASE IN SHIFTER WILL SHIFT THE AGGREGATE DEMAND CURVE
I *Policy variables*	
Government spending	Right
Tax rates	Left
Transfers	Right
Bank reserves	Right
II *Other shifters*	
Profit and income expectations of business and households	Right
The foreign price level	Right

SHIFTERS OF AGGREGATE SUPPLY	AN INCREASE IN SHIFTER WILL SHIFT THE AGGREGATE SUPPLY CURVE
I *Short-run*	
Wages	Up (left)
Profit margins (markup factors)	Up (left)
Raw material prices	Up (left)
II *Long-run*	
The capital stock	Down (right)
The labor force	Down (right)
Technology	Down (right)
Profit expectations	Down (right)

* This section contains optional material which can be omitted without loss in continuity throughout the rest of the text.

marginal costs shifts the aggregate supply curve up; anything that decreases firms' marginal costs shifts the aggregate supply curve down. It should be noted that the long-run shifters (such as a technological advancement which increases the productivity of both labor and capital or an increase in the labor force) shift the entire aggregate supply curve to the right. Of course, this means that the full-employment level of output also expands to the right.

In our model, we have assumed that *expectations* about prices and interest rates are constant. Obviously, these expectations can be important shifters of either the aggregate demand curve or the aggregate supply curve. We will take these effects into account in the next chapter. As preparation for that discussion, you should try to improve your understanding of what has been developed to this point by working through several exercises which involve changes in some of the variables listed in Table 13-4.

CUTTING TAXES

In Figure 13-6, we show a situation at point A where the economy is operating at less than full employment. Let us assume that a decrease in tax rates is enacted to stimulate aggregate demand and move the economy to

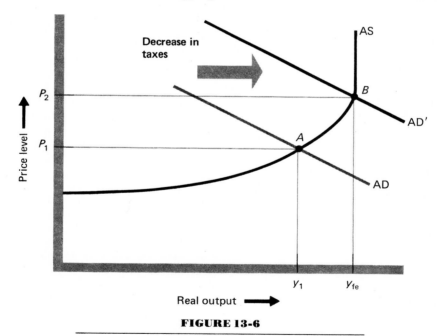

FIGURE 13-6

A cut in taxes will increase aggregate demand. If the tax cut is initiated when the economy is operating below full employment, the result will be a rise in output *and* a rise in prices. What will happen if the tax cut is initiated when the economy is operating at full employment?

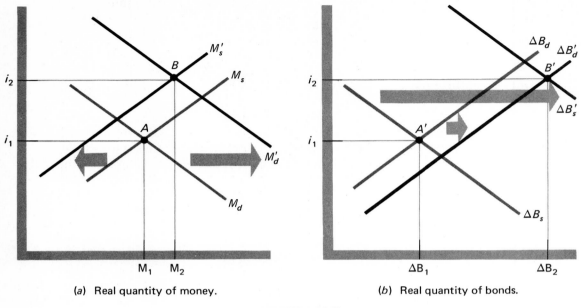

(a) Real quantity of money.   (b) Real quantity of bonds.

FIGURE 13-7

A decrease in taxes will raise interest rates.

full employment. Before the tax decrease, the price level is at P_1 and output is at y_1. After the tax decrease has caused an increase in demand, we move to point B, where prices have increased to P_2 and output to full-employment y_{fe}. Since we have assumed that output does not increase any further once full employment is reached, any additional increase in demand will lead only to increases in prices but no further increases in real output. Also, recognize that on the horizontal axis it is real output (output in constant dollars) that is being measured. Nominal output is real output multiplied by the price level.

Figure 13-7 shows how the same reduction in taxes will affect interest rates in the money and bond markets. Again, we assume that real values are being measured on the horizontal axis. Thus M is the nominal quantity of money divided by the price level and ΔB is the nominal quantity of new bonds divided by the price level. A reduction of taxes will lead to an increase in real income from y_1 to y_{fe}, in Figure 13-6. This will shift the money demand curve in Figure 13-7a to the right [recall that $M_d = f(\overset{-}{i}, \overset{+}{Y})$]. At the same time, rising income will shift the curve representing the demand for new bonds in Figure 13-7b to the right because at higher income we will have higher saving and thus a higher demand for bonds ($\Delta B_d = f(\overset{+}{i}, \overset{+}{Y})$). However, because taxes are reduced while government spending remains the same, the government will have to increase its debt to maintain the same level of spending. This will shift the curve for the supply of bonds to the right.

What about the curve representing the money supply? Rising prices will shift the money supply curve to the left. This is because we assume that the Federal Reserve sets the nominal supply of reserves. As long as there is no change in Federal Reserve policy, the nominal supply of reserves does not change. Any increase in prices must reduce the real value of the banking system's reserve base.

A reduction in the real quantity of reserves will shift the money supply curve to the left. Thus we see that a decrease in taxes with no change in monetary policy will be expected to bid up interest rates. This is true both because the demand for money will rise and also because rising prices will reduce the real supply of money at any given interest rate.

INCREASING RESERVES

Let us take another example. Assume that rather than cutting taxes, the Fed. increases the supply of reserves in the banking system. This will increase aggregate demand because falling interest rates stimulate more consumption and investment. In Figure 13-8, we again show the aggregate supply and aggregate demand curves; we also show that output is increased

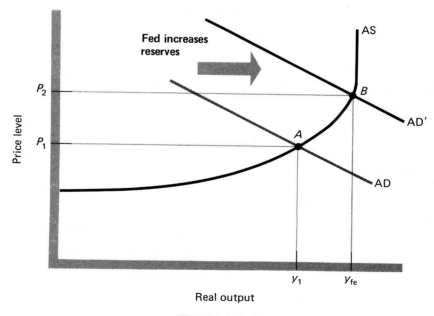

FIGURE 13-8

An increase in bank reserves resulting from Federal Reserve monetary policy will increase aggregate demand. In this case the result is a rise in the price level and a rise in real output.

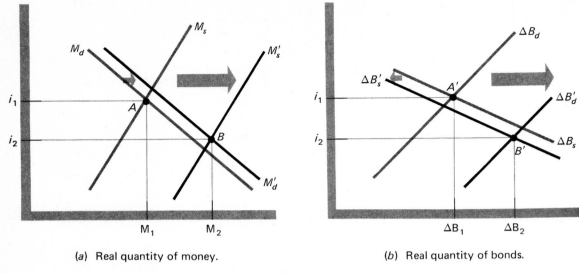

(a) Real quantity of money.

(b) Real quantity of bonds.

FIGURE 13-9

An increase in reserves will lower interest rates.

from y_1 to y_{fe} and the price level is increased from P_1 to P_2. The result is the same as in Figure 13-7.

However, let us examine what happens in the money and bond markets as a result of the increase in reserves. Let us look first at the bond market in Figure 13-9. An increase in income will increase saving and increase the demand for new bonds. Thus the demand curve must shift right. What about the supply of bonds? Rising income will increase government tax receipts. Since we assume that government spending remains the same, the government deficit must fall. This will shift the curve for the supply of bonds to the left. Thus the interest rate must fall from i_1 to i_2. The actual quantity of bonds may rise or fall depending on which curve shifts most. In our example bonds outstanding increase to ΔB_2.

In our diagram for the supply and demand for money, we see that rising income increases the demand for money. At the same time, the expansionary monetary policy of the Fed has also shifted the supply curve of money to the right. However, despite the fact that both curves shift right, we still know that interest rates must fall. This is because interest rates have fallen in the bond market and the interest rate that equates the supply and demand for bonds must also equate the supply and demand for money.

Thus, the basic difference between our two examples is that monetary policy works primarily through reducing interest rates; this, in turn, increases expenditures by stimulating spending among households and businesses. A tax cut, on the other hand (as well as an increase in government spending) works directly through income to increase spending. Assuming that monetary policy remains constant (that there is no change in reserves), this rising spending must bid up interest rates. Again, in both cases we are assuming initial situations of less than full employment. The interested reader can verify that an increase in taxes will decrease income, decrease interest rates, and decrease the price level; a decrease in the supply of reserves will lead to a decrease in income, an increase in interest rates, and a decrease in the price level.

A RISE IN THE PRICE OF OIL

Let us look at one more example. Let us assume an upward (and leftward) shift of the aggregate supply curve as a result of an increase in raw material prices such as the quadrupling of the price of crude oil which occurred in 1974. Figure 13-10 shows the effect on aggregate supply and demand. In this case, the supply curve shifts up as a result of rising costs of production.

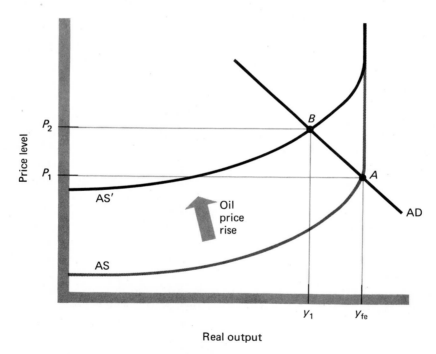

FIGURE 13-10

A rise in the price of oil (raw materials prices), other things being equal, will increase costs of production and shift the supply curve left. Producers will now demand higher prices to produce the same level of output (or, put another way, they will be willing to produce less output at the same price level). Given aggregate demand, the shift in supply will raise prices and lower output (and thus increase unemployment).

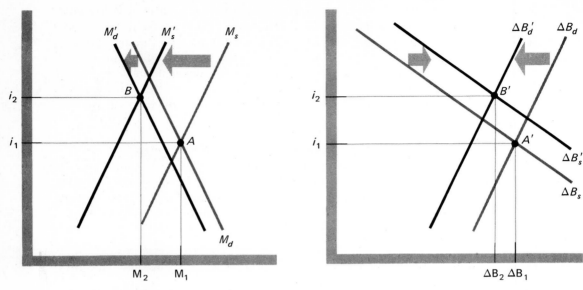

(a) Real money balances.

(b) Real quantity of new bonds.

FIGURE 13-11

An increase in the price of oil will raise interest rates.

The demand curve does not change. The price level increases from P_1 to P_2 and output falls from y_{fe} to y_1. Here we have a classic case of cost-push inflation — prices rise because costs rise — and unemployment rises.

In this case, what happens in the money and bond markets? This is shown in Figure 13-11. Let us look at the bond market first. The demand for bonds must shift left because of falling income and thus falling saving. What about the supply of bonds? Falling income leads to falling tax receipts for the government and, for any given level of government expenditures, a rise in the government deficit. The effect is a rightward shift in the bond supply curve from ΔB_S to $\Delta B_S'$. Thus we see that interest rates must rise from i_1 to i_2. The actual quantity of new bonds may increase, decrease, or not change depending on which curve shifts more.

Next, look at the money market. Falling income will reduce the demand for real money balances, shifting the demand curve from M_d to M_d'. What about the supply of money? Assuming no change in monetary policy (a given nominal supply of reserves), rising prices will reduce the real value of the quantity of reserves and shift the money supply curve to the left. Since the interest rate that equates money demand and money supply must be the same as the one that equates bond demand and bond supply, we know that the new solution must be at i_2, a higher interest rate, and M_2, a reduced real quantity of money.

Thus we see that an increase in raw material prices has a contractionary effect in two ways. First, it increases costs of production; second, it reduces demand because rising prices reduce the real value of money balances. (This is a movement up the aggregate demand curve.)

13-9
SUMMARY OF MAJOR POINTS

1

Our aggregate model of the economy is based on the behavior of the household, business, government, and foreign sectors. The individual spending, saving, and borrowing decisions made by each sector interact with one another, and the interaction of all these decisions throughout the economy affects the demand for and supply of money, bonds, goods, and labor.

2

Interest rates are determined by two things: the demand for money by the various sectors and the supply of money resulting from the behavior of banks and the Federal Reserve. The primary determinant of money demand is the level of aggregate expenditures (or income); the primary determinant of the money supply is the level of bank reserves furnished by the Fed. As a result, interest rates depend on income or expenditures (positively) and reserves (negatively).

3

Surplus sectors are net demanders of bonds; deficit sectors are net suppliers of bonds. The interest rate that equates the supply and demand for money will also equate the supply and demand for new bonds.

4

Aggregate demand for goods and services (aggregate expenditures) is the summation of demands by the individual sectors. The individual sector demands are a function of interest rates, government spending, and tax rates. Since interest rates depend on reserves and expenditures, the aggregate demand for goods and services is related to reserves, government spending, and tax rates.

5

Aggregate demand is negatively related to the general level of prices. This is because increases in prices reduce the real value of government expenditures, increase the effective tax rate, reduce the real value of money balances, and reduce net exports. Increased taxes and reduced real money balances reduce consumption expenditures by households.

6

The short-run aggregate supply curve traces out a positive relationship between the price level and the supply of output offered by producers. At full employment, the short-run supply curve becomes vertical; rising prices will not induce firms in the aggregate to produce more output because resources (such as labor) in the economy are already being fully utilized at this point. The major short-run shifters of the supply curve are wage rates, raw material costs, and profit margins. In the long run, the supply curve is also shifted by growth of the capital stock, growth of the labor force, and technological improvements.

7

The aggregate supply curve combined with the aggregate demand curve determines the general level of prices and output. For any given level of output, there will be a corresponding level of unemployment.

8

At less than full employment, an increase in demand due to expansionary fiscal policy will lead to rising interest rates; an increase in demand due to expansionary monetary policy will lead to falling interest rates. It should be emphasized that these are the short-run effects; the longer-run effects examined in the next chapter can be quite different.

9

An upward shift in the aggregate supply curve will, in the short run, lead to rising prices, rising interest rates, and rising unemployment.

13-10
REVIEW QUESTIONS

1   Explain why we expect the demand for money to be negatively related to the market interest rate.

2   In 1978, interest rates rose even though the money supply and bank reserves grew about 7½ percent. How can this be explained?

3   Each of the following may be true or false. Explain why the statement is true or false.

   a An increase in income will lead to an increase in interest rates.

   b An increase in the supply of bank reserves will lead to a decrease in interest rates.

   c An increase in interest rates will lead to an increase in business investment.

   d Aggregate expenditures are a positive function of the interest rate.

e The supply of new bonds is a positive function of the interest rate.

f The demand for new bonds is a positive function of income.

4   We expect the aggregate demand curve for goods and services to be a negative function of the general price level. Discuss several reasons why.

5   The aggregate supply curve indicates that the price necessary to induce firms to expand output (production) increases at an increasing rate as output is increased. Explain why.

6   Explain how each of the following will effect (1) the price level, (2) aggregate output, (3) unemployment, and (4) the interest rate. Assume an initial position of less than full employment.

  a An increase in government spending
  b An increase in wage rates
  c A decrease in the supply of bank reserves
  d An increase in the productivity of workers
  e An increase in profit margins

7   "Once the economy is at full employment, increases in bank reserves (and the money supply) will be inflationary." Discuss this statement.

8   Explain how the Federal Reserve can *veto* a fiscal policy action that the Congress has enacted.

13-11
SUGGESTED READINGS

1   For an introductory treatment of the supply and demand for money, see Campbell McConnell, *Economics*, 7th ed. (New York: McGraw-Hill, 1978), chap. 15 and pp. 662–664. For more advanced discussions, see David Laidler, *The Demand for Money* (New York: Harper & Row, 1977); Charles Baird, *Macroeconomics* (Chicago: Science Research Associates, 1973), chaps. 10–11; William Branson and James Litvak, *Macroeconomics* (New York: Harper & Row, 1975), chaps. 4 and 12, and Rudiger Dornbusch and Stanley Fischer, *Macroeconomics* (New York: McGraw-Hill, 1977), chaps. 4, 7, and 8.

2   For a treatment of the aggregate expenditure model, see McConnell, op. cit., chap. 12; Baird, op. cit., chaps. 5–6, Branson and Litvack, op. cit., chap. 3, and Dornbusch and Fischer, op. cit., chap. 3. The aggregate supply and demand model is developed in Branson and Litvak, op. cit., chap. 9, and Dornbusch and Fisher, op. cit., chaps. 11–13. For a more detailed treatment of the labor market, see Branson and Litvak, chaps. 7–8, and Dornbusch and Fisher, chap. 15.

14

INFLATION AND UNEMPLOYMENT

A recession [or inflation] is like an unfortunate
love affair. It's a lot easier to talk your way in
than it is to talk your way out.

Bill Vaughn

14-1
UNDERSTANDING INFLATION
AND UNEMPLOYMENT: A BEGINNING

Over the past decade, the rate of inflation has tended to rise on average and
unemployment has fluctuated in a fairly wide range. Our aim is to identify
and analyze the factors which have contributed to this economic instability.
Of course, we shall be particularly interested in the role of monetary policy.

In Chapter 13, we studied the determinants of the supply and demand
for real output, money, and bonds, which, in turn, determined the level of
real output, employment, prices, and interest rates. That analysis was static;
there was no explicit treatment of the dynamic relationship—that is, the
relationship over time—between the key variables determining aggregate
supply and demand. For example, we were concerned with the factors
which shifted the aggregate demand for output toward or away from full employment. This focus on increases or decreases in the levels of key variables was a necessary first step in our analysis.

The next step is to consider dynamic analysis where we take explicit account of the rate of change in the various key variables. This is a more realistic analysis where we will be looking at increases or decreases in the growth rate of key variables. For example, we shall be interested in how the

STATIC VERSUS DYNAMIC ANALYSIS

The analysis in Chapter 13 concentrated on comparing the effects of different *levels* of key economic variables. For instance, an increase in the level of government spending would shift the aggregate demand curve to a new equilibrium income point on the aggregate supply function. By comparing the new equilibrium income level to the old one, we showed the effects of the government spending increase. Comparing one equilibrium point with another is called *comparative static analysis*. This helps to clarify the interrelationships between key economic variables and financial variables. But "real world" discussions in economics are not concerned only with the level of the variables; rates of change over a time period are more relevant. For instance, in discussing prices, it is not the level of prices that is the focus of most discussions but rather the rate of change in price levels or the rate of inflation. Policymakers want to know and discuss whether inflation will be 10 percent over the next year or some other figure, either higher or lower.

Dynamic analysis focuses on the rate of change in variables over some time period, usually a month, quarter, or year. Newspaper accounts today do not simply state that prices are rising; rather, the emphasis is on the *rate* of increase of prices, usually at an annual rate. A headline like "Prices rising 7 percent annually" (or some other number) is reporting on the annual rate of change. In this chapter our focus will be on dynamic analysis, or the rate of change in key variables.

The student should note that in this analysis we discuss increases and decreases in the growth rate, say, of inflation or GNP. To be sure that you have a clear idea of this concept, let us use an example: Assume that real GNP grew at an annual rate of 6 percent in the last year. If we expect that real GNP will grow by 4 percent in the forthcoming year, there will be a *decrease* in the growth rate or rate of change. On the other hand, an expected 9 percent growth rate in GNP would indicate an *increase* in the growth rate.

growth rate of the money supply is related to the inflation rate, the growth rate of real output, and the unemployment rate. (You will be happy to know that the analysis developed in Chapter 13 will go a long way toward uncovering the nature of this and other relationships.)

In the next section, we will employ the aggregate supply-and-demand framework, which we learned in the last chapter, to analyze the relationship between inflation and unemployment as well as their causes. These two problems have plagued our economy for many years; that is why they play a prominent role in the discussion, formulation, and execution of policy.

14-2
THE RELATIONSHIP
BETWEEN INFLATION AND UNEMPLOYMENT

First, some fairly straightforward definitions. The rate of inflation is equal to the increase in prices (as measured by the consumer price index, for example) expressed as a percentage of the level of prices. Algebraically, this can be expressed as $\Delta P/P = \dot{p}$. (A dot over any letter or symbol in this chapter will indicate that we are referring to the rate of change of the particular variable, in this case, $\Delta P/P$.)

As for the unemployment rate, we know from our discussion of aggregate supply (and the production function) that, if the other factors of production and the wage rate are given and constant, there is a unique level of employment for each level of real output.

Let N_{fe} = the level of employment which produces "full-employment" output y_{fe}

N_1 = an employment level less than full employment, which produces output y_1

$N_{fe} - N_1$ = number of workers unemployed U at output level Y_1

$$u_1 = \frac{N_{fe} - N_1}{N_{fe}} \text{ or unemployment rate}$$

where u_1 is the unemployment rate at employment level N_1. It is the ratio of unemployed workers ($N_{fe} - N_1$) to the full-employment labor force N_{fe}.[1]

Now that we have the key concepts defined, let us move to the relationship between inflation and unemployment in the short run.

---

[1] This is consistent with the general equation found in Section 13-6, $U = f(y_{fe} - y_{actual})$. If y_{actual} falls relative to y_{fe} (that is, if $y_{fe} - y_{actual}$ gets larger), then N_{actual} falls relative to N_{fe} and U increases. The full-employment level of output is the output which could be produced if all factors of production were fully employed. This concept is often referred to as "potential output" and is discussed in the Appendix to this chapter.

THE SHORT-RUN CASE:
SHIFTING AGGREGATE DEMAND CURVES

In the short run, with wages given (constant), the aggregate supply curve can be represented by AS_1 in Figure 14-1. Given a particular level of taxes, government spending, and bank reserves—see Equation (13-13)—we can also fix the aggregate demand curve as AD_1. The interaction of supply and demand yields a short-run equilibrium at point A. What we have is a snapshot of the economy. Now let us suppose that, as time passes, aggregate demand grows at a steady rate, perhaps reflecting the growth in bank reserves. Over time, as demand increases from AD_1 to AD_2 (assuming a given supply curve), the new short-run equilibrium is at point B. As demand increases further to AD_3 in the next time period, the equilibrium is at point C. Note that we are assuming the same-size shift in the demand curves. This is demonstrated in that the horizontal distance between AD_1 and AD_2 is equal to the horizontal distance between AD_2 and AD_3 per unit of time.

As the demand curve shifts in equal amounts with a given supply curve, we can measure the change in price levels or, more importantly, the rate of inflation. This is presented in Figure 14-2, where we can see that the price level, measured on the vertical axis, goes from P_1 to P_2 to P_3 with each sub-

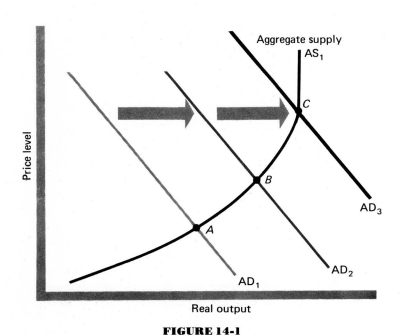

FIGURE 14-1

As aggregate demand grows along a stable aggregate supply curve, equilibrium moves from point A to point C.

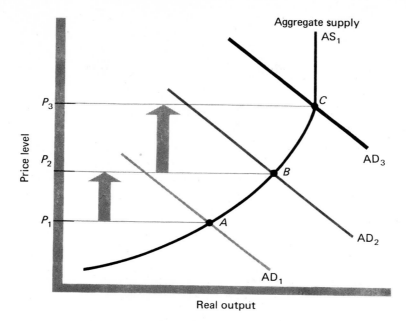

FIGURE 14-2

The rate of inflation in moving from point A to point B is $(P_2 - P_1)/P_1 = \dot{p}_{12}$. This is less than the rate of inflation in moving from point B to point C, which is $(P_3 - P_2)/P_2 = \dot{p}_{23}$. Hence, as the full-employment level of output is approached, identical increases in demand will result in larger rises in prices.

sequent shift in the aggregate demand curve (corresponding to equilibrium points A, B, and C, respectively). The rate of inflation as the price level moves from P_1 to P_2 is $(P_2 - P_1)/P_1 = \dot{p}_{12}$. As demand increases further, the rate of inflation is $(P_3 - P_2)/P_2 = \dot{p}_{23}$. You will note from Figure 14-2 that $(P_3 - P_2)$ is greater than $(P_2 - P_1)$. The rate of inflation, therefore, in going from point B to point C is greater than the rate in moving from point A to point B.

The interesting result is that because of the upward-sloping short-run supply curve, the growth of aggregate demand will lead to an increase in the rate of inflation as full employment (y_{fe}) is approached ($\dot{p}_{23} > \dot{p}_{12}$).

The shifts in the demand curve with the supply curve given also increase the level of real output. This is shown in Figure 14-3, as the equal-size shifts in the aggregate demand curve increase the level of output from y_1 to y_2 to y_{fe}. In this short-run model, output can increase only if employment rises and therefore unemployment falls.

At output y_1 in Figure 14-3 the level of employment is N_1; at output y_2, it is N_2; at output y_{fe}, it is N_{fe}. The rate of unemployment at output levels y_1, y_2, and y_{fe} (or equivalently at equilibrium points A, B, and C, respectively) is given as follows:

$$u_1 = \frac{N_{fe} - N_1}{N_{fe}}$$

$$u_2 = \frac{N_{fe} - N_2}{N_{fe}}$$

$$u_{fe} = \frac{N_{fe} - N_{fe}}{N_{fe}} \text{ or full employment}$$

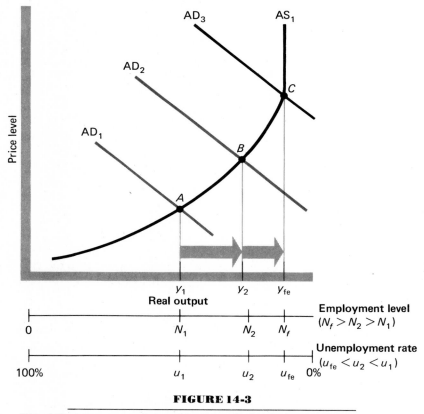

FIGURE 14-3

The shifts in aggregate demand increase the level of output and the level of employment. Consequently, the level of unemployment is reduced. As the full-employment level of output is approached, identical increases in demand will result in smaller rises in output. In our example, as demand is increased, two things happen: the rate of inflation increases and the rate of unemployment decreases.

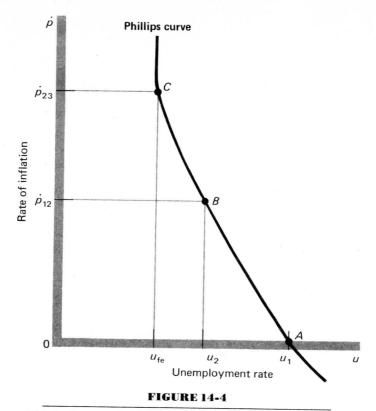

FIGURE 14-4

This is the so-called Phillips curve which depicts an inverse relationship between inflation and unemployment. As the economy moves toward full employment (U_{fe}), the rate of inflation accelerates (in fact, since the curve gets steeper, the inflation rate increases at an increasing rate).

Notice that the rate of unemployment at y_1 will be higher than the rate of unemployment at y_2; that is, $u_1 > u_2$.[1] The shifts in AD increase the level of output and the level of employment. Consequently, the rate of unemployment is reduced. Furthermore as the full employment level of output y_{fe} is approached, identical increases in demand result in smaller rises in output. In fact, as AD increases in our example, two things happen—the rate of inflation $\dot{p}$ rises and the rate of unemployment u falls. Furthermore, as the full-employment level of output is approached (that is, as we move from point A to B to C), identical increases in demand result in *larger*

[1] Note that we do not put a dot over u. This is because it does not represent a rate of change over time as does the inflation rate $\dot{p}$. Rather it represents the ratio of the number of unemployed workers to the labor force. Sharp readers will also note that our equations imply that unemployment is zero at u_{fe}. In practice, of course, we do not ever have 100 percent employment (0 percent unemployment). Today economists usually argue that full employment corresponds to an unemployment rate of about 5½ percent. This apparent contradiction in terms used by economists will be cleared up in Chapter 17 (we hope!).

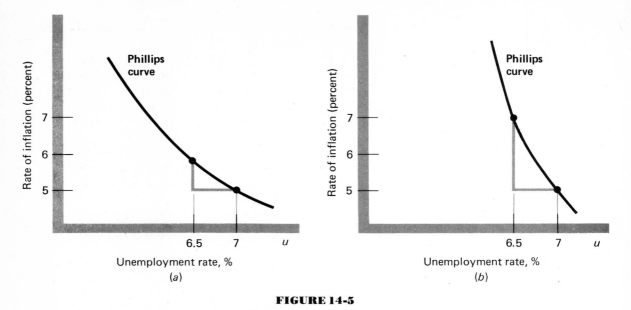

FIGURE 14-5

The Phillips curve in (*b*) is drawn with a steeper slope than that shown in (*a*). The steeper slope of (*b*) means that the trade-off between inflation and unemployment is worse. In (*b*), a drop in the unemployment rate from 7 percent to 6½ percent brings about a 2 percent rise in the inflation rate. In (*a*), a similar drop in the unemployment rate brings about a ½ percent rise in the inflation rate.

increases in prices and *smaller* increases in output (and therefore smaller declines in unemployment). Once full employment is reached, increases in demand will raise only prices, not output. We can express the relationship between inflation and unemployment implied by the above analysis as $\dot{p} = f(\bar{u})$, which simply states that the rate of inflation is a negative function of the rate of unemployment.[1]

We can transpose the rate of inflation and the unemployment rate consistent with points A, B, and C of Figures 14-2 and 14-3 onto a diagram such as Figure 14-4. On the vertical axis we plot the inflation rate and on the horizontal axis the unemployment rate. At point A, the inflation rate is assumed to be zero (since this is where we began our analysis at price level P_1 and equilibrium point A in Figure 14-2) and the unemployment rate is u_1 (this is the rate of unemployment consistent with producing a level of output equal to y_1 at equilibrium point A in Figure 14-3). At point C, on the other hand, we show the inflation rate to be $\dot{p}_{23}$ when we are at full employment u_{fe}. The other points are similarly derived. The relationship between inflation and unemployment shown in Figure 14-4 has come to be known as

---

[1] Recall, of course, that the rate of unemployment is, in turn, a function of aggregate supply and aggregate demand.

the *Phillips curve.*[1] This curve suggested to policymakers and economists that there was a trade-off between inflation and unemployment; one had to trade off—that is, be willing to accept—inflation in order to lower unemployment or to accept more unemployment to lower inflation. The Phillips curve expresses an interdependent relationship between unemployment and inflation that poses a dilemma for policymakers: *less unemployment is possible only at the cost of greater inflation.* Hence, this *trade-off* between these two related policy goals exposes conflicts in setting policy objectives.[2]

Because the goals of full employment and price stability are not simultaneously achievable, attempts to move the economy closer to one goal will necessarily move it further away from the other goal. The degree to which one objective must be given up to obtain a little bit more of the other is measured by the slope of the Phillips curve. The steeper the slope of the curve, the more inflation rises for any drop in the unemployment rate. This is demonstrated in Figure 14-5.

THE SHORT-RUN CASE:
SHIFTING THE AGGREGATE SUPPLY CURVE

The derivation of the relationship between inflation and unemployment was based on the assumption of a given supply curve, while the demand curve was allowed to shift. Suppose we reverse the assumption and hold the level of demand constant while shifting the aggregate supply curve to the left. A possible cause of such a shift would be a rise in the wage rate; see Equation (13-16). In this case, as the supply curve shifts left, prices increase and output decreases. To see this, let us work through, as we did for the shifts in the demand curve, the graphical analysis.

Figure 14-6 shows, with a given demand curve, equal-size shifts to the left of the supply curve. The first aggregate supply curve AS_1 is shown intersecting the aggregate demand curve at point A, which is assumed to be the full-employment level of real output y_{fe}. The second supply curve AS_2 intersects the aggregate demand curve at B, and equilibrium point B gives a level of output of y_2. The third shift to the left gives aggregate supply schedule AS_3 and equilibrium point C. At this equilibrium point, the level of output is y_3.

As we demonstrated previously, each level of output gives a unique level of employment (unemployment) in the economy. As real output falls from the y_{fe} output, the level of employment also falls; consequently, the rate of unemployment u rises.

Figure 14-7 concentrates on what happens to the price level and hence

[1] A British economist named A. W. Phillips published some empirical work in 1958 which traced out a similar relationship. See A. W. Phillips, "The Relation Between Unemployment and the Rate of Change in Money Wage Rates in the United Kingdom, 1861–1957," *Economica* (November 1958), 284–299.

[2] We have drawn the Phillips curve in Figure 14-4 crossing the horizontal axis thereby showing that at some high rate of unemployment the rate of price change would actually be negative.

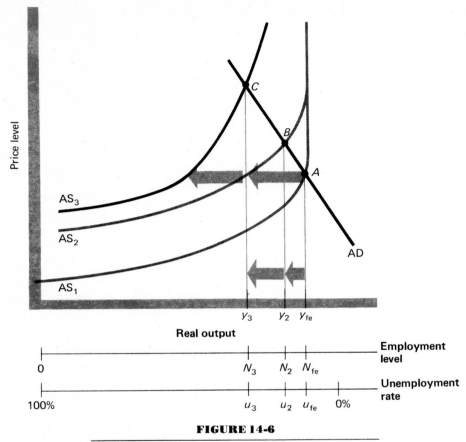

FIGURE 14-6

As the aggregate supply curve shifts upward and to the left because of, say, a rise in the wage rate, real output and employment fall and unemployment rises. The arrows show these to be equal-size shifts in the supply curve.

the inflation rate as the aggregate supply curve shifts upward and to the left. At each subsequent equilibrium point, the level of prices is higher.[1] As we showed previously, the rate of inflation at each equilibrium point is the rate of change in prices or $\Delta P/P$. As the supply curve shifts from AS_1 to AS_2 to AS_3, the rate of inflation *rises*. In other words,

$$\frac{P_3 - P_2}{P_2} = \dot{p}_{23} > \frac{P_2 - P_1}{P_1} = \dot{p}_{12}$$

---

[1] We have drawn Figure 14-7 with the shift in the supply curve not affecting the full-employment level of output. This is because we assume technology is given in the short run. In reality, as wages or raw material prices rise, full employment output may fall. For example, an increase in oil prices may make some business plants and equipment inefficient—that is, too costly to operate.

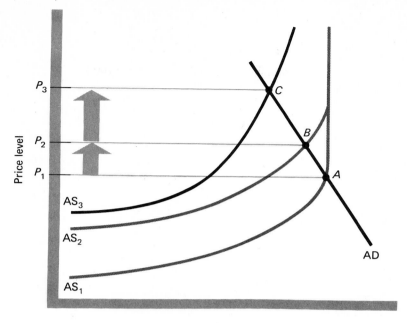

FIGURE 14-7

As the supply curve shifts back, the level of prices rises at an increasing rate, exhibiting a rise in the inflation rate. The rate of inflation as the economy moves from point A to point B is $(P_2 - P_1)/P_1 = \dot{p}_{12}$. This is less than the inflation rate as the economy moves from point B to point C, which is $(P_3 - P_2)/P_2 = \dot{p}_{23}$.

The result shown in Figure 14-7 is a classic example of cost-push or supply-side inflation. In other words, the inflation arises from increases in costs (such as wage rates or raw material prices) which shift the supply curve.

Just as we did with shifting demand curves, we can trace out the relationship between inflation and unemployment with shifting supply curves. The inflation rate as supply shifts from AS_1 to AS_2 is $(P_2 - P_1)/P_1 = \dot{p}_{12}$; as supply shifts from AS_2 to AS_3, the inflation rate becomes $(P_3 - P_2)/P_2 = \dot{p}_{23}$. (See Figure 14-7.) The corresponding unemployment rates are u_2 and u_3. (See Figure 14-6). Since employment is falling (unemployment is rising), u_3 must be greater than u_2. We can plot these coordinate points on a graph. In other words, we can see from Figures 14-6 and 14-7 that inflation rate $\dot{p}_{12}$ and unemployment rate u_2 are generated at equilibrium point B, and that inflation rate $\dot{p}_{23}$ and unemployment rate u_3 are generated at equilibrium point C. These points are plotted and connected (together with the initial equilib-

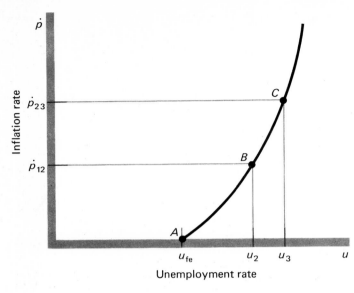

FIGURE 14-8

With an upward-shifting supply curve, the curve depicting the trade-off between the inflation rate and the unemployment rate is positively sloped.

rium point A) on Figure 14-8. From this analysis, we would conclude that as inflation increases, unemployment is also increasing; hence the relationship between these variables is now positive $\dot{p} = f(\overset{+}{u})$.

The analysis above, which shows the relationship between $\dot{p}$ and u to be either positive or negative, suggests that the exact relationship between inflation and unemployment is uncertain. What can be said about it? At a minimum, you ought to be able to convince yourself that when demand is increasing relative to supply (demand-induced inflation), we expect the inflation rate to be a negative function of the unemployment rate; as unemployment increases, inflation falls, and conversely. Alternately, when costs of production are being pushed up relative to demand, causing an upward shift in supply, inflation may increase as unemployment increases. If both supply and demand are shifting, the relationship between unemployment and inflation is ambiguous. It really depends on which curve is shifting faster.

Actual data on inflation and unemployment for the United States over the past 15 years are plotted in Figure 14-9. As you can see, the actual relationship does not look at all like we might expect the Phillips curve to look. To develop a more realistic view of the factors affecting the relationship between unemployment and inflation over time, we need to extend the analysis.

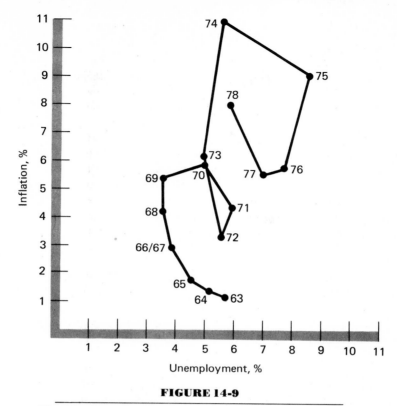

FIGURE 14-9

The data for inflation and unemployment. Note that the data show elements of both a positive and a negative relationship between inflation and unemployment.

THE LONGER-RUN CASE

As time passes, two major forces affect the aggregate supply curve and the full-employment level of output. On the one hand, the labor force and the capital stock will be growing, reflecting the growth in population and capital accumulation (investment) as well as technological breakthroughs. These factors will raise the productivity of new and existing labor and capital inputs. All these factors will tend to shift the aggregate supply curve to the right. If the aggregate demand curve were fixed, prices would fall and output would rise. This is demonstrated in Figure 14-10. On the other hand, the other factors affecting aggregate supply—such as wages, profit margins, and raw material prices—could be rising, causing aggregate supply to shift to the left. For a fixed demand curve, this would generate a rise in prices and a fall in output. This is demonstrated in Figure 14-11.

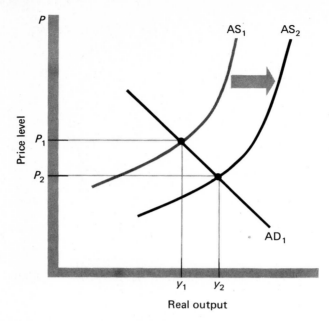

FIGURE 14-10

Rightward-shifting aggregate supply causes prices to fall ($P_2 < P_1$) and output to go up ($y_2 > y_1$). The aggregate supply curve shifts to the right over time due to growth in the capital stock and population as well as to technological breakthroughs that increase productivity.

It is the net effect of these two sets of conflicting forces which will determine the position of aggregate supply, which, in turn, determines prices and output for any given demand curve. To understand the relationship between the inflation rate and the unemployment rate, we need to know what can or will happen to aggregate supply.

To simplify matters considerably, let us assume that profit margins and raw material prices are constant (Hooray!) and that the labor force and capital stock grow at a steady rate. Given these assumptions, the net effect on the supply curve (and therefore prices and output) over time will mainly be a result of the growth in wages, which pushes supply in one direction, and the growth in productivity due to technological innovation, which pushes in the other direction.

We can write a fairly simple yet extemely informative equation which brings together the major factors affecting the growth in wages:

(14-1)
$$\dot{w} = f(\overset{+}{\dot{p}^e}, \overset{-}{u})$$

where $\dot{w}$ = rate of growth of wages

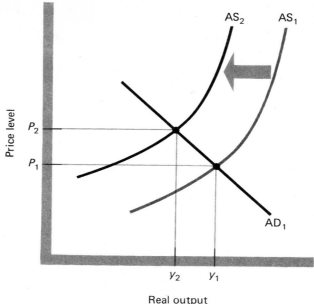

Price level

AS_2 AS_1

P_2

P_1

AD_1

y_2 y_1

Real output

FIGURE 14-11

Leftward-shifting aggregate supply causes prices to increase
$(P_2 > P_1)$ and output to fall $(y_2 < y_1)$. The aggregate supply
curve shifts to the left over time due to rising wages, profit
margins, and/or raw materials prices.

$\dot{p}^e$ = **rate of inflation expected in the future**[1]
u = **unemployment rate**

Equation (14-1) indicates that the rate of increase in wages will depend
on the unemployment rate and the expected rate of inflation.[2]

In general, we would expect the rate of unemployment u and the growth
of wages $\dot{w}$ to be negatively related. Rises in unemployment will frequently
reflect falling demand for output and therefore also for labor as firms attempt to cut costs in the face of reduced revenue. With existing workers
being laid off and new members of the labor force having a difficult time
finding jobs, it seems reasonable to believe that those left on the job will
have a more difficult time securing large wage increases. On the other
hand, if unemployment is falling as firms respond to increased demand for

---

[1] The superscript ^{e} refers to an expected or future value of a variable. It should be noted that $\dot{p}^e$
depends in part on current and past rates of inflation. This is discussed in Appendix A to this
chapter.

[2] Of course, some miscellaneous factors, such as the bargaining power of unions, play a role in the
determination of the growth of wages. For this discussion, we shall abstract from these factors.

output by increasing employment, labor markets tighten and workers feel encouraged to seek larger wage increases.

As for expected inflation $\dot{p}^e$, we would find wages growing faster as expected inflation—a measure of the expected cost of living for workers—rises. Workers are primarily interested in their real wages—that is, the real purchasing power of the income they earn. The higher past or current inflation, the more likely it is that some (perhaps most) workers' real wages (and therefore real standards of living) have not risen as fast as the workers had expected or hoped. In some cases, real wages may have decreased. Such developments will encourage workers to bargain for wage increases which make up for lost ground—that is, anticipated increases in real wages that were eroded by inflation. Similarly, the higher the inflation rate expected in the future, the higher the current wage demands to protect workers' real incomes.

Will rising wages shift the aggregate supply curve to the left? As mentioned earlier, this depends on the growth of labor productivity (that is, the rate of growth of output per unit of labor). If productivity grows ($\dot{p}r$) as fast as wages, marginal costs of production and, therefore, the aggregate supply curve will not be affected by the rise in wages. This is worth remembering: if the rise in wages is equal to the rise in productivity, marginal costs will remain constant.[1] If firms' markups m over costs remain constant, the schedule of prices required to induce business to produce various levels of output is unaffected; thus the supply curve does not shift. However, if wages rise faster than productivity ($\dot{w} > \dot{p}r$), there will be upward pressure on prices. Equation (14-2) shows this relationship. Here the rate of inflation is equal to the rate of wage growth, as determined by the factors in Equation (14-1), minus the rate of productivity growth.[2]

$$\text{(14-2)} \qquad\qquad \dot{p} = \dot{w}(\overset{+}{\dot{p}^e}, \overset{-}{u}) - \dot{p}r$$

If we assume that $\dot{p}r$ is constant, we see that the relationship between $\dot{p}$ and $\dot{u}$ now depends on what happens to wages $\dot{w}$ due to changes in $\dot{p}^e$. It is to this, the effect of $\dot{p}^e$ on the inflation/unemployment relationship, that we now turn. You may want to take a breather before moving on. You deserve one.

THE SHORT- AND LONG-RUN VIEWS COMBINED

Now we can begin to pull things together. Equation (14-1) tells us that for any given unemployment rate, the rate of increase in wages will depend on

[1] If other inputs are ignored, marginal cost is equal to the wage rate multiplied by the additional labor needed to produce an additional unit of output. If the wage rate rises by, say, 3 percent, but the productivity of workers also rises 3 percent—meaning 3 percent less labor is needed to produce an additional unit of output—then marginal cost will not be affected by the rise in wages.

[2] To be complete we could add another term to equation (14-2) to account for the effect of changes in raw material prices or profit margins on the inflation rate. Increases in either will tend to increase the inflation rate.

how fast and to what degree wages respond to expected inflation. For example, with 5 percent expected inflation ($\dot{p}^e = 5$ percent), there might be a 6 percent wage increase ($\dot{w} = 6$ percent). In other words, the rate of increase in wages depends on what labor expects the inflation rate to be.[1]

Equation (14-2) tells us that for any given unemployment rate and with productivity growth assumed constant, the rate of inflation will vary positively with the *expected* rate of inflation. To trace the response of the current inflation rate $\dot{p}$ to the expected inflation rate $\dot{p}^e$, we need to know a little more about how $\dot{p}^e$ affects the growth of the wage rate $\dot{w}$.

In Figure 14-12 we trace the effects of wages responding to actual and to expected inflation. Initial equilibrium is at point A, where AD$_1$ intersects AS$_1$. Now suppose that demand increases from AD$_1$ to AD$_2$. This will lead to an increase in prices to P_2 and a new equilibrium at B. However, an equilibrium at point B *assumes* that wages *fail* to respond to the increase in prices. If wages *do* respond, this will shift the aggregate supply curve upward and to the left.

On the assumption that wages do respond to price increases, we have drawn AS$_2$ in Figure 14-12. The new equilibrium is now point C. However, equilibrium at point C would exist only if wages do not respond fully to the rise in expected prices. If wages respond fully to the rise in prices, the economy would move to an equilibrium at point D. Points D and A have the same output levels and therefore also the same employment levels. They differ only in that prices and nominal wages at point D are higher than at point A. Since wages and prices have increased by the same rate, this will not affect the demand for labor by firms. At the same real wage (w/P), the same quantity of labor will be employed. Both points B and C imply a reduction in real wages as demand increases.

In general, to the extent that wages respond to actual and anticipated inflation, the increase in output and decrease in unemployment that accompany a rise in aggregate demand will be smaller; the increase in prices—and therefore inflation—will be larger.[2] In other words, as wages respond to actual and anticipated inflation, the closer to point D will be the ultimate or final (long-run) equilibrium point; point B will only be a short-run equilibrium.

---

[1] The expected *real* wage of labor is defined as (w/P) where w is the nominal wage rate and P is a price index. The rate of growth of real wages is ($\dot{w} - \dot{p}$). For example, if wages are expected to increase by 8 percent per annum and prices by 6 percent per annum, real wages will grow by 2 percent per annum (ignoring taxes). On the other hand, if anticipated inflation is 12 percent per annum, then real wages are, in the example given here, expected to decline by 4 percent per annum.

[2] During the 1970s, economists came to use the term "stagflation" to refer to the simultaneous existence of above-average unemployment and inflation rates; the economy was "stagnating"—growing slowly—and yet inflation persisted. Such a state of affairs can be explained with the simple graphs developed to this point. In particular, if $\dot{w}$ responds quickly and significantly to increases in $\dot{p}$ generated by policy-induced increases in aggregate demand, then, in Figure 14-12, the economy will move from a point like A to a point like D.

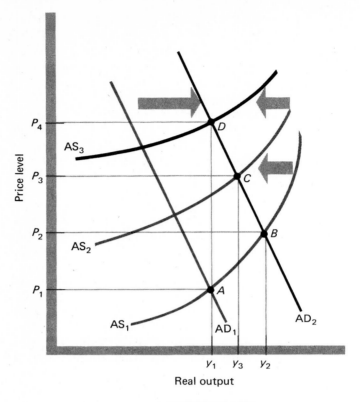

FIGURE 14-12

With aggregate demand increasing from AD_1 to AD_2, the price level rises to P_2 and output to y_2. The new equilibrium will be at point B if wages do not respond to increased prices: the supply curve remains stable as demand shifts. If wages respond to actual and anticipated inflation, this will shift the aggregate supply to the left. The larger the extent of the response of wages, the farther upward and to the left the aggregate supply curve will shift.

EXPECTED INFLATION AND THE PHILLIPS CURVE

The implication of labor adjusting their wage rates to expected inflation has great import for the concept of the Phillips curve we derived in Figure 14-4. When we derived this curve, we assumed implicitly that laborers did not recognize that rising prices were eroding their real incomes. That is, the aggregate supply curve did not shift leftward. In other words, the Phillips curve in Figure 14-4 was derived assuming that $\dot{p}^e = 0$. Since we have now dropped that assumption and expect workers to seek wage increases to restore their real incomes, we should expect that the relationship between inflation and unemployment as traced by the Phillips curve of Figure 14-4 no longer is correct. In point of fact, there is a different relationship between inflation and unemployment for each different value of $\dot{p}^e$.

We can emphasize this point by analyzing Equation (14-2). We reproduce Equation (14-2) here, assuming that productivity growth ($\dot{p}r$) is constant.

$$(14\text{-}2a) \qquad\qquad \dot{p} = \dot{w}(\overset{-}{u}, \overset{+}{\dot{p}^e}) - \dot{p}r$$

If we assume further that u is constant, then the value of $\dot{w}$ will depend on $\dot{p}^e$; the greater $\dot{p}^e$ is the greater $\dot{w}$ becomes. Of course, the growth rate of $\dot{w}$ affects inflation ($\dot{p}$). Hence, given u, the greater $\dot{p}^e$ is, the greater $\dot{p}$ becomes. Another way of expressing this conclusion is that *the same unemployment rate would correspond to different inflation rates given different values of $\dot{p}^e$.* In Figure 14-12, points A and D demonstrate this conclusion. At these equilibrium points, different expected inflation rates are associated with the same output level and therefore unemployment rate.

SHORT- AND LONG-RUN PHILLIPS CURVES

Once economists began to take the role of expected inflation into consideration in the determination of the growth in wage rates, it was clear that it would be necessary to modify the Phillips curve analysis that we derived earlier. We can assume that as workers recognize a rising inflation rate, that will affect future inflation—that is, when $\dot{p}^e$ is increasing workers will seek increased wages to restore their real incomes. In response to this development, economists now talk about a family of Phillips curves, each of which are short-run curves corresponding to different expected rates of inflation. The *position* of each short-run curve depends on the expected rate of inflation; the higher the expected rate of inflation, the higher the short-run Phillips curve.

These short-run curves intersect a long-run curve. The long-run curve and short-run curves intersect where expected inflation equals the actual rate of inflation ($\dot{p}^e = \dot{p}$). This means that every point on the long-run curve is where expected inflation equals actual inflation.

Figure 14-13 should help to nail down the points we are trying to make. Here we have drawn a long-run curve (PC$_{lr}$) and a family of short-run curves (PC$_0$, PC$_3$, PC$_6$, PC$_9$). Each of the short-run curves corresponds to an expected rate of inflation of zero, 3, 6, and 9 percent, respectively. (That is, $\dot{p}^e$ takes on the values from zero to 9). Notice that the position of each short-run curve depends on the value of $\dot{p}^e$ or the anticipated or expected inflation; the higher $\dot{p}^e$, the higher the short-run Phillips curve. Also note that the point at which each short-run Phillips curve cuts the long-run curve is where the expected and actual rates of inflation are equal. For example, PC$_0$, the short-run Phillips curve corresponding to a zero rate of expected inflation, intersects the long-run curve PC$_{lr}$ at point A, where actual inflation is zero. Similarly PC$_6$, the short-run curve corresponding to an ex-

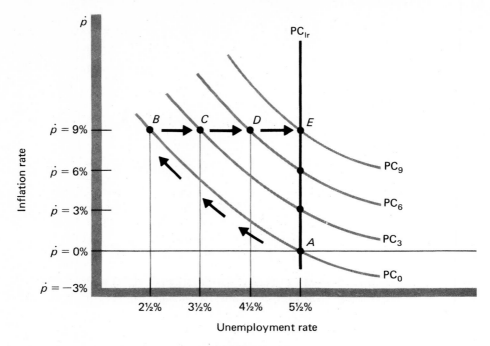

FIGURE 14-13

While aggregate demand is stimulated to lower the unemployment rate to 2½ percent, the actual inflation rate rises to 9 percent as the economy moves along the Phillips curve PC_0. This will bring about adjustments in inflationary expectations, which will lead to shifts in the short-run Phillips curve. The economy will follow the path $ABCDE$ to the new equilibrium, point E, where unemployment is the same as it was initially, but inflation is higher than it originally was.

pected rate of inflation of 6 percent, intersects the long-run Phillips curve at the actual inflation rate of 6 percent.

Let us assume that the economy is initially at point A, where the unemployment rate is 5½ percent and actual and anticipated inflation is zero. Now suppose policymakers think that an unemployment rate of 5½ percent is too high and they engineer an expansion in aggregate demand. This might move the economy to point B; thus a lower unemployment rate of 2½ percent is "bought" by an increase in the rate of inflation from zero to 9 percent. Although the inflation process is complex, one way that the movement from A to B could occur is that the expansion in demand could initially lead to an increase in product prices. There is general agreement among economists that product prices tend to respond to increased demand more rapidly than money wages. With prices rising more rapidly than nominal wages, real wages fall and producers expand output and employment, thereby reducing unemployment to 2½ percent as the economy moves along the short-run Phillips curve PC_0. In essence, the policymakers have reduced unemployment while increasing the actual rate of inflation.

However, this stimulation and reduced unemployment rate may be short-lived. The *actual* inflation rate after the increased demand is 9 percent, not zero. Workers negotiating wages when the economy was at point A are surprised by the acceleration of inflation; it was not anticipated! Over time, as inflation persists at the 9 percent rate, workers will adjust their expectations to the actual inflation rate (that is, $\dot{p}^e$ will rise gradually to 9 percent) and they will begin to incorporate these price expectations into their wage bargaining.[1] As $\dot{p}^e$ rises, first to 3 percent, then to 6 percent, and then to 9 percent, the short-run Phillips curve shifts to the right. Each shift moves the unemployment rate, given a 9 percent inflation rate, back to the right. From point B, the economy moves to point C, corresponding with an unemployment rate of 3½ percent. Next the economy moves to point E, corresponding with an unemployment rate of 4½ percent. Ultimately, the economy moves to point E, corresponding with an unemployment rate of 5½ percent. The result is that we end up at a point like E in Figure 14-13 rather than a point like B.[2]

At point E, the unemployment rate is the same as at point A, and the inflation rate is higher than at point A. Rather than ending up on the short-run Phillips curve PC_0 at point B, we have instead ended up on the long-run curve PC_{lr} at point E. The long-run curve allows for the adjustment of inflation expectations to actual inflation, the resultant rise in money wages, and the shift of aggregate supply.[3]

The vertical long-run Phillips curve suggests that there is no long-run trade-off between inflation and unemployment. In the long run the economy will settle at the full employment level of unemployment—called the "natural rate of unemployment." Inflation can be anywhere on the long-run Phillips curve. The policy implications are straightforward; once the economy reaches the natural rate, stimulative policies only lead to higher inflation. In our example, the inflation rate of 9 percent is consistent with an unemployment rate of 2½ percent in the short run, but an unemployment rate of 5½ percent in the long run.

A corollary of this finding is that policy designed to lower the unemployment rate below the "natural rate of unemployment," which is determined by the structure of the labor market, the characteristics of the labor force,

---

[1] The idea that price expectations played an important role in the *location* of the short-run Phillips curve was first advanced by Milton Friedman in "The Role of Monetary Policy," *American Economic Review* (March 1968), 7–11.

[2] The rise in money wages lifts the real wage and therefore real costs of production back toward their preinflation level. As a result of the rise in real wages, employers are induced to cut back employment, thus reversing at least in part the initial downward movement in unemployment.

[3] All this could be related back to our shifting aggregate supply and demand curves. We will not burden you with the details. It is sufficient to be conversant with the determinants that shift the aggregate supply and demand curves.

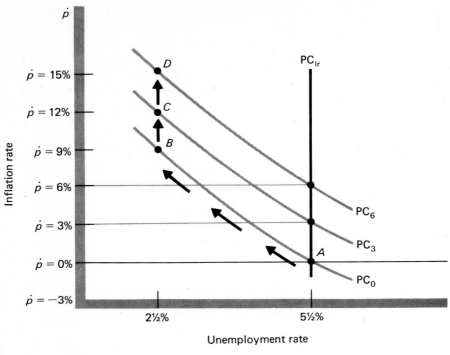

FIGURE 14-14

Holding the unemployment rate at 2½ percent can only be
accomplished through a continuing acceleration of inflation
(points *ABCD*).

the growth of the labor force, and so forth, can only succeed as long as
actual inflation *exceeds* expected inflation. This is demonstrated in Figure
14-14, where we plot again our long-run Phillips curve and our family of
short-run curves. Let us assume that the policymakers stimulate aggregate
demand and reduce the unemployment rate to 2½ percent. Once the 9
percent actual inflation is anticipated and adjusted for in wage bargaining,
we would expect the economy to move along the path described in Figure
14-13, back to an unemployment rate of 5½ percent on the long-run Phillips curve. The only way the policymakers could keep the unemployment
rate at 2½ percent would be to *continue to stimulate* aggregate demand.
If they did this, then the economy would move along the path shown in Figure 14-14. With each shift in the short-run Phillips curve, the actual inflation rate would rise as long as the policymakers insisted on maintaining the
unemployment rate at 2½ percent.

One important implication of the above analysis is that once inflation
gets going and people begin to adjust their expectations of inflation upward,

there is considerable *momentum* built into the inflationary process. This is important to recognize because it means that if policymakers try to *lower* the inflation rate by reducing aggregate demand, the initial effect will be to increase the unemployment rate, perhaps significantly. While the inflation rate will fall as time passes, the initial (short-run) effects of reduced demand on prices will be moderated by the upward pressure on prices emanating from continuing increases in wages. Over time as unemployment rises, wage gains will become smaller and the decline in inflation will be more dramatic.

It seems that policymakers have some worrisome issues to weigh when formulating and implementing policy. An in-depth discussion of these issues is reserved for Part V; however, in the next section, we shall look at some of the implications of this analysis.

14-3
THE POLICY IMPLICATIONS
OF INFLATIONARY EXPECTATION

In the years immediately following the "discovery" of the Phillips curve (say, 1958–1967), the dominant view within the economics profession was that there existed a reasonably stable short-run Phillips curve which policymakers could use as a *quantitative* guide for policy. More specifically, the presumption was that policymakers could execute policies that would put the economy on the short-run curve and move it along that curve. Economists recognized that there were shifts in the short-run curve and that there might be a steeper (perhaps vertical) long-run curve; but the economists frequently downplayed these things on the presumption that they were of relatively minor importance over the time span—say four years or less—relevant to monetary and fiscal policymakers.

More recently, economists have developed considerable skepticism concerning the use of the Phillips curve as a quantitative guide for policy. Most economists now believe that various factors besides policy actions —such as changes in raw material prices, the productivity of labor, profit margins, and price expectations—can shift the aggregate supply-and-demand functions over the short run as well as the long run. The net result of such short-run shifts is an unstable and therefore unreliable short-run Phillips curve. An unreliable short-run Phillips curve is *at best* a qualitative guide to the short-run response of inflation and unemployment to changes in aggregate demand brought about by changes in monetary and fiscal policy.[1]

---

[1] Some economists would go further and argue that as the public have come to understand and learn to live with inflation, they have adjusted much more quickly to changes in actual and anticipated inflation. The implication is that the longer-run relationship between inflation and unemployment begins to assert itself in a much shorter period of time than previously was the case. "The long run is now!"

The implications of this discussion for monetary policy can be tentatively stated here and will be pursued in more detail later.

1

Once the public believes that inflation will persist, monetary policy actions will not easily lower the rate of inflation in the short run. Expectations of future price increases will raise wage demands and push up prices charged by firms. It could also lead the public to try to "beat" the expected price increases by buying before prices rise. This would increase their demand for goods and services over and above what it would have been otherwise. Such effects will increase the upward pressure on prices and thus partially offset, for a time at least, any policy actions designed to restrict the growth in aggregate demand and reduce inflationary pressures.

2

If the economy is operating below full employment, policy actions designed to raise the growth of aggregate demand will lower the unemployment rate and put upward pressure on prices. Over time, as labor markets tighten and price expectations are revised upward, the rate of inflation will accelerate. Once the rate of inflation accelerates, the problems outlined in the preceding paragraph become more evident.

It seems that, as a policymaker, you should either leave the economy alone in the short run or perform masterful doctoring so as not to trigger inflationary expectations. Is the former strategy an option? Is the latter feasible? These and other issues will be addressed in Part V.

14-4
APPENDIX A—THE
FORMATION OF PRICE EXPECTATIONS*

The expected rate of inflation *is* a major determinant of the interaction between aggregate supply and aggregate demand; therefore, it is also a major determinant of the relationship between inflation and unemployment. The important factor is how fast the public adjust their expectations to actual inflation. The slower and less complete this adjustment is, the slower

---

* This section contains optional material which can be omitted without loss of continuity throughout the rest of the text.

the response of wages and the more likely we are to observe a negative rather than a positive relationship between the rate of unemployment and inflation.

The weight of current research on the formation of price expectations suggests that the public do not adjust their expectations instantaneously. However, the evidence also suggests that as the public have come to develop an understanding of the process of inflation, the lag in adjusting their expectations has shortened considerably.

Considerable work has been done in recent years on the way in which the public form expectations in general and price expectations in particular. Equation (14-3) brings together the factors which this research suggests are important in determining expectations of future inflation.

$$(14\text{-}3) \qquad \qquad \dot{p}^e = f(\overset{+}{\dot{p}_L},\ \overset{+}{\dot{c}^e},\ \overset{+}{\dot{AD}^e})$$

where $\dot{p}^e$ = expected rate of inflation
$\dot{p}_L$ = a weighted average of current and past rates of inflation which measures the recent inflation experience
$\dot{c}^e$ = expected growth in costs of production (such as raw material prices or labor costs)
$\dot{AD}^e$ = expected growth in aggregate demand (as indicated by the growth of bank reserves, government expenditures, and so forth)

This equation suggests that the expected rate of inflation is dependent first on the public's experience with inflation—the actual (or realized) rates of inflation ($\dot{p}_L$). We measure this experience as a weighted average, but it is most likely that the rate of inflation in the recent past (say the last one to two years) is more influential in forming expectations about the future than inflation in the more distant past. Thus more recent years are weighted more heavily than earlier years. For example, if prices had been rising by about 5 percent per year for a decade and in the most recent two years by about 6 percent, then—all other factors being equal—the public will probably expect inflation in the coming year to be closer to 6 percent than to 5 percent.

Other factors that contribute to the formation of price expectations include the effect of expected changes in costs of production (will the price of oil rise or fall?) and in aggregate demand (will policy be expansionary or contractionary?). In trying to forecast and anticipate the future, it is unreasonable to believe that the public will take only the past into consideration. To follow up on the illustration above, if the public expect a large rise in the price of oil, government expenditures, or bank reserves in the coming year, they may adjust their expectation of inflation up to, say, 7 percent.

14-5
APPENDIX B—
POTENTIAL OUTPUT AND
GROWTH OVER THE LONG RUN*

Throughout most of this chapter, we have assumed that the size of the labor force and the capital stock were fixed. Thus the levels of employment and output consistent with full employment N_{fe} and y_{fe} were also constant. The aggregate supply curve turned vertical at y_{fe}, since y_{fe} represented economic capacity (the maximum level of output which could be produced). This is termed the *potential output* of the economy. In a long-run model, it must be recognized that potential output can be increased by growth of the labor force, capital accumulation, and technological improvements. In terms of our previous analysis, these factors will, over time, shift aggregate supply to the right, increasing the *level* of potential output.[1]

During a recession, output growth falls and usually becomes negative for a time. With the labor force growing but the growth in demand for labor slowing or even contracting, unemployment will of course be rising. As actual output growth slows or falls and potential output continues to grow, a "gap" is opened up between the actual level of output and potential output.[2] During an expansion, actual output can grow faster than potential output because of the gap opened up during the recession. In fact, the only way for the gap to be closed is for actual output to grow faster than potential output.

In Figure 14-15 we have drawn aggregate supply and demand curves which shift to the right so as to produce a steady rate of output growth equal to the growth of potential output at full employment, and a steady (constant) rate of inflation.[3]

Unfortunately, actual output does not grow steadily and at the same rate as the potential growth rate. And inflation has tended to fluctuate widely around a rising trend. We can, however, think of steady growth as a target toward which policymakers attempt to move the economy. Of course, in the real world, a variety of factors in addition to policy actions affect supply and demand. Furthermore, policymakers may not choose the "appropriate" growth rates of reserves and government expenditures or the "appropriate" structure of tax rates. As a result, nonsteady growth is the more typical case

---

* This section contains optional material which can be omitted without loss of continuity throughout the rest of the text.

[1] Significant increases in wages, raw material prices, or profit margins could be retarding the rightened shift and/or be shifting the supply curve up as it shifts right.

[2] This gap is often referred to as the "Okun gap." Arthur Okun, now of the Brookings Institution, developed the concept of the output gap when he was a member of President Kennedy's Council of Economic Advisors. By the way, you know you have really "made it" in economics, as in any social science, when your name is attached to some line, point, curve, or such.

[3] This result requires that the P and y axes be logarithmic scales.

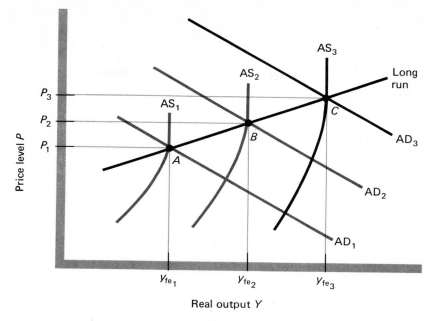

FIGURE 14-15

Beginning at an initial equilibrium point A, which is a short-run equilibrium point at full employment, aggregate demand and potential output are shown growing at the same rate. This results in a steady rate of inflation and a steady rate of growth in real output. The broad line connecting each of the short-run equilibrium points yields the long-run steady growth rate of the economy.

and inflation and unemployment vary over time around the steady growth rate trend. In the policy chapters of Part V, we shall look at the behavior of the policymakers in some detail and at the problems they face in making "appropriate" decisions.

14-6
SUMMARY OF MAJOR POINTS

1

In the short run, increases in the growth of aggregate demand (reflecting, say, stimulative monetary policy) will tend to lower the unemployment rate and raise the rate of inflation.

2

A sudden and significant surge in costs of production (reflecting, say, an increase in the price of oil) will tend to raise unemployment and inflation in the short run.

3

The "Phillips curve" relates the unemployment rate and the rate of inflation. In general, this relationship will depend on the interaction between movements in aggregate demand and aggregate supply. In the short run as aggregate demand rises, unemployment will tend to fall, and inflation will rise (the relationship is negative). However, as time passes and the public observes a tightening of labor markets and rising prices (which adversely affect their real incomes), demands for higher wages (in excess of productivity gains) will become more prevalent. The adverse effect on costs of production and therefore on the aggregate supply function will tend to put further upward pressure on prices and reverse—at least in part—the initial drop in unemployment. To the extent that wages respond to actual and anticipated inflation, the decline in unemployment that accompanies a rise in aggregate demand will be smaller and the inflation rate will be higher.

4

In the short run, factors such as contractual arrangements and government regulations make the structure of wages and prices sticky or rigid. Over the long run, such rigidities dissipate. This means that the long-run Phillips curve, which reflects the adjustments discussed in the preceding paragraph, is vertical. The worsening of the trade-off as time passes, along with the apparent instability of the short-run Phillips curves, has led many economists to argue that the Phillips curve is an unreliable guide for policymakers.

5

The expected rate of inflation is a major determinant of the interaction between aggregate supply and aggregate demand and therefore $\dot{p}^e$ is also a major determinant of the short- and long-run relationship between inflation and unemployment.* Research suggests that although expectations about future prices are based on a weighted average of current and past rates of inflation as well as on expectations about future changes in aggregate supply and demand, such future price expectations are formed slowly and with a lag. This lag in adjustment along with the institutional rigidities discussed in the preceding paragraph, suggests that we will probably observe in *the short run* a negative relationship between changes in the unemployment rate (brought about by changes in aggregate demand) and the inflation rate.

* Refers to the Appendixes (optional material).

6*

The level of output which could be produced if all factors of production were "fully employed" is referred to as "potential output." The rate of growth in potential output will depend on the growth of the labor force, capital formation, and productivity. Policymakers try to implement monetary and fiscal policy actions which will result in steady growth of aggregate demand at a rate consistent with the growth rate of potential output. This would keep the economy operating at or near full employment with little or no inflation. Unfortunately the more normal state of affairs is unsteady growth with cyclical fluctuations in inflation and unemployment. The key question is how policymakers can deal with these fluctuations and to what extent policy itself tends to cause them.

14-7
REVIEW QUESTIONS

1 What is the Phillips curve? How and why does the short-run relationship between inflation and unemployment differ from the relationship in the longer run?

2 The original Phillips curve is a very useful quantitative guide to policymakers." Discuss this statement.

3 Discuss briefly how the public's expectations about future inflation affect the aggregate supply curve.

*4 Discuss the major factors affecting the public's expectations about future inflation.

*5 Distinguish between the potential and actual rate of real GNP and explain the relationship between them during recessions and expansions.

6 In 1972–1973, economic activity accelerated, unemployment fell, and inflation began to drift up. During 1973–1974, monetary and fiscal policy became more restrictive and OPEC raised the price of oil by 400 percent. Economic activity slowed significantly in late 1974 and fell sharply in early 1975, as the economy fell into a deep recession. Unemployment rose and inflation slowed. Monetary and fiscal policy became increasingly stimulative

* Refers to the Appendixes (optional material).

as 1975 progressed. Economic activity recovered and GNP expanded through the end of 1978. Over this three-year period, unemployment gradually declined and inflation, especially in late 1977 and 1978, rose. Using the analysis developed in this and the previous chapter, draw a series of graphs that depict the movements in aggregate supply and demand and inflation and unemployment from 1972 to 1978. Explain intuitively what is happening on each.

14-8
SUGGESTED READINGS

1   For an excellent, nontechnical treatment of the Phillips curve see Thomas Humphrey, "Changing Views of the Phillips Curve," *Economic Review*, Federal Reserve Bank of Richmond (July 1973), 2–13.

2   For an excellent, nontechnical treatment of inflation see Thomas Humphrey, "Some Current Controversies in the Theory of Inflation," *Economic Review*, Federal Reserve Bank of Richmond (July–August 1976), 8–19.

3   The concept of potential output, its relationship to actual output, and the relevance of this comparison for policymakers is discussed in the *Economic Report of the President* (Washington: 1979), 72–76.

THE STRUCTURE
OF INTEREST RATES

Creditors have better memories than debtors.

James Howell

15-1
INTEREST RATES EVERYWHERE!

Through all the preceding chapters, we have frequently assumed that only one kind of interest-yielding financial asset is traded in financial markets. We referred to this financial asset with the catch-all term "bond." This simplifying assumption allowed us to make a further one—that there is only one interest rate, called "the" interest rate. These simplifications allowed us to study the determinants of the level of the interest rate, as we did in Chapters 13 and 14. Now, we are prepared to become more realistic and take into account the many different types of financial assets and interest rates.

Financial analysts have isolated and identified four factors as primarily responsible for determining the relationship among interest rates on different types of financial assets. These four factors are (1) term to maturity, (2) risk of default, (3) tax treatment, and (4) marketability. The first factor—term to maturity—affects the relationship among interest rates (that is, the yields from different financial assets) in various ways. There are many and complex theories about how term to maturity affects the structure of interest rates. Let us attack and discuss this tougher factor first, holding the other factors constant.

15-2
INTEREST-RATE DIFFERENTIALS:
THE ROLE OF TERM TO MATURITY

To examine how interest rates differ only with respect to term to maturity, see Table 15-1. This table shows the interest rates on U.S. Treasury securities of different maturities—from one-year to ten-year terms to maturity—on two different dates—September 8, 1977 and January 2, 1979. Figure 15-1 plots the relationship between the interest rates and their terms to maturity for each of these two dates.

The *yield curve* is a graphical representation of the relationship between yields (interest rates) on particular securities and their terms to maturity. Two yield curves are plotted in Figure 15-1.

Notice that on January 2, 1979, the one-year Treasury bond yield (interest rate) was 10.53 percent, while the yield on ten-year Treasury bonds was 9.16 percent. Thus the slope of the yield curve at that time was slightly negative, meaning that yields declined as the term to maturity increased. In contrast, on September 8, 1977, the yield curve had a positive slope, which means that yields rose with term to maturity.

TABLE 15-1
INTEREST RATES ON TREASURY SECURITIES

SEPTEMBER 8, 1977		JANUARY 2, 1979	
TERM TO MATURITY (YEARS)	INTEREST RATE (PERCENT)	TERM TO MATURITY (YEARS)	INTEREST RATE (PERCENT)
1	6.37	1	10.53
2	6.54	2	9.98
3	6.72	3	9.62
5	6.96	5	9.33
7	7.14	7	9.23
10	7.28	10	9.16

SOURCE: U.S. Treasury.

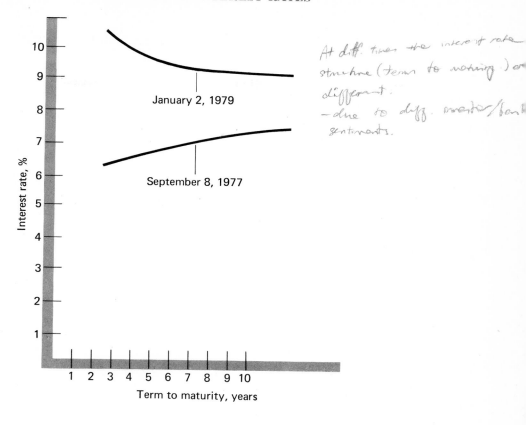

At diff. times the interest rate structure (term to maturity) are different.
– due to diff. investor/bank sentiments.

FIGURE 15-1

The yield curve shows the relationship between interest rates on particular types of securities and their terms to maturity. The yield curve for September 8 had a positive slope (yields rose with term to maturity), while the January 2 yield curve had a negative slope (yields fell with term to maturity). Various theories have been advanced to explain the _term structure of interest rates_.

The shape and slope of the yield curve is called the _term structure of interest rates_. What causes it to change shape over time?

Much has been written to explain the term structure of interest rates, but it all can be boiled down to three basic theories: the _expectations_ theory, the _liquidity preference_ theory, and the _segmented markets_ theory. To simplify our explanations of these theories, we shall assume that there are only two types of Treasury securities—those with a "short" term to maturity and those with a "long" term to maturity.

CRACKING THE CODE
IN THE TREASURY SECURITIES MARKET

In Chapter 12, we cracked the code in the corporate bond and stock transactions reports in the financial pages of the major United States newspapers. Now we thought you might be interested in learning how to read the reports of transactions in the Treasury securities market.

Treasury securities are particularly important because they are the basis of data from which most yield curves are drawn.

To understand how to read the accompanying table of transactions that occurred on March 9, 1979 (taken from *The Wall Street Journal* of March 12, 1979), let us take a look at the circled line. Under "rate" (first column) is listed "9¼s." This is the coupon rate, and it indicates that the holder of this security receives $9.25 for each $100 (face or par value), usually in semi-annual installments.

The maturity date (second column) is 1982, May. This simply indicates that the security will mature in May of 1982.

Following the maturity date is the letter "n." This indicates that the security is a note. The only distinction between notes and bonds is that the original maturity (maturity when issued) for notes is ten years or less, while that for bonds is over ten years.

The next two columns give the "bid" and "asked" prices. The bid price is the price the dealer is willing to pay to acquire this security; the asked price is the price the dealer is asking to sell the security. Prices are quoted in thirty-seconds. Thus 100.7 bid means $100^7/_{32}$ or $100.21875 per each $100. (Hence for a $1000 bond, the bid price is $1002.1875.) The asked price is 100.11 which means $100^{11}/_{32}$ or 100.34375 per $100. (For a $1000 bond, the asked price is $1003.4375).

The column labeled "bid chg" shows that the bid for this particular government security was down $^2/_{32}$ at the close of business on March 9, 1979, compared with the previous trading day.

The last column gives the yield to maturity on this note. It is 9.12 percent on an annual basis. Recall that the yield to maturity takes into account the return to the investor of both the coupon yield and the price appreciation or depreciation between the time when the security is bought and when it matures. In this case, there will be a slight depreciation at maturity; the security is selling at a slight premium (that is, the market price of $1002.1875 exceeds the face value of $1000).

Friday, March 9, 1979
Over-the-Counter quotations; sources on request.
Decimals in bid-and-asked and bid changes represent
32nds; 101.1 means 101 1/32. a-Plus 1/64. b-Yield to call
date. d-Minus 1/64. n-Treasury notes.

Treasury Bonds and Notes

Rate	Mat.	Date	Bid	Asked	Bid Chg.	Yld.
6s,	1979	Mar n..............	99.22	99.26+	.1	9.55
5⅞s,	1979	Apr n..............	99.13	99.17+	.1	9.25
7⅞s,	1979	May n..............	99.18	99.22....		9.46
6⅛s,	1979	May n..............	99.3	99.7 +	.1	9.63
6⅛s,	1979	Jun n..............	98.24	98.28....		9.85
7¾s,	1979	Jun n..............	99.9	99.13+	.1	9.63
6¼s,	1979	Jul n..............	98.17	98.21+	.1	9.79
6¼s,	1979	Aug n..............	98.12	98.16....		9.84
6⅞s,	1979	Aug n..............	98.20	98.24....		9.86
6⅝s,	1979	Aug n..............	98.13	98.17....		9.91
6¾s,	1979	Sep n..............	98.5	98.9 +	.1	9.91
8½s,	1979	Sep n..............	99.7	99.11+	.2	9.75
7¼s,	1979	Oct n..............	98.7	98.11 −	.1	10.00
6¼s,	1979	Nov n..............	97.15	97.19+	.1	10.02
6⅝s,	˙˙79	Nov n....... ..	97.21	˙˙ ˙˙		9.˙˙
7s	19͏81	˙˙	9͏˙	97.2͏6 −		˙˙
˙˙s,	1981	Sep	˙.26	93.30....		9.48
7s,	1981	Nov n..............	94.7	94.11....		9.44
7¾s,	1981	Nov n..............	96.1	96.5 −	.1	9.40
7¼s,	1981	Dec n..............	94.22	94.30....		9.35
6⅛s,	1982	Feb n..............	92.8	92.16 −	.1	9.10
6⅜s,	1982	Feb...............	92.20	92.28 −	.2	9.21
7⅞s,	1982	Mar n..............	96.7	96.11 −	.1	9.28
7s,	1982	May n..............	93.26	94.2 −	.1	9.19
8s,	1982	May n..............	96.25	97.1 ...		9.09
9¼s,	1982	May n..............	100.7	100.11 −	.2	9.12
8½s,	1982	Jun n..............	97.7	97.11 −	.1	9.20
8⅛s,	1982	Aug n..............	96.25	96.29 −	.1	9.20
8¾s,	1982	Sep n..............	97.17	97.21 −	.1	9.16
7⅛s,	1982	Nov n..............	93.14	93.18 −	.1	9.22
7⅞s,	1982	Nov n..............	95.24	95.28 −	.2	9.22
9⅜s,	1982	Dec n..............	100.15	100.19 −	.3	9.19
8s,	1983	Feb n..............	96.3	96.7 −	.1	9.17
9¼s,	1983	Mar n..............	100.1	100.3 −	.3	9.22
7⅞s,	1983	May n..............	95.15	95.19 −	.1	9.17
3¼s,	1978-83	Jun..............	82.6	83.6 −	.6	7.98
7s,	1983	Nov n..............	91.24	91.28 −	.4	9.18
7¼s,	1984	Feb n..............	92.14	93.18 −	.1	9.17
6⅞s,	1984	Aug..............	88.14	88.30....		9.00
7¼s,	1984	Aug n..............	91.28	92 −	.4	9.15
8s,	1985	Feb n..............	95.8	95.12+	.1	9.02
3¼s,	1985	May..............	76.12	77.12 −	.10	7.95
4¼s,	1975-85	May..............	79.20	80.20 −	.2	8.32
8¼s,	1985	Aug n..............	95.20	95.24 −	.6	9.14
7⅞s,	1986	May n..............	93.12	93.16 −	.1	9.12
˙˙	1986	....	93.24	93.28 −	.8	9.˙˙
8⅞s,	˙˙	Aug..............	˙˙	˙˙˙.4 ˙		9.08
8⅝s,	1993	Nov..............	96.2	9˙...−	.8	9.08
9s,	1994	Feb..............	99.10	99.12 −	.5	9.08
4⅛s,	1989-94	May..............	76.10	77.10+	.2	6.50
3s,	1995	Feb..............	76	77 −	.4	5.13
7s,	1993-98	May..............	83.6	84.6 −	.4	8.71
3½s,	1998	Nov..............	76.2	77.2 −	.2	5.41
8½s,	1994-99	May..............	95.2	95.10 −	.6	9.01
7⅞s,	1995-00	Feb..............	89.2	89.10 −	.8	9.03
8⅜s,	1995-00	Aug..............	93.16	93.24 −	.5	9.04
8s,	1996-01	Aug..............	90.2	90.10 −	.10	9.01
8¼s,	2000-05	May..............	92.14	92.22 −	.6	8.98
7⅝s,	2002-07	Feb..............	86.12	86.20 −	.6	8.93
7⅞s,	2002-07	Nov..............	90.18	90.26 −	.10	8.75
8⅜s,	2003-08	Aug..............	93.14	93.22 −	.6	8.99
8¾s,	2003-08	Nov..............	97	97.2 −	.10	9.04

n— Treasury notes.

U.S. Treas. Bills

Mat	Bid Discount	Ask	Mat	Bid Discount	Ask	Mat	Bid Discount	Ask	Mat	Bid Discount	Ask
3-15	9.93	9.69	7- 5	9.51	9.41	5-10	9.59	9.45	8-30	9.54	9.48
3-22	9.96	9.72	7-12	9.54	9.42	5-17	9.58	9.44	9- 6	9.53	9.51
3-29	9.93	9.65	7-19	9.54	9.42	5-24	9.56	9.42	9-18	9.53	9.45
4- 3	9.72	9.44	7-24	9.56	9.44	5-29	9.55	9.41	10-16	9.53	9.43
4- 5	9.79	9.55	7-26	9.54	9.42	5-31	9.57	9.47	11-13	9.53	9.43
4-12	9.80	9.58	8- 2	9.54	9.44	6- 7	9.52	9.50	12-11	9.54	9.44
4-19	9.75	9.67	8- 9	9.54	9.44	6-14	9.53	9.41	1- 8	9.52	9.44
4-26	9.72	9.54	8-16	9.56	9.44	6-21	9.51	9.39	2- 5	9.51	9.43
5- 1	9.59	9.41	8-21	9.56	9.46	6-26	9.51	9.37	3- 4	9.48	9.46
5- 3	9.60	9.46	8-23	9.55	9.47	6-28	9.48	9.36			

Whenever the security sells at a premium, the yield to maturity is less than the coupon rate. Can you explain why the yield to maturity exceeds the coupon rate when the security sells at a discount (market price is less than the face value)? *bec at maturity you'll get + face value higher → yield↑*

Quotations for Treasury bills are also shown in the accompanying table. When issued, all Treasury bills carry maturities of one year or less. Unlike notes and bonds, which pay interest in semiannual installments (by way of the coupons), Treasury bills are issued at a discount from par—that is, at a price less than $100 per $100 of face or par value. The investor pays, say, $99 and at maturity receives $100.

Look at the circled bill quotation. The maturity date of the bill is 4-5, which means April 5, 1979 (we know it is 1979 because no bills carry maturities of more than one year). Dealers are bidding 9.79 percent for the issue and asking 9.55 percent. These bid and asked quotations are in terms of annual yield. Unlike the note and bond quotations which were in terms of prices, bill quotations are expressed in terms of annual yield (this is all part of a conspiracy to make cracking the code difficult). The higher yield (on the bid side) means that a lower price is being offered by the dealers to buy the Treasury bill and the lower yield on the asked side indicates that the dealer is selling the bills at a higher price (remember the inverse relationship between security yields and security prices, page 241).

THE EXPECTATIONS APPROACH

To understand the expectations theory about the term structure of interest rates, let us begin by assuming that you have funds to lend and that the current yield on a one-year security—a "short"-term security—is 5 percent per year and the current yield on a two-year security—a "long"-term security—is 6 percent per year. Now suppose that you and everyone else with funds available to lend expect that the yield on short-term (one-year) securities will be 9 percent one year from now. Assuming that you have no preference as to holding one-year or two-year securities, that is, you do not have a preference for either short- or long-term securities, which would you acquire now? (The assumption of indifference to short- or long-term securities is quite important, as we shall see later.) You will acquire the security with the highest expected rate of return. But which of the two—the one-year or the two-year—gives the highest expected rate of return?

The answer is arrived at in two simple steps: (1) calculate the return from acquiring the one-year security now plus the expected return from a one-year security one year from now; then (2) compare it with the 6 percent return you would earn by acquiring the two-year security now. The two consecutive one-year securities would be expected to yield an average rate of return of (5 percent + 9 percent)/2 = 7 percent. From the lender's viewpoint, *two consecutive one-year short-term securities will be more attractive than the long-term security as long as the average of the current short-term yield and the expected short-term yield is greater than the current long-term yield*. Note that *the key to the choice here is the expected short rate in the future*.

The above strategy based on expectations was developed from the demand side of the market for bonds, that is, from the point of view of the lender. But do not forget, there is also a supply side of the market for bonds. The expectations of the borrower are also very important. Suppose you need funds for two years and the choice is between selling a security for two years with an interest rate of 6 percent per year versus selling a one-year security at 5 percent per year now and selling another one-year security one year from now at an *expected* 9 percent rate. What would you do? Presumably, you would sell a two-year security with an annual interest rate of 6 percent rather than sell two consecutive one-year securities having an expected average annual interest rate of 7 percent.

When borrowers believe that the average of current and future interest rates on "shorts" exceeds the rate on "longs," they will increase their current supply of "longs," thus tending to raise the interest rate on the latter. That is, borrowers will want to sell two-year bonds, thus increasing their supply and thereby requiring higher interest rates to be paid on them to clear the market.

Taken together, the effects of investor and borrower expectations on the demand and supply for securities, respectively, determine the structure of interest rates. According to the expectations approach, we should expect the long-term interest rate to be the average of current plus expected future short-term rates. One can, in fact, examine the term structure and extract from it the exact level of future expected short rates.

To illustrate: examine the one-year and two-year rates for September 8, 1977, in Table 15-1. If long rates are the average of current and expected short rates, this means that the two-year rate—6.54 percent—is the average of the current one-year rate—6.37 percent—and the expected one-year rate one year from now. Simple algebra reveals that (if the theory is correct) this future expected short rate must be 6.71 percent:

(a) The current one-year rate = 6.37 percent.
(b) The implicit one-year rate expected to prevail one year from now = x (this is what we are solving for).
(c) The average of the current one-year rate and the one-year rate expected to prevail one year from now = 6.54 percent.
(d) Therefore $(6.37 + x)/2 = 6.54$ and $x = 6.71$ percent.

With reference to the yield curves shown in Figure 15-1, the expectations approach would interpret the shape of the January 2 curve as indicating that investors expect future short-term rates to decline. Since the two-year rate is below the one-year rate and the two-year rate is (according to the expectations theory) the average of the current one-year rate and the one-year rate expected one year from now, the one-year rate expected to prevail one year from now must be less than the current one-year rate. The shape of the September 8 yield curve indicates that investors expected future short rates to rise. Can you explain why?

Some important assumptions implicit in the expectations theory are as follows: (1) transactions costs associated with buying or selling securities are negligible; (2) lenders (and borrowers) as a group have no preference between longs and shorts (or, saying the same thing in another way, longs and shorts are close substitutes for one another); and (3) market participants have similar expectations as to the future course of interest rates.

As you might suspect, the following approaches to the explanation of the term structure of interest rates take some exception to one or more of these assumptions.

THE LIQUIDITY PREFERENCE APPROACH

The liquidity preference approach to the term structure of interest rates is a variation of the expectations approach. The basis of the liquidity preference approach is that most people recognize that we live in an uncertain world and that most borrowers and lenders are risk-averse.

What does this have to do with interest rates? In general, lower risk is associated with short-term securities; long-term securities are considered to carry a higher risk.[1] Therefore, risk-averse investors would prefer short-term rather than long-term investments. In addition, short-term investments are more liquid, and risk-averse investors will have a preference for liquidity.

To understand better the ideas of risk aversion and liquidity preference, think for a moment about your life. You are fairly certain about what you will do tomorrow, but what can you say about what you will be doing ten years from now? The same kind of reasoning applies to expectations about future interest rates. Investors may feel secure about estimates of interest rates in the immediate future, but they do not feel as confident about estimates into the distant future; for distant estimates, errors in estimation are more likely. This increased chance of error means an investor feels that more risk is associated with the purchase of long-term securities than with short-term securities. Hence, the liquidity approach suggests that investors prefer short-term securities.

---

[1] We are not referring to the risk of default (covered later on in the chapter). The risk we are concerned with here is the possibility of an unexpected *rise* in interest rates which will *lower* the price of long-term securities.

WHAT IS RISK AVERSION?

Risk-averse investors (and we assume most are) will avoid assets with higher risk vis-à-vis assets with lower risk if the expected returns are the same. Suppose a lender is in the process of deciding which of two financial assets (A or B) to acquire. Assume the expected rate of return on both assets over the next year is 10 percent. However, suppose the *probability* of earning 10 percent on asset A is 1 (100 percent), but the probability of earning 10 percent on asset B is only ½ (50 percent) and there is a ¼ (25 percent) chance the return on asset B will be zero and ¼ (25 percent) chance the return on asset B will be 20 percent. The expected return on both assets is 10 percent. (You calculate the expected return by multiplying the potential return by the probability of that return: asset A (10 percent × 1.0 = 10 percent); asset B (10 percent × ½ + 0 percent × ¼ + 20 percent × ¼ = 10 percent).

In this example, the possible variance of the return on asset B makes it more risky; thus the risk-averse investor will prefer asset A.

In general an investor would only be willing to acquire risky assets if the expected return exceeds the return available on low-risk assets. For bearing additional risk, lenders must be rewarded with higher returns paid by the borrowers who issue risky securities.

For example, suppose the current one-year interest rate, the current two-year rate, and the one-year rate expected one year from now all are 5 percent. According to the expectations theory, the yield curve would be flat and investors (lenders) would be indifferent between one-year versus two-year bonds. However, the preceding discussion implies that our risk-averse investor would *prefer* to acquire the one-year bonds—that is, the investor is *not* indifferent. If the investor bought the two-year bonds, he or she would run the risk that the one-year rate next year could actually be higher than the estimate of 5 percent. For instance, suppose the one-year rate next year turned out to be 6 percent instead of 5 percent. If rates were to increase next year, the price of the two-year bond with one year to maturity would have to fall (a capital loss) to equate its rate of return with the higher rate on a *new* one-year security. If the investor had to sell the two-year bond at the end of the first year, the realized rate of return would

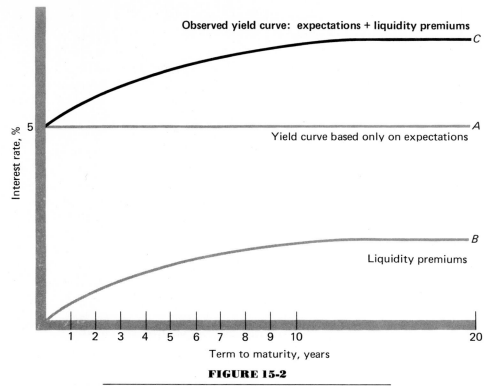

FIGURE 15-2

Liquidity premiums and term to maturity. Because long-term securities are usually less liquid and more risky than short-term securities, risk-averse investors must be "bribed" to buy them with liquidity premiums which rise with term to maturity.

be less than anticipated at the time of purchase—the 5 percent earned the first year minus the capital loss. Of course, if the two-year bond is held to maturity, there would be no actual capital loss, but the actual rate of return will be lower than two one-year securities would have generated. Also, remember that a bondholder may need funds and therefore may have to liquidate the bond before maturity. If this were the case, an actual capital loss could be incurred. Such possibilities give rise to a preference for liquidity.

What all this implies is that investors must be "bribed" with a sweetener to buy long-term securities. This sweetener is referred to as a *liquidity premium*, which can be illustrated with the help of Figure 15-2. Suppose the current short rate and expected short rate were both 5 percent. The expectations approach suggests that the yield curve would be flat (curve A). However, we just implied in the preceding discussion that bond sellers have to offer an interest premium to get investors to buy bonds having long-term maturities. The size of the premiums is presumed to rise with the term to maturity. Curve B in Figure 15-2 depicts the size of such interest premiums—liquidity premiums—at each maturity. Curve C represents the yield curve actually observed: the components of the total yield (curve C) are the interest-rate expectations (curve A) and the liquidity premiums, represented by the liquidity preference curve (curve B).

By way of contrast, note that the expectations approach would explain the shape of the yield curve depicted by curve C as one which indicates that market participants expect rates to rise over time.

The previous discussion looks to the demand side of the market. But let us not lose sight of the behavior of the suppliers of debt, which is implied by the liquidity approach. *If liquidity premiums exist, this means that borrowers are willing to pay them.* But why would borrowers be willing to pay more to borrow for two years than they expect to pay by borrowing for one year now and for one year a year from now? Here again risk aversion and uncertainty play the key roles. There is some chance that one-year rates will be higher one year from now than the one-year rates are now. If higher-than-expected rates were to materialize next year, then borrowing for one year now and refinancing one year from now would prove to be more expensive than borrowing for two years now. Also, the firm could suffer some difficulty in the coming year, which might reduce its credit rating and make it difficult to acquire funds one year from now. By borrowing long term, the probability of such problems can be reduced.

In sum, the fact that yield curves have almost always been positively sloped over the past twenty-five years has suggested to many that liquidity premiums do, in fact, exist. Theoretical considerations on both the supply and demand side of the securities markets and a variety of empirical studies seem to support such a judgment.[1]

THE SEGMENTED MARKETS APPROACH

A third approach to explaining the relationship between the structure of interest rates and the term to maturity is the segmented markets approach. This approach emphasizes the fact that many market participants do not consider shorts and longs as close substitutes for one another.

For example, life insurance companies prefer long-term assets. The liabilities of life insurance companies—payments due to the beneficiary upon the death of the insured—are also long-term and quite predictable (given data on life expectancy and so on). Therefore, life insurance companies tend to match the long terms of their liabilities with long-term assets. Life insurance companies do not need much liquidity; therefore they do not need many short-term assets, preferring long-term assets instead.[2]

[1] Early work in this area was carried out by Reuben Kessel. See his *The Cyclical Behavior of Interest Rates* (National Bureau of Economic Research, 1965), Occasional Paper no. 91.

[2] The segmented markets approach is sometimes referred to as the "institutional" approach, since it focuses on the behavior of particular institutions with regard to asset-liability choice. It is also called the "hedging pressure" approach, since by matching maturities of assets and liabilities (assuming the yield on the former exceeds that on the latter), an institution is hedging against an adverse movement in the yield on asset holdings.

Banks, on the other hand, are presumed to value liquidity because of the possibility of volatile deposit flows. Hence, banks would prefer short-term assets.

Corporations tend to finance inventories in short-term markets (bank loans and commercial paper) and to finance purchases of new equipment and the construction of new plants in long-term markets (stocks and bonds). The point of these examples is that many institutions have preferred maturities or *habitats* in the market. For these institutions, shorts and longs are poor substitutes for one another. If that is the case, then the market for shorts is essentially separate from the market for longs. Another way of looking at it is that the overall market for securities can be *segmented* into long and short markets. Interest rates in each segment will then respond to supply and demand pressures in that segment. The other approaches—the expectations approach and the liquidity preference approach—tend to view the long and short markets as integrated. Of course, "segmented" does not mean *totally* separate or independent; it does mean that the greater distance there is between the maturity of one security and the maturity of another, the less substitutable they are for each other.

COMBINING THE VARIOUS APPROACHES

There is little doubt that many borrowers and lenders have preferred maturities, creating market segmentation. Nevertheless, the short and long markets are not watertight compartments. Furthermore, expectations about the future course of interest rates do play a role in portfolio choice.

Burton Malkiel, an expert on the term structure of interest rates, has said: "Segmentation must be reinterpreted to mean simply that many buyers and sellers must be paid differential premiums to induce them to move from their preferred maturities."[1] In general, there is a continuum of investors and borrowers along the maturity spectrum who engage in portfolio actions that link together the yields on shorts and longs. As Malkiel argues: "These investors provide the links in a continuous chain tying together all maturity sectors of the bond market, and ensure that expectations play an important role in shaping the yield curve."[2]

While longs and shorts are not good substitutes for one another in many borrower and lender portfolios, research has demonstrated that expectations do affect portfolio choice and that many investors are willing to switch habitats (preferred maturities) if the interest rate differential (bribe) is "large enough."

---

[1] Burton Malkiel, *The Term Structure of Interest Rates: Theory, Empirical Evidence, and Applications* (Morristown, N.J.: General Learning Press, 1970), p. 21.
[2] Ibid., p. 22.

In combining the three approaches to explaining the term structure of interest rates, we can view the current long-term rate of interest i_L as being a function of the current short rate i_s, the expected path of future short rates i_s^e, and liquidity premiums l.

$$\text{(15-1)} \qquad\qquad i_L = f(\overset{+}{i_s}, \overset{+}{i_s^e}, \overset{+}{l})$$

The relationship between the current long-term rate of interest and each of the determinants is given by the sign over the variables. We would expect current long rates to rise if current short rates rise, if investors revise their expectations about future short rates upward, or if liquidity premiums rise. Each of these factors is positively related to the long-term rate of interest.

Assuming for simplicity that $l = 0$, two key questions should be addressed if Equation (15-1) is to have any real meaning: (1) what is the quantitative impact of a change in i_s on i_L and (2) what determines i_s^e?

The answer to the first question can be seen best through a simple example. Ignoring liquidity premiums, the rate on, say, twenty-year securities would be equal to the average of the current short (one-year) rate and the expected path of the short rate over the next nineteen years. Assuming that $i_s = 5$ percent and this rate is expected to prevail over the next nineteen years (that is, $i_s^e = 5$ percent), it must follow that $i_L = 5$ percent. Now suppose the current short rate rises to 6 percent *but* i_s^e remains at 5 percent; then $i_L = 5.05$.

(a) i_L = twenty-year security = average of current short rate and expected short rates over next nineteen years

(b) Original case $i_L = \dfrac{5 + (19 \times 5)}{20}$

$$i_L = \frac{100}{20} = 5 \text{ percent}$$

(c) New case $i_L = \dfrac{6 + (19 \times 5)}{20}$

$$i_L = \frac{101}{20} = 5.05 \text{ percent}$$

Although i_s has risen by one percent (5 to 6), i_L rises by only .05 percent (5 to 5.05). Since the change in current short rates affects only the first term in a sequence of twenty, the change in i_L is one-twentieth of the change in i_s. Note that the key assumption responsible for this result is that changes in i_s do not cause participants in the financial market to revise their expectations about future short rates (i_s^e).

In reality, changes in current short rates, along with other factors, do affect expectations about the future course of short rates. This, in turn, affects long rates. Experience suggests that, on average, long rates (say the rate on twenty-year bonds) change by about one-fourth to one-third of the change in short rates.

This brings us to the second question—what determines i_s^e? It seems sensible to believe, and considerable research has shown, that market participants take into account the past and present when forming their expectations about the future. To be more specific, the past movement of interest rates, the current state of the economy, and the actions (past and present) of fiscal and monetary policymakers all affect expectations about short-term interest rates. These can be illustrated by example.

If current short-term rates are at historically high levels, then this may be one piece of information leading investors to believe that short-term rates will fall in the future. If the economy is entering a recession, participants may believe that the forthcoming fall in credit demands—the mirror image of which is a fall in the supply of securities—will lead to a fall in future short rates.

Finally, if the rate of inflation has been rising or is expected to rise, market participants may expect interest rates to be under upward pressure in the future as borrowers and lenders adjust their behavior to the higher expected inflation. The relationship between inflation and interest rates is important; let us examine this issue more closely.

15-3
INTEREST RATES AND INFLATION

It is now widely agreed that actual inflation *and* expectations of inflation in the future affect interest rates—both long- and short-term. The nature of this relationship can be illustrated with a simple example.

If you were to lend your friend $100 today and she agreed to pay it back one year from now with 5 percent interest ($100 + $5), you might consider yourself $5 richer and a shrewd financier. Your $100 of capital would have earned $5 of nominal interest income for you. However, if during the year the inflation rate were 5 percent, the real value of your capital plus interest would be exactly the same as the real value of your capital at the beginning of the year. In fact, if the inflation rate were greater than 5 percent, your friend would be paying you back dollars one year from now which would buy less goods and services than they would today. The shrewd financier in this case would be your friend, not you!

Hence it would seem clear that when you make a loan, you should be concerned about two things: *nominal interest*—how many dollars you will receive in the future in return for lending now—and *inflation*—how much these dollars will be worth upon repayment (the purchasing power of the dollars). An investment bearing even a relatively high market interest rate may not be attractive to lenders if, due to price inflation, the dollars which are later repaid have less purchasing power than the dollars originally lent.

The implication of all this is that the market (or stated) interest rate—something called the *nominal* rate—is not an adequate measure of the *real* return on an investment unless there is assurance of price stability. Rather, the appropriate measure of the *real* interest rate (real return) is the return on an investment corrected for changes in the purchasing power of money. *The real interest rate is calculated by subtracting from the nominal market yield on the investment the rate of price inflation expected to prevail in the period until maturity.* For example, if an investor expected inflation of 4 percent, then an investment bearing 7 percent nominal interest will be expected to yield only 3 percent in real terms. If expected inflation were 7 percent, the investment bearing 7 percent nominal interest would yield nothing in real terms and investors who are not victims of "money illusion" —valuing money for itself rather than for what it will buy—will not invest. Wise investors will concern themselves with the market interest rate only insofar as it enters their calculation of the real interest rate.

Another way of viewing this is that the market interest rate (nominal rate) is composed of two parts—a real interest rate plus an inflation premium. The inflation premium will be adjusted in response to changes in current and expected inflation rates, raising or lowering the overall market rate of interest.

The first economist to analyze statistically the relationship between inflation and real and market rates of interest was Irving Fisher—a prominent early-twentieth-century economist. The available evidence, such as that shown in Figure 15-3, does show that market rates of interest are highly correlated with inflation and inflationary expectations.

The reasons for this correlation are not complicated. Suppose the commercial paper rate is 9 percent and the current and expected rate of inflation is 7 percent. This means that the expected real interest rate is 2 percent. What happens if firms revise their expectations of future inflation upward to 10 percent? If the commercial paper rate remains at 9 percent, they would expect the real rate—the real cost of borrowing funds—to be minus 1 percent. Such a good deal should lead to a considerable increase in the demand for funds. The rise in demand should begin to put upward pressure on the commercial paper rate. What about lenders of funds in the commercial paper market? Initially, they would have expected a real return of 2 percent $(9 - 7 = 2)$. If lenders also revise the expectations of inflation upward to 10 percent, it seems reasonable to presume that an expected real return of minus 1 percent would make them less willing to lend and thus reduce the supply of funds available in the commercial paper market. The reduction in supply would also put upward pressure on the commercial paper rate.

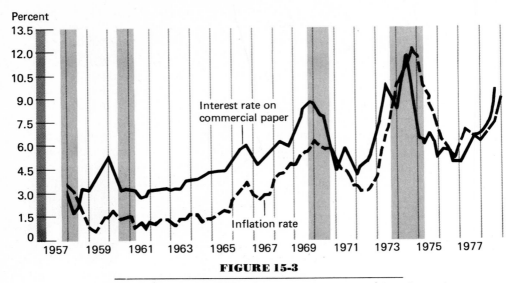

FIGURE 15-3

The inflation rate equals the year-over-year percent change in
the Consumer Price Index. When inflation accelerates, market interest rates usually rise.

In sum, expectations of inflation affect portfolio decisions that determine the demand for and supply of funds. Since interest rates respond to
changes in demand and supply and inflation affects demand and supply,
expectations of inflation affect interest rates—both long- and short-term.

15-4
RATE DIFFERENTIALS:
RISK, LIQUIDITY, AND TAXES

The previous section dealt with interest rates on securities that were alike
in every respect except one—term to maturity. Now we will extend our discussion and examine the relationship among interest rates on securities
with the same term to maturity but that differ with regard to default risk,
liquidity (marketability), or taxability.

DEFAULT RISK

The term "default risk" refers to the probability of a debtor defaulting, that
is, not paying the principal and/or the interest due on an outstanding debt.
The two major credit-rating agencies, Standard & Poor's and Moody's, evaluate a borrower's probability of default and assign the borrower to a particular risk class. With this information, a lender can determine to what degree
a borrower will be able to meet debt obligations. Both Standard & Poor's
and Moody's distinguish among nine different types of borrower risks. Table
15-2 reproduces the nine credit ratings with a brief description of each.

TABLE 15-2
CREDIT RATINGS

MOODY'S	GENERAL DESCRIPTION	STANDARD & POOR'S
Aaa	Best quality, the smallest risk	AAA
Aa	High quality	AA
A	Higher medium grade	A
Baa	Medium grade	BBB
Ba	Lower medium grade, having speculative elements	BB
B	Lacks characteristics of desirable investment	B
Caa	Poor standing	B
Ca	Highly speculative	B
C	Lowest grade (in default)	D

In the case of business firms, the credit-rating agencies examine the pattern of revenues and costs experienced by a firm, its leverage ratio, its past history of debt redemption, and the volatility of the industry, among other things.[1] A firm with a history of strong earnings, low leverage, and prompt debt redemption would get an Aaa rating. Firms that have experienced net losses, have rising leverage, and have missed some loan payments would get a Baa or lower rating.

United States government securities are viewed as relatively riskless. That is, most investors would assign a zero probability to the federal government going broke; after all, the government has broad powers to tax to cover any debt.

Because United States government securities are riskless, they are not even rated. They are assumed to come above the AAA or Aaa ratings. If investors are indeed risk-averse, they would expect to get a higher yield from an AAA- or Aaa-rated security than from a government security of the same maturity. (Remember that risk aversion implies that a higher expected return is necessary to induce an investor to accept more risk.) Obviously, we can take this one step further: for securities having the same maturity, an AA or Aa security would be expected to yield more than a less risky AAA or Aaa security, a BBB or Baa security would be expected to yield more than an A security of the same maturity, and so on down the credit ratings shown in the table.

To illustrate the relationship between default risk and yield, see Figure 15-4, which shows the spread between the interest rate on AAA- and Baa-rated municipal bonds. Note that the spread varies considerably from year to year. There are two basic reasons for this. First, all investors can become more risk-averse at particular points in time. This means that lower-rated

---

[1] The agencies also assign ratings to securities issued by state and local governments. Factors considered would include the tax base, the level of outstanding debt, the current and expected budget situation, the growth in spending, etc.

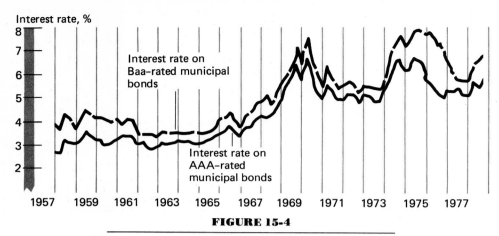

FIGURE 15-4

The spread between Baa-rated municipal bonds and AAA-rated bonds widened considerably during 1974–1975 as the financial problems plaguing some municipal governments (like New York City) became more generally known.

bond issuers will have to pay a larger risk premium to borrow (the spread widens). Second, the supply of low-rated issues relative to the supply of high-rated issues can change. We would expect the spread between the two to narrow when the supply of AAA issues grew relative to the supply of Baa issues and vice versa.

A dramatic example of the first point can be seen by examining in Figure 15-4 the AAA to Baa spread in the municipal market in 1974–1975. Note that the spread widened considerably. This occurred because the profound financial problems confronting New York City became public knowledge and investors became increasingly fearful that New York City would default on its outstanding securities. This development had direct effects on the yields of New York City bonds in the secondary market and had indirect effects on the yields of bonds of other municipalities. Other major cities (such as Philadelphia, Cleveland, and Boston) were experiencing similar financial problems. All this led investors to reevaluate the creditworthiness of many municipal bonds, especially the lower-rated ones. All this was occurring as the economy was sliding into its worst post-World War II recession, a fact that worsened the difficult financial problems facing many debtors. With municipal tax revenues declining, is it any wonder investors demanded higher yields on bonds issued by lower-rated municipalities?

LIQUIDITY OR MARKETABILITY

In Chapter 12, we spent considerable time discussing and analyzing the various sectors of the financial markets (municipal, corporate, government, etc.) and the behavior of dealers and brokers who "make markets" in the various securities. We pointed out that the quality of the secondary market for securities varied directly with the willingness of brokers and dealers to make markets in particular types of securities. Not surprisingly, the willingness of market makers to perform this function is determined by how much profit they can earn. And their profitability is a function of the volume of transactions in the market they make.

How does this affect the liquidity of a security and how does liquidity affect yields? "Liquidity," as you may remember, refers to the time and cost involved in exchanging an asset for money. To illustrate, a Treasury security is quite liquid. There is an active, high-quality secondary market reflecting the large number of market makers, the large number of buyers and sellers, and the large volume of issues outstanding (approximately $850 billion in 1979). As you might expect, a government security is much more liquid than a small, infrequently traded corporate issue, even if the corporate issue is highly rated.

Securities having the same maturity and the same quality but different liquidities will have correspondingly different rates of return. The less liquid securities will offer higher rates of return. Investors want to be compensated for the lower liquidity of an asset.

TAXABILITY

The last major feature influencing the structure of interest rates is the taxability of securities. As you may know, interest income earned from bonds issued by state and local governments is exempt from the federal income tax.[1] This means, for example, that if you are in the 50 percent federal income tax bracket, a 4½ percent interest rate on a municipal bond is equivalent to a 9 percent interest rate on, say, a taxable corporate bond; after taxes, both yield 4½ percent. The tax-exempt status of municipal bonds makes them quite attractive to taxpayers in high tax brackets. This is one reason why commercial banks and casualty insurance companies, which are both financial intermediaries and subject to the 46 percent corporate income tax, have traditionally been heavy purchasers of municipal securities.[2]

How does the yield on tax-exempt securities relate to the yields on other types of securities? You might begin to answer by guessing that the yield on tax-exempt municipal bonds would be equal to the yield on similarly rated corporate bonds minus the average tax rate of municipal bond purchasers multiplied by the corporate yield. For example, suppose the rate on AAA-rated corporate bonds is 9 percent and the average tax rate of buyers

---

[1] It is also true that interest earned on federal government securities is exempt from state and local income taxes.

[2] For commercial banks, there is an additional factor at work. There is often subtle pressure to purchase the securities issued by municipalities in the immediate geographical area. With the banks' resources—that is, deposits—coming from the local citizens, such purchases are viewed as an investment in the community the bank serves, an investment that demonstrates the goodwill and intentions of the bank.

is 50 percent, meaning that half the interest income will be taxed away. If the only difference between the corporate bond and a AAA-rated municipal bond is that the interest on corporate bonds is taxable, while the interest on the municipal bond is not, we would expect buyers to prefer the municipal securities to the corporate bonds as long as the rate on municipal bonds exceeded 4½ percent. If the yield on municipal bonds equaled 4½ percent, investors would be indifferent since the corporate bond yields 4½ percent $(9 - .5 \times 9 = 4½)$ after taxes. What if the average tax rate of buyers of municipal securities is only 40 percent; what yield on municipal bonds would leave investors indifferent between our 9 percent corporate bond and a municipal bond? We hope that you understand why the answer is 5.40 percent.

Unfortunately, the relationship between taxable and tax-exempt yields is not quite so simple. In general the yield on municipal securities will be somewhat higher than one might expect after projecting the average tax rates of buyers. If you followed the last section on liquidity and marketability, you should be able to guess why. For the most part, the quality of the secondary market in municipal issues is not quite as good as the secondary market for corporate issues. As a result, municipal securities possess somewhat less liquidity than other types of securities.

15-5
THE STRUCTURE OF
LONG-TERM RATES: A SUMMARY

We can summarize in equation form the major factors that affect the structure of interest rates. We will expand Equation (15-1) to include the risk class of the issuer r, the taxability of the issue t, and the marketability of the issue as reflected in the liquidity premium l, as developed earlier. The expanded equation containing all the determinants of the long-term rate of interest i_L is presented in Equation (15-2):

(15-2)
$$i_L = f(\overset{+}{i_s}, \overset{+}{i_s^e}, \overset{+}{l}, \overset{+}{r}, \overset{+}{t})$$

As we can see by the signs over the variables, there is a positive relationship between each of the determinants and the long-term rate of interest.

15-6
MOVEMENTS IN LONG AND
SHORT RATES OVER THE BUSINESS CYCLE

All interest rates tend to move together over time, and they tend to show a definite cyclical pattern. All interest rates tend to rise as economic activity picks up (from the trough of a recession to the next business cycle peak) and to fall as economic activity slows (from the business cycle peak to the recession trough).

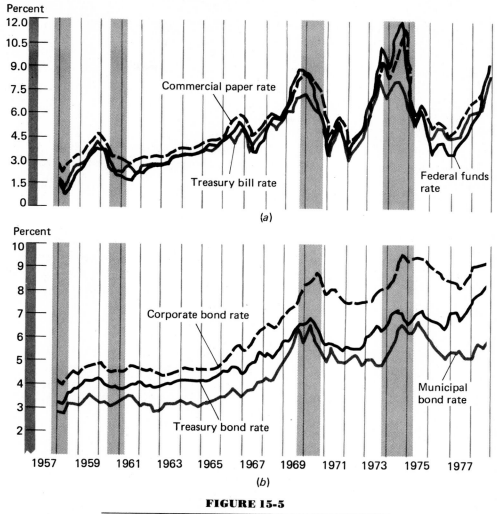

FIGURE 15-5

(a) Short-term interest rates. (b) Long-term interest rates.

To illustrate, part *a* of Figure 15-5 shows three interest rates—on federal funds, Treasury bills, and on commercial paper—over the past twenty years; part *b* shows the rate on corporate bonds, municipal issues, and Treasury bonds over the same period.

Several things emerge from these figures: (1) the rates on particular types of short-term instruments move quite closely with other short rates, and the same goes for longs; (2) short and long rates vary together, although the movement in short rates is considerably larger than the movement in long rates; (3) interest rates show a definite cyclical pattern, rising and falling according to economic activity.

15-7
SUMMARY OF MAJOR POINTS

1

The yield curve is a graphical representation of the relationship between yields (interest rates) on particular securities (such as Treasury securities) and their terms to maturity.

2

The expectations approach to explaining the shape of the yield curve—the "term structure" of interest rates—suggests that current long rates are equal to an average of the current short rate and the expected short rates during the life of the security.

3

According to the expectations approach, if future short rates are expected to rise, then current short rates will be below current long rates and the yield curve will be upward-sloping. If future short rates are expected to fall, then current short rates will exceed current long rates and the yield curve will be downward-sloping.

4

The liquidity preference approach suggests that investors must be rewarded for giving up liquidity. This means that even if current short rates are equal to expected future short rates, the current long rate will exceed the current short rate by a liquidity premium. This means that long-term rates will be determined by current short-term interest rates, expected short-term rates, and liquidity premiums.

5

The current and expected rates of inflation have an important effect on current and expected market interest rates. The higher the rate of inflation (now or in the future), the higher will be interest rates.

6

The structure of interest rates differs not only with regard to the term to maturity but also the risk-averseness of borrowers and lenders, the quality of the secondary market, and the tax situation of the security.

7

For any given maturity, securities with higher degrees of risk will have higher yields; investors must be rewarded for bearing additional risk.

8

Movements in interest rates show a definite cyclical pattern: they rise in recoveries and fall in recessions.

15-8
REVIEW QUESTIONS

1 Indicate whether each of the following is true, false, or uncertain. Explain why or under what conditions the statement is true, false, or uncertain.

a An upward-sloping yield curve indicates that investors expect future short rates to rise.

b A downward-sloping yield curve indicates that investors expect future short rates to fall.

c A flat yield curve indicates that investors expect future short rates to remain constant.

d The preference for liquidity ensures that short rates will, in general, be below long rates.

2 Explain why securities issued by different corporations will have different yields even when issue date and maturity are the same.

3 Explain why municipal securities pay lower yields than corporate securities even though they may be less liquid and more risky.

4 Explain why the rate of inflation and interest rates are highly correlated.

5 Why is the yield curve usually negatively sloped around a peak in the business cycle and positively sloped around a trough?

6 "High interest rates mean that monetary policy is restrictive." Analyze this statement.

15-9
SUGGESTED READINGS

1 For an excellent review of the literature on the term structure of interest rates, see Burton Malkiel, *The Term Structure of Interest Rates* (Morristown, N.J.: General Learning Press, 1970).

2 For a complete, readable, and well-done textbook treatment of the structure of interest rates, see James Van Horne, *Financial Market Rates and Flows* (Englewood Cliffs, N.J.: Prentice-Hall, 1978). For a more advanced treatment, see J. Light and W. White, *The Financial System* (Homewood, Ill.: Irwin, 1979), chaps. 8–10.

3 For more on the relationship between inflation and interest rates (and the answer to Question 6 above), see Mark Willes, "Are Interest Rates Too High?" *Quarterly Review*, Federal Reserve Bank of Minneapolis (Fall 1978), 1–3.

THE EXCHANGE RATE
AND THE BALANCE
OF PAYMENTS

Business fortunes are made on the ability to
forecast changes in the values of national currencies, while political futures become frayed
as a result of these changes.

Robert Aliber

16-1
WORLD FINANCIAL TRANSACTIONS AND YOU!

The parties in a domestic financial transaction use the same kind of
money—dollars. For financial transactions between parties in two different
countries, it is not that simple; they use different kinds of money. That
means that for financial transactions between parties in two different countries, the money of one of the countries must be converted into the money of
the other.

For example, an auto dealership in the United States imports automobiles made in a factory in West Germany and sells them in the United
States. The auto dealership receives dollars from its customers in the

United States. The United States firm would prefer to make payments in dollars for the autos it imports from the factory in West Germany. The West German factory, on the other hand, would prefer to receive marks in payment for the autos it delivers to the United States. The West German firm wants to be paid in marks because it must pay the costs to produce the autos (such as wages to its employees) in marks; the West German firm cannot pay its costs in dollars. This being the case, the United States importer will need to exchange dollars for marks to pay for the West German autos. But—*how many* dollars need to be exchanged for marks to pay for the West German autos? Does one dollar equal one mark? One dollar equal two marks? Two dollars equal one mark?

Up through Chapter 15, we assumed that the dollar was the only means of payment in the United States economy and also throughout the world. However, for our analysis to be more realistic, we must introduce the different world monies—the Japanese yen, the British pound sterling, the West German mark, and others. We must also introduce and examine the factors affecting the exchange value—that is, the purchasing power of one national money relative to another.

As we did in Chapter 7, we will simplify our analysis of international financial transactions by assuming a two-country model—the United States and the rest of the world. Also, we will analyze the factors affecting the value of the United States dollar relative to the value of the means of payment in the rest of the world, which we shall call the *keg*.[1] As we shall see, the determinant of the relative value of the two currencies will be the exchange rate.

> The *exchange rate* is the number of units of domestic money
> needed to acquire one unit of foreign money; it is the price one
> must pay to acquire foreign money. For example, if the dollar-
> keg exchange rate is $2, this means that you have to pay $2 to get
> 1 keg, or 1k. Conversely, from the foreign point of view, the
> keg-dollar exchange rate must be ½ k—that is, you have to pay
> ½ k to get $1.

To understand how the exchange rate between the dollar and the keg is determined—that is, for example, how it comes to be $2 today and, say, $2.50 next month—we need to examine the factors affecting the interna-

---

[1] There is no real need to extend our analysis beyond two national monies; the general framework we will develop is directly applicable to the more complex relationships among all national monies. To illustrate, suppose we knew $1 was equivalent to 2k and that 2k were equivalent to 4 marks. Then it must follow that $1 is equivalent to 4 marks. This "transitivity" allows us to confine our analysis to two monies.

tional supply of and demand for both currencies. We shall refer to the market where foreign monies are traded or exchanged as the "foreign currency market"—some people call it the "foreign exchange market."

16-2
THE DEMAND FOR FOREIGN CURRENCIES

The demand by United States residents for foreign currency, which is the United States demand for kegs, is derived from the demand by United States residents for foreign goods, services, and securities. In other words, the *United States demand for kegs* in the foreign currency market depends on the *United States demand for imports*. If the United States demands, or buys, foreign goods, services, or securities, the United States must have kegs to pay for them. How do domestic purchasers get kegs? In general, United States purchasers will have to supply dollars in exchange for kegs. This being the case, the demand for foreign currency (kegs) in the United States reflects a willingness to supply domestic currency (dollars) in exchange.[1]

GOING OVERSEAS

Suppose you had an upcoming trip abroad for which you need marks. You might call your local bank in Nashville, Tennessee, and place a buy order for marks. Most likely your local bank does not have a foreign currency department. As a result, your local bank in Nashville will probably call its correspondent bank in New York (a larger bank that provides it with various services) and will place the order for the marks with the correspondent bank's foreign currency department.

In the United States, most transactions in foreign money are executed by the foreign currency departments of the largest commercial banks—most particularly those located in New York City. The foreign currency market is not centralized physically in one building, as is the New York Stock Exchange. Rather, the foreign currency market's participants—such as banks and firms all around the world—are linked together by telephone and telex. (This is referred to as an "over-the-counter" market.) The large banks in New York function as dealers in foreign currencies. As foreign currency dealers these banks (1) stand ready to

---

[1] Happily the analysis is symmetrical: the demand for dollars in the rest of the world reflects a willingness by foreigners to supply kegs. As above, such demand is related to the *foreign* demand for United States goods, services, and securities—that is, *United States exports* of real and financial assets.

Foreign Exchange

Tuesday, November 28, 1978

Prices for **foreign banknotes**, as quoted on the last business day (in dollars):

	Buying	Selling	Buying Yr Ago
Argentina (Peso)	.00095	.0011	.0015
Australia (Dollar)	1.08	1.16	1.07
Austria (Schilling)	.069	.072	.06
Belgium (Franc)	.03	.034	.026
Brazil (Cruzeiro)	.041	.0521	.05
Britain (Pound)	1.88	1.98	1.77
Canada (Dollar)	.84	.86	.88
China-Taiwan (Dollar)	.024	.0278	.022
Colombia (Peso)	.0235	.0253	.02
Denmark (Krone)	.17	.19	.15
Egypt (Pound)	1.32	1.43	1.28
Finland (Markka)	.23	.25	.23
France (Franc)	.21	.23	.19
Greece (Drachma)	.027	.029	.021
Hong Kong (Dollar)	.20	.2110	.20
India (Rupee)	.095	.124	.07
Indonesia (Rupiah)	.0017	.00242	.0016
Italy (Lira)	.0011	.0013	.00100
Japan (Yen)	.0049	.0053	.0038
Malaysia (Ringgit)	.40	.4637	.34
Mexico (Peso)	.04	.05	.04
Netherlands (Guilder)	.46	.49	.40
New Zealand (Dollar)	.82	1.0775	.78
Norway (Krone)	.18	.20	.17
Pakistan (Rupee)	z	z	.03
Philippines (Peso)	.1230	.1355	.11
Portugal (Escudo)	.019	.023	.02
Singapore (Dollar)	.41	.4693	.34
South Korea (Won)	.0014	.00207	.0013
Spain (Peseta)	.013	.015	.011
Sweden (Krona)	.21	.23	.19
Switzerland (Franc)	.55	.58	.44
Thailand (Baht)	.0450	.0495	.04
Turkey (Lira)	.0320	.04	.03
Uruguay (Peso)	.13	.1507	.15
Venezuela (Bolivar)	.2270	.2330	.22
West Germany (Mark)	.51	.53	.43

Supplied by one major New York bank.
z-Not available.

buy or sell foreign currencies at the prevailing market price—
that is, the prevailing exchange rate—and (2) maintain an inventory of various foreign currencies. The New York bank may be willing to buy marks at 51 cents per mark (bid price) and sell them at 53 cents per mark (offer or asked price). Accordingly, the cost to you would be 53 cents per mark multiplied by the number of marks you need.

If you knew how to read the tables in *The Wall Street Journal,* you could anticipate the cost to you for the marks or whatever foreign currency you wanted to buy. We have reproduced the foreign exchange table from *The Wall Street Journal* for November 28, 1978. This table gives us, in dollars, the prices of the major foreign currencies of the world.

For instance, the New York commercial bank will buy a mark from you for 51 cents (look at West Germany, under the buying column), and it will sell a mark to you for 53 cents (look under the selling column). It is interesting to note that on November 28, 1977 (the third column), the bank was buying marks for 43 cents. Do you understand the implication of this? It means that if a hotel room in West Germany cost 100 marks per night in 1977, then an American traveler in 1977 would have paid $43 for the room. In 1978, if the cost of the hotel room in West Germany is still 100 marks, it will cost the American traveler $53. The trip is more expensive in 1978 than it was in 1977 because the value of the dollar has declined relative to the mark.

DETERMINANTS OF DEMAND

The *demand* for kegs D_k is a "derived demand"—that is, derived from the demand of United States residents for foreign goods and assets. The demand for kegs reflects a willingness to supply dollars $S_\$$ in exchange for the kegs. These relationships can be summarized by the following expressions:

(16-1) $D_k = f$ (United States imports of foreign goods, services, and financial assets)

        $S_\$ = f$ (United States imports of foreign goods, services, and financial assets)

        $D_k = S_\$$

In Chapter 7, we studied the variables that influenced United States demand for foreign goods, services, and assets. In that chapter, we specified seven determinants of the demand for imports of goods, services, and financial assets. These seven determinants are:

Y_{US} = United States income
P_{US} = price of United States goods
P_f = price of foreign goods
i_{US} = rate of return in the United States
i_f = rate of return in foreign countries
Z = tastes and other special factors
x = expectations

Since the demand for foreign currency or kegs is derived from the United States demand for imports, these seven determinants are also the determinants of the demand for kegs. Hence, we can write a behavioral equation for the demand for kegs D_k similar to the equations developed in Chapter 7.

(16-2) $D_k = f(\overset{+}{Y}_{US}, \overset{+}{P}_{US}, \overset{-}{P}_f, \overset{-}{i}_{US}, \overset{+}{i}_f, \overset{?}{Z}, \overset{?}{x}) = S_\$$

The signs over the symbols show the relationship between each determinant and the demand for kegs.

Let us review the relationship between each determinant and the demand for imports, which we now know is also the demand for kegs or any foreign currency.

United States income Y_{US} will be positively related to the demand for kegs. An increase in United States income Y_{US} will raise the demand for goods, services, and securities produced in the United States *and* produced abroad. The demand for foreign goods, services, and securities implies a demand for kegs to pay for these products.

Prices in the United States P_{US} will also be positively related to the demand for kegs. If P_{US} rises and everything else remains the same, then United States residents will be induced to buy foreign goods, since foreign goods will be cheaper than the same goods made in the United States. On the other hand, if P_f rises, United States residents will be less inclined to buy foreign goods.

The rate of return in the United States i_{US} will be negatively related to the demand for kegs. Higher rates of return in the United States relative to the rest of the world will lead to an increased demand for United States securities and a decreased demand for foreign ones. The less the demand for foreign securities, the less the demand for kegs to pay for or buy those securities. On the other hand, higher rates in the rest of the world i_f will increase the demand for foreign securities and, therefore, the demand for foreign kegs.

Finally, consumer tastes, availability of domestically produced substitutes, and a host of other miscellaneous factors Z and expectations x will affect the demand for kegs. As discussed in Chapter 7, the effect of these factors depends on particular circumstances.

THE EXCHANGE RATE
AND THE DEMAND FOR KEGS

In addition to these seven determinants, there is one more determinant of the demand for kegs that we did not yet discuss. It is the exchange rate ER. The exchange rate represents the number of dollars you must pay for each keg, which, of course, affects the demand for kegs. To see the relationship between the demand for kegs and the exchange rate, we must begin with a formula that translates the *keg price* of foreign goods (for example, the price of a foreign car in foreign currency, or kegs) to the *dollar price* of foreign goods (the price of that same foreign car in United States dollars).

Equation 16-3 presents this formula.

(16-3)
$$P_f^\$ = P_f^k \times \text{ER}$$

where $P_f^\$$ = dollar price of foreign goods
P_f^k = keg price of foreign goods
ER = exchange rate

An example may help illustrate how this formula works. Suppose the dollar-keg exchange rate is $3—it takes $3 to purchase 1k—and the keg price of a foreign auto is 5000k. Then, using Equation (16-3), it must follow that the dollar price of the auto $P_f^\$$ in the United States is $15,000 ($15,000 = 5000k × $3/1k).[1]

You will notice from Equation (16-3) that two things can change the dollar price of a foreign good $P_f^\$$. It can change because the exchange rate ER changes or because the keg price P_f^k changes. For example, if the exchange rate goes from $3 to $3.60, the dollar price of the auto could rise to $18,000 [$18,000 = 5000k × ($3.60/1k)]. In this example, the keg price of the car remained the same at 5000k, but the price of kegs increased from $3 to $3.60 each. If the exchange rate remained constant but the keg price of the car rose, for example, to 5500k, then the dollar price of the auto would be $16,500 ($16,500 = 5500k × 3/1k).

For our purposes in this chapter, we are concerned about the exchange rate and what causes it to change. In particular, we can see from Equation (16-3) that a rise in the exchange rate will raise the dollar price of foreign goods $P_f^\$$ and, thereby, make foreign goods more expensive in the United States. The more expensive the foreign goods, other things remaining the same, the less will be the United States demand for those goods. Obviously then, the less the demand for foreign goods, the less the quantity of kegs demanded.[2] Hence, the relationship between the demand for kegs and the exchange rate is negative.

(16-4)
$$D_k = f(\overset{-}{\text{ER}})$$

DERIVING THE DEMAND FOR KEGS

We will work through an example deriving the demand for kegs as a function of the exchange rate. To do this, let us assume that all other factors influencing the demand for kegs remain constant. In other words, all the factors in Equation (16-2) are held constant; for simplicity, that means only ER in Equation (16-4) is allowed to vary. Further, assume that the only goods traded between the United States and the rest of the world are foreign-made automobiles. Columns 1 and 2 in Table 16-1 show the quantity of autos demanded at three different dollar prices of the foreign cars. One hundred foreign autos are demanded in the United States when the price of each is $6000; at $4000 each, 150 autos will be demanded; and at $8000

[1] A variant of the formula in Equation (16-3) could be used to express dollar prices of United States goods in keg terms: $P_{US}^k = P_{US}^\$ × 1/ER$, where $P_{US}^\$$ = the price of United States goods in dollar terms and P_{US}^k = the price of United States goods in terms of kegs. We will express prices in dollar terms throughout.

[2] One real-world example that might help illustrate the point is the exchange rate between the United States dollar and the Swiss franc. Over the last few years, the value of the dollar relative to the Swiss franc has dropped precipitously; that is, the exchange rate has risen and it takes more dollars to buy one Swiss franc. Hence Swiss-made products (like Swiss watches) are very expensive in the United States and not affordable by many United States citizens.

TABLE 16-1
UNITED STATES DEMAND FOR FOREIGN AUTOS

(1) DOLLAR PRICE OF FOREIGN AUTOS	(2) QUANTITY OF FOREIGN AUTOS DEMANDED IN THE UNITED STATES AT ALTERNATIVE PRICES	(3) POINT PLOTTED IN FIGURE 16-1
$4000	150	C
6000	100	B
8000	50	A

each, 50 autos will be demanded. The relationship between the price and quantity is plotted in Figure 16-1.

The second step is to derive the demand for kegs from the United States demand for foreign autos. Let us assume that the price of autos in foreign countries is fixed at 2000k. Because the foreign (keg) price is fixed, the dollar price of foreign autos in the United States will change only if the dollar-keg exchange rate changes.

Remember how this works from Equation (16-3). When the keg price of the auto is 2000k and the exchange rate is $2, then the dollar price of the autos is $4000 [2000k × ($2/1k)]. When the dollar-keg exchange is $3, the dollar price is $6000 = [2000k × ($3/1k)]. When the dollar-keg exchange rate is $4, the price is $8000 = [2000k × ($4/1k)]. These calculations are shown in columns 1, 2, and 3 of Table 16-2. These columns show us that changes in the exchange rate will change the dollar price of foreign goods.

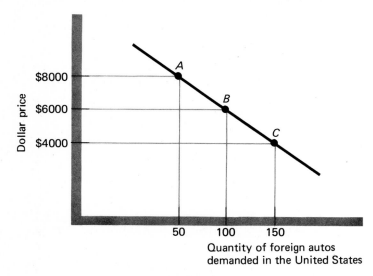

FIGURE 16-1

The demand for foreign autos in the United States is a negative function of the dollar price of these autos.

TABLE 16-2
DEMAND FOR FOREIGN MONEY RELATED TO DEMAND FOR
TRADED GOODS AND THE EXCHANGE RATE

(1) KEG PRICE OF AUTOS	(2) ALTERNATIVE DOLLAR/KEG EXCHANGE RATES	(3) DOLLAR PRICE OF AUTOS AT ALTERNATIVE EXCHANGE RATES (COL. 1 × 2)	(4) DEMAND FOR KEGS AT ALTERNATIVE EXCHANGE RATES (COL. 2, TABLE 16-1 × (COL. 1, TABLE 16-2)	(5) POINT PLOTTED IN FIGURE 16-2
2000k	$2/k	$4000	300,000k	C′
2000k	$3/k	$6000	200,000k	B′
2000k	$4/k	$8000	100,000k	A′

By comparing column 3 in Table 16-2 with columns 1 and 2 in Table 16-1, we can determine how many foreign autos will be demanded in the United States at the alternative dollar prices implied by the different exchange rates (column 2, Table 16-2). For example, at an exchange rate of $3, the dollar price of foreign autos is $6000 and the quantity of autos demanded is 100. At an exchange rate of $4, the dollar price of foreign autos is $8000 and only 50 cars are demanded.

Now it is a simple step to derive the demand for kegs from the demand for autos. We need to multiply the number of autos demanded at each alternative exchange rate by the keg price of autos (column 4 of Table 16-2 = column 2, Table 16-1 multiplied by column 1, Table 16-2). For example, at an exchange rate of $3, which gives a dollar price of foreign autos in the United States of $6000, the quantity of autos demanded is 100. The

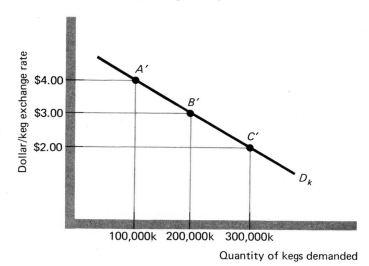

FIGURE 16-2

The demand for kegs is a negative function of the exchange rate (dollar price of kegs).

number of autos (100) multiplied by the keg price of 2000k per auto gives a total of 200,000k needed to purchase the autos (100 autos multiplied by 2000k per auto).

The final results of these calculations are plotted in Figure 16-2. As you can see, the higher the dollar price of kegs, the less will be the quantity of kegs demanded. What does this mean? The higher the dollar price of kegs, the more expensive are foreign goods in the United States and, therefore, the less will be the demand for foreign goods in the United States. In other words, Figure 16-2 plots a demand curve for kegs where the quantity of kegs demanded is a negative function of the exchange rate—the dollar price of kegs.

16-3
THE SUPPLY OF FOREIGN CURRENCIES

Figure 16-2 shows only the demand curve for kegs. And where there is a demand curve, there obviously must be a supply curve! You can expect that the supply of kegs S_k is derived from a *foreigner's* demand for United States goods and securities. As foreigners buy United States goods, they pay for these goods by supplying kegs and demanding dollars. The supply-of-kegs function would include those variables which influence the demand for imports by foreigners or, more directly, those variables which influence United States exports of goods, services, and securities.

(16-5) $S_k = f$(foreigner's demand for United States goods, services, and financial assets)

$D_\$ = f$(foreigner's demand for United States goods, services, and financial assets)

$S_k = D_\$$

DETERMINANTS OF SUPPLY

The supply of kegs (and demand for dollars) is given by Equation (16-6).

(16-6) $$S_k = f(\overset{+}{Y_f},\ \overset{-}{P_{US}},\ \overset{+}{P_f},\ \overset{+}{i_{US}},\ \overset{-}{i_f},\ \overset{?}{Z},\ \overset{?}{x}) = D_\$$$

The seven determinants are as follows:

Y_f = foreign income
P_{US} = price of United States goods
P_f = price of foreign goods
i_{US} = rate of return in the United States
i_f = rate of return in foreign countries
Z = tastes and other special factors
x = expectations

How do these variables affect the supply of kegs by foreigners? The higher the income in the foreign country Y_f, the greater the demand for United States goods and securities and, hence, the greater the supply of kegs. Higher prices in the United States P_{US} would decrease the foreign demand for United States goods and, hence, the foreign supply of kegs. Again, higher prices in the foreign country P_f relative to United States prices would lead to more foreign demand for United States goods and more kegs supplied. Higher yields in the United States i_{US} would lead to increased demand for United States securities and hence an increased supply of kegs. Finally, higher yields in the foreign country i_f would reduce the supply of kegs, while the effects of tastes Z and expectations x would depend on the particular circumstances.

THE EXCHANGE RATE AND THE SUPPLY OF KEGS

Besides these variables, the supply of kegs is also a function of the exchange rate. The higher the dollar price of kegs, the greater will be the quantity of kegs supplied (see graph in Figure 16-3). This reflects the fact that as the dollar price of kegs rises, United States goods become less expensive in foreign countries and foreigners will demand more of them. To illustrate, suppose a United States computer sells for $120,000. At an exchange rate of $3, the keg price to foreigners is 40,000k. If the exchange rate rises to $4, the keg price will fall to 30,000k and computers will be cheaper to foreigners.

We would expect the lower keg price of computers to increase the quantity of computers demanded and therefore to increase the quantity of

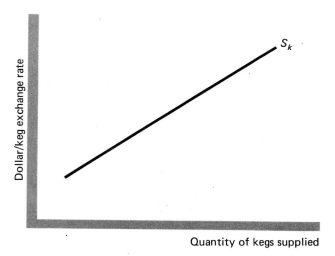

FIGURE 16-3

The supply of kegs is a positive function of the exchange rate (dollar price of kegs).

dollars demanded *and* the quantity of kegs supplied. Hence the relationship between the supply of kegs and the exchange rate is positive.

$$(16\text{-}7) \qquad\qquad S_k = f(\overset{+}{\text{ER}})$$

This relationship is graphed in Figure 16-3.

In sum, a rise in the dollar-keg exchange rate will decrease the quantity of kegs demanded (since the dollar price of foreign goods in the United States will have risen) and increase the quantity of kegs supplied (because the keg price of United States goods in foreign markets will have fallen).

16-4
THE EXCHANGE RATE
AND THE BALANCE OF PAYMENTS

The demand-and-supply functions for kegs, which we developed in the preceding sections, can now be plotted together to determine the equilibrium quantity of kegs demanded and supplied at the equilibrium exchange rate. This is plotted in Figure 16-4. So you do not lose sight of the behavior underlying these functions, we have also cooked up Figure 16-5. Before you go on, make sure you understand clearly the flows depicted in Figure 16-5.

Figure 16-4 can be analyzed just like any supply-demand diagram. For example, if for some reason the exchange rate were held at $1.50, then the demand for kegs would be greater than the supply for kegs and we would have disequilibrium in the foreign currency market. To return to equilibrium, market forces would require the exchange rate to rise to $2.

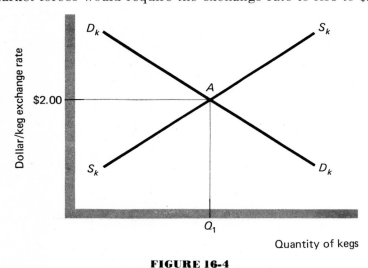

FIGURE 16-4

The supply and demand for kegs will determine the dollar/keg exchange rate.

FIGURE 16-5

The foreign currency market facilitates world trade.

SUPPLY = DEMAND
AND THE BALANCE OF PAYMENTS

What does it mean when the supply of kegs is equal to the demand for kegs? At point A in Figure 16-4 the quantity of kegs demanded to consummate United States importation of goods, services, and securities from the foreign country is exactly equal to the quantity of kegs supplied to consummate the exportation of goods, services, and securities from the United States to the foreign country. This means that the *net value* of transactions in goods, services, and securities between the countries is zero. Put more formally, the following set of market-clearing or equilibrium conditions will hold:

$$(16\text{-}8) \quad \begin{array}{ll} (a) \quad D_\$ = S_\$ & (d) \quad D_k = S_k \\ (b) \quad D_\$ - S_\$ = 0 & (e) \quad D_k - S_k = 0 \\ (c) \quad D_\$ - S_\$ = \text{BOP}_{\text{US}} = 0 & (f) \quad D_k - S_k = \text{BOP}_f = 0 \\ \multicolumn{2}{c}{(g) \quad \text{BOP}_{\text{US}} = \text{BOP}_f = 0} \end{array}$$

The set of conditions in Equation (16-8) look far more imposing than the simple information they convey. As foreigners import more goods, services, and securities from the United States, they will demand more dollars. United States residents supply dollars to foreign countries by importing goods, services, and securities from abroad.

When foreign demand for dollars $D_\$$ is greater than United States supply $S_\$$, the United States balance of payments BOP_{US} is in surplus. When the United States imports more than foreigners import, $D_\$$ will be less than $S_\$$ and the United States BOP_{US} will be in deficit. If $D_\$ = S_\$$, then it must follow that the desires of foreign and domestic residents match perfectly. It also means that our balance of payments equals zero, or $\text{BOP}_{\text{US}} = 0$.

Since we are assuming that there is only the United States and the rest of the world (representing the foreign economy), if $BOP_{US} = 0$, it must also follow that the foreign balance of payments BOP_f is also equal to zero.

Now let us examine this from the other side. A demand for kegs reflects imports by United States residents of foreign goods, services, and securities. A supply of kegs reflects foreign residents importing United States goods, services, and securities. If D_k is greater than S_k, then BOP_f will be in surplus; if D_k is less than S_k, BOP_f will be in deficit. If $D_k = S_k$, the desires of foreign and United States residents coincide such that $BOP_f = 0$.

The conditions expressed in Equation (16-8) tell us that when the supply and demand for kegs are equal to each other, as at point A in Figure 16-4, the balance of payments for each country in our two-country model (the United States and the rest of the world) is zero.

CHANGES IN THE EXCHANGE RATE

So long as the exchange rate is free to move, it will eventually equate the supply and demand for a currency. Whenever there tends to be a deficit or surplus in the BOP, it cannot persist for long. For example, let us assume that the United States demand for kegs tends to exceed the supply of kegs at the prevailing exchange rate. The adjustment to this "disequilibrium" will be a rise in the dollar price of kegs. This, in turn, will raise the dollar price of foreign goods in the United States (depressing imports) and lower the price of United States goods in the rest of the world (increasing exports). The adjustment will continue until $D_k - S_k = 0$ and $BOP_{US} = 0$.

To understand the underlying cause of changes in the exchange rate, it is necessary to know what causes shifts in the supply and demand for foreign currencies. This is exactly the information we covered in the last section. For example, a change in any of the variables in Equation (16-2) will shift the demand-for-kegs schedule in the direction indicated by the sign above each variable. (A positive sign indicates that changes in the determinant shift the function to the right, a negative sign indicates a leftward shift.)

To illustrate, let us begin from point A in Figure 16-6, where $D_k = S_k$ and $BOP_{US} = 0$. Now let inflation accelerate faster in the United States relative to inflation in the rest of the world. Since P_{US} rises, two things will happen. The demand for kegs will shift to the right (to D_k') as United States demand for foreign goods rises. And the supply of kegs will shift to the left (to S_k') as foreign demand for United States goods declines. As households and firms adjust to the change, both the demand and supply shifts will reinforce one another and generate a *fall* in the value of the dollar—that is, an *increase* in the dollar price of kegs (point B).[1]

---

[1] Note that the quantity of kegs supplied and demanded at point B need not be equal to the supply and demand at point A. All that is required is equality between D_k and S_k at each equilibrium point.

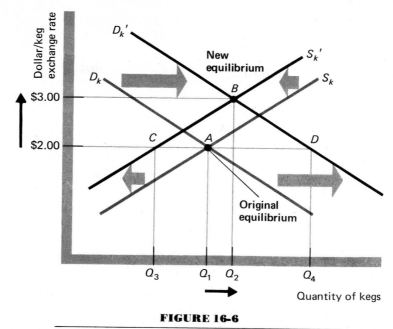

FIGURE 16-6

An increase in inflation in the United States relative to the rest of the world will increase the United States demand for foreign goods and assets and, therefore, increase the demand for kegs as demonstrated by a shift to the right of the D_k curve. At the same time, the foreign demand for United States goods will decrease, and hence the supply of kegs will decrease as shown by a shift to the left of the S_k curve. Both shifts will generate an increase in the dollar price of kegs.

The exchange rate adjusts to a new equilibrium following a "shock" or disturbance to the original equilibrium, because households and firms adjust their spending and saving decisions. In general, a change in relative prices, rates of return, or income will induce domestic and foreign residents to rearrange their portfolios—their *stock*—of real assets, financial assets, and money. This stock-adjustment process will take the form of changes in the *flow* of spending on domestic as well as foreign goods, services, and financial assets.

MOVEMENTS IN EXCHANGE
RATES OVER THE SHORT AND LONG RUN

Two terms often employed in describing exchange rate movements over time are *depreciation* and *appreciation*.

A rise in the dollar price of kegs is referred to as a depreciation of the dollar, since you now need more dollars to purchase one keg. The depreciation of the dollar is simultaneously accompanied by an appreciation of the keg; you need less kegs to purchase one dollar. As our domestic currency depreciates, the demand for United States goods and assets in foreign markets rises and the United States demand for foreign goods and assets falls. Thus, just as the value or purchasing power of the United States dollar is inversely related to the United States price level ($1/P_{US}$), the value or purchasing power of the dollar in the rest of the world is inversely related to the exchange rate ($1/ER$). If the ER rises from $2 to $3, each dollar buys less kegs and therefore less foreign goods and services; that is, the international purchasing power of the dollar has declined.

Over the longer run (several years), economists generally believe that the growth in real income (output) and prices in the United States vis-à-vis other countries will have the predominant influence on the demand and supply of kegs and, therefore, the dollar exchange rate. As a long-run norm, it is thought that *purchasing-power parity* must exist between two monies.

PURCHASING POWER PARITY

What do we mean by "purchasing-power parity"? As usual, an example should help to illustrate the concept. Suppose a bushel of wheat cost $2 in the United States and 1k in foreign countries. Assume the exchange rate is $1 ($1 = 1k). United States residents could use $2 to buy 1 bushel of wheat in the United States *or* they could use the $2 to purchase 2k and then buy 2 bushels of wheat from foreign countries. Since the purchasing power of the dollar is higher internationally then domestically, there is an incentive to import foreign goods, in this case wheat; as a result, the United States would be running continual balance-of-payments deficits.

Assuming the price of wheat in the United States and in foreign countries does not change, the only way for the keg and the dollar to have equal purchasing power in terms of goods (in this case wheat) is for the exchange rate to rise to $2. When this happens, $2 will buy 1 bushel of wheat in the United States or it will buy 1k, which also will buy 1 bushel of wheat. At this point, we have purchasing-power parity between the keg and the dollar in purchasing wheat.

If the dollar prices of all goods in the United States are twice as high as the foreign prices of similar foreign goods, then we would expect over the longer run the international value of the dollar to be roughly half that of the keg ($2 = 1k or, from the foreign point of view, ½k = $1). In general, the long-run equilibrium exchange rate between the currencies of two countries depends on the price levels in each country. The nature of this dependence will be discussed in Chapter 21.

Over the short run, a variety of factors affect the exchange rate. One particular factor which plays an important role in determining the exchange rate is expectations. For example, expectations influence the exchange rate through their impact on investor decisions to buy or sell *securities* in domestic and foreign financial markets. To illustrate the point, suppose the Federal Reserve embarks on a policy to slow the growth of aggregate demand in order to lower the United States inflation rate. In the short run, such a policy would slow the growth of bank reserves and increase interest rates. Against this background, it seems likely that investors, noting the rise in interest rates i_{US} in the United States relative to world interest rates, would be more inclined to purchase United States securities than before this action. While there could also be some short-run effects of such a policy action on the demand for goods, experience suggests that there is a longer lag between such actions and their impact on exports and imports of goods. On balance, we would expect the dollar to appreciate relative to the keg as the supply curve for kegs shifts to the right (foreigners demand more United States securities) and the demand curve for kegs shifts to the left (United States residents demand less foreign securities).

16-5
FIXED EXCHANGE RATES
AND THE BALANCE OF PAYMENTS

Thus far we have assumed that the exchange rate is free to move and therefore to equate (bring into balance) the demand and supply of foreign monies. However, if governments interfere with the functioning of the market by holding (pegging or fixing) the exchange rate at a specific value, then, in the face of developments causing shifts in the supply of or demand for foreign currency, the BOP will move into deficit or surplus.

To illustrate this possibility, suppose prices in the United States P_{US} rise, causing the shifts in D_k and S_k in Figure 16-6 described earlier. Also, suppose that the United States and foreign governments are committed to maintaining the dollar/keg exchange rate at $2. Ignoring for the moment how the government can do this, note that, before the shifts, an exchange rate of $2 equated the demand and supply for kegs $(D_k = S_k)$. Now, after the shifts, the demand for kegs Q_4 is greater than the supply of kegs Q_3 at an exchange rate of $2—with the excess of demand for kegs over the supply of kegs equal to $Q_4 - Q_3$ or to the distance CD. What does this mean in terms of BOP_{US}?

It means that United States demand for foreign goods and securities, which determines the demand for kegs, is greater than the foreign demand for United States goods and securities, which determines the supply of kegs. This means BOP_{US} is in deficit. This deficit must be financed, and—as was pointed out in Chapter 7—the government will wind up financing it by reducing its holdings of international reserves (gold, SDRs, and foreign currencies) by the equivalent of the difference between the demand for kegs minus the supply of kegs.

A major characteristic of the international monetary system over the period from the end of World War II until the early 1970s had been the unwillingness of governments to allow exchange rates to move freely. The reasons for this unwillingness—which involve economic and political considerations—will be examined in Chapter 21. The period of fixed exchange rates was characterized by the existence of persistent deficits in the BOP of various countries, such as Britain and the United States, and resulted in continuing declines in their international reserve holdings. The persistent deficits (and the persistent surpluses in other countries) eventually led to the breakdown of the fixed exchange-rate system.

Since 1973, exchange rates have been more flexible, although they have not been allowed to move freely to equate supply and demand in the foreign currency market. As discussed above, over the longer run we would expect that the relative inflation rates among countries will have a pervasive influence on exchange-rate movements (purchasing-power parity). Accordingly, since 1973, we would expect that those countries which have experienced high inflation rates (and other associated political-social-economic problems) have also experienced a depreciation of their currencies relative to the dollar. On the other hand, countries such as West Germany have

TABLE 16-3
INFLATION RATES IN THE UNITED STATES AND GERMANY*

	UNITED STATES	GERMANY
1973	6.2%	6.9%
1974	11.0%	7.0%
1975	9.1%	5.9%
1976	5.8%	4.5%
1977	6.5%	3.9%
1978	7.6%	2.6%
Average of past six years	7.7%	5.1%

* As measured by the consumer price index for each country.

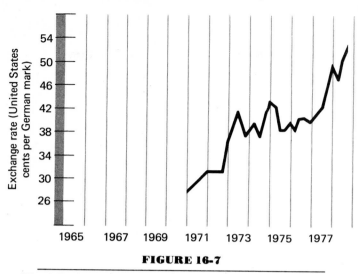

FIGURE 16-7

The dollar has depreciated relative to the German mark during the 1970s.

experienced relatively low inflation rates over this period. We would expect that the value of their currencies have appreciated vis-à-vis the dollar. The inflation rates for the United States and West Germany over the past five years are shown in Table 16-3; Figure 16-7 plots the exchange rate between the dollar and the mark. Can you explain why the dollar has depreciated vis-à-vis the mark?

When we get to Chapter 21, we will be prepared to discuss how and why governments intervene in foreign currency markets to affect the exchange rate. At that time, we will discuss in considerable detail the structure of and changes in the international monetary system over the past thirty years.

16-6
SUMMARY OF MAJOR POINTS

1

To pay for foreign goods purchased, we must convert dollars to foreign currencies. Likewise, foreigners must convert their currencies to dollars to purchase and pay for our goods. The dollar price of obtaining a unit of a foreign currency is called the exchange rate.

2

The demand for foreign currencies is derived from our demand for foreign goods, services, or financial assets.

3

The supply of foreign currencies is derived from foreign demand for our goods, services, and financial assets.

4

The dollar price of foreign goods can be calculated by multiplying the foreign price of foreign goods by the exchange rate between the dollar and the foreign currency. If foreign prices of foreign goods are constant while the exchange rate increases, then the dollar price of foreign goods will rise.

5

The exchange rate between the dollar and foreign currencies is determined by the demand for foreign currencies and the supply of foreign currencies.

6

If the demand for foreign currencies rises relative to the supply of foreign currencies and exchange rates are allowed to fluctuate freely, the exchange rate will rise; that is, it will take more dollars to purchase one unit of foreign currency.

7

If exchange rates are allowed to fluctuate freely, the demand for foreign currencies will always be brought into balance with (be equated to) the supply of foreign currencies. This means that the balance of payments is always equal to zero.

8

Over the longer run, the exchange rate between two currencies will be determined largely by relative rates of inflation in the countries. The exchange rate will move over time until purchasing-power parity exists between the two currencies.

9

Over the short run, a variety of factors—including the expectations of domestic and foreign residents concerning future monetary and fiscal policy actions, future interest rates, and future inflation rates—will affect exchange rates.

If exchange rates are not allowed to move freely to equate the supply of and demand for foreign currencies, some nations will experience balance of payments surpluses while others will experience balance of payments deficits. From the end of World War II until the early 1970s, exchange rates were *not* allowed to move freely and the United States experienced a growing balance of payments deficit.

16-7
REVIEW QUESTIONS

1   Twenty years ago the dollar price of a German mark was about 25 cents; today, it is about 50 cents. How do you think this has affected the dollar price of Volkswagens in the United States?

2   After identifying the various factors affecting the demand for and supply of foreign currencies, explain how changes in five of the factors affecting supply and five of the factors affecting demand could lead to a depreciation of the dollar vis-à-vis foreign currencies (the keg).

3   Explain carefully why the balance of payments is always equal to zero if exchange rates are free to move to equate the supply of and demand for foreign currencies.

4   Suppose the United States wanted to reverse the depreciation of the dollar relative to the mark, shown in Figure 16-7. What policy actions would you recommend? Explain how these actions would affect the exchange rate between the dollar and the mark. Do you see any problems associated with actually implementing these policy actions?

5   Explain what we mean by "purchasing-power parity." Why do we expect purchasing-power parity to exist in the long run if exchange rates are flexible?

16-8
SUGGESTED READINGS

1   For a good, concise presentation on the workings of the foreign currency markets, see Roger Kubarych, *Foreign Exchange Market in the United States*, Federal Reserve Bank of New York (August 1978).

2   For a readable and short article on the relationship of United States inflation and the corresponding decline in the foreign-exchange value of the dollar, see Douglas Mudd, "Movements in the Foreign Exchange Value of the Dollar During the Current U.S. Expansion," *Review*, Federal Reserve Bank of St. Louis (November 1978), 2–7.

FIVE

STABILIZING THE ECONOMY: MONETARY, FISCAL, AND INTERNATIONAL POLICIES

In Part V, we introduce the policy tools and describe how they are supposed to help stabilize the nation's economy. We will examine these various policy tools, how they are used, how they affect the economy, and why things often go wrong.

But before we do that, we will study what stabilizing the economy means and how to specify the stabilization goals which guide policymaker decisions. The goals of policy derive partly from the workings of the democratic political process and partly from what theory and experience suggest is attainable. If the goals can be agreed upon, the process of stabilizing the economy is somewhat less complicated although by no means simple. Once the goals are established, the next step is to agree on the policy actions to attain those goals. The policy issues become these: (*a*) how do we reach the goal agreed upon (what means, route, or path do we choose) and (*b*) how do we know—having set forth on a path leading to the agreed-upon goal—that we are in fact on course?

The situation here is like that of a sailor setting out for London from New

York. Clearly, the sailor knows where he wants to go—that is, the goal is established. Further, in this case the path or course to be followed can be chosen from a limited number of alternatives. However, once having chosen the course, the sailor must continually determine whether the sailing vessel is on course. Tides, winds, and currents will alter the direction of the vessel, and frequent adjustments are required in order to reach the final destination.

Implementing economic policy poses the same kinds of problems. A goal must be established, a path to the goal must be chosen, and—once on the path—the economy must be constantly monitored for deviations from the chosen course so that any errors can be corrected.

Chapter 17 introduces the major issues involved in specifying and pursuing the goals of economic policy. As we will see, the goals of policy are agreed upon only in general terms. For example, everyone agrees that unemployment should be kept "low." But not everyone agrees on what that means specifically. Is four percent unemployment "low" enough? Five percent? Six percent? How about zero percent?

One factor that should be kept in mind as we investigate these issues is that the list of policy goals *and* the actions taken to try to achieve them derive from our knowledge of the structure of the economy. In general, if the economic goals are to be meaningful, they ought to be attainable. What is attainable depends in large part on the workings of the economy and on our *understanding* of them. This is one of the reasons why we have, in this text, investigated the structure of the economy before specifying the goals of policy and the instruments of the policymakers.

Figure V-1 outlines the major elements defining the relationship between the policymakers and the rest of the economy. The diagram shows that policymakers have various policy goals. The Fed—the monetary policymaker—has monetary tools such as open market operations, reserve requirements, and the discount rate; the federal government—the fiscal policymaker—has fiscal tools such as tax rates and government spending levels. The policymakers use these tools to affect the behavior of banks and the public, thereby exerting a certain amount of control over such key variables in the economy as inflation and unemployment.

If you continue to follow the arrows in the diagram, you will see that the policy tools affect spending and saving decisions within the structure of the economy and that those decisions affect inflation and unemployment. These two key economic variables are the measuring rods that indicate how well the economy is being stabilized. A look at the actual measures of these two variables at any point in time, comparing them with the desired values or goals for these variables, will indicate to the policymaker whether or not the economy is on course. By monitoring movements in the key variables, the policymakers get some feedback on what is happening in the economy and how well the economy is being stabilized.

If a given policy action is not having its expected impact, then policymakers—observing this—may decide to change policy, thereby initiating another round of effects on the structure and key variables.

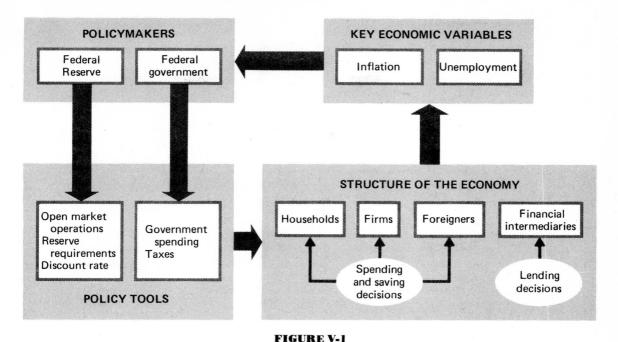

FIGURE V-1

Policymakers and the economy.

Note that in Figure V-1 we are considering both monetary and fiscal policymakers. Chapters 18 and 19 are devoted to studying the monetary policymakers. We shall study the Fed's organization, the behavior of policymakers, and the policy issues they face. Chapter 20 focuses on fiscal policymakers.

The last chapter of the text, Chapter 21, introduces additional complications that policymakers face daily. First, there is the increasingly important interrelationship between domestic and international factors and the effect this has on the stability of the domestic economy and on the consciousness of policymakers. In the 1950s and 1960s, it was believed that when the United States sneezed, Europe caught cold—but not the other way round. Events of the 1970s have shown that the United States economy is vulnerable in a variety of ways to changes in the world situation (did someone say oil?) and that we are unable to ignore international concerns in formulating and implementing policy.

In examining the theory and practice of policymaking, it is important to recognize the underlying premises which condition the behavior of policymakers. In general, policymakers believe that the economy is unstable; that is, in the absence of stabilization policy, the economy will fluctuate from recessions and high unemployment rates to overexpansion and high rates of inflation. As shown in panel (a) of Figure V-2, policymakers believe that some index of economic activity (such as the growth rate of real output) will fluctuate in a wide range in the absence of any policy actions. Ideally, policymakers should

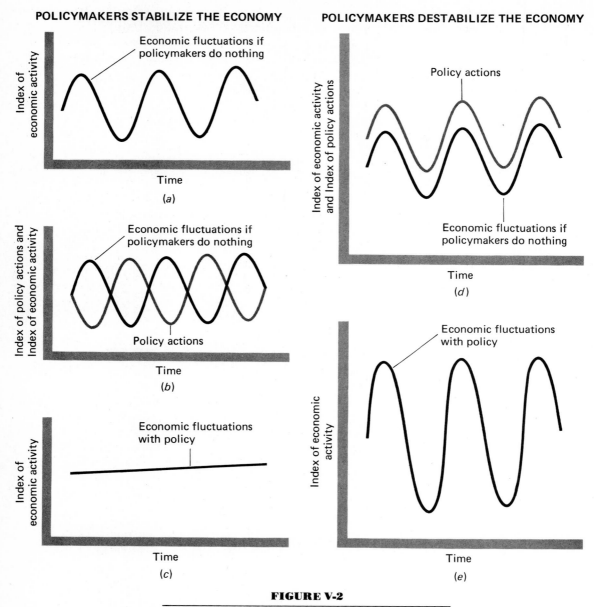

FIGURE V-2

The theory and practice of economic policymaking.

manipulate their tools so as to offset the fluctuations in economic activity. Thus, as shown in panel (*b*), some index of policy actions (like the rate of growth of bank reserves, the money supply, or government expenditures) should fluctuate so as to counteract the fluctuations in economic activity. The hoped-for result is shown in panel (*c*) where the economy is stabilized.

Of course, things do not necessarily work out this way in practice. It is possible—and this is something we will investigate in this part of the text—that stabilization policy might not offset economic fluctuations but actually might aggravate them, leading to even wider swings in the economy than would occur if there were no policy. This situation is illustrated in panels (*d*) and (*e*). If this were the case, stabilization policy would be not the remedy but rather part of the problem. There are economists who believe that the economy is inherently stable and that swings in economic activity flow mainly from unnecessary and unsuccessful attempts at stabilization.

As usual, reality lies somewhere between the two extremes depicted in panels (*c*) and (*e*) of Figure V-2. Over the past forty years, some fluctuations in economic activity were caused by policymakers and some potential fluctuations were alleviated or eliminated by policymakers. By examining what policymakers do and why they do it, this part of the text should help you see why they have not done a better job.

17

ECONOMIC GOALS: WHAT ARE THEY, WHO SETS THEM, AND HOW ARE THEY PURSUED?

When two men agree on everything, one of them is doing all the thinking.

Sam Rayburn

17-1
GUIDES FOR GOVERNMENT POLICY

Since the Depression of the 1930s United States economic policy has been based on the premise that we live in an unstable market system which can and should be stabilized. We are now prepared to examine how economic policies designed to stabilize the economy are adopted, who adopts them and why, and how they work . . . or do not work.

To begin our study of economic policies, let us recall that in Chapter 6 we saw that economic policies are designed to do one of three things: allocate resources, distribute income, or stabilize the economy. In this and the following chapters, we shall be mainly concerned with policies designed to stabilize the economy. But we must also remember that policies designed to affect income distribution (for example, food stamps) or resource allocation (such as various types of regulatory policies implemented by the Federal Trade Commission, Interstate Commerce Commission, etc.) often have an effect on the stability of the economy. We will look at how the side effects of other "microeconomic" policies affect stabilization. And we will also look at how policies designed to stabilize can cause instability. In this latter respect, both the patient (the economy) and the doctor (the policymaker) need some critical study by us, the students of the economy and policy-making.

In formulating and implementing (executing) policy, the makers of policy are guided by certain economic goals. Let us start our study of policy by defining the economic goals that our society has established and toward which the policymakers ought to strive.

17-2
THE ECONOMIC GOALS
OF STABILIZATION POLICY

As a society, our goals are based on our values, which are translated into goals through the political process. Let us look at an example of how our values are the basis of our goals. As a society, we are concerned about the level of unemployment because we believe that the unemployed are in the process of seeking work. We do not believe the unemployed are just lazy and shiftless. This belief is an important underlying factor in the policy to maintain a low level of unemployment. Another example is our perception of the "proper" role of government in American society. Today, unlike a hundred years ago, society believes it proper for government to involve itself as a stabilizer and regulator of the economic system. If the laissez faire philosophy of the nineteenth century prevailed today—that is, the notion that because the economy is inherently stable, the best government is the least government—you would not need to study this section of this text (nor would it be written).[1]

If we start from the premise that our economic goals should be reasonable and attainable targets, our actual choice of economic goals depends in part on how much we understand about how the economy works and how it can be influenced by policy. The question is: how do we as a society decide what is reasonable and attainable?

---

[1] Of course, there has been and will continue to be discussions about the proper size of government and, therefore, the optimal degree of government involvement or intervention in society. In the late 1970s, this issue has been a particularly hot one. Such discussions have been generated by the rise in total government spending and taxes.

As we acquire greater knowledge of how the economic system works, we consequently learn how alterations here and there affect its performance. Some conditions, events, and developments that were once regarded as inevitable—such as severe recessions—are now considered controllable to some degree. However, whether stabilization policy is in fact brought to bear on a particular problem depends partly on the economic literacy of the nation. If the electorate (the voters) does *not* regard an economic development, say high unemployment, as inevitable but rather something that government policy can affect and solve, then pressure is exerted through the political process to "do something." On the other hand, if the public did not understand or expect that an economic problem could be solved, political action might not be forthcoming.

There are dozens of economic goals we could strive for. Examples would include full employment, greater equality in income distribution, and economic freedom, to mention just a few. On some of these goals, such as income distribution, there is some controversy. Nevertheless, most economists and policymakers agree that our macroeconomic goals are "full" employment, "sustained" economic growth, "reasonable" price stability, and international "balance" or "equilibrium."

WARNING

The quotation marks around the adjectives above are there to emphasize the imprecision of these *qualitative* goals. The flowery rhetoric used in discussing and analyzing our economic goals can hide the promise and pitfalls of policy actions behind a cloud of ambiguity. In trying to pierce this cloud, some points covered in earlier chapters should be helpful. In particular our discussion of the structure of the economy in Chapter 14 and our brief discussion of the impact of political and economic factors on policy decisions should make you a little skeptical of our government's ability to be all things to all people.

Having specified the general economic goals, which cannot be measured precisely, we should point out that they are not ends in and of themselves but only the means of achieving underlying social goals. In the words of Walter Heller, a former Chairman of the President's Council of Economic Advisers:

"Full" employment of our human and material resources. The term "full employment" stands as a proxy, as it were, for the fulfillment of the individual as a productive member of society, for the greater equality that grows out of giving every able-bodied worker access to a job, and for a national determination to demonstrate that a market economy, based on freedom of choice, can make full and productive use of its great potential.

"Sustained" economic growth, our proxy for a rising standard and quality of life at home, and an everbroadening base for our economic and political leadership abroad.

"Reasonable" price stability, our proxy for equity between fixed and variable income recipients and, in today's outward-looking economy, a vital condition for maintaining our competitive position in world markets without trade restrictions.

International "balance," our proxy for promoting an international economic setting in which there will be free movement of people, commerce, and finance across national boundaries, and scope for expansionary domestic policies.*

* Walter E. Heller, *New Dimensions in Political Economy* (New York: Norton, 1967), pp. 59–60. We have made minor changes in Heller's terminology to conform with ours.

With the above discussion as background, we can now begin to analyze the relationship between goals and policymaking in more detail.

17-3
MODELING SOCIETY'S
ECONOMIC OBJECTIVES

Although we realize that society's economic goals are not precisely measurable, we do know that the economic well-being of society depends on how well it achieves its economic objectives. For instance, consider the objective of price stability. The better inflation is controlled, the better off society will be. This relationship can be expressed as:

$$(17\text{-}1) \qquad\qquad S = f(\bar{\dot{p}})$$

where S is a measure of the satisfaction or the utility society receives from achieving its economic goal to control inflation and $\dot{p}$ measures the actual inflation rate (remember, a dot over a letter indicates a rate of change in percent). Because S represents satisfaction or utility received, the relationship is called a *utility function*. A minus sign is put over $\dot{p}$ to indicate that the relationship between $\dot{p}$ and S is negative; the utility function simply tells us that the higher the inflation rate, the less satisfaction or utility society experiences. The lower the inflation rate (that is, the more the economic goal of controlling inflation is achieved), the more satisfaction society receives.

The *degree* of dissatisfaction (or disutility) experienced will depend on how much the actual inflation rate exceeds the objective (where the objective is the inflation rate deemed consistent with "reasonable" price stability). Let us denote $\dot{p}^*$ as the inflation rate representing the goal of price stability. Then the difference $(\dot{p} - \dot{p}^*)$ would measure the gap between the inflation rate objective and the actual inflation rate. This difference would represent the society's failure to achieve "reasonable" price stability, resulting in a loss of utility or satisfaction.

If we expand Equation (17-1) to include the four economic goals we discussed in the previous section, the expanded utility function might look as follows:

$$(17\text{-}2) \qquad S = f(\overset{-}{\dot{p} - \dot{p}^*}, \overset{-}{u - u^*}, \overset{-}{\dot{y} - \dot{y}^*}, \overset{-}{\text{BOP} - \text{BOP}^*}, Z)$$

where $\dot{p}$, u, $\dot{y}$ and BOP each represent the measure of actual inflation $\dot{p}$, unemployment u, economic growth or output growth $\dot{y}$, and our international position BOP, respectively. The starred (*) variables represent the desired economic goals of "reasonable" price stability, "full" employment, "sustained" economic growth, and international balance. The Z stands for everything else that yields satisfaction but which we are ignoring here while we focus solely on the four primary economic goals.

The utility function in Equation (17-2) links the economic goals represented by the variables in the equation to the supposed overall objective of policymakers—to maximize society's satisfaction. The utility function also helps us to identify and study the problems policymakers face in setting and pursuing these goals. For example, we can examine things like:

a How are $\dot{p}$, u, $\dot{y}$, and BOP measured?
b What are the desired values of u^*, $\dot{p}^*$, $\dot{y}^*$, and BOP*?
c What are the relative weights that are assigned to each of the goals? Does missing the unemployment goal by 2 percent subtract the same amount from society's total satisfaction as missing the inflation goal by 2 percent?

The answers to these questions are the substance of the next several sections.

17-4
MEASURING THE KEY VARIABLES

Before we can analyze how economic goals are set, we first have to understand how they can be measured. In this section we will briefly explore how the four major economic goals that deal with prices, unemployment, economic growth, and international balance can be measured.

PRICES

A number of indexes are used to measure price changes. (The general method used to compute these indexes was described in Chapter 2.) These indexes are frequently discussed in the media. The most popular are the *Consumer Price Index* (CPI), which measures prices consumers pay at the retail level, and the *Producer Price Index* for finished goods (PPI), which measures prices at the wholesale level. The PPI is sometimes referred to as the "wholesale price index." Each of these indexes has its shortcomings. Nevertheless, they are often used in combination to analyze the degree of inflation in the economy.[1]

The PPI measures the general price level for finished goods, which are goods ready for sale to retailers. Because the PPI reflects price movements at the earlier stages of the production-distribution process, it is more immediately responsive to changing economic pressures than other price indexes. However, changes in the PPI are closely followed by similar changes in consumer prices.

[1] A broader (more comprehensive) measure of price changes than either the PPI or CPI is the GNP implicit price index (sometimes called the "GNP deflator"). This index is derived from the GNP accounts and it measures the general price level of all final goods and services (including government) produced during a specified period. The index suffers, however, from a number of technical factors in its compilation which limit its accuracy. Also, the index is published quarterly and hence has much less value as a measure of the timing of inflation than either the CPI or PPI, both of which are published monthly.

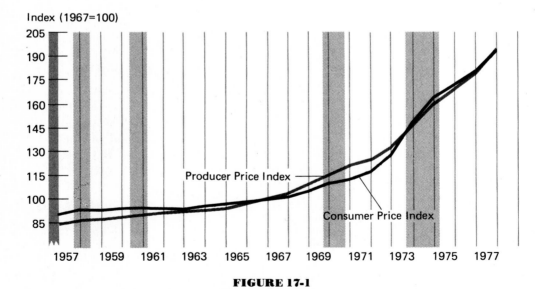

FIGURE 17-1

The long-run relationship between consumer (retail) prices and producer (wholesale) prices. Year to year, the correlation between movements in the CPI and PPI is quite high.

A close look at the data, especially over the long term as indicated in Figure 17-1, does show that consumer prices (as measured by the CPI) and producer prices have basically similar long-term profiles.

However, month-to-month changes in the PPI are not perfectly correlated with current or subsequent changes in the CPI. One reason the correlation is not perfect is that the PPI, which measures prices of commodities at their first level of transactions, may not measure the prices actually charged (producers may offer retailers discounts on the prices charged). In addition, the retail markup on a product may vary over the business cycle, altering the relationship between the PPI and CPI. For instance, during an expansionary phase, the retail price markup might be 10 percent over the wholesale price; during a downturn in the economy, the markup might only be 5 percent.

The CPI is the price index that is most widely employed as a measure of price inflation. In general, the CPI is designed to measure the changes in the average price of a representative sample of goods and services purchased by all urban consumers in the United States.[1] Its importance as a measure of the cost of living has increased markedly in the last decade. Upward movements in the CPI trigger wage adjustments in many labor contracts and benefit adjustments in social security and government pensions.[2]

Although the CPI is often used as a measure of the cost of living, it may often not be a precise gauge of changes in the cost of living. The CPI may be inaccurate because it measures only the cost of purchasing a given *set* of goods in fixed quantities. For instance, the CPI at present measures the cost of purchasing 400 items which were selected in 1972–1973. Over time, however, consumers change the kinds of items they buy. They substitute among goods and services because of changes in relative prices, tastes, and incomes. For example, consumers may buy more wheat germ or bean sprouts today instead of other goods. This substitution of food items in the family budget would mean that the CPI basket does not reflect actual consumer purchases. Rather, the CPI tells us what it cost today to buy the goods we were actually buying in the base year. However, since tastes and qualities of goods change only slowly and the base-year bundle of goods is updated periodically, the rate of change of the CPI is still the most widely used measure of inflation.

---

[1] Actually, the Bureau of Labor statistics publishes two CPIs. One covers all urban consumers and the other covers all urban wage earners and clerical workers. The former index reflects the spending patterns of about 80 percent of all consumers and covers—in addition to wage earners—the self-employed, professionals, the retired, the unemployed, and the poor. When the CPI was last under review, some users proposed dropping the wage-earner index in favor of the broader index which had more coverage and was more useful as a measure of general inflation. Labor unions objected, fearing that a broader index, being less representative of the spending patterns of their members, would not fully reflect price changes of things they buy.

[2] Cost of living adjustments (COLA) were first negotiated in 1948 by General Motors and the United Automobile Workers. Automatic increases in wages tied to the CPI have since become increasingly common. At present, about 8.5 million union workers are covered by COLA.

As we proceed, remember that the inflation rate (the rate of change of prices) over any period (month, quarter, or year) is always expressed as a percentage change (usually at an annual rate). For example, suppose the February CPI was 110 and the March CPI is 111. The change in index points is 1.0, which is equal to a percent change of 0.9 (percent change = the change in index points over the period divided by the level of the index at the start of the period = 1/110 = .009).

$$
\text{March inflation rate}
\begin{cases}
= \dfrac{\text{March CPI} - \text{February CPI}}{\text{February CPI}} \\[2mm]
= \dfrac{111 - 110}{110} = 1/110 \\[2mm]
= .009 \\[2mm]
= .9 \text{ percent}
\end{cases}
$$

To annualize this monthly figure you have to multiply by 12, resulting in an annual inflation rate of 10.8 percent in March.

$$
\text{Adjusting one-month (March) inflation rate to an annual rate}
\begin{cases}
= 12 \text{ months} \times .9 \text{ percent per month} \\[2mm]
= 10.8 \text{ percent}
\end{cases}
$$

UNEMPLOYMENT

Statistics on the labor force, employment, and unemployment are derived from a monthly survey known as the Current Population Survey which originated in 1940. This survey of approximately 47,000 households is the largest monthly survey in the world. To be counted as part of the labor force, a person must be 16 years old, working or currently available for work, *and* have engaged in some form of job-seeking activity within the past four weeks. By definition, the labor force is equal to those employed plus those unemployed. Note that if you are out of work but not engaged in some form of job-seeking activity, you are not counted as part of the labor force and, therefore, not counted as unemployed. To be counted as unemployed, you must be part of the labor force as just defined but without a job.

LOOKING BEHIND
THE UNEMPLOYMENT RATE

A popular myth is that unemployment is experienced by the same kinds of people for long stretches at a time. For most of the unemployed, this is not true. *There is a pool of unemployed and people enter and leave the pool frequently for a variety of reasons.* Thus, unemployment over a year, for example, is generally experienced by many different kinds of people, each individual being unemployed for a relatively short period.*

Table 17-1*A* shows the *duration* of unemployment (the number of weeks out of work) at two very different stages of the business cycle; May 1975 was close to a cyclical trough and May 1978 was three years into the subsequent economic recovery. Near the trough, the average duration of unemployment was longer, reflecting a larger proportion of unemployed persons who had been out of work for fifteen weeks or more. Note that in both May 1975 and May 1978, more than half of the unemployed had been out of work for less than fifteen weeks. This suggests that most unemployment reflects a variety of persons entering and leaving the pool of the unemployed.

Table 17-1*B* presents data on the reasons for being unemployed for the same two periods. As you might expect, the per-

TABLE 17-1A
DURATION OF UNEMPLOYMENT

PERCENTAGE UNEMPLOYED FOR	MAY 1975	MAY 1978
Less than 5 weeks	34.7	48.1
5 to 14 weeks	26.9	29.6
15 weeks or more	38.3	22.3
Average duration in weeks	14.8	12.1

TABLE 17-1B
REASON FOR UNEMPLOYMENT

	MAY 1975	MAY 1978
Job losers (layoffs)	57.5	42.5
Job leavers (quits)	9.2	13.5
New entrants	9.6	14.8
Reentrants	23.5	29.2

SOURCE: *Employment and Earnings* (Bureau of Labor Statistics, U.S. Department of Labor, published monthly).

centage of persons unemployed who are laid off declines as the economy recovers. When the economy improves, perhaps reflecting stimulative monetary and fiscal policy, there are fewer layoffs. However, this tendency, which will lower the unemployment rate, is offset to some degree by a tendency for "quits" to increase. In an improved economy, there are more alternative job opportunities. Formerly "discouraged" job seekers reenter the labor force. That is, persons who had been searching for work but became discouraged, gave up, and hence left the labor force, start looking for work again. These latter developments often contribute to some sluggishness in the downward movement of the unemployment rate during an economic recovery.

* The unemployment rate u can be expressed in terms of the annual frequency of unemployment F and the average annual duration of unemployment D. More specifically, $u = F \times D$. To illustrate, if the average member of the labor force is unemployed once every four years for 13 weeks, then $F = {}^1/_4$ per year and $D = {}^{13}/_{53}$ per year, or $u = {}^1/_4 \times {}^{13}/_{52} = {}^1/_{16} = .0625 = 6{}^1/_4$ percent of the labor force is unemployed. Anything which increases the frequency or duration of spells of unemployment will, in turn, increase the unemployment rate.

All of us would probably agree that everyone who seeks a job should be employed. We would also agree that this represents full employment. But the policymaker charged with the task of achieving full employment is faced with a complex problem. For example, as shown in Table 17-1*B*, unemployed persons can be divided into four major groups based on their *reason* for being unemployed. They are:

1

"Job losers," people who have been laid off either permanently or temporarily

2

"Job leavers," people who voluntarily quit or left their employment

3

"Reentrants," people who previously worked at a full-time job, left the labor force, and now wish to return to work

4

"New entrants," people who are looking for their first jobs

In what order should the policymaker be concerned about these categories? To a great extent, the answer depends on judgments as to what constitutes an economic hardship and how unemployment may contribute to economic hardship. For some people, an economic hardship is where unemployment means not having the necessities—the three basic elements of food, clothing, and shelter. Others see economic hardship as a relatively low standing in the income distribution. Still others consider an unemployed person, even someone who has adequate income from other sources, to be experiencing psychological hardship. Further, many people believe that long spells of unemployment among teenagers are especially damaging to their development as responsible citizens.

Thus, there is no single way of analyzing unemployment, measuring it, and correcting it to satisfy everyone. As a result, one economist has proposed groupings of unemployment indicators, identified by the symbols U1 to U7, which illustrate a range of value judgments from a very narrow definition of unemployment to a very broad definition. These groupings are shown in Figure 17-2.

The official unemployment rate regularly published for all those in the labor force age sixteen and over, as described above, is labeled U5. It does not involve a value judgment regarding a person's family or marital status, relative need for work, or personal (demographic) characteristics. It only requires that a person be out of work and seeking a job.

The *unemployment rate* is computed by dividing the number of unemployed persons by the labor force. For example, if the labor force totals 102 million, 7 million of whom are unemployed, the unemployment rate is equal to ($7/102 = .0686$) 6.9 percent.

We will not review all the definitions here, but to show the contrast in the range of definitions of unemployment let us review U2 and U6. The first of these, U2, measures the percent of unemployed persons who lost their last jobs, "job losers." Some analysts might prefer U2 as the measure of the unemployment rate because they believe unemployment is more serious (more of a hardship) for workers who are laid off.

Other analysts might prefer U6, which is more inclusive than U2 or the official unemployment rate U5. To compute U6, half of the number of unemployed persons seeking part-time work and half of the number of part-time workers who would prefer full-time work are added to the number of unemployed included in U5. The rationale here is that part-time workers who would prefer full-time work should be counted as at least partially unemployed and, similarly, that unemployed persons seeking only part-time work should be given half weight (instead of full weight).

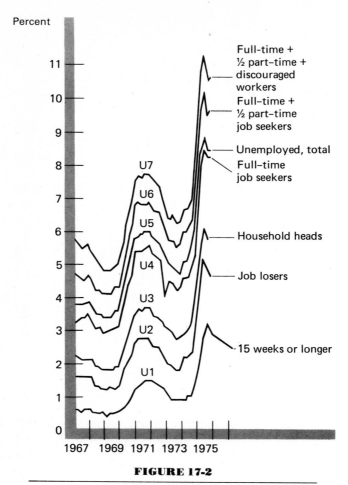

FIGURE 17-2

Seven ways to measure unemployment. (*Source:* Julius Shiskin, *Labor Force and Unemployment*, Washington, D.C.: Bureau of Labor Statistics, U.S. Department of Labor, Report 486, 1976.)

Our reason for reviewing these different measures of unemployment is to suggest that there is no single "true" measure of unemployment; rather, there are many different measures reflecting different points of view about the economic and psychological hardships imposed by unemployment. Nevertheless, policymakers have to choose one of these measures; U5 is the measure currently in use.[1]

---

[1] In the fall of 1979 a blue ribbon Commission on Employment and Unemployment Statistics issued their final report. It contained numerous recommendations designed to improve the data. It remains to be seen what if any changes the government will adopt.

ECONOMIC GROWTH

When we speak of economic growth, we are referring to the growth of output of goods and services. We saw earlier (Chapters 13 and 14) that if the economy is not operating at the full-employment level policymakers can raise aggregate demand so as to raise output and employment. If the economy is operating at the full-employment level, the actual level of output being produced is equal to the potential level of output which could be produced. At this point, economic growth or increases in potential and actual output would be determined by three things: (1) the growth in the availability of capital and labor to produce goods, (2) increases in the productivity of these factors of production, and (3) the growth in aggregate demand. Potential output grows as a result of growth of the labor force, capital stock, and of productivity; it is basically determined by *supply* —the more resources (factors of production) there are, or the more productive they are, the more output *could* be produced. Actual output produced depends on the growth of aggregate demand and the growth of potential output. If potential output grows but demand does not, the economy will stagnate as actual output grows more slowly than potential output. Similarly, if the economy is already at full employment and aggregate demand grows faster than potential output, inflationary pressures will intensify.

The goal of economic growth and the goal of full employment are often viewed as complementary. If the government enacts policies designed to maintain full employment this is likely to have a beneficial effect on economic growth. To illustrate the opposite case, assume the Congress raises the corporate income tax. We would expect that the business sector would decrease its investment in new plant and equipment. Remember that investment is a component of aggregate demand in the short run but that it adds to productive capacity and potential economic output in the long run. If investment is curtailed in response to short-run policy actions, then potential output will be that much less in the long run. Thus policies affecting aggregate demand in the short run may adversely affect aggregate supply in the long run.

Perhaps the most common measure of economic growth is the rate of increase in real national income (or output) as measured by the Department of Commerce (real GNP). However, the goal of economic growth and the way it is measured implies "The more real output growth, the better." In other words, everyone is better off if we can increase the size of the pie (total output) that is divided among us. But this attitude toward economic growth ignores the effect of growth on the environment and the depletion of natural resources. Economists concerned about pollution and, more generally, the "quality of life" have begun to question the desirability of trying to achieve high rates of economic growth. Here, as elsewhere, there are disagreements over the priority this goal should receive in designing policy. You should recognize, however, that if the pie does not grow, the standard of living in the United States will also not grow.

INTERNATIONAL BALANCE

In Chapters 7 and 16, we introduced the foreign sector and showed how transactions between domestic sectors and the foreign sector affect the balance of payments and the exchange rate. Some economists define international balance in terms of both the balance of payments and the exchange rate: if the exchange rate is stable *and* the balance of payments is equal to zero, the United States is neither gaining nor losing international reserves. While such a solution does represent a kind of balance between the domestic and foreign economies, it is too restrictive a definition. In general, the government should take actions that encourage the international trading of goods, services, and securities. Such actions may involve exchange rate changes and a balance of payments that is not always equal to zero. Unfortunately there is no simple way to measure this objective. About the best we can do is identify those actions which discourage trading and reduce the economic benefits that accrue to the United States.

Like economic growth, improving the international situation is a long-term goal. It can be achieved only over the long run. The relationship between the attainment of the international objective and the attainment of other economic objectives is complex. Chapter 21 is devoted to a discussion of this relationship.

17-5
WHAT ARE THE DESIRED VALUES FOR THE KEY VARIABLES AND WHAT IS THE RELATIONSHIP AMONG THEM?

We have just discussed how to measure price changes, unemployment, growth, and our international economic position. We can now ask: What are the *desired* values for each of these variables that will indicate the economic goals represented by them? That is, what should be the values of each of the starred variables in the utility function Equation (17-2)?

If we tried to get everyone to agree on an answer to this question, we would be resoundingly unsuccessful. Imagine that you have been appointed the economic czar of the United States and you are asked to implement a policy to achieve our economic goals. Being a most benevolent czar, you ask the people to give you desired numerical values for the starred variables in

It is important to recognize that the consensus of opinion on the appropriate economic goals for policymakers to pursue begins to crumble as more specificity is introduced into the definition of economic goals. No one is against full employment! But once we give more specificity to what we mean by "full employment," there is less agreement among the interested parties. Within the political arena, agreement on the economic goals among many individuals and groups who hold divergent views can apparently be secured only through generalizations. Two prominent scholars summarize the issue this way:

> We have a political process precisely because people have multiple goals that somehow must be reconciled into a single course of government action. This resultant course of action may be called a policy, but that term is misleading if it is regarded as implying one mind, one will, and one theory. Legislation *requires* ambiguity in the statement of goals so that coalitions can be formed in support of it, and each group can believe that the legislation serves its own specific purposes.*

* M. Rein and S. White, "Can Policy Research Help Policy?" *The Public Interest* (Fall 1977), 123 (emphasis added).

the utility function. The response will be quite varied. Different political leaders will offer quite different values for each of the variables, as will many of the political interest groups. Some might suggest an inflation rate of 7 percent as quite "reasonable" because they assign a high priority to minimizing unemployment and believe that a 7 percent inflation rate is consistent with low unemployment.[1] Others might suggest a zero inflation rate, as they assign a high priority to maintaining maximum purchasing power and a relatively low priority to the unemployment goal. As you receive answers to your request for specific values from the many and varied interests throughout the country, it will become obvious to you that no single value can be easily assigned to each of the starred variables in the utility function. What this simply means is that people have different views of the structure of the economy and different judgments about the priorities that should be assigned to each goal.

Given no clear-cut direction by the people as to what specific numerical values for each of the economic objectives to aim for, you will be faced, nev-

[1] Implicit in such a statement of course is the belief that it is more important to attain the unemployment goal than the goal of price stability. This raises another issue—which goal is more important to achieve; and that is interrelated with the issue of the desired numerical values for the key variables.

ertheless, as the economic czar, with the prospect of pursuing stabilization policy. As a policymaker who is cognizant of the people's interests, you will now have to make some choices of your own. These choices will have to be consistent with the broad economic goals and they must always remain within the bounds of what the majority of the people want, or else you might be evicted from your position. In fact, you probably will develop the diplomatic and political technique of avoiding specific answers and instead give answers in such terms as "full employment," "reasonable price stability," and so forth.[1]

It would, of course, be naive to suggest that "good" policy procedures require everyone to agree on everything and that all policy discussions must be models of clarity and logic. Nonetheless, we should ask ourselves and consider over the next few chapters whether or not a vague and broad approach to policymaking is, in effect, one of the major problems tending to contribute to poor policymaker performance.

17-6
ASSIGNING PRIORITIES:
INFLATION VERSUS UNEMPLOYMENT

Even if policymakers could agree on how to measure inflation, unemployment, and the other key variables *and* they could decide on the desired values (goals) for these variables, at least one problem would still remain: should each goal get equal weight or should we assign a higher priority (weight) to one goal and a lower priority to others?

Those economists and policymakers who believe that different weights should be assigned to different goals typically believe that the costs to society—called the welfare costs—of, say, high inflation are different from the costs of high unemployment. Those who think the costs of inflation exceed the costs of unemployment, believe that the inflation goal should get top billing; those who believe that the costs of unemployment exceed the costs of inflation believe that the unemployment goal should be assigned the highest priority. To get some feel for the issues involved, let us examine briefly the costs of inflation and unemployment.

The welfare costs of inflation depend critically on whether the inflation

---

[1] A recent attempt to specify the goals in greater detail was a bill introduced in Congress entitled The Full Employment and Balanced Growth Act, popularly called the Humphrey-Hawkins bill. This was a general economic policy bill intended to supplement the 1946 Employment Act and to define more precisely the economic goals of our nation. The initial bill was rather specific, but the version passed by Congress in mid-October 1978 was extremely watered down and mostly an empty gesture. The bill passed promises a simultaneous reduction of unemployment to 4 percent and of inflation to 3 percent by 1983, a balanced budget, a trade surplus, and—for good measure—higher farm subsidies. A little something for everybody!

is fully anticipated or not. If an inflation is unanticipated, it can redistribute income and wealth from one group to another. For example, under unexpected inflation, debtors gain at the expense of creditors. If the rate of inflation is not fully anticipated, the interest cost to the borrower, and therefore the interest return to the lender, will be lower in real terms than the return expected when the loan contract was made. For another example, if wages lag behind prices, real wages fall and firms benefit; labor loses, firms gain. More generally, as an unanticipated inflation progresses, the resulting changes in relative prices are associated with a redistribution of income and wealth. If the inflation were fully anticipated, we would expect wages and interest rates to reflect the coming inflation. This anticipation would mean that inflation would not have as much effect in redistributing income and wealth, as described above. But people on nominal fixed incomes would still suffer, of course; they might be able to anticipate inflation but they would be unable to do anything about it.

Briefly, these are some of the ways in which unanticipated inflation can redistribute income and wealth within the private sector. Unanticipated inflation can also generate distributive effects between the private and public sectors. We saw in an earlier chapter that the federal government is a constant debtor. Therefore, inflation reduces the real value of the government's outstanding debt. In addition, the progressive nature of our tax system results in an increase in real tax rates when prices and nominal incomes rise. Inflation (even if anticipated) serves, in effect, as a government tax on the private sector. This means that the government can raise revenue by "inflating." (See the example in Chapter 13.)

Inflation can also adversely affect the production of goods and services. On the demand side, inflation can generate uncertainty and discourage investment. It can also raise current consumption and lower saving as households adopt the maxim "buy today; tomorrow it will cost more." On the supply side, resources are wasted in economizing on cash balances, gathering information more frequently, changing price lists, and so forth. More generally, the advantages of a smooth-functioning monetary system (discussed in Chapter 2) are sacrificed when the purchasing power of money is declining rapidly.

All of these effects of inflation make the economic system less efficient, induce institutional and social pressures, and increase government intervention. In other words, they contribute toward a highly unstable economic environment.

Many economists view the preceding analysis of the effects of inflation as one-sided. They believe that billions of dollars of output are forever lost when actual output falls short of potential output—that is, when the actual unemployment rate exceeds the unemployment rate thought to be a proxy for "full" employment. Assessing high costs to unemployment (and relatively low costs to inflation) is also often the result of what might be called a humanistic approach to the inflation-unemployment problem. Elliot

Liebow, a noted anthropologist, puts it this way: "The question is not simply how much more unemployment we can stand, but whether we can stand, through deepening unemployment, a deepening of the race and class divisions that are already threatening to tear our society apart."[1] Liebow is even more specific: ". . . behind much of what presents itself to us as family instability, dependent women and children, violence, crime, and retreatist life styles, stand men and women, black and white, who cannot support themselves and their families."[2] The dilemma facing policymakers should now be clearer.

17-7
POLICYMAKING

How do policymakers behave when there are disagreements among different groups concerning the *specifics* of defining desired goals and assigning priorities among them? In the vernacular, they "hang loose." Quite bluntly, it is difficult to find any policymaker—monetary or fiscal—who would be willing to state publicly any definite numerical values for an economic objective or to be very exact on the priorities among economic objectives. Policymakers do assign specific values and make such choices. But what we are trying to say is that political necessity requires policymakers to avoid, as much as possible, making any specific public statements. In other words, we must distinguish between what policymakers *say* and what they actually *do* to analyze economic policymaking.

For the policymaker, the problem is not just defining a goal or selecting among goals. If it were that easy, all the policymaker would have to do is set an economic goal and select the policy to achieve it. That is, if we desire to achieve goal Y, we put into operation policy X and presto, goal Y is achieved. For it to be that easy, policymakers would have to know and understand the precise underlying structure of the economy. Unfortunately, there is considerable uncertainty (and therefore disagreement) within the economics profession and policymaking circles over the exact structure of the economy, giving rise to disagreements on things like:

1

The path or route that policy should take to reach objective Y

2

The time lag between policy action and its effect on key variables

3

The impact that a given change in a policy tool has on the key variables

---

[1] E. Liebow, "The Human Cost of Unemployment," in A. Okun (ed.), *The Battle Against Unemployment* (New York: Norton, 1972), p. 2.
[2] Ibid., p. 11.

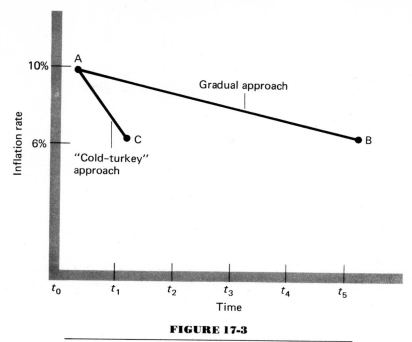

FIGURE 17-3

If inflation is high, policymakers generally might consider two alternative strategies to lower the rate of inflation to a more "reasonable" level. Each will have a different impact in the short run on unemployment and the growth of output.

In addition, when making policy decisions it is also important to consider the "initial conditions" and the "planning horizon." The ease or difficulty in reaching the destination of a journey depends partly on where you start. For example, a long-term goal of reducing inflation when the starting point is a 10 percent inflation rate might be approached by setting a series of short-term inflation objectives, each lowering the inflation rate in successive steps. The debates over economic policy often revolve around the size of the steps—that is, how fast to move toward a long-term goal.

Figure 17-3 is a graph that represents this idea of successive short-term objectives toward achieving a long-term goal. On the vertical axis is plotted the inflation rate, and time is plotted on the horizontal axis. The initial condition is at point A, a 10 percent inflation rate in period t_0. The policymaker may set out on a gradual approach to a targeted 6 percent inflation rate. Doing it gradually will require a series of short-term steps over five time periods (from A to B) before attaining a 6 percent rate. The alternative is to go "cold turkey" in the first period and to pursue a restrictive policy that brings inflation immediately to 6 percent (from A to C).

According to our analysis in Chapter 14, the "cold turkey" approach would obviously have an adverse effect on unemployment; unemployment would rise. Policymakers, not wishing to antagonize organized labor and others concerned with the unemployment goal, might therefore be more likely to opt for a gradual approach toward reducing inflation. Of course, there are less gradual and more gradual approaches to the target, and it is disagreement over such matters that makes for grand economic debates!

After setting a long-term goal, policymakers must regularly evaluate it and perhaps change or adjust that goal somewhere along the line. For example, it might very well happen that as we move toward less inflation, we change direction and concern ourselves with, say, unemployment. Hence, we never reach our original long-term inflation goal; rather, we change paths and objectives.

Thus far, we have seen that the economic policymaker's job is to choose goals consistent with society's goals, establish priorities among them, and define each goal statistically as well as possible. The policymaker must also choose the path toward each goal, being aware of initial conditions, the planning horizon, and the possibility of changing, adjusting, or abandoning goals. Who said a policymaker couldn't walk and chew gum at the same time?

To understand these issues better, we will develop in the next section a general model of how policymakers behave.

17-8
UNDERSTANDING POLICYMAKER BEHAVIOR

Policymakers select a set of long-term goals which are broadly consistent with the long-term goals of society. Presumably, the policymakers' satisfaction or utility from achieving these long-term goals is directly related to and derived from society's satisfaction or utility in achieving the same goals. The goals must be consistent because policymakers, although given rather broad discretion in making policy over the short run, are not immune from the political process. The fiscal policymakers—Congress and the President—can eventually be voted out of office if they are not pursuing the long-term goals of society. The monetary policymaker is isolated from the direct electoral and political process by its so-called independence (discussed in Chapter 18). Therefore, for the monetary policymaker, the political pressure is indirect. This indirect pressure is brought to bear on the Fed through breakfast at the White House, appearances before congressional committees, and other similar day-to-day events.

Policymakers' goals are really long-term goals which are used to guide short-run decisions. Hence, to understand the policymakers' actions, we need to examine their short-term behavior. Two general approaches or theories of behavior have been postulated to explain the actual behavior of policymakers. One approach is to assume that policymakers are informed, idealistic "guardians of the general good." Such policymakers would pursue policies that maximized society's welfare and thus clearly would act for the public good.

Another, quite different approach is to assume that policymakers are primarily concerned with their own welfare. That is, they are more interested in staying in power than in the welfare of society. In the words of Anthony Downs, who proposed this theory, a policymaker should be regarded as "an entrepreneur selling policies for votes instead of products for money."[1] In this view, their behavior is designed to maximize political support. Instead of being idealistic guardians of the public good who are guided by the desire to maximize social welfare, elected policymakers are viewed as *vote maximizers*, just as producers are profit maximizers.

The model we are discussing here leads to the conclusion that stabilization policy *can* become "strongly colored by the specific features of the political system, in particular by short-term vote-getting considerations, and that the business cycle therefore becomes a mixture of economic and political forces interacting with each other."[2]

In an ideally organized political system, politicians' pursuit of their own self-interest would tend to achieve the public interest through the workings of the political process. Unfortunately, the political system, like the economic system, is far from ideal. There is no single "public interest" in America, but rather many interests which often compete against one another. The net result in the view of many analysts is that policymaking is strongly influenced by political considerations rather than considerations relating to economic stability. Is it any wonder many believe cyclical instability is often induced (or exacerbated) by the government?

The issues we have raised here and in earlier sections on policymaking will be elaborated on in subsequent chapters. We will study both monetary and fiscal policymakers and integrate the role of political and economic factors into our study of their decision making. As we do so, however, remember that even if we set the political considerations aside, policymakers' control over the business cycle is very imperfect. There are several reasons for this. First, any shocks to the domestic economy can frustrate the best-conceived plans for control of the business cycle. Such shocks can include such things as an oil embargo, a poor crop of anchovies in Peru, or a major labor-management dispute in the United States. Second, although our level of understanding of the functioning of the economy has improved markedly over the past twenty-five years, it nevertheless remains limited in key areas. This uncertainty means that any action under consideration by policymakers could ultimately turn out to be the wrong move. The resulting concern, in turn, leads to some caution and

[1] Anthony Downs, "An Economic Theory of Political Action in a Democracy," *Journal of Political Economy* (April 1956), 137.
[2] Assar Lindbeck, "Stabilization Policies in Open Economies with Endogenous Politicians," *American Economic Review* (May 1976), 14.

timidity in pursuing various policies. This risk-averse characteristic of the policymaking process means that there are lags not only in recognizing the possible need for action but also in making the decision to take action. When these "recognition" and "decision" lags are added to the "impact" lag—that is, the time between the action and its impact on the economy—it is not hard to see why policy actions might often turn out to be "too little, too late." In general, control of the business cycle is imperfect because of the delicate balancing (compromising) of the interests and opinions of various organizations which challenge the wisdom and authority of the national government and often succeed in modifying both the actions of policymakers and the effects of such actions.

17-9
SUMMARY OF MAJOR POINTS

1

Our economic goals are guides used by policymakers in formulating and implementing policy actions.

2

The primary goals of stabilization policy are full employment, reasonable price stability, sustained economic growth, and international stability.

3

The utility or satisfaction society derives from its stabilization policy actions can be viewed as a function of the gap between the desired and the realized value of each of the variables representing the various stabilization goals. A reduction in the gap for any one goal (assuming the gap has not widened for the other goals) will increase the utility or satisfaction of society.

4

Some of the goals may conflict, at least in the short run. Moving closer to our growth goal may move us further away from our inflation goal. Thus, society must "weigh" each of the goals. These weights will differ depending on the attitudes and the political philosophy of the party in power. A Republican administration might prefer low growth and low inflation. A Democratic administration might prefer high growth, even at the cost of high inflation.

5

For each of our policy goals, there are many ways of measuring whether it has been achieved or not. Even if we agree on the appropriate measure of the variable for an economic goal, there is still disagreement on the appropriate policy target (numerical value) for the variable in question.

6

Even if we can specify numerical values for our targets, we still have the problem of developing policies to achieve those targets. First, the desired policy may not be politically feasible. Second, even if the political system can enact the desired policy, administrators may not be able to achieve the targets set forth by the policymakers.

7

The structure and workings of the economy are not perfectly known. This means that any given policy action may not give the desired policy result.

8

The primary objective of political policymakers is probably to maximize their political support. In an ideal, well-organized political system, policymakers maximizing their own political support would also ensure maximization of society's welfare (well-being). Unfortunately, the political system (like the economic system) contains many impediments to the achievement of this social optimum.

17-10
REVIEW QUESTIONS

1   The federal government can be both a stabilizing and a destabilizing influence in the American economy. Explain this seeming paradox.

2   Some stabilization goals conflict with each other, others are complementary. Explain how this complicates the job of specifying values for target variables that are used to measure the achievement of our stabilization goals.

3   There are many measures of inflation, many measures of unemployment, many measures of growth, many measures of international stability. Discuss some of the problems involved in specifying which measures to use for policy purposes.

4   If there is a trade-off between unemployment and inflation, how do we decide which is the lesser evil?

5   Discuss the interrelationships between achieving short-run and long-run stabilization goals.

6   Achieving the short-run goal of low inflation may not contribute to

achieving our desired long-run growth rate. Explain why this could be the case.

7 As the economy recovers from a recession and stimulative monetary and fiscal policies are enacted, the unemployment rate often falls rather slowly. Explain the reasons for this phenomenon.

8 Identify the costs to society of unanticipated inflation.

9 In the short run, investment spending is an important component of aggregate demand. Explain how policies designed to reduce aggregate demand in the short run may have an adverse effect on economic growth in the long run.

10 Suppose you are Chairman of the Federal Reserve System and, like everyone else, desire "full employment" and "reasonable price stability." Denote these goals by u^* and $\dot{p}^*$. Assume you have one policy tool—denote it by X. What are the problems involved in setting X so that your goals can be achieved over time?

17-11
SUGGESTED READINGS

1 For a discussion of the political process and policy formation, see Randall Bartlett, *Economic Foundations of Political Power* (New York: Macmillan, 1973), chaps. 1, 2, 7, and 11, and Anthony Downs, *Economic Theory of Democracy* (New York: Harper & Row, 1957), chaps. 1, 2, and 3.

2 A readable integration of the academic, political, and policymaking systems can be found in M. Rein and S. White, "Can Policy Research Help Policy?" *The Public Interest* (Fall 1977), 119–136, and R. Lombra, "Policymaking and Policy Advice: Economic, Political, and Social Issues," in *The Political Economy of Policymaking* (Beverly Hills, Calif.: Sage, 1979), pp. 13–34.

THE FEDERAL RESERVE: WHO DOES WHAT

There have been three great inventions since the beginning of time: fire, the wheel and central banking.

Will Rogers

18-1
"STOCK PRICES SLUMP ON FEAR OF FED MOVES"

This was a recent headline on the financial page of a major newspaper. The story went on to discuss why the Dow Jones industrial average (an index of stock prices) dropped 10 points the previous day. On this occasion, many financial observers believed that stock prices fell due to anticipated monetary policy actions that might slow the growth rate of money and raise interest rates (the cost of borrowing). Of course, monetary policy does not affect only the prices of stock. We have seen in earlier chapters that changes in interest rates and bank reserves induce firms, households, banks, and foreigners to alter their behavior (that is, adjust their portfolios). The task now before us is to study the tools available to the policymakers and to analyze in some detail how monetary policy affects the behavior of various sectors in the economy.

Our study of the Federal Reserve System is divided into two chapters. In this chapter we look at the organization of the Fed and the policy tools of the Federal Reserve System. This includes an analysis of the administrative (power) structure within which policy decisions are formulated. In the following chapter, we study how monetary policy actions are transmitted to the economy. We will take an especially careful look at the mechanism which links Fed monetary policy actions to the financial system and ultimately to unemployment, inflation, and economic growth. This is called the *transmission mechanism*. Once we understand the nature of the transmission mechanism, we will be in a better position to examine the factors (economic *and* political) which affect the actual behavior of the monetary policymakers. The emphasis here is on what the Federal Reserve does in formulating and implementing policy and why it acts as it does. In Chapters 9 and 10, we analyzed the role of the supply of bank reserves in determining the supply of money; in Chapters 13 and 14, we saw how bank reserves affected interest rates, prices, output, and employment. Throughout these chapters we did not explain how the changes in reserves were effected or what generated such changes. By establishing a link between the objectives of monetary policy, the actions resulting from that monetary policy, and the anticipated state of the economy, we will be able to see more clearly the underlying rationale of various policy actions.

18-2
THE FEDERAL RESERVE:
THE ORGANIZATIONAL STRUCTURE

A few years ago, a public opinion poll in one of the weekly news magazines reported that the Chairman of the Board of Governors of the Federal Reserve System was considered the second most influential person in the United States, topped only by the President. This poll reflected something about the importance of the Federal Reserve System and monetary policy in our lives.

The Federal Reserve System was created by Congress in 1913 to avoid the banking crises that had periodically plagued the United States economy, the most recent of which had been the banking crisis of 1907— Congress moved slowly back then too! The main purpose of the Federal Reserve was simple. It served as a central bank which could lend funds to commercial banks during periods of liquidity strains and thus provide these banks with the cash necessary to avoid insolvency.[1] This concept

---

[1] For an excellent monetary history and a summary of the events leading up to the legislation establishing the Federal Reserve, see Milton Friedman and Anna Jacobson Schwartz, *A Monetary History of the United States, 1867–1960* (Princeton, N.J.: Princeton University Press, 1963), chap. 4.

was referred to in the 1913 legislation as providing an "elastic currency," and it is today often referred to as "the lender of last resort" function.

Over time, the original purposes of the Federal Reserve Act have been modified. In the midst of the Great Depression, it was clear that the limited scope and powers of the Federal Reserve System were not up to handling the nearly 8000 bank failures which occurred during the 1930–1933 period. Additional policy tools and regulations were needed. In the Banking Reform Acts of 1933 and 1935, many of these tools and regulations were provided. For instance, it was during this period that the Fed was given enlarged power to vary reserve requirements, to set margin regulations on stock market collateral, and to prohibit the payment of interest on demand deposits.

The most significant change that occurred during this period involved the underlying role of the Federal Reserve, that is, the Fed's purpose and objectives. The existing economic environment, the changing view of the role of government policy, and the new legislation all moved the Fed into a new era. That is, the Federal Reserve System became a full-fledged central bank. It was charged with contributing to the attainment of the nation's economic and financial goals through its ability to influence the availability and cost of money and credit in the economy. Let us first identify the major parts of the Federal Reserve System and then discuss the role of each.

BOARD OF GOVERNORS

The core of the Federal Reserve System is the Board of Governors, located in Washington, D.C. The Board consists of seven members appointed by the President with the advice and consent of the U.S. Senate. Members of the Board are appointed for fourteen-year terms which are arranged so that one term expires every two years. The long tenure and staggered terms were designed to help insulate the Board from day to day political pressures.[1] In theory, the President of the United States, serving four years, would be able to appoint only two of the seven on the Board, thus preserving the type of independence of judgment enjoyed by the Supreme Court. (In actuality, deaths and early resignations of Board members have permitted recent Presidents to name about one new Board member a year.) We might also note that Board members cannot be reappointed and can be removed from office only under extraordinary circumstances. (It has never happened.)

The President appoints (with the advice and consent of the Senate) one of the seven to be Chairman and one to be Vice Chairman. The choice of Chairman is crucial, for experience shows he (there has not yet been a she)

---

[1] The concern about political pressure on the central bank was well founded in the early history of banks in the United States. For instance, see Bray Hammond, *Banks and Politics in America from the Revolution to the Civil War* (Princeton, N.J.: Princeton University Press, 1957).

FEDERAL RESERVE BANKS

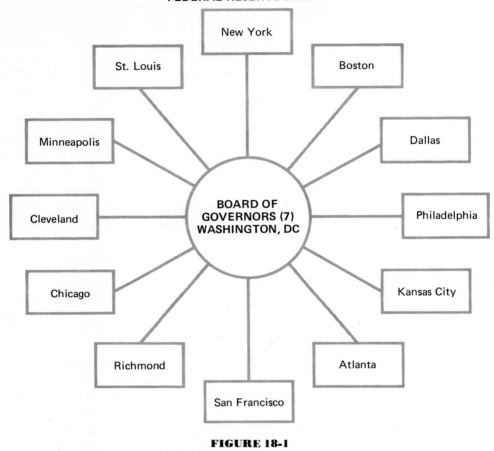

New York

St. Louis

Boston

Minneapolis

Dallas

BOARD OF
GOVERNORS (7)
WASHINGTON, DC

Cleveland

Philadelphia

Chicago

Kansas City

Richmond

Atlanta

San Francisco

FIGURE 18-1

The nation is divided into *twelve* districts. Each district is
served by a Federal Reserve bank located in a large city in the
district. The Board of Governors for the whole Federal Reserve
System is located in Washington, D.C.

becomes the chief spokesman for the Fed and thus a strong force in United
States economic policymaking.

FEDERAL RESERVE BANKS

The original Federal Reserve Act divided the nation into twelve districts.
Each Fed district is served by a Federal Reserve bank located in a large city
in the district. Thus, as shown in Figure 18-1, we have the Federal Reserve
Bank of Boston, the Federal Reserve Bank of New York, and so on, respectively, for Philadelphia, Richmond, Cleveland, Atlanta, Chicago, Dallas,

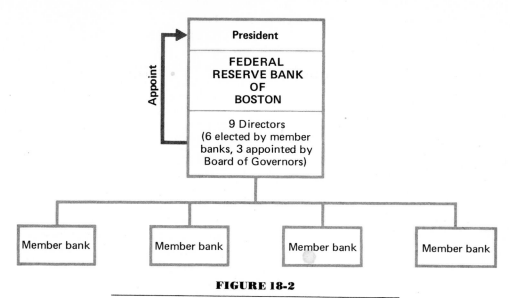

FIGURE 18-2

Commercial banks which are members of the Fed within the district served by the Federal Reserve Bank of Boston elect six directors of the Reserve bank. The Fed's Board of Governors appoints three additional directors. The directors appoint the President of the Federal Reserve Bank of Boston.

Kansas City, St. Louis, Minneapolis, and San Francisco.[1] As discussed in Chapter 8, all commercial banks which are national banks (federally chartered) must join the Federal Reserve System. State-chartered banks may or may not join. As shown in Figure 18-2, the member banks within a Reserve bank district (say, the Boston district) elect six of the nine directors of that Reserve bank and the Board of Governors appoints the other three. These directors, in turn, appoint the president and other officials of that Reserve bank.

The reason why the original Federal Reserve Act created twelve reserve banks (and the election of directors by member commercial banks) was to decentralize policymaking authority. We will see later that, over time, the desire to decentralize authority has been frustrated by the increased concentration of policymaking authority in Washington.

FEDERAL ADVISORY COUNCIL

The Federal Advisory Council is composed of twelve individuals (often prominent bankers), one from each of the Federal Reserve districts. As its name suggests, the Advisory Council's power is very limited. It meets sev-

[1] Geography buffs who will not sleep until they see the boundaries of each district are referred to a handy map included in a number of texts on the principles of economics and each issue of the *Federal Reserve Bulletin.*

eral times a year with the Board of Governors to provide advice on economic and banking matters. Federal Reserve insiders say that the Advisory Council serves little useful function. They say it serves mainly as a medium for public relations and the exchange of information. We do hear that the cocktails after the meetings are great!

FEDERAL OPEN MARKET COMMITTEE

The Federal Open Market Committee (FOMC) is the principal policy-making body within the Federal Reserve System; it formulates and implements monetary policy. The twelve-person membership of the FOMC includes all seven members of the Board and five of the twelve Federal Reserve Bank presidents. The President of the New York Federal Reserve Bank (which as we shall see executes policy in accord with the FOMC's instructions) always holds a seat on the FOMC and is a permanent voting member. The remaining four seats are filled by the other Reserve Bank presidents serving one-year terms on a rotating basis. It should be noted that although only five Federal Reserve Bank presidents have voting rights on the FOMC at any one time, all twelve presidents (and their senior advisers) attend FOMC meetings and participate in the discussions. By law, the FOMC determines its own internal organization. By tradition, it elects the Chairman of the Federal Reserve Board as Chairman of the FOMC and the President of the New York Reserve Bank as Vice Chairman of the FOMC. With the Board having seven of the twelve votes, perhaps you can see why most of the policymaking authority resides in Washington.

The FOMC meets in the strictest security in Washington every four to five weeks, usually on the third Tuesday of every month. Thirty days after the meeting, the FOMC publishes a summary of its meeting, called the "Record of Policy Actions," in the *Federal Reserve Bulletin*.[1] Included in the Record is the "Policy Directive," which is usually a two- to four-paragraph statement. This statement represents a digest of the meeting, states the policy consensus of the FOMC, and sets forth the operating instructions (or directive) to the Federal Reserve Bank of New York regarding the conduct of open market operations. New York is the center of the United States financial system. Since monetary policy affects the economy by working its way through the financial system, it is logical that the New York Fed should execute policy on behalf of the entire Fed.

In the 1950s and 1960s, the "Policy Directive" was a very unclear statement. For example, it was not unusual for the directive to instruct the New York Fed to maintain "an even keel tipped on the side of ease" or to "lean

---

[1] The secrecy of the contents of the meeting and the delay in publishing a summary of the actions contributes to the mystique surrounding monetary policy. It is also a sore spot with Congress, especially in light of the Freedom of Information Act. The Fed is, in fact, sensitive to this, because it has, over time, shortened the lag for releasing the "Record of Policy Actions" to thirty days from ninety days.

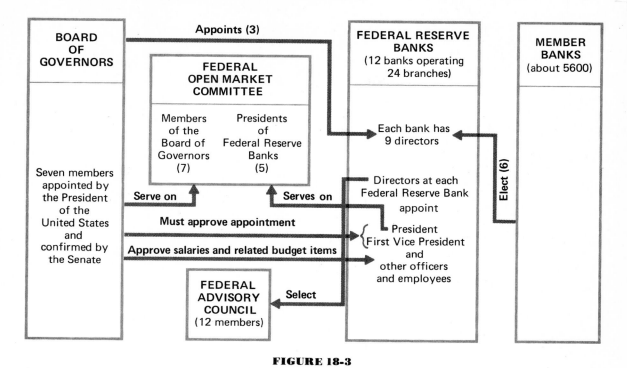

FIGURE 18-3

Organizational structure of the Federal Reserve System.
(*Source:* Adapted from *The Federal Reserve System—Purposes and Functions*, Washington, D.C.: Board of Governors, 1974.)

against the wind." Such broad and vague instructions gave the New York Fed little guidance and considerable freedom in executing policy. However, since the beginning of the 1970s, the directive has become much more precise. It now includes specific values for various strategic target variables. For example, the directive might specify that open market operations over the coming month should be conducted so as to achieve M1 growth of 4 to 6 percent, M2 growth of 11 to 13 percent, and a federal funds rate of 9½ to 10 percent. Since such actions can affect current and future economic and financial conditions, economists, financial investors, and professional portfolio managers read the "Record of Policy Actions" and the "Policy Directive" very carefully.[1]

We have cooked up (with some help) Figure 18-3 to help you get an overall picture of the organizational structure of the Fed. After we discuss the instruments or tools which the Fed has at its disposal, we will have more to say about who does what within the organization.

[1] Excerpts from a "Record of Policy Actions" are reprinted as an appendix to Chapter 19.

18-3
THE FED'S POLICY TOOLS[1]

Before we can discuss how the Fed forms monetary policy and puts it into action and why in general the Fed does what it does, we must examine the tools available to Fed policymakers and the way in which these tools are used. As shown in Figure 18-4, open market operations are at the top of the list of tools, followed by the discount rate, reserve requirements, Regulation Q interest-rate ceilings, margin requirements, and a rather innocuous tool called "moral suasion."

OPEN MARKET OPERATIONS

The buying or selling of United States government securities by the New York Federal Reserve Bank on behalf of the whole Federal Reserve System and under the guidance and direction of the FOMC constitutes far and away the most important day-to-day monetary policy tool.

The buying and selling of securities by the Fed is referred to as *open market operations* (OMO).

In general, OMO affect the quantity of reserves in the banking system and the level of interest rates, particularly short-term interest rates such as the federal funds rate and Treasury bill rates. (We say "affect" because changes in other factors, discussed in the Appendix, can have an impact on both reserves and interest rates. Remember, throughout our discussion of monetary policy, that the Fed is only part of the picture, albeit a crucial part. Regarding interest rates, for example, although the Fed is a major determinant of the supply of funds available, the level of interest rates will depend on the factors affecting the demand for funds as well as the supply.)

Write the following rule on your arm so you won't forget it: *when the Fed buys securities, bank reserves rise; when the Fed sells securities, reserves fall.* Since so much depends on this rule, let us trace out the mechanics of the relationship between OMO and bank reserves *R*. Suppose the Fed wants to add $1000 to the supply of reserves in the banking system. The *trading desk* at the New York Fed, which is run by the *manager* of the Fed's portfolio of securities (the trading desk manager is the individual at the New York Fed directly charged with executing OMO and carrying out the FOMC's instructions), will buy $1000 of securities and pay for these by issuing a check to the seller. Assuming the seller deposits the check in a

---

[1] The terms "instruments" and "tools" are often used interchangeably when discussing policy. Think of the Fed's tools or instruments as being analogous to the surgical instruments used by doctors.

```
┌─────────────────────────────────────────┐
│                                         │
│         THE FED'S TOOLS                 │
│  ─────────────────────────────────────  │
│                                         │
│  Open market operations                 │
│                                         │
│  Discount rate                          │
│                                         │
│  Reserve requirements                   │
│                                         │
│  Regulation Q interest rate ceilings    │
│                                         │
│  Margin requirements                    │
│                                         │
│  Moral suasion                          │
│                                         │
└─────────────────────────────────────────┘
```

FIGURE 18-4

These are the tools (or instruments) the Fed can use in trying to
stabilize the economy.

bank, say HLT National Bank, the bank will "clear" the check through the
Federal Reserve's check processing network. (This process is described in
the Appendix and Figure 18-9.) In this case, HLT will send the check to the
Federal Reserve bank in its district. The Fed in turn will credit HLT's
deposit balance at the Fed. (As noted in Chapter 8, commercial bank reserves can be held in two forms—vault cash or deposits at the Fed.) Given
this set of transactions, the relevant *changes* on everyone's balance sheet
will be as follows:

Fed		Public		HLT National Bank	
ASSETS	**LIABILITIES**	**ASSETS**	**LIABILITIES**	**ASSETS**	**LIABILITIES**
+$1000 securities (from public)	+$1000 deposits of member banks (HLT)	−$1000 securities +$1000 deposits (at HLT)		+$1000 reserves (at Fed)	+$1000 deposits (of public)

After the open market operation, the Fed has $1000 more securities and
the public has $1000 less securities. In return for selling the securities to
the Fed, the public gets a $1000 check from the Fed, which it deposits in
HLT National. The deposit is an asset for the public and a liability for the
bank. The bank, after sending the check to the Fed for collection, will have
its deposit balance at the Fed—a component of its reserves—credited.

Those of you with good memories will recall that in Chapter 9, where we
developed the relationship between changes in bank reserves and the
money supply, the illustration began with $1000 in deposits (and reserves)
being dropped on the doorstep of HLT National Bank (see Table 9-1). At the

time, we urged you not to worry about where the $1000 came from; we would deal with it later. The preceding discussion fulfilled our promise, showing you how the Fed can inject reserves (deposits) into the banking system. Holding other things equal, this injection will (as discussed in Chapters 9 and 10) affect bank behavior and therefore interest rates and the volume of bank assets and liabilities. We shall have much more to say on how the Fed guides its OMO and how these actions affect the economy; they are so important that the whole next chapter is devoted to OMO.

THE DISCOUNT RATE
AND MEMBER-BANK BORROWING

The discount rate is a highly visible, but less important, Fed policy instrument. The discount rate is the interest rate the Fed charges member banks for borrowing reserves directly from the Fed.

Holding other factors constant, bank reserves are increased when banks borrow from the Fed. We say that the discount rate is a "visible" policy instrument because changes in the discount rate are often well publicized (for example, on the evening news broadcast), unlike day-to-day OMO, which are followed closely only by a small group of experts in the financial system.

The setting of the discount rate is the general responsibility of the Reserve banks, although it can only be changed by the Board of Governors. The process works as follows: The Directors of the Reserve banks meet regularly and review matters relevant to administering the Reserve banks, including the discount rate. If the Directors see the need to recommend a change in the rate, they forward their recommendation to the Board of Governors, who evaluate it and either approve or disapprove the change. The ultimate authority to change the discount rate resides with the Board. In recent years, they have frequently disapproved requests for rate changes, and it is rumored that they have solicited requests for rate changes from Reserve banks when they wanted to change the rate and no requests were in hand. Is there any doubt about who calls the shots?

Changes in the discount rate can have several possible effects on bank behavior and the economy. The most obvious effect involves changes in the cost of borrowing reserves from the Fed—increases in the discount rate raise the cost of borrowing, while decreases lower it. Holding other factors constant, we would expect an increase in the rate to lead to a drop in the volume of member-bank borrowing from the Fed. Conversely, a rise in member borrowing would be expected following a decrease in the discount rate. Of course, in the real world other factors are hardly ever constant, and bank decisions to borrow or not borrow from the Fed will be based not on one but on several considerations.

The Fed views borrowing by banks as a privilege, not a right accorded members of the System. Since it is a privilege, the Fed urges banks to borrow only when other alternatives are not available. This sentiment is spelled out in the Fed's Regulation A, which specifies the permissible size of loans, their frequency, and the reasons for which member banks may borrow. It is here that the Fed's *discount policy* is laid out.[1] The rules make it clear that borrowing from the Fed is, under normal circumstances, to be for short periods, preferably no more than a few days or weeks. Banks that borrow frequently—say for eight consecutive weeks or for thirty out of thirty-five weeks—can be examined by the Fed's team of auditors. The Fed views the borrowing privilege as a means for member banks to deal with temporary liquidity needs which may be caused, for example, by unexpected deposit outflows or an unexpected surge in loan demands. The key word is "temporary." If a member bank borrows persistently, the Fed begins to think that the bank's management is either consciously violating the provisions of Reg A, cannot handle the liquidity pressures, or may have a chronic problem affecting its profitability and perhaps its solvency (its ability to pay off or redeem its liabilities). It is at this point that the Fed will step in. If the Fed feels that the borrowing privilege is being abused, it can deny the bank's request to borrow.

The main reason that banks do borrow occasionally (as the Fed expects them to do) is to acquire enough reserves to meet the Fed's reserve requirements at the close of business each week.[2] To illustrate, suppose HLT Bank is fully loaned up (that is, it has no excess reserves), the Fed's reserve requirement is 10 percent, and HLT's balance sheet is as follows:

HLT National

ASSETS	LIABILITIES
$50,000 reserves $450,000 loans and securities	$500,000 deposits

[1] Borrowing from the Fed requires collateral. This can be supplied in two ways. One is to sell securities to the Fed. This is called "discounting." Another method is to present the Fed with a promissory note secured by securities. This is called an "advance." While most borrowings from the Fed today are advances, the early days of the System saw banks borrowing at the Fed by discounting. Hence the term "discount policy."

[2] The details of reserve requirements will be explored in the next section.

So far, so good; HLT has $500,000 of deposit liabilities and, given that the reserve requirement is 10 percent, it has just enough reserves ($50,000) to meet its requirements. It also has $450,000 of loans and securities; the balance sheet balances! Now suppose a depositor walks in and withdraws $10,000. HLT loses deposits and reserves. The bank now has a problem: it has $490,000 of deposits, the Fed requires it to hold reserves equal to 10 percent of its deposits ($49,000), but it only has $40,000 of reserves. To meet its reserve requirement, it will have to come up with $9000 of reserves. One obvious possibility is to borrow the reserves from the Fed.

HLT National

ASSETS	LIABILITIES	
$ 50,000 reserves 450,000 loans and securities	$500,000 deposits }	Initial situation
−$10,000 reserves	−$10,000 deposits }	Effect of deposit withdrawal
$ 40,000 reserves 450,000 loans and securities	$490,000 deposits }	New situation; bank is short of required reserves

HLT National

ASSETS	LIABILITIES	
$ 40,000 reserves $450,000 loans and securities	$490,000 deposits }	Bank is short of required reserves
+$9,000 reserves	+$9,000 borrowing from Fed }	Effect of borrowing from the Fed
$ 49,000 reserves $450,000 loans and securities	$490,000 deposits $ 9,000 borrowing from Fed }	Bank now has enough reserves to meet Fed requirements

Whether or not HLT (or any bank) will borrow from the Fed when it needs reserves will depend mainly on the cost of borrowing from the Fed relative to the next best alternative borrowing source. Like anyone else, banks try to borrow where it is cheapest. Since the federal funds market (the market where banks trade reserves among themselves) is the major alternative to borrowing directly from the Fed, the volume of bank borrowing from

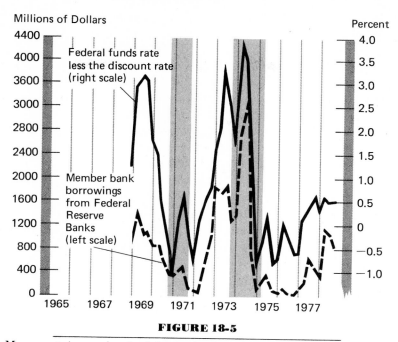

FIGURE 18-5

Movements in member-bank borrowing from the Fed are mainly a function of the difference between the cost of borrowing reserves in the federal funds market (the federal funds rate) and the cost of borrowing reserves directly from the Fed (the discount rate). As the federal funds rate rises relative to the discount rate, borrowing directly from the Fed becomes more attractive and member bank borrowing rises. (*Source:* Federal Reserve.)

the Fed is closely tied to the difference between the federal funds rate and the discount rate. This is illustrated in Figure 18-5, where we plot member-bank borrowing on the right vertical axis and the federal funds rate minus the discount rate on the left vertical axis. The higher the federal funds rate is relative to the discount rate, the cheaper it is to borrow from the Fed; therefore we would expect bank borrowing from the Fed to rise when the differential widens and to fall when the differential narrows.

The point is demonstrated quite clearly in Figure 18-5 for the calendar year 1974. You will note that during this year the federal funds rate rose relative to the discount rate. Correlated closely with this widening of the differential was a significant increase, to over $3 billion, in the volume of reserves borrowed. Conversely, in 1976–1977, when the differential was actually negative, the volume of bank borrowings from the Fed was relatively small.

LENDER OF LAST RESORT

You may wonder why there is any borrowing at all when the discount rate exceeds the funds rate (when the differential is negative). At any point in time (when the differential is positive or negative), there may be a number of banks in serious financial difficulty. If this is generally known in the financial system, other banks will be unwilling to lend these troubled banks reserves through the federal funds market. Accordingly, the banks who need reserves have no real alternative to borrowing from the Fed. The Fed will lend to them as a "lender of last resort" and try to assist the banks in overcoming their difficulties. Under extreme circumstances, the Fed (along with the FDIC) can replace a bank's management or declare the bank insolvent and close it. It is generally agreed that the Fed's willingness to perform this emergency function maintains confidence in the financial system and stabilizes the economy.

It is argued by some monetary economists that normal (as opposed to emergency) bank borrowings from the Fed raise a potential problem for monetary policy. These economists criticize discount policy because it permits banks to escape the effects of monetary restraint.

In fact, these critics refer to discount policy as an "escape hatch." The argument is simply that during periods of monetary restraint, when the Fed is using OMO to slow the growth of reserves and encourage a rise in interest rates, banks can avoid the restrictive effects of open market operations by borrowing from the Fed. Defenders of discount policy prefer to view such borrowings as a "safety valve." They see the offsetting effect as moderate and, in fact, helpful to the monetary authorities. They liken the member-bank borrowing to a brake on an automobile. With a brake, you can drive the car at a higher rate of speed than you can without a brake. Hence, although the discount mechanism seems to weaken monetary controls, it actually strengthens them by making it possible to use open market operations more vigorously. For critics of the discount mechanism, it is more like a defective clutch than a brake. The slipping clutch retards the rate of speed of the automobile; it does not help the automobile go faster at all. Further, these critics of the discount mechanism see a brake in an automobile as a discretionary tool, which is not analogous to the discount mechanism.[1] The impetus and initiative for borrowing resides with the member banks.

[1] Warren Smith, "The Instruments of General Monetary Control," *National Banking Review* (September 1963), 47–76.

It would be fair to say that most economists do not regard member-bank borrowing as a serious problem for monetary control. Economists generally believe that the Fed has the power and flexibility to achieve its policy objectives, even in the face of the "leakage" due to the discount mechanism. Banks cannot borrow indefinitely, and the size of each borrowing is limited. Furthermore, the Fed can adjust the discount rate so as to discourage borrowing. In fact, research shows that the Fed adjusts its discount rate to changes which have already occurred in open market rates, such as the federal funds rate.

The *federal funds rate* is the rate set in the market for federal funds. Federal funds are essentially reserves that banks trade among themselves for periods of one day (or sometimes several days). Banks that need reserves will demand them, while banks that do not need reserves immediately will supply them. The Fed can have a profound effect on the rate banks pay for borrowing reserves because it can essentially determine the supply of reserves. For example, by increasing the supply of reserves relative to the demand, the Fed can engineer a drop in the federal funds rate. More on this key short-term interest rate later.

It is often said that changes in the discount rate "cause" changes in other short-term interest rates. A careful review of the data suggests the relationship is the reverse; changes in short-term interest rates cause changes in the discount rate. Suppose the federal funds rate rises significantly relative to the discount rate as the Fed, through its OMO, slows the growth of reserves. As the spread between the funds rate and discount rate widens, banks will be encouraged to borrow from the Fed. Such borrowing will offset, at least in part, the slowing of the growth in reserves intended by the Fed. The remedy is for the Fed to adjust the discount rate upward and thus to discourage borrowing from the Fed. Clearly, the change in the discount rate follows rather than leads the change in the funds rate (and other short-term interest rates). The close relationship between the discount rate and the federal funds rate is shown in Figure 18-6.

In recent years, the discount rate and the Fed's discount policy have not been the main focus of monetary policy. However, from time to time the discount rate has been raised with great fanfare and publicity. The purpose of the announcements of these increases in the discount rate was to represent to the public (domestic and foreign) the Fed's resolve to fight inflation. Such psychological warfare is thought by most economists to be of limited value.

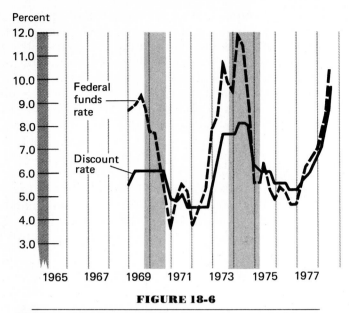

FIGURE 18-6

The federal funds rate and the discount rate are highly correlated. For the most part, this reflects the tendency for the Fed to adjust the discount rate so as to "keep it in line" with the funds rate.

RESERVE REQUIREMENTS

The third monetary policy instrument is reserve requirements on bank liabilities, which, for the most part, consist of demand deposits, time deposits, and savings deposits.[1] We saw in Chapters 9 and 10 how reserve requirements affect the money supply and the ability of banks to expand their loans and holdings of securities. The higher the level of reserve requirements, the less excess reserves per dollar of deposits are available for lending (acquiring earning assets) and, hence, the greater the cost of deposits to banks. If reserve requirements on demand deposits were 15 percent, then banks could lend up to a maximum of 85 cents on a $1 demand deposit. They would hold 15 cents as required reserves and, of course, would be earning no explicit return on this 15 cents. If the reserve requirement were 10 percent, banks would hold 10 cents. They would lend 90 cents. Therefore, an additional 5 cents could be earning interest for the bank; hence the cost of the deposit to the bank is reduced.

[1] As discussed in Chapter 8, banks do have nondeposit liabilities, and some of them are subject to reserve requirements. For simplicity, we shall ignore them here.

Changes in reserve requirements are a potentially powerful monetary policy tool because small changes in the requirements can greatly increase or decrease the volume of excess reserves in the banking system. For example, if banks are currently holding $30 billion of reserves, all of which are required, and the reserve requirement is 10 percent, we know that total deposits are $300 billion. If the Fed were to cut the reserve requirement by ½ percent to 9½ percent, this would, in effect, free $1.5 billion of reserves from the grip imposed by reserve requirements and lower the overall cost of deposits. Those newly released excess reserves could be lent by banks. The analysis is symmetrical; a rise in reserve requirements will lower excess reserves and raise the cost of deposits.

There are other reasons why the Fed has tended not to use the reserve requirement tool very much in recent years. Chief among them is the so-called *membership problem*. The reserves which member banks are required to hold can be kept either in the bank's vault as cash or on deposit at a Reserve bank. Whatever the location of the reserves, they are non-interest-bearing assets which member banks must maintain. They are, in effect, a tax imposed on member banks for belonging to the Fed. As discussed briefly in Chapter 8, nonmember banks are state-chartered and regulated by state banking authorities. In many states, the reserve requirements imposed by the state are more lenient than those imposed by the Fed; in some states the reserve requirements are lower, and also in some states interest-bearing assets, such as Treasury bills, may be used to satisfy the requirement.

With the rise in the general level of interest rates since World War II and the significant and historic jumps in interest rates in the 1970s, the opportunity cost of holding sterile non-interest-bearing reserves increased. It is no wonder then that over time, an increasing number of banks have decided to give up their membership in the Federal Reserve System. One vivid indication of this exodus is the drop in the percent of all commercial banks which are members of the System; in 1945, 49.1 percent of all banks belonged to the Fed, as compared with about 38 percent in 1978. Another indication is that the share of total bank deposits that are under the control of member banks has fallen from about 86 percent in 1945 to about 72 percent in 1978. These data are plotted in Figure 18-7.

The declining membership concerns the Fed for several reasons. First, it might impair the Fed's ability to control the money stock through open market operations which bring about changes in the reserves of member banks. We have seen in earlier chapters that changes in bank reserves are a major tool of monetary control. Second, declining membership can impair the Fed's ability to estimate the volume of money, bank reserves, total loans extended by banks, and other financial data. Only member banks are required to report, on a weekly basis, data on reserves, deposits, and so on. As member banks account for a smaller share of the banking system, these data become poorer estimates of the current status of the banking and

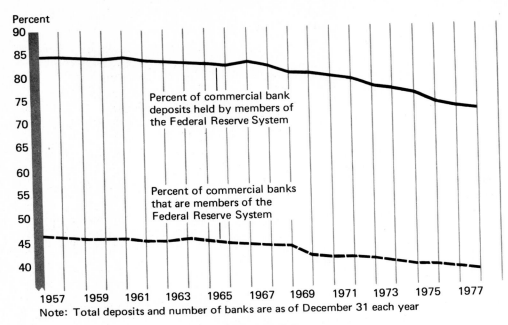

FIGURE 18-7

The ratio of member banks to total commercial banks has been dropping for some time. In part, this reflects a growing number of banks which have decided to give up their membership in the Fed. The result is that member banks account for a smaller share of total deposits in the United States than previously. [*Source:* R. A. Gilbert, "Utilization of Federal Reserve Bank Services by Member Banks: Implications for the Costs and Benefits of Membership," *Review*, Federal Reserve Bank of St. Louis (August 1977), p. 2.]

financial system. Before policymakers can decide where to go with policy, it is important that they know, as clearly as possible, where they are.[1]

In view of the membership problem, the Fed has been reluctant to raise reserve requirements in recent years, even though such a rise might have helped to slow the growth of the money supply and moderate inflationary pressures in the economy. Increasing the implicit tax could very well accelerate the decline in membership. As a result, reserve requirements have

[1] As mentioned in Chapter 8, the decline in membership in the Federal Reserve System is a hot political issue. Congressional hearings were held on the issue in early 1979. The proposals made to Congress have included the suggestion that all banks be members of the System; that the Fed pay interest on required reserves; that reserve requirements be lowered; that member banks be allowed to hold required reserves in secure, highly liquid interest-bearing assets; and so forth. By the time you read this, one of these proposals (or a variant thereof) may have become law.

been on the back burner.[1] Can you now see more clearly why we argued earlier that OMO were the major policy tool?

OTHER MONETARY CONTROLS: REGULATION Q

Besides the major monetary tools discussed in the preceding sections, the Fed has a variety of other tools that can have considerable influence on banks and financial markets. One of these is Regulation Q. As discussed in Chapters 8 and 11, this regulation allows the monetary authorities to establish a maximum interest rate that commercial banks (and thrift institutions) may offer depositors on time deposits and savings deposits.[2] The original purpose of Regulation Q was to limit the use of interest rates as a way of competing for depositors. It was believed that if banks were allowed to compete aggressively for funds, they would be tempted to engage in "rate wars." Banks would raise rates payable to depositors, which, in turn, would raise borrowers' costs to astronomical levels; it might also cause banks to seek high-yielding but risky and unsound business loans to cover the high cost of funds and still earn a profit.

The theory of the banking firm discussed in Chapter 10 should convince you that if Regulation Q were repealed, such behavior would be unlikely to develop. In general, banks seek to maximize profits subject to constraints regarding the liquidity and safety of their portfolios. Therefore banks would offer depositors rates on time deposits and savings deposits that are consistent with the return available on assets and that do not violate those constraints.

Even though the original justifications for the ceiling do not hold much water, the Fed did, on occasion, find the Regulation Q ceilings to be important in engineering an economic slowdown. The years 1966, 1969, and 1974 offer excellent examples of the economic impact of the ceilings. Each year was characterized by strong inflationary trends, strong business demands for loans, and rising interest rates. As money-market rates moved above the Regulation Q ceilings, disintermediation ensued. This reduced the availability of funds to businesses, home buyers, and so forth and contributed to the economic slowdown which followed.

[1] There are several subtleties regarding reserve requirements that are worth noting. At present, the structure of reserve requirements is quite complex—they vary by size of bank and type of deposit. For example, the reserve requirement on demand deposits for the largest banks is 16¼ percent, while for the smallest banks it is 7 percent; the requirement for all banks on savings deposits is 3 percent, while the requirement for all banks on time deposits with four or more years to maturity is 1 percent. See *The Federal Reserve System—Purposes and Functions*, for a discussion of the (somewhat dubious) rationale for this complex structure of requirements. You should also note that the volume of required reserves banks are required to hold in a given week (the bank week—the so-called statement week—runs from Thursday through Wednesday) is computed by taking the level of deposits on banks' balance sheets two weeks previous and multiplying them by the appropriate reserve requirement. This system of "lagged reserve accounting" is discussed in some detail by Albert Burger, *The Money Supply Process* (Belmont, Calif.: Wadsworth, 1972).

[2] The Fed sets the rates for member banks, the Federal Deposit Insurance Corporation sets them for nonmember banks, and the Federal Home Loan Bank Board sets them for savings and loan associations. An interagency committee coordinates the ceiling-setting process.

As discussed in Chapters 8 and 11, the incentive to innovate around the interest-rate ceilings led to several things: the development of nondeposit sources of funds, the suspension of the Q ceilings on large CDs, and the growth of money-market (or liquid asset) mutual funds. The days of Regulation Q are numbered. Although in the past it was part of the "cutting edge" of monetary policy, market innovations have reduced its usefulness. There are also serious questions regarding whether or not the ceilings are fair to everyone (the ceilings obviously discriminate against the small saver). All this indicates that the ceilings will probably fade away eventually. The introduction of money-market certificates in mid-1978 might be viewed as the first step in this process.

MARGIN REQUIREMENTS

Margin requirements, another little-used tool, govern the extent to which purchasers of common stock can finance their purchases by borrowing. The Fed's power to influence such borrowing directly grew out of the stock market crash of 1929. The general feeling was that the speculative boom which caused the rise in stock prices preceding the crash was fueled by extensive borrowing. When stock prices fell, the holders of the stocks suffered huge capital losses and could not pay off their loans. Those who had lent the funds—the banks, brokers, and dealers—were left with all the defaulted loans. As a result, they failed too, adding to the economic and financial collapse.

In retrospect, the Fed felt it should have had at its disposal a tool to make credit harder to come by in the stock market. The result was the development of margin requirements, which the Fed may vary between 25 and 100 percent. The requirement specifies the percentage of the price of the stock that a purchaser must come up with; the rest can be borrowed. Thus, if the margin requirement is 75 percent, the purchaser can borrow only 25 percent of the total purchase price.

MORAL SUASION

If all else fails, the Fed tries moral suasion. Moral suasion is not a clearly defined policy tool, but there is no doubt that there have been times, when the Fed feels it is warranted, that a letter or statement has been sent to member banks urging them to pursue a certain policy in the national interest. Generally, such letters or statements ask banks to restrict the rate of growth of loans. The Fed's "persuader" is a slightly veiled threat to examine the banks' records or possibly deny credit at the discount window.

A typical use of moral suasion occurred in September 1966, when the president of each Federal Reserve Bank wrote the member banks in that bank's district. The essential part of the letter stated, "The System believes that the national economic interest would be better served by a lower rate of expansion of bank loans to business" and that "this objective will be kept in mind by the Federal Reserve Banks on their extensions of credit to member banks through the discount window." The message was clear. Another example of moral suasion is a 1973 letter from the Chairman of the Board of Governors. This letter, sent during a period of strong inflationary trends, suggested that banks should be more cautious in extending lines of credit to businesses. The letter also warned these banks that stringent bank examination procedures would be employed to enforce this suggestion.

Economists have little confidence in the effectiveness of such actions; they all agree that it is good politics and demonstrates the Fed's concern about the economy, but few believe that banks or other participants in the financial system alter their behavior in any significant way in response to such "jawboning."

18-4
WHO DOES WHAT WITHIN THE FED?

Having spelled out the Fed's organizational structure and identified the various tools available to Fed policymakers, we will now show which group within the Fed has primary responsibility for each tool. Figure 18-8 shows the division of responsibility within the Fed. As you can see in the diagram, the Board of Governors determines reserve requirements, the discount rate, margin requirements, and the Regulation Q interest-rate ceilings.[1] The FOMC (made up of the seven Board members and five of the twelve Federal Reserve bank presidents) directs open market operations.

Clearly, the Board swings the most weight within the Federal Reserve System. As shown earlier on Figure 18-3, the Board even exercises general budgetary control over the Reserve banks. Remember the golden rule: "He who has the gold rules!" The Reserve banks deal directly with the member banks. In dealing with member banks, the Reserve banks administer discount policy; they are an important part of the nation's check-clearing system (discussed in the Appendix) and play an important educational role by providing banks and the public with information on Fed policy and the workings of the financial system and the economy.

Thanks to a former member of the Board who has written a book about the Fed, we can be even more specific about where the power to make policy within the Fed lies. Sherman Maisel estimated that the Chairman of the

---

[1] Not shown on the figure are the many regulatory and supervisory responsibilities carried out by the Fed. In general, the Board is responsible for the overall soundness of the banking and financial system and for implementing various pieces of legislation relating to borrowing and lending which the Congress has passed and charged the Fed with executing. Examples would include truth in lending, fair credit standards, regulation and supervision of bank holding companies, and so forth. Obviously, the Board is kept very busy with matters other than monetary policy.

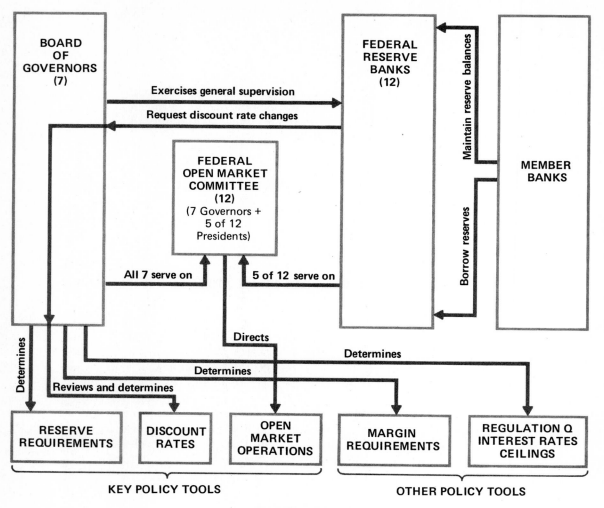

FIGURE 18-8

Who does what within the Fed? Note carefully how all important decisions are made either by the Board or by the FOMC. (*Source:* Adapted from *The Federal Reserve System—Purposes and Functions*, Washington, D.C.: Board of Governors, 1974.)

Board of Governors (and FOMC) had about half the power pie.[1] Perhaps now you can see why this individual is such a powerful figure in United States policy circles.

[1] Sherman Maisel, *Managing the Dollar* (New York: Norton, 1973), p. 110. This book is highly recommended.

18-5
THE FEDERAL RESERVE SYSTEM: AN INDEPENDENT WATCHDOG, CONVENIENT SCAPEGOAT, OR CUNNING POLITICAL ANIMAL?

The Federal Reserve System is a United States government agency whose primary responsibility is stabilization policy. However, the Fed is just one of many agencies of the government which also try to stabilize the economy. Others include the Council of Economic Advisers, the Department of the Treasury, and the Office of Management and Budget. Each of these agencies, unlike the Fed, is under the direct control of the executive branch of government. For example, the President can fire at any time the Chairman of the Council, the Secretary of Treasury, and the Budget Director.

The Federal Reserve was established by Congress as an *independent agency*. It is independent because of the way it is structured. For one thing, each member of the Board is appointed to a fourteen-year term, so that once appointed, a member of the Board does not have to defend his or her actions to the Congress, the President, or the public. Also, the Fed does not need or get an appropriation from Congress. This is because the Fed makes its "way" from the interest income it earns on loans to member banks and its holdings of government securities. Last, the Fed is exempt from many provisions of the Freedom of Information Act and "government in the sunshine" legislation (legislation which calls for government policy to be made in meetings open to the public). As a result, Fed policymakers usually meet in secret to formulate policy.

Nevertheless, the Fed is not completely outside the government; it is firmly embedded in our political system. In the short run, however, the Federal Reserve does not take orders from anyone in the executive or legislative branch of government. Its decisions regarding monetary policy are, in theory, not constrained by the whims of the President or Congress or by partisan politics. We say "in the short run" because, in the long run, Congress can pass laws that the Fed must obey; it could abolish the Fed altogether. We think it fair to say that the Fed is aware of these possibilities and behaves accordingly.

Ever since the Fed was created, politicians and academics have debated the desirability of Federal Reserve independence. The controversy has been largely focused on the degree to which the Fed should alter its policy in response to "suggestions" from the Congress or the President. Obviously, the more responsive the Fed were, the less independent it would be. The continuing debate over this issue in part reflects the frustration expressed by the President and some members of Congress in their often unsuccessful efforts to enact fiscal policy actions designed to attain our economic goals. In recent years, this frustration has led to several attempts to make the Fed more responsive to the Congress. The Fed saw such moves as a serious threat to its independence and vigorously fought off overt efforts to clip its wings.

Those who support independence do so mainly on the grounds that anything less than independence will inject "politics" into monetary policy operations. This argument was put forth eloquently by Arthur Burns, former Chairman of the Board of Governors, in a commencement address at Jacksonville University in 1977:

> In most countries around the world central banks are in effect instrumentalities of the executive branch of government—carrying out monetary policy according to the wishes of the head of government or the finance ministry. That is not the case in this country because the Congress across the decades has deliberately sought to insulate the Federal Reserve from the kind of political control that is typical abroad. The reason for this insulation is a very practical one, namely, recognition by Congress that governments throughout history have had a tendency to engage in activities that outstrip the taxes they are willing or able to collect. This tendency has generally led to currency depreciation [inflation], achieved by strategems ranging from clipping of gold and silver coins in earlier times to excessive printing of paper money or to coercing central banks to expand credit unduly in more modern times.

To Representative Henry S. Reuss (Chairman of the House Committee on Banking, Currency, and Housing), the independence of the Fed, despite the eloquent words of Chairman Burns, is inconsistent with democracy. Representative Reuss sees it this way:

> In these days of government in the sunshine, it would be hard to imagine the following scene: A board of twelve men meets behind closed doors once a month to decide the nation's fiscal policy.
>
> Seven of them have been chosen by the President, five by representatives of banking and big business. At this particular meeting, they review the nation's economic condition and decide that what's needed is a hike in taxes and a

cut in federal spending. The next morning, their decisions are quietly put into effect. Thirty days later, they issue a summary of the meeting telling the country what they did.

Fiscal policy, fortunately for the nation, is not really made that way. Taxing and spending decisions are debated thoroughly, in a tug of war between the executive and legislative branches. But we allow monetary policy to be shaped in a way that closely fits the scene just described.*

* Henry S. Reuss, "A Private Club for Public Policy," *Nation* (October 6, 1976), 370.

It is argued that the President and Congress are held accountable for the state of economic conditions. If unemployment is rising and inflation is rampant, it is the President and Congress who will be driven from office at election time. Because the President and the Congress are responsible for economic policy, they should have all the tools at their disposal. More generally, opponents of Fed independence argue that monetary policy, like other government policies, should be controlled by people directly responsible to the electorate.

The kinds of reforms that opponents of the Fed's independence would like to see include (1) a change in the way members of the FOMC are selected, particularly the five voting members who are Reserve bank presidents and who have been selected by the Reserve bank directors to sit on a public policymaking board; (2) a change in the makeup of the boards of directors of the Reserve banks;[1] and (3) a requirement that the Fed be more open with Congress and the public about its policies. With the Fed often projecting the idea that monetary policy is too complicated for the public and the Congress to understand, or that secrecy is essential to successful policy, it should not be surprising that Congressional representatives are suspicious. They want to open up the process of formulating monetary policy to examine and debate it.

Proponents of continuing the Fed's independence argue that politicians are interested in getting elected and reelected, and this means that they are short-run maximizers; they do not take the long view. This could be disastrous if the long-run impacts of policy are different from the short-run impacts. For instance, to please the electorate, politicians might pursue a stimulative monetary policy resulting in an expansion of economic activity, even though the longer-run impact of this policy might accelerate inflation.

Long-time observers of the political-economic wars believe that this de-

[1] A study by the staff of the House Banking Committee concluded that the directors are "representative of a small elite group which dominates much of the economic ills of this nation."

419

bate (over whether or not the Fed should be independent) is more form than substance. On the one hand, it is argued that Congress finds the current system quite convenient. If the economy performs badly, the Congress can blame the Fed for what went wrong and tell the public that the Fed, insulated by its independence, would not respond to Congress's call to "do the right thing." Scapegoats are convenient—if monetary policy were responsible to Congress, then who would there be to blame? On the other hand, there is considerable evidence that the Fed is in fact heavily influenced by political factors. Thus, the Fed's independence is in part an illusion. This is another dimension of what we have referred to earlier as "the political economy of policymaking," a theme we shall pursue in the next chapter.

18-6
APPENDIX—THE FED'S
BALANCE SHEET AND BANK RESERVES*

We will examine the consolidated balance sheet for the entire Federal Reserve System. This will help us to see how the Fed affects the volume of reserves in the banking system. The consolidated balance sheet for the whole Federal Reserve System is shown in Table 18-1. Let us first make sure that we understand each major category of assets.

Gold and Special Drawing Rights (SDRs) Certificate Account This account reflects the Fed's holdings of international reserves, discussed in Chapters 7 and 16. Changes in this account involve fairly complex transactions among the Fed, the Treasury, International Monetary Fund, and foreign governments. Nevertheless, it will suffice if you recognize that acquisitions of gold, SDRs, or foreign currency will raise international reserves in the United States and this asset account for the Fed; conversely, sales of gold, SDRs, and foreign currency will lower international reserves and this asset account for the Fed.

Loans These are loans made by the various Federal Reserve banks to commercial banks. As discussed in the text, the rate charged on such loans is the discount rate.

Securities These are the government and agency securities that the Fed acquires or sells through its open market operations. The Fed can buy or sell securities in either of two ways. First, it can buy or sell outright. An outright trade, other things equal, represents a permanent addition or subtraction of reserves from the banking system. Second, the Fed can buy or sell through what is called the *repurchase agreement* (RP). This is an arrangement whereby the New York Fed agrees to buy securities from the securities

---

* This section contains optional material which can be omitted without loss of continuity throughout the rest of the text.

TABLE 18-1
CONSOLIDATED BALANCE SHEET OF THE FED
(Billions of dollars)

		OCTOBER 26, 1977	OCTOBER 25, 1978	CHANGE OVER THE YEAR
Total Assets		$133.7	$156.2	$22.5
Gold and SDR certificate account		12.8	13.0	.2
Loans		1.2	1.8	.6
Securities		107.1	127.4	20.3
Outright	105.4		122.4	
RP	1.7		5.0	
Float		4.0	4.9	.9
Other assets		8.6	9.1	.5
Total Liabilities and Capital		133.7	156.2	22.5
Federal Reserve notes		88.6	97.9	9.3
Deposits of member banks		28.2	34.7	6.5
Deposits of U.S. Treasury		6.4	11.7	5.3
Other liabilities and capital		10.5	11.9	1.4

SOURCE: *Federal Reserve Bulletin*, Consolidated Condition statement for Federal Reserve Banks. See "Glossary: Weekly Federal Reserve Statements," Federal Reserve Bank of New York, for all you could ever want to know about the Fed's balance sheet and other Fed statistical releases.

dealers with whom it regularly does business,[1] and the dealers agree to repurchase the securities on a specific day in the near future. Most RPs are for one day, but from time to time they run for up to seven days. By using the RP, the Fed can increase reserves temporarily, other things equal, for a specific period of time.

As discussed in Chapter 12, (nonbank) dealers are highly leveraged firms that generally borrow funds to finance their holdings (inventory) of government securities. An RP, from the dealer's point of view, is a method by which the Fed finances the dealer's inventory of securities. The dealer is not really giving up ownership of the security when it is sold temporarily to the Fed, since it will be available to the dealer to sell when the RP matures.

The New York Fed can also execute the opposite of an RP, called a *reverse RP* or matched sale-purchase transaction. In this case, the Fed agrees to a temporary sale of securities to dealers which is matched by an agreement to repurchase the securities on a specific day in the near future. Again, most reverse RPs are for one day. Such transactions temporarily reduce reserves

---

[1] The Fed's OMOs are executed with government security dealers (see Chapter 12) which the New York Fed has certified as fit to make markets in such securities and to conduct business with the Fed. There are about thirty such dealers; about half of them are departments of large commercial banks and the rest are nonbank dealers (such as Salomon Brothers and Merrill Lynch).

in the banking system. You will see in a few moments how RPs can come in handy.

Float   This asset item arises from the accounting conventions underlying the Fed's check-clearing procedures. Suppose you live in New York and you send a check for $100 drawn on your account at a New York City bank to your mother who lives in Chicago. She receives the check and deposits it in her bank account. Her bank credits her demand deposit balance and sends the check to the Federal Reserve Bank of Chicago for collection. At this point for her bank, the check becomes a cash item in the process of collection. The Chicago Fed will send the check to the New York Fed, which will return the check to your bank. At that point your demand deposit account will be debited. For the two commercial banks (yours and hers), the Fed will complete the transfer of funds arising from the check by increasing the deposit account (reserves) of the Chicago bank at the Chicago Fed and lowering the deposit account (reserves) of the New York bank at the New York Fed. When all these transactions are completed, the total amount of deposits and reserves in the banking system will, other things equal, be as it was before. The difference will be in the location of the deposits and reserves (commercial bank deposits at Fed banks). Chicago will have gained and New York will have lost deposits and reserves. Because of the time it takes to transfer the check physically, the Fed will typically credit the Chicago commercial bank's account at the Chicago Fed before it debits the account of the New York bank at the New York Fed. This means that for a short time (usually a day), the deposit and reserves in question appear on the balance sheets of both banks. All this is shown in Figure 18-9. As a result, the Fed is, in effect, providing credit to the banking system through this procedure.[1] As electronic technology is applied to the check-clearing process, we would expect the volume of float to fall.[2]

Now that we have sorted out the major asset accounts, let us briefly examine the major liability and net worth entries.

Federal Reserve Notes   Federal Reserve notes are the paper money in circulation. These notes constitute about 90 percent of the currency in circulation in our economy. The other 10 percent of the total currency in circulation consists mainly of coins minted by the Treasury.

Deposits of Member Banks   As we have already learned, member banks may hold reserves in the form of vault cash or in the form of deposits at the

---

[1] All this is analogous to the way in which individuals use "float." Many of us write checks and send them off to pay bills and so forth, even though at that specific moment we do not have enough funds in our account to cover the check. Knowing that it takes time for the check to "clear," we plan to add funds to our accounts in time to cover the check.
[2] On the Fed's balance sheet, float is actually the difference between cash items in the process of collection (an asset) and deferred-availability cash items (a liability). The asset item always exceeds the liability item because the Fed credits the deposit (reserve) account of the bank sending a check for collection to the Fed before it debits the deposit (reserve) account of the bank on which the check is drawn.

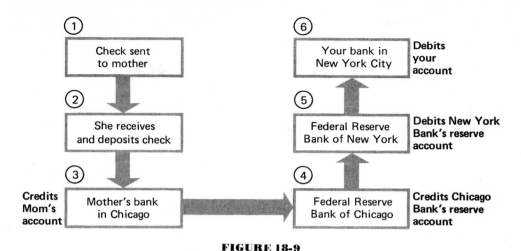

FIGURE 18-9

The Fed's check-clearing system. The arrows show the movement of the check through the system. Since this all takes time *and* the Chicago Fed will credit the Chicago bank's account before the New York Fed debits the New York bank's account, each commercial bank will temporarily have use of the same funds—this is float. When the process is complete, the Chicago bank will have more funds and the New York bank less funds.

Fed. Such deposits, which account for the majority of bank reserves, are assets for the banks and liabilities for the Fed. These deposit balances are held at the bank's district Reserve bank, and they rise or fall as the Fed credits or debits the bank's balance.

Deposits of U.S. Treasury This is the Treasury's money account. The Treasury pays its bills by writing checks on its deposit balance at the Fed. When this happens, Treasury deposits decline. If tax receipts rise (as they do around major tax dates, such as April 15) or the Treasury issues and receives payment for securities to finance a deficit, the Treasury's deposits at the Fed will rise. The level of Treasury deposits rises and falls with the ebb and flow of government receipts and expenditures.

THE BANK RESERVE EQUATION

With all the relevant items defined, the first thing to notice about Table 18-1 is that the largest asset item is the securities account and the largest liability accounts are Fed notes and deposits of member banks. The second thing to notice is that, although the values of all items on the balance sheet change somewhat over time, the largest and therefore the most significant changes occur in the largest items.

To bring together all the key items that affect bank reserves, including OMO, we can develop the *bank reserve equation*. This equation is derived by rearranging the Fed's balance sheet. We know that total assets TA equal total liabilities and capital TL:

(a) $$TA = TL$$

On the liability side of the Fed's balance sheet, we have currency issued by the Fed C, Treasury deposits TD, member-bank deposits—which, if we ignore vault cash, is equal to total reserves R—and all other liabilities and capital OL.

(b) $$TL = C + TD + R + OL$$

Rearranging terms, we can express reserves in terms of the other items.

(c) $$R = TL - C - TD - OL$$

Using equation (a), we can rewrite equation (c) substituting TA for TL:

(d) $$R = TA - C - TD - OL$$

Total assets are equal to the gold and SDR account, reflecting international reserve holdings IR, plus loans L, plus government securities held GS, plus float F, plus other assets OA.

(e) $$TA = IR + L + GS + F + OA$$

The final step is to substitute equation (e) into equation (d) which gives us the bank reserve equation:

(f) $$R = IR + L + GS + F + OA - C - TD - OL$$

$$
\text{Reserves} = \begin{cases}
+\text{IR international reserves} \\
+L \text{ loans} \\
+\text{GS government securities} \\
+F \text{ float} \\
+\text{OA other assets} \\
\\
-C \text{ currency} \\
-\text{TD Treasury deposits} \\
-\text{OL other liabilities}
\end{cases}
$$

Increases in these items raise bank reserves.

Increases in these items lower bank reserves.

Changes in any of the items with a plus sign before them will raise bank reserves, while changes in any of the items with a minus sign before them will lower bank reserves.[1] Note that all the items with plus signs are from the asset side of the Fed's balance sheet, while the items with minus signs are from the liability side of the Fed's balance sheet.[2]

CAN THE FED CONTROL BANK RESERVES?

We saw in this chapter how changes in government securities held—which come about through open market operations—and loans to member banks directly affect bank reserves. Let us take a simple example to see how factors other than the Fed's holdings of securities and loans to member banks affect the volume of reserves in the banking system.

Suppose it is tax time (April 15) and you owe the government money. You will write a check and send it in to the Internal Revenue Service (a branch of the Treasury). As this check is cleared, your deposit account at your bank and your bank's deposit account at the Federal Reserve will be lowered and the Treasury's account at the Fed will be raised. Assuming that the Treasury holds on to the funds for a time, the net result of this series of transactions is that deposits and reserves in the banking system will be lower!

To thicken the plot, suppose the Fed, given its current policy stance, does not want reserves and deposits to decline. What can it do? The answer is that it can purchase securities to offset the impact on the commercial banking system of the rise in the Treasury's desposits. In general, these so-called "defensive" OMO are designed to offset movements in other factors in the bank reserve equation so as to maintain existing conditions in the banking system. Since the Fed does not change its policy stance each day but the other factors in the bank reserve equation are always changing, the Fed conducts a massive amount of day-to-day "defensive" OMO, usually in the form of RPs. Over time the Fed will alter its policy stance and conduct "offensive" OMO (mainly in the form of outright purchases or sales) designed to change conditions in the economic and financial system; the latter are our primary focus of interest.

In sum, even though a variety of factors can affect the volume of reserves in the banking system, the Fed's powerful tool, OMO, enables it to offset the impact of these other factors and thus "have its way" with bank reserves.

---

[1] Some economists (particularly monetarists) prefer to work with a concept called the "monetary base" rather than bank reserves. The base B is defined as total reserves plus currency in circulation. Analytically, this only requires us to rearrange equation (f) by moving currency to the left-hand side:

$$R + C = IR + L + GS + F - TD - OL = B$$

From this point on, the analysis would proceed in the same way. See Albert Burger, *The Money Supply Process*, for more on the monetary base.

[2] The plus items are sometimes called "factors supplying reserves" or "sources of reserves," while the minus items are called "factors absorbing reserves" or "uses of reserves." A table in the *Federal Reserve Bulletin* reports the data in this fashion.

18-7
SUMMARY OF MAJOR POINTS

1

The Federal Reserve System was established by an act of Congress in 1913. The original act was modified and strengthened in 1935 following the economic and financial collapse of the Great Depression.

2

The Board of Governors, located in Washington, D.C., is the core of the Federal Reserve System. It is composed of seven members appointed by the President (with the approval of the Senate) for fourteen-year terms. The terms are staggered so that one expires every two years. The President appoints one of the governors as Chairman.

3

The country is divided into twelve districts. Each district is served by a Federal Reserve bank located in a large city within the district. The framers of the original Federal Reserve Act hoped to decentralize policymaking authority within the Fed through the creation of Reserve banks.

4

The Federal Open Market Committee (FOMC) is the chief policymaking body within the Fed. It is composed of twelve members: the seven members of the Board of Governors and five of the twelve presidents of the Reserve banks. The president of the New York Federal Reserve Bank is a permanent voting member, and the other four slots rotate yearly among the remaining eleven presidents.

5

The FOMC directs open market operations (OMO), the major tool for effecting monetary policy. These operations involve the buying or selling of government securities—actions which affect the volume of reserves in the banking system as well as interest rates. When the Fed buys securities, this increases bank reserves and puts downward pressure on short-term interest rates, particularly the federal funds rate. This, in turn, encourages bankers to expand loans and therefore expands deposits (the money supply).

6

The "Record of Policy Actions," which is a summary of the monthly meetings of the FOMC, is released to the public about thirty days after a meeting. It contains the "Policy Directive," the set of instructions regarding the conduct of OMO, which is issued to the New York Fed. The New York Fed, located at the center of the nation's financial markets, executes OMO on behalf of the FOMC and the entire Federal Reserve System.

7

The discount rate is the rate the Fed charges member commercial banks for borrowing reserves from their district Federal Reserve bank. Since the Fed views borrowing as a privilege rather than a right, banks are encouraged to borrow only when absolutely necessary and only for short periods of time. In deciding whether or not to borrow, banks will compare the cost of borrowing reserves in the federal funds market with the Federal Reserve's discount rate. The higher the federal funds rate relative to the discount rate, the larger the volume of borrowing from the Federal Reserve by member banks. In recent years, the Fed has tended to adjust the discount rate in response to changes that have already occurred in open market rates (for example, the federal funds rate).

8

The Fed has a very complicated structure of reserve requirements. These requirements, which specify the volume of reserves banks must hold against deposits, vary with the type of deposit and size of bank. The Fed has been reluctant to raise reserve requirements in recent years, even though such actions might have helped fight inflation, because the lower reserve requirements imposed by many states have contributed to a continuing exodus of banks from the Fed. The decline in Fed membership raises potential problems for monetary control; as of this writing, the membership problem is the subject of a number of bills pending before the Congress.

9

Other Fed tools for effecting monetary policy include Regulation Q, which sets the maximum interest rates banks can offer the public on certain types of time and savings deposits; margin requirements, which specify the percentage of the value of common stock which the buyer must pay directly (the rest can be borrowed); and moral suasion, which is "jawboning" of member banks by the Fed.

10

There is an ongoing debate as to whether or not the Fed should continue to operate as an independent government agency. The Fed and others argue that independence is essential to the pursuit of economic stability. Opponents argue that such independence is inconsistent with our democratic form of government. Others observe that the Congress and the President find the Fed a convenient scapegoat when the economy deteriorates. They further believe that the Fed is really not all that independent; it does respond to political pressure.

18-8
REVIEW QUESTIONS

1 Discuss the policymaking structure of the Fed. Who does what? Why does most of the power rest with the Board of Governors and in particular with the Chairman?

2 Explain how OMO can increase reserves in the banking system.

3 How does the discount rate affect borrowing by member banks from the Fed? How does the Fed set the discount rate?

4 What is the membership problem? Why is the Fed worried about it?

5 Why is Regulation Q less effective today than in the early and mid-1970s?

6 Why is it said that the Fed is independent?

7 Do you think the Fed should be more independent, less independent, or left as it is? Defend your answer.

8 The Fed is often called "the lender of last resort." What does this mean?

*9 Discuss the different types of OMO. Why does the Fed do so many RPs?

*10 Can the Fed control bank reserves? Defend your answer.

* Refers to material covered in the Appendix.

18-9
SUGGESTED READINGS

1   You can get a highly readable description of the Fed and its varied activities right from the horse's mouth, Board of Governors of the Federal Reserve System, *The Federal Reserve System—Purposes and Functions* (Washington, D.C.: 1974).

2   For more on the ins and outs of OMO see Paul Meek, *Open Market Operations* (New York: Federal Reserve Bank of New York, 1973). He is one of those at the New York Fed charged with executing OMO, so he knows of what he writes.

3   A number of years ago the Fed conducted a major study of its discount policy. In 1971 and 1972, the results were published by the Board in three volumes under the title *Reappraisal of the Federal Reserve Discount Mechanism*. Since we have never been accused of modesty, those interested in knowing more about how the Fed sets the discount rate and how it affects the financial system are referred to R. Lombra and R. Torto, "Discount Rate Changes and Announcement Effects," *Quarterly Journal of Economics* (February 1977), 171–176.

4   Readers interested in material which elaborates on the issues covered in the Appendix can consult, *Modern Money Mechanics* (Chicago: Federal Reserve Bank of Chicago, 1978). (As noted earlier, most of the Federal Reserve material is free on request.)

5   Those looking for a real treat are referred to two articles by Edward Kane (one of our favorite authors): "The Re-Politicization of the Fed," *Journal of Financial and Quantitative Analysis* (November 1974), 743–752, and "Good Intentions and Unintended Evil: The Case Against Selective Credit Controls," *Journal of Money, Credit and Banking* (February 1977), 55–69. The first examines the degree of political influence on Fed actions and the second explains why regulations, such as Regulation Q, spring leaks over time and fail to have the effects desired by policymaking. Read these!

19

THE FEDERAL RESERVE: THE FORMULATION AND IMPLEMENTATION OF POLICY

Monetary policy is among the most discussed
but least understood of all major influences on
the economy.

Sherman Maisel

19-1
POLICYMAKING: ART OR SCIENCE?

In Chapter 18 we examined the structure of the Federal Reserve System
and the tools the Fed uses to execute monetary policy. We saw that the
FOMC was the key policymaking body within the Fed and that open market
operations (OMO) were the most important tool the Fed had. In this chapter we will study how the Federal Reserve System employs its power to
try to stabilize the national economy—that is, how the Fed goes about pursuing the economic goals of "full employment, low inflation, and sustainable economic growth." We begin by examining the way in which monetary

policy is conveyed to the rest of the economy—the transmission mechanism. We will discuss the effects of monetary policy on the economy in more detail than appeared in Chapters 13 and 14. In those chapters, we simply assumed a change in reserves and argued that through its effects on the money supply and interest rates, a change in reserves would increase or decrease aggregate demand for goods and services in the economy. Here we will analyze in some detail why the Fed engages in open market operations (that is, changes the amount of bank reserves) and how these actions affect economic activity.

We shall focus on what the Fed actually does or tries to do. Ferreting this out is not as easy as it may seem. What the Fed *says* it does is often not exactly the same as what the Fed *is* doing or has done. As discussed in Chapter 18, the Fed must exist in a political environment. This leads the Fed to say that it has in the past, is now, and will in the future do the right thing. In other words, because the Fed exists in a political environment, it is reluctant to admit that it goofed when it has made a mistake.

Monetary policymaking is not an exact science; policymakers have occasionally made mistakes which contributed to economic instability rather than alleviated it. Accordingly, in the course of our examination we should recognize that despite monetary policymakers' good intentions, they may be unsuccessful and fail to achieve the economic goals laid out in Chapter 17. Their failures may be explained by such things as a defective approach to policymaking, political constraints, or a defective fiscal policy which overrides monetary policy. We shall see that the "doctors" at the Fed face a variety of problems in diagnosing the "patient," deciding on the proper treatment, administering the treatment, and monitoring the patient's response. As a result, to understand the failure of the economy (the patient) to stay well, we must examine carefully the Fed's policy procedures and the way in which the Fed's actions affect the economy.

19-2
THE TRANSMISSION MECHANISM

Have you ever stacked a series of domino tiles in such a way that when you tip the first one, it falls, causes the second tile to fall, and so on—the motion rippling through the stack until they have all fallen. The thrust that tips over the first tile is transmitted to the second and the second transmits the motion to the third until the original thrust is transmitted through the entire stack of tiles.

As shown in the domino illustration and Figure 19-1, the transmission mechanism for monetary policy works somewhat similarly. That is, such an action, specifically OMO, is transmitted through the financial system to the economy.

In simplest terms, the transmission mechanism can be thought of as starting with policymakers using one of their tools (such as OMO). This

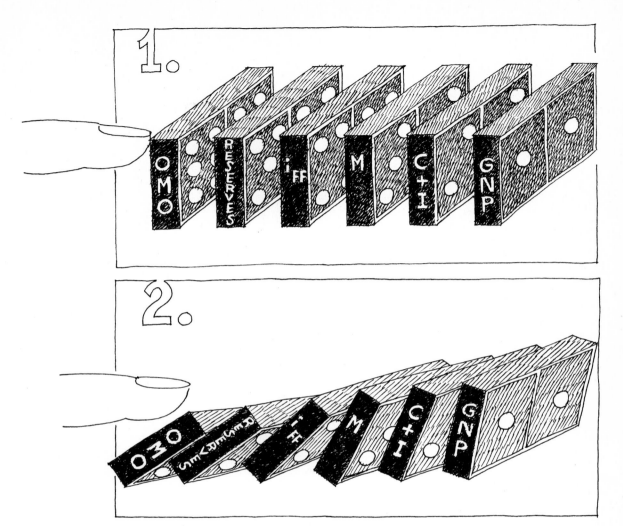

The structure of the economy—which encompasses the financial system and the markets for goods and services and factors of production—links the Fed's chief policy instrument OMO to the overall pace of economic activity (GNP). When the Fed initiates an open market operation, this action is "transmitted" through the economy by a series of linkages or channels. An open market operation first affects bank reserves which in turn alters the federal funds rate. The change in the funds rate and bank reserves will lead to changes in other interest rates and the money supply. These changes within the financial system will in turn affect the spending plans of households (consumption) and firms (investment), and thus will affect GNP.

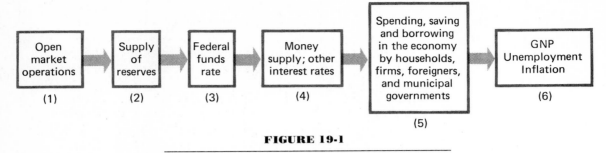

FIGURE 19-1

The linkages between monetary policy and domestic economic activity.

policy action will affect the financial system and the behavior of the various sectors (the structure of the economy), all of which in turn affects economic activity. A more specific and detailed representation of the linkages between monetary policy and economic activity is presented in Figure 19-1. Here we see that (1) an OMO (say, a purchase of securities by the Fed) will (2) increase the supply of reserves in the banking system, which will (3) lower the federal funds rate and other interest rates and (4) lead to an expansion in the money supply. We would expect such developments to (5) stimulate spending in the economy and thus (6) raise GNP, put upward pressure on prices, and perhaps lower unemployment. Economists have identified three channels through which the changes in reserves and the federal funds rate ultimately bring about the aforementioned changes in economic activity: the cost-of-capital channel, the net-worth (or wealth) channel, and the credit-availability channel. You can think of these channels as lying behind the spending, saving, borrowing box (5) in Figure 19-1. Let us examine each of these more carefully.

COST-OF-CAPITAL CHANNEL

Suppose banks, households, and firms had planned their portfolios before the Fed executed any OMO. How would the Fed's actions change the status of everyone's portfolios? Let us start by assuming that the Fed's OMO increases the supply of reserves, which is promptly followed by a resulting decline in the federal funds rate. The next thing that happens is that banks will find the cost of funds has declined and that they have more reserves than they are required to hold. They will want to earn interest on this excess supply of reserves. Banks will adjust to this situation in two ways: (1) they will purchase securities (such as Treasury and municipal securities) in financial markets and (2) they will expand their loans to consumers and businesses.

If everyone else in the economy was happy with the status of their portfolios before the Fed increased the supply of reserves, how do the banks accomplish these two adjustments which are aimed at putting their excess reserves to work? To accomplish the first adjustment, banks will simply have to offer higher prices to buy the public's securities. For example, banks might offer $1100 for bonds that originally sold for $1000 and are now in the hands of the public. The higher price would induce holders to part with their bonds and sell them to the banks. Given the inverse relationship between prices and interest rates (yield to maturity) on existing securities, the banks' actions will lower interest rates in the marketplace.

To accomplish the second adjustment—expanding loans in order to put excess reserves to work—banks will also have to induce the public to alter their portfolios. How can they do that? Banks can simply lower the interest rates on their consumer and business loans.

As the banks make these adjustments, their actions will tend to lower the interest rates, most noticeably on short-term securities, particularly short-term Treasury bills. With the Treasury bill rate lower than other short-term interest rates, the public will increase its demand for these other securities. Thus, the rates on these other securities will also fall. The close substitutability among short-term securities ensures that the structure of rates will move into line with the lower federal funds rate. With current short-term interest rates falling and perhaps the Fed's actions creating expectations of lower short-term rates in the future, there will be a tendency for long-term interest rates also to decline somewhat. (Recall our discussion of the term structure of interest rates in Chapter 15; long-term rates are determined not only by current short-term rates but also by short-term rates expected to prevail in the future.)

The end result of these several effects is that the cost of capital will have fallen. This ought to encourage firms to increase their investment spending on plant and equipment, encourage households to increase their spending on durable goods and housing (the mortgage rate will also have declined), and perhaps induce state and local governments to increase their capital expenditures. All in all, the Fed's OMO will clearly result in an increase in aggregate demand for goods and services in the economy.

HOUSEHOLD-NET-WORTH OR WEALTH CHANNEL

The household-net-worth or wealth channel operates through the change in the *value* of asset holdings induced by the Fed's OMO. Such changes in wealth are expected to affect the spending-saving decisions of households—and we have already learned that household spending-saving decisions affect output, employment, and prices.

Once again, let us assume that the Fed increases the supply of reserves through open market purchases. The increase in reserves leads to a reduction in interest rates which, in turn, raises bond prices, *and* stock prices. Why do stock prices also rise? As interest rates fall, the current actual yield on bonds falls relative to the current expected yield on equities (where the expected yield on equities is the ratio of dividends to the price of common stock and any expected capital gains). Suppose that before the Fed's OMO, the yield on bonds was 9 percent and the expected yield on equities was also 9 percent. When bond yields drop to, say, 8¾ percent after the Fed's OMO, the higher expected yield on equities will attract investors. Since investors consider equities and bonds to be substitutes for one another, the public will react to the drop in the rate of return on bonds by increasing their demand for equities. This will raise stock prices.[1] Overall, the rise in bond and equity prices means that the total value of financial assets held by the public increases, or, in other words, the public is made wealthier by the expansion in bank reserves.

The increased wealth of households leads them to increase their spending, thereby increasing business sales. Tracing this further, we would expect a rise in sales to lead firms to increase inventories and capacity utilization. In the short run, we would expect an increase in the hours worked and in the number of workers employed. This will give a further boost to sales. Over time, we would expect rising sales and increased capacity utilization to encourage a rise in investment spending (new plant and equipment). In sum, the rise in household wealth is believed to have a powerful, positive effect on household spending decisions and, as a result, also on business spending.

CREDIT-AVAILABILITY CHANNEL

When we discussed the cost-of-capital channel and the household-wealth channel we assumed that equity prices and interest rates were free to adjust in order to equate changes in supply and demand for financial assets. For example, when the supply of loans increased relative to the demand for loans, we assumed that interest rates would fall. However, many studies have shown that monetary policy influences the economy not only through adjustments in interest rates—the price of credit—but also by changes in the nonprice terms of credit. Changes in nonprice terms affect the availability of credit. Examples of these nonprice terms of credit are compensating balance requirements (the volume of deposits firms must hold with banks as a condition for the bank granting a loan or providing other services), standards of creditworthiness, size of down payments, maturity of loans, and required pledges of collateral. All these terms can play a part in an agreement between lenders and borrowers. When financial intermediaries use these nonprice terms to determine who gets loans and who does not, they are ra-

---

[1] A more formal explanation would follow from the notion that equity prices are equal to the discounted present value of the sum of firms' expected future earnings. When interest rates fall, the rate used to discount the stream of future earnings falls; this raises the present value and hence equity prices. The Fed's actions may also lead financial investors to raise their expectations of firms' future earnings. This will also raise the present value of firms and therefore raise stock prices. We might also note that the rise in equity prices lowers the cost of financing through the issuance of equity by firms, and this reinforces the effects of falling interest rates on the cost of capital to firms.

tioning credit. In a period of restrictive monetary policy when interest rates are rising and the growth in bank reserves is slowing, banks ration their credit. That is, banks could require larger compensating balances as a condition for a loan; or, as often happens in the market for home mortgages, banks will require a home buyer to make a larger down payment to obtain a mortgage. For example, the required down payment on a house might rise from 20 to 30 percent, or on a car loan from 10 to 25 percent.

As long as interest rates—the price of credit—are free to increase, the price of credit primarily allocates credit. When and where usury ceilings prohibit increases in the price of credit, it is the nonprice terms of credit that allocate credit. In general, as interest rates rise, the nonprice terms of credit will also rise, which will reduce the availability of credit to prospective borrowers and hence reduce spending in the economy.

Historically, the mortgage market provided the best example of the credit-availability channel's power in the transmission mechanism of monetary policy. Whenever market interest rates rose above the Regulation Q ceilings at banks—and, more importantly, at the thrift institutions—*disintermediation* would occur; that is, depositors, seeking the higher yields available on market securities, would shift their funds from the intermediaries to the open market. This would reduce the volume of funds these intermediaries had available to lend. They would respond by raising mortgage rates (to the extent possible) and by tightening the nonprice terms of loans. Because there was less credit available to builders for construction loans and home buyers for mortgage loans, activity in the housing industry would obviously be restrained. However, as discussed in Chapters 11 and 18, the advent of money market certificates in 1978 reduced the disintermediation financial intermediaries experienced as market interest rates rose. This development, along with a growing tendency for states to eliminate or raise usury ceilings, reduced the need for intermediaries to ration credit by altering the nonprice terms. As a result, the credit-availability channel is now somewhat less important than it once was.

A SUMMING UP

These three channels represent the various complex linkages between Fed policy actions and economic activity. The representation is far from exact, but in an economy where GNP is well over $2 trillion, it is really the best we can hope for. Many agree with the following comment by Milton Friedman and Anna Schwartz: "We have little confidence in our knowledge of the transmission mechanism, except in such broad and vague terms as to constitute little more than an impressionistic representation rather than an engineering blueprint."[1] This statement suggests that economists and policymakers should not overestimate how much they think they know about the way the economy reacts to policy actions.

[1] Milton Friedman and Anna Schwartz, "Money and Business Cycles," *Review of Economics and Statistics* (February 1963), suppl. 1, 55.

19-3
LAGS IN MONETARY POLICY

Now that we know something about monetary policy and the three channels through which it affects the economy, let us consider *how long* it takes for monetary policy to work its way through the three channels. For policymakers, knowing how long it takes for policy to influence the economy is important if monetary policy is to stabilize the economy.

Before we begin to discuss time lags in monetary policy, examine Figure 19-2 for a few moments. We are now ready to begin our explanation of time lags. Note that in this figure, which is a kind of time chart, the total lag is the time between the moment when the economy begins to need corrective action even though no one may have yet noticed the need (point A) and the moment when whatever policy action was taken has it fullest effect on the economy (point E). You can also note from the diagram that the total lag can be decomposed into two lags—an inside lag and an outside lag.

THE INSIDE LAG

The inside lag is the amount of time that elapses between the point when there is a need for policy action (point A) and the point when policymakers actually take action (point D). For instance, if in January inflation begins to accelerate, but it is not until July that a policy is decided upon and put into action to moderate the inflation, the inside time lag is six months. This inside lag (the lag internal to the policymaking process) is usually thought of as consisting of three parts: the recognition lag, the decision lag, and the action lag. The recognition lag is the time that elapses between the origin of a need for action (point A) and the recognition of that need (point B). For

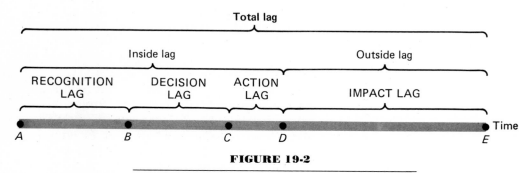

FIGURE 19-2

The policy lag. The economy begins to need corrective action at point A, but the need is not recognized. At point B in time, the need for corrective action is recognized and policymakers begin to think about what that corrective action should be. At point C, policymakers have decided what policy action is needed and they plan to put that policy into effect. By point D, the policy has been implemented. By point E in time, the policy action has begun to have a significant effect on the economy.

example, if the economy is in need of action in January but the need is not recognized until February, the recognition lag is one month. The decision lag is the time that elapses from the recognition point (point B) until policymakers decide what to do (point C). The action lag is the time that elapses from the decision point until policymakers actually put a new policy into effect to correct the problem in the economy. For instance, if the Fed recognizes the need for action in February, takes until June to decide what to do, and takes no action before July, the decision lag is four months and the action lag is one month.

WHY IS THE INSIDE LAG NOT A MATTER OF DAYS INSTEAD OF MONTHS?

Recognition lags of several months exist for a number of reasons. One of the most important reasons is that policymakers often have difficulty figuring out exactly what is going on in our complex economy. The policymaker relies on weekly, monthly, and quarterly data on such variables as retail sales, industrial production, the unemployment rate, and so forth. Of course, it takes time to collect, process, and assimilate these data. Furthermore, data spanning one month do not make a trend. A rule of thumb to help detect a trend is this: three successive monthly changes in the same direction in a data series (for example, the rate of inflation as measured by the Consumer Price Index coming in at 4 percent, 5 percent, and then 6 percent over a three-month period) are necessary to indicate a trend in that series. To make matters worse, movements in one type of indicator frequently give signals that contradict what another indicator is showing. It is no wonder, then, that policymakers—or, more accurately, their staffs of data researchers and analysts—are constantly sifting through the data available on the state of the economy, looking for any signals that might call for a change in monetary policy. All this is very much analogous to a skipper in a yachting race who is always checking the wind, the height of the seas, and the current, looking for any possible signals that might require a change in rudder or sail in order to keep on the best course.

Apart from policymakers' difficulties in detecting exactly what is going on in the economy, there is another reason for the lag in recognizing what is going on. We live in a democracy which is also a bureaucracy, and this means that there are meetings to attend, personalities to deal with, memos to write, memos to evaluate, more meetings to go to, memos about the follow-up meetings . . . you get the point.

If, after all this, it is recognized that some sort of policy action should be taken, the entire memos-meetings-more memos-more meetings cycle starts all over again in an attempt to decide precisely what should be done. And this is one of the reasons for the decision lag. Action cannot come until there is some agreement on what action should be taken.

As for the action lag, this encompasses the time from the decision (point

C) until action is taken (point *D*). This is not usually a long interval, especially in the case of monetary policy.

THE OUTSIDE LAG

Once policymakers change policy, there is a time lag between when the new policy action is introduced (point *D*) and when that action begins to affect the economy (point *E*). This is called the impact lag, which is external to the policymaking process. That's why it is also called the outside lag. To illustrate, in July the Fed might undertake open market operations to increase the supply of reserves relative to demand, but it may be January before effects on the unemployment rate are felt. In this case, the outside lag is six months. The duration of the outside lag is due to the structure of the financial system and the structure of the economy. The increased reserves must first work their way through the banking system and financial markets and then into the spending decisions of households and firms.

THE TOTAL LAG: HOW LONG?

The duration of the inside lag is thought to be relatively short for monetary policy—perhaps on the order of three to six months.[1] This is due mostly to the fact that the FOMC has a strong staff and meets monthly. When the economic environment begins to change, the FOMC usually becomes aware of what *might* be happening in fairly short order (say three months). As we shall see later, however, the FOMC is often reluctant to react vigorously to emerging developments. Disagreements within the FOMC, a fear of making mistakes, and the political environment within which they must operate all contribute to a "go slow" approach which delays action to some extent. This means that the decision lag may also be several months. As for the action lag, with the New York Fed capable of conducting OMO each business day, once a new course for policy is set, the lag in implementing that policy is virtually zero.

Estimates of the length of the impact lag, which makes up the lag beyond the policymaking process (the outside lag), vary widely. The Federal Reserve sometimes implies that the lag is almost zero—change policy today and watch the economy respond tomorrow! In contrast, Milton Friedman's research led him to conclude that the impact lag is *long* and *variable*, averaging about 1 to 1½ years. He argued that the length and variability of the lag made it difficult to predict exactly when a particular monetary policy action would have its effect on the economy. He concluded that policymakers would contribute most to economic stability by pursuing his monetary rule. This rule called for the Fed to use its tools so as to achieve a constant (stable) growth rate of the money supply.

---

[1] In contrast, the inside lag for fiscal policy is considered to be quite lengthy because of the often lengthy congressional debates which precede any action. More on this in Chapter 20.

THE RATIONALE FOR FRIEDMAN'S MONETARY RULE

If the impact lag is long and variable, policymakers would not be able to judge when a particular action would ultimately have an effect on economic activity. Hence, policymakers could not be certain that their actions would, in fact, stabilize economic activity. As discussed in the introduction to this part of the text, it is conceivable that when policy actions finally do begin to affect economic activity, the circumstances which motivated the original actions may have changed and some new action will be needed. However, if the lag is long, it is really too late to affect the current situation. For these reasons (along with the inside lag discussed above), Friedman does not favor conscious efforts on the part of policymakers to change monetary policy in response to emerging economic developments. He would *replace* monetary policy made at the *discretion* of policymakers with a *monetary rule*. The rule would call for a constant (stable) rate of growth in the money supply consistent with the long-run growth rate of real output in the economy. The specific rule follows from the quantity theory of money discussed in Chapter 11. Given the equation of exchange $MV = Py$, if velocity V is constant and the long-run rate of real output growth is, say, 3 percent, then if the money supply M grows at a 3 percent rate, we can, according to this view, forget about inflation; prices P will be stable. Since the growth of money will not vary, "Monetary policy can prevent money itself from being a major source of economic disturbance."[*] Friedman believes that adjusting policy to current developments ignores the existence of the impact lag and increases the probability of policy being procyclical rather than countercyclical. This is just another way of saying that policy may be destabilizing rather than stabilizing.

[*] Milton Friedman, "The Role of Monetary Policy," *American Economic Review* (March 1968), 12.

Most economists believe the truth on the length and variability of the lag lies somewhere between the two extremes that are represented by Friedman and the Fed. Two economists, John Kareken and Robert Solow, have put it this way:

Monetary policy works neither so slowly as Friedman thinks, nor as quickly and surely as the Federal Reserve itself seems to believe. . . . Though the *full* results of policy changes on the flow of spending may be a long time coming, nevertheless the chain of effects is spread out over a fairly wide interval. This means that *some* effect comes reasonably quickly, and that the effects build up over time so that some substantial stabilizing power results after a lapse of time of the order of six or nine months.*

* John Kareken and Robert Solow, "Lags in Monetary Policy," in Commission on Money and Credit, *Stabilization Policies* (Englewood Cliffs, N.J.: Prentice Hall, 1963), p. 2.

In recent years, most research studies of available data on the impact lag confirm the view expressed by Kareken and Solow. Figure 19-3 depicts the typical lag estimated by researchers. After the Fed purchases, say, $100 million of securities (an OMO), the resulting rise in bank reserves will begin to affect the financial system and economic activity. The initial effects (in the first six months) on spending are relatively small; but over a six- to

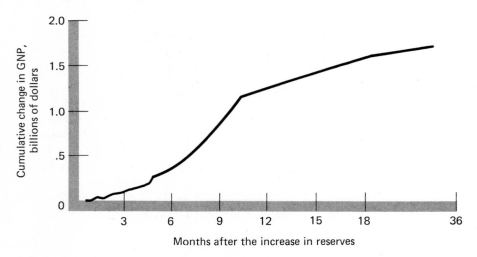

FIGURE 19-3

Cumulative effects of a $100 million increase in bank reserves on GNP. The initial effect on GNP of a $100 million open market operation that raises bank reserves is rather small. However, the effect over six to twelve months is considerable, and this effect continues to cumulate through the third year after the policy action.

twelve-month period, the impact on GNP is considerable and virtually all the effect is felt by the end of the third year.[1]

DEALING WITH THE LAG

In formulating and implementing monetary policy, the policymakers must be aware of the various time lags discussed above. Diagnosing the problem takes time, deciding on the treatment takes time, and it takes time for the treatment to work. Policy actions cannot be instantaneously formulated, implemented, and effective. The problems these lags create for policymakers attempting to stabilize the economy are compounded by the fact that policymakers must make policy without perfect knowledge of either the transmission mechanism or precisely how long it takes for policy to be transmitted to the economy. The longer the lags and the more uncertainty policymakers face, the less likely it is that policy will be stabilizing. Faced with such problems, policymakers have developed a policy strategy which relies on intermediate targets. Let us find out what these intermediate targets are all about.

19-4
POLICYMAKING AND INTERMEDIATE TARGETS

The concept of an intermediate target for policymakers to aim at can be highlighted with the help of the accompanying illustration on page 444.

Fed policymaking follows our illustration rather closely. The Fed's ultimate objective is to achieve the goals discussed in Chapter 17. These final targets of policy actions are defined in terms of desired outcomes for variables measuring inflation, unemployment, and economic growth.[2] As discussed above, these variables are only remotely (distantly) related to the Fed's instruments. This remoteness exists both in terms of time (remember the time lags) and in terms of distance, in the sense that these variables are at the end of a long, complicated transmission mechanism, imperfectly understood by policymakers. Recognizing the problem, and convinced that it needs something to guide its actions, the Fed uses its policy tools—chiefly OMO—to hit some intermediate target which it believes is closely related to the final target. The basic idea is that hitting the intermediate target will improve the chances of hitting the final target. (An obvious corollary worth remembering for later reference is that failure to hit the intermediate target will probably result in a failure to hit the final target.)

---

[1] See, Michael Hamburger, "The Lag in the Effect of Monetary Policy: A Survey of Recent Literature," in *Monetary Aggregates and Monetary Policy* (New York: Federal Reserve Bank of New York, 1974), pp. 104–113, and the literature cited therein.
[2] We will ignore international objectives for now.

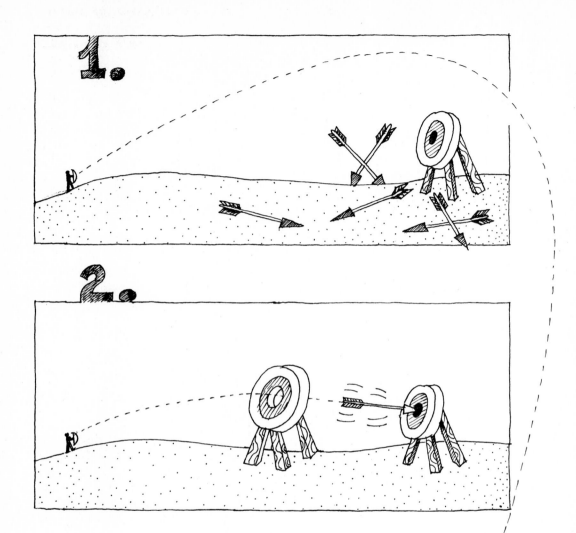

Why an intermediate target? Suppose you were holding a bow and arrow and desired to hit the center of a target that you could barely see way off in the distance. The bow would be your instrument and the target you really wanted to hit would be your final target. Because of the distance and poor visibility you might have great difficulty hitting the final target. One strategy you might consider to accomplish your objective would be to select an intermediate target—a clearly visible target between you and the less visible final target. The idea is to align the intermediate target between you and the final target in such a way that if you hit the center of the intermediate target, your arrow will continue on and strike the final target.

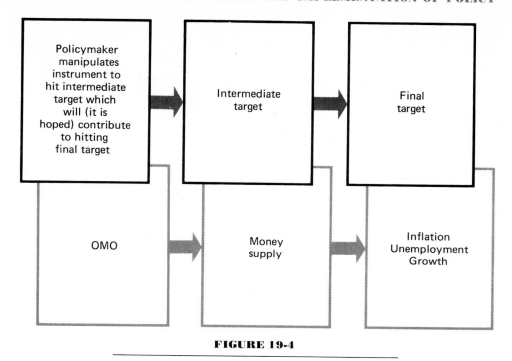

FIGURE 19-4

Instruments, intermediate targets, and final targets.

SELECTING THE
INTERMEDIATE TARGET: THE ISSUES

Much of the research on monetary policy over the past decade has been concerned with trying to determine which variable the Fed should use as an intermediate target. The candidates have tended to fall into two categories: monetary aggregates and interest rates. Within each category there are many specific candidates: short-term interest rates; long-term interest rates; bank reserves; M1; M2; M3; and so forth.

Since our focus is on what *is* rather than on what *ought* to be, we will not delve deeply into this debate. There are some key points, however, which do need to be mentioned. Most researchers have agreed that *a good intermediate target should be controllable by the Fed;* that is, by manipulating its policy tools, the Fed ought to be able to hit the desired value of the intermediate target (where the desired value could be 6 percent growth in M1, if that were the target, or a corporate bond rate of 9 percent, if that were the target). In the context of the illustration, if the archer could not hit the intermediate target, the whole exercise would not be worth undertaking. Researchers also believe that *the relationship between the intermediate target and the final target should be reliable.* More specifically, particular values for the intermediate target should result in values for the final targets which can be predicted with a reasonable degree of accuracy. Again, in terms of our illustration, if hitting the bull's-eye of the intermediate target often led to missing the final target, then the intermediate target would be useless.

THE MONEY SUPPLY
AS THE INTERMEDIATE TARGET

While academic researchers debated these issues, the Fed was faced with the ongoing task of making policy. Over most of the 1950s and 1960s, the Fed did not really have a well-defined strategy which linked its policy tools to its final targets. Instead, it tended to focus on "conditions in the money market." The condition of the money market was vaguely defined in terms of the level of short-term interest rates, excess reserves held by banks, and borrowing by member banks from the Fed. When the Fed wanted to "stimulate" the economy, it would engage in actions to "ease" or "loosen" money-market conditions—to lower short-term rates, raise excess reserves, and lower member-bank borrowing. When the Fed wanted to "restrain" the economy, it would engage in actions to "tighten" money-market conditions—to raise short-term interest rates, lower excess reserves, and raise member bank borrowing.

Economists eventually criticized this so-called strategy for many reasons. For example, even though the Fed could, in effect, control money-market conditions, economists argued that changes in such conditions were not related reliably to the final targets. The vagueness and imprecision of the strategy was also criticized. Jack Guttentag, a former Fed economist and now a professor, put it this way:

> **The main weakness of the strategy is its incompleteness, i.e., the fact that the Federal Open Market Committee (FOMC) does not set specific quantitative target values for which it would hold itself accountable for . . . any . . . "strategic variable" that could serve as a connecting link between open market operations and system objectives. . . .***

> *** Jack Guttentag, "The Strategy of Open Market Operations," *Quarterly Journal of Economics* (February 1966), p. 1.

As the 1960s wore on and the actual performance of the economy reinforced the notion that the Fed's approach to policymaking was flawed, policymakers began to pay more attention to criticisms like Guttentag's. Policymakers began to give more serious consideration to developing a complete strategy (policy tool → intermediate target → final target). The result of this evolutionary process, which was heavily influenced by monetarists' research, was that, in 1970, the Fed adopted the money supply as an intermediate target. As Figure 19-4 shows, the Fed directs its OMO toward hitting a particular growth rate of the money supply which it expects, in turn, will contribute to achieving the final targets.

The next section develops in some detail how the Fed guides its OMO toward the money supply and the final targets and why it does what it does.

19-5
THE FORMULATION OF MONETARY POLICY

To sort out what the Fed does and why it does it, we will divide our discussion into two parts. We will first discuss the *long-run phase* of policymaking—that is, how the Fed selects its "long-run" (twelve-month) target growth rate for the money supply and how this target is revised as time passes. The second part of our examination of the formulation of policy focuses on the *short-run phase* of policymaking—that is, how the Fed formulates policy each month to achieve the twelve-month target.

THE LONG-RUN PHASE

As discussed in Chapter 18, Fed policymakers, specifically the FOMC, meet monthly, usually on a Tuesday just after the middle of the month. Several times a year the Fed focuses on formulating its long-run strategy. That is, the Fed selects the rate of monetary growth for the coming twelve months which it believes will be most consistent with its final targets. For example, at January's meeting, the FOMC might focus on selecting a targeted rate of monetary growth for the coming year. (The targeted growth rate would be calculated from the average level of the money supply in the fourth quarter of the previous year—October, November, and December—through the fourth quarter of the current year.) The long-run growth rate selected will normally be reevaluated and, if necessary, revised at subsequent meetings.

How is the desired long-run growth rate of the money supply arrived at? The process underlying the selection begins several weeks before the January meeting, when the Fed's staff develops its economic forecasts twelve to eighteen months into the future for those variables of major concern to policymakers: GNP, the Consumer Price Index, and the unemployment rate. These projections are developed with the aid of such devices as statistical models of the economy, surveys of consumer and business spending plans, and the best judgment of the Fed's staff. The Fed bases its forecasts on assumptions about factors which determine prices, output, and employment but which are *not* under Fed control (for example, OPEC price increases and fiscal policy). The Fed also assumes a growth rate of the money supply—a factor the Fed can control and which is important in determining

A MODEL OF THE LONG-RUN PHASE

As we pointed out in Chapter 17, policymakers can be viewed as acting so as to maximize utility. As shown in Equation (19-1), policymaker utility or satisfaction S is a function of the deviation of the actual values of the target variable T^A from the desired values of these variables T^*.

$$(19\text{-}1) \qquad S = f(T^A - T^*)$$

The further that actual inflation, unemployment, and economic growth deviate from the desired values for these variables, the lower will be the policymaker's and society's well-being or utility.

In attempting to minimize the difference between T^A and T^*, policymakers are constrained by the structure of the economy and other factors (such as fiscal policy) which affect the target variables. The constraint imposed by the structure implies that if the Fed wants to take actions, say, to lower inflation, these actions must work their way through the economy (remember the transmission mechanism). Since this takes time and may raise unemployment in the short run, the Fed cannot solve the inflation problem instantaneously and may find that agressive anti-inflation actions move the economy further away from its "full" employment goal. Equation (19-2) summarizes the structure of the economy and the way in which monetary policy and other factors determine the target variables.

$$(19\text{-}2) \qquad T^A = f(M_L, F_L)$$

The actual values of the target variables (for example, the unemployment rate and the consumer price index) are a function of the current and past (lagged) money supply M_L, current and past fiscal policy, and all other factors F_L affecting the target variables.

The decision the Fed faces can now be summarized with the aid of Equations (19-1) and (19-2). Given F_L and T^*, the Fed must evaluate the staff's forecasts and choose the M for the coming year that results in an outcome for the T^A that comes closest to the T^*.

overall economic activity. The growth rate of the money supply assumed is generally the long-term target rate in force at the time of the projection, say 5 percent.

Following the development of the base forecast, the Fed's staff also often prepares one or more alternative forecasts for evaluation by the policy-makers. These alternative scenarios are derived assuming different rates of monetary growth than the rate (say 5 percent) underlying the base forecast. The purpose of this exercise is to identify the implications of, say, a 4 or 6 percent rate of growth in the money supply over the coming year as compared with the 5 percent rate in the base forecast. The FOMC at its meeting evaluates these alternative scenarios in terms of how close each comes to achieving its final targets and selects a particular money supply growth rate as its target for the forthcoming year.

THE RELATIONSHIP BETWEEN
THE LONG- AND SHORT-RUN PHASES

Having selected a desired long-run growth rate for the money supply over the next twelve months—we will use 5 percent for illustrative purposes—the Fed must now guide its OMO monthly so as to achieve the desired long-run monetary growth path. It is important to recognize that there are an infinite number of monthly and quarterly patterns of monetary growth that could turn out to average 5 percent over a full year (for example, 5 percent at an annual rate each month, zero percent for six months and 10 percent for six months, or three months each of 7 percent, 6 percent, 4 percent, and 3 percent growth). As will be shown, the monthly pattern chosen by the Fed will generally depend upon the interest rate and the recent behavior of the money supply vis-à-vis the long-run desired growth path.

The relationship between the short- and long-run growth rates for the money supply is illustrated in Figure 19-5. Assume that a 5 percent long-run growth path for the money supply was adopted in January and that, by the February meeting, the money supply was well above the level consistent with the desired 5 percent long-run path. Under these circumstances, three (or more) alternative paths for the short-run money supply growth rate are normally considered by the Fed. Each alternative is designed to return the growth rate to the long-term path, but each requires successively longer adjustment periods. (Currently, the control period for the Fed's short-run strategy is two months: in December, the control period is December–January; in January, it is January–February, and so on). A rapid return to the long-run path may require slowing down the growth rate to 2 percent in the February–March control period (alternative A). Alternatively, a growth rate of 3 percent in the February–March control period and in several successive periods would return the money supply to the long-run path in June (alternative B). A 4 percent growth rate in February–March and in the following months would return the money supply to the long-run path in August (alternative C). The process underlying the selection of these alternative paths—that is, forming monetary policy in the short run—and the execution of policy are discussed in the following sections.

THE SHORT-RUN PHASE

To understand the short-run phase of policymaking, we need to examine how the Fed formulates policy from month to month to achieve the long-run, twelve-month monetary targets. In general, the short-run phase involves selecting a short-run growth rate for the money supply that is consistent with the long-run target and developing an operating procedure to achieve the twelve-month growth path.

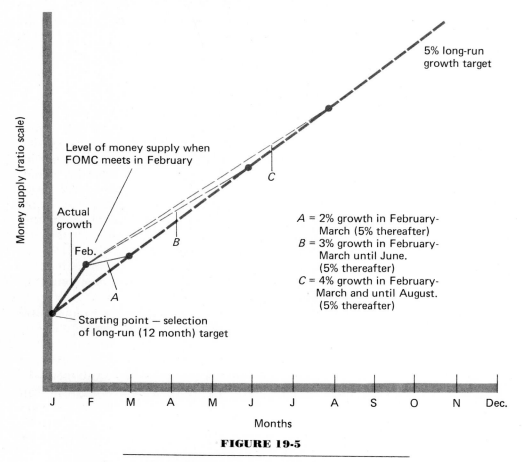

FIGURE 19-5

Suppose the FOMC decided in January to pursue a long-term (twelve-month) target calling for a 5 percent growth in the money supply. In February, they find that actual growth has exceeded the target. The question the FOMC must resolve is how to return to the long-term target path. Paths *A*, *B*, and *C* are three alternatives they might consider.

The Fed has a choice between two alternative operating procedures. One is to aim at a prescribed level of the *federal funds rate* which can be linked to a growth rate of money. The other is to focus on the growth rate in *bank reserves* which can also be related to money growth rates. Both approaches and variables are interrelated, as we will see.

Throughout the 1970s, the Fed choose an operating procedure which was based on the relationship of the federal funds rate to the money supply. Late in 1979, however, it announced a change in its operating procedure: henceforth it would focus on bank reserves as a means of achieving its money supply targets. To understand the trials and errors of the Fed's experience in the 1970s and why the Fed decided to alter its procedure, we will examine the Fed's attempt to control money with the federal funds rate and then show how this procedure has been modified in the recent switch to controlling money with bank reserves. The reserve approach to the short-run phase is presented in Section 19-8.[1]

OPERATING PROCEDURE:
A FEDERAL FUNDS RATE APPROACH

Throughout the 1970s the Fed tried to control monetary growth by manipulating the federal funds rate. The federal funds rate is an interest rate which is determined—you guessed it—in the federal funds market. In earlier chapters, we learned that the federal funds market is where commercial banks trade reserves; banks with "excess" reserves sell them to banks with "deficient" reserves. In general, the federal funds rate—the "price" for acquiring reserves—is determined by the net demand for reserves relative to the net supply. Since OMO conducted by the Fed are the ultimate determinant of the supply of reserves in the banking system, the Fed can, in effect, control the federal funds rate.

Each month, the staff prepares for the FOMC's consideration a set of alternative short-run (two-month) growth rates for the money supply.[2] Associated with each alternative short-run growth rate for the money supply will be a level for the federal funds rate. The federal funds rate is the key variable on which to focus.

Given the existing long-run growth target for the money supply (selected at, say, the January meeting) and the current level of the money supply relative to the path consistent with that target as shown in Figure 19-5, the staff might produce a set of alternatives for FOMC consideration at its February meeting as shown in Table 19-1.

The first row of the table contains alternative short-run growth rates

---

[1] As we go to press, it is impossible to tell how serious the Fed is and how long the change in procedure will last. The announced alteration in Fed procedures may turn out to be the most significant development regarding monetary policy in a generation or another example of the Fed saying one thing and doing another. Only time will tell. In the meantime, understanding Fed policy will require familiarity with past and current procedures.

[2] We will use the present tense throughout rather than the past tense.

TABLE 19-1
SHORT-RUN ALTERNATIVES
(For February–March period)

	A	B	C
Money supply growth (percent change at seasonally adjusted annual rate)	2	3	4
Federal funds rate	8	7	6

that are expected to return the money supply to its long-run path. The second row contains the level of the federal funds rate that the staff believes is necessary to achieve the various money supply growth rates in the first row. The columns are the alternatives. Alternative A, for example, would indicate that, to achieve a 2 percent money growth rate and to return to the long-run path by March (as shown in Figure 19-5), the level of the federal funds rate required would be 8 percent.[1]

How does the Fed's staff derive the federal funds rate consistent with each money supply alternative?

The federal funds rate, shown in the second row of Table 19-1, is derived with the help of a money demand function. Recall that in Chapter 13 we pointed out that the demand for money M_d could be expressed as a function of income Y and the short-term interest rate i_s. This can be written in general form as,

$$M_d = f(\overset{+}{Y}, \overset{-}{i_s})$$

or it can be written as a mathematical equation:

(19-3) $$M_d = aY - bi_s$$

where a and b are coefficients. The Fed staff is endowed with a massive computer, many talented economists, and all the relevant data, enabling it to calculate estimates of a and b, the coefficients in the money demand function. With estimates of the coefficients a and b and a projection of income from the long-run phase of policymaking, the staff can solve the money demand equation for the level of the short-term interest rate consistent with a particular level of the money supply as well as for any particular growth rate in the money supply.

Algebraically, we can rearrange Equation (19-3) to get:

(19-4) $$i_s = \frac{aY - M_d}{b}$$

---

[1] We will see later that a reserve approach to monetary control will add a third row to Table 19-1— the various growth rates of reserves consistent with the alternative money supply growth rates.

Suppose we have estimates of a and b and we also have a projection of Y. We know the level of the money supply in January (remember, the FOMC is meeting in February) and we can calculate the level of the money supply in March which would yield the annual growth rates over the February–March period shown in the first row of Table 19-1. For example, if $M = \$400$ billion in January, the March levels of M—which would yield 2 percent, 3 percent, and 4 percent annual rates of growth, respectively—are $\$401.3$ billion, $\$402$ billion, and $\$402.6$ billion.[1] Armed with all this data, we can solve Equation (19-4) for the interest rate i_s—or, more specifically, each value of the federal funds rate—consistent with each of the alternative rates of money supply growth.

Following the old adage that a picture can be worth a thousand words, let us see how the federal funds rates can be derived graphically for each of the alternative growth rates or each of the money supply levels resulting from the three alternative growth rates.

SLOPE AND MONEY DEMAND

To appreciate what follows it is necessary to understand what the slope of a line represents. The slope of the line in the graph below tells us how much money demand M_d changes when the

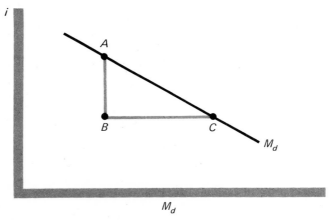

interest rate i changes. For example, if we move from point A to point C on the money demand function, $\Delta M_d = BC$ and $\Delta i = AB$. The slope therefore is AB/BC (remember, rise over run). Note that the slope in this case is negative AB is negative, BC is positive, and a negative number divided by a positive number is negative).

When the interest rate rises, money demand falls: and when the interest rate falls, money demand rises.

---

[1] These levels of money supply growth are calculated as follows: Taking the 3 percent annual growth as an example and going backward, ($402 − $400)/400 = the percent change in the money supply over the two-month period February–March = .005. To get an annual rate of growth, this figure must be multiplied by 6 (since there are six two-month periods in a year). The result is .005 × 6 = .03, or 3 percent. The other figures are derived in a similar fashion.

The line M_d in Figure 19-6 represents the staff's estimate of the position and slope of the money demand function in January; the slope is defined by the coefficient b, which reveals how much M_d changes when i_s changes. If the level of M was $400 billion in January and the prevailing federal funds rate was 6 percent, point J represents the starting point for the construction of row 2 in Table 19-1. Given that the staff has a projection of the near-term rise in income Y over the next two months and also knows the coefficient a—that is, the staff knows how much M_d changes for any change in Y—the staff can estimate the rightward shift in M_d, say M'_d. The rest is easy. If the federal funds rate were to remain at 6 percent, the staff would expect $M = \$402.6$ billion in March (point C), implying an annual rate of growth over the February–March period of 4 percent (alternative C in Table 19-1). Similarly, if the federal funds rate were to rise to 7 percent, the staff

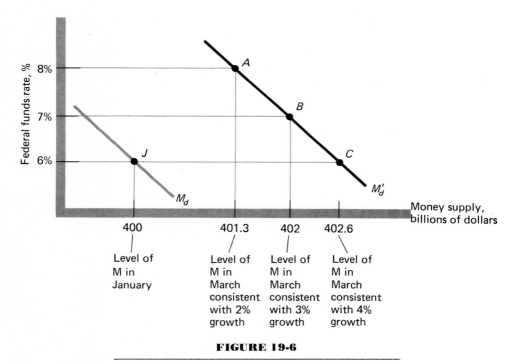

FIGURE 19-6

How the staff derives the federal funds rate consistent with alternative outcomes for the money supply. The staff estimates the position and slope of the money demand function in January and then forecasts the rightward shift in the function (to M'_d) that will occur over the February–March period as income grows. Any given federal funds rate, say 7 percent, will then be expected to be associated with a particular outcome for the money supply (in this case $402 billion).

would expect the level of money demand to be lower and therefore the rate of monetary growth, at 3 percent to be lower as well. Trace through for yourself what happens if the federal funds rate is 8 percent.

Selecting the Short-Run Alternative The various short-run federal funds rate–monetary growth rate alternatives appear in the "blue book," which is prepared monthly by the Fed staff for the FOMC's consideration.[1] Each alternative is accompanied by a discussion of how it relates to the long-run target path and a discussion of the conditions that might develop in financial markets. The latter tries to answer such questions as: How might the volume of offerings (new issues) in the corporate and municipal bond markets rise or fall under each alternative federal funds rate? How will other interest rates and stock prices be affected? How will the Treasury's debt-management operations be affected? How might international financial markets and the exchange rate between the dollar and foreign currencies be affected? How will deposit flows to thrift institutions and the mortgage market be affected?

When the FOMC meets, it examines each of the alternative federal funds rates, debates the ramifications of each, and then selects one of them. The selection of a particular federal funds rate and short-run target for money supply growth completes the formulation phase of monetary policy.

Summing Up the Formulation Phase To summarize the process of formulating monetary policy, the Fed first picks a long-run growth rate for the money supply that it believes will help to achieve its ultimate objectives—sustainable economic growth and low rates of unemployment and inflation. It then selects a short-run money supply path consistent with the long-run desired path and picks an operating procedure, i.e., either a funds rate approach or a reserves approach. In the 1970s the Fed used a funds rate approach and picked the federal funds rate thought to be consistent with the achievement of the short-run—and, therefore, the long-run—money supply trajectory. This completes the *formulation* phase of policy-making.

As for the *implementation* of policy, discussed in Section 19-6, the Fed then conducts its OMO—buying or selling securities to increase or decrease the supply of reserves in the banking system—so as to maintain the federal funds rate at its specified level. This is the monetary policy process, as shown in Figure 19-7.

Looking at Fed policy from a different perspective, there is a chain of

---

[1] This is top secret—so don't tell anyone. It is called the blue book because it is a set of documents bound together with a blue cover!

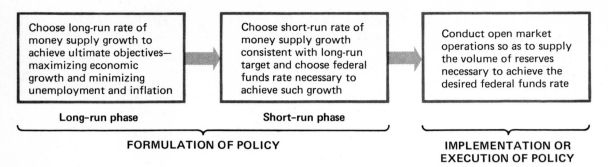

| Choose long-run rate of money supply growth to achieve ultimate objectives—maximizing economic growth and minimizing unemployment and inflation | Choose short-run rate of money supply growth consistent with long-run target and choose federal funds rate necessary to achieve such growth | Conduct open market operations so as to supply the volume of reserves necessary to achieve the desired federal funds rate |

Long-run phase   **Short-run phase**

FORMULATION OF POLICY   **IMPLEMENTATION OR EXECUTION OF POLICY**

FIGURE 19-7

The monetary policy process under a federal funds rate approach.

cause and effect which links Fed policy to its ultimate objectives. This set of linkages, referred to as the "transmission mechanism" for monetary policy, shows how policy is transmitted to the economy. When the Fed engages in OMO, this has an immediate effect on the supply of bank reserves and the federal funds rate. Changes in bank reserves and the federal funds rate have an effect on the cost and availability of funds in the banking system, in other financial intermediaries (such as savings and loans associations), and in financial markets.

Thus changes in bank reserves and the federal funds rate affect the money supply and other interest rates (for example, rates on consumer and business loans). Such changes, in turn, alter the volume of spending on goods and services by households, business firms, foreigners, and municipal governments; over time, all that spending affects GNP, unemployment, and the rate of inflation.

19-6
THE IMPLEMENTATION OF MONETARY POLICY UNDER A FEDERAL FUNDS RATE APPROACH

Once the FOMC makes its policy decision, the Fed (specifically, the Federal Reserve Bank of New York) must conduct OMO to achieve the short-term targets. Given the alternative selected by the FOMC, say alternative B from Table 19-1, the Fed will conduct its OMO to achieve a 7 percent federal funds rate. The FOMC expects that these actions will produce a February–March money supply growth rate of 3 percent.

The general relationship between the federal funds rate desired by the Fed i_{FF}^* and the money supply target M^* is represented by Equation (19-3):

$$(19\text{-}3) \qquad\qquad i_{FF}^* = f(M^*)$$

The Fed selects the level of the federal funds rate it believes is consistent with achieving a particular rate of monetary growth and will direct its

OMO toward achieving that level of the federal funds rate. The final link in our analysis is to show how OMO and the actual federal funds rate i_{FF} are related.

We already know that the federal funds rate is determined in the federal funds market, where banks buy and sell reserves. More specifically, the federal funds rate is determined by the net demand for reserves by banks—with some banks selling reserves and some banks buying, what matters is the net demand—and the supply of reserves determined by the Fed. As in all markets, if the demand exceeds the supply, i_{FF} will rise; if the supply exceeds the demand, i_{FF} will fall.

The total supply of reserves is under the direct control of the Fed.[1] In particular, changes in reserves ΔR will directly reflect OMO, since $\Delta R =$ OMO. If the Fed wants to lower i_{FF}, it will purchase securities and therefore raise the supply of reserves relative to demand; if the Fed wants to raise i_{FF}, it will sell securities and therefore lower the supply of reserves relative to demand.

Given the linkage between OMO and changes in the supply of reserves, and the linkage between changes in the supply of reserves and the federal funds rate, once the FOMC has selected a desired level of the federal funds rate i_{FF}^*, the Fed's OMO will be a function of the difference between the actual level of the federal funds rate i_{FF} and the desired level i_{FF}^*.

$$(19\text{-}4) \qquad \Delta R = \text{OMO} = f(\overset{+}{i_{FF} - i_{FF}^*})$$

In particular, if the actual level of the federal funds rate exceeds the desired level—if $i_{FF} > i_{FF}^*$—the Fed will buy securities, thereby increasing the supply of reserves relative to demand and lowering i_{FF}. On the other hand, if the actual level of the funds rate is below the desired level, the Fed will sell securities, thereby lowering the supply of reserves relative to the demand and raising i_{FF}.

The relationship between OMO, the supply of reserves, the demand for reserves, and i_{FF} can be illustrated graphically, as shown in Figure 19-8. The demand for reserves by banks is a negative function of the interest rate. As the funds rate falls, banks demand more reserves, since the cost of acquiring funds falls. A lower cost of the funds that banks borrow would enable the banks to lower their loan rates, thus raising the public's demand for funds (money). For all these reasons, the demand for reserves R_d is downward-sloping in Figure 19-8.[2]

One of the basic things the FOMC staff assumes in projecting the growth in money and the federal funds rate necessary to achieve that growth is the notion that the demand for money, as shown in Figure 19-6,

---

[1] The appendix to Chapter 18 discusses this point in some detail.
[2] The demand for reserves can be thought of as a "derived demand"—that is, it is derived from the public's demand for funds. This is analogous to a firm's demand for labor, which is derived from the public's demand for the firm's output. The loans made and securities purchased are the output of banks and reflect the public's demand for money.

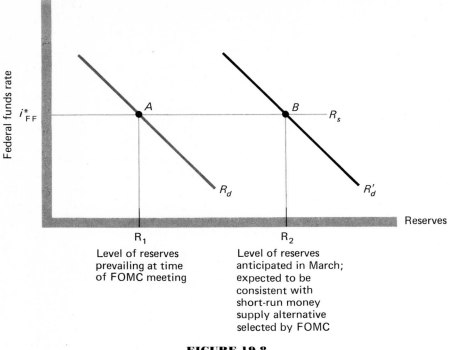

FIGURE 19-8

Bank demand for reserves will shift to the right (R_d to R_d') as income grows and the public increases its demand for funds. The Fed will "peg" the federal funds rate at the level they desire (i_{FF}^*) by supplying reserves "elastically" at this rate. This means that the supply-of-reserves function (R_s) is horizontal and the actual quantity of reserves R_2 will be determined by the demand for reserves.

will gradually shift from M_d to M_d' as income grows over the February–March period. As a result, the demand for reserves will shift gradually from R_d to R_d'. As the demand for reserves grows, the Fed aims to increase the supply of reserves through OMO. This is accomplished by *supplying reserves elastically* at the desired level of the federal funds rate. Supplying reserves "elastically" means that the Fed will supply all the reserves necessary to keep the actual federal funds rate i_{FF} equal to i_{FF}^*. If $i_{FF} > i_{FF}^*$, more reserves will be supplied; if $i_{FF} < i_{FF}^*$ less reserves will be supplied. In effect, the horizontal dotted line running from i_{FF}^* becomes the supply of reserves function and the actual quantity of reserves in the banking system is determined by demand—that is, by the demand for reserves and money by banks and the public.

If everything works out right, the Fed will end up at B in Figures 19-6 and 19-8 and achieve its desired rate of growth of the money supply. However, we can assure you that if the last few years demonstrate anything, it is that everything rarely works out right.

MISSING THE MONEY SUPPLY TARGETS

If the demand for money at a given federal funds rate turns out to be greater or less than the Fed had estimated, then the actual money supply will also be, respectively, greater or less than desired. With the Fed "pegging" the federal funds rate,—not allowing the rate to change—it is supplying all the reserves banks are demanding at this particular level of the funds rate. Since bank demand for reserves reflects the public's demand for money, the Fed is also supplying all the money the public demands at this funds rate level. For example, in Figures 19-6 and 19-8, if M_d, and therefore R_d, shift further to the right than estimated—that is, further than M_d' and R_d'—then the actual growth in money and reserves will exceed the Fed's short-run target. But what would explain such an error in the Fed staff's estimate of money demand? There are several possibilities: the staff could be working with faulty estimates of the money demand function; the money demand function could have shifted randomly; or there could have been an error in the staff's estimate of income, which was *the* major input to estimating the level of the federal funds rate consistent with the desired rate of money growth. The last possibility is the major problem. If income grows more rapidly than estimated by the Fed, the demand for money and reserves at the prevailing level of the federal funds rate, will be higher than expected and the Fed will, at least initially, supply enough reserves and money to prevent the funds rate from rising.

Unfortunately, if it supplies more reserves and money, the Fed allows monetary policy to be *procyclical;* that is, the excessive expansion of the supply of money and reserves will tend to reinforce and exacerbate the cyclical upswing in economic activity. Ideally, this is not what the Fed should do. Rather, the Fed should take actions that dampen or alleviate cyclical swings in the economy.

THE FED'S SHORT-RUN RESPONSE
TO MISSING THE MONEY SUPPLY TARGETS

There is, *in theory,* a mechanism which limits the procyclical movement in reserves and money *between* FOMC meetings. This aspect of the implementation of policy is summarized in the following equation:

$$(19\text{-}5) \qquad \Delta i_{\text{FF}}^* = f(\overset{+}{M} - M^*)$$

Between FOMC meetings, the Fed can adjust the target level of the federal funds rate in response to deviations of the actual money supply M from its target M^*. In particular, if incoming data show that $M > M^*$, the Fed can raise i_{FF}^* by slowing the growth in the supply of reserves relative to the growth in demand. Similarly, if incoming data show that $M < M^*$, then the Fed can lower i_{FF}^* by raising the growth in reserves relative to the growth in demand.

INTEREST RATE MOVEMENTS AND THE MONEY SUPPLY STATISTICS: THE ART OF FED WATCHING

Each week the Fed receives, analyzes, and publishes data on the money supply. These data, which are usually published late Thursday afternoon, are carefully scrutinized by financial analysts all around the country (and the world). The data are usually discussed in some detail in the Friday edition of *The Wall Street Journal* and other leading newspapers. Why all the fuss? Because these "Fed watchers" are looking for some indication of the Fed's next policy move, since any such move is likely to have important effects on the financial system in general and interest rates in particular. For example, if the Fed receives data which suggest that the money supply is growing much faster than it desires, it will consider raising the federal funds rate. Fed watchers (many of whom are ex-employees of the Fed) understand this. As a result, when the published data show a large increase, Treasury bill rates, commercial paper rates, CD rates, and even some bond rates will often rise during subsequent days, in anticipation of Fed actions to slow the growth of reserves and raise the federal funds rate. As discussed in Chapter 15, expectations about the future course of interest rates are importantly influenced by anticipations of what the Fed is up to.

The Fed expects an increase or decrease in the funds rate to decrease or increase, respectively, the demand for money. At the same time the change in bank reserves and the funds rate will alter the supply of money by changing the reserve position of banks and the rates on bank deposits and earning assets. In other words, the change in the federal funds rate (and the growth of reserves) is designed to narrow the difference between M and M^*.

Perhaps we have just given you the idea that the Fed's response to apparent deviations in the growth of the money supply from specified target growth is straightforward, mechanical, and precise, as suggested by Equation (19-5). It is not all that precise, as we will now show.

19-7
ACTUAL POLICY IN THE 1970S: THE ROLE OF UNCERTAINTY AND CONSTRAINTS ON INTEREST-RATE VOLATILITY

The Fed does not aim at single, specific desired values for the federal funds rate and for the money supply; the Fed actually aims at ranges of values. For example, with reference to alternative B in Table 19-1, the entry for money supply growth might be 2 to 4 percent and the corresponding entry for the federal funds rate might be 6¾ to 7¼ percent. The range for the federal funds rate is a self-imposed constraint by the Fed on the degree to which it will allow the rate to vary between monthly meetings. Since changes in the federal funds rate affect other interest rates, particularly short-term rates, the Fed's constraint also indirectly limits the monthly variation in other interest rates. The range for the money supply is a *range of tolerance* which explicitly recognizes two things: that there is an inherent short-run volatility in the growth of the money supply and that it is difficult to control this growth very precisely. There is another way to view the range for the money supply: if the target is difficult to hit, make it bigger!

If the incoming data on the money supply following a monthly Fed meeting indicate a growth rate that does not fall within the specified range of growth rate values, then the Fed will react. For example, suppose the FOMC at its January meeting selected a range for the growth of the money supply of 2 to 4 percent and a range for the funds rate of 6¾ to 7¼ percent, expecting a 7 percent federal funds rate (the midpoint of the funds rate range) to produce 3 percent money supply growth (the midpoint of the money growth range). If incoming data suggest that the money supply is expanding at a 4 percent rate (the upper end of the range), the Fed will probably sit tight and keep the funds rate at 7 percent. This expansion of the money supply over the January–February period is shown in Figure 19-9. Should actual money supply growth exceed the range, the Fed would reduce the supply of reserves relative to the demand and thereby raise the federal funds rate. The reduced supply of reserves and resultant higher interest rates will help get monetary growth back within the long-run range.

If money supply growth is below the range, the Fed increases reserves, thus lowering the federal funds rate; increased reserves and lower interest rates will help get money growth back up within the tolerance range. In our example, if incoming data suggested that the money supply was expanding at, say, a 7 percent rate, the Fed might slow the growth of reserves relative to demand so as to raise the funds rate to 7¼ percent (the upper end of its range).

Unfortunately, research has suggested and actual experience in the 1970s has verified that the Fed's range of allowable variations in the federal funds rate is too narrow to adequately control money supply growth. The volatility of the money supply over the short run and the Fed's desire to

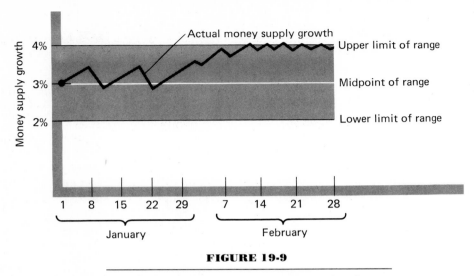

FIGURE 19-9

The growth of the money supply remains within the range.

moderate movements in the federal funds rate and other interest rates have caused the Fed to miss the money supply target in about half the two-month control periods over the past few years. As shown in Table 19-2, actual growth in the money supply (column 4) was either greater or less than the desired range (column 3) in six out of twelve control periods. It appears that, over the short run, the Fed has not been able to achieve precise control over money growth. It has, however, kept within its federal funds rate target range. It must be concluded that the rather loose control over short-run money growth reflected the Fed's own unwillingness during this period to take actions necessary to achieve more precise control.

Why was the Fed unwilling to take actions necessary to achieve more precise control over monetary growth? Many observers attribute the Fed's timidity to political and economic forces. The policy record for the 1970s shows that policymakers are risk-averse and, whenever possible, they try to avoid taking actions with considerable uncertainty attached to their outcomes. They also avoid highly visible and politically sensitive actions. The money supply, for example, is an abstract concept that the public, the Congress, and the President do not identify with. In fact, most people would probably argue "The more money the better!" Interest rates, on the other hand, are highly visible, and when they rise, the Fed is immediately identified as the culprit. Understandably, then, whenever money supply growth was exceeding the desired range, there was a tendency to moderate or postpone any upward movement in interest rates.

The justifications for the Fed's moderate approach generally fall into two areas. First, economic data on sales, inventories, the money supply,

TABLE 19-2
SHORT-RUN ALTERNATIVES SELECTED IN 1977†

(1) DATE OF MEETING	(2) TWO-MONTH CONTROL PERIOD	(3) DESIRED RANGE FOR MONEY SUPPLY GROWTH	(4) ACTUAL MONEY SUPPLY GROWTH	(5) DESIRED RANGE FOR FEDERAL FUNDS RATE	(6) ACTUAL FEDERAL FUNDS RATE
Jan. 18, 1977	Jan.–Feb.	3–7	3.1	4¼–5	4.60–4.72
Feb. 15, 1977	Feb.–Mar.	3–7	3.1	4¼–5	4.62–4.74
Mar. 15, 1977	Mar.–April	4½–8½	13.0	4¼–5¼	4.60–4.77
April 19, 1977	April–May	6–10	10.4	4½–5½‡	4.82–5.34
May 17, 1977	May–June	0–4	2.6	5¼–5¾	5.31–5.45
June 21, 1977	June–July	2½–6½	11.4	5¼–5¾	5.33–5.43
July 19, 1977	July–Aug.	3½–7½	11.9	5¼–6‡	5.45–5.94
Aug. 16, 1977	Aug.–Sept.	0–5	6.6	5¾–6¼	5.97–6.10
Sept. 20, 1977	Sept.–Oct.	2–7	9.7	6–6½	6.35–6.50
Oct. 18, 1977	Oct.–Nov.	3–8	5.3	6¼–6¾	6.42–6.58
Nov. 15, 1977	Nov.–Dec.	1–7	3.1	6¼–6¾	6.49–6.55
Dec. 20, 1977	Dec.–Jan.	2½–8½	7.4	6¼–6¾	6.65–6.78

† During 1977, actual money supply growth was outside the Fed's desired range in six of the twelve control periods.
‡ Upper limit of range raised between meetings to figure shown.
SOURCE: Federal Reserve. Data for the money supply are expressed as seasonally adjusted annual rates of growth averaged over the two-month control period. The range for the Federal funds rate and the actual outcome apply to weekly averages during the inter-meeting period.

and so forth are often quite erratic and do not clearly indicate the direction in which the economy is moving (remember the recognition lag). This causes policymakers to delay their response to apparent changes in these variables until more information (that is, more months of data) is available to confirm such changes.[1] The second justification is somewhat illusory: the Fed believes it can eventually get back to the long-run growth path. Accordingly, the Fed nearly always chose a slow, gradual return to the long-run path since it involved a smaller rather than larger rise in the interest rate over the near term. With gradualism being the watchword, actual growth in the money supply was often off the desired short- and long-run paths. In sum the Federal Reserve was not exercising its fullest control over monetary growth, and has, unfortunately, contributed to a loss of control over economic activity and to the persistence of inflation.

Fed policymakers have to operate in a difficult environment. They never know for sure where the economy is and where it is headed, they do not

---

[1] Another reason for the Fed's delayed response is that it sets a target range for M2 as well as M1 and sometimes the actual growth of M1 is outside its target range, while the growth of M2 is within its range. With the monetary aggregates giving off conflicting signals, the policymakers tend to react cautiously.

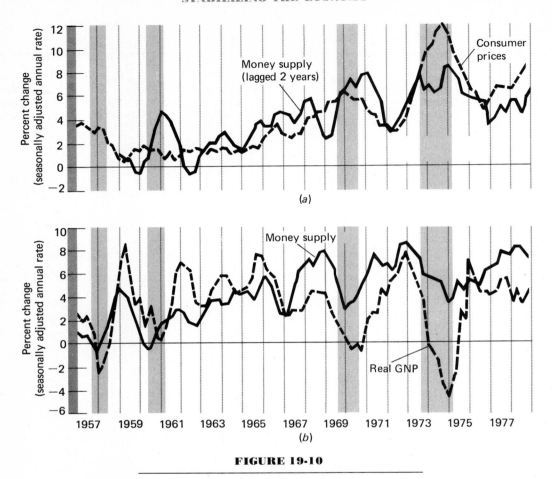

FIGURE 19-10

(*a*) The rising trend in the growth of the money supply has been matched by a rising trend in the rate of inflation. (*b*) Cyclical swings in money growth have been matched by cyclical swings in real economic activity (GNP).

know *precisely* how their actions affect economic activity, and they do not know *precisely* how long it takes for their actions to be effective. The probability of policy being procyclical (destabilizing) rather then countercyclical (stabilizing) is enhanced by such problems. Layered on top of all this uncertainty are various political constraints tied to certain economic realities. More specifically, as discussed in Chapter 14, policy actions designed to stimulate aggregate demand will tend to raise output and lower unemployment in the short run and raise prices over the longer run. This tendency, along with the fact that political figures are most interested in short-run developments, has contributed to the deterioration of policymakers' ability to contain inflation. Once inflation becomes embedded in the economic system, policy actions specifically designed to moderate inflationary pressures will, in the short run, be associated with rises in the unemployment rate—a bad! Only over the longer run will inflation abate—a good![1]

These economic and political realities, combined with the Fed's approach to policymaking have caused the Fed, willingly or unwillingly, to contribute to the rise in the rate of inflation over the past ten years. As shown in the top panel of Figure 19-10, the rising trend in monetary growth has been matched by a rising trend in the rate of inflation. As for the short run, cyclical swings in money growth, as shown in the bottom panel of Figure 19-10, have been matched by cyclical swings in economic activity. How are these relationships to be explained? Many economists would argue that the Fed followed a "seat of the pants" approach to making monetary policy. They would also argue that the Fed did not and does not sufficiently appreciate the paramount role of money supply growth in determining our economic destinies. Because of this, its policies in the 1970s were procyclical in the short run and inflationary in the long run.

Some economists would also argue that short- and long-run fluctuations in the rate of inflation and the rate of economic growth are the result of many forces (such as fiscal policy, OPEC price decisions, wage changes, and growth of productivity) in addition to monetary policy. The presumption is that once one of these other factors, say fiscal policy, changes, the Fed gets dragged along. The "accommodative" policy (that is, a policy that accommodates rather than offsets the economic effects of changes in these other factors) is thought to be the joint result of the political and economic factors discussed above.

As 1979 wore on the Fed became increasingly aware of serious problems with its operating procedure. At the same time a deterioration in economic conditions was helping to forge a political consensus that some new approaches to policymaking (both fiscal and monetary) were called for. The Fed reacted to the pressure (some would say it seized the opportunity) by adopting a new operating procedure.

19-8
CHANGING THE OPERATING PROCEDURE:
A RESERVE APPROACH TO MONETARY CONTROL

In the fall of 1979, with the price of gold reaching a historic high of over $400 per ounce, with the value of the dollar falling precipitously in the foreign currency market, and with the inflation rate at 13%, policymakers were understandably quite concerned about the stability of the economy.

---

[1] The analysis underlying this distinction between short- and long-run effects was discussed in Chapter 14. Reread that discussion to gain a better understanding of this distinction.

Early in 1979, the Fed had established a money supply growth target of 1½ to 4½ percent. As the year progressed, the Fed had adjusted the federal funds rate upward as it tried to slow monetary growth to choke off inflation. But the figures on monetary growth exhibited rather startling increases; from March through September money supply growth was about 9 percent— well in excess of the Fed's target. What was happening? The Fed's operating procedure, which focused on the federal funds rate, was permitting a demand-determined increase in the volume of reserves and the money supply.

If the Fed employs the funds rate approach to monetary control, it pegs the federal funds rate at a level believed consistent with its money supply target by supplying all the reserves (and money) that banks (and the public) demand at this rate. However, as shown in Figure 19-11, if there is an unexpected shift in the demand for reserves by banks (reflecting an increase in the demand for money by the public) to, say, R'_d, this would lead to a reserve supply of R_2 at i^*_{FF}. The supply function for bank reserves is thus horizontal, and any unexpected shift in demand induces changes in the quantity of reserves. During 1979, credit demands were booming and banks increased their reserve demands to accommodate their customers' needs. The Fed in turn accommodated the banks and money supply growth overshot the Fed's targets.

An alternative approach and operating procedure for the Fed to follow is to focus on the supply of bank reserves. We know from Chapter 9 that the money supply can be thought of as the product of the level of reserves and the money multiplier. Hence, if the Fed has a desired money supply M^*, it could estimate the money multiplier m, and then divide the money multiplier into the desired money supply to come up with the quantity of reserves R^* consistent with M^*.[1] Such an approach to the formulation and implementation of policy can be expressed as follows:

$$(19\text{-}6) \qquad\qquad R^* = f(M^*)$$

$$(19\text{-}7) \qquad\qquad OMO = f(R^* \overset{+}{-} R)$$

Equation (19-6) tells us that the desired level of reserves R^* is a function of the desired money supply M^* and Equation (19-7) tells us that the Fed's open market operations are a function of the difference between the actual and desired level of reserves. If actual reserves are below desired reserves $(R^* > R)$, the Fed will buy securities; if actual reserves exceed desired reserves $(R > R^*)$, the Fed will sell securities.[2] If you feel that this approach

[1] If $M = m \cdot R$, then $M^*/m = R^*$.
[2] Remember Fed purchases increase reserves and Fed sales decrease reserves.

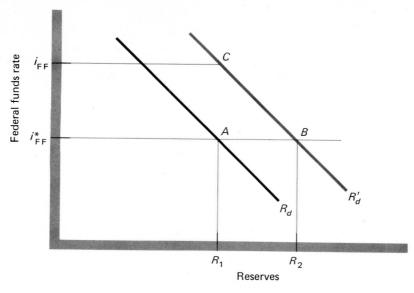

FIGURE 19-11

Under a funds rate approach to money supply control the Fed expects a particular funds rate, say i^*_{FF} to be consistent with a desired money supply target M^* and a particular level of reserves, say R_1. If the demand for money, and therefore bank demand for reserves, increases unexpectedly to R'_d, the result would be that the actual money supply would exceed M^* and actual reserves R_2 would exceed R_1. The equilibrium would be at point B and the quantity of reserves and money supply would be demand-determined. Under a supply approach to monetary control, an increase in money demand and reserve demand would lead to a rise in the actual federal funds rate to i_{FF}, but no increase in the quantity of reserves. The equilibrium would be at point C and the federal funds rate would be demand-determined.

—a reserve approach—is a more direct approach to controlling the money supply, you are right on the button!

Just to be sure it is all reasonably clear let's see how the reserve approach would affect Figure 19-11. Assume that R_1 is the desired level of reserves. If the demand for reserves by banks is R_d, then the supply and demand intersect at funds rate i^*_{FF}. However, if the demand for reserves shifts unexpectedly to R'_d, then the funds rate will be i_{FF}. If the Fed is using a reserve approach, then the supply curve for reserves is a vertical line at the desired reserve level and the funds rate is demand-determined. An approach or operating procedure which focuses on reserves is a supply approach to monetary control and this is the approach that monetarists have advocated for a long time. In a nutshell, the monetarists believe that there is less slippage between reserves and money supply growth than between the federal funds rate and money supply growth. Put another way, they believe the multiplier is easier to predict and is subject to less fluctuation than the relationship between the funds rate and the money supply.[1]

Now what has all this got to do with the fall of 1979? As we were saying in the first paragraph of this section, the Fed's operating procedure, which focused on the funds rate, was leading to a procyclical monetary policy as the demand for reserves was increasing. The new chairman of the Fed, Paul Volcker, announced on October 6, 1979, a series of steps that the Fed hoped would reverse the direction policy had been taking. The Fed argued that moderating inflation and restoring faith in the dollar required "bold action." The most significant part of the announcement was that the Fed intended to change its operating procedure from a funds rate approach to a reserve approach. Since credit demands were still strong, the implication was clear: interest rates were going to rise significantly as the Fed was going to allow rates to seek their own level. Following the Fed's announcement, interest rates rose to historic levels, the stock market plunged, and everyone braced themselves for a difficult period. Apparently, the Fed meant business.

The early political reactions to the Fed's moves were quite supportive. The White House was encouraging, as were many key Congressional and business leaders.[2] *The Wall Street Journal* called the Fed's moves "the most hopeful economic policy development in over a decade." The general response appeared to reflect an emerging consensus in the country that something serious should be done about inflation. Within the economics profession, monetarists, in particular, expressed hope that the Fed would stick to the supply approach, but having a sense of history and knowing the Fed's actions often have not matched its rhetoric, they were expressing some caution. Ira Kaminow put it this way:

> **If the fundamental cause of monetary excesses has been a technical inability to control money, then a technical solution of the sort adopted on October 6 may well succeed. The old money control procedures were extremely imprecise and a shift to control through bank reserves could easily improve precision and give**

---

[1] Note that both the funds rate and reserve approaches give identical results when the demand curve for reserves is R_d. The problems arise, and the two approaches are not equivalent, when the demand for reserves (and money) varies unexpectedly.

[2] We don't mean to imply that everyone was happy! The real estate industry for one was expressing concern. Also, Lane Kirkland, the successor to George Meany as head of the AFL–CIO criticized the Fed's actions, saying they "are the wrong move at the wrong time and will not solve the problem."

the Federal Reserve added ability to slow money growth and inflation in an orderly fashion.

But there are those who believe that inflation impulses go deeper than Fed technique. Economic aspirations are soaring past our ability to deliver. And when the political process directly or indirectly presses the Fed to chase unattainable goals for economic growth, the central bank responds with the printing press. Political pressures of course need not be as obvious as direct orders from the President or Congress. Fed officials are hardly immune from the more subtle influences of the political mood and climate in the country.

If excessive money growth has been a response to recurring political pressures for expansive policy, then the October 6 package did nothing to get at fundamental causes of inflation. It neither relaxed the pressures nor increased the Fed's ability to resist them. To the contrary, the package responds well to the political mood of the moment and so offers no particular hope that overexpansion is not again around the corner if the politics begin to push that way.*

> * Ira Kaminow, "The Fed May Not Have Shed Its Easy-Money Bias," *American Banker* (October 24, 1979), p. 4.

How long will the Fed stick to this new operating procedure? Will there be a recession? A credit crunch? Disaster in the housing industry? Will high interest rates save the dollar? Will the 1980 elections affect the ultimate outcome of this policy? As we go to press, these are just some of the questions being asked about the future. By the time you read this text, many of the answers to these questions may be available. The analysis presented in this chapter should enable you to understand better why things turned out as they did.

19-9
APPENDIX A—THE FED'S RECORD OF POLICY ACTIONS*

As discussed in the text, the FOMC meets each month to formulate policy. The "Record of Policy Actions" is a summary of the deliberations and discussions at each meeting and is published in the *Federal Reserve Bulletin*.

---

* This section contains optional material which can be omitted without loss of continuity throughout the rest of the text.

The following excerpts are from the "Record of Policy Actions" for the FOMC meeting held July 18, 1978, published in the September 1978 *Bulletin*.

The first exerpt (with our comments in the brackets) relates to the *long-run phase* of the formulation of policy discussed in the text.

At this meeting the Committee reviewed its 12-month ranges for growth in the monetary aggregates. At its meeting in April 1978 the Committee had specified the following ranges for the period from the first quarter of 1978 to the first quarter of 1979: M-1, 4 to 6½ percent; M-2, 6½ to 9 percent; and M-3, 7½ to 10 percent. The ranges being considered at this meeting were for the period from the second quarter of 1978 to the second quarter of 1979.

The Committee members differed principally in their preferences for the 12-month range for M-1: A majority favored retention of the existing range, while a member favored an increase in its upper limit. In the case of the broader aggregates, most members expressed a preference for retaining the existing ranges; one member suggested that the lower limits be reduced by ½ of a percentage point, yielding ranges of 6 to 9 percent for M-2 and 7 to 10 percent for M-3.

An increase in the upper limit of the range for M-1 was advocated on the expectation that, over the coming year, growth of M-1 would have to exceed the 6½ percent upper limit of the existing range, as it had over the past year, if strains in the financial markets were not to be so severe as to threaten an economic downturn. In this connection it was emphasized that the high rate of inflation in prospect for the quarters immediately ahead was attributable in part to governmental actions and to some strong forces in the private sector that were not likely to be moderated appreciably by the stance of monetary policy. In these circumstances, it was argued, the Committee ought to raise the upper limit of the range for M-1 to allow for a growth rate that—given upward cost pressures on prices—was more nearly consistent with the generally anticipated rate of growth in real and nominal GNP for the year ahead and that, consequently, was more likely to be achieved.

[Note here that someone on the Committee is suggesting the Fed should accommodate more inflation to avoid recession.]

Several arguments were advanced in favor of retaining the existing range of 4 to 6½ percent for M-1. First, M-1 growth in the second quarter—at an annual rate of 9½ percent, on a quarterly-average basis—had exceeded the upper limit of the Committee's range by a considerable margin, so that retention of the existing range for the year from the second quarter of 1978 to the second quarter of 1979 would allow for growth considerably faster than 6½ percent over the five-quarter period beginning the first quarter of 1978. Second, for *a considerable period of time growth in M-1 on the average had exceeded the range adopted by the Committee and a reduction of growth to a rate within the existing range would be an important step toward moderating inflation.* Also, such a reduction would have a positive effect on the economic outlook.

Moreover, any increase in the range could be misleading: Such an action, no matter what reasons might be offered for it, was likely to be interpreted both in this country and abroad as a signal of a shift in System policy toward less emphasis on fighting inflation. Since that was not the case, it would be consistent to retain the existing range, although the rate of growth over the period might be around the upper limit of the range.

[Note here the decision to retain the existing range but the expectation that actual money growth might be at the high end of the range instead of at the middle of the range. This suggests that the FOMC is reluctant to really try to slow money supply growth.]

At the conclusion of its discussion the committee decided to retain the existing ranges for the monetary aggregates. It was agreed that the longer-run ranges, as well as the particular aggregates for which longer-run ranges were specified, would be subject to review and modification at subsequent meetings. It was also understood that short-run factors might cause growth rates from one month to the next to fall outside the ranges anticipated for the year ahead.

[What short-run factors?]

The next excerpt covers the *short-run phase* of the formulation of policy.

In the discussion of policy for the period immediately ahead, the members differed mainly in their views as to whether, and to what degree, additional firming in money market conditions should be sought during the next few weeks for the purpose of restraining monetary growth in coming months. No sentiment was expressed for easing money market conditions.

[Most see a need for the federal funds rate and other interest rates to rise to slow money growth; the question is how much and when. Note the caution; "let's go slow."]

Several members proposed that for the time being operations be directed toward maintaining the money market conditions currently prevailing. It was argued that, in light of increased uncertainties in the economic outlook, such a "pause" would afford the Committee an opportunity to evaluate additional evidence on the current situation and outlook. It was suggested that, coming on top of the considerable firming in money market conditions over the past year or so, *further significant firming would risk bringing on a recession.* It was also observed that the restraining effects of the rise in interest rates over the past month had not yet been fully felt and that any firming that might be appropriate could be achieved at a later time.

On the other hand, a number of members favored a prompt further firming of money market conditions. Such a course was needed, it was suggested, to bring growth in M-1 within the Committee's longer-run range.

In considering the ranges for the annual rates of growth in the monetary aggregates to be specified for the July–August period, the members took account of the indications that growth in M-1 might accelerate in July. Most members preferred ranges of tolerance for growth in M-1 over the 2-month period extending from a lower limit of 4 or 5 percent to an upper limit of 8 or 9 percent. One favored a high range, from 5 to 10 percent, and another a lower range, from 3 to 7 percent. For M-2, most members favored ranges extending from 6 or 7 percent to 10 or 11 percent; one member preferred a range of 5 to 10 percent.

With respect to the Federal funds rate, most members favored ranges centered either on 7¾ percent, the midpoint of the 7½ to 8 percent range specified at the June meeting, or on the somewhat higher level that had developed in the most recent days.

At the conclusion of the discussion the Committee decided that operations in the period immediately ahead should be directed toward maintaining the weekly-average Federal funds rate within a range of 7¾ to 8 percent. The members agreed that, in deciding on the specific objective for the Federal funds rate, the Manager should be guided mainly by the relation between the latest estimates of annual rates of growth in M-1 and M-2 over the July–August period and the following *ranges of tolerance:* 4 to 8 percent for M-1 and 6 to 10 percent for M-2.

[Note how large the bull's-eye is.]

It was also agreed that if, giving approximately equal weight to M-1 and M-2, their rates of growth appeared to be close to or beyond the limits of the indicated ranges, the Manager should raise or lower the objective for the funds rate in an orderly fashion within its range.

At the conclusion of the meeting, the FOMC issues a "Policy Directive" to the Federal Reserve Bank of New York. This document guides the conduct of OMO between FOMC meetings. This particular directive summarized the exerpts included above.[1]

To see how things went between the July and August meeting, the following is excerpted from the "Record of Policy Actions" for the August 15, 1978 meeting of the FOMC (published in the October *Bulletin*).

Following the July 18 meeting the Manager of the System Open Market Account sought bank reserve conditions consistent with a weekly-average Federal funds rate somewhat above 7¾ percent. Data that became available throughout the inter-meeting interval suggested that growth in the monetary aggregates over the July–August period would be well within the Committee's ranges and the Manager continued to seek conditions consistent with a Federal funds rate within a range of 7¾ to 8 percent. The average rate during the inter-meeting period was about 7⅞ percent.

[1] You can read the actual directive; *Federal Reserve Bulletin* (September 1978), 753–755.

Things did not go so smoothly during the next month. Read the rest of the "Record" for the August 1978 meeting (in the October 1978 *Bulletin*) to see what the FOMC decided and then go to the November 1978 *Bulletin* and read the description of what went on between the August and September FOMC meetings (pages 850–851). The money supply grew considerably faster than desired and the response was to slow the growth in reserves and raise the federal funds rate.

19-10
APPENDIX B—DOES THE FED CONTROL INTEREST RATES?*

A popular *misconception* is that the Fed controls or determines interest rates, particularly short-term interest rates. Given that the Fed can control the federal funds rate, this view is usually supported by evidence such as that contained in Figure 19-12a. Since movements in the federal funds rate (which reflect, at least in part, the Fed's OMO) are highly correlated with the commercial paper rate, changes in the federal funds rate *cause* changes in the paper rate. In this view, the Fed stands at the top of a pyramid—it changes the funds rate, and this change spills over into other interest rates throughout the economy.

To put it bluntly, this is a myopic, shortsighted view of how interest rates are determined. As we have discussed several times throughout the text, interest rates are determined by Fed policy (which affects the supply of funds) *and* a variety of other factors—such as income (which affects the demand for funds) and inflation (which through its effect on expectations can influence both lenders' willingness to supply funds and borrowers' willingness to demand funds). Figure 19-12b shows the relationship between the inflation rate and the commercial paper rate; Figure 19-12c shows the relationship between short-term borrowing by businesses (loans from banks and commercial paper issued) and the commercial paper rate.[1] Clearly, one could also make the claim that changes in inflation and the demand for funds by firms "cause" changes in the commercial paper rate.

Happily, there *is* a way to tie the three panels of Figure 19-12 together. When aggregate demand rises (say, because of past changes in monetary and fiscal policy), income will rise and there will be upward pressure on prices. The rise in the demand for goods and services will be accompanied by a rise in the demand for funds to finance additional spending. As banks try to accommodate the demands of their customers for more funds by expanding their loans and holdings of market assets (such as commercial

---

* This section contains optional material which can be omitted without loss of continuity throughout the rest of the text.

[1] Those with good memories will remember that short-term borrowing by firms is closely related to their holdings of inventories (flip back to Chapter 5).

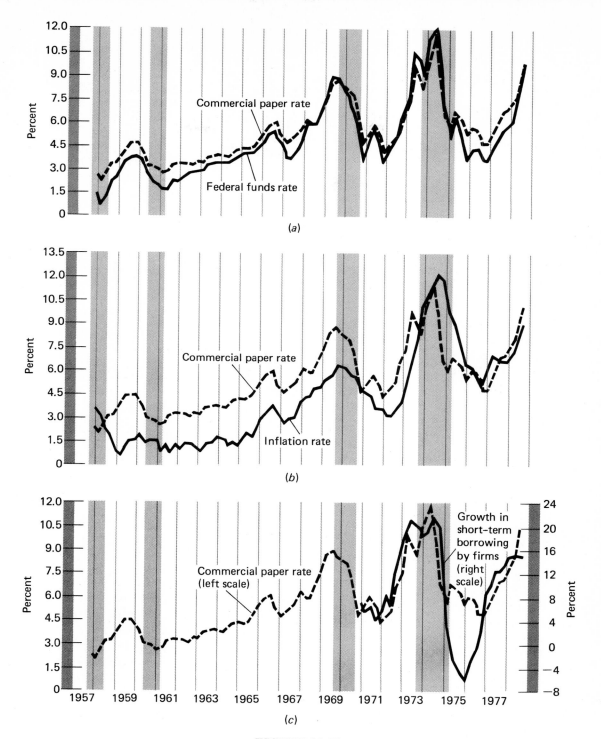

FIGURE 19-12

Relationships among interest rates, inflation, and credit demands. —all related

paper), they will bid for additional reserves in the federal funds market. If the rise in income, and therefore the demand for money and reserves, exceeds the rise underlying the targeted federal funds rate and money supply growth desired by the FOMC, the Fed will initially supply the additional reserves necessary to support the expansion in credit being extended by banks. As time passes, the Fed will notice that the money supply is rising faster than desired. With banks expanding loans and purchasing securities, they will be "creating" additional demand deposits. The reasons for the excessive growth in money will gradually become evident as data are released on retail sales, industrial production, inflation, and so forth. In this environment, the Fed will raise the funds rate, and other short-term rates will rise in response.

This view of how interest rates are determined is analogous to an inverted pyramid, with the economy at the top and the federal funds market and the Fed at the bottom. The various factors affecting the supply of and demand for federal funds (exclusive of current Fed actions) all converge on the financial system in general and banks in particular. The pressures generated by such developments alter bank behavior in the federal funds market and, in the absence of Fed action, the funds rate would adjust to changes in the demand for funds relative to the supply. If credit demands are expanding, the upward pressures on the funds rate (and other interest rates) will intensify. The Fed can, in the short run, pour enough reserves into the economy to forestall significant interest rate increases. Over the longer run, however, as money growth and inflation accelerate, the Fed will change its policy stance and interest rates will rise. You can work out the opposite case—suppose aggregate demand and income fall?

19-11
SUMMARY OF MAJOR POINTS

1

The transmission mechanism for monetary policy is like a stack of dominoes—if you tip over the first one, you start a process in which all the dominoes fall in sequence. In general, when the Fed conducts open market operations, the effects are transmitted to bank reserves, the federal funds rate, the money supply, and also other interest rates. These effects on money and the financial system affect GNP, unemployment, and inflation.

2

Monetary policy affects spending through its effects on the cost of capital, wealth, and credit availability.

3

There is a substantial time lag involved in the formulation, implementation, and ultimate effectiveness of monetary policy. The inside lag consists of the recognition lag, the decision lag, and the action lag. The outside lag consists of the impact lag. Once a monetary policy action is taken, its effect on economic activity is not immediate. The action will work its way through the transmission mechanism and, as time passes, the effect on economic activity will cumulate. Research suggests that the inside lag averages three to six months and the outside lag is at least six months.

4

The length of the total lag, along with its variability, and the difficulty associated with pinning down the transmission mechanism, have led some economists (such as Milton Friedman) to suggest that the Fed adopt a monetary rule.

5

Although policymakers have rejected the monetary rule, they do use the money supply as an intermediate target.

6

In the long-run phase of policymaking, the Fed selects the rate of growth in the money supply—its intermediate target—over the coming year which it believes is most consistent with full employment and low inflation, its final targets.

7

In the short-run phase of policymaking, the Fed selects a short-run target for the money supply growth rate which it believes is consistent with the long-run money growth target. At the same time the Fed selects a target for the federal funds rate. By directing its open market operations toward this desired level of the federal funds rate, the Fed expects to achieve its money supply targets.

8

In implementing policy, the Fed will conduct its open market operations so as to achieve the desired level of the federal funds rate. The Fed will supply additional reserves (buy securities) if the actual funds rate exceeds the desired level; it will reduce the supply of reserves (sell securities) if the actual rate is below the desired level.

9

If incoming data suggest that actual growth in the money supply is exceeding the target, the Fed will slow the growth of reserves and raise the federal funds rate. When it appears that monetary growth is falling short, the Fed increases reserves and lowers the funds rate.

10

In the 1970s, the Fed tended to delay its policy response to emerging undesirable economic developments. The existence of uncertainty and political pressure often contributed to procyclical (destabilizing) actions and a rise in the rate of inflation.

11

In October 1979 the Fed announced a switch in its operating procedure from a federal funds rate approach to a reserves approach. The change is designed to improve the Fed's control over money supply growth.

12*

The Fed affects but does not control interest rates. The Fed responds to pressures which have converged on the financial system, and its actions interact with other factors (such as price expectations) affecting the supply of and demand for funds.

19-12
REVIEW QUESTIONS

1   Describe the transmission mechanism of monetary policy.

2   Describe each of the lags in monetary policy. Why are they so long?

3   Why does the Fed use the money supply as an intermediate target?

4   How does the Fed choose the target for the money supply growth rate through the coming year? Why does the Fed staff produce an economic forecast?

5   Why does Milton Friedman advocate a monetary rule? What rule does he advocate?

6   How do the short-run (two-month) money supply targets relate to the long-run (yearly) targets?

7   How did the Fed go about trying to achieve the money supply target in the 1970s?

* Refers to the Appendix (optional material).

8 Why did the Fed miss the money supply target so often in the 1970s?

9 "The secular acceleration in the rate of inflation between 1960 and 1980 was *caused* by the Fed." Evaluate this statement.

10 Go read the bond markets column and any other stories on interest rates in the last five or ten issues of *The Wall Street Journal* and explain how actual or anticipated Fed actions have affected financial markets.

11 In earlier chapters (Chapter 13 in particular), we showed how an increase in reserves and the money supply lowered interest rates. Assuming we did not lie to you, why is it that when participants in the financial market notice a large rise in reserves and the money supply, interest rates often rise?

12 Explain the supply (reserves) approach to money supply control.

*13 "The Fed controls interest rates." Evaluate this statement.

19-13
SUGGESTED READINGS

1 The best group of readings available on monetary policy is contained in Thomas Havrilesky and John Boorman, *Current Issues in Monetary Theory and Policy* (Arlington Heights, Ill.: AHM Publishing, 1980). There are articles on the transmission mechanism, lags, the strategy of monetary policy, the role of the money supply, and so forth.

2 Another good book of readings on monetary policy well worth exploring is Ronald Teigen, *Readings in Money, National Income, and Stabilization Policy* (Homewood, Ill.: Irwin, 1978).

3 Every year the Fed produces an *Annual Report* and every three months or so there is a lead article in the *Federal Reserve Bulletin* on recent financial developments. Both contain descriptions of the deftness with which monetary policy has been carried out. After reading this chapter, you should be better able to read between the lines of such policy discussions and have some feel for how policymakers could have improved their performance.

* Refers to the Appendix (optional material).

20

FISCAL POLICY AND THE ELUSIVE QUEST FOR ECONOMIC STABILITY

> Government behavior will always reflect two
> important facts: first, governments cannot know
> for certain what they should do, and secondly,
> they cannot know for certain what they are
> doing.
>
> Randall Bartlett

20-1
THE OTHER GANG IN TOWN

Monetary policymakers meeting in the main offices of the Federal Reserve on Constitution Avenue are not the only folks in Washington interested in economic stability. There is another gang in town that, in theory, is also interested in economic stability. The President and the executive branch of government plus Congress are charged with the determination of fiscal policy. Fiscal policy actions by the government may reinforce or offset the monetary policy actions being taken by the Fed.

Fiscal policy, like monetary policy, is an important part of the government stabilization effort; but in a textbook on money and the financial system, only a brief treatment of fiscal policy is possible. In this chapter, we want to focus on how fiscal policy is formulated and implemented. We will also analyze the effects of fiscal policy on financial variables and on economic activity. Most important to our study of money and the financial system is the interrelationship between fiscal and monetary policy. The questions are as follows: Do monetary and fiscal policy represent a coordinated effort to achieve our economic goals? Do monetary and fiscal policymakers pursue actions which conflict? Do fiscal policymakers often pursue policies which destabilize the economy and then "persuade" the supposedly independent Federal Reserve to accommodate? Have these possibilities in mind as you read on; by the end of the chapter, you should be in a better position to understand why it has proved so difficult to achieve economic stability.

20-2
FORMULATING FISCAL POLICY

One basic difference between fiscal policy and monetary policy is this: the Fed is the only body that formulates and puts monetary policy into effect. However, there is no single government body that formulates and implements fiscal policy. Instead, the executive and legislative branches of government are jointly responsible for formulating fiscal policy. They jointly determine and implement fiscal policy designed to stabilize the economy in the following way.

The President, with the assistance of the Secretary of the Treasury, the Director of the Office of Management and Budget, and the Council of Economic Advisers *recommends* fiscal policy—that is, how much taxation and government spending is needed to stabilize the economy.

The Congress, with the assistance of the Congressional Budget Office and its various committees—such as the Joint Economic Committee, the House Ways and Means Committee, and the Senate Finance Committee—*enacts* fiscal policy.

Separating the power and authority to formulate fiscal policy as shown in Figure 20-1 makes this a slow and time-consuming procedure. In fact, the process is even more cumbersome than meets the eye. As discussed in Chapter 6, government policies that are enacted usually represent compromises among the various power centers that actually determine government policy—the President, the Congress, the government bureaucracies, the organized special-interest groups, and the electorate. The President may recommend policy and the Congress may be charged with enacting policy, but the policies which eventually emerge will in fact represent compromises among the interested parties. Such compromises take time to develop.

For example, let's assume that inflation accelerates and the President has decided to tighten fiscal policy in order to decrease aggregate demand

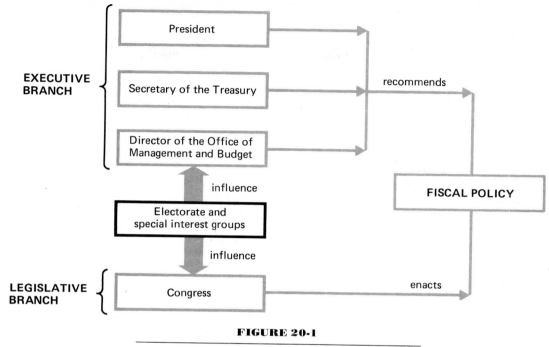

FIGURE 20-1

The formation of fiscal policy.

and reduce inflation. This means that the President, in consultation with his economic advisers (the Secretary of the Treasury, the Budget Director, and the Council of Economic Advisers) must come up with a fiscal program to recommend to Congress. This fiscal program must take into account the political realities of what Congress will accept and, to some degree, what the government bureaucracy will accept. If the plan requires a change in tax policy, this proposal is submitted to the House Ways and Means Committee and the Senate Finance Committee.

The House and Senate committees will each hold their own hearings to obtain testimony from tax experts, concerned interest groups, and government agencies. Each committee then attempts to put together a fiscal program and enact it as legislation. The trick is that the fiscal program must balance the various competing interests and still be acceptable to the President and Congress. But before it reaches that point, each house—the House and the Senate—must vote on a fiscal program put in the form of legislation. A problem that usually develops is that the fiscal programs put together and passed by each house are usually not the same. So then what happens? The bills must then go to a conference committee made up of representatives of both houses who attempt to work out the differences between the two versions of the bill. When the conference committee comes up with an agreed upon bill, it must go back to both houses for final passage and then to the President for his signature.

It takes a long time to formulate fiscal policy. In terms of our discussion of lags in formulating and implementing policy in Chapter 19, this means that fiscal policy suffers from a long *inside lag*. The time between the point at which the economy is in need of some fiscal action and the stage at which a final decision is actually made and carried out is sometimes so long that many economists believe fiscal policy to be essentially unworkable as a stabilization tool. They argue that compromises are difficult to forge, often weaken the effect of the intended policy, and frequently reflect political rather than economic considerations.

POLITICAL CONSIDERATIONS

Fiscal policy decisions are inevitably political as well as economic. They are political because spending and tax programs affect particular sectors of society. We cannot just increase or decrease taxes; we must decide *whose* taxes to increase or to decrease. Obviously, different groups in society have different views as to who should pay for what or who should get the benefits. For instance, if a tax increase is necessary, who should pay the increase? Should it be just households or should it also include the business sector? Should lower-income families be excluded from a tax increase? And how do we define low income? The same issues arise in making spending decisions. We must decide whether to spend or not to spend on national defense, education, highways, and many, many other possible programs. The final outcomes of both spending and taxing decisions are usually the result of a compromise among the various competing public and private interests that have access to the political decision-making process.

An illustration of the difficulties associated with proposing changes in fiscal policy was provided by the initial reactions to President Carter's proposed budget for fiscal year 1980 (October 1, 1979, through September 30, 1980). The President, concerned about accelerating inflation, proposed a budget he called "lean and austere." One senator's reaction to the budget was as follows: "This budget is an economic iceberg set to sink the taxpayer." A representative from Illinois (a farm-product state) said he was particularly bothered by a budget cut in the export credit program, which extends loans to foreign countries so that they can buy United States farm products. A congressman from New Jersey threatened to introduce legislation to continue a program that Carter reduced—at twice the spending level proposed by the President! The President of the American Nurses Association said the Carter budget would cut nursing education and "ultimately health care will suffer." The Americans for Democratic Action said "there will be cuts in crucial programs which provide services to the poor."

The Republicans, looking forward to the 1980 presidential election, argued that the budget proposed by Carter was inflationary. The often confusing rhetoric on budgets is nicely summarized by Eugene McCarthy (former United States senator) and James Kilpatrick (newspaper columnist): "They are regularly identified by those who propose them as lean and sober, generally as tight, sometimes as frugal and austere, often as bareboned. They usually are seen by others as padded, bloated, and larded with fat."[1]

As discussed in Chapter 6, *most* changes in government policy regarding taxes, transfers, expenditures, or regulation are directed toward allocative or distributive goals rather than primarily toward stabilization goals. Special-interest groups, government agencies, and Congressional committees are usually interested in specific problems and naturally seek out specific solutions. Some are interested in housing for the poor and elderly, others in improving health care, some in a new submarine for the Navy, while others are in favor of higher incomes for farmers. The problem is that, taken together, policies pursued to accomplish these laudable objectives may very well contribute to economic instability. For instance, do senators from the Midwest know or care that raising price supports for agricultural commodities and imposing acreage restrictions or import restrictions to raise the price of agricultural goods and raise farm income will also lead to higher consumer prices, which, in turn, raise payments tied to the "cost of living"—wages, pensions, food stamps allotments, and so forth? It is well understood by the senators that their reelection depends primarily on what they can do to help farmers in their own states, not on what happens to inflation throughout the country. And before you criticize this attitude, ask yourself whether you would do otherwise.

The fact is that elected fiscal policymakers (the President and the Congress) are interested in improving society's welfare *and* in getting reelected. Spending more and taxing less is likely to make at least some members of society better off in the short run and to enhance the policymakers' chances of being reelected. This explains why fiscal policymakers focus primarily on short-run developments; look for quick, popular remedies for problems; and pay little attention to the longer-run, often unintended cumulative effects of such remedies.

The theme developed above—which we call the political economy of policymaking—is an essential ingredient if one is ever to understand what policymakers do or fail to do.

---

[1] *A Political Bestiary* (New York: McGraw Hill, 1978), p. 24. This is a funny, entertaining book; we recommend it highly.

20-3
ECONOMIC EFFECTS OF FISCAL POLICY

When one is assessing the economic effects of fiscal policy, it is helpful to distinguish between its *direct effects* on incomes and expenditures and its *indirect effects* on these variables. Changes in tax rates have a direct effect on taxes paid by households and firms and thus alter the income received by these sectors. Changes in household or firm incomes, in turn, affect their spending decisions. Changes in government spending also have a direct effect on income and expenditures, since government spending is a component of GNP.

The indirect effects of fiscal policy on overall income and expenditures in the economy result from the fact that all spending by the government must be financed. If the government's budget is balanced initially—that is, if government expenditures are equal to government receipts—and the government raises expenditures or cuts taxes, it will incur a deficit. The deficit will be financed by selling bonds. As we shall see, the increase in the supply of bonds will have an effect on the general level of interest rates prevailing in the financial system. Changes in interest rates will, in turn, have some effect on spending decisions in the economy. Thus fiscal policy affects economic activity directly through its impact on incomes and expenditures and indirectly through its impact on the financial system.

Let us examine these several effects in more detail by looking at the mechanism for the transmission of fiscal policy.

CHANGES IN TAXES: DIRECT EFFECTS

We learned in Chapter 13 that changes in taxes affect aggregate demand in the economy. In particular, a cut in taxes increases demand while a rise in taxes lowers demand. To make sure you understand this relationship, let us work through an example. Suppose the economy is operating well below full employment (with actual output well below potential output) and the government enacts a general cut in individual and corporate income taxes. The cut in taxes will immediately and directly raise the current disposable income of households and the current net income (income after taxes) of businesses. If the tax cut is expected to be permanent, it will also raise future expected disposable income of households and future expected net income of businesses. This rise in current and expected future incomes will encourage households to increase their consumption spending and encourage firms to expand their investment spending. Taken together, the rise in spending plans will increase aggregate demand (the aggregate-demand curve in Chapter 13 shifts to the right). The rise in demand will raise output and prices. The closer the economy is to full employment, the larger will be the rise in prices and the smaller the rise in output.

Of course, the government does not have to enact a general cut in taxes to stimulate aggregate demand. It could, for example, decide to enact an investment tax credit.

A *tax credit* is a subtraction from the tax one would otherwise pay. Typically, the government legislates tax credits when it wants to encourage the public to engage in certain types of expenditures. For example, in recent years Congress has provided a 15 percent tax credit for homeowners who add insulation to their homes. If your normal tax bill is, say, $4000 and you spend $1000 for more insulation, your actual tax bill would be $3850. You are allowed to deduct 15 percent of the expenditures on insulation (up to a maximum of $2000) from your tax bill. Thus your tax credit will be $150 and your tax bill is $4000 − $150 = $3850. The government wants to encourage the public to use less energy. By allowing the tax credit, it in effect lowers the price of insulation to the purchaser. The lower price should increase the demand for insulation. From the government's viewpoint, increasing the amount of insulation in homes is one way to help accomplish its energy-saving objective.

The *investment tax credit*, as its name suggests, is a credit provided to firms for adding to their stock of plant and equipment. Hence the idea is to stimulate investment. The tax credit in effect lowers the price of capital goods and therefore ought to encourage firms to expand their operations. The credit is currently 10 percent. This means that if a new machine costs, say, $1000, the firm gets a $100 credit, lowering its taxes payable by this amount. In effect, the machine costs the firm $900 instead of $1000.

An investment tax credit should raise investment demand and and therefore aggregate demand. Over the longer run, this credit will contribute to rises in the capital stock and therefore increases in aggregate supply and economic growth.

So much for the direct effects of tax changes. Let us look briefly at the direct effects of changes in government spending.

CHANGES IN GOVERNMENT SPENDING: DIRECT EFFECTS

When the government decides to buy a new missile or to hire new government employees, the money spent accrues to the missile company or to the new employees in the form of higher incomes. As was the case above, the higher incomes will tend to stimulate investment spending by firms and consumption spending by households. Thus changes in government spending directly affect aggregate demand by changing total expenditures and thus income, which, in turn, effects demand by households and firms.

FINANCIAL EFFECTS OF FISCAL POLICY

As discussed earlier (particularly in Chapter 6), government spending G minus government tax receipts T equals the government deficit D_g:

$$(20\text{-}1) \qquad\qquad G - T = D_g$$

Any government deficit must be financed by issuing (supplying) government bonds in the financial market. Financing the deficit is one facet of the government's debt management.

DEBT MANAGEMENT

The U.S. Treasury is responsible for managing the debt of the government. The Treasury essentially conducts two types of financing operations: (1) it must *finance* the current deficit by issuing new debt and (2) it must *refinance* old issues of debt reflecting past deficits that are maturing. In financing the current deficit and retiring maturing debt, the Treasury must consider the timing of the sale of new issues and what maturity distribution of securities should be issued. In other words, how many notes, bills, and bonds should be issued and when should they be issued?

The Treasury is by far the largest single borrower in financial markets. To minimize the disruptions that its financing operations can cause in the market, the Treasury has "regularized" a large part of its financing activity. By this we mean that the Treasury announces its borrowing intentions well in advance and tends to borrow at regular intervals. For example, every Monday, the Treasury sells Treasury bills carrying three- and six-month maturities. These weekly sales of bills are used by the Treasury to refinance bills which are maturing—say, $5.8 billion—and to help finance part of the current budget deficit. The latter is done by selling, say, $6 billion of bills on Monday. Of this $200 million will be used to cover the current budget deficit and the rest will be used to pay off the $5.8 billion of maturing bills.

Check the last several issues of *The Wall Street Journal*; it regularly reports the announcements and results of Treasury financing operations.

In general, the government's deficit is equal to the change in bonds ΔB_{sg} supplied by the government:

(20-2) $$D_g = \Delta B_{sg}$$

If the government lowers taxes or raises expenditures, this will increase the deficit and thus increase the supply of bonds in the economy. As discussed in Section 13-4 of Chapter 13, an increase in the supply of bonds (reflecting an increase in the demand for funds by the government) will tend to raise interest rates on government securities. The rise in interest rates on government securities will, in turn, encourage a rise in interest rates on other securities—such as corporate bonds, municipal bonds, and perhaps even mortgages. Did you ask why? As the yield on government securities rises, investors seeking higher returns will be attracted to these securities. Some will rearrange their portfolios by selling, say, corporate bonds and buying government bonds. This *substitution* will tend to raise the rate on corporate bonds (lower the price).

Why are we interested in this financial effect of fiscal actions? The rise in interest rates generated by the government's deficit financing will tend to *crowd out* some private borrowers such as firms, households, and municipal governments. All this means is that the rise in rates will induce some who had planned to borrow *and* spend to cancel, postpone, or alter their spending and borrowing plans. More specifically, the rise in rates will tend to lower investment spending by some firms and lower consumption spending by some households. Thus fiscal policy has an *indirect* effect on aggregate demand through its effect on interest rates.

In the example we have been following, the direct effects of the rise in government spending or cut in taxes raise aggregate demand, while the indirect effects lower aggregate demand. What matters, of course, is the net effect. Most research on the topic suggests that the net effect depends importantly on how far the economy is from full employment (the effect on output is more positive the further we are from full employment), how sensitive consumption and investment spending are to changes in interest rates (the effect on output is more positive the less sensitive are consumption and investment to changes in interest rates), and the monetary policy that accompanies the fiscal policy. Given our focus on money and the financial system as well as Fed policy, the last determinant of the effect of fiscal policy should be examined more closely.

THE FED'S MONETARY POLICY AND CROWDING OUT

To state the issue directly: The Fed can pursue policies that prevent crowding out and thus can allow the fiscal policy actions discussed above to have a significant, positive effect on aggregate demand and therefore on output and prices. How can the Fed do this? All the Fed needs to do is buy enough government securities—that is, conduct enough OMO—to keep interest rates from rising. Remember that the deficit increases the supply of bonds; by increasing the demand for bonds directly and providing reserves for commercial banks that can also increase their demand for bonds, the Fed can, at least in the short run, keep interest rates from rising. If rates do not rise, the crowding out discussed above will not occur.

> **The Fed heads off crowding out by increasing the supply of reserves and money in the financial system. In terms of our room example, as Uncle Sam tries to enter the room, the Fed takes actions which enlarge the size of the room so that all households and firms planning to borrow, as well as Uncle Sam, can be accommodated.**

The reasoning above can also be turned on its head: the Fed can pursue policies that guarantee crowding out and thus can prevent fiscal policy actions from having any significant effect on aggregate demand, and therefore on output and prices. (Can you explain how?)

You should now be able to see something that you might not have understood before reading the above discussion: the effect of fiscal policy on the economy depends very much on monetary policy. Figure 20-2 summarizes the transmission mechanism for fiscal policy, specifically a rise in government spending. The figure and discussion above suggest the need for us to look a bit closer at the relationship between fiscal and monetary policy.

20-4
THE RELATIONSHIP
BETWEEN FISCAL AND MONETARY POLICY:
COORDINATION OR CONFLICT?

Ideally, we would hope that our fiscal and monetary policymakers embraced the same goals, assigned similar priorities to each, and coordinated their policy decisions. Operationally, this would mean that there were open lines of communication between the various decision makers so that each was fully informed of what the other was doing and planned to do. Any disagreements on what needed to be done to stabilize the economy could then be ironed out before policy actions were implemented.

As we pointed out in Chapters 18 and 19, the Fed is an independent agency. This means that it can, at least in theory, pursue a policy that conflicts with the thrust of fiscal policy. Suppose the Fed, intent on lowering the inflation rate, was pursuing a restrictive policy while fiscal policymakers, intent on lowering the unemployment rate and raising economic growth, were pursuing a stimulative policy. It does not take much imagination to see that this particular conflict between policymakers will not contribute to the achievement of economic stability.

In the above case, conflict between policymakers was bad; is conflict ever good? The answer is yes. Suppose fiscal policymakers were enacting

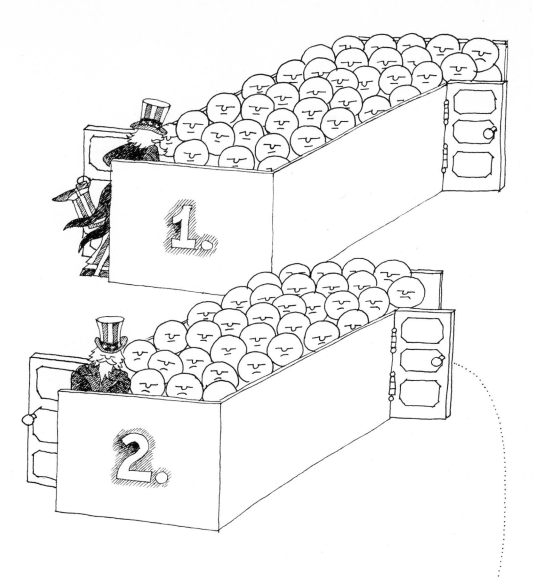

What we mean by "crowding out" can be seen by visualizing a 6- by 12-foot room with a door at the front and another at the rear. This room is full of people, all of whom demand some space. If the room is already full and Uncle Sam comes through the front door—Uncle Sam can always demand space—then someone must be pushed out the rear door. In the financial markets, this is done through a rise in interest rates which alter the borrowing and hence spending plans of both the household and business sectors.

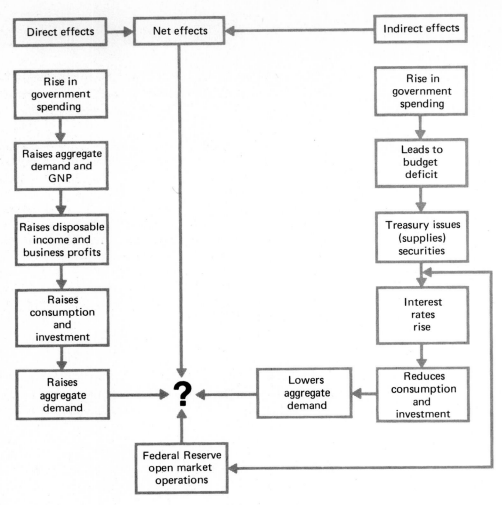

FIGURE 20-2

The transmission mechanism for fiscal policy. The *net* effect of fiscal policy on aggregate demand and therefore on the economy will depend on the direct and indirect effects of fiscal actions. If, for example, the government increases its spending, this will *directly* raise GNP and aggregate demand and lead to further increases in aggregate demand through the rises in consumption and investment induced by increases in household disposable income and business profits. Offsetting the direct effects to some degree will be the *indirect* effects. Assuming the government budget was initially in balance, the rise in spending will lead to a budget deficit and therefore to an increase in bonds supplied (sold) by the government. This will tend to raise interest rates which in turn will have some depressing effect on aggregate demand through the impact of rising rates on consumption and investment. The strength of this offsetting, indirect (financial) effect will depend in part on what the Federal Reserve does. If, for example, the Fed buys securities (open market operations), bank reserves will rise, and the rise in interest rates, and thus the strength of the indirect effect, will be reduced.

policies destined to create economic instability. Ideally, in this case we would not want the Fed to coordinate its policy with the President and the Congress; the economy would be better off if the Fed engaged in actions which reduced the destabilizing effect of the fiscal policy actions.

The problem such conflicts create is perhaps obvious; the Congress and the President get very testy when the Fed appears to be in effect "vetoing" fiscal policy. As a result, the Fed is often under considerable pressure to "accommodate" fiscal policy, whether this policy is contributing to economic stability or not. The term *accommodate* refers to actions that the Fed can take to moderate the crowding out which can accompany fiscal actions. As discussed in the last section, a rise in government spending financed by the selling of bonds will, among other things, put upward pressure on interest rates. If the Fed buys bonds, it can relieve the upward pressure on interest rates and thus stave off the crowding out of consumption and investment which would otherwise occur. If the fiscal actions were inappropriate, the accommodation by the Fed (and resulting rise in reserves and the money supply) would reinforce the economic effects of the fiscal actions. This suggests that poor fiscal policy may be one of the factors contributing to the Fed's failure to hit its money supply targets, discussed in the last chapter. All in all, the chances of achieving our economic goals are considerably reduced when the Fed accommodates poorly designed fiscal policies.

In sum, it is a mistake to consider monetary and fiscal policies as independent of one another. There is a complex, ongoing interaction among all policymakers. The potential for conflict among monetary and fiscal policymakers always exists; thus political and economic compromises are common. Unfortunately, given the impatience of policymakers and their interest in the shorter-run effects of policies, such compromises can lead to economic instability over the longer run.

20-5
THE SEARCH FOR NEW POLICIES

With policymakers failing to achieve the economic stability they and the nation desire, some economists and policymakers have suggested that conventional monetary and fiscal policies by themselves may not be sufficient to achieve our economic goals. This naturally gives rise to research directed at uncovering new policies to deal with our economic problems. Among the most popular alternatives developed and, in fact, used in the United States and several foreign countries are wage and price controls.

WAGE AND PRICE CONTROLS

These are a whole host of actions taken by governments to try to reduce or eliminate increases in wages and prices. By restraining wages and prices, governments hope to moderate inflationary expectations and reduce wage increases in excess of productivity gains (which shift the aggregate supply curve in Chapter 13 to the left). These controls run the gamut from outright *freezes* of wages and prices, to *mandatory controls* (which place a ceiling on the increase in wages and prices), to *voluntary controls* or guidelines which the public is asked to honor as it sets prices or negotiates wage contracts. All these types of controls are sometimes referred to as *incomes policies*, since the control of wages and prices affects the incomes of households and firms.

These controls are typically invoked (or seriously considered) when government policymakers observe a significant acceleration in the rate of inflation and are unwilling to run the risk (both political and economic) of a serious recession. We have learned earlier (in Chapters 13 and 14) that slowing the rate of inflation would require policymakers to slow the growth in aggregate demand. The short-run effects of a slowing in the growth of demand are likely to include a rise in the unemployment rate and a reduction of economic growth. The drop in the inflation rate will come later. Since people are unwilling to wait that long (impatience again) and unwilling to accept a recession, the imposition of controls on wages and prices is obviously an attractive alternative.

The record of wage and price controls is not impressive. Research suggests that such controls, by themselves, have not been very successful in moderating inflation in the United States or in other countries.

Some economists argue that such controls treat the symptoms of the problem rather than the principal causes—overly expansive monetary and fiscal policies—and that policymakers make matters worse by viewing such controls as a substitute for appropriate monetary and fiscal policies. A frequently mentioned metaphor nicely illustrates this point. Visualize a pot full of water on a gas stove with the burner on. Suppose the water is boiling and you want to prevent it from spilling over. One approach might be to put a lid on the pot and try to hold the steam and water back. Does anyone think this will work for very long? Another possibility is to turn the heat down and thereby lower the temperature of the water. The worst of all possible combinations would be to put the lid on *and* turn the heat up. You can be quite sure that the lid would blow off.

Wage and price controls are the counterpart to the lid in our illustration; the people turning the flame up or down are the fiscal and monetary policymakers; and the height and intensity of the flame represent the actual effects of conventional monetary and fiscal policies on the economy—the pot of water.

The United States experimented with wage and price controls from 1971 to 1973 and from 1978 at least until this text went into print. Some suggested readings at the end of this chapter review the record. It is not good. The lid cannot be held on for long, especially when the heat is being turned up.

Perhaps policymakers somewhere, sometime will design wage-price controls in concert with appropriate monetary and fiscal policies which will moderate inflation without a recession. In the meantime, the search for alternatives will continue and governments will experiment with various types of wage and price controls.

OTHER NEW POLICIES AND DILEMMAS

New policies are not restricted to wage-price or incomes policies. In recent years there have also been various proposals aimed at increasing aggregate supply. The best known are various tax cut proposals that would cut income taxes significantly over a three-year period. The proponents of these tax cuts support this policy not because it will increase demand but because they believe that over time it will increase supply. Thus, such cuts are intended to reduce rather than increase inflationary pressures. The argument of the supporters is that a major tax cut will increase work incentives as well as the incentive of businesses to invest and savers to save. All of this will increase capital accumulation and increase productivity. Most economists agree that the short-run effects of such tax cuts would be to increase demand. There is considerable disagreement over the longer run effects on aggregate supply. If such a program is to be tried, it would be desirable to try it during a time of economic slack when the short-run effects would be less likely to be inflationary.

While the merits of various tax cuts have been debated, some economists have noted that in recent years price increases have been led by four major items: costs for energy, food, housing, and medical care. These economists argue that *restrictive fiscal and monetary policies will have little short-run effect* on any of these items. Thus, there has been increasing attention paid to microeconomic policies aimed at dealing with these specific sources of inflationary pressure. As yet there has emerged no economic or political consensus as to the appropriate policies for dealing with these problems. We can, however, expect major debates over how to contain these costs in the coming years.

20-6
APPENDIX A—THE BURDEN OF
THE NATIONAL DEBT*

When people hear that our national debt—that is, the total amount of United States government debt outstanding—is about $850 billion, one question that inevitably comes up is: "Is this enormous national debt a *burden* that will have to be paid off by future, still unborn generations of Americans?" With our current population at about 210 million persons, every man, woman, and child in the nation in effect owes somebody $4047.62. Do you feel poorer now that we have informed you of your share of the debt burden? Let us examine the issue more closely.

If each of us owes that much money, to whom do we owe it? For every creditor there must be a debtor; for every debit there is a credit. To answer the question, let us suppose that all holders of government bonds are Americans. In this case the debt is, in effect, owed to ourselves! The net burden

---

* This section contains optional material which can be omitted without loss of continuity throughout the rest of the text.

on society is nil. There are, of course, distributional effects within society; those that own the bonds will be receiving interest income and those without bonds will be paying taxes to pay that interest income. The bondholders are better off and the taxpayers without bonds are worse off; on balance, however, there is no current net burden on society.

In assessing the burden of the debt, one must keep in mind the fact that the debt comes into existence and rises when the government's spending exceeds its receipts. What does the government purchase? In general, it purchases resources (factors of production) which enable it to produce goods and services provided to the public—for example, national defense, education, and highways. Thus, in exchange for the debt, we get benefits in the form of goods and services provided by the government. Obviously, the debt looks less burdensome when we recognize these benefits. A sizable portion of the current debt resulted from deficits incurred during World War II; if you think this debt is a burden on society, consider what would have happened if the government had not spent and incurred these deficits. Of course, if the government spends money frivolously or its spending crowds out private spending and generates considerable inflation, then the notion that the debt in some way burdens society is more credible.

The debt can be burdensome in another way. In the discussion above, we assumed that the outstanding debt is all owed to Americans. This, of course, is not true. Our discussion in earlier chapters pointed out that a growing share of the debt is owed to foreigners—about 20 percent in mid-1979. Thus we owe part of the debt to foreigners (such as OPEC) rather than to ourselves. The debt owed to foreigners is a financial claim they have on future United States wealth. When they exercise these claims, our national wealth will be reduced and future generations will bear that burden. This is one aspect of the growing importance of international considerations in the United States; accordingly, we shall devote Chapter 21 to a discussion of international economic policy.

20-7
APPENDIX B—THE FULL-EMPLOYMENT
BUDGET DEFICIT (OR SURPLUS) AS A
MEASURE OF FISCAL POLICY*

The Federal government's *actual* budget deficit or surplus is measured by the difference between government expenditures and receipts. If the government enacts no new spending programs and does not change policy regarding taxes or transfers, the actual budget will automatically move into deficit when the economy enters a recession and into surplus when the economy enters an inflationary boom. To see why this is the case, suppose that the budget is initially in balance; expenditures are equal to receipts. Holding government purchases of goods and services constant, when the

* This section contains optional material which can be omitted without loss of continuity throughout the rest of the text.

economy moves into a recession, income falls. The fall in income leads to a fall in tax receipts and a rise in transfer payments—for example, unemployment compensation—which push the federal budget into deficit. We would not want to use the emerging deficit as an indicator that fiscal policy had turned "stimulative"—that is, as an indicator of conscious actions taken by policymakers to raise aggregate demand and therefore overall economic activity. By assumption, fiscal policymakers have done nothing!

Clearly an alternative measure of the thrust of fiscal policy is needed. Movements in the *deficit or surplus of the full-employment budget* provide such a measure. This deficit or surplus is *not* the difference between *actual* government expenditures and receipts; it is the difference between expenditures and receipts that would exist *if* the economy were operating at full employment. The relationship between the actual and full-employment budget concepts is illustrated in Figure 20-3. Study this figure and the caption which accompanies it.

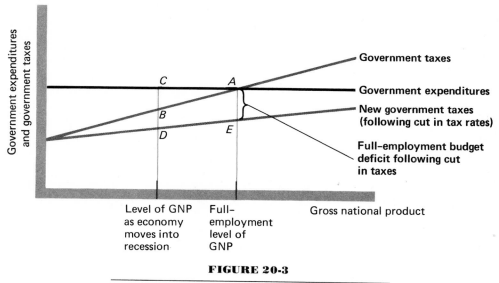

FIGURE 20-3

If the economy is operating at full employment, the actual and full-employment budgets are balanced; government expenditures are equal to tax receipts at point *A* (we will ignore transfer payments for simplicity). Now suppose the economy enters a recession and the government initially does nothing to reverse the decline in income. The actual budget which was balanced at point *A* will move into a deficit equal to the distance *BC*. Is fiscal policy stimulative? The answer is no because the full-employment budget is still in balance. We would only conclude that fiscal policy had turned stimulative if, for example, the government cut tax rates, shifting down the tax function. A cut in tax rates means that the government's tax receipts will be lower at every level of income. The actual budget deficit will rise to *CD*, and now the full-employment budget *AE* is in deficit. The movement in the full-employment budget from balance to a deficit has correctly captured the stimulative thrust of fiscal policy.

You should now be able to see why the actual deficit is a misleading indicator of fiscal policy and why, say, a cut in tax rates or a rise in government expenditures will move the full-employment budget toward a deficit.

In general, if the full-employment budget moves into deficit, this is an indicator of a stimulative fiscal policy. If the full-employment budget moves into surplus, this is an indicator of a restrictive fiscal policy (that is, fiscal policy actions being pursued to reduce aggregate demand).

AN ILLUSTRATION

The contrast between the actual and full-employment budget concepts was vividly demonstrated in 1974–1975. The United States economy entered a recession in late 1973. As 1974 proceeded, the downturn in economic activity gradually worsened. Initially, fiscal policymakers did very little in response (Watergate was occupying them and inflation was worsening). The actual budget moved into a deficit which grew larger as the months passed. The full-employment budget, reflecting the lack of action by fiscal policymakers, was about in balance. Finally, in early 1975, with the unemployment rate over 9 percent, the policymakers cut taxes and raised spending. The full-employment budget moved from balance to a $50 billion deficit. This action, along with the Fed's monetary policy, helped propel the economy upward.

Data on the full-employment budget are published regularly by the Federal Reserve Bank of St. Louis, the Council of Economic Advisers, and the Congressional Budget Office.

20-8
SUMMARY OF MAJOR POINTS

1

The President recommends fiscal policy actions. The Congress enacts fiscal policy.

2

Fiscal policy decisions inevitably reflect both economic and political considerations. Decisions to alter government spending or taxes will affect specific groups or sectors of the economy. Those groups adversely affected will try to minimize the effects, while those benefiting will try to ensure maximum gains. The final policy decisions will reflect compromises among the various competing groups within and outside the government.

3

Most government policy actions are directed primarily toward allocative or distributive goals rather than toward stabilization goals. In many cases the longer-run, unintended effects of such actions bring about more, rather than less, economic instability.

4

Increases in government spending directly raise GNP and induce further increases in GNP by affecting consumption and investment. Reductions in taxes directly raise the income of firms and households, in turn increasing consumption and investment and thus GNP. These are the direct effects of fiscal policy.

5

There are also indirect effects of fiscal policy. If the government raises its spending or cuts taxes, there will be an increase in the government deficit, requiring the Treasury to increase the supply of government securities sold (supplied). The increase in supply will tend to raise interest rates and discourage some consumption and investment. The rise in interest rates induced by the fiscal policy actions will crowd out some private spending. The net effect of fiscal policy on GNP will depend on the strength of the direct effects relative to the strength of the indirect (financial) effects.

6

The Federal Reserve can significantly influence the net effect of fiscal policy on the economy. For example, if it buys securities (remember open market operations) when the Treasury sells them, it can prevent the rise in interest rates and the subsequent crowding out. Unfortunately, "accommodating" the Treasury can help to make the Fed miss its money supply targets and contribute to economic instability over the longer run.

7

The United States government and governments around the world have experimented with various forms of wage and price controls as a cure for inflation. Many economists believe that such controls treat the symptoms of the inflation problem rather than the underlying causes. The record provides little evidence that controls by themselves have actually cured or helped to cure the inflation problem.

20-9
REVIEW QUESTIONS

1   Why does it take so long to formulate fiscal policy?

2   Provide a list of government programs designed to accomplish objectives related to the allocation of resources or distribution of income which may, in some way, contribute to economic instability (that is, inflation, unemployment, low rates of economic growth, and international imbalances).

3   What are the financial effects of fiscal policy and how do these effects relate to crowding out?

4   The U.S. Treasury is charged with managing the federal debt. What does this entail?

5   How is it that the Fed can determine how effective fiscal policy actions will be?

6   "Wage-price controls can be used in place of conventional monetary and fiscal policy actions to reduce inflation." Evaluate this statement.

*7   "A deficit in the federal budget indicates that fiscal policy is stimulative." Evaluate this statement.

20-10
SUGGESTED READINGS

1   For a stimulating argument on how current economic analysis creates a political bias toward deficits and inflation, see James M. Buchanan and Richard E. Wagner, *Democracy in Deficit: The Political Legacy of Lord Keynes* (New York: Academic Press, 1977).

2   We would also recommend Edward R. Tufte, *Political Control of the Economy* (Princeton, N.J.: Princeton University Press, 1978). In this book, Professor Tufte examines the effects of politics on economic decisions. He analyzes the role of elections and political parties in deciding who gets what, when, and how in the economic arena.

3   A very readable summary of fiscal policy—what it is, its promises, and its pitfalls—is presented in *Understanding Fiscal Policy*, (Washington, D.C.: Congressional Budget Office 1978).

4   More advanced investigations of fiscal policy are available in most intermediate texts on macroeconomics. We would recommend Rudiger Dornbusch and Stanley Fischer, *Macroeconomics* (New York: McGraw Hill, 1978), chaps. 10 and 19; see chap. 16 for discussion of wage and price controls.

5   For more on tax policy and investment, see Andrew Abel, "Tax Incentives to Investment: An Assessment of Tax Credits and Tax Cuts," *New England Economic Review*, Federal Reserve Bank of Boston (November/December 1978), 54–63, and Carl Palash, "Tax Policy: Its Impact on Investment Incentives," *Quarterly Review*, Federal Reserve Bank of New York (Summer 1978), 30–36.

* Refers to the Appendix (optional material).

21

THE UNITED STATES IN THE WORLD ECONOMY

Before I built a wall, I'd ask to know what I was walling in or walling out.

Robert Frost

21·1
"DOLLAR TAKES BEATING IN FOREIGN CURRENCY MARKET AS U.S. INFLATION ACCELERATES"

Newspaper headlines like this indicate that there is a considerable degree of interaction between the United States economy and foreign economies. The interaction has become so great that many people—like the U.S. Congress, the President, the U.S. Treasury Department, and the Federal Reserve—are spending considerable time analyzing world economic and financial developments and their implications for United States policy. As you read this, important international policy actions are undoubtedly being discussed or implemented. Happily, we have already covered much of the material we need in order to examine and understand such actions.

In Chapter 7 we examined the foreign sector and the determinants of the United States balance of payments, although we simplified our study of these things by assuming that there were no policy actions either by the United States or by foreign governments. In Chapters 13 and 14 the foreign sector was combined with the household, business, and government sectors to derive the behavioral relations that determine income, prices, and financial variables such as interest rates and the money stock. We dealt with the different world monies in Chapter 16, where we examined the foreign currency market and the determinants of the exchange rate between the dollar and foreign currencies. Finally, in Chapters 17, 18, and 19, we examined monetary and fiscal policy actions aimed primarily at internal objectives (inflation, unemployment, and growth).

To round out our analysis of the relationship between the United States and the rest of the world, we will examine international policy in this chapter. We will examine how international policy actions along with domestic policy actions affect the economic and financial environment, not only in the United States but also in the rest of the world.

One underlying theme of this chapter is the interaction between political and economic forces. Political scientists have for some time understood the role of economics in the foreign policy stance of our nation. An example of this relationship is the United States move in the mid-1970s toward closer ties with the Arab countries. Few would deny that this dramatic policy shift away from unquestioned support for Israel was related in a significant way to the 1973 OPEC oil embargo, the fourfold rise in the price of oil in 1974, and the United States' increasing dependence on oil imported from OPEC. (In 1970, 25 percent of the oil consumed in the United States came from OPEC; in 1979, this figure has risen to 45 percent.)

Economists have been somewhat slower in recognizing the considerable role that power politics plays in international economic policymaking. Economic theory may tell us that banning the exportation of computers to the Soviet Union or the importation of cigars from Cuba or X-rated movies from Sweden results in a less than optimal allocation of United States and world resources. But optimum allocation of resources is probably of little consequence in the chambers where policy is made.

In general, the interaction of political, social, and economic forces is important in studying the foreign sector. However, the primary focus in this chapter will be the international monetary system and the political and economic forces which have shaped it. We will first examine the international monetary system as it was when there were fixed-exchange rates between currencies. There are two reasons for this approach: (1) the current system of flexible exchange rates evolved out of the flaws in the fixed-exchange-rate system and (2) the current system still retains some of the aspects of the old system.

21-2
A LOOK AT THE OLDEN DAYS:
THE FIXED-EXCHANGE-RATE SYSTEM

During the Depression-plagued 1930s, international trade and finance was in considerable disarray. Thousands of banks in the United States and around the world failed (went bankrupt) and chaotic economic conditions resulted. To try to improve things, individual countries implemented various policy actions, but these interfered with the exchange of goods, services, and financial assets around the world. Many countries believed that their internal depression was caused by forces generated outside their own economies. Accordingly, they tried to insulate their economies from such outside forces by restricting the flow of goods and capital to and from other countries. Trade began to fall off, and so did the economic well-being of all countries. Gradually, countries began to recognize the folly of insulating themselves economically, and they saw the need to reform the international monetary system. Unfortunately, the progress toward a more sensible system was delayed by the outbreak of World War II and the nationalistic tendencies that accompanied it. This was hardly the best time for the nations of the world to agree on anything!

Finally, in 1944, as World War II was ending, the leading industrial and trading nations gathered at Bretton Woods, New Hampshire, to devise what everyone hoped would be a more stable international financial system. One outgrowth of this conference was the establishment of the International Monetary Fund—commonly referred to as the IMF—a kind of United Nations of international trade and finance.[1] Note that we use the analogy of the United Nations rather than the often used analogy of a world central bank. As at the United Nations, the major countries call the shots in the IMF; the IMF cannot implement any major programs or policy actions without the agreement of these countries. In addition, the IMF does not have the power or tools to materially affect the supply of money and credit around the world. The IMF is not a world central bank.

Let us examine—mainly from the United States' point of view—the workings and implications of the fixed-exchange-rate system formally implemented in 1947 by agreement of the IMF member countries.

The agreement provided for the reestablishment of *fixed* rates of exchange between foreign currencies and the convertibility of foreign currencies held by governments into gold. It was hoped that these steps would restore confidence in the international financial system.[2] It was thought that

---

[1] See J. Keith Horsefield et al., *The International Monetary Fund*, (Washington, D.C.: IMF, 1969), for a review of the establishment, evolution, and the functioning of the IMF.

[2] In the 1800s, most of the countries of the world had adopted the "gold standard" and fixed exchange rates. As mentioned above, however, the lack of agreement among countries and the economic environment led many to abandon the standard whenever it was convenient. See Leland Yeager, *International Monetary Relations: Theory, History, and Policy* (New York: Harper & Row, 1976), chaps. 15–19 (and the literature cited therein), for more information on the evolution and collapse of the gold standard.

flexible rates—that is, rates allowed to move in response to shifts in the supply of and demand for currencies—created uncertainty for those engaged in international trade and finance. (This notion is akin to the discussion in Chapter 3 of the effects of risk and uncertainty on portfolio decisions.) Assuming that firms and individuals are risk-averse, a fluctuating exchange rate—which allows the value of one currency to change relative to another and therefore alters prices of foreign goods and financial assets—could adversely affect international transactions by increasing the risk of capital losses. For example, if someone purchased foreign assets which cost 100k when the dollar-keg exchange rate was $2 (it takes $2 to buy 1k), the total dollar outlay would be $200. If the exchange rate were to fall to $1 by the time our investor decided to sell the foreign assets for kegs and exchange the kegs for dollars, the investor would only get $100 back—a capital loss. It was thought that many people, faced with such risks, would be less willing to engage in international transactions.

As for the convertibility of gold, many countries experiencing trade deficits and capital outflows had suspended convertibility from time to time in the 1930s so as to limit their loss of international reserves. Fear that a currency could not be converted to gold often impeded trade because few countries would want to accept a foreign currency if its convertibility— viewed as an indicator of the "soundness" or value of that currency—was in doubt. In sum, it was hoped that fixed rates of exchange between currencies and ready convertibility would lead to the removal of barriers to imports and that, as a result, world trade and finance would prosper.

Well, how did it all work out for the United States? The short answer is that for many years, because of the role of the dollar in international trade and finance and the resulting willingness of foreigners to accumulate massive financial claims on the United States, it appeared to work well. From a long-run point of view, however, the system allowed the United States to neglect the evolving "fundamental imbalance" in its economic relationships with the rest of the world. The result of this trend and similar developments in other countries was a breakdown of the fixed-rate system and a move toward flexible exchange rates.

21-3
THE FUNCTIONING OF THE
FIXED-RATE SYSTEM:
THEORY AND PRACTICE

The objective of the system of fixed exchange rates was to foster high employment around the world and the efficient allocation of world resources through the encouragement of free trade. At the time, economists believed that a fixed-rate system would create an environment fostering trade; the uncertainty caused by the fluctuating value of one currency in terms of another would be eliminated.

THE ADJUSTMENT MECHANISM:
HOW IT WAS SUPPOSED TO WORK

Among the so-called rules of the fixed-rate system (sometimes called the "rules of the game") was the notion that *the domestic money stock and interest rates would be affected by balance of payments surpluses or deficits.* A United States balance of payments deficit generated by rapid domestic inflation, for example, would be expected to lead to a decline in United States international reserve holdings. Let us illustrate this important point.

Remember from Chapters 7 and 16 that the balance of payments BOP is equal to the sum of net exports NX and the balance on capital account BKA, which, in turn, must equal the change in international reserves ΔIR. In equation form,

$$(21\text{-}1) \qquad BOP = NX + BKA = \Delta IR$$

A United States deficit resulting from an acceleration of inflation in this country meant that our international payments for imports of goods and securities would exceed our receipts from the exportation of goods and securities. With purchasing-power parity upset (see Section 16-4), the surplus countries would, in the first instance, accumulate United States dollars equal to the excess and then present dollars to the United States in exchange for gold or some other international reserve asset. (Actually, foreigners would bring the dollars to their central bank and exchange the dollars for their own domestic currency. The central bank would then present the dollars to the United States in exchange for gold.) Surplus countries converting United States currency into gold would lower the international reserve holdings of the United States and increase their own international reserve holdings. The decline in international reserves held by the United States—a factor affecting the reserve base of the domestic banking system (see the Appendix to Chapter 18)—would, in turn, cause a decline in both bank reserves and the United States money stock as well as a rise in interest rates.[1] These developments would be expected to slow economic activity somewhat, reducing the demand for imports and moderating the rise in domestic prices.[2] It was thought that these favorable effects on the balance of trade would be reinforced by capital inflows (financial investments by foreign countries) induced by the increase in domestic interest rates.

As for the surplus countries, the rise in their international reserve holdings would increase their domestic reserve base and money supply, lowering their interest rates. This would stimulate economic activity and put upward pressure on prices, increasing the demand for imports of goods and inducing capital outflows.

It was hoped that the end result of these several effects would be a move

[1] Visualize the fall in IR as causing a leftward shift of the money supply function in Chapter 13.
[2] Visualize the fall in reserves and money as causing a leftward shift of the aggregate demand function in Chapter 13.

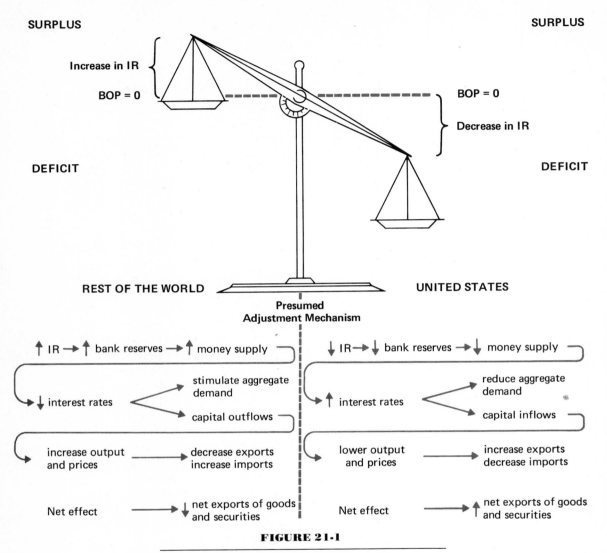

FIGURE 21-1

In theory, a country experiencing a BOP deficit would be losing IR and a country experiencing a BOP surplus would be
gaining IR. The movement in IR would, in turn, be expected
to initiate an adjustment in domestic economic and financial
conditions that reduced the deficit and the surplus.

back toward purchasing-power parity, reducing both the existing BOP deficit in the United States and the surplus in the rest of the world. As Figure
21-1 shows, it was expected that changes in United States and foreign holdings of IR which unbalanced the scale would set in motion forces which
would lead to the reestablishment of purchasing-power parity and BOP

equilibrium—usually defined as BOP = 0. These forces would restore balance by reducing the United States deficit and the foreign surplus.[1]

HOW IT WORKED OUT

The IMF recognized that this type of adjustment mechanism might fail to work because of a "fundamental disequilibrium" in the balance of payments. In such a situation, changes in IR and the associated effects on the domestic economy would not be powerful enough to correct the imbalance; the scale in Figure 21-1 would still remain tipped even after large changes in IR holdings.[2] In this case, the IMF rules allowed for a change in the fixed rate of exchange for a country's currency: a country with a *persistent* deficit would devalue or depreciate its currency, while a country with a *persistent* surplus would allow its currency to appreciate. *Thus, fixed exchange rates did not necessarily mean constant rates for all time.*[3]

In practice, *an orderly change in exchange rates in response to persistent foreign-sector imbalances proved difficult to engineer.* Not the least of the problems was how to define objectively a "fundamental disequilibrium."[4] Political considerations generated many impediments to any change in the fixed rate. For example, a devaluation was often viewed as an overt sign that a country was declining as an economic power, that the present prime minister's economic policies had been a failure, and so forth. Anyone doubting this point is urged to read the reaction of the political opposition in England each time the pound sterling was devalued in the late 1960s and early 1970s. Remember that under the constitutions of many foreign countries, a president or prime minister does not necessarily serve out his or her term; resignation of the existing government and a call for new elections because of a financial crisis is not unheard of.

Within any country the political dialogue on balance of payments deficits or surpluses—and the need (or lack of need) for adjustments in the exchange rate—always revolved around several important economic realities.

On the macroeconomic side, there is the fact that it was quite possible, under the fixed rate system, for a conflict to exist between a country's domestic economic objectives and its objectives with respect to the rest of the world. In other words, a conflict between internal and external objectives might arise. Suppose that country X was running a balance of payments deficit, its international reserves were minimal, and domestic economic activity was depressed (high unemployment, little economic growth, and so

---

[1] Countries also frequently imposed tariffs, quotas, or capital controls in an attempt to alter the flow of international transactions. More on this later on.

[2] The adjustment mechanism might not work because of severe structural problems in the economies of the relevant countries, the onslaught of a war which generated large financial outflows, or an unwillingness on the part of the relevant countries to honor the rules of the game (an unwillingness to allow ΔIR to fully affect domestic bank reserves, the money supply, and interest rates). More on this below.

[3] For example, between 1948 and 1967, the exchange rates of 97 of the 109 IMF member countries changed at least once relative to the dollar.

[4] A working definition might be a persistent (or chronic) deficit or surplus in a country's BOP.

forth). Domestic considerations call for expansionary policy while balance of payments considerations call for restrictive action. The political party in power would be under pressure from the IMF and its international creditors to devalue its currency and to pursue a restrictive monetary and fiscal policy, while the political opposition at home would be emphasizing the unfavorable domestic implications of such actions.

On the microeconomic side, *changes in exchange rates can have important effects (unfavorable as well as favorable) on key industries or sectors within a country.* For example, country X would find its importers opposed to devaluation, since devaluation would raise the domestic price of imported goods; exporters would be in favor of the devaluation, since it would lower the prices of its goods in foreign markets.

ONE CRISIS AFTER ANOTHER

The result of the contradictions inherent in the fixed-rate system was a never-ending series of international monetary crises. For the fixed-exchange-rate system to work, the countries of the world had to be willing to accept whatever would happen to their domestic economies as a result of adjusting to international economic imbalances. More specifically, countries had to pursue similar domestic policies which produced comparable rates of inflation. If purchasing-power parity among currencies was not preserved over time, the payments imbalances associated with the fixed rates of exchange would grow. Since few countries were willing to coordinate their domestic policies, the inclination was to avoid adjustment in the face of emerging BOP problems. As a country's foreign-sector deficit grew and its international reserves declined, a devaluation of its currency became more and more inevitable. Such expectations engendered large international speculative flows out of the currency. Remember, a speculative monetary transaction is one where the transactor expects and is willing to bet on a "favorable" change in the price of a security or a currency. In this case, the speculator sold country X's currency at the fixed rate, expecting to be able to repurchase it in the near future at a cheaper rate. The result would be a quick capital gain.

To illustrate, suppose that the dollar-keg exchange rate is $2 now, but that many expect it to rise to $2.50 soon. Such expectations encourage speculators to sell dollars and purchase kegs in the foreign currency market. If you sell $100,000 now, you receive 50,000k. If the dollar-keg exchange rate moves to $2.50, you can then sell the 50,000k for $125,000. The resulting capital gain on this series of transactions would be $25,000. Not bad!

Country X, now experiencing speculative capital outflows on top of its existing deficit, would argue that world speculators were wrecking its economy; government officials would say a devaluation was out of the question. The hard reality would be that country X would be losing international reserves IR rapidly. Finally, after several secret meetings among world finance ministers to determine the "appropriate" change in the exchange rate, country X's currency would be devalued.

During the 1950s and 1960s, the international economic and financial position of the United States deteriorated. How was it that for a long time the United States avoided devaluation of the dollar and for the most part ignored the foreign sector? Did the United States break the rules of the game? Was the United States calling the shots? Let us see how the fixed dollar exchange rate was maintained and what the implications were.

21-4
THE PROCESS USED TO
FIX THE DOLLAR
EXCHANGE RATE

In the international trading of goods, services, and financial assets, just as in domestic trading, the value of items sold must ex post (after the fact) be identically equal to the value of items purchased. In terms of the examples we have been using, this means that the quantity of dollars used to purchase kegs must be equal to the quantity of dollars purchased with kegs. At point A in Figure 21-2, the quantity of dollars spent on foreign currency re-

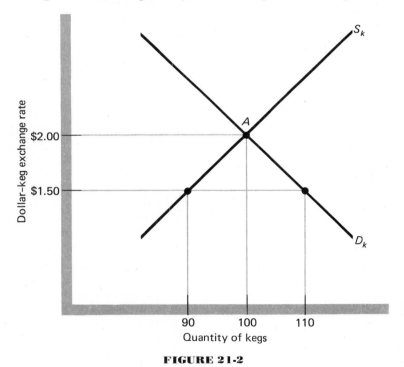

FIGURE 21-2

At an exchange rate of $2, the quantity of kegs demanded (100) equals the quantity of kegs supplied. This also means that the quantity of dollars supplied to purchase the kegs ($200 = $2 × 100) is equal to the quantity of dollars purchased with kegs.

sulting from the demand for kegs equals 2×100; this also equals the quantity of dollars purchased with foreign currency resulting from the supply of kegs. However, ex ante (before the fact), there is no reason to believe that, at any given dollar-keg exchange rate ER (such as $1.50), the quantity of kegs United States residents plan to buy (demand for kegs) will be equal to the quantity of kegs foreigners plan to sell (supply of kegs). At an ER of $1.50, as shown in Figure 21-2, $S_k = 90$ and $D_k = 110$. That is, demand exceeds supply; $110 > 90$ or $D_k > S_k$. The ex post equality between supply and demand will come into being as a result of some *adjustment mechanism* that eliminates the ex ante discrepancy between supply and demand. In a competitive market where prices are free to change, an excess of demand relative to supply at any given price will set in motion forces (in this case portfolio adjustments) that will eventually result in a higher price. More specifically, a rise in price will reduce the quantity demanded and increase the quantity supplied to the point where supply is equal to demand. However, in a system of fixed exchange rates, the price of one foreign currency in terms of another is held constant. The price does not adjust to "clear" the market—that is, eliminate an ex ante imbalance between supply and demand. This being the case, what adjustment mechanism brings about the ex post equality between the supply of and demand for kegs?

INTERVENTION BY THE UNITED STATES

For analytic purposes, we have defined the balance of payments BOP as equal to net exports NX plus the capital account balance BKA. We also know that, ex post, payments of United States residents to the rest of the world must equal receipts from the rest of the world; a BOP deficit, for example, must somehow be financed. We already pointed out that a United States BOP deficit means a decrease in United States holdings of international reserves IR. (Note that we are, for the moment, ignoring actions *foreign* governments may take.) In terms of Equation (21-1), the ex post equality of international payments and receipts—or put another way, the equality between the international supply and demand for dollars and kegs—means that the sum of $NX + BKA - \Delta IR$ must always net out to zero. Thus, if the demand for kegs exceeds the supply at the fixed exchange rate—meaning that the demand for kegs by United States residents (supply of dollars) to purchase foreign goods, services, or financial assets exceeds the supply of kegs by foreign residents (demand for dollars) to purchase United States goods, services, or financial assets—then the result will be a United States BOP deficit. To produce an equilibrium between international payments and receipts, United States government holdings of kegs or some other international reserve asset will decline. The decrease in IR will be exactly equal in value to the excess of keg demand over keg supply, which is also equal to the BOP deficit.[1]

Exactly how does the United States finance its BOP deficit? One possibility, which we have already discussed, is that foreigners first accept dollars and then present the dollars to the United States government in exchange for gold or some other international reserve asset. Another possibility is direct *intervention* by the United States into the foreign currency market.

Intervention is an activity engaged in by the United States government or foreign governments. Usually a nation's central bank —the Fed in the United States, the Bank of Japan in Japan, and so forth—acting on behalf of the government, conducts the actual intervention operations. In general, "intervention" refers to the central bank's buying (or selling) of a foreign currency in the foreign currency market and simultaneously selling (or buying) its domestic currency. For example, the Fed on behalf of the United States government might sell Japanese yen and purchase dollars. As discussed below, these operations are usually designed to limit the movement in the exchange rate that would otherwise occur in the absence of such intervention.

In Chapter 16, we briefly discussed the foreign currency market. We pointed out that this market was an over-the-counter market "made" by the foreign currency departments of large commercial banks in New York, London, and other major financial centers. Brokers and dealers in this market continually receive offers to buy (demand) and sell (supply) various currencies. If the "buy" orders exceed the "sell" orders at the current exchange rate between two currencies, the broker or dealer, like every good auctioneer, will call out a higher price. If there are more sell orders than buy orders, the auction price will be lowered.

The Federal Reserve Bank of New York has a trading desk for operations in the foreign currency market just like the trading desk for operations in the domestic securities market discussed in Chapter 18. The manager of this desk and the staff monitor developments in the foreign currency market. If the United States is on a fixed-exchange-rate system and the quotations by the dealers and brokers in the foreign currency market indicate that the dollar is beginning to depreciate (that is, the exchange rate for

---

[1] To get a better grasp on this discussion, reread Sections 16-2 through 16-5 and then reread the last few paragraphs above.

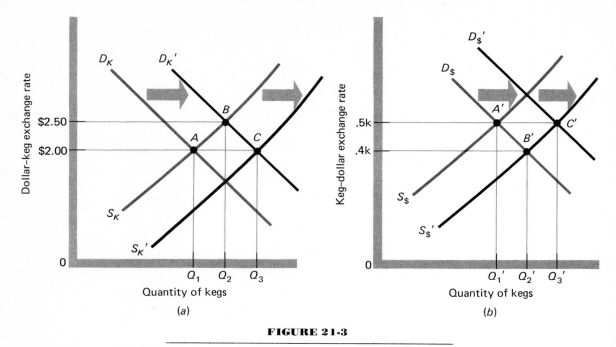

FIGURE 21-3

Intervention. (a) Foreign currency market for kegs. (b) Foreign currency market for dollars. Initially, the foreign currency market for kegs is in equilibrium at point A. When the Fed raises aggregate demand in the United States, one of the effects will be an increased demand for foreign goods, services, and securities by United States residents. This will increase the demand for kegs from D_k to D'_k. In the absence of any intervention, the exchange would rise to $2.50; the dollar would depreciate. To counteract this rise, the Fed will supply (sell) kegs in the foreign currency market, shifting the supply of kegs from S_k to S'_k. The foreign currency market returns to equilibrium at point C, with the exchange rate unchanged.

the dollar is, say, rising from the fixed rate of $2 to $2.50 per keg), then the New York Fed would be prepared to intervene directly in the market by offering to buy enough dollars and sell enough kegs from its portfolio of international reserve assets to maintain the dollar-keg exchange rate at $2.

The two panels in Figure 21-3 illustrate graphically how intervention works. In panel (a), the initial equilibrium in the foreign currency market—that is, the market for kegs in our two-country world—is shown at point A, where the exchange rate equals $2, quantity equals Q_1, and the demand D_k and supply S_k curves intersect. For illustrative purposes, the foreign currency market in the rest of the world—that is, the market for dollars—is shown in panel (b). Remember that the supply of kegs is the mirror image of the demand for dollars, and the demand for kegs is the mirror image of the supply of dollars. The equivalent equilibrium position in the market for dollars is point A'—the exchange rate is equal to .5k (the inverse of the dollar-keg exchange rate), the quantity is equal to Q_1' (which must equal Q_1 multiplied by the dollar-keg exchange rate).[1]

Now let us assume that the Federal Reserve conducts its domestic open market operations so as to stimulate the economy. We would expect the rise in bank reserves and the money supply, along with the drop in short term interest rates, to increase aggregate demand. The initial effect will be a rise in prices and output in the United States, which will also raise United States demand for foreign goods and securities. This would be depicted in panel (*a*) by a rightward shift in the demand for kegs from D_k to D_k' and in panel (*b*) by a rightward shift in the supply of dollars from $S_\$$ to $S_\$'$. In terms of Equation (16-2) we have a rise in Y_{US} and P_{US} and i_{US} would fall.[2]

If exchange rates were free to vary, the increase in our demand for foreign goods and securities (other things remaining the same) would result in a depreciation of the dollar, with a new equilibrium at point B in panel (*a*), the exchange rate moving from \$2 to \$2.50, an appreciation of the keg—point B' in panel (*b*), and an exchange rate of .4k. The new keg rate is the inverse of the dollar-keg rate (.4 = $^1/_{2.50}$). The impending balance of payments deficit would not occur because of the adjustment in the exchange rate.

Under a fixed rate system, the New York Fed would sell (supply) kegs from its portfolio of international reserves; this would result in a rightward shift of the curve in panel (*a*) for the supply of kegs S_k' and the curve in panel (*b*) for the demand for dollars $D_\$'$. How many kegs (dollars) must the Fed supply (sell) and how many dollars must the Fed demand (purchase)? Given the assumptions of our example, this can be stated precisely—the distance AC in panel (*a*) equals the quantity ($Q_3 - Q_1$) which equals the quantity of kegs supplied; the distance AC also equals the decrease in United States holdings of international reserves; and distance AC also equals the balance of payments deficit generated by the stimulative monetary policy. Thus, in this example, the Federal Reserve, in effect, finances the BOP deficit.

In the Appendix to Chapter 18, it was pointed out that the Federal Reserve's portfolio of international reserve assets is a factor affecting the reserve base of the United States banking system. This being the case (in the absence of another action), bank reserves and the money stock would shrink somewhat as a result of the Fed's sale of kegs in the foreign currency market. Remember, the Fed is selling kegs and demanding dollars, and the individual who purchases the kegs must pay for them with a check denominated in dollars drawn on a United States bank. When the Fed receives the check, it

---

[1] Again, to reinforce your understanding of this, reread Section 16-5.
[2] There would also be some negative effect on foreign demand for United States goods and securities, resulting in a leftward shift of the S_k function in panel (*a*) of Figure 21-3. We will ignore this to keep the diagram simple.

debits the bank's deposit balance at the Federal Reserve, which is part of the bank's reserves. The bank, in turn, will debit the depositor's balance. As is true of any decrease in reserves available to the banking system, this would lead to declines in the supply of money and credit. In terms of an earlier discussion (Chapter 13), this would be a leftward shift in the money supply function.

STERILIZATION

The decline in the money supply would counteract the original actions taken by the Fed to stimulate domestic economic activity. To avoid the undesired economic and financial effects this might generate, the New York Fed's domestic trading desk would offset the negative effects of a foreign currency operation on the domestic reserve base by buying United States government securities—an operation which adds to bank reserves.[1] This is often referred to as "sterilizing" the foreign sector imbalance. What we mean by this is that the domestic economy is insulated or buffered from the financial effects of the BOP deficit.

The concept of sterilization is important and will be referred to again later on in the chapter. Note here, however, that the rules of the fixed rate system are being violated when a country consistently sterilizes, since its reserve base and money stock are not being altered by BOP deficits or surpluses.

INTERVENTION BY FOREIGNERS

We can use Figure 21-3 again to demonstrate a type of adjustment mechanism that is quite similar to United States intervention in the foreign currency market—*intervention by foreign governments in the market*. Again, suppose the Fed stimulates the domestic economy by increasing bank reserves through open market operations. As time passes, foreign central banks—observing a depreciation of the dollar (appreciation of the keg)—could demand dollars in the foreign currency market (supply kegs). Graphically, the result will be the same as depicted before, when the United States intervened: the demand for dollars $D'_\$$ will shift to the right and the supply of kegs S'_k will also shift to the right by enough to keep the exchange rate constant. In this case, the foreign central banks will, in effect, finance United States balance of payments deficits.[2]

---

[1] You might write down balance sheets (T accounts) for the public, banks, and the Federal Reserve and trace out these various transactions to be sure you follow each step. All the details on intervention are spelled out in the following article: Anatol Balbach, "The Mechanics of Intervention in Exchange Markets," *Review*, Federal Reserve Bank of St. Louis (February 1978), 2–7.

[2] Frequently, governments would try to affect directly the flow of international payments. For example, a country experiencing BOP deficits might impose tariffs and quotas on imported goods and controls on capital outflows. Such policies were designated to preserve the fixed exchange rate and eliminate the deficits by reducing the demand for foreign currencies (that is, shifting D_k to the left). See any good international economics textbook—such as Klaus Friedrich, *International Economics* (New York: McGraw Hill, 1974)—for further discussions of tariffs, quotas, and other controls.

"Sterilization" refers to operations undertaken by the central bank to counteract the effect that movements in international reserves would have on the reserve base of the domestic banking system. As the sketch depicts, a BOP deficit would generate a decline in IR, which would lower the supply of reserves in the United States banking system (the bathtub). The Fed offsets this decline by purchasing government securities—that is, conducting open market operations—thus pouring reserves back into the banking system.

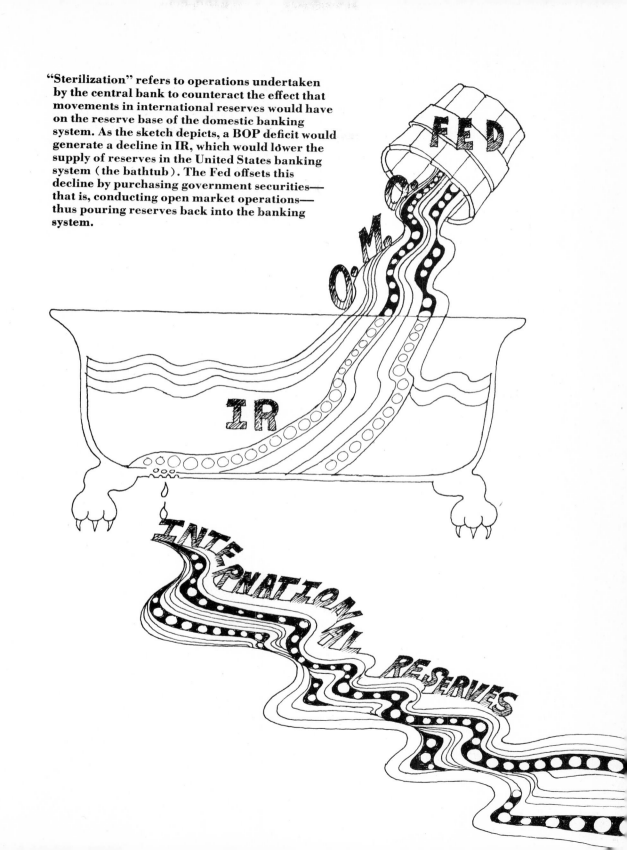

In terms of our balance of payments equation $BOP = NX + BCA$, the capital inflow that results from the purchase of dollars by foreign central banks will exactly offset the BOP deficit that emerged in the United States as a result of the domestic monetary policy action. The increase in dollar holdings by foreigners is a capital inflow, since it represents exports of a financial claim on the United States.

The net result of the foreign intervention is that foreign central banks sterilize for the United States and, in effect, finance the United States BOP deficit. There is no effect on the reserve base of the United States banking system and the domestic and international trading desks of the New York Fed can take the day off. Why are foreigners willing to do this? The motivations are several. As discussed in Chapter 7, foreigners may desire to acquire dollars because of (1) planned future purchases from the United States, (2) the dollar's status as a reserve currency around the world, or (3) the attractive investment opportunities offered by United States financial markets. In addition, countries with large export sectors may be unwilling to allow an appreciation of their currencies because it would raise the prices of their goods in foreign markets and thereby weaken their competitive position.

Before leaving the theoretical world and returning to the real world, where we can examine what actually occurred over the fixed-exchange-rate period, two other details must be mentioned.

First, the foreign monetary authorities, in acquiring dollars in foreign currency markets, more often than not invested these dollars in the United States. Why hold non-interest-bearing dollar balances? These investments were mostly in the short-term area (under one-year maturity) and usually were in the form of the purchase of U.S. Treasury securities.[1] Of course, some countries still converted their dollar holdings into gold.

Second, the increase in dollar holdings (or, more precisely, the increase in the holdings of assets denominated in dollars) raised foreign international reserve holdings and, therefore, the reserve bases of the banking systems in foreign countries. In contrast to the situation in the United States, the monetary authorities in various foreign countries often found it difficult to sterilize the effect of the increase in the reserve base. In general, different institutional arrangements characterizing the domestic financial systems in many of these countries, and the size and degree of "openness" of these countries vis-à-vis the United States (where "openness" refers to the size of the foreign sector relative to domestic sectors) accounted for the inability of foreign monetary authorities to sterilize completely. The key implications of this latter point will become clearer later on.

---

[1] The intervention by foreign central banks, and the resulting increase in their holdings of U.S. Treasury securities, has been spectacular over the last decade. In 1968, foreign official accounts (central banks and governments) held $12.4 billion of the $356.2 billion of total United States debt outstanding (3.5 percent). By the end of 1978, foreign official accounts held $133 billion of the $783 billion of debt outstanding (17 percent). Not only do foreigners finance our BOP deficits, they also help to finance our federal budget deficits!

21-5
THE MOVE TO FLEXIBLE RATES

Throughout the 1960s, the international competitive position of the United States in trade weakened. Put more formally, there was an erosion in the degree of comparative advantage the United States possessed previously in the production of various goods. The most immediate reasons for this deterioration were an increase in inflation and wage rates in this country relative to the rest of the world and technological advances in other countries which further improved their competitive positions in world trade. In a more general sense, the combination of large budget deficits resulting from a very expansive fiscal policy, the Vietnam war, and an overly accommodative monetary policy played a key role. On the fiscal side, for example, there was a major tax cut in 1964; at the same time, the United States was becoming increasingly involved in the Vietnam war, which required enormous spending for arms. As for monetary policy, the growth of the money stock trended up over the decade. While unemployment fell, the inflation rate gradually increased. With income rising in the United States and United States prices rising faster than world prices, imports were stimulated relative to exports. These forces tending to reduce net exports were worsened by capital account developments. United States industry, recognizing profitable investment opportunities in the rest of the world, built new plants and shifted financial resources away from the domestic economy. Such capital outflows also contributed to BOP deficits.

In sum, over the 1960s, United States net exports steadily fell. Reflecting this trade-induced erosion in international receipts relative to payments and rising capital outflows, United States holdings of international reserves fell as foreigners converted their dollar proceeds into gold and the United States sold foreign currencies in the market to maintain the fixed rate of exchange between the dollar and other world monies. At the same time, claims on the United States by foreign governments rose dramatically, as they also intervened in foreign currency markets to maintain fixed exchange rates. With the United States importing more goods and securities than it exported, the tendency in the foreign currency market was for the dollar to depreciate relative to other currencies. Foreign governments supplied their currency and demanded dollars to offset this tendency. The dollars these governments acquired were then invested in the United States, mainly in United States government securities. As you can see from Figure 21-4, in the late 1960s, these financial claims held by foreign official institutions—foreign governments and foreign central banks—began to exceed the stock of IR held by the United States by an increasing margin. In terms of what we discussed in previous sections, the *adjustment mechanism* at work through at least 1971 involved changes in international reserves as opposed to changes in exchange rates. The quantity of international reserves held by the United States declined, while the quantity of IR held by foreigners rose by that and more, reflecting their direct intervention

FIGURE 21-4

Throughout the 1960s, the international economic position of
the United States deteriorated. The BOP deficits were financed by declines in United States holdings of IR and by the
intervention of foreign official institutions in foreign currency
markets to acquire dollar claims on the United States.

in foreign currency markets to maintain the fixed rates of exchange and the
transfer of IR from the United States to foreigners.

It does not take much training in economics or finance to figure out one
reason why this system could not last: the United States was buying up
foreign goods and securities with dollars. In effect, the printing of money
and other financial claims became our most important export industry (the
exporting of financial claims on the United States). When the debt of any
individual or corporation continually rises, questions crop up about the
debtor's ability to redeem the outstanding claims with goods or other assets
of equal value. Then there is mounting pressure from the creditors to improve the balance sheet by reducing the outstanding debt, cutting costs,
and so forth. The rising dollar claims held by foreigners bred a similar kind
of pressure on the United States to improve its international payments situation and revealed some of the glaring inconsistencies inherent in the
fixed-rate system.

In addition to the effect on trade, the rising United States inflation rate
added to the payments problem in another way. To the extent that the rise
in the inflation rate was unanticipated, interest returns on United States
financial assets held by foreigners did not fully compensate the holders of

these claims for the ongoing erosion in the dollar's purchasing power. Creditors become very testy when this happens and gradually become more reluctant to accept such claims.

Another problem, not so well understood at the time, was that the United States was, in effect, calling the economic shots for most of the world. If the United States stimulated the economy relative to other countries, the rise in domestic income and the price level would tend to move its BOP into deficit. As a result, foreign governments would accumulate IR. This, in turn, would raise the reserve bases and money stocks in foreign countries, which would tend to stimulate their economies. This phenomenon tended to lead to a synchronization of the business cycle in the United States and the rest of the world.

The dictionary defines "synchronization" as a process whereby events happen together—that is, coincide or coexist. In speaking of synchronization of the business cycle in the United States and the rest of the world, we mean that when the United States economy was booming, this tended to coincide with a booming economy in the rest of the world. Similarly, when the United States was experiencing a recession, this tended to coincide with recessions in other countries. The synchronization was explained by the fact that the United States is an important purchaser of goods and services from foreigners; when the United States economy was booming, United States demand for foreign goods would rise, tending to stimulate foreign economies; when the United States slipped into a recession, United States demand for foreign goods would fall, tending to depress foreign economies. The rise and fall in United States demand would generate increases and decreases, respectively, in the IR holdings of foreigners and therefore tend to raise or lower foreign money supplies. In short, the United States affected aggregate demand in foreign countries. This is why many economists argued that the United States was the hub of the world economic wheel and could export inflation as well as recession.

Despite the problems, tensions, and contradictions of the existing system, no one wanted to bite the bullet. The United States was not prepared to put the domestic economy through the wringer to correct its "fundamental imbalance" with the rest of the world. The IMF could do little without United States cooperation but tried various patchwork devices to save the fixed-rate system. These included the creation of special drawing rights (SDRs)—a new international reserve asset created and distributed to member countries to aid in the financing of BOP deficits and, at the same time, reduce the international monetary system's dependence on gold and the United States dollar. As trade increased, the demand for international reserves also increased. The need for international reserves is closely related to the transactions demand for money: as expenditures rise, the need for transactions balances rises as well. Through the late 1960s, the United States BOP deficits provided the bulk of the increase in the IR around the world. If IR could come from another source, the "need" for dollars would be reduced.

Despite such efforts, recurring crises characterized the international monetary environment. Eventually, politicians became aware of the flaws in the system (economists had been writing about the problem for years) and began to see the need for greater flexibility in exchange rates.

THE COLLAPSE OF THE
FIXED-RATE SYSTEM

In August 1971, as part of this economic program to moderate inflation and correct the "fundamental imbalance" in the United States' international economic position, President Nixon suspended the official convertibility of dollars into gold and urged foreign countries to allow their currencies to float and presumably to appreciate vis-à-vis the dollar. The year 1971 had been a tough one in foreign currency markets, especially for the dollar. As 1970's big jump in liabilities to foreigners (shown in Figure 21-4) suggests, foreign governments had been intervening on a massive scale during the year to preserve the fixed rates of exchange. Until this time, despite the problems the dollar was having, the United States had consistently argued that a dollar devaluation was out of the question.

Following Nixon's action, attempts were made to reestablish fixed rates at the new exchange rates prevailing in the marketplace. At the same time, the band of permissible fluctuation in a currency's value around the new rates was widened. Previously, exchange rates were allowed to fluctuate in a range of ± 1 percent around the fixed rate. In this period, the band was widened to $\pm 2\frac{1}{4}$ percent. Only when the rate began to move outside this band would intervention be called for. However, as time passed, the new fixed rates for a number of currencies could not be kept even within the limits of the wider bands. This should come as no surprise to you. As long as governments pursued monetary and fiscal policies that diverged from one another, interest rates, inflation rates, and incomes across countries would differ. Such differences would induce changes in the supply of and demand for currencies around the world, and that made it very difficult to control exchange rates within specified limits. Finally, in early 1973, most of the major countries allowed their currencies to float. By floating, the countries of the world could pursue divergent domestic economic policies.

They could get off the wheel the United States had been spinning. The interdependence (or synchronization) of United States and foreign business cycles which had accompanied fixed rates could be replaced by a degree of independence.

21·6
FREELY FLUCTUATING VERSUS FLEXIBLE EXCHANGE RATES

It would be a mistake to conclude that since early 1973 the international monetary system has been characterized by *freely fluctuating exchange rates —that is, a system where exchange rates are allowed to respond freely to changes in the supply of and demand for various currencies, and governments do not intervene in foreign currency markets. A more accurate description of the system is that rates have been flexible; that is, rates have been allowed to vary, but there has been substantial intervention over time by some countries* and the value of some currencies has been held relatively close to that of other currencies (this is called "managed floating"). For example, some European countries have developed a system whereby each of their respective currencies floats vis-à-vis the dollar but is held roughly fixed in value relative to the others.[1] The point of all this is that the more intervention there is, the closer we are to the old fixed-rate days.

Through the mid-1970s, the IMF tried to work out new articles of agreement that would govern international monetary relations. However, just as in the United Nations, it was difficult to engineer agreement among countries with very different political-economic-social objectives and in different stages of economic and political development. In the meantime, each country simply chose the exchange rate system that seemed to suit it best: some floated freely, some floated with intervention, and some fixed their rates. Robert Solomon, former senior adviser on international developments at the Fed, states clearly the implications of each country doing its own thing: ". . . international monetary reform has been put on a back burner, now being regarded as an evolutionary process. . . ."[2] As for the United States, it has intervened relatively little, and—although other major trading nations have from time to time intervened substantially—the value of the dollar relative to other key currencies has, over time, been allowed to change considerably.

The flexibility in exchange rates would appear to have come just in time.

[1] Initially this was called a "joint float." In 1979, an attempt was made to formalize the joint float into a European Monetary System. The rationale for the System was to strengthen the economic and political ties among European nations as well as the economic and political power of the nations as a group vis-à-vis the United States. As this text goes to press, there is no hard evidence that such a system is working or can work. Can the French, Germans, Italians, British, and so forth really be expected to agree on common economic policies?

[2] Robert Solomon, in R. Hinshaw (ed.), *Stagflation—An International Problem* (New York: Marcel Dekker, 1977), p. 68.

The United States experienced double-digit inflation and then the most severe recession of the postwar period in 1974–1975. While many countries also experienced inflation and recession over this period, reflecting the universal effects of the OPEC oil price rise and the similarity of policy responses by individual governments, the flexibility in rates helped most countries to avoid the severe problems that could have developed under the old fixed-rate system.

21-7
SOME CONTEMPORARY ISSUES INVOLVING INTERNATIONAL ECONOMIC AND FINANCIAL RELATIONSHIPS

THE EFFECTIVENESS OF MONETARY POLICY

The movement to flexible exchange rates has strengthened the effect that monetary policy has on the domestic economy. Suppose the Federal Reserve decides to *stimulate* aggregate demand by buying government securities. This will lower the federal funds rate and increase the growth of the reserve base and the money stock. The fall in United States interest rates relative to world interest rates ought to induce capital outflows from the United States and therefore decrease the demand for dollars (supply of kegs) in the foreign currency market. If United States and foreign governments do not intervene, the resulting depreciation of the dollar would tend to lower the prices of United States goods in foreign markets and to raise the prices of foreign goods in the United States. This ought to decrease import demand and raise export demand, increasing net exports. Since $Y = C + I + G + NX$, it must follow that higher net exports increase total aggregate demand. The implication is that the effect of monetary policy actions will be magnified (or at least not hindered) under a system of flexible exchange rates.

The additional increase in aggregate demand accompanying the stimulative monetary policy action is not an unmixed blessing, however. There is some evidence that the resulting depreciation of the value of the dollar increases the pressure on prices in the United States relative to what would happen in the short run under a fixed-rate system. Given that institutional rigidities (contracts, for example) prevent wages and prices in the United States from falling in the short run, the rise in import prices puts upward pressure on domestic prices. For example, some imported goods are inputs to the production of United States goods; as import prices rise, this raises the costs of production in the United States and encourages United States producers to raise their prices. This upward pressure is reinforced by the impact of increased demand for United States exports. At a microeconomic level, it is, of course, true that individual prices and industries will be affected in the short run. When the exchange rate shifts, importers and exporters of particular goods and producers of close substitutes for traded goods can experience significant changes in the demand for their goods. Of course, the firms and industries that are hurt will make the most noise and try to convince politicians of the need to do something about the exchange rate or to insulate them from foreign competition.[1]

REGULATORY AND SUPERVISORY POLICY

In 1974, the Franklin National Bank failed. At the time, it ranked twentieth in size among banks in the United States. The bank's downfall was caused in part by a movement in exchange rates that generated large capital losses on its holdings of foreign currency. Not surprisingly, this event greatly increased policymakers' concern over the undesirable effects flexible exchange rates could have on balance sheets. The FDIC, the Comptroller of the Currency, and the Fed—under pressure from the Congress—increased their surveillance of banks' foreign activities and tightened various regulations to better control banks' exposure to adverse international developments. The Financial Accounting Standards Board (FASB)—an independent organization that sets standards and guidelines for the accounting profession—also responded and issued a rule (FASB #8) that requires corporations to show on their income statements profits or losses that include capital gains or losses on foreign assets and liabilities. With exchange rates for some currencies moving in a wide range over fairly short periods of time, this rule has had an important effect on the reported earnings and financial management of large corporations.

The flexibility of rates has made life more difficult for a corporation treasurer. Suppose a United States corporation agrees to sell ten computers to another country and the contract calls for the price to be denominated in kegs and requires payment and delivery in ninety days. Let us assume the current dollar-keg exchange rate is $2 and the agreed-on price is 500,000k per computer. What happens if the dollar-keg exchange rate moves to $1.50 by the time the payment is made? Instead of receiving 5k million worth $10 million, the United States corporation will receive 5k million worth only $7.5 million. Risk of such a capital loss could induce the United States corporation to engage in a

[1] The call for tariffs or quotas often emanated from such discussions. See Michael Michaely, *Theory of Commercial Policy: Trade and Protection* (Chicago: University of Chicago Press, 1977); *Changing Patterns in Foreign Trade and Payments*, ed. by Bela Balassa (New York: W. W. Norton, 1978), and the literature cited therein for a good discussion of the theory and "political economy" surrounding this issue.

transaction in the *forward or futures market in foreign currencies*. This market is analogous to the futures market in commodities and certain types of financial instruments. In this example, the United States corporation can *hedge* against the adverse movement in the dollar-keg exchange rate described above by selling kegs in the forward market for delivery in ninety days. Of course, there are a variety of other things the corporation can do; many new payments practices have evolved in the changed international environment.*

* For a description of these practices see Charles Henning, William Pigott, and Robert Scott, *International Financial Management* (New York: McGraw-Hill, 1978), chaps. 15–16; and Ronald McKinnon, *Money in International Exchange* (New York: Oxford University Press, 1979), chap. 4.

Another dimension of policymakers' concern has involved the large volume of United States bank loans to foreign countries, particularly the less developed countries (LDCs). Many of these countries have experienced large increases in their trade deficits as a result of the huge rise in the price of oil. The need to finance these deficits and the LDCs' lack of international reserves IR gives rise to a demand for loans to pay their oil bills.

United States financial institutions have played an important role in *recycling* the funds the OPEC nations have earned. The OPEC countries lend part of their surplus funds to United States banks in the form of time deposits (CDs), for example, and the United States banks, in turn, lend to the LDCs. The policymakers say they are concerned about this because the United States banks performing this financial intermediation are bearing all the risks of default by the LDCs; in addition if the OPEC nations removed their funds from United States banks for some reason, a liquidity crisis could be generated. As to the risks, it should be noted that the banks are presumably earning an intermediary profit which compensates them for the risk involved. With regard to the possible liquidity problem, individual banks could borrow directly from the Fed if such a sudden deposit outflow were to occur. In addition, if you have acquired some appreciation for the integration of world financial markets by this point, you might wonder where OPEC would put the funds. If it is the Eurodollar market, the United States banks could, in effect, recover the deposits by borrowing there.

Policymakers have been pressuring the IMF to play a bigger role in the recycling of OPEC funds. They want the IMF to be *the* intermediary—borrowing from OPEC and lending to LDCs. In recent years, the IMF has, in fact, moved in this direction.[1]

[1] See the annual report of the IMF for a discussion of their various lending facilities.

21-8
SUMMARY OF MAJOR POINTS

1

International economic policy decisions reflect economic and political forces.

2

The agreement among the major nations of the world at Bretton Woods in 1944 established the International Monetary Fund and provided for the reestablishment of fixed rates of exchange among currencies as well as official convertibility of currencies into gold.

3

Given that over the long run exchange rates between currencies will be determined by purchasing-power parity, fixed exchange rates are only viable as long as countries experience comparable rates of inflation.

4

An important rule underlying the fixed-rate system was that BOP surpluses or deficits and the resulting inflow or outflow of international reserves would be allowed to affect the domestic money supply and interest rates. It was thought that if policymakers in one country stimulated their own economy and thus raised their output and prices relative to other countries, a domestic BOP deficit and outflow of international reserves would ensue. The presumed international adjustment to the rise in IR in the surplus country would be a rise in the domestic money supply, a fall in interest rates, and therefore an increase in aggregate demand. A fall in IR in the deficit country would cause a fall in the domestic money supply, a rise in interest rates, and a decrease in aggregate demand. The net economic impact of these several effects was expected to equalize the rates of inflation (and economic growth) across countries over time, thereby preserving the system of fixed exchange rates between currencies.

5

Under the "rules" of the fixed-rate game, nations would have to gear their domestic policy actions so as to maintain (or reestablish) equilibrium in their balance of payments position. In effect, this meant that nations would have to surrender some of their sovereignty (their freedom to make policy independent of policy made by other nations). The frequent conflicts between domestic and international policy objectives led many countries to violate the "rules."

6

The IMF provided for a change in a nation's exchange rate if its BOP position was in "fundamental disequilibrium." Such changes were difficult to engineer because of a variety of political problems, and this contributed to frequent international monetary crises through 1971.

7

The actual mechanism used to fix exchange rates involved intervention in foreign currency markets by the Federal Reserve and foreign central banks. If the dollar began to depreciate on foreign currency markets, the Fed would be prepared to buy dollars and foreign central banks would be prepared to sell foreign currencies. The United States did not allow the drop in its IR (when it did the intervening) to affect domestic bank reserves. The Fed conducted offsetting open market operations in domestic markets to "sterilize" the BOP deficit and IR outflows.

8

The contradictions inherent in the fixed-rate system led to its inevitable collapse in the early 1970s and to a floating-rate system.

9

Under a floating-rate system, countries are free to pursue independent domestic policies (policies that are not directly dependent on international developments and the BOP). The exchange rate will adjust to differences in policy and therefore to inflation and economic growth across countries. For example, if the United States implements a monetary and fiscal policy that produces higher growth and inflation here than in the rest of the world, purchasing-power parity would be maintained by a depreciation of (fall in the value of) the dollar in foreign currency markets.

10

As is often the case, the system hardly ever works as well in practice as it does in theory. In the last few years, many foreign central banks have continued to intervene heavily in foreign currency markets (so-called "managed" floating) to moderate the appreciation of their currencies vis-à-vis the dollar. In addition, the depreciation of the dollar—which raises import prices in the United States—appears to have worsened inflationary pressures over the short run.

11

Despite the problems, a system of flexible exchange rates is probably here to stay. It is easier to allow exchange rates to adjust than it is to get a group of different countries to agree on common economic policies and comparable rates of economic growth and inflation.

21-9
REVIEW QUESTIONS

1   Discuss briefly or define the following terms: intervention, sterilization, the Bretton Woods agreement, FASB rule #8.

2   Explain how purchasing-power parity between currencies would be maintained under a system of fixed exchange rates.

3   Explain why the fixed-exchange-rate system broke down in the early 1970s.

4   Explain how purchasing-power parity between currencies would be maintained under a system of flexible exchange rates.

5   How have foreign official institutions come to hold such a large portion of U.S. Treasury debt?

6   Assume you are a corporate treasurer in charge of domestic and international financial transactions. Suppose you expect the dollar to appreciate vis-à-vis the German mark but to depreciate against the yen over the next ninety days and you have to make payments to German and Japanese suppliers within the next ninety days. What would you do to minimize the cost of these payments?

7   Now that you have worked out Question 6, how would you, as the treasurer, form your expectations about the future course of exchange rates? How would you factor in monetary policy?

21-10
SUGGESTED READINGS

1   There are two books on international monetary issues written by men who have been close to the action in international policymaking over the last twenty years: Robert Solomon, *The International Monetary System 1945–1976* (New York: Harper & Row, 1977); and Charles Coombs, *The Arena of International Finance* (New York: Wiley, 1976). Solomon was senior adviser to the Board of Governors of the Fed and the FOMC on international matters and Coombs ran the international trading desk at the New York Fed.

2   We can also recommend several broader treatments of United States international economic policy actions which take careful account of political issues: Stephen Cohen, *The Making of U.S. International Economic Policy* (New York: Praeger, 1977), and Joan Spero, *The Politics of International Economic Relations* (New York: St. Martin's, 1977).

3   We pointed out in the text that, in other nations, institutional arrangements and the conduct of monetary policy frequently differ from those in
the United States. The following book pursues these differences in some
detail: Donald Hodgman, *National Monetary Policies and International
Monetary Cooperation* (Boston: Little, Brown, 1974).

4   A recent textbook with many details on international financial markets
is highly recommended: Gunter Dufey and Ian Giddy, *The International
Money Market* (Englewood Cliffs, N.J.: Prentice Hall, 1978). Another very
readable book which cuts through the jargon which often permeates international financial discussions is Robert Aliber, *The International Money
Game* (New York: Basic Books, 1976).

5   The IMF regularly publishes *International Financial Statistics*. It contains the key data necessary to compare and contrast economic developments among nations.

6   For more on how the changing world financial situation affects commercial banking, see Warren Moskowitz, "Global Asset and Liability Management at Commercial Banks," *Quarterly Review*, Federal Reserve Bank of
New York (Spring 1979), 42–48.

GLOSSARY

A

aggregate demand (AD) Total expenditure on final goods for a given period. Equal to consumption, plus investment, plus government spending, plus net exports.

aggregate demand curve Relation between real output demanded and the general level of prices.

aggregate supply (AS) Total value of output produced during a given period.

aggregate supply curve Relation between real output supplied and the general level of prices.

appreciation Increase in value of one currency unit in relation to another. When used to describe dollar exchange rate movements, this term means that the value of the dollar relative to a foreign currency has risen, i.e., it takes fewer dollars to buy a unit of the foreign currency.

arbitrage Practice of buying an asset in one market (at a lower price) and selling it in another market (at a higher price).

asked price Price at which market makers (brokers and dealers) offer to sell a particular security.

automatic transfer service (ATS) System of automatic transfers from savings deposits to demand deposits to cover a customer's overdraft.

B

balance on capital account (BKA) Net change in the value of securities issued by the United States to the rest of the world: The sale of United States securities in a given period minus the purchase of foreign securities equals the United States net export of securities.

balance of payments (BOP) Net difference between payments from the rest of the world for United States goods, services, and securities purchased by foreign residents and payments to the rest of the world for foreign goods, services, and securities purchased by United States residents.

balance of trade   Difference between the dollar value of United States exports of goods and services to the foreign sector and the dollar value of United States imports from the foreign sector (sometimes called net exports).

basis point   Equal to 1/100 of 1%; used in referring to interest rate movements. If the interest rate on a bond rises from 6 to 6.25 percent, the rate has risen 25 basis points.

bearer bond   Bond which is presumed to be owned by the person who holds it; the owner's name is not on record with the issuer. Such a bond carries detachable interest coupons. Interest is collected by presenting a coupon for the interest period to the issuer's agent or the bondholder's bank.

bid   Price that market makers offer to pay when they purchase a particular security. (The bid price is lower than the asked price).

bond   Written promise by the issuer to repay a fixed amount of borrowed money on a specified date and to pay a fixed annual rate of interest in the meantime, generally at semiannual intervals.

broker   Person or firm acting as an intermediary or go-between in arranging trades for buyers and sellers of securities, commodities, or real estate.

budget constraint   During any given period a spending unit's spending or saving decisions are constrained (limited) by its current budget.

C

capital market   Financial markets where securities with original maturities of more than a year are traded.

certificates of deposit (CD)   Time deposits issued in designated denominations and with fixed maturity dates. Generally the term CD is used to refer to large denominations—over $100,000.

comparative static analysis   Analysis which compares one equilibrium point with another.

compensating balance   Portion of a loan to a firm that the bank holds as a compensation (in addition to the interest rate) for the bank's willingness to make the loan (or provide other services) to the firm.

compounding   Growth in the value of a financial asset as a result of interest earned on the original principal and on the reinvested interest.

consumption Expenditure by households on goods and services.

consumption function Relation between aggregate consumption and aggregate disposable income (holding other variables constant).

convertible bond Corporate bond which may be converted at the option of the holder into a stated number of shares of the corporation's common stock. Essentially, this is a contract which gives the lender (creditor) the option to become an owner (shareholder).

correspondent banking Business arrangement between two banks for one to provide the other with special services such as check clearing or financial investment advice.

coupon Certificate of interest attached to a bond which represents the interest the borrower promises to pay the bondholder (usually in semiannual installments) on a specified date; detached for presentation for payment.

coupon rate (yield) Annual rate of interest, which the borrower promises to pay the bondholder, expressed as a percentage of the face or par value. The coupon rate equals the coupon payment in dollars divided by the par value of the bond.

credit union share drafts Checklike instruments written against interest-bearing accounts in credit unions (in order to transfer funds to third parties).

crowding out Term used to describe the possibility that borrowers in the private sector (e.g., households and firms) may be pushed or rationed out of financial markets when the federal government borrows to finance its deficit.

current yield Annual interest a bond pays divided by the current price of the bond. For example, bond A pays $80 annually; today its price is $920, therefore, the current yield = 80/920 = .087 = 8.7 percent.

D

dealer Person or firm acting as a principal (i.e., a buyer or seller) in the buying and selling of securities.

debenture Bond which is not secured by a particular asset but instead is backed by the general credit of the issuing corporation. Most corporate bonds are debentures.

demand deposit (D) Deposit at a commercial bank which is payable by the bank on demand. Commonly known as checking accounts.

depreciation (devaluation) Decrease in value of one currency unit in relation to another. When used to describe dollar exchange rate movements, this term means that the value of the dollar relative to a foreign currency has fallen; i.e., it takes more dollars to buy a unit of the foreign currency.

direct finance Loan by a surplus unit directly to a deficit unit (avoiding the financial intermediaries).

discount Difference between the current market price of a bond and its face value when the price is lower than the face value. For example, a bond with a face value of $1000 whose current market price is $900 is selling at a $100 discount.

discounting Means of calculating the present value of the future stream of expected returns generated by an asset.

disintermediation Withdrawal of funds from intermediaries by households in order to acquire claims in the financial markets directly.

disposable income (Y_d) Personal (household) income minus personal taxes; amount of funds the household sector has available for consumption and saving.

dual banking system Term arising from the fact that in the United States banking system some banks are chartered by the federal government and other banks are chartered by state governments.

dynamic analysis Analysis that focuses on the rate of change in variables over some time period.

E

electronic funds transfer system (EFTS) System whereby payments are made by banks to third parties via electronic commands.

endogenous Variable that is determined within the model.

equilibrium Condition in the economy (or a market) from which there is no tendency to deviate.

Eurodollars Dollar-denominated deposits held in foreign banks or branches of American banks overseas.

ex-ante Planned or desired values of a variable; for example, planned consumption expenditure represents desired consumption at some expected level of income.

ex-post Realized value of a variable; for example, realized consumption expenditure.

excess reserves (XR) Reserves a bank holds above and beyond required reserves.

exchange rate (ER) Number of units of domestic money needed to acquire one unit of foreign money.

exogenous Variable that is determined outside the model.

exports (E) Value of United States goods and services demanded by the rest of the world.

F

federal funds market   Trading of reserves (mainly) among banks; typically banks with excess reserves lend them temporarily to banks that need reserves.

federal funds rate (i_{FF})   Interest rate that is charged for borrowing federal funds.

Federal Reserve notes   Paper currency in circulation issued by the Federal Reserve.

financial asset (financial claim)   Asset which is a claim on money for the holder; a promise to pay money (a liability) for the issuer. Bonds, stocks, notes and currency are financial assets for the holders.

financial intermediaries   Financial institutions which transfer funds from ultimate lenders (savers) to ultimate borrowers (deficit units).

financial investment   Change in holdings of financial assets over a given period.

fiscal policy   Government taxing or spending policy used to stabilize the economy.

float   Reserves in the banking system that are created through the accounting conventions underlying the Fed's check-clearing procedures.

flow concept   Variable (such as income) which is measured over some period of time.

fractional reserves banking system   Banking system where banks must hold some fraction (between 0 and 100 percent) of their volume of deposits as reserves.

full employment   Level of employment defined to correspond to full use of the labor force at existing wage rates. This allows for frictional and structural unemployment and the level would usually correspond to about 5½% unemployment.

full-employment deficit (or surplus)   Estimate of what the government budget deficit (or surplus) would be if the economy were at full employment.

full-employment output (Y_{fe})   Aggregate output produced when the economy is at full employment.

G

government spending (G)   Purchases of goods and services by federal, state, and local governments.

gross national product (GNP)   Total value of all final goods and services produced during a given time period.

I

imports (M) Foreign goods and services demanded by and sold to the United States.

income Earnings per period; for the economy, income is total wages, salaries, rent, interest, and profit.

indirect finance Claim acquired by a surplus unit on a financial intermediary which, in turn, finances a deficit unit.

inflation Rate of increase in the general level of prices (such as the consumer price index); usually quoted at an annual rate.

intermediation Transfer of funds from surplus to deficit units via the services of a financial intermediary.

international reserve assets Internationally acceptable means of payment; currently they include SDRs, gold, and foreign currencies.

investment Expenditures on new plant, equipment, and inventories.

L

leverage ratio (L) Ratio of a firm's long-term debt to equity.

liability management Bank's management of its liability structure to increase its source of funds or to reduce its costs of funds.

liquidity premium Premium required by investors to hold longer-term securities which are less liquid than shorter-term securities.

M

marginal Term used by economists to refer to the extra (additional) increase in some variable.

marginal efficiency of investment (MEI) Rate of return on an investment project that a firm might undertake.

M1 Currency plus demand deposits held by the public; the most commonly used measure of the money supply.

M2 Currency plus demand deposits plus time and savings deposits at commercial banks; another measure of the money supply.

monetarist Economist who believes that the dominant determinant of prices and the level of economic activity is the rate of growth of the money supply.

monetary policy Policy by the Federal Reserve aimed at controlling interest rates and/or the money supply in order to stabilize economic activity.

money market Market where securities with original maturities of one year or less are traded.

money market certificates Time deposits with six-month maturities that carry a maximum yield tied to the rates on six-month Treasury bills.

N

near-monies Highly liquid stores of value that possess many of the characteristics of money; examples are savings accounts, savings and loan shares, and Treasury bills.

negotiable orders of withdrawal (NOW) Interest-bearing accounts that allow a holder to withdraw or transfer funds by writing a negotiable order of withdrawal payable to a third party (thus functioning as means of payment similar to demand deposits).

net exports (NX) Foreign purchases of United States goods and services (United States exports) minus United States purchases of foreign goods and services (United States imports).

net taxes (T) Total tax receipts minus total transfer payments.

nominal Value of a variable measured in current dollars.

nonprice terms of credit Terms of credit, other than interest rates, which affect the ability of a borrower to borrow. Such terms include the size of the down payment on the loan, the length of the repayment period, and the amount or type of collateral required.

note Shorter-term security which generally matures in less than ten years.

O

open market operations (OMO) Buying or selling of government securities by the Federal Reserve to affect the reserve base of the banking system: buying increases reserves, selling decreases reserves.

opportunity cost Forgone alternative; for example, when one holds money, one forgoes the explicit interest return that could be earned by putting the money in a savings account.

P

par value (face value) Principal amount of a bond; the amount of money due at maturity—usually $1000 per bond.

portfolio Stock of financial assets and liabilities in an account at a given point in time.

premium Difference between the current market price of a bond and its value at maturity when the price is higher than the par or face value. For example, a bond with a face value of $1000, whose current market price is $1100, is selling at a $100 premium.

present value Current worth (or value) of future returns. Since a dollar today is worth more than a dollar in the future (because it can be lent out and earn interest), future returns are discounted by an appropriate interest rate to compute their current worth.

primary market Market where new issues of securities are bought or sold.

prime rate Interest rate a bank charges its most creditworthy customers.

productivity Measure of output per hour worked.

R

rate of return on investment Discount rate that makes the income stream of an asset equal to the present cost of the asset. *See also* Marginal efficiency of investment.

real assets Assets of a tangible nature, such as an automobile, home, television set, factory, or land.

real output Nominal output divided by a price index or output measured in dollars of constant purchasing power.

Regulation Q Federal Reserve regulation that sets a maximum interest rate which banks can offer on time and savings deposits.

repurchase agreement Arrangement whereby the New York Fed agrees to buy securities from a dealer with the proviso that the dealer repurchase them on a specific day in the near future.

required reserves (RR) Reserves which by Fed regulation banks are required to hold. The required reserves are a percentage of deposits.

retained earnings (current) (RE) That portion of current corporate income which is not paid out as dividends or taxes but instead is retained within the corporation for reinvestment.

reverse repurchase agreement Arrangement whereby the Fed agrees to a temporary sale of securities to a dealer with the proviso to repurchase them.

risk-averse Descriptive term for, say, borrower behavior where the borrower avoids the riskier of two assets when the yields are the same.

S

saving (S) Disposable income minus consumption equals saving.

savings Net stock of financial assets held by a household; equal to total financial assets minus total financial liabilities.

secondary market Market where outstanding issues are bought and sold by owners and purchasers. Such transactions may be made either over-the-counter or through an organized exchange.

special drawing rights (SDRs)   Assets issued to member countries of the International Monetary Fund. Often called "paper gold" since SDRs are an acceptable means of international payments.

spread   Difference between what a dealer pays for a security (the bid price) and the price at which the dealer offers to sell it (the asking price).

stabilization policy   Fiscal or monetary policies designed to stabilize economic activity.

stagflation   Simultaneous occurrence of inflation and unemployment.

sterilization   Central bank actions designed to insulate a nation's money supply against being influenced by inflows or outflows of international reserves.

stock concept   Variable which is measured at some point in time.

surplus sector   Sector whose current income minus current expenditures is positive.

surplus unit   Individual units in the household, business, government, or foreign sector whose current receipts exceed current spending.

syndicate   Group of underwriters.

T

tax credit   Credit against the tax owed; a $12 tax credit reduces one's tax liability by $12.

tax deduction   Usually a reduction in the amount of income which is taxable. For example, a three-martini lunch costing $12 is deductible from income. If, say, a person is in the 50% tax bracket, there is a $6 reduction in taxes.

transfers   Government payments for which no productive service is performed in the current period; examples are social security payments, welfare benefits, and veterans benefits.

U

underwriters   Market makers who agree to buy from the issuer securities which they then sell (distribute) to individual and institutional investors.

unemployment   Portion of the workforce that is unemployed at current wage rates.

unemployment rate (u)   Ratio of unemployed workers to the total workforce.

usury ceiling   State-imposed ceiling or maximum interest rate that can be charged on loans by financial intermediaries.

V

value added   Increase in the value of a product during a particular production process; equal to the value of output produced by a firm minus the costs of goods and services purchased from other firms.

velocity of money (V)   Ratio of GNP for a given year to the stock of money.

W

wealth (net worth)   Value of assets minus the value of liabilities at a point in time.

Y

yield curve   Graphical representation of the relationship between interest rates on particular securities and their terms to maturity.

yield to maturity   Average annual rate of return (sometimes called the internal rate of return) on an investment (or security) if it is held to maturity.

INDEX

INDEX